A BIBLE HANDBOOK

TO THE

ACTS

OF THE

APOSTLES

MAL COUCH
General Editor

kregel
PUBLICATIONS

Grand Rapids, MI 49501

A Bible Handbook to the Acts of the Apostles
Mal Couch, General Editor

For more information about Kregel Publications, visit our web site at www.kregel.com.

Cover design: Nicholas G. Richardson
Book design: Frank Gutbrod

Photograph and illustration credits:
p. 12, Temple model, Jerusalem, *Kregel Publications*
p. 34, The Apostle Peter, Lateran Museum, Rome, *Dr. Paul L. Maier*
p. 72, "The Crucifixion," *Gustave Doré*
p. 82, Columns in the Forum, Rome, *Kregel Publications*
p. 92, Relief carving from Smyrna, *Kregel Publications*
p. 102, The Apostle Paul, Lateran Museum, Rome, *Dr. Paul L. Maier*
p. 109, Temple model, Jerusalem, *Kregel Publications*
p. 120, Grain harvest, Israel, *Kregel Publications*
p. 157, "The Descent of the Spirit," *Gustave Doré*
All other maps and illustrations, Frank Gutbrod, *Kregel Publications*

Library of Congress Cataloging-in-Publication Data
    A bible handbook to the acts of the Apostles / Mal Couch, general editor.
        p.   cm.
    Includes bibliographical references (p.).
    1. Bible. NT. Acts—Criticism, interpretation, etc.
    2. Bible. NT. Acts—Theology.   I. Couch, Mal.
BS2625.2.B46   1998   226.6'06—dc 21   98-44660
                                                        CIP.
ISBN 0-8254-2360-0

Printed in the United States of America

1 2 3 4 5 / 03 02 01 00 99

TABLE OF CONTENTS

Tongues

5

FOREWORD

As a young pastor just out of seminary, I did not appreciate the book of Acts. I heard others speak with glowing words about how much the book blessed them. But not me. This recorded history by Dr. Luke was the key to showing how God brought salvation to the world. But to a novice Bible student, the book was overloaded with twists and turns. It had too much narration and, to my (apparently) immature mind, it was too complicated to keep me awake. This is a terrible confession for one who believes, without reservation, in the inspiration by the Holy Spirit for the writing of Acts. Despite this firm theological confirmation, I resolved to avoid teaching from the book.

Then a few years ago the contents and drama of Acts seemed to explode before my eyes. To me, the book began to read like the exciting adventure it is. I believe what enticed me to look again at Acts was a burning concern about what is happening today in the church. As confusion has grown like weeds, New Age philosophies lifted their ugly heads in some of the teachings within congregations that historically were evangelical. I decided to go back to the source of our New Testament faith and rethink the book of Acts. What lessons could I learn afresh from the struggles of those who gave their very lives for the gospel of Jesus Christ? What lessons are there for the turmoil and confusion that engulf the larger world of conservative churches?

As I read and translated Acts, I found I could not put down the book. Time-honored principles and practices began to pour off its pages. I found myself learning anew how Paul dealt with those who hated Christ and rejected the gospel. I discovered again the great practical pillars of the church, which were laid down as the Holy Spirit began to transform lives in city after city in the Greek world. Even though Acts is a transitional narration, the lessons for today are innumerable for our generation of Bible teachers, missionaries, and pastors. I trust this theology and survey of Acts may renew for others a revitalized sense of mission and urgency as we see our world growing ever more intolerant toward the Lord Jesus Christ and His saving grace.

Mal Couch
General Editor

CONTRIBUTORS

Paul Benware, Th.M., Th.D., is a professor at Philadelphia College of the Bible, Langhorne, PA.

Mal O. Couch, M.A., Th.M., Th.D., Ph.D., is founder and president of Tyndale Theological Seminary and Biblical Institute, Fort Worth, Texas.

Thomas Figart, Th.M., Th.D., is Distinguished Professor Emeritus at Lancaster (Pennsylvania) Bible College.

Arnold Fruchtenbaum, Th.M., Ph.D., is a conference speaker and founder of Ariel Ministries. He lives in Tustin, California.

Robert Lightner, Th.M., M.L.S., Th.D., is visiting professor of theology at Tyndale Theological Seminary.

Steven McAvoy, Th.M., Th.D., is director of the Institute for Biblical Studies, Lake Oswego, Oregon.

Russell L. Penney, M.A., D.Sc., Th.D., is Professor of Missions at Tyndale Theological Seminary and Biblical Institute.

Randall Price, Th.M., Ph.D., is professor of theology and Bible at Liberty Baptist Theological Seminary and founder and president of World of the Bible Ministries, Inc., San Marcos, Texas.

ADDITIONAL RESEARCHERS AND WRITERS

Cris Cone, M.A., Ph.D. candidate, is professor of Bible at Tyndale Theological Seminary and Biblical Institute.

Bobby Hayes, M.A., Ph.D. candidate, is associate professor at Tyndale Theological Seminary and Biblical Institute.

Tom Henderson, M.A., D.Min., is a pastor and instructor at Tyndale Biblical Institute.

Todd Virnoche, M.A. candidate, is a researcher at Tyndale Theological Seminary and Biblical Institute.

Part 1

THE THEOLOGY OF
THE BOOK OF ACTS

The book of Acts contains a rich harvest of theological themes and revelation about God's new program, the dispensation of grace, sometimes called the dispensation of the church. Through the inspiration of the Holy Spirit, Acts opens with new directions set forth, as the gospel goes beyond Israel to the world. Though there are new revelations about the gospel that progressively unfold throughout the book, one must still view Acts as a history of a transition from the dispensation of law to the church age.

Because of this transition, many of the doctrines of Acts are in their formative stage. For example, though we see the baptism of the Holy Spirit in Acts, not every detail needed to help us understand its significance is given. In Acts the filling of the Holy Spirit seems to be a sovereign work of the Spirit to achieve specific results. But in Paul's Epistles, the filling of the Spirit is mentioned only in Ephesians 5:18, where Paul attaches a command that the believer "allow" the Spirit to work. New things taking place in Acts will become normative for the church age as the New Testament unfolds.

Because of the transition, one must realize that a lot of events are taking place with the Old Testament Law as the backdrop. The priesthood and temple are still in operation. Jerusalem is still central in key events, though progressively Antioch, Syria, becomes the headquarters of the new movement known as Christianity.

Part 1 examines the maturing process of the early church in Acts. Particular attention is paid to the work of the Holy Spirit and the growth and polity of the church as a collection of local assemblies and as the corporate body of Christ. Apostolic authority, deacons, and elders are analyzed. This section will look at the role of the temple in early Acts, the progressive rejection of Christ by the Jews, the coming judgment on the nation, and the providential spread of the gospel beyond Palestine to the cities of Greece and Rome.

Chapter 1

INTRODUCTION

Author and Authenticity

Almost all of church history ascribes both the Gospel of Luke and the Acts of the Apostles to Luke, an extraordinary physician, historian, and missionary. We know for certain that he was a Gentile and that his Greek name was *Loukas* with the Latin equivalent of *Lucanus*. From Acts we learn that he was a Gentile and that he was a physician (Col. 4:11, 14), but how and when he began the profession is not known. Some scholars debate whether Luke was a pure Gentile or a non-Jewish Semite. The majority believe he was simply a Greek. As the Gospel of Luke and the book of Acts are studied, it is certain that the author, Luke, was an educated and able writer, researcher, and observer. He had a thorough knowledge of Greek literature and language.

From Luke 1:2, the apostle tells us he was not an eyewitness concerning the things he reports nor a minister from the beginning. He joined the apostle Paul at Troas and sailed with him and his companions to Macedonia (Acts 16:10–11). In fact, from chapter 16, Luke continually comes in and out of the Acts narration with the personal note of "we" and "us." Obviously, he was involved in many occasions in the drama of the founding of Christianity.

At one point, Luke went with Paul to Philippi but apparently did not share in his persecution (16:25–17:1) nor did he leave the city with the apostle Paul, because suddenly the narrative turns to "they," as he describes what went on in the city. Luke reappears at the end of Paul's third missionary journey (20:6). The first-person plural "we" is used in the narrative from that point through the end of the book.

Why did Luke not experience the same persecution as Paul and Silas? It can only be speculated that, being in an honorable profession and a Gentile, he escaped the wrath of angry crowds and officials who were intolerant of Jews. Luke clearly was faithful to the apostle Paul until the end (2 Tim. 4:11). In the last glimpse of him, Paul refers to him as "the beloved physician" (Col. 4:14) and "fellow-laborer" (Philem. 24).

Theodore the Lector (early sixth century) states the tradition that Luke was a painter, but this cannot be substantiated. Some say Luke was a Syrian from Antioch and that he was with the disciples before the conversion of Paul. A third-century quote says Luke had neither wife nor children and that he died in Bithynia "at the age of seventy-four, filled with the Holy Ghost."[1] But history is not certain when or where the apostle died. Gregory of Nazianzus (330–389) says he became a martyr under emperor Domitian, but that view is not unanimous with all accounts. This view also states that his bones were carried from Achaia to Constantinople and buried there in the twentieth year of Constantius.[2]

Place in the Canon

The church has for centuries labeled this book "The Acts of the Apostles," though no one believes this is the official title given by the Holy Spirit. Sometimes the word *Acts* can mean the "decrees or laws," but more than likely here it has to do with the "activities" and ministries of the apostles. Some object to the title and believe it should be ascribed "The Acts of the Holy Spirit." It is interesting to note, however, that the book concentrates on the works of Peter and Paul, as directed and guided by the Spirit of God.

From the human standpoint, it was Peter who opened the gospel frontier to the Jews and Gentiles, and Paul focused mainly on the Gentile world. However, in Acts, Paul continually encounters Hellenistic Jews, with many accepting the gospel and some violently rejecting it. Since these two men had the most important roles in founding the church, it is helpful to possess a permanent record of their efforts.

Acts holds a secure place in the New Testament canon. The early church Fathers were unanimous about the historicity and accuracy of this work, mentioning it and quoting from it continually and confidently. The authority for Acts rests on the same foundations as does Luke's gospel.

Date of Writing

Many see Luke and Acts as one book in two parts. And most would say that when Luke finished his gospel account, he continued writing his Acts chronicles. Albert Barnes notes:

> As the history [in Acts], however, is continued to the second year of the residence of Paul at Rome (Ac. xxviii. 31), it was evidently written about as late as the year 62; and as it makes no mention of the subsequent facts in the life of Paul, or of any other event of history, it seems clear that it was not written much after that time.[6]

Barnes further mentions that some fix the date and place at around 63 in Rome. A minority hold that the work was penned in Alexandria, Egypt, but there is no factual evidence for this.[7] A more critical position argues that Acts was written by some later, anonymous scribe around 115–30. But few seriously believe this late date can be defended. A more common liberal or critical date nominated is 80–95. Luke would not likely be the author so late.

However, if written after 70, the book could not easily have avoided all reference to the fall of Jerusalem. Internally, there are a number of reasons for dating the book as early as 61. Most compelling is the situation of the Jews, who are still portrayed as having enough spiritual and political power to influence Roman courts against Christians. Richard Longenecker further argues:

> And why would Luke after that time want to argue before a Gentile audience that Christianity should be accepted as a "religiolicita" because of its relation to Judaism? True, Vespasian and Titus waged their war against the Jews of Palestine, and particularly against their Zealot leadership, without mounting a general persecution against Diaspora Jews or imposing official restrictions on them. Yet in the eyes of the Roman world Palestinian Judaism was largely defunct after A.D. 70.[8]

Longenecker notes that assumptions made by the author of Acts show ignorance of what happened when hostilities broke out in Palestine between Jewish Zealots and the Roman Tenth Legion in 66 and also the Neronian persecutions that began in 65. Internal evidence indicates a composition of no later than 64.[9]

Internal Dating

It is difficult to determine exact dates within the structure of Acts. Some events can be clearly placed. Most agree that King Herod Agrippa died around 44 (Acts 12) and that the famine mentioned during Claudius's reign happened between 46 and 48. By working with fixed dates, certain deductions are possible. Two crucial problems regarding Paul's ministry help establish a time line, Paul's visit to Jerusalem (Gal. 2) and the procuratorship of Festus. Based on the latter one can establish approximate dates for Paul's Caesarean imprisonment and his arrival in Rome.

Few scholars agree on the internal dating of Acts but the date for chapter 1 seems to have the fewest arguments. There are only two alternatives for the date of the crucifixion of Christ, which would also be representative of the first chapter of Acts.[3] W. J. Conybeare, J. S. Howson, and Harold Hoehner prefer 33 as the date of the death of Christ and the beginning of the church.[4] James Boyer believes Acts begins in 30. Therefore, there are differences among these scholars regarding the internal chronology of Acts. For the purposes of this book in part 3, the chronology established by Boyer will be used for dating events covered by the book of Acts. Where references are made to Old Testament dates, the work of John C. Whitcomb will be used.[5]

Audience

Both the Gospel of Luke and Acts are addressed to a Greek named Theophilus (Luke 1:1–4; Acts 1:1–2), whose name means "loved of God." Little is understood about this man, but what is known is most compelling. R. C. H. Lenski believes that Luke collected all the facts about the life of Jesus before he began his gospel account. As an educated man, Lenski argues, this research project became a golden opportunity to herald the truth about the Lord.[10] And then Luke encountered Theophilus.

Many believe Luke could have sent Theophilus the Gospel of Mark but that the account was too short. Thus, a more detailed record was called for. Both the Gospel and the book of Acts are written in a refined Koine or even near-classical Greek. By the many Old Testament quotes in the *Septuagint* (hereinafter *LXX*), Theophilus could appreciate the wording.

Some have thought the name was not addressed to one individual but to any "friend of God." The majority opinion still sees this man as a specific, and more than likely wealthy, aristocrat. Luke uses *"most excellent"* or *"most noble" (kratistos)*, an honorary title of those holding official rank or social status and position. It is used when addressing the procurator of Judea (Acts 23:26; 24:3; 26:25). The word is related to the Greek noun *kratos* meaning "power, rule, sovereignty." Obviously, Theophilus was a man of distinction and possibly authority. Since Luke does not use this title in Acts 1:1, many are led to believe Theophilus had become a believer in Christ, since Christians in the early church did not use *kratistos* in addressing each other.[11]

There is evidence that Luke, to a degree, wrote his Gospel to prove partially that Jesus and His disciples were not dangerous to Rome. Some think that Theophilus might have been a Roman official. It seems doubtful by the language of Luke 1 that he was a believer. Luke said that he had "compile[d] an account of the things accomplished among us" from those who were eyewitnesses. He had "investigated everything carefully from the beginning, to write it out for you in consecutive order, most excellent Theophilus; so that you might know the exact truth about the things you have been taught" (vv. 1–4). T. E. Provence adds:

> The former translation is consistent with an understanding of Theophilus as a non-Christian Roman official concerned about the political effects of the new faith. According to this view, Theophilus would have gotten some information about Jesus and His followers, . . . perhaps not all of it positive. Luke's purpose in such a case would have been to win him over to a more favorable view of Christianity, . . . even to faith.[12]

Theme and Purpose

Concerning the theme and purpose, Robertson Nicoll writes:

> Not only the aim but the purpose and contents of the book are set forth, . . . in the Preface, chap. i. 1–8. The prophetic words of the Lord in verse 8 implicitly involve a table of contents: "Ye shall receive power when the Holy Ghost," etc., ii. 1–13; "witnesses unto me" (1) "in Jerusalem," ii. 14–viii. 1, and (2) "in all Judaea and Samaria," viii. 2–xi. 18, (3) "and to the uttermost part of the earth," xi. 19–xxviii. . . . The writer closes with the end which his aim required, the preaching of the Gospel in Rome, the capital of the world, the metropolis of the human race, without hindrance.[13]

Another view of the theme of Acts is described by Lenski:

> Luther regarded Acts as a beautiful mirror in which one beholds the truth: *Sola fides justificat*. The fathers likewise admired the contents of the book, noting the great variety of subjects and the immense value of each: the great testimony in regard to the apostolic doctrine and the church; the fundamental outline of church government, church discipline, and church organization; an arsenal full of artillery against the antichrist; a laboratory full of remedies against all soul-destroying errors of faith and offenses in conduct; a larder stocked with all kinds of food for faith, patience, and hope; an inspiration for love and all its works; a very treasury of learning and right doctrine.[14]

Though Lenski's wording is colorful and descriptive, he may have missed Luke's dramatic and painful transition from the dispensation of Law to the revelation and dispensation of the church. Lenski's lofty words may have also overlooked the practical theological direction for Luke's book. In the first few verses of this book the apostle tells how the Lord had "given orders" "to wait" for the baptizing work of the Holy Spirit that was promised to come upon the disciples. When the Spirit moved on them, they were "all filled" [controlled, made complete] by the Spirit and became bold by His power in order to testify of Jesus.

In many ways the "acts" of the Holy Spirit is the theme of this writing! The Spirit of God would carry out His purposes mainly through the apostles Peter and then Paul. The Holy Spirit worked through Jesus in giving Him the directives for the apostles (1:2). The Spirit would also baptize the disciples (1:5), come *upon* them (1:8), prophesy (1:16), and give them words to speak (2:4). The Spirit would also be "poured forth" on various individuals (2:17), could be resisted (7:51), bestowed upon others through the apostles' authority (8:18), dramatically move a disciple such as Philip from one place to another (8:39), comfort (9:31), and give revelation through visions (10:19). The Spirit could command Peter to do certain things by speaking directly to him (11:15), indicating such things as a coming famine (11:28), grant joy (13:52), forbid an act such as speaking (16:6), come to individuals for special purposes (19:6), and testify to specific people (20:23). He could even work through others, providentially appointing overseers (20:28).

The work of the Spirit most often mentioned in Acts is his control over the lives of believers for the purposes of God. This is referred to in the English translations as "filling." The Greek *pimplēmi* is used to describe this work of the Spirit in 2:4; 4:8, 31; 5:17; 9:17; 13:9. John Walvoord comments:

> The Greek word *pimplēmi* is found eight times used in this connection (Luke 1:15, 41, 67; Acts 2:4; 4:8, 31; 9:17; 13:9). Another form of the same verb, *plēroō*, is found twice in reference to the filling of the Spirit (Acts 13:52; Eph. 5:18). In addition to the two verbs used to express the idea, the adjective *plērēs* is used in four instances (Luke 4:1; Acts 6:3; 7:55; 11:24). . . . The doctrine of the Holy Spirit is subject to gradual unfolding in the Acts, certain aspects of His ministry being subject to the immediate agency of the apostles. In the doctrine of the filling of the Holy Spirit, however, every instance fully sustains the premise that this ministry is found only in Christians yielded to God. [15]

The Spirit fills or controls those believers who are yielded. In his Epistles Paul shows in more detail how the Spirit works in the child of God during the church age. In both Acts and the Epistles, His dwelling is seen as permanent. By the obstruction of the believer, He may be grieved (Eph. 4:30) and quenched (1 Thess. 5:19).

Besides recording the dynamic work of the Spirit of God in Acts, Luke also works hard to point out that the early church was not in a hostile relationship with the imperial Roman government, particularly at first. As the book closes, a spiritual war is going on with the Jewish leaders. As the key character of the waning chapters, Paul is told he would bear witness in Rome (23:11; 28:23). We know as the author of Acts could not, that his would be the final voice that would convict and call Israel before she was scattered in the Jewish wars and the Temple destruction. Acts ends abruptly as Paul pronounces a final judgment upon the nation from the *LXX* version of Isaiah 6:9–10: "For the heart of this people has become dull, and with their ears they scarcely hear" (Acts 28:27a). His final words were: "Let it be known to you therefore, that this salvation of God has been sent to the Gentiles; they will also listen" (28:28).

Dispensational Transitions of Acts

The book of Acts is an historical narrative of the first few decades of Church history. However, it is not merely a record of history. As a theological historical narrative, it is a history obviously being developed through the sovereign outworking of God's purpose.

It is a book of transitions of many things and an historical account of the shift from the dispensation of the law to the dispensation of grace. It is a great missionary book recording the founding, the spread, and the history of the first thirty years of the Church. For that reason, the key word in the book is *witness*, which is found twenty times. This witness of the gospel is seen in its basic movement from east to west: Jerusalem to Antioch to Ephesus to Rome.

The value of the book lies in several areas: spiritual (it provides many spiritual lessons, chief among them deals with the issue of how one should respond to persecution); historical (early Church history); biographical (the acts of Peter and Paul); missionary (the spread of the gospel); dispensational (from Law to Grace); pneumatological (acts of the Holy Spirit); and, doctrinal (doctrine found in propositional statements). On the last point, the key element to remember is that the main purpose of the book of Acts is to record history and not develop doctrine; and doctrine must not be developed from historical events alone. Thus, the final word for church doctrine must be authenticated in the church Epistles.

The Seven Transitions of Acts

It is possible to discern at least seven transitions in the book of Acts.

The first transition is *historical* as it moves from the Gospels to the Epistles. The Gospels record the theological history of the life of Jesus of Nazareth, focusing primarily on His three-year public ministry, culminating with His death and resurrection. The Epistles develop the theological implications of Christ's life and death. Luke sets out the ramifications of the gospel for the world, for Israel, for the Gentiles, for the Church, and for the individual believer in both the present and the future.

Besides giving the historical origin of the Church, Acts serves as a bridge between the Gospels and the Epistles. It serves as the background for ten of the thirteen Pauline Epistles: Romans (Acts 19:21–22); 1 and 2 Corinthians (Acts 18:1–16); Galatians (Acts 13:14–14:28); Ephesians and Colossians (Acts 19:1–20:35); Philippians (Acts 16:11–40); 1 and 2 Thessalonians (Acts 17:1–9); and Philemon (Acts 18:22–23).

The book of Acts provides us with the historical account of how the apostles were able to overcome the deep shock of Jesus' death, realizing that their new mission was to proclaim the gospel to the Jew first and also to the Gentile.

The second transition is *religious*, from synagogue to church. In the Gospels, the Temple and the synagogues are prominent, with the church mentioned only twice in Matthew (16:18; 18:17), but even then it was viewed as something still future. The synagogue continues in the book of Acts, but now a new entity comes into being—the church. In Acts, synagogue and church coexist, but the synagogue is increasingly the gathering place of unbelieving Jews, whereas the church is viewed as a gathering of believing Jews and Gentiles. Paul regularly attended synagogue services, but as the book of Acts shows, this had primarily an evangelistic purpose.

A third transition is *God's program from Israel to the Church*. For the dawning age, God ceases to deal with Israel nationally, except in judgment, and the prospect of judgment is strong in the book of Acts as destruction prophesied by Jesus was anticipated. It does not mean that God has "cast off Israel" irrevocably; rather He now works primarily with the remnant of Jewish believers.

Jewish and Gentile believers make up the church. The remnant of Israel is both part of Israel the whole and the Jewish wing of the church, but God's salvation program is now primarily being worked out through the church, the body of Jewish and Gentile believers. This is to continue until the Gentiles to be saved are in the kingdom (Rom. 11:25). The book of Acts deals with the beginnings of the calling out of the Gentiles to have a people for His name (Acts 15:14).

The fourth transition is *theological*, from Christ being present to the Holy Spirit being present. The first chapter of Acts opens up with Jesus still physically present in His resurrection body. The chapter records His physical, visible departure from earth to take His seat at the right hand of God the Father until God makes His enemies the footstool of His feet (Ps. 110:1).

The fifth transition is *pneumatological*, from the Spirit being *with* believers to the Spirit being *in* believers. John 7:39 states that a new manifestation of the Spirit's ministry will follow Christ's ascension. The promise is that those who believe will receive the Spirit in a way not experienced heretofore, but the Holy Spirit is not yet given because Jesus is not yet glorified. That glorification occurs at His ascension.

The sixth transition is *national,* from Jews to Gentiles. As the book of Acts opens, virtually all believers are Jewish. The few Gentile believers had been proselytes to Judaism, and that is the way things stood through the first nine chapters of the book of Acts. In chapter ten, through Peter's preaching at the house of Cornelius, for the first time uncircumcised Gentiles who were not proselytes to Judaism entered the church.

The seventh transition is *dispensational,* from law to grace. This is not to say that there was no grace under the law any more than it means there is no law under grace. The grace of God was manifested in many ways throughout the history of the Old Testament. Furthermore, in the dispensation of grace, we certainly must follow the law of Christ.

Purpose of the Transitional Period

Why was a transitional period necessary? The answer is: To reach the Old Testament saints with the gospel. "Old Testament saints" means those who were saved under the previous dispensation. It must be remembered that all those who were saved and still living before the cross did not suddenly lose their salvation after the cross until they accepted the death of Christ for their salvation.

As of Acts 2, the new content of faith for salvation were the three points of the gospel as explained by the apostle Paul: (1) Christ died for our sins; (2) He was buried, the evidence of His death; and, (3) He rose again on the third day (1 Cor. 15:1–4). This is the content of the gospel, and this is what one must believe and trust to have salvation. However, that was not the content of faith prior to Acts 2. In the Gospels, we read of the apostles' traveling throughout the Land of Israel preaching the "gospel," but the gospel in the Gospels is not of the same content as found in 1 Corinthians 15:1–4. The Gospels stress that Jesus is the Messianic King, in whom one must trust to receive salvation. It should be noted that Jesus did not clearly proclaim His coming death to the apostles until Matthew 16:21. Yet even before that we find the apostles proclaiming the gospel. Obviously, the gospel they preached did not include the substitutionary death of Christ. When He finally told them about His death, not only did it take them by surprise but also they did not fully understand what He was saying.

How long did the transition last? One answer is that it lasted until all those died who were born and had come to faith under the law. But the transition may have been fading from Acts 23 on. For example, Paul might have had in mind a witness to the Jews by participating in a purification ritual. Paul does not compromise the gospel, but he performs a ceremony that the Jews still living under the law could respect. But from this event on, Jewish issues seem to be left behind.

The Jewish Historical Background

Most books on the book of Acts focus primarily on the Roman historical background dealing with the Roman emperors who were on the throne in the period covered by the book of Acts (Tiberius, Gaius or Caligula, Claudius, and Nero). Under Nero, Peter and Paul were martyred. Introductions to the book of Acts also deal with local rulers, such as Pontius Pilate, Agrippa I, Felix, Festus, and Agrippa II. This is not to negate the importance of this background and certainly no one can fully understand the book of Acts without understanding the Roman background.

But, to understand fully the dispensational importance, one must focus on the Jewish background, especially going back to the gospel period. The primary gospel writer, important for our study in the Jewish background to the book of Acts, is the Gospel of Matthew, but other gospel writers also add knowledge to this frame of reference. The key passage is found in Matthew 12:22–45.

Closely connected with God's kingdom program is the first coming of the Messiah. Both John the Baptist (Matt. 3:1–2) and Jesus (Matt. 4:17) came proclaiming that the kingdom of heaven was at hand. Neither John nor Jesus nor the gospel writers recording these events tried to define the nature of this kingdom, obviously expecting the audience to understand what they meant by that term; and well they might since Jewish audiences had common knowledge of the Old Testament and understood the nature of the messianic kingdom.

Even covenant theologians of all stripes admit that the common Jewish understanding of the kingdom in first-century Israel was that of a literal earthly kingdom centered in Jerusalem and ruled by the Messiah. The obvious origin of such a view was the literal understanding of the Old Testament prophets. If either John or Jesus meant something totally different, on which all covenant theologians insist, then why did neither explain such a distinction from the beginning? The very fact that they did not shows that the common Jewish understanding of the coming kingdom was correct.

> Suddenly in Matthew 3 John the baptizer, the Lord's forerunner, appears on the scene. His message was, Repent, for the kingdom of heaven is at hand. What does the word kingdom mean here? It certainly cannot be some spiritual kingdom in the hearts of people. That kingdom was always present. Furthermore, the fact that John never explained what the term meant when the Jews clearly expected an earthly kingdom would imply that he was expecting the same type of kingdom.[16]

However, the common Jewish understanding that all Israel has a share in the age to come was an incorrect one and so both John and Jesus proclaimed that the need to repent for righteousness was the means of entering the kingdom. Furthermore, to see the messianic kingdom established in their day required Israel's acceptance of Jesus as the Messianic King.

> "The gospel of the kingdom" proclaimed by Christ in Matthew 9:35 must be the same as that preached by Him in 4:23. It was the good news of the nearness of the kingdom and freedom of access by repentance. The kingdom was proximate in two senses. First, the Messiah was here on earth, and second, the kingdom's coming was contingent on Israel's response to her Messiah.[17]

The Kingdom and Dispensationalism

When He was rejected, a key change took place in the kingdom program. Stanley Toussaint has stated the dispensational viewpoint quite well:

> Very often the dispensationalist school of interpretation will refer to "the offer of the kingdom" to Israel. By this is meant the contingency of the coming of the kingdom to Israel in the first century based on Israel's acceptance of Jesus as its Messiah. This concept is clearly found in the New Testament. For instance, Peter states the coming of the Messiah rests on Israel's repentance (Acts 3:19–21). The Lord Himself said that John the Baptist could have been the fulfillment of the Elijah prophecy of Malachi 4:5–6 if Israel had repented (Matt. 11:14). . . .
>
> However, dispensationalists may want to clarify their terminology. The New Testament does teach the contingency of the coming of the kingdom premised on the response of the Jews. But every Israelite wanted the kingdom to come. To say Christ offered the kingdom to Israel is true, but it leaves the impression the Jews did not want the kingdom to come. It would be far better to say Jesus offered Himself as Israel's Messiah and the coming of the kingdom was contingent on their acceptance or rejection of Him.[18]

John 11:1–57

The resurrection of Lazarus recorded in John 11:1–44 is the presentation of the first sign of Jonah. Jesus raised others from the dead, yet all of the other resurrections are covered in just a few verses. Here John used forty-four verses to give great detail about the resurrection of Lazarus. Why? This is the sign of Jonah that Jesus had promised. In verse 42, Jesus made it clear that Lazarus was raised for the Jewish multitudes: "And I knew that thou hearest me always; but because of the people standing around I said it, that they may believe that thou didst send me."

Then in verses 45–46 there is the response of the Jews: "Many therefore of the Jews, who came to Mary and beheld that which he did, believed in him. But some of them went away to the Pharisees, and told them the things which Jesus had done."

Many Jews responded correctly to this first sign of Jonah and believed that Jesus was who He claimed to be, but the others still wanted some kind of word or decision from their leaders, and so they reported to the Pharisees what Jesus had done. Since this was the sign Christ had promised them, they responded to the challenge in verses 47–50 and 53:

> Therefore the chief priests and the Pharisees gathered a council, and were saying, "What are we doing? For this man is performing many signs. If we let him go on like this, all men will believe in him, and the Romans will come and take away both our place and our nation." But a certain one of them, Caiaphas, who was high priest that year, said unto them, "You know nothing at all, nor do you take into account that it is expedient for you that one should die for the people, and that the whole nation should not perish. . . . So from that day on they planned together to kill Him.

Verses 54–57 give the results of the Sanhedrin verdict. First, Christ went into hiding for a short period because the hour of His death was not yet come (v. 54). Second, the people still raised questions about the resurrection of Lazarus (vv. 55–56). Third, the Sanhedrin's verdict filtered down to the masses: "Now the chief priests and the Pharisees had given commandment, that, if any man knew where he was, he should show it, that they might take him" (v. 57).

Thus, they sought an opportunity to put Him to death. The rejection of the messiahship of Jesus that occurred in Matthew 12 culminated in John 11 with a decree of death hanging over the person of Jesus. The first sign of Jonah, the resurrection of Lazarus, was officially rejected by the Sanhedrin.

With the announcement of the commitment of the unpardonable sin, the destruction of Jerusalem now became the coming judgment for the rejection. The nation and city of Jerusalem would be destroyed as a result of Israel's national rejection of the Messiah (Matt. 23:38; Luke 24:20–24).

Luke 19:41–44

Further light is shed on the nature of the unpardonable sin in the rejection of the messiahship of Jesus in Luke 19:41–44. This passage is in the context of the triumphal entry of Jesus into Jerusalem. Thousands of Jews cried, "Hosanna, blessed is He that comes in the name of the Lord." This shout had clear messianic overtones, based upon the messianic context of Psalm 118:26. The Jewish masses proclaimed His messiahship as He approached Jerusalem. However, the Jewish leaders had already committed the unpardonable sin. Judgment had already been set upon that generation. Since the sin was unforgivable, there was no way of alleviating that judgment.

Dispensational Purposes of Acts

The dispensational purposes of Acts can be further seen in the various reasons for which the book of Acts was written. The purposes of the book of Acts can be divided into four categories.

First are *historical purposes*:

1. to trace the first thirty years of Church history as the Messiah was now building His Church in accordance with His own prophecy;
2. to trace the spread of the gospel from Jerusalem to Rome in fulfillment of the Great Commission;
3. to trace the growth of the Church through the summary statements found in Acts 2:47; 5:14; 6:7; 9:31; 12:24; 16:5; and 19:20; and
4. to record Israel's rejection of the second sign of Jonah, the resurrection of Jesus, at which point the gospel begins to go out to non-Jews.

Second is the *theological purpose*, to authenticate the new faith as a work of the Holy Spirit. This authentication by the Holy Spirit is seen in 1:5–8; 2:1–47; 5:1–11; 6:5; 8:14–17; 10:44–47; 13:1–4; and 19:1–7.

Third is an *apologetic purpose* to prove that the new movement was well received by civil governmental officials. Roman leaders either give it a hearing or ignore it, but they do not oppose it (for example, Sergius Paulus, the officials of Philippi, Gallio, the Asiarchs of Ephesus, the town clerk of Ephesus, Felix, Festus, and Agrippa).

Fourth is an *eschatological purpose*—the development of the mystery of the kingdom program. In Matthew 13, Jesus introduced the mystery kingdom as a new facet of God's kingdom program put into effect as a result of the rejection of the messianic kingdom. The mystery kingdom program actually begins in Matthew 13, but the book of Acts reveals its further development.

One more area worth mentioning in the dispensational importance of the book of Acts is how it relates to the issue of Israelology. The book of Acts teaches six points here.

1. Israel as a nation did reject the messiahship of Jesus; therefore, that generation was under divine judgment (2:22–23, 36; 3:13–18; 4:10–11);
2. the second coming was preconditioned on Israel's acceptance of the messiahship of Jesus, and until Israel accepts Him there will be no second coming (3:19–20);

3. nevertheless, someday Israel will make that decision and the kingdom will be restored to Israel (1:6; 3:21);
4. Hebrew and Gentile Christianity are both valid expressions of the new faith (15:1–29);
5. circumcision is valid for Jewish believers (16:1–3); and
6. the doctrinal teaching of Romans 1:16 is affirmed. The gospel is to the Jew first. In keeping with that principle, Paul is always careful to go to the Jew first (13:5, 14; 14:1; 16:11–13; 17:1–2, 10, 16–17; 18:1, 4, 19; 19:1, 8; and 28:17).

Necessity of the Transition

In Luke's gospel, the earliest intimation of transition from Law to Grace comes in Luke 5:33–35, when people came to Jesus to ask:

> "The disciples of John often fast and offer prayers; the disciples of the Pharisees also do the same; but yours eat and drink." And Jesus said to them, "You cannot make the attendants of the bridegroom fast while the bridegroom is with them, can you? But the days will come; and when the bridegroom is taken away from them, then they will fast in those days."

Just how much of this was understood at that time is questionable, but in Luke 9:18–22, which is parallel to Peter's confession of Christ in Matthew 16:16 and Jesus' response in 16:17–21, He clearly states that "the Son of man must suffer many things, and be rejected by the elders and chief priests and scribes, and be killed, and be raised up on the third day." In Luke 17:22–25, immediately after prophesying of His coming "as lightning," (v. 24) Jesus said, "But first He must suffer many things and be rejected by this generation." In Luke 19:11–27 Jesus "spoke a parable because he was near Jerusalem, and because they thought that the kingdom of God should immediately appear" (v. 11). This parable deals with a nobleman who "went into a far country to receive for himself a kingdom and to return" (v. 12).

The significant point in all these passages, as well as others, is that there was supposed to be an immediate transition from the dispensation of law to the dispensation of the kingdom, but the kingdom was rejected: "We will not have this man to reign over us" (Luke 19:14). This was indeed a rejection, not a postponement of the kingdom. However, it did provide the occasion for the fulfillment of the perplexing prophecies of a suffering Messiah, and for the transition from the dispensation of Law to the dispensation of Grace, since "the law was given by Moses, but grace and truth came by Jesus Christ" (John 1:17).

The Ministry of the Holy Spirit

Ministries of the Holy Spirit must be consideration in the transition from law to grace: regeneration, indwelling, sealing, filling, baptism, and distribution of spiritual gifts.

Regenerating

This is the work of the Holy Spirit by which He imparts eternal life to the sinner who believes in Christ. Though the actual Greek word *palingenesia* ("born again") is used only in Titus 3:5, to refer to the new life in salvation and in Matthew 19:28 to refer to the new life to be imparted to the creation in the millennium, the *doctrine* of the new birth was taught by Jesus in John 3 using the verb *gennaō* with the adverb *anō*, which is translated "to be born again," or "to be born from above."

Jesus expected Nicodemus to know of the doctrine of the new birth from the Old Testament. As far back as 1 Samuel, King Saul is spoken of in words that certainly correspond to the new birth. Though King Saul had mental problems later in life, attempting to kill his own son Jonathan and David and finally committing suicide, his earlier life is often forgotten. He was chosen by God, not by the people, and was anointed as king by Samuel. Samuel said to Saul, "Then the Spirit of the Lord will come upon you mightily, and you shall prophesy with them and be changed into another man. . . . Then it happened when he turned his back to leave Samuel, God changed his heart" (1 Sam. 10:6, 9a).

Or, perhaps Jesus was thinking of Ezekiel 11:19–20: "And I shall give them one heart, and shall put a new spirit within them . . . that they may walk in My statutes and keep My ordinances, and do them. Then they will be My people, and I shall be their God." Or Ezekiel 36:26–27a, "Moreover, I will give you a new heart and put a new spirit within you. . . . And I will put my Spirit within you."

Though neither word for regeneration is used in the book of Acts, it is significant to observe Acts 11:15–18 when Peter reviewed his experience of the great sheet let down from heaven. It was meant to signify that God is no respecter of persons as far as salvation is concerned. Peter says that the Holy Spirit fell on the Gentiles, giving them the same gift as He did to the Jews who had believed on the Lord Jesus Christ.

Indwelling

In the New Testament sense, indwelling is the work of the Holy Spirit whereby He enters the body of the believer, so that it becomes the temple of the Holy Spirit (1 Cor. 6:19) forever (John 14:16). Does this constitute a transition from the Old Testament concept of the indwelling of the Holy Spirit? Leon Wood associates Old Testament regeneration with indwelling: "Regeneration is a momentary act when spiritual life is imparted to a sinner. It happens instantaneously. Indwelling, on the other hand, only begins then. . . .

Indwelling means that this relationship continues from that point on."[19] Then he associates the sealing of the Holy Spirit with indwelling. "It is His continued indwelling that makes certain the eternal security of the believer. . . . It is the fact of the permanent indwelling of the Holy Spirit that constitutes the sealing of the believer."[20]

Wood also associates the departure of the Holy Spirit from Saul in 1 Samuel 16:15 as merely a loss of empowerment, not a loss of indwelling.[21] He obviously does not distinguish regeneration, indwelling, and sealing as different; rather, they are the beginning, continuing, and permanence of one extended act of the Holy Spirit in both Old and New Testaments.

The use of such significant words as "In whom," "within whom," and "entered into" indicates that the Holy Spirit did indeed indwell certain men in the Old Testament, but the recorded number of such individual believers is so limited that it is not possible to conclude that every believer was indwelled. There simply is no evidence of such a permanent indwelling. To the contrary, it is said on separate occasions that the Spirit entered into Ezekiel (Ezek. 2:2; 3:24). How could this be if Ezekiel was permanently indwelled?

We conclude, therefore, that there is a transition in the book of Acts regarding the indwelling of the Holy Spirit. In light of what has been presented above, the indwelling of the Holy Spirit can be characterized as *repetitive* in the dispensation of law, but in the church age He is permanently *resident* in each believer. Christ's promise in John 14:16–17 becomes clear as He makes the distinction, "He abides with (Gk. *par*) you and shall be in *(en)* you" (v. 17b).

Sealing

This is described as the guarantee, or "pledge (Gk. *arrabōn*), of our inheritance, with a view to the redemption of God's own possession, to the praise of His glory." (Eph. 1:14; cf. 2 Cor. 1:22; Eph. 4:30). The Holy Spirit Himself becomes this guarantee that our bodies will be redeemed by the One who purchased us with His own blood (Acts 20:28). Since there is no mention of such a work of the Holy Spirit in the Old Testament, are we to assume it was so? Several things assure the eternal nature of Old Testament salvation:

> *Eternal security.* Isaiah 32:17: "And the work of righteousness will be peace, and the service of righteousness, quietness and confidence forever." It has often been claimed that the actual words, *eternal security* do not occur in the Bible. But consider the following from the Hebrew lexicon as the verb *batach* is defined: "To be secure, to fear nothing for oneself; the opposite of *ya're*, "to fear." Used in a good sense of the security of the righteous Isa. 12:2 'I will trust *(batach)* and not be afraid *(ya're).*'" On the same page the noun form is defined, "*betach*: Security, Isa. 32:17, without danger and fear; safely."[22] Two significant translations of Isaiah 32:17 come first,

from Keil and Delitzsch: "And the effect of righteousness will be peace, and the reward of righteousness rest and security forever."[23] The Berkeley Version, lesser known than some other modern versions, translates 32:17: "And the fruit of justice will be peace, and the effect of righteousness rest and security forever."[24]

Eternal salvation. Isaiah 51:6: "Lift up your eyes to the sky, then look to the earth beneath; for the sky will vanish like smoke, and the earth will wear out like a garment, and its inhabitants will die in like manner, but my salvation shall be forever [Heb. *olam*], and my righteousness shall not wane."

Everlasting name. Isaiah 56:5c: "I will give them an everlasting name, which will not be cut off."

Everlasting life. Daniel 12:2: "And many of those who sleep in the dust of the ground will awake, these to everlasting life, but the others to disgrace and everlasting contempt."

We conclude that there *is* a transition from the Old Testament to the New Testament with regard to the specific sealing ministry of the Holy Spirit. Even though the actual word *sealed* is not used on the Day of Pentecost, it is quite clear that the Holy Spirit Himself was given as a gift at that time. Even as Peter said in Acts 11:17a, "God gave to them the same gift as He gave to us also after believing in the Lord Jesus Christ." The Holy Spirit is the gift as well as the seal, given on the Day of Pentecost, and to all church saints who believe thereafter!

Filling

Two New Testament verbs are translated *"fill"* with regard to the work of the Holy Spirit. One is *pimplēmi,* used twenty-four times, twenty-one of which are in Luke and Acts. In Luke 1:15, 41, 67, it refers to the filling of John the Baptist and his parents with the Holy Spirit. In Acts 2:4, on the Day of Pentecost all the disciples were filled with the Holy Spirit and began to speak in other languages. Later, in 4:8 Peter was *"filled"* and in 4:31 all the disciples were *"filled."* In 9:17 and 13:9 the word refers to Paul. Thayer's lexicon lists all these verses under the definition "What wholly takes possession of the mind is said to fill it."[25] Practically the same definition is given to the second verb, *plēroō;* "to pervade, take possession of one's heart," John 16:6; Acts 5:3, and in Eph. 5:18 "to diffuse throughout one's soul."[26] In each of these cases, the idea of control is present. Another author, referring to Acts 13:52, stated, *"plēroō* also implies that a man is completely controlled and stamped by the powers that fill him."[27]

One adjective, *plērēs,* comes from the same root as *plēroō* and means "full of, abounding in, wholly occupied with, completely under the influence of or affected by."[28] It is used of Jesus in Luke 4:1, "full of the Holy Spirit"; of the seven in Acts 6:3, "full of the Spirit and of wisdom"; and of Barnabas in Acts 11:24a, "full of the Holy Spirit and of faith."

Most of these definitions show that the filling of the Holy Spirit denotes His influence in, and control over, the lives of individual Christians. But there are occasions where the two verbs are used in other ways. Two examples will suffice: In Luke 1:15 the angel spoke concerning John the Baptist, "he shall be filled (*pimplēmi*) with the Holy Spirit, while yet in his mother's womb." This immediately distinguishes filling from regeneration, indwelling, sealing, and baptism of the Holy Spirit, since no baby is born saved. Yet this child could be controlled by, and be under the influence of, the Holy Spirit from his mother's womb.

In like manner, Jehovah could say of Jeremiah in the Old Testament, "Before I formed you in the womb I knew you; and before you were born I consecrated you; I have appointed you a prophet to the nations" (Jer. 1:5). In Jeremiah's case, "sanctified" (Heb. *kadash*) has the idea of being set apart for a task. Again, it is the divine influence and control over a life even before salvation.

The other verb, *plēroō*, is used in Acts 5:3 when Peter asked Ananias, "Why has Satan filled your heart to lie to the Holy Spirit?" Since there is no reason given to assume that Ananias and Sapphira were unbelievers, the inference is that this is a case of Satanic influence from the outside, just as Satan could attempt to "sift" Peter in Luke 22:31. *Plēroō* is also used in Eph. 5:18, where a full definition of "filling" can be demonstrated.

Our conclusion, then, concerning whether there was a transition in the filling of the Holy Spirit from law to grace is twofold. First, the actual words for filling and for the coming of the Holy Spirit upon certain believers mightily seem to refer to miraculous powers. These include the sign gifts of the apostolic age. There also are numerous admonitions to seek God, to walk in His ways, and to keep His Word, all directed generally to every believer. These are the equivalents of the Old Testament saint who is filled with the Spirit. Terminology may differ, but this particular work of the Holy Spirit is the same in every dispensation.

Baptizing

According to 1 Corinthians 12:12–13, the proper definition of the baptism of the Holy Spirit is His work by which every believing sinner is placed into the body of Christ, the church, as a member. These verses indicate the universality of this baptism for every member, the time of it as past (at the moment of salvation), and the equality of Jews, Gentiles, bond or free in this body. Galatians 3:27 adds that we have been baptized "into Christ" and "have put on Christ" then adds the equality of male and female (v. 28) to what was said in 1 Corinthians 12:13.

The two occurrences in the book of Acts refine the definition by designating the time when this ministry of the Holy Spirit began. In His post-resurrection appearances to the apostles, Jesus commanded them to "wait for the promise of the Father, which, saith he, ye have heard from me. For John truly baptized with water, but ye shall be baptized with the Holy Spirit not many days from now" (Acts 1:4–5). This immediately takes us back to John 14:16–17, where the original promise was given: "And I will pray the Father, and he shall give you another Comforter, that he may abide with you forever; even the Spirit of truth, whom the world cannot receive, because it seeth him not, neither knoweth him; but ye know him; for he dwelleth with you, and shall be in you."

When the promise is referred to in Acts 1:5, Christ gives one of the results accompanying that residence, namely, the baptism of the Spirit. His only explanation is to compare it with John's baptizing in water. A few sentences later, Christ adds still another blessing of the coming of the Holy Spirit: "But you shall receive power when the Holy Spirit has come upon you" (Acts 1:8a). Literally, the participle (*elthontos*) is "Having come upon you" (*eph hymas*). This power, in turn, is defined as the filling of the Spirit: "And they were all filled (*eplēsthēsan*) with the Holy Spirit" (2:4), resulting in the miraculous ability to speak in foreign languages (2:5–11).

Acts 11:15–18 is the only other place in the book of Acts where the baptism of the Holy Spirit is mentioned. The occasion is Peter's recognition of Gentile salvation; and he uses some significant phrases to describe what happened: "And as I began to speak, the Holy Spirit fell on them, as He did upon us at the beginning" (v. 15). When was this beginning? Obviously it was on the Day of Pentecost. Specifically, what began? Again, it is obvious that it is the beginning of the church, the body of Christ.

Vengeance and the Book of Acts

Another purpose of the book of Acts is to dramatize the buildup of the coming vengeance spoken of by Jesus in the Olivet Discourse. Many scholars miss this theme, but the connection is made by noting Luke's account of the Lord's words about the coming fall of Jerusalem and the destruction of the temple (Luke 21:22–24).

Before examining this section, we must address the dating of Luke's gospel and the book of Acts again (see pp. 13–15). Most scholars see the two books as two parts of one narration (see p. 13) and often refer to the historical record of Luke-Acts. Commentator William Hendriksen writes:

> Luke cannot have finished [Acts] before the year 62. As to the latest probable date, here we must be careful. It is sometimes said that since Paul must have been released [from Roman imprisonment]

about A.D. 63 or soon afterward and Acts ends with Paul still in prison, the book must have been written not later than the year 63, for if Luke had known about Paul's release he would probably have mentioned it.[29]

Hendriksen then notes:

Conclusion: the book of Acts was probably written before the middle of the year 64. A reasonable guess would be A.D. 63. And since Luke-Acts is really a single work, the date when Theophilus received the Third Gospel cannot have been much earlier—probably "sometime during the period A.D. 61–63."[30]

Thus the gospel of Luke was probably written toward the end of the events taking place in Acts. The apostle Luke was witnessing firsthand the headstrong spiritual hardness of the Jewish people. He saw the hatred of the leaders of Jerusalem toward the apostles and the gospel. He noted how believers were suffering from the persecution of the leading zealous Jews in the city of Jerusalem.

As Luke probably read Matthew's account of the Olivet Discourse, and additionally interviewed various disciples as to what Jesus actually said on that occasion, he noted that Matthew did not give details about the fall of Jerusalem or the temple. And yet in the complete account, as finally recorded by Luke, the Lord clearly refers to a coming vengeance upon that city.

Why did Matthew not go on and record Christ's words about Jerusalem and the temple's soon fall? After all, the Lord hinted at it as He began the Olivet narrative. "Do you not see all these things [of the temple]? Truly I say to you, not one stone here shall be left upon another, which will not be torn down" (Matt. 24:2b). One theory put forth is only a conjecture. Since Matthew wrote around A.D. 45, he may have avoided being offensive to the Jews by leaving out Christ's vivid description of the impending doom of the city and temple. But almost twenty years had passed since Matthew wrote. And now as Luke penned his gospel, he could understand this prophecy of destruction soon coming upon Jerusalem. Luke saw firsthand the emotional encounter of Paul and the Jews of Rome. He heard the apostle's condemnation: "The heart of this people has become dull. . . ." (Acts 28:27).

In Luke's account of the Olivet Discourse, he begins, as does Matthew, with a warning of the Tribulation events (21:5–11). But at 21:12, Luke takes a sidetrack by reporting these words of Christ: "But *before all these things*, they will lay their hands on you and will persecute you, delivering you to the synagogues and prisons, . . ." Note the word *before* would mean before the Tribulation. How long before, none of the disciples knew. Luke then brings in Jesus' words about Jerusalem: "But when you see Jerusalem surrounded by armies, then recognize that her desolation is at hand" (v. 20). He quotes the Lord's words about "great distress" and "wrath" to this people (v. 23). All of this He calls the "days of vengeance" (v. 22).

Luke concludes his "vengeance" section with "and Jerusalem will be trampled underfoot by the Gentiles until the times of the Gentiles be fulfilled" (v. 24). This vengeance section is inserted in the narration. Verse 25 continues the description of tribulational cosmic disturbance so dramatically portrayed by Christ:

Tribulation

- "There will be great earthquakes, . . . great signs from heaven" (21:11).

Destruction of Jerusalem

- "But before all these things, they will lay their hands on you and will persecute you" (v. 12a).
- "It will lead to an opportunity for your testimony" (v. 13).
- "When you see Jerusalem surrounded by armies, . . . recognize that her desolation is at hand" (v. 20).
- "These are days of vengeance, in order that all things which are written may be fulfilled" (v. 22).
- "There will be great distress upon the land, and wrath to this people" (v. 23b).
- "Jerusalem will be trampled underfoot by the Gentiles until the times of the Gentiles be fulfilled" (v. 24b).

Return to Tribulation

- "There will be signs in sun and moon *and stars*" (v. 25a).
- "The powers of the heavens will be shaken" (v. 26b).

Second Coming of Christ

- "Then shall they see the Son of Man coming in a cloud with power and great glory" (v. 27).

The Jerusalem destruction and vengeance section, then, is verses 12–24. This could very well tie into the close of the book of Acts in which Paul says, "The Holy Spirit rightly spoke through Isaiah the prophet to your fathers, saying, 'Go to this people and say, "You will keep on hearing, but will not understand"'" (28:25b–26a). The book of Acts then closes with "this salvation of God has been sent to the Gentiles; they will also listen" (v. 28).

The Greek word for "vengeance or punishment" *(ekdikasis)*[31] comes from the verb *dikaioō*, often translated "justify, do justice, vindicate."[32] With the preposition *ek*, the word carries the thought of "justice coming forth" as retribution in response to some specific crime. Fourteen times in the New Testament the verb and the noun are translated as "vengeance" or "revenge."

God is bringing upon Israel revenge for her harsh rejection of the gospel. With the witness of the apostles and of the thousands of Jews who had accepted Christ as Savior and had suffered great persecution for their faith, the children of Israel of that generation built a mountain of wrath that would come down upon their heads in 70. The Jews were not at war with just Christians; they were at war with the Lord! And "God's vengeance on his enemies is a compensation for those who suffer persecution."[33]

Some commentators see this vengeance alluded to in the book of Hosea, especially chapter nine. The prophet writes, "The days of punishment have come, the days of retribution have come; . . . because of the grossness of your iniquity, and because your hostility is so great" (9:7). With a dispersion in mind, Hosea cries, "My God will cast them away because they have not listened to Him; and they will be wandering among the nations" (v. 17).

Could it be that the book of Acts demonstrates this "vengeance" of which Hosea and other prophets speak? Henry Alford writes of the distinct result of "the divine anger, as that which shall befall this nation [of Israel]."[34] Albert Barnes adds:

> Judgment had been threatened by almost all the prophets against [Jerusalem]. They had spoken of its crimes and threatened its ruin. Once God had destroyed Jerusalem and carried the people to Babylon; but their crimes had been repeated when they returned, and God had again threatened their ruin.[35]

Lenski notes that the word *vengeance* has the thought of "the handing out of justice."[36] It is the vindication or retribution for the sin of unbelief and for Jerusalem's crimes against the gospel and for "her complete and final rejection by God."[37]

Chapter 2

THE CHURCH AND THE BOOK OF ACTS

The Beginning of the Church

The Jewish Feast of Pentecost

The significant events recorded in Acts 2 took place on the Jewish festival day of Pentecost. The term *pentecost (pentekostos)* is the Greek word for "fiftieth." This festival was celebrated on the fiftieth day after the presentation to the Lord of the first sheaf of grain of the spring harvest.

Before 70, the fifty days were reckoned from the first Sunday after the Passover feast. This method of reckoning would always place the feast of Pentecost on a Sunday, which therefore establishes the coming of the Holy Spirit and the beginning of the church in Acts 2 on a Sunday.

In the Old Testament this feast is spoken of in a number of places with a variety of names. It is referred to as the "feast of weeks" in Exodus 34:22 and Deuteronomy 16:10; it is called the "feast of harvest" in Exodus 23:16; and it is known as the "day of the firstfruits" in Numbers 28:26. The celebration is most often referred to as the Feast of Weeks (Heb. *shavuot*). This festival was, therefore, initially a national spring harvest celebration. In later Judaism it became the anniversary of the giving of the law to Moses at Mount Sinai, which is not an unreasonable possibility in light of the time notation given in Exodus 19:1.

The Day of Pentecost in Acts 2

When the Lord Jesus ascended to heaven ten days before Pentecost, He commanded the apostles to wait in Jerusalem until He had sent to them the promised "Helper," the Holy Spirit (John 14:16–17, 26; 16:7–15). Earlier in His ministry Jesus had clearly stated that the Holy Spirit would not be given until He Himself was glorified (John 7:37–39). The Spirit's unique presence and ministries were absolutely essential for the fulfilling of the commission to go into the world and make disciples from all of the nations. Without the presence and power of the Holy Spirit with them, the apostles would be unable to obey Christ's command and their efforts would have ended in failure. With a total of 120 people, the apostles waited and prayed for the next ten days after the Ascension of Christ. While the Lord Jesus did not specifically state that the Spirit would be sent at the festival of Pentecost, the apostles seem to be expecting something to happen on that day, as Acts 2:1 might read: "And when the day of Pentecost was finally come." But, whether they anticipated something happening on the day of Pentecost, great events did happen that day.

The Beginning of the Church

First, the church of Jesus Christ began on Pentecost. Until the Holy Spirit came that day with His new and expanded ministries, the church did not exist. It could not exist until the Head of the body, Jesus Christ, had risen from the dead, ascended to heaven and had sent the Holy Spirit (Eph. 1:22–23). According to the apostle Paul, a believer enters into the church, the body of Christ, through the Spirit's ministry of baptism (1 Cor. 12:12–13). That ministry of the Holy Spirit had not existed.

Before He ascended to heaven, the Lord Jesus promised that the apostles and the other believers would be baptized by the Holy Spirit in just a few days (Acts 1:5). Although this baptizing work of the Holy Spirit is not specifically mentioned in the Acts 2 account, it is certain from Acts 11:15–16 that such a ministry did occur for the first time on Pentecost.

Therefore, on Pentecost the apostles and all other believers in Jesus Christ were placed into the church. Since this is the very first occurrence of the Spirit's work of baptism (placing individuals into the body of Christ) and since there is no other way of entering the church, this is the beginning of Christ's church.

Since the initial baptizing work of the Spirit on Pentecost, all who believe in Jesus Christ as Savior are baptized by the Holy Spirit at the moment they are regenerated by the Spirit. There is no genuine believer in Christ who has not been baptized by the Holy Spirit.

The Coming of the Spirit

Second, on Pentecost the Holy Spirit came to fulfill His new role and ministries. Being omnipresent, the Holy Spirit was always present and active in the world. Through the lens of the New Testament, His activities in the Old Testament can be observed. But if the Holy Spirit has always been at work in the world, what did Jesus mean when He told the apostles in the upper room that He would send the Spirit? The Spirit would come in the sense of having new ministries related to the church (such as baptism), as well as expanded ministries to believers in Christ (such a permanent, universal indwelling). So on the day of Pentecost the Holy Spirit came in the sense of beginning in His new role in relationship to the church.

The Signs of the Spirit

A practical problem for the apostles was how to know when the Holy Spirit had really come. Since the Spirit is invisible, how would the apostles and the rest of the 120 believers know for sure that He had indeed come? It could not rest on the feeling of one person or on the testimony of several or the speculations of a small group. His coming had to be clear, objective, and unmistakable to the senses of all who were there. And so it was.

According to Acts 2:1–4, there were four evidences that the Spirit had come.

1. The sound of a violent wind was heard.
2. "Tongues like fire" were observed resting on each person.
3. Each believer was filled with the Holy Spirit.
4. They spoke in other languages.

It should be noted that Christ sent the Holy Spirit into the world just once. What happened on Pentecost is not repeated. This introduction of the Holy Spirit is not the normal pattern for the church.

Rushing Wind

The first evidence that the Holy Spirit had come was the sound like a violent, rushing wind. The sound was so great that it "filled the whole house" where the believers had gathered. The Spirit's work of regeneration was symbolized by the wind in Ezekiel's vision of the dry bones (Ezek. 37:1–14). In that vision, Ezekiel prophesied to a valley filled with dry bones representing the nation of Israel. As he spoke, the bones came together and a skeleton was made. Then flesh grew on the bones and a lifeless corpse could be seen. Ezekiel then prophesied to the wind and called it to blow on the bodies.

This wind (the Spirit of God) was seen as the life-giving breath of God filling Israel and giving it spiritual life. Most likely, this vision of Ezekiel was in Jesus' mind as He spoke with Nicodemus about the need to be born by means of the Spirit picturing the Spirit's work like the wind (John 3:8). Jesus then chided Nicodemus for being a notable teacher in Israel and yet not understanding this basic truth from the Old Testament (John 3:10).

Tongues of Fire

The Spirit's coming was visual as well as audible. The various languages spread as a rapidly moving fire across all those gathered. People were hearing the gospel in their own language. Fire denotes the divine presence as in the burning bush experience (Exod. 3:2–5).

Filling with the Spirit

Each person in the room was filled. This evidence of the Holy Spirit's coming was probably less obvious than the first two but was real and identifiable nevertheless. "Filling" with the Spirit simply means that they were all controlled by the Holy Spirit. In the New Testament, there are two works of the Spirit. The main kind of filling has to do with progressive controlling of the believer as he yields to the Lord (Eph. 5:18). This is a progressive, lifelong activity for the believer.

A second kind of filling has to do with the Spirit's temporary controlling of a person for unique ministry situations. This is seen in a number of places in the book of Acts and was apparently indicated by unusual boldness and wisdom in difficult ministry situations (e.g., 4:8, 31; 13:9). This filling can be repeated, as is seen in the case when Peter was controlled by the Spirit on Pentecost and then in other ministry situations. This was the filling that took place on Pentecost. Though less obvious to the senses, the Spirit's presence would have been seen in a new attitude of boldness toward the task at hand (similar to Acts 4:31). Those present would have recognized this change amongst those in their gathering. Though it is not clear, it may be that this filling in preparation for the upcoming ministry situation was also evidenced in their ability to speak in tongues. But it should be noted that nowhere else are filling and speaking in tongues connected.

Speaking in Other Languages

Speaking in other languages was an evidence of the Holy Spirit's coming. There is some debate over whether only the apostles spoke in tongues. The text is not clear. But since the purpose of tongues speaking at this instance was to validate the arrival of the Holy Spirit, and since all 120 experienced the first three evidences, it seems reasonable to assume that all 120 in the room not only heard the tongues speaking but also spoke in tongues.

This supernatural ability to speak in tongues was yet another confirmation that the Holy Spirit had come in His new role. But of these four evidences of the Holy Spirit's coming, the speaking in tongues has generated the most controversy. In order to arrive at some conclusions regarding what took place on the day of Pentecost in the matter of the tongues speaking, it is important to define the gift and understand why it was given.

What Is Speaking in Tongues?

The ability to speak in tongues was the ability to speak in known human languages that were unknown to the speaker. This definition is arrived at by noting that the word for tongue (glōssa) is used in the New Testament for the physical organ of the tongue, but it frequently refers to language or speech. At the first manifestation of the gift in Acts 2, Luke carefully described the nature of the gift. When he stated that they "began to speak with other tongues" (Acts 2:4), he used the normal word for language (glōssa). He underscored that known human languages were involved when he used the word dialect (dialektos) and then proceeded to tell his readers what languages were being spoken (vv. 6, 8).

Those who heard the tongues speaking on the day of Pentecost were Jews who had been part of the great dispersion of Israel. These had returned to the city of Jerusalem from many parts of the world to celebrate the feast of Pentecost. These Jews, expecting to hear Hebrew and Aramaic, were amazed to hear unschooled Galileans speaking Gentile languages fluently. According to Luke, every person was amazed by the phenomenon because "they were each one hearing them speak in his own language" (2:6). These languages were from almost every part of the Gentile world, both major languages and dialects. These Jews heard that day known languages, not ecstatic utterances.

From the words used and from the context itself, it is abundantly clear that the tongues speaking in Acts 2 had to do with known human languages that were unknown to the ones who spoke. It is a solid rule of biblical interpretation that the meaning of clear passages must determine the meanings in obscure passages. Acts 2 is a passage which clearly describes the gift of tongues.

The matter of tongues speaking is not really dealt with a great deal in the Scriptures. Luke in the book of Acts and Paul in the book of 1 Corinthians give our pertinent information on this phenomenon. The only other passage where tongues is specifically mentioned is Mark 16, where it is said that believers would speak with "new tongues." Robert Gromacki observes:

> Assuming that the passage is genuine, the usage of the adjective kainos rather than its synonym neos is noteworthy . . . kainos refers to the new primarily in reference to quality . . . whereas neos refers to the recent. It is admitted by all that the phenomenon of speaking in tongues did not occur in the Old Testament or Gospel periods and that it first happened on the day of Pentecost (Acts 2). Therefore, if speaking in tongues had involved unknown languages never spoken before, Christ would have used neos (new in time).

But since He used *kainos*, this must refer to foreign languages which were new to the speaker, but which had been in existence before.[1]

What About Ecstatic Utterances?

Our understanding of tongues comes from Luke and Paul. Both use *glōssa* for the gift of tongues. Luke and Paul were close companions and laborers for Christ for many years. Both used the same word to describe the same gift. There is no evidence that their definitions of *glōssa* differed in any way. And there is no evidence that the tongues speaking that occurred on the day of Pentecost differed from the tongues speaking that took place at Corinth. Tongues were known human languages.

Since Acts 2 is the first place where the phenomenon occurs, and it is described in detail there, and since there is no further definition or description later on, it must be concluded that the gift of tongues is the supernatural ability to speak in a human language that is unknown to the speaker.

It has been suggested that Paul allows for a second kind of tongues when he speaks of the "tongues of angels," that is, ecstatic utterances (1 Cor. 13:1). However, the word *glōssa* is not used to speak of ecstatic utterances in any other place, and such a definition here would be against the established meaning of the word. Even if *glōssa* were used of ecstatic utterances, that does not establish the fact that this is what is meant by the tongues of angels. That would be a rather large leap in logic because we do not know if angels speak in a language that is significantly different from human languages. Could it be that they speak in one of our *human languages?*

Anytime angels speak in the Bible it is in a language that is known to the human hearers, even in the case of the apostle John, who heard them speak in heaven in the book of Revelation. Furthermore, it must be remembered that the apostle Paul is using hyperbole (hypothetical exaggeration) in 1 Corinthians 13. In that chapter, he is simply emphasizing the essential place of love in the use of spiritual gifts. He states that, even if he knew everything or gave his body to be burned and he did it without love, then such matters would be without value.

The fact of the matter is that Paul did not know everything, did not give his body to be burned, and did not speak in an angelic language. It is unwise to build a doctrinal position on hypothetical exaggeration, particularly when it makes one go against the established meaning of words. It is best to conclude that the gift of tongues is the ability to speak in known human languages which are unknown to the speaker and to avoid the inclusion of ecstatic utterances in the definition.

Was Tongues Speaking a Sign?

Once it is seen that the gift of tongues has to do with known human languages and not ecstatic utterances, then the purpose can be more easily discerned. As Acts 2 is the only place in the Scriptures where tongues is defined, so 1 Corinthians 14 is the only place in the Scriptures where the purpose of tongues is discussed. Here Paul taught the Corinthian church that prophecy was a greater gift than tongues because the church could be edified through prophecy. He noted that when the church assembles together everything should be done for the purpose of edification (1 Cor. 14:26).

In the midst of this discussion concerning what is best for the church when it meets together, he instructed them regarding the purpose for the gift of tongues (1 Cor. 14:20–22). He evidently suspected that some of the Corinthian believers would not respond in a positive way to his teaching on tongues, so he began this segment with an exhortation for them to be mature in their thinking. In 14:22, he told them that the gift of tongues actually functioned as a sign, rather than as a means of edification. Since tongues were given as a sign, this raises two important questions: (1) To whom are tongues a sign? and (2) Of what are tongues a sign? In seeking to understand the purpose of the gift, it is necessary to answer these two questions.

First, to what people are tongues given as a sign? The text clearly states that tongues are a sign to unbelievers (14:22). So it would seem that the apostle rules out the gift of tongues as a sign to Christians that might indicate anything about their spirituality, blessing, or fellowship with God. It is instead, he says, a sign to unbelievers. One would assume that any and all unbelievers were the subject if Paul had not narrowed it by quoting from the prophet Isaiah. Specifically, tongues speaking is a sign for the unbeliever who is an Israelite. This conclusion is based on Paul's focus on "this people" (14:21). He quotes Isaiah 28:11, which in context is speaking to the unbelieving nation of Israel. The nation of Israel again and again had heard the Lord's word spoken to them in the Hebrew language but had not paid attention. The Lord would now speak to them in the language of foreigners. In his commentary on the book of Isaiah, Edward J. Young writes:

> God will speak to the nation in a language that it does not know. They had regarded His speaking through the prophet as so much nonsense; as a matter of fact, He would now speak to them in such a way that they would not understand, but would only hear sounds which seem to them as vain babblings. It is probably correct to see here a reference to the coming of the Assyrians, whose language, naturally, the Judahites would not understand . . . The thought then is that God will speak to Judah by means of people who speak a language different from that of the Jews. . . . It will be a message directed to "this people." In this designation we are brought again in memory to the commission which God had given to the prophet. When he speaks to "this people" they will not hear. They mock his words, confident in their own wisdom, and for that reason God

will speak to "this people" by means of a language or tongue that they will not understand. From this point on Judah is to come under the domination of foreign peoples. In speaking to the people in a tongue which they do not understand, the Lord is not acting capriciously, for He had already spoken in clear tones to them, pointing out the true way to peace and rest.[2]

In understanding Paul's statement on the purpose of tongues, it is important to realize that tongues are not a sign to believers, nor are they a sign to unbelievers generally. Specifically, they are a sign to unbelievers in the nation of Israel. It is to this special group of people that tongues are a sign.

What do tongues signify? It is usually thought that tongues signal blessing or God's favor. But the Old Testament reveals that the opposite is true. The languages of foreigners had special significance to the nation of Israel. In Deuteronomy 28:49 God warned Israel that disobedience would bring discipline, such as drought or plagues. But if Israel refused to respond to these disciplinary actions and repent, then a final discipline would take place. Foreign nations would conquer them. They would hear the language of foreigners. Isaiah built on this basic truth from the Mosaic law code when he warned Israel and Judah in his day. He warned that since they would not listen to *God's voice spoken through* Hebrew-speaking prophets, they would certainly listen when foreigners invaded the land and "spoke" to them in their unintelligible tongues.

Hence, rejecting the words of God which bring repose, they are willing to obey the words of those who speak another tongue, and whose yoke is not easy nor their burden light. Thus, the unbelieving, ungrateful nation hastens on to the destruction, which, by its own apostasy, it has invited.[3]

Isaiah's words were fulfilled when Assyria took Israel captive and Babylon subjugated Judah. This Old Testament context is a key to understanding the phenomenon of tongues speaking. Tongue speaking had Old Testament roots, something the Corinthian believers did not understand. So Paul taught the Corinthian Christians that tongues were a sign of coming judgment on unbelieving Israel.

Tongues and a Warning

In the Old Testament God always extended warning and grace to Israel before bringing judgment. The same was true in the New Testament. The nation of Israel in the days of Christ once again demonstrated a hardened heart of unbelief. The message from God came in power and with great clarity from Messiah Himself. But Israel did the unthinkable. They rejected their own Messiah and participated in His murder, refusing to accept His marvelous words and mighty authenticating miracles.

In light of Israel's willful rejection and terrible unbelief, Jesus pronounced judgment on that generation of Israel (cf. Matt. 23:33–39). He declared that they were more wicked than their ancestors and they would be judged. Judgment did indeed come on that generation, but this time God's rod of discipline was the Roman Empire. On Pentecost, when the speaking in tongues first appeared, Peter not only preached to the Jewish people that Jesus was the Messiah but also warned them to separate themselves from that condemned generation (Acts 2:40). The tongues were a gracious sign of warning to Israel that judgment was on its way. Judgment did come in 66–73 in the Roman wars, and Israel once again heard the tongues of foreigners.

Paul's Use of Tongues

So why did Paul use the gift of tongues so extensively? Understanding its purpose as a sign of coming judgment to unbelieving Israel, he probably used it in synagogue after synagogue as he traveled over the world in Jewish evangelism. God graciously gave him the ability to speak in the native tongue of the area which would serve as a powerful sign to the Jews living there. It would be a sign with roots in the Old Testament. Paul's hearers should have understood the significance. In that context it fits the expressed purpose of the gift and, furthermore, it was yet another sign to the Jews who were constantly looking for authenticating signs (1 Cor. 1:22). For further discussion of the work of the Holy Spirit, see part 2 of this book, "A Theology of the Holy Spirit in Acts" and "The Works of the Holy Spirit in Acts."

The Organized Church in Acts

Apostles

After Jesus' earthly ministry and ascension, the most important individuals left to carry on His work in the world were the apostles. The establishing of the church, the reception of the church's doctrine, and the spread of the gospel of Christ were largely dependent on the apostles. Since the apostles cast such a large shadow over the New Testament, it is essential to understand what we can about them and the ministry that was given to them.

What Is an Apostle?

The Greek word apostolos simply means "one sent forth." In older Greek literature it was a maritime or military term. A naval fleet dispatched on some expedition was called "the apostle." But in the Greek world before the New Testament the term was never used of a personal representative or emissary. Numerous terms were used for religious messengers or representatives, but apostle was not one of them.

When Jesus selected twelve men to associate closely with Him and to represent Him, He gave them the title *apostles*. Jesus clearly did not borrow the word from current Greek thought. And yet it does not seem that Jesus was using this term in an entirely new way. The evidence is that He was simply adopting a word then in current use among the Jews. The Jewish use of *apostle* carried with it the idea of one who was an official delegate of another. That usage is well known from literature after the fall of Jerusalem. But since it is highly unlikely that they borrowed it from the hated Christians, it was probably in use in Jesus' day. Likely He simply adopted a familiar term. In Jewish usage, an apostle held a highly responsible position with power and authority to act for the sender.[4] And while this context is valuable to our understanding, it is the use of the word in the New Testament that decisively establishes its meaning and theological significance in relationship to the church.

From the almost eighty uses of the word "apostle" (mainly by Luke and Paul), it can be concluded that an apostle was one sent with authority to represent another.[5] The word carries with it the idea of a special commission and special empowerment as one spoke and acted with the authority of the sender. The apostles of Christ were granted great power and authority, with which they authenticated their message and laid the foundation of Christ's church (Luke 9:1–6; 2 Cor. 12:12).

So an apostle is one sent by Christ with authority to represent Him. In passing, it should be noted that an apostle is distinct from a disciple. While it is true that the words were used of the same individuals, they are not synonymous. A disciple *(mathētēs)* is simply a "follower or learner." Jesus had thousands of disciples, and it was from among His many disciples that He selected the twelve apostles (Luke 6:12–13).

The Twelve Apostles

When Jesus established the office of apostle, He selected twelve men to fill it. These twelve men had been with Him since the days of John the Baptist and had, therefore, seen Jesus' miraculous works and heard His insightful and authoritative teachings. Each would be a witness of His resurrection (Acts 1:22–23). The twelve apostles are listed in four different passages of Scripture (Matt. 10:2–4; Mark 3:16–19; Luke 6:14–16; Acts 1:13).

The ranks of the Twelve were soon reduced to eleven with the defection and death of the traitor, Judas Iscariot. After the ascension of Christ it was the clear conviction of Peter and the others that this vacancy needed to be filled immediately. They saw it as a subject of Old Testament prophecy (Acts 1:16–26; cf. Pss. 69:25; 109:8). Two qualified men who had seen the resurrected Christ and had been with Jesus from the beginning of His ministry were set forth as possible replacements. The apostles left the decision to the Lord in the casting of lots, and Matthias was chosen to replace Judas Iscariot.

It has been the opinion of some that Paul, not Matthias, was truly God's choice to the be twelfth apostle. But Paul never claimed to be one of the Twelve. Rather, he viewed his apostleship as distinct (cf. Gal. 1:11–17; 2:2–9). Also, it is difficult to believe that Peter and the rest of the apostles would have made such a bold move in replacing Judas Iscariot simply on their own initiative. Instead, they saw their action as a fulfillment of Scripture, which would seem to suggest that this was something the Lord Jesus instructed them to do.

The Apostle Paul

Though not one of the Twelve, Paul must be seen as a true apostle of Jesus Christ. Clearly and forcefully he declared that he was an apostle, equal in authority with the Twelve (1 Cor. 1:1; 9:1–5; 2 Cor. 1:1; 11:5; Gal. 1:1–2:15; 2 Tim. 1:1, 11). Luke also presented Paul as a true apostle of Jesus Christ. Luke, who had spoken often of the twelve apostles, did not restrict the use of the word *apostle* to just the Twelve but expanded it to include Paul (e.g., Acts 14:4, 14).

Although Paul did not accompany Jesus during His ministry (which was a requirement to be one of the Twelve), he did see the resurrected Lord Jesus. Paul did not have a vision on the Damascus Road but actually saw the risen Christ that day (cf. Acts 9:3–7, 17; 22:6–9; 26:12–16; 1 Cor. 15:8). Although he was untimely born (1 Cor. 15:8), he nevertheless was a true apostle of Christ.

Other Apostles

The term *apostle* attaches to others as well. They may not have been as prominent as Paul or the Twelve, but that does not automatically mean that they held an inferior rank. Other factors are involved in making such a determination. One such individual who is classified as an apostle is Barnabas.

As Luke records the missionary activity of the early church, he refers to Barnabas and Paul as apostles, treating them as equals. In fact, Luke places Barnabas ahead of Paul in his discussion (cf. Acts 14:4, 14). Later on, Paul himself sees Barnabas as an associate in his apostleship to the Gentiles (cf. Gal. 2:1–9) and as one holding the office of apostle (cf. 1 Cor. 9:5–6).

Another possible apostle is James, the Lord's brother. James became a prominent part of the Jerusalem church and seems to be included by Paul in the ranks of the apostles as an equal with Peter (cf. Gal. 1:19). James is individually mentioned as one eyewitness of the resurrection of Christ but, at the same time, he is also included in the group of apostles (1 Cor. 15:7). James could have been like Paul in that he was an apostle who was untimely born (1 Cor. 15:8).

It is quite likely that the term was applied to many others besides these fifteen. If the concept was restricted to just these men, why were early churches fooled by some who claimed to be apostles but were not. That there were false apostles who brought confusion into the church is seen in several passages (2 Cor. 11:13–15; Rev. 2:2). The early church apparently allowed for some flexibility in the use of the term, although Paul and the Twelve seem to be especially esteemed as apostles of Christ.

The Scriptures speak of the "gift" of an apostle (Eph. 4:11), which also seems to suggest a larger group than Paul and the Twelve. Paul uses the term to describe Junia and Andronicus (Rom. 16:7) and the Lord's brothers (1 Cor. 9:5). However, in regards to these individuals the word is apparently used in a broader sense of being authorized messengers of the churches (see 2 Cor. 8:23; Phil. 2:25).

A case can be built that these are apostles in the sense of being authorized messengers of the churches but not authoritative representatives of Jesus Christ (like the Twelve). These individuals certainly did not have the same influence or status as Paul and the Twelve.

The Extent of the Apostolic Office

What were the requirements for those apostles who had official authority? Several things had to be true before one could legitimately claim to be an apostle of Jesus Christ. First, they had to have been called by Christ Himself. The very idea of one being an authoritative representative of another would point to this. The direct hand of the Lord is seen in the selection of the Twelve (Luke 6:12–13), the choice of Paul (1 Cor. 15:8; Gal. 1:1), and the replacement of Judas by Matthias (Acts 1:21–26). Of course, without any scriptural verification it can only be speculated whether this was true of Barnabas and James, the Lord's brother.

Second, it was necessary that an apostle actually saw the resurrected Lord Jesus. Since the resurrection of Christ is foundational to the faith, he had to be able to testify from firsthand knowledge to this fundamental reality (Acts 1:21–23; 1 Cor. 9:1; 15:7–9).

Third, he had to be able to demonstrate the "signs of a true apostle," which was the ability to work miracles and demonstrate works of power (Matt. 28:18–20; Acts 2:43; 5:12; 2 Cor. 12:12; Heb. 2:4). These demonstrations of power validated the claim that they were authoritative representatives of the Lord Christ.

There is no compelling evidence for the idea of apostolic succession. The only apostle who was ever replaced was Judas Iscariot by Matthias and that was necessary to complete the ranks of the Twelve (cf. Matt. 19:28; Rev. 21:14). Later when James, who was one of the Twelve, was put to death by Herod Agrippa I (Acts 12:1–2), the church did not replace him. And there is no record of any other apostle being succeeded at death.

If apostolic succession was required and needed, Paul, for example, certainly would have addressed the crucial matter of his apostolic replacement when he clearly was facing death (2 Tim. 4), but he does not even hint at such a thing. It also should be noted that, in light of the requirements for a true apostle, no one after the first century could qualify. No one since that time has seen the risen Christ, and no one could have been with the Lord Jesus during His earthly ministry. Also, it must be remembered that one who claims the office of an apostle must be able to work the supernatural signs of a true apostle. The inability to perform sign miracles clearly shows that such claims are false.

So it is necessary to conclude that there are no apostles in the church today. Nor are any needed, for their work was foundational in nature. Theirs was a gift and a ministry of establishing the church and its doctrine (John 14:26; 16:12–13; Eph. 2:20). Once the church had been established on a proper foundation and the Scriptures for the church had been given and authenticated, the foundational ministry was completed. These facts should caution us not to dilute the concept of an apostle by viewing those who do missionary work today as modern apostles.

Did Peter occupy a primary place among the apostles? Jesus addressed Peter and said "upon this rock I will build My church" (Matt. 16:16–19). If one interprets the "rock" as a personal reference to Peter, the primacy of Peter has been taught. In an attempt to avoid this conclusion, some have suggested that the "rock" refers to Peter's great confession about Christ, while others have reasoned that it refers to Christ Himself. However, it is probably best to take the statement at face value as an actual reference to Peter.

But it is necessary to understand that the Lord extended the application beyond Peter to the other apostles (cf. Matt. 18:18; John 20:21–23). And Paul, in the progress of revelation, made it clear that the church would be built on all of the apostles, not just Peter (Eph. 2:20).

It is true that the Lord did have a special role for Peter in initially opening the door into the church, first to the Jewish nation, then to the Samaritans, and finally to the Gentiles (cf. Acts 2:5–47; 8:14–17; 10:1–48; 15:7). But the idea that Peter had a position as Christ's unique representative on earth was foreign to Peter and the rest of the apostles and is absent from the writings of the New Testament (e.g., Gal. 2:11–14; 1 Peter 5:1–5). In fact, at the Jerusalem Council (Acts 15), James, not Peter, played the more significant role.

Elders

Believers share a basic equality in Jesus Christ (Gal. 3:28). There are no superior or inferior members of Christ's church. The wonderful truth of the equality of our position in Christ, however, does not rule out the fact that there are different functions and positions established by the Lord of the church. In the church are offices which some occupy and others do not. The primary office of the local church is that of the elder.

The Elder in the New Testament Church

The first mention of the elder in the church (Acts 11:30) lacks any definition or description. This strongly suggests that already there was a clear understanding of the position and function. This understanding would have come from the association with the Jewish synagogue as well as from the role of the elder throughout the Old Testament. The first churches organizationally resembled the synagogue and were made up of Jewish believers and established by Jewish apostles. So the idea of an elder would have been common to all of them.

In the Old Testament, elders functioned in various leadership roles. They almost always functioned as a collegiate body or council, either of a tribe or a city or of a special group such as the priests. They were judges, counselors, and advisers who had a significant influence and authority in Israel. The "elders of the people" are shown in Scripture to have a strategic place in national life. While the term *elder* did point to men who were older in age, its focus was primarily on their maturity, which included great wisdom and important life experience (e.g., Exod. 3:16, 18; 19:7; 24:1,7; Deut. 19:12; 21:19; 22:16–18; 25:7; Josh. 24:31).

It can be concluded, therefore, that the concept and origin of the office of elder in the church was influenced by the Old Testament and by the synagogue. However, the church, which began on the Day of Pentecost, and the synagogue, with its roots back in the Old Testament, are distinct entities, and there are some differences between them. It is the general nature of the elder as one who guided with wisdom and led with authority that was brought into the church from the Jewish community.

Titles of the Office

The New Testament uses two words for the office of elder. The word *elder (presbyteros)* and *bishop* or *overseer (episkopos)* are used synonymously (cf. Acts 20:17, 28; Titus 1:5, 7; 1 Peter 5:1–2). The word *elder* emphasizes the maturity of the man, both in spiritual matters and life experience. This emphasis would be quite similar to that of the Jewish concept of elder derived from the Old Testament. The words *bishop* or *overseer* emphasize function, signifying guardianship over others and focusing on the general responsibility of the leader for spiritual oversight over the local church.

That these two words are used interchangeably shows us that bishop and elder do not describe different offices. The idea that these are two different offices began after the first century and is not supported by the use of the words in the New Testament.

A third word is often included in the discussion of this primary office of elder and that is the word *pastor (poimēn)*. This word focuses on the shepherding functioning of the elders' work (1 Peter 5:1–2). However, the word itself occurs only once and that in reference to the spiritual gift of pastor-teacher (Eph. 4:11). The term *pastor,* though in common usage in the church today, is not actually an interchangeable term with "elder" and "bishop."

A person could possess the spiritual gift of pastor-teacher and not hold the office of elder. Conversely, one could be an elder and not have the spiritual gift of pastor-teacher. However, all elders have a pastoral role as they shepherd the flock of God.

The Duties of Elders

There are four primary responsibilities of elders in the local church. First, they are to *give guidance*. Elders are leaders and leaders are to lead (1 Tim. 5:17; Heb. 13:7, 17; 1 Peter 5:1–3). It is the shepherds, not the sheep, who presumably have the spiritual wisdom and experience to give good direction to the church. This, of course, does not mean that they are to "lord it over" the church, but neither are they simply "representatives" of the people.

Second, the elders are to *teach* their people the Word of God (Acts 20:28; 1 Peter 5:1). "Feeding the flock" is a primary responsibility and activity of the elder, which is why one of his qualifications is that he must be "able to teach" (1 Tim. 3:2). Elders are not simply administrators but rather handlers of the Word of God. This does not mean that every elder must have the spiritual gift of teaching and be able effectively to teach large groups of people. It does mean that every elder knows the Scriptures and can bring them accurately to bear upon the issues facing the people in the church.

Third, the elders are to *protect* the flock from doctrinal error and from practical error (Acts 20:28–30; 2 Tim. 2:24–3:17; Titus 1:10–16). Once again, this assumes that an elder is knowledgeable of the Scriptures and thus able to detect that which is contrary to God's will and Word. Failure to detect error can have disastrous results for the church.

Fourth, the elders are to *have general oversight* of the life of the church. They are responsible for all that pertains to the life and ministry of the church (Acts 20:28). This does not mean that elders are to *do* everything but they are ultimately *responsible* for everything.

The Selection of Elders

According to Acts 20:28, elders are selected by the Holy Spirit for the responsibility of leading the church of Christ. The Lord is the Head of the church and He ultimately is the One who raises up its leaders.

Elders are to be selected and to serve on the basis of the qualifications set forth in the Scriptures. First Timothy 3 and Titus 1 give some twenty qualifications for elders.[6] As these qualifications are considered, several points need to be kept in mind. First, these are requirements that the Lord Himself established. The church cannot set them aside or replace them with others of its own choosing. This requires, of course, that the church know the requirements when selecting its elders.

Second, the church must realize that no man will ever fully and completely fulfill these requirements. In regard to these qualifications, no elder will ever reach full development or have a perfect balance. So while the standard must be viewed with all seriousness, a balance between the ideal and real life must be maintained.

Third, no one qualification is said to be more important than the rest. Paul, for example, does not say that "above all else, a man must have such and such qualification." The church has had the tendency to elevate some qualifications above others, but the text of Scripture does not do this.

Fourth, it is the current life of the elder that is to be kept in view, not his past. Paul states that an elder "must be" these things. He does not say that these things must always have been true. This is a significant point because past sins and inadequacies do not, therefore, remove one from the possibility of being an elder. If the past were in view, no one would ever qualify for the position of elder.

The New Testament is not clear on the actual guidelines for appointing elders. When elders were selected for the churches established on Paul's first missionary journey, it is said that Paul and Barnabas selected them (Acts 14:23). The word for select *(xeirotoneō)* in New Testament times simply meant "to select" or "to appoint." There is nothing in the word or in the passage which would indicate that the churches themselves participated in the appointments.

In Titus 1:5, Paul instructed Titus to "appoint" *(kathistēmi)* elders in every church. This word is used of the appointment of the high priest, where no election was involved (Heb. 5:1; 8:3). Clearly Titus was responsible for the job of selecting elders, but there is no indication of the process involved. It is also used of the selection of the seven men to help the apostles (Acts 6:3), where the apostles made the final decision after some involvement by the church. While democratic elections may seem normal to those raised in a democracy, it is not set forth in the New Testament.

The Number of Elders

James speaks of calling for the "elders of the church" when one was sick, which would seem to suggest that the call was being made to a plurality of elders in a single church (James 5:14). There are a number of other references which point to a plurality of elders in the church (cf. Acts 11:30; 15:2, 6, 22–23; 16:4; 20:17, 28; Phil. 1:1; 1 Thess. 5:12–13; 1 Tim. 5:17; Heb. 13:17; 1 Peter 5:1). Two scripture passages are in the singular (1 Tim. 3:1–2; Titus 1:5–7). In these passages, leadership qualifications are the subject, and when Paul speaks here of the elder in the singular, he is using a generic reference to the elder as type.

In discussing the matter of singularity or plurality of elders, it should also be remembered that the synagogue did set the pattern for the local church in a number of ways. Synagogues had a plurality of elders. Also, in the Old Testament a plurality of elders can be seen, since they always functioned as a council or a group. Elders are not shown to have authority individually.

The Authority of Elders

Responsibility and leadership require authority. Unless elders have authority, they could not possibly carry out their duties as required by the Scriptures. The Head of the church, Jesus Christ, has all authority (Matt. 28:18–20). He has delegated authority to those who are to carry out His will and His work. The purpose of this authority is preeminently to build up and strengthen those who are being led (2 Cor. 10:8; 13:10). It is also given to deal with sin and failure within the ranks of the church (2 Cor. 13:1–3). The authority of elders is pictured in the book of Revelation, where the twenty-four elders are seen sitting on thrones (e.g., 4:4; 5:8, 11, 14; thrones symbolize authority in the book of Revelation). Furthermore, in the Old Testament the elders of Israel clearly had authority.

The Lord Jesus taught that two kinds of leadership authority are needed for effective leadership. One kind of leadership authority comes from the position that is being occupied and the other is derived from serving others (Mark 10:35–45). When in balance, the best kind of leadership authority will be demonstrated.

Deacons

The title *deacon* is used in a great variety of ways in the church today. In some churches, one who is a deacon holds the most important governing position in the church, while in other churches deacon is a position without much authority and is clearly a lesser office.

In the New Testament, the word deacon *(diakonos)* means "servant." This word, along with the verb "to serve" *(diakoneō)* and the noun "service" *(diakonia),* is used about 100 times in the New Testament and is translated according to the general idea of serving or ministering.

The Origin of the Office

It is commonly thought that Acts 6 was the beginning of the office of deacon. In this passage, the apostles found themselves overwhelmed by the problem of distributing food for needy widows in the church. Recognizing that valuable time was being taken away from their praying and preaching, they recruited seven men to address this need and to relieve them of this burden. Were these the first deacons? Probably not. These men were called alongside the apostles to deal with a temporary crisis in the Jerusalem church.

We can probably say that Acts 6 provides a primitive model of church leadership that would be developed more fully later. Perhaps these seven can be considered prototypes of deacons. Some time during the next twenty years of the church's history, the office of deacon became part of the church's organizational structure.

The first clear reference to the office of deacon is found in Philippians 1:1 where the apostle Paul addresses the elders and the deacons of that church along with the rest of the believers. About two years after Paul wrote to the Philippians, he wrote to Timothy at Ephesus and gave the qualifications for one who would be a deacon in the church (1 Tim. 3:8–13). These letters were written in the early 60s and indicate that the position of the deacon was well known and well established in the church.

The Duties of the Office

There is considerable information concerning the elders' duties and responsibilities but little about the duties of the deacon. Traditionally, the office of deacon has been primarily concerned with the material needs and ministries of the church. This is based largely on the model found in the Acts 6 passage as well as the term *deacon* itself, which points back to the idea of waiting on tables. While ministry in the area of financial matters and material things is an appropriate realm for the deacon, it is probably unnecessary to restrict them to that kind of ministry.

The lack of precision in the Scriptures related to their responsibilities probably allows flexibility in their service. It would seem likely that the service and ministry of the deacon would be defined by the needs of the church as perceived by the elders. They would function as assistants to the elders and could serve in meeting the spiritual as well as the material needs of the assembly.

The Qualifications for the Office

The Scriptures require high standards for the deacon, as they do for the elder (1 Tim. 3:8–10, 12–13). Deacons also are to be spiritually mature, having been tested and approved in the experiences of life. They should manage their households and their own personal lives well and should be knowledgeable and committed to the truth of God. The main difference between the elder and the deacon has to do with being able to teach the Word of God. The ability to teach the Word is required of the elder but not of the deacon. Aside from this difference, it is clear that the qualifications were high for those who would be given the privilege and the responsibility to serve Christ as deacons in His church.

The Number of Deacons

The New Testament, as well as the practice of the early church, consistently points to a plurality of deacons in the church. Though some have argued that there should always be seven deacons (based on Acts 6), this unnecessarily restricts churches which differ greatly in size and ministry needs. There is no fixed number, but there is plurality.

Peter and the Keys of the Kingdom

Though it would be through the apostle Paul that the full meaning and revelation of the church would come, Jesus first uses the word in Matthew 16:18.

Not only is the term *church* (Gk. *ekklēsia*) first used here in the New Testament but also in its context it is used in the technical sense of the coming of the new dispensation of grace that would replace the dispensation of law.

In the context, the Lord is preparing His disciples for His coming death. "From that time Jesus Christ began to show His disciples that He must go to Jerusalem and suffer many things from the elders and chief priests and scribes, and be killed and be raised up on the third day" (Matt. 16:21). Just prior to that, He had asked His disciples, "Who do people say that the Son of Man is?" (v. 13). The phrase *Son of Man* means "The Son related to humankind." This is a powerful description of the Messiah, who would represent humanity in the presence of God the Father.

Peter answered the Lord first by saying, "Thou art the Christ, the Son of the living God" (v. 16). In these words Peter confirmed that he understood that Jesus was the Anointed King (the Christ) and that He was somehow related to deity ("the Son related to God," Ps. 2). The Lord then called Peter "blessed" because the Father in heaven had revealed these truths to him (v. 17).

Jesus then spoke these important words:

> And I also say to you that you are Peter, and upon this rock I will build My church; and the gates of Hades shall not overpower it. I will give you the keys of the kingdom of heaven; and whatever you shall bind on earth shall be bound in heaven, and whatever you shall loose on earth shall be loosed in heaven. (Matt. 16:18–19)

Before examining the various parts of these two verses, it is important to point out that Jesus raises two different subjects in the passage. The first subject has to do with Christ building His church; the second subject has to do with the kingdom of heaven. Grammatically, these two issues can be separated. *Church* in Matthew 16:18 and *kingdom* in verse 19 may not be identical in meaning.[7] Lenski says that these words become clearer when we note that "the keys" belong to the kingdom of heaven. This kingdom is not identical with "my church" in verse 18.[8] D. A. Carson concurs: "The two words belong to different concepts, the one to 'people' and the other to 'rule' or 'reign.'"[9]

By examining the passage carefully, one can easily see that two distinct subjects are in view: "I will build My church," and "I will give you the keys of the kingdom of heaven." One would think that somehow if the two were the same, the passage might read something like "I will build My church and give to you, Peter, its keys." Or, "My church is the kingdom I have been teaching about all along." Or still, "Peter, you will be the head over My kingdom, the church." But no such hint is given, either in this context or in the history of the founding of the church, recorded in the book of Acts.

To get a complete answer in regard to this passage of Scripture, it is helpful to ask a series of questions.

- Who or what is the "rock"?
- Who had a greater role in reaching the Gentiles at Rome?
- What is the "kingdom of heaven"?
- What do "binding" and "loosening" mean?
- What are the earliest views about the passage in the early church?
- What has been the most common Roman Catholic view of Matthew 16?
- What are the changing Roman Catholic views of Matthew 16?

Who or What Is the "Rock"?

Peter's name, *Petros*, is a masculine word in Greek. The phrase "upon this the rock [*petra*]" is actually feminine. Jesus in no way is calling Peter "the girl rock"! Notice that "this the" is feminine. This must be referring back to something already said, but it certainly is not pointing back to the disciple Peter! It must also be pointed out, however, that the feminine form of "rock" can be referring to something said or indicated that in itself is not feminine. The most logical explanation is that it refers to Peter's statement, "Thou art the Christ, the Son of the living God" (v. 16). Jesus acknowledges Peter's words, "flesh and blood did not reveal this to you, but My Father who is in heaven" (v. 17).

> Jesus purposely uses two Greek words which, though not identical, are closely related in meaning. What he said was, "You are petros, and upon this petra I will build my church," meaning, "You are a rock, and upon the rocky ledge (or cliff) of the Christ, 'the Son of God the living' who was revealed to you and whom you confessed, I will build my church." If Jesus had intended to convey the thought that he was going to build his church on Peter he would have said, "and on you I will build my church."[10]

Conclusion: the church is to be built upon the person of Christ, not upon the disciple Peter.

Who Had a Greater Role in Rome?

Since Rome was the capital of the Gentile world, the question is raised as to the primacy of Peter in that city. Paul makes it continually clear in his writings that he was the apostle sent to the pagan world. This, of course, does not mean that Paul and Peter ministered exclusively to the two different groups, Jews and Gentiles. Many times in the ministry of Paul he was witnessing to his Jewish brothers. Likewise, Peter often found himself sharing the gospel with Gentiles.

But since the early church was made up of more Gentiles than Jews, one would expect Paul to be the head of the church, if God had so appointed a human figure to hold that position. After Paul's first missionary journey, he shared with the church at Antioch how God used him to open a "door of faith to the Gentiles" (Acts 14:27), and that by his mouth the Gentiles "should hear the word of the gospel, and believe" (15:7).

When the Jews refused the truth at Corinth, Paul swore that from then on he would go to the Gentiles with the truth of Jesus (18:6). The Lord Himself had told the apostle, "I will send you far away to the Gentiles" (22:21). Paul made it clear he was the apostle to the Gentiles (Rom. 11:13). In contrast, Peter makes it clear that his primary role was among the Jews, though scattered over the known world (1 Peter 1:1).

If Peter was to be the head of the church, as Roman Catholicism contends, why is this not mentioned elsewhere in the development of the New Testament? Observes Edward Denny, when Paul writes of Christ as the Head of the church, "He makes no mention of any visible head; had one been appointed by Christ he would have been of necessity compelled to mention here the fact."[11] Denny continues,

> St. Paul throughout his teaching as to the Unity of the Body, which is the Church, never in the remotest way alludes to any necessity for there being a visible head to that portion of the mystical Christ which is here on earth. . . .
>
> Further, that St. Paul, *the* Apostle, as he is designated by the Fathers, for example, by St. Augustine and St. Chrysostom, was entirely ignorant of the existence in the Church of any office superior to that which he held himself, . . .
>
> Moreover, when the Acts of the Apostles is examined there is no reference, explicit or implicit, to any visible Head of the Church, who as Supreme Pastor governed the Church.[12]

What Is the "Kingdom of Heaven"?

In almost all instances, the expressions *kingdom of God* and *kingdom of heaven* refer to the coming millennial reign of Christ on earth. That this kingdom then goes on into eternity following the one-thousand-year reign of Christ is agreed upon by most dispensationalists. The focus of the *kingdom-of-God* issue can be discovered in the Gospels. John, Mark, and Luke use the expression *kingdom of God* exclusively. Yet Matthew used the phrase *kingdom of heaven* some thirty times and *kingdom of God* only three times.

In the view of most premillennialists and dispensationalists, the two expressions clearly point to the Davidic covenant and the millennial reign of David's Son, Jesus the Messiah! For example, David points out, "[The Lord] has chosen my son Solomon to sit on the throne of the kingdom of the Lord over Israel" (1 Chron. 28:6b). And Christ will come through Solomon's line. Though it is the Lord's kingdom (29:11), it is still bequeathed to David's sons and established forever (28:7–8).

Since Peter will help launch the church in Acts 2, what does it mean that he will be given the keys to the kingdom of heaven, especially since that kingdom is not the church? Isaiah 22:20–23, a passage not directly related to the issue, may shed some light on the question.

As Israel faces the terror of the Assyrians during the kingship of Judah's king Hezekiah (approx. 701 B.C.), Isaiah the prophet points out that God would place his servant Eliakim in Jerusalem with a certain great prophetic spiritual authority. "He will become [like] a father to the inhabitants of Jerusalem and to the house of Judah. Then I will set the key of the house of David on his shoulder, when he opens no one will shut, when he shuts no one will open" (vv. 21–22).

Almost exactly like Eliakim, Peter would be given a certain open-ended authority over the city of Jerusalem and over the people of Judah, in regard to an issue of judgment in their acceptance and rejection of the gospel message. This authority, if it can be called that, also reflects upon great issues with the house of David and the kingly line. After all, it was Israel's king that was crucified by His own people for their own sins. As Peter preached, the people made judgments against the kingdom and their king.

For example, Peter cried out to the people of Jerusalem, "Repent, . . . that your sins may be wiped away, in order that times of refreshing may come from the presence of the Lord; and that He may send Jesus, the Christ appointed for you, whom heaven must receive until the period of restoration of all things about which God spoke by the mouth of His holy prophets . . ." (Acts 3:19–21).

This is clearly a kingdom offer, though Peter certainly did not know God's timetable for the coming millennial reign. In theory, Peter was unlocking or opening. He was living out the voice of God! And before the Sanhedrin Peter cried out, "[Jesus] is the one whom God exalted to His right hand as a Prince and a Savior, to grant repentance to Israel, and forgiveness of sins" (5:31). Note how Peter focuses on the Messiah's work as Savior for Israel, the Jewish people!

In time, the message of Christ would slip away from the Jews. Peter's work of judgment against the people would be over. The gospel message would then go to the Gentiles. Israel would be cut off and scattered.

What Does the Binding and Loosening Mean?

Returning to the question of *binding* and *loosening*, a closer examination of Matthew 16:19 is important. The text best reads: "I will [future tense] give you the keys of the kingdom of heaven; and whatever you should bind [aorist, active, subjunctive] on earth shall itself have been bound [Perfect, passive, participle] in heaven, and whatever you should loose [aorist, active, subjunctive] on earth shall itself have been loosed [perfect, passive, participle] in heaven."

By the use of two perfect passive participles, the Lord seems to be saying that what Peter does here on earth, with the Jews, with a reference to a kingdom message most applicable to them, the apostle is but carrying out what God has already determined in heaven to be done. Peter is but an instrument of judgment against the Jews that has been previously determined by the Lord. Thus, Peter is the Lord's visible instrument of judgment, but the final active authority still rests with God. Thus, he really does not have what is normally called "authority." He is a providential instrument against the Jews and their view of the kingdom of heaven. Once they have been judged through the "instrument" Peter, the work of the Lord through the church increases, as is shown in the book of Acts.

Is this interpretation correct? Though there are some differences of opinions, many great Bible scholars think so. Carson, for example, observes, "when the perfect participle is given its full force in the Matthean passages, the periphrastic future perfect in 16:19 becomes 'whatever you bind on earth shall have been bound in heaven, and whatever you loose on earth shall have been loosed in heaven' (similarly for 18:18). Thus, as [the grammarian] Mantey insisted, there is no evidence for "sacerdotalism or priestly absolution" in the NT."[13]

Therefore, the church on earth carries out heaven's decisions. Heaven is not ratifying the church's decisions.

What Are the Earliest Views?

A survey of patristic writings shows that seventeen of the early church fathers felt the passage means that the church was built on Peter. This includes Origen and Jerome.

A second view of the church fathers was that the church was built on all the apostles, not simply upon Peter. But a majority of forty-five of the church fathers felt, according to Denny, " that these words are to be understood of the Faith which St. Peter had confessed, that is, that this Faith, this profession of faith, by which we believe that Christ is Son of the living God, is the eternal and immovable foundation of the Church."[14]

This is by far the more common interpretation, and it is attested to by the Eastern church fathers Gregory of Nyssa, Cyril of Alexandria, Chrysostom, Theodoret, and Theophylact. It is supported by such Western fathers as Hilary, Ambrose, Augustine, and Gregory the Great.

That the rock was Peter would not be fully espoused until Siricius, bishop of Rome, in 385 wrote a letter to the bishop Himerius of Tarragona, Spain, arguing for the primacy of Peter.

Though it is a faulty hermeneutical argument, Denney believes it can be stated that the interpretation that Christ is the Rock does not take away from the third interpretation, held by most of the fathers, that it is upon Peter's confession that the church rests. In fact, some feel that both views are acceptable. Denny explains:

Hence Dionysius the Carthusian gives the two interpretations as equally expressing the meaning of the words, saying, "And upon this rock, that is, upon the firmness and foundation of his Faith [i.e., upon that of Peter], or upon this Rock which thou hast confessed, that is Myself, the chief corner-stone, the lofty mountain of which the Apostle says other foundation can no man lay, etc.[15]

But one of the major rules of biblical interpretation is that there is almost always just one meaning for a given passage. It would be rare for two very distinct ideas to be embedded in one sentence or short paragraph.

The weight of early church history points to the fact that most church fathers believed that Christ's statement in regard to the rock has to do with Peter's confession of who Jesus really is. It is upon that confession that the church will be built.

What Is the Roman Catholic View?

Since around 1860, the Catechism of Father Joseph Deharbe has been recognized as the most important doctrinal statement for Catholics throughout North America. Thousands of Catholics cut their teeth on this little volume that carried the imprimatur of John Farley, the Archbishop of New York. According to this book, on the basis of Matthew 16, Christ appointed Peter to be the Supreme Head of His church.[16] Deharbe notes: "We learn from this, 1. That Christ built His Church upon Peter, as upon the true foundation-stone; 2. That He gave him in particular the keys of the Kingdom of Heaven; and 3. That He commissioned him alone to feed His whole flock."[17]

In the Roman Catholic catechism the question is asked, "Who followed Peter upon his death?" The answer:

> The Councils, as well as the Fathers of all ages individually have unanimously and most decidedly, by word and deed, acknowledged in the Roman Popes the Primacy and Supremacy of St. Peter. The Ecumenical Council of Florence (1438) referred to "the Decrees of the General Councils, and the Ecclesiastical Statutes," when it declared "that the Bishop of Rome (the Pope) possessed the Primacy over the whole universe; that he was the Successor of the Prince of the Apostles, St. Peter, and the true Vicegerent of Jesus Christ, the Head of the whole Church, . . . and whoever refused to recognize the Pope as the Head of the Church was at all times considered by all the faithful as an apostate."[18]

The Catholic Church is serious about the Matthew 16 passage of Scripture. From this it builds an overwhelming system that is meant to control the religious life of all under the church's power. And this power starts with Peter and comes down to every Pope ever placed in office.

The Catechism of Father Deharbe points out that it is easy to find the visible church because perceptible marks have been left that the world can see. Because of this, all who deny the church are "under pain of eternal damnation" if they do not listen to her.[19] "Non-Catholic Religious Societies" (Protestant denominations) are not true because they have no common Head (such as the Pope), and because their founders are not holy."[20] As well, they "have rejected many articles of faith and means of sanctification, as, for example, the Sacrifice of the Mass and most of the Sacraments."[21] The people in these groups are lost "Because they cannot produce from among themselves one Saint, confirmed as such by his miraculous power."[22]

The Catechism continues and warns that all must adhere to the decisions of the church. And when the Pope speaks for the church, he speaks infallibly. "The General Council of the Vatican, in 1870, defined that the Pope is infallible when he teaches the church *ex cathedra*."[23]

Contrary to what the Catholic Church tries to convey today, non-Catholics do not stand much of a chance for salvation unless they come back into the fold of the Mother Church: "From the beginning whoever obstinately refused to accept and believe a doctrine of Catholic Faith, when so declared *ex cathedra* by the Pope, was always cut off from the communion of the Church, and condemned as a heretic."[24]

> All those who by their own fault are Heretics, i.e., who profess a doctrine that has been condemned by the Church; or who are Infidels—that is, who no longer have nor profess any Christian faith at all; and 2. All those who by their own fault are Schismatics— that is, who have renounced, not the doctrine of the Church, but their obedience to her, or to her Supreme Head, the Pope.[25]

Further, a heretic is one by his own fault, who knows about the Catholic Church, is convinced of her truth, but does not join her. But more, he could know her, if he searched, but through indifference and other culpable motives, neglects to do so.[26] And apart from the Church there is no salvation. "Every one is obliged, under pain of eternal damnation, to become a member of the Catholic Church, to believe her doctrine, to use her means of grace, and to submit to her authority."[27]

From the words of Jesus in Matthew 16, the Catholic Church has constructed a system that confines its followers to its own deadly path. In Peter, power was transferred from bishop to bishop, through the centuries, that has created a mountain of belief from which there is no room for challenge nor is there an escape. Those who do not believe all that the Church says are lost. But there are some changes in the wind that will prove to be a deeper and more subtle trap for those not familiar with Catholic strategy.

What Is the Changing Roman Catholic Interpretation?

After the first three or four centuries, developing Roman Catholicism held that the Catholic Church is the kingdom of heaven, or kingdom of God. Theologically, this is *amillennialism*. But in the theological writings of the modern church there is an attempt to change this Kingdom idea. How far this will go is not certain. In the 1286-page work *Catholicism* (1994) by Father Richard P. McBrien, new thoughts emerge about a Kingdom yet future that is related to, yet separate from, the earthly church. McBrien writes, "Insofar as the Church offers a credible witness to the truth, it will arouse the world to a 'living hope' in the coming of the Kingdom of God."[28]

He then quotes Catholic theologian Karl Rahner, who states, "The Church is not itself the Kingdom of God."[29] Another theologian, Edward Schillebeeck, writes, "The Church is committed to the coming Kingdom of God, but it is not yet in possession of the Kingdom. The Church is still on the way, in history, searching tentatively for solutions to the problems of human existence."[30] He goes on to say that when the church finds the solutions, the world can be fully "humanized."

To many recent Catholic theologians, the church is seeking a parallel path to the world, "critically involved in the building of the world and the progress of the nations."[31]

McBrien further writes,

> The Church is necessary for the world as a sacrament, an efficacious sign and instrument of God's redemptive activity in Jesus Christ, leading toward the final Kingdom of God. . . . The Church is necessary for those individuals who are in fact called by God to acknowledge the Lordship of Jesus and to collaborate with him in the coming Kingdom of God.[32]

McBrien also admits that it was Augustine who first identified the Church with the Kingdom.[33] But twentieth-century Catholic theology insists that the church and the kingdom are not the same. The kingdom, they say, will be the product of divine and human initiative and collaboration. It will have political and social dimensions.[34] It will be fully manifested in the future. In the meantime, the Eucharist represents the Kingdom and even "anticipates" it. McBrien says, "The Catholic Church has never officially defined the meaning of the Kingdom of God. The Second Vatican Council overcomes the separation between general and individual eschatology, links the present and the future, and establishes a fundamental unity between the earthly and the heavenly."[35]

By what has been written so far by McBrien, it is not impossible that this could evolve into an imminent and near millennial view of a coming Kingdom. If this happens, a clash could be anticipated in the future between the promised Jewish millennial kingdom and the kingdom of the Catholic Church on earth.

Thus, the open warfare and conflict with the false prophet, who could be the Pope, and the people of God, as described in the book of Revelation. And the Pope would be loyal to and standing behind the "political and social dimensions" of the kingdom of the antichrist!

The keys to the kingdom given to Peter has to do with his role of judgment of the Jewish nation and their notion of the reign of the Messiah. Wherever Peter went, he convicted the Jewish leaders about their rejection of Jesus as their Savior and Messiah. Peter was but the instrument in the hands of a sovereign God to carry out this opening and closing of doors (loosening and binding) spiritually for that generation of the Jewish people.

The Church is not that kingdom. But the Church is build upon the statement of Peter as to the divine person of the Lord. New Testament history seems best to support these views.

In great error, the Catholic Church has created a primacy of Peter from the Matthew 16 passage to support their political structure.

Messianic Jewish Issues in Acts

The Sabbath

The Sabbath was the sign, seal, and token of the Mosaic covenant. As long as that covenant was in effect, the Sabbath law was mandatory. Dispensationalism teaches that, since the law of Moses has been rendered inoperative, the Sabbath command no longer applies. Covenant theologians with their inconsistent insistence that the law of Moses is still in effect, also insist that the Sabbath law applies. However, they totally ignore exactly what Moses wrote about how to keep the Sabbath and they even change the day of the week, which the law of Moses does not allow. Many Jewish believers also insist on mandatory Sabbath keeping. Though they base it on the Law of Moses, they at least retain it with the seventh day of the week.

In the book of Acts, the Sabbath is mentioned nine times. The first time (1:12) it is used to measure the distance between Jerusalem and the Mount of Olives (a Sabbath day's journey, about three thousand feet). All other references relate to the Sabbath observance in the synagogue (13:14, 27, 42, 44; 15:21; 16:13; 17:2; 18:4). No conclusions can be drawn about mandatory Sabbath-keeping for Jewish or Gentile believers on the basis of these passages. These passages refer to Jewish unbelievers in the synagogue service and say nothing about the meeting of the church.

This is not to deny that there were Jewish believers present in synagogues during the period of Acts. But there is no command in the book of Acts for Jewish believers to hold corporate worship on the Sabbath. Furthermore, Jewish believers' presence in the synagogue was not the meeting of the church.

There are, of course, many reasons Jewish believers may have continued to observe the Sabbath as a day of rest, especially within the land of Israel. These may have been for reasons of habit, social pressure, fear of sanctions, missionary policy (as in the case of Paul), conservative leadership in Jerusalem, and personal theological convictions.

There are two other passages in the book of Acts that may have a bearing on the question of the Sabbath. The first is Acts 15:1–29, which records the proceedings of the Jerusalem Council. Initially, the issue was circumcision of the Gentiles (v. 1), but later it expanded to include the keeping of the Law of Moses (v. 5). Peter states in 15:10: "Now therefore why do you put God to the test by placing upon the neck of the disciples a yoke which neither our fathers nor we have been able to bear?"

In this context, the "yoke" is clearly the Law of Moses. If the Jews ("neither our fathers nor we") were unable to keep the law, there is no reason to force it upon the Gentiles and ask them to do what even the Jewish believers could not do. It is obvious that neither circumcision nor even Sabbath keeping was laid upon the Gentile believers to keep. Peter's statement implies that neither are these things obligatory for Jewish believers any more.

Sunday

A few things should also be said about Sunday, since covenant theologians often insist that Sunday is now the Sabbath and Sabbath laws apply to it.

In many circles it has been taught that Sunday worship universally began only in 321 with the Law of Constantine, or in 364 with the Council of Laodicea. However, the contributors to *From Sabbath to Lord's Day* have shown with excellent documentation that Sunday worship was a very universal practice of all churches outside Israel by the beginning of the second century. They also clearly point out that in those early days, while Sunday was viewed as a day of worship, it was not viewed as a Sabbath.

What later church councils did was ratify a practice already common, and only then did they begin to apply the Sabbath rules to Sunday. In the beginning it was not so. Sunday was a day of worship but not a day of rest. As church history developed, more and more Sabbath laws from the Old Testament were applied to Sunday, and this concept is present to this day. So many speak of the "Christian Sabbath," or the "Sunday Sabbath."

However, it is no more correct to speak of a "Christian Sabbath" than a "Jewish Sunday." Charles Hodge, in his *Systematic Theology*, goes to great lengths to insist that all of the Ten Commandments still apply, including the fourth commandment. He also insists, with no scriptural evidence, that the fourth commandment now applies to the first day of the week and not the seventh. His evidences are all derived from the Old Testament, and he insists that the United States government issue laws that will require Sunday observance on a society that may not even believe. His arguments, taken from the Law of Moses, ignore the seventh-day emphasis of that same law.

Even dispensationalists, who should know better, fall into the same trap. Merrill F. Unger, for example, wrote in his Bible dictionary:

> As the Sabbath commemorates God's creation rest, the first day speaks of Christ's resurrection. The seventh day marks God's creative rest. On the first day Christ was unceasingly active. The seventh day commemorates a finished creation, the first day, a finished redemption. In the present dispensation of grace, Sunday perpetuates the truth that one-seventh of one's time belongs to God. In every other particular there is contrast.[36]

Sunday is never called the Sabbath in the New Testament but always the first day of the week. Nor is it ever called "the Lord's Day." Although the early church fathers certainly used that term for Sunday, it was not so used in the New Testament.

The one place where that term appears is Revelation 1:10, and there is no reason to assume that this day was a Sunday. There is good reason to believe it was not. In this passage, the term "Lord" in the Greek text is not a noun but an adjective. It would be better translated as a *lordy* day. It does not refer to a specific day of the week such as the Sabbath, Saturday, or Sunday. Rather, it was a day in which John was enraptured by prophetic and divine ecstasy and received divine revelation. It was a day in which he fell under the control of the Holy Spirit and was given prophetic inspiration. For him it was, indeed, "a lordy day."

It is true that by the second century churches observed Sunday as a day of worship. It is also clear that the Pauline churches in the first century observed the first day of the week as a day of worship. This is rather apparent from Acts 20:7–8, 11:

> And upon the first day of the week, when we were gathered together to break bread, Paul discoursed with them, intending to depart on the morrow; and prolonged his speech until midnight. And there were many lights in the upper chamber where we were gathered together. . . . And when he was gone up, and had broken the bread, and eaten, and had talked with them a long while, even till break of day, so he departed.

Evidence is strong that the practice of the church meeting on the first day of the week actually began with Jewish believers within Israel itself. Since Jewish believers continued to attend the synagogue and temple on Saturday mornings, they needed another time to gather together, and did so on the first day of the week. In Jewish timetables, the first day of the week begins at sundown and not at midnight on Saturday. While they did meet on the first day of the week, it was Saturday night.

The Sabbath is a time of eating, so Jews generally do not fast before or on the Sabbath. The question is, why not fast at any time on the day after the Sabbath? The answer is, to avoid showing any respect to the day regarded as special by the Nazarenes. The significance of this quotation is that Jewish believers were worshiping on the first day of the week. M. Max Turner states:

> We must conclude that it is barely imaginable that first-day Sabbath observance commenced before the Jerusalem Council. Nor can we stop there; we must go on to maintain that first-day Sabbath observance cannot easily be understood as a phenomenon of the apostolic age or of apostolic authority at all.
>
> If an apostolic decision was made after the council on so important a matter as this, it would not have been an easy decision to reach and it would inevitably have left its mark in the Epistles and in Acts. But as we have seen, Acts is silent on the issue and Paul's handling of controversies involving the Law and the Sabbath makes it difficult to believe that he knew of any Sabbath transference theology.[37]

The Use of Israel in the Book of Acts

Covenant theologians boldly state that the church is the new Israel and sometimes make it sound as if that claim is an obvious foregone conclusion of the New Testament. Some covenant theologians have written that the terms *Israel* and *the church* are used interchangeably. Such a claim simply does not correspond with the way the term Israel is used throughout the New Testament, including the book of Acts.

In the New Testament, the term *Israel* is used a total of seventy-three times. Twenty of these uses are found in the book of Acts. The following is a list and summary of those passages:

- Acts 1:6b. "They were asking Him, saying, 'Lord, is it at this time You are restoring the kingdom to Israel?'" The disciples had ethnic Israel and not the church in mind in this context.
- Acts 2:22. Peter addresses an unbelieving Jewish audience and states, "Men of Israel." Contextually, this could hardly be the Church.
- Acts 2:36. "Therefore let all the house of Israel know for certain that God has made Him both Lord and Christ—this Jesus whom you crucified." This is the same audience as in 2:22.

- Acts 3:12. Peter again addresses unbelieving Jews with the words, "Men of Israel."
- Acts 4:10. Peter has ethnic Israel in view when he declares to "all the people of Israel" that the lame man was healed in the name of Jesus.
- Acts 4:27. Israel is listed along with the Gentiles as guilty of the crucifixion.
- Acts 5:21. A reference to the "senate of the sons of Israel" who were unbelievers.
- Acts 5:31. Peter offers "repentance to Israel." Israel is in unbelief at this point.
- Acts 5:35. Gamaliel addressing the Sanhedrin states, "Men of Israel."
- Acts 7:23, 37, 42. Stephen makes historical references to Israel of the Exodus.
- Acts 9:15. God declares that Paul will proclaim the gospel "before the Gentiles and kings and the sons of Israel." This is a reference to unbelieving Jews.
- Acts 10:36. Peter refers to the historical fact that Jesus came to preach the gospel to Israel, the majority of whom did not believe the message.
- Acts 13:16. Paul addresses an unbelieving Jewish audience as "Men of Israel, and you who fear God."
- Acts 13:17. Paul refers to the historical Israel of the Exodus.
- Acts 13:23. Paul mentions the historical fact that a Savior had come to the Jews.
- Acts 13:24. Paul refers to the historical fact that John the Baptist preached repentance to Israel.
- Acts 21:28. The mob who attacked Paul is referred to as "Men of Israel."
- Acts 28:20. Paul declares that he is chained for the messianic hope of Israel.

In not one instance in Acts does the term *Israel* refer to the church. The book of Acts offers no support for any concept of a theology of transference or a theology of replacement. In Acts, both Israel and the church exist side by side, without any confusion as to their distinctive identities.

Signs, Wonders, Miracles, and Healings

There is a common misconception taught in some circles that believers in general in the history of the book of Acts were doing miracles, signs, and wonders. The impression is given that signs and wonders was the normal experience of every church in the apostolic period and that believers in general were performing these signs and wonders. However, a careful look at the actual miracles performed in the book of Acts shows that within this book, the only ones performing miracles, signs, and wonders were the apostles or apostolic legates, those upon whom the apostles laid hands for special missions. Acts 2:43 sets the tone for what is true throughout the book of Acts: "And fear came upon every soul: and many wonders and signs were done through the apostles" (KJV).

Peter, John, and the Lame Beggar

The next miracle recorded is that of the healing of the lame beggar by the apostle Peter in Acts 3:1–11. It was obviously an apostolic miracle and set the stage for Peter's second sermon, as recorded in the book of Acts. As a result of this incident, the two apostles were arrested and threatened by the Sanhedrin. After being released, they led an apostolic prayer meeting in which they prayed in Acts 4:29–30, "And now, Lord, take note of their threats, and grant that Thy bondservants may speak Thy word with all confidence, while Thou dost extend Thy hand to heal, and signs and wonders take place through the name of Thy holy Servant Jesus."

The apostles asked for God to look upon the threats against them for the purpose of intervening against those threats. They prayed for the boldness to continue speaking, despite threats, and they prayed that their message might be confirmed by signs and wonders. The prayer was answered in verse 31, which states that they spoke the word of God with boldness.

Peter and the Rest of the Apostles

Acts 5:12–16 states:

> And at the hands of the apostles many signs and wonders were taking place among the people; and they were all with one accord in Solomon's porch. But none of the rest dared to associate with them; however, the people held them in high esteem. And all the more believers in the Lord, multitudes of men and women, were constantly added to their number; to such an extent that they even carried the sick out into the streets, and laid them on cots and pallets, so that when Peter came by, at the least his shadow might fall on any one of them. And also the people from the cities in the vicinity of Jerusalem were coming together, bringing people who were sick or afflicted with unclean spirits: and they were all being healed.

The account begins by describing the apostolic signs (v. 12a). This again shows that it is not true that believers in general were doing miracles and signs and wonders in the book of Acts but only the apostles and those who were apostolic legates, those who were appointed by the laying on of hands by the apostles, who were able to do it. This fact had come out four times before: 2:43; 3:6–7, and 4:22 and 33. This ability was not given to believers in general, but was evidence of apostolic authority. Just preceding this event was the story of the deaths of Ananias and Sapphira. The church had been purged, and God was at work through the apostles.

Many people chose neither to believe nor to join the Jewish believers. This may have been due to fear of persecution and fear of discipline. There had already been one persecution against the church, and the second was soon to begin. And the case of Ananias and Sapphira must have been frightening to those outside the body. Nevertheless, they were of good report among the general population.

Verse 15 records that Peter, in particular, had healing abilities. Although all the apostles had apostolic authority and apostolic power to perform miracles, Peter was the head apostle, the one with the keys to the kingdom. His ability was recognized as extraordinary even among the apostles and by the people who carried their sick to where he might pass. But the reputation of all the apostles spread. The tense in verse 16 means that multitudes "kept on coming" from Jerusalem and nearby cities. Two types of need are mentioned here. Some needed healing from physical problems, and some needed freeing from demonic oppression.

Every person who came was healed because the apostles had authority to heal, regardless of the faith of the person who came to them. This authority to heal was part of the larger package of apostolic authorities and powers. The tense used means they were healed one at a time, and this was constantly being repeated. This is certainly not true of faith healers today. Faith healers cannot do what these apostles did, although they claim to be doing the same thing; not everyone who comes to these faith healers walks away healed.

Stephen

The next case is that of Stephen. In Acts 6:1–6 we have the account of the appointment of the first deacons of the church of Jerusalem, among whom was Stephen. The appointment is recorded in Acts 6:6 with prayer and the laying on of hands. Thus, they became apostolic legates. As a result, Acts 6:8 states: "And Stephen, full of grace and power, was performing great wonders and signs among the people." The ability of Stephen to perform signs and wonders evidently came after his appointment by the apostles; it accompanied apostolic authority. In every case where miracles are performed in Acts, they are done either by an apostle or by an apostolic legate, a person who was appointed to do so by the laying on of hands by an apostle.

Peter, Aeneas, and Tabitha

The next record, one that shows the necessity of apostolic presence, is in Acts 9:32–43, where we have two accounts of healings by Peter. First is the healing of Aeneas in Acts 9:32–35. The second account is that of the resurrection of Dorcas, or Tabitha, in Acts 9:36–43. While Peter was still at Lydda, where he had healed Aeneas, Tabitha, or Dorcas, had died in Joppa (or Jaffa). The text makes it clear that she was among believing disciples.

If it was possible for believers in general to do these miracles, then it should have been possible for these disciples to heal Dorcas before she died, or to raise her from the dead after she died. However, they had no such power, nor does the text even imply that it was due to any lack of faith on their part. But when they knew that Peter was close by in Lydda, they quickly fetched him to come to Joppa, and then Peter raised her back to life.

Paul and Barnabas

In Acts 13:6–12, we find Paul, as he begins his missionary journeys, also exercising apostolic authority in signs and wonders. Among the first recorded events is his judgment upon Elymas the sorcerer, by striking him blind. This was done by apostolic authority.

Barnabas, Paul's colaborer on his first missionary journey, is also classed among the apostles. What they did together along apostolic lines is recorded in Acts 14:3–4:

> Therefore they spent a long time there speaking boldly with reliance upon the Lord, who was bearing witness to the word of His grace, granting that signs and wonders be done by their hands. But the multitude of the city was divided; and some sided with the Jews, and some with the apostles.

The miracles were not being done on the basis of the law, but on the basis of grace through faith. Here, again, only the apostles were able to do these signs and wonders. This led to the fact that in Iconium, the multitude of the city were divided. Some were on the side of the unbelievers and some were on the side of the apostles. Use of the plural form shows that both Paul and Barnabas were referred to as apostles, and both were exercising apostolic miracles.

The role of Paul and Barnabas exercising apostolic signs and wonders was used as a witness in the Jerusalem council in Acts 15:12: "And all the multitude kept silent, and they were listening to Barnabas and Paul as they were relating what signs and wonders God had done through them among the Gentiles."

Here, again, it is these apostles who are credited with performing signs and wonders, and not believers in general. On the contrary, believers in general in the church of Jerusalem were to conclude from this that these men had apostolic authority and were being used by God to establish Gentile churches in spite of their uncircumcision.

The Uniqueness of Paul

Acts 16:16–18 records the exorcism of the soothsaying woman, but again done through the authority of the apostle. Note also 19:11–12:

> And God was performing extraordinary miracles by the hands of Paul, so that handkerchiefs or aprons were even carried from his body to the sick, and the diseases left them and the evil spirits went out.

These two verses record unique miracles performed by the apostle Paul, as was the case with the apostle Peter (5:15). But these were wrought especially by the hands of Paul. It was part of his apostolic authority. This phrase again shows that such powers were limited to the apostles and their legates in the book of Acts. Miracles were not performed by believers in general.

Ananias of Damascus

In all of the above examples recorded in the book of Acts, without exception, miracles, signs, and wonders were performed by either apostles or apostolic legates. The only possible exception to the rule is the case of Ananias of Damascus, whom God used for the purpose of healing the apostle Paul's blindness. This account is recorded in Acts 9:10–18:

> Now there was a certain disciple at Damascus, named Ananias; and the Lord said to him in a vision, "Ananias." And he said, "Behold, here I am, Lord." And the Lord said unto him, "Arise and go to the street called Straight, and inquire at the house of Judas for a man from Tarsus named Saul, for behold, he is praying, and he has seen in a vision a man named Ananias come in, and lay his hands on him, that he might regain his sight." But Ananias answered, "Lord, I have heard from many about this man, how much harm he did to Thy saints at Jerusalem; and here he has authority from the chief priests to bind all who call upon Thy name." But the Lord said to him, "Go, for he is a chosen instrument of Mine, to bear my name before the Gentiles and kings and the children of Israel; for I will show him how much he must suffer for My name's sake." And Ananias departed and entered the house, and after laying his hands on him said, "Brother Saul, the Lord Jesus, who appeared to thee on the road by which you were coming, has sent me, so that you may regain your sight, and be filled with the Holy Spirit." And immediately there fell from his eyes something like scales, and he received his sight; and he arose and was baptized.

The account of Ananias of Damascus begins with the call of Ananias. The church by then had already spread as far as Damascus, and Ananias was among the Damascus believers. The Lord's message came to him in a vision. God called Ananias by name and Ananias responded: "Behold, here I am, Lord," probably using the Hebrew version, *Hineni*, meaning "Here am I."

Though he was blind, Paul could see a vision. In his vision, Ananias laid hands on Paul as the means of his healing. So Ananias received a special appointment to act out what God had already promised. By the hands of Ananias, Paul would receive his sight, which he lost on the road to Damascus.

The Laying on of Hands

The laying on of hands in the book of Acts both departs from and is similar to the practice of laying on of hands in the Old Testament and the Gospels. It is similar in that it is both multipurpose or multidimensional, and that it shares some of the same purposes or usages. It departs from the past in that certain usages are omitted in Acts and new ones added. Even so, the basic significance or implication of the laying on of hands remains the same.

The basic idea behind the laying on of hands is somewhat fluid. It appears to involve the concepts of identification, separation, and communication and/ or transference. And while all of these concepts may be implied in any given case of the laying on of hands, often one is more prevalent than the others, depending upon the purpose or occasion that calls for the laying on of hands.

While it is said that the practice of the laying on of hands was not peculiar to the Jews,[38] its practice in the book of Acts has its roots in Jewish tradition. We are concerned here with the religious, ceremonial rite of laying on of hands. Strictly speaking, the laying on of hands can have a broad range of meaning. Literally, every time one person lays or puts his hand upon another person, there is a "laying on of hands."

Outside of the Gospels there are thirteen New Testament references to the ritual laying on of hands. Three other references involve the hands in a metaphorical or literal sense (though without *epitithēmi*, "lay or put on").[39] These appear to have some bearing on the meaning of the laying on of hands.

Occurrences in Acts

3:7. The first reference is to the hands, though not to the ritualistic practice, and is for healing. Peter takes the hand of the lame man and brings him to his feet.

6:6. Though it is grammatically possible to hold that the congregation who chose the seven lay hands upon them, it is more probable grammatically and contextually that the apostles are placing hands on the seven.[40] The apostles had the authority of Christ to consecrate. By the laying on of hands, the seven receive their office by apostolic appointment.

8:17. Though Philip brought the gospel to the Samaritans with signs and wonders (Acts 8:5–8), it is the apostles Peter and John who lay hands on them that they might receive the gift of the Holy Spirit.

8:18 (noun form); *8:19* (verb form). Simon's offer to buy the apostolic prerogative to lay hands on others was a moral and spiritual affront to the Holy Spirit. But the theological significance of this passage is the inseparable association of the apostles to their high office and incontestable authority. The absurdity of Simon's offer to buy this authority, which is given only by Christ to His apostles, highlights the exclusivity of the privilege. The apostles *could* not pass on or confer on another either the office of apostleship or the apostolic authority and ability.

9:12. Ananias is commissioned in a vision to lay hands on and heal Saul. Nothing is said here about the Holy Spirit.

9:17. In obedience to his commission, Ananias lays hands on Paul and offers him both healing and filling with the Holy Spirit. What is meant by the command to be "filled with the Holy Spirit"? Either Paul *receives* the outpoured Spirit, as did the disciples on Pentecost (Acts 2:4; cf. 2:38; 8:15–17; 11:15; 19:2–6), or, having already received the Spirit he is empowered or emboldened by the repeatable "special filling" (see pp. 28–29).

13:3. Simeon, Lucius, and Manaen—who are *not* said to be apostles—lay hands on Barnabas and Saul, who are (later) said to be apostles. It could be argued that Simeon, Lucius, and Manaen, were in fact apostles. They are among the "prophets and teachers" in the church at Antioch (Acts 13:1). There is no mention here that any were apostles, but we know that Barnabas and Saul were (Acts 14:4, 14). On the other hand, Barnabas and Saul are not said to be apostles until *after* they are "set apart" by the laying on of hands by Simeon, Lucius, and Manaen (13:3) and "sent out by the Holy Spirit" (13:4). However, Paul traces his apostleship to the Damascus Road experience, not to the Antiochan commission (1 Cor. 9:1; Gal. 1:11–24). If Paul was already an apostle when he was set apart for their work (13:2), why not Barnabas? And if Barnabas, why not Simeon, Lucius, and Manaen?

19:6. Paul encounters disciples of John the Baptist (19:3). Whether they were believers in an Old Testament sense may be uncertain (see pp. 29–30). They were not believers in a New testament or post-Pentecost sense, for Paul had to explain Jesus to them (19:4), after which they were baptized in the "name of the Lord Jesus" (19:5). Then Paul "laid his hands upon them [and] the Holy Spirit came upon them, and they began speaking with tongues and prophesying" (19:6). There is no ambiguity here. This is the efficacious use of the laying on of hands that was strictly an apostolic prerogative.

28:8. Paul confers neither the Holy Spirit nor the sign gifts in this instance. It is an efficacious use of the laying on of hands in that it brings healing to Publius's father.

At no time in the book of Acts is the efficacious use of the laying on of hands ever exercised by one who is not an apostle. Apart from the references to healing (3:7, possibly, and 28:8), the consistent purpose seems to be the apostolic conferral of the Holy Spirit or the ability to do signs and wonders. The apostles alone possessed the ability to confer the Spirit or the sign gifts. This ability (the efficacious use of laying on of hands) to confer the Holy Spirit or sign gifts appears to have been exclusively an apostolic prerogative.

Chapter 3

THE PERSON OF JESUS CHRIST IN ACTS

The Name *Jesus*

Yeshua, or *Joshua*, means in Hebrew "Jehovah saves" (for notes on the Hebrew and Greek forms of the name, see chapter summaries under 1:1). Though there is no direct Old Testament connection between the name *Jesus* and the messianic prophecies, the concept of the Messiah as Savior is found in prophetic sense in Isaiah 53:11–12: "My Servant will justify the many, as He will bear their iniquities. . . . He Himself bore the sin of many, and interceded for the transgressors." Though *Yeshua* became a common name, it had specific significance to Jesus Christ throughout the entire New Testament. In Acts Jesus is mentioned seventy times with the designation *Christ* (*Christos*, "Messiah") added some fourteen times and with the name *Christ* standing alone seventeen times. More often than not, the name is attached to some additional designation, as the following examples indicate.

"A Nazarene"

This identification refers to the place where Jesus was raised, the city of Nazareth (Matt. 2:23). Though there was no such city named in the Old

Testament, there is a prophetic play on words taken from Isaiah 11:1, where the future Messiah is described as a branch (Heb. *netzer*) coming forth from Jesse, David's father. *Netzer* is closely related phonetically to *Nazareth*, and Christ is described as "a Nazarene" six times. Nathanael voiced the common prejudice when he asked, "Can any good thing come out of Nazareth?" (John 1:46), but in Acts the word became a designation of blessing! The lame man was healed in the name of Jesus Christ the Nazarene (Acts 3:6; 4:10), and the Lord identified Himself to the murderer Saul with "I am Jesus the Nazarene, whom you are persecuting" (Acts 22:8).

"The Crucified One, the Savior"

This is a crucial truth in the book of Acts, though Luke focuses more on the aftermath of the Lord's death, specifically His resurrection and ascension. With great emotion, Peter cries forth, "Therefore let all the house of Israel know for certain that God has made Him both Lord and Christ—this Jesus whom you crucified" (2:36). The crucifixion, of course, was for the sins of Israel and the world, whereby Jesus would be declared Savior! "From the offspring of [David], according to promise, God has brought to Israel a Savior, Jesus" (13:23). McGarvey comments:

> In this brief sentence Paul skillfully introduces Jesus as the promised Son of David who was to deliver Israel (Ps. lxxxix. 19–37), and also states the time of his public appearance, in accordance with the Gospel narratives, as immediately after the close of John's (the Baptist) ministry. Thus he fixes attention not upon the time of his birth, but upon the time that God "brought him to Israel as a Saviour."[1]

In Peter's second sermon to his people (Acts 2:22–36), he boldly stresses that the Jews were the human agency in Christ's death. He says this Man "you nailed to a cross by the hands of godless men and put Him to death" (v. 23b). He adds to this that God's sovereignty was mysteriously behind the death of the Lord. He was "delivered up by the predetermined plan and foreknowledge of God" (v. 23a). Thus His death was not simply a twist or accident of history.

"The Resurrected One"

Luke focuses heavily on this truth, indicating that the resurrection is absolutely essential to the doctrine of personal salvation. Peter argues that, since Christ must reign on David's throne, He must come forth from the grave. His argument comes from Psalm 16:10: "For Thou wilt not abandon my soul to Sheol; neither wilt Thou allow Thy Holy One to undergo decay." By these words David was speaking of his son, the Messiah, as David "looked ahead and spoke of the resurrection of the Christ" (Acts 2:31). The resurrection is again mentioned in regard to the apostles who "were giving witness to the resurrection of the Lord Jesus" (4:33), and God who had fulfilled His promise "to our children in that He raised up Jesus" from the dead (13:33–34). "But He whom God raised did not undergo decay. Therefore let it be known to you, brethren, that through Him forgiveness of sins is proclaimed to you" (vv. 37–38). In this passage salvation is tied to the resurrection.

As Paul would note later, without the resurrection there is no deliverance from sin: "If Christ has not been raised, your faith is worthless; you are still in your sins" (1 Cor. 15:17). As Paul went forth later with the gospel, the resurrection of Jesus was to him the essential heart of the issue of salvation. The Epicureans and Stoics he encountered labeled Paul an idle babbler because "'He seems to be a proclaimer of strange deities,'—because he was preaching Jesus and the resurrection" (17:18c). But some Greeks seem to have had an open curiosity about the resurrection. They asked: "May we know what this new teaching is which you are proclaiming? For you are bringing some strange things to our ears; we want to know therefore what these things mean" (17:19b–20).

Later in Acts, it is clear how far removed the Roman magistrate Festus was from such events as Christ's resurrection when he reported to King Agrippa that the Jews simply "had some points of disagreement with [Paul] about their own religion and about a certain dead man, Jesus, whom Paul asserted to be alive" (25:19). But being a Roman citizen, Paul appealed to be sent to Rome for a fair trial. There, the truth of the resurrection of Jesus would travel even farther into the Gentile world and, in time, bring thousands to Christ through the witness of the apostle Paul to this miracle from God.

"The Christ, the Anointed"

The Greek word *Christos* is equivalent to the Hebrew *he Maschioch*, "the Anointed One, or Messiah." The name comes from one of the most messianic of Old Testament passages, Psalm 2. In this Psalm, David prophesies of the nations and rulers of earth conspiring against the Lord and against His Anointed (v. 2; *LXX* Gk., *Christos*). But the Lord will speak with terror to the nations, with the coming Tribulation (v. 5), but He will ultimately install His king "upon Zion (in Jerusalem), My holy mountain" (v. 6). In paragraph two of the psalm, the Lord sends His Son to the earth to someday receive His inheritance, at which time He will rule the nations with a rod of iron (vv. 7–9). The world is to "worship the Lord with reverence" (v. 11) and take refuge in the Lord's Anointed lest God is angry and men perish in the way (v. 12).

In Acts, as persecution against the apostles begins, the Christians recognize that the resistance of the world was prophesied in Psalm 2 (Acts 4:25–26). As well, Peter realizes for certain that the resurrection has affirmed Jesus as the Anointed who would someday reign on David's throne (2:36). Christ was appointed for the Jews (3:20) and marked out to suffer for sins (3:18).

By this name, men are to believe and be baptized (2:38; 5:42). As well, in the name of Jesus Christ, many miracles and healings take place in Acts (4:10; 9:34; 16:18).

To identify Jesus as Messiah, the Anointed, is crucial for witness to the Jews. They have waited for the coming Son of David. Through the Holy Spirit, Peter and the disciples dramatically convince the Jews concerning Jesus. The conversion of Saul/Paul begins another phase of apologetic witness. He immediately begins to confound the Damascene Jews "by proving that this Jesus is the Christ" (9:22). Lenski well observes:

> "Proving that this one is the Christ," the Messiah promised by the Scriptures, indicates how the Jews were confounded. Those proofs were conclusive, overwhelming, and silenced the opponents. Then the same thing happened that had occurred in the case of Stephen; unable to refute the argument, these opponents resolved to kill the man who presented it.[2]

"The Lord"

The designation *Lord* is ultimately a reference to Daniel 7:9–28 where Jesus, as the Son of Man, enters the throne room of God following His ascension and receives all dominion, authority and kingdom "under the whole earth" (vv. 14, 27): "His kingdom will be an everlasting kingdom, and all the dominions will serve and obey Him." At his death, Stephen sees Jesus standing at the right hand of God the Father (Acts 7:55) and cries out, "Lord Jesus, receive my spirit" (7:59).

That Jesus is now seated at the right hand of God the Father is one of the great neglected doctrines of Scripture. Daniel saw Him presented to the Father (the Ancient of Days) as the "Son of Man" (Dan. 7:13), or "the son who is related to mankind" by His human incarnation and then by His bodily ascension as described in Acts 1:9. The attending angels prophesied that He would return in like manner (bodily and in power) "in just the same way as you have watched Him go into heaven" (v. 11).

Peter refers to Jesus as the One who is seated next to His Father when he quotes Psalm 110:1: "The Lord said to my Lord, 'Sit at My right hand, until I make Thine enemies a footstool for Thy feet'" (Acts 2:34b–35). Jesus is made (Gk. *poieō*, "declared, designated, established") by His obedience, to be both the Lord *(Kyrios)* and the Christ, the Messiah, who is yet to reign on earth on David's throne (v. 36). The Lord is presently seated at the right hand of the Father. He will reign on the Davidic throne in the future as the Messiah. That there are two thrones is clearly stated in the book of Revelation. Jesus said: "He who overcomes, I will grant to him to sit down with Me on My throne, *as I also overcame and sat down with my Father on his throne*" (3:21, emphasis added).

"The Holy One"

When Peter healed the man born lame, he made it clear that it was done in the name of the Holy One "you disowned . . . and asked for [instead] a murderer to be granted to you" (3:14). Peter makes sure they understand that *Holy One* is the name of Jesus, by whose power the lame man walked (3:16).

In Old and New Testaments the word *holy* (Heb. *kodesh*, Gk. *hagios*) is a profound concept, something that is special, even unique, "that which is to be set aside." In both testaments, the verb is generally translated "to sanctify." The word *holy* is one of the most commonly used words in Scripture, especially in describing the attribute of God. Concerning the word as used in the Old Testament, Robert Baker Girdlestone writes:

> The point involved in every case is relation or contact with God. Thus the Sabbath day was holy because God rested thereon, and it was to be set apart by Israel as a pledge that He had sanctified or set apart the people to Himself (Exod. 31.13); . . . God Himself was regarded as holy, i.e., as a Being who from His nature, position, and attributes is to be set apart and revered as distinct from all others.[3]

In the Gospels, Jesus is referred to as "the Holy One" in several important passages. The unclean spirit that had such violent control of a tormented man cries out "Have You [Jesus] come to destroy us? I know who You are— the Holy One of God!" (Mark 1:24). Peter in his great testimony of the Lord proclaims, "And we [the disciples] have believed and have come to know that You are the Holy One of God" (John 6:69). The angel, in announcing to Mary that she will be the mother of Jesus the Savior, explains, "the Most High will overshadow you; and for that reason the holy offspring shall be called the Son of God" (Luke 1:35).

The New Testament passages refer to Psalm 16, David's messianic song. "For Thou wilt not abandon my soul to Sheol; neither wilt Thou allow Thy Holy One to undergo decay" (v. 10). This passage is quoted by Peter (Acts 2:25–28) to show that King David spoke as a prophet regarding Jesus (2:32). Paul applies the quotation directly to Jesus in Acts 13:35: "He whom God raised did not undergo decay."

"The Righteous One"

As Jesus is called "the Holy One" in Acts 3:14, He is also called "the Righteous One" (*dikaios*) in the same verse. In both expressions, the deity of the Lord is clearly in view. For as God is called "the Holy One" in many Old Testament passages (e.g., Isa. 10:20; 30:12; 41:20), so He is referred to as "the Righteous One" (e.g., Deut. 32:4; Ps. 119:138; Jer. 12:1).

The word *righteous* or *righteousness* has in view certain legal demands and the fact that God is the ultimate Judge, with requirements that must be fulfilled. The concept of righteousness belongs more to the ideal of salvation. Righteousness mediated by faith is the universal reality of salvation, according to Romans 10:4.[4]

As God is described as morally righteous in character, likewise is Jesus, being God, so portrayed. New Testament prophets and personalities certainly refer to Christ's righteousness with His deity in mind. Stephen says the fathers of the Jews killed the prophets "who had previously announced the coming of the Righteous One, whose betrayers and murderers you have now become" (Acts 7:52). Ananias tells Saul as he ministers to him, "The God of our fathers has appointed you to know His will, and to see the Righteous One, and to hear an utterance from His mouth" (22:14). As used theologically of Jesus, these texts tell us that our Lord is sinless in an absolute sense. Thus Christ did not die for His own sins; instead, He went to the cross to bear our transgressions.

"The Prince"

Acts and Hebrews coin a most unusual description of Jesus, the *archēgos* ("prince"). The term is related to a family of words translated "beginning" *(archē)*, "chief or high one," as in chief priest *(archiereus)*. It is interesting that this unusual word, *archēgos*, is used twice in Acts and twice in Hebrews in contexts that are very Jewish.

Before his fellow Israelites, Peter has proclaimed Jesus "the Holy One" and "the Righteous One" (3:14) whom the people had put to death but who was also "the Prince of life" (3:15). In his great sermon before the Sanhedrin, Peter refers to Psalm 110:1, where the Messiah is seated at the right hand of the Father. He again refers to Christ as a Prince and a Savior: "The God of our fathers raised up Jesus, whom you had put to death by hanging Him on a cross. He is the one whom God exalted to His right hand as a Prince and a Savior, to grant repentance to Israel, and forgiveness of sins" (5:30–31).

Is the writer of Hebrews quoting the apostle Peter when he writes that God is perfecting *(teleioō)* or maturing through sufferings Jesus who is "the author ("Prince," *archēgos*) of their salvation" (2:10)? In 12:2, the author of Hebrews writes of "fixing our eyes on Jesus, the author ("Prince," *archēgos*) and perfecter of faith, who for the joy set before Him endured the cross, despising the shame, and has sat down at the right hand of the throne of God." Like Peter, the writer of Hebrews quotes Psalm 110:1. Preferring to translate *archēgos* as "Author" in Acts 3:15, R. C. H. Lenski writes:

> To this climax there is added the paradox, "you killed the Author of life." How can life's own Author be killed? One might ask further, "How can Jesus become the Author of life by being killed?" This is one of those great Scriptural statements that cannot be brushed aside . . . [as] mere verbal play. "The Author of life" is a divine name for the person of Jesus, yet something human is predicted of him.[5]

"The Judge"

The apostle Peter told Cornelius and his household that Christ was appointed by God to be the Judge (*kritēs*) "of the living and the dead" (Acts 10:42). In contrast, Peter goes on and says that all the prophets bear witness of Him, that "everyone who believes in Him receives forgiveness of sins" (v. 43). Thus Jesus is both the One who will determine salvation but He Himself provides the sacrifice that gives salvation. It seems as if the apostle James repeats this truth when he wrote ". . . behold, the Judge is standing right at the door" (James 5:9). This would be a rapture passage because James says the Lord's coming is at hand (v. 8) and therefore believers should not be complaining against each other (v. 9). In other words, He could come suddenly while the believer is alive and they would be taken before Him to be judged as to how they treated the fellow Christian.

Paul substantiates Christ's coming to judge the believer. Again the rapture is in view because Paul hints it could happen as he was anticipating the return of Jesus. "In the future there is laid up for me the crown of righteousness, which the Lord, the righteous Judge, will award to me on that day; and not only to me, but also to all who have loved His appearing" (2 Tim. 4:8).

Concerning Christ as Judge, on Acts 10:42 Barnes notes:

> The doctrine of the New Testament is, that those who are alive when the Lord Jesus shall return, . . . will be caught up in vast numbers like clouds, to meet him in the air, without seeing death, 1 Th. iv. 16, 17. Yet before this they will experience such a change in their bodies as shall fit them for the judgment and for their eternal residence—a change which will liken them to those who have died, and have risen from the dead. What this change will be, speculation may fancy, but the Bible has not revealed. See 1 Cor. xv. [6]

"The Prophet"

Both Peter and Stephen recognize that Jesus is the great Prophet whom Moses predicted would someday arrive on the scene of Israel's history. In Deuteronomy 18, Moses warned Israel in the Wilderness to avoid those who practice divination and witchcraft (v. 10). Moses probably knew that in time the nation would fall prey to a swarm of false prophets. He added: "The Lord your God will raise up for you a prophet like me from among you, from your countrymen, you shall listen to him" (v. 15).

In Peter's poignant sermon at the temple, he reminds the Jews that God sent Jesus, the One the prophets preached (Acts 3:20). Likewise, the Lord would send the promised Prophet spoken of by Moses. A warning then follows: "And it shall be that every soul that does not heed that prophet shall be utterly destroyed from among the people" (v. 23). Peter acts as a prophet himself because this judgment indeed fell on his generation and on all who rejected the Lord Jesus.

Stephen, in his final message to his Jewish brothers, also quotes Deuteronomy 18:15. He reminds his listeners that the nation, when beginning their wandering in the wilderness, spoke against Moses, just as his own generation was speaking against Jesus (Acts 7:37–41). Stephen comments on the Israelites' unwillingness to obey Moses. They had repudiated him and turned their hearts back toward Egypt (v. 39). Stephen cuts the Jews in his conclusion that the fathers had killed those who had announced the coming Messiah, and now his listeners had betrayed and murdered the Messiah himself (v. 52). It was then that the crowd dragged Stephen out of the gates of Jerusalem and stoned him to death (vv. 57–60). They wanted nothing to do with the Prophet.

"The Servant"

Peter explains in Acts 3 that Moses looked forward to the great Prophet, Jesus. He reminded his audience that the prophets had predicted "these days," when God would raise up His Servant to reach all the families of the earth. And yet the gospel first would come to the nation of Israel "to bless you by turning every one of you from your wicked ways" (vv. 24–26). While Peter speaks, the captain of the temple accosts him and John because the Sadducees are "greatly disturbed" that Peter and John are teaching the resurrection of "the Servant Jesus" (4:2). Peter had said earlier that with the resurrection God "glorified His servant Jesus" (3:13). After being arrested and released, Peter again refers to Christ as the Lord's "holy servant Jesus" (4:27, 30).

Before the Pharisees in Matthew 12:17–22, the Lord applies to Himself Isaiah 42:1–4, which reads in part: "Behold, My Servant, whom I uphold; My chosen one in whom My soul delights. I have put My Spirit upon Him; He will bring forth justice to the nations." Isaiah also speaks of this same Servant as the future King who "will be high and lifted up, and greatly exalted" (52:13) and who, as "My Servant, will justify the many, as He will bear their iniquities" (53:11).

"The Son of David"

The Gospels contain many references of Christ as the Son of David (Matt. 1:1; 9:27; 21:9; Luke 1:32; 3:31; 18:38–39; 20:41). This substantiates Jesus' position in the line of the kings of Israel. David is from the monarchical tribe of Judah. Physically, Mary is a daughter of David. Joseph, too, is a descendant of David and, legally, Joseph is the "adoptive" father of Jesus. Though not a blood relative through Joseph, the adoptive relationship established hereditary legal rights for a child as securely as did paternity in Jewish society. Matthew puts it this way: "To Jacob was born Joseph the husband of Mary, by whom was born Jesus, who is called Christ" (Matt. 1:16).

The apostle Paul focuses on the importance of the lineage of Christ when speaking at the synagogue in Pisidian Antioch. He noted "the offspring (*spermatos*) of this man [David], according to promise, God has brought to Israel a Savior, Jesus." (Acts 13:23). On this verse, Lenski observes:

> This . . . statement that Jesus was "from the seed" of David ought to give pause to all those who deny that Mary was a lineal descendant of David and refuse to understand Luke's genealogical table (Luke 3:23, etc.) as being that of Mary. . . . Paul speaks of both the birth or descent of Jesus and of his office. "According to promise" even connects the two, for it was God's promise that one of David's blood should be the Savior, 2 Sam. 7:16; Isa. 11:1; Jer. 23:5, 6; Zech. 3:8; Luke 1:32, 33.[7]

It is through the covenant with David that the Messiah must come (2 Sam. 7:12–17). The angel Gabriel tells Mary that the One born "will be great, and will be called the Son of the Most High; and the Lord God will give Him the throne of His father David; and He will reign over the house of Jacob forever; and His kingdom will have no end" (Luke 1:32–33).

Since the new covenant is the focus in Acts, the Davidic reign is not given heavy priority. The kingdom has been postponed. As the apostles in Acts realize this fact, they concentrate on the issue of salvation through Christ. His reign is another issue and is yet far future.

"The Son of God"

Though a key issue in the Gospels, the fact of the sonship of Jesus is almost an understood fact in Acts. The expressions *the Christ, the Son of Man,* and *the Son of David* are mentioned often in this book. The Jewish people were aware that these phrases taught that the Messiah was also "the Son of God." As well, they knew the major Old Testament passage was Psalm 2. Here the Lord says, "Thou art My Son, today I have begotten Thee" (v. 7). This Son of God is also the promised "Anointed" (Christ) in verse 2.

Paul quotes Psalm 2:7 in his sermon at Pisidian Antioch, where he focuses on Jesus, who is the offspring of David (Acts 13:23), the one who was put to death by Pilate (v. 28), raised from the dead (v. 30), and would never again decay (v. 37). Paul argues that God had to raise Him from the grave because He is the begotten Son of God: "And we preach to you the good news of the promise made to the fathers, that God has fulfilled this promise to our children in that He raised up Jesus, as it is also written in the second Psalm, 'Thou art My Son; today I have begotten Thee'" (Acts 13:32–33). John Polhill writes:

> Jesus was indeed the Son of God from all eternity and recognized as such throughout his earthly life (Luke 1:35; 3:22; 9:35). But it was through the resurrection that he was exalted to God's right hand, enthroned as Son of God, and recognized as such by believing humans. It was through the resurrection that he was declared Son of God with power (Rom. 1:4).[8]

"The Son of Man"

Jesus applies the title *Son of Man* to Himself more than any other title recorded in the Gospels. This title's origin is Daniel 7 and the prophecy of the "Son of Man" brought before the throne of God and given an "everlasting dominion" (7:13–14). This passage must be connected to Psalm 110:1, in which David's Lord *(Adonai)* is told to sit at the Father's right hand in heaven "until I make Thine enemies a footstool for Thy feet." The scenario seems to be as follows: At the ascension of Jesus, He entered the throne room of His father and is presented as the "Son related to Humankind." He became a man, died for humanity, was given dominions and kingdoms, and is seated now until His enemies are subjugated.

Psalm 110:1 is quoted five times in Acts. Following the resurrection and ascension, notes Peter, Jesus is "exalted to the right hand of God" (2:33), after being instructed to do the same by the Father (v. 34). The Lord is exalted to that position as the Prince and Savior, "to grant repentance to Israel, and forgiveness of sins" (5:31). And as Stephen is dying from the stoning by the Jews, he sees heaven open and Jesus, the Son of Man, "standing at the right hand of God" (7:55–56).

Finally, it is clear in the interrogation of Jesus before Caiaphas before His crucifixion that the Jews considered the terms *Son of Man, Son of God,* and *Christ* to be equivalent (Matt. 26:63–64). The Jews also realized that somehow the Son of Man was related to deity. When Jesus told the high priest, "You shall see the Son of Man sitting at the right hand of Power, and coming on the clouds of heaven" at His return, Caiaphas "tore his robes, saying, 'He has blasphemed!'" (v. 65). This is why the Jews rushed Stephen when he saw the *Son of Man* at God's right hand. The crowd went mad and "cried out with a loud voice, and covered their ears, and they rushed upon him with one impulse" (Acts 7:57).

The book of Acts uses almost every name that defines the Lord Jesus. Not only are the names brought to the minds of the disciples but also the importance and significance of each reference is understood. All the names have powerful prophetic urgency. The names of Christ act as pieces of a puzzle that fit together to reveal a larger picture of His glory and majesty.

Chapter 4

THE USE OF PROPHECY IN ACTS

The pulsing heartbeat of the book of Acts is the fulfillment of Old Testament prophecy. Acts is the culmination, the climax, of many of the most important promises made in the older Book. But prophecy in Acts is used in other ways besides historical fulfillment. Luke frequently quotes Peter, Paul, and others as they use prophetic utterance for literary and theological purposes. It is helpful to examine some of those uses.

The Covenants

The Abrahamic Covenant

The Abrahamic covenant is the driving force of the Bible and is extremely important in the development of the book of Acts. What God lays forth in this promise to Abraham and His children forms the glue that holds the Bible together. The initial verses of the covenant are found in Genesis 12:1–3, where God makes predictions about three issues. He tells Abraham: (1) go to the land I will show you, (2) and I will make you a great nation, (3) and I will bless you, and I will use you to bless all the nations. God divides one covenant into three critical parts that deal with a land, a seed or nation, and a blessing. From this, three subcovenants are expounded and explained throughout the Old Testament:

1. the Palestinian covenant, dealing with the land promises to Abraham's children;
2. the Davidic covenant, focusing on David and his "ultimate" Seed, the Messiah; and
3. the new covenant, expanding and explaining the blessing of the Abraham covenant.

Of the Abrahamic covenant, Enns writes:

> God's method of fulfilling the Abrahamic Covenant is literal, inasmuch as God partially fulfilled the covenant in history: God blessed Abraham by giving him the land (Gen. 13:14–17); God blessed him spiritually (Gen. 13:4, 18; 14:22, 23; 21:22); God gave him numerous descendants (Gen. 22:17; 49:3–28). The important element of the Abrahamic Covenant, however, demands a future fulfillment with Messiah's kingdom rule. (1) Israel as a nation will possess the land in the future. Numerous Old Testament passages anticipate the future blessing of Israel and her possession of the land as promised to Abraham. Ezekiel envisions a future day when Israel is restored to the land (Ezek. 20:33–37, 40–42; 36:1–37:28). (2) Israel as a nation will be converted, forgiven, and restored (Rom. 11:25–27). (3) Israel will repent and receive the forgiveness of God in the future (Zech. 12:10–14). The Abrahamic Covenant finds its ultimate fulfillment in connection with the return of Messiah to rescue and bless His people Israel.[1]

Acts often refers to Abraham, and the Abrahamic covenant is at the core of Peter's argument in 3:25, in which Peter mentions specifically the covenant of Abraham and points to Genesis 12:3 and 22:18: "And in your seed (Abraham) all the families of the earth shall be blessed." Peter reminds his own generation that they are the sons of the prophets, "and of the [Abrahamic] covenant which God made with your fathers." From this he argues in 3:26, "For you first, God raised up His Servant, and sent Him to bless you by turning every one of you from your wicked ways."

Peter, Stephen, and then later Paul realize the importance of going back to the roots of the nation and observing again how God developed His plan around the ancient patriarch. Abraham and God's covenant with him are reminders of the continuity by which the living God developed a plan that had a culmination in their day. And though they are a privileged people, the Lord will still deal with their sin and rejection of His promised Son! Though the covenant is not directly mentioned again in Acts, there are other important references to the patriarchs who were recipients of its blessing. For example, Peter stated: "The God of Abraham, Isaac, and Jacob, the God of our fathers, has glorified His servant Jesus, the one whom you delivered up, and disowned in the presence of Pilate, when he had decided to release Him" (3:13).

In his defense, Stephen rehearses how the Lord blessed the nation in the past. Stephen refers to the land aspect of the covenant when he said, "The God of glory appeared to our father Abraham when he was in Mesopotamia, before he lived in Haran, and said to him, 'Depart from your country and your relatives, and come into the land that I will show you'" (7:2b–3). Stephen notes that at first God gave him no inheritance in the land and yet promised that later it would be the possession of his descendants (v. 5).

Stephen then mentions the sign of the covenant, circumcision, and how it would verify and confirm the sons of Jacob (v. 8). He refers to the tomb purchased by Abraham, where Jacob was laid to rest (v. 16). He looks back again to Abraham as the fatherly source of the nation, even as they exploded in numbers while in captivity in Egypt (v. 17).

Finally, when speaking about the great prophet Moses, Stephen reminds the Jews how the Lord said to the great lawgiver, "I am the God of your fathers, the God of Abraham and Isaac and Jacob" (v. 32).

The apostle Paul goes further, directly connecting his generation and Abraham and the fact that, through him, salvation has finally been realized in the coming of Jesus Christ. "Brethren, sons of Abraham's family, and those among you who fear God, to us the word of this salvation has been sent out" (13:26). Though this is Paul's only mention of the father of the nation in Acts, he clearly intertwines Abraham, his descendants, and the coming of Christ the Savior.

The Palestinian/Land Covenant

This covenant is mentioned only in passing in Acts. Since in Acts the final dispersion of the Jews from the land is now about to take place (in A.D. 70), Stephen refers to it briefly (7:4–7). And since the full promise of blessings are being postponed for the Jews, it only makes sense that this covenant is barely referred to. But Stephen looks back in history and says, Abraham, you will "come into the land that I will show you" (v. 3), and "God removed [Abraham] into this country [Canaan] in which you [Jews] are now living" (v. 4), and "He promised that He would give [the land] to him as a possession, and to his offspring after him" (v. 5). By mentioning offspring, Stephen places a judgment on the heads of those standing before him. Despite the rejection of Christ by the Jews in Acts, this promise will be fulfilled by some future believing generation!

The Davidic Covenant

"It is God's promise to David," according to J. W. McGarvey, "that indicates David's greater Son will be the One through whom this future kingdom will be inaugurated (2 Sam. 7:12–16). In this magnificent statement God promises David that His dynasty, issuing in Messiah, will never be terminated and Messiah's kingdom rule will be forever." [2]

Son of God

Immediately upon his conversion, Saul, filled by the Holy Spirit, begins speaking of this Davidic covenant and the fact that Jesus is the Son of God (Acts 9:20; see pp. 80–81). The Jews recognize this as Psalm 2:7 and a key reference to the Davidic covenant.

The Messiah, the Christ

The Davidic covenant and Psalm 2 are also important to Peter. After they are threatened and released by the elders and chief priests, Peter and John in Acts 4:25–26 quote Old Testament references to the "rulers" gathering together against the Lord and against His Christ. They see it as a fulfillment of the prophecy that God's holy servant Jesus was turned upon by "Herod and Pontius Pilate, along with the Gentiles and the peoples of Israel" (v. 27). This is also part of Saul's message after his conversion. Before all the Jews living in Damascus he proves the prophecy that "Jesus is the Christ" (9:22). He repeats this prophetic proof at Thessalonica (17:3) and at Ephesus, "for he powerfully refuted the Jews in public, demonstrating by the Scriptures that Jesus was the Christ" (18:28).

As the Jews at Pisidian Antioch resist the message of Paul and Barnabas, the apostles quote the great messianic prophecy of Isaiah 49:6: "I have placed You [the Messiah] as a light for the Gentiles, that You should bring salvation to the end of the earth" (13:47). Not only do they apply that directly to Christ but also, as His servants, they feel compelled to be His emissaries. Paul and Barnabas must have seen this moment at Antioch as providential. Now they know that God has begun to turn away from the Jews and toward the Gentiles. They boldly told the Jews that they were unworthy of eternal life and that "we are [now] turning to the Gentiles" (v. 46). As they left the city, "they shook off the dust of their feet in protest against them" (v. 51).

Kingdom of God

This is one of the most frequently recurring prophetic themes found in the Old Testament. Though the doctrine of the kingdom is implicit in many prophecies, it is also implied in a multitude of contexts. One has but to study the orthodox Jewish rabbis as they comment on the prophecies to see the great number of verses that are clearly kingdom references. Christian commentators, especially dispensational premillennialists, concur with much of the biblical exegesis of the orthodox rabbis when they speak of kingdom glories when the Messiah reigns.

Remember that Acts is the history of the transition from kingdom expectations to the new work of building the church; yet, the kingdom of God is often alluded to throughout the book. However, what is interesting is how it is *not* referred to in Acts. (1) The kingdom is never made a synonym for the church, (2) no details are given as to what was said about the kingdom, and (3) the kingdom is never seen as some mystical or spiritual aspect of the church age.

The book of Acts opens with Jesus teaching the apostles about "the kingdom of God" (1:3). Whatever He was teaching specifically, they were still looking for the promised physical restoration of "the kingdom to Israel" (v. 6). The Lord sidesteps their kingdom question and speaks of something new that will be initiated by the Holy Spirit to empower the disciples as his witnesses (vv. 7–8).

It is interesting that He does not say, "You have it all wrong! There will not be a promised earthly kingdom as prophesied in the Old Testament. The church will take the place of the kingdom!" Throughout Acts, the kingdom concept is left intact, but the reader feels the impact from the explosion of the "new" thing. The new covenant prompted by the Holy Spirit spreads out beyond the nation of Israel. But the kingdom of God as a yet future viable promise for restored Israel is still there in Acts.

For example, though not knowing God's timetable, Peter refers to the prophecy of the Christ someday sitting on David's throne (2:30). Before that can happen, Peter sees Jesus' resurrection in the prophecy of Psalm 16:8–11: "For Thou wilt not abandon my soul to Hades, neither wilt thou allow Thy Holy One to see the pit" (vv. 10–11).

In Samaria, Philip was preaching "the good news about the kingdom of God and the name of Jesus Christ" (8:12). Paul took that message to the Jews at Ephesus (19:8). Later, meeting with the elders of Ephesus, he reminded them that he had indeed been faithfully preaching the kingdom (20:25). If the church was now in a spiritual sense the kingdom, the apostles had ample opportunity to explain that as they taught. But the doctrines of the church and the kingdom are clearly kept separate throughout the book of Acts.

This separation is made clear in the context of 28:31 as Paul is described as "preaching the kingdom of God, and teaching concerning the Lord Jesus Christ with all openness, unhindered." McGarvey notes that two subjects are in mind because preaching was done mainly with the unsaved and teaching was for the believers.[3] The question that surely lingers among the apostles is when the earthly messianic kingdom would come. Paul certainly understands that the tribulation must come before the arrival of the kingdom (2 Thess. 2:1–12).

Acts 14:22 clearly points to the separation of the kingdom from the church. Paul and Barnabas went about Antioch and other cities teaching, "Through many tribulations we must enter the kingdom of God." If they were already in the body of Christ, the church, how could they be yet still entering the kingdom? The Word of God clearly teaches that the destiny of church saints will be the earthly one thousand-year reign of Christ.

Though not radical premillennialists, both A. T. Robertson and R. C. H. Lenski understand that the kingdom mentioned in 14:22 is not the church, but rather something future and beyond that present moment, in the context of Acts. They clearly understand that the church is not the kingdom. On this verse Robertson writes: "Paul frankly warned these new converts in this heathen environment of the many tribulations through which they must enter the Kingdom of God (the culmination at last)."[4] Though Lenski thinks the kingdom of glory is in view, he still makes an important distinction in that we are not yet in that kingdom: "The kingdom of glory is referred to, God's and Christ's eternal glorious, heavenly rule. The thorns prick us as we climb upward to that kingdom, but the roses await us there."[5] Though not in agreement with premillennialists, these men still see these kingdom passages in Acts as distinct from the church.

Three key prophetic passages in Acts picture the kingdom that will in the future be restored. Peter urges the Jews to repent "that He may send Jesus, the Christ appointed for you, whom heaven must receive until the period of restoration of all things about which God spoke by the mouth of His holy prophets from ancient times" (3:20–21). This is the millennial time of refreshing (v. 19). Not knowing God's timetable, Peter believes the kingdom may come soon. One thing is for certain—he speaks of the kingdom as separate from what was happening at that moment with the church.

At the Jerusalem Council (15:1–29), James noted how God "first" took from among the Gentiles a people for His name. Then James introduces his quotation from the prophet Amos (Amos 9:11–12) with the words "after these things." To what things does James refer? Notes in the *New Scofield Study Bible* make this comment: "James quoted from the *LXX*, which here preserved the original text. Amos 9:11 begins with the words "in that day." James introduced his quotation in such a way as to show what day Amos was talking about, namely, the time after the present world-wide witness (Acts 1:8), when Christ will return."

David's fallen tabernacle is the earthly dynasty that is yet to come when the Messiah returns. Since this is yet future, there is no way it can be the present church age! Richard N. Longenecker, writing in *The Expositor's Bible Commentary*, well notes:

> In the end times, James is saying, God's people will consist of two concentric groups. At their core will be restored Israel (i.e., David's rebuilt tent); gathered around them will be a group of Gentiles (i.e., "the remnant of men") who will share in the messianic blessings but will persist as Gentiles without necessarily become

Jewish proselytes. It is this understanding of Amos' message, James insisted, that Peter's testimony has affirmed, the result being that the conversion of Gentiles in the last days should be seen not as proselytizing but in an eschatological context.[6]

Is Christ on David's Throne?

Some try to say that Christ is now on David's throne, thus the kingdom is here in the church in a certain spiritualized way. The passage used is Peter's message, 2:22–36, which actually is presenting two different doctrines. Because Christ is the Holy One (v. 27), He has been "raised up again" (v. 32), which gives Him the right to reign on David's throne (v. 30). He has therefore been "made" or declared the "Christ" (v. 36). But because He has ascended into heaven and sits at the Father's right hand (v. 34) He is designated "the Lord." The reference is to Daniel 7:13–14, which says the Messiah will someday be given all universal authority, an "everlasting dominion." Because of this, Jesus the Son of Man sits at the Father's right hand (Ps. 110:1) and has been declared "the Lord" (2:34, 36). In Greek, "made . . . both Lord and Christ" means the two are actually two distinct happenings or events. To be declared Lord places Jesus at the right hand of the Father; to be declared the Christ means He has the right to someday reign on David's throne in Jerusalem. The throne of the Father in heaven is not the future Davidic throne on earth! The Lord Jesus prophetically states, "He who overcomes, I will grant to him to sit down with Me on My throne, as I also overcame and sat down with My Father on His throne" (Rev. 3:21).

The New Covenant

The new covenant has its origins in the Abrahamic covenant. Notice God's promise in Genesis 12:3 to bless the nation and all others through the nation. Enns writes:

> Jeremiah envisioned a future day when God would restore the fortunes of Israel and bring them back into the land (Jer. 30:3). This would be an eschatological restoration for it would follow the time of great tribulation for Israel (Jer. 30:7). Jeremiah prophesied the rebuilding of Jerusalem in that future day (Jer. 30:18–24) and the resultant kingdom blessings (Jer. 31:1–12). The blessing of Israel in that future day would be based on the New Covenant that God would make with Israel (Jer. 31:31–34). That New Covenant is made with the nation Israel (Jer. 31:31) and will be in contrast with the Old Covenant, the Mosaic Covenant, which could not produce righteousness in the people.[7]

The new covenant includes the forgiveness of sins (Jer. 31:34) and the indwelling of the Holy Spirit (Jer. 31:33; Ezek. 36:27). When Jesus broke bread and partook of the wine with the disciples at Passover, He alluded to the fact that His impending death would ratify the new covenant: "This cup which is poured out for you is the new covenant in My blood" (Luke 22:20).

Though the new covenant is given first to Israel, and ultimately will be fulfilled when the kingdom is restored, the church now shares the benefits of that covenant. This in no way makes the church Israel. God still has a distinct national program for the Jewish people. They will not enter that kingdom with its blessings until they have personally accepted Jesus as their Savior and King. For now, during this dispensation, the believers in Christ are the "servants of a new covenant, not of the letter [the Law], but of the Spirit; for the letter kills, but the Spirit gives life" (2 Cor. 3:6).

The Coming of the Spirit

Many facets of the new covenant are mentioned in Acts. And many prophecies about the covenant are fulfilled in the book. The baptism of the Holy Spirit prophesied by the Lord (1:4–5) seems to fulfill the promise of being cleansed by the Spirit in Ezekiel 36:25–27. "*Then I will sprinkle* [Heb. *zarak*, "slosh"] clean water on you, and you will be clean. . . . And I will put My Spirit within you and cause you to walk in My statutes." Though Ezekiel promises this washing for regathered Israel, the church now receives the "spill-over" blessings of the cleansing and Spirit indwelling.

Before His ascension, Jesus also predicted the empowerment of the Holy Spirit, through the new covenant, for the disciples: "But you shall receive power when the Holy Spirit has come upon you; and you shall be My witnesses" (1:8). This would happen in conjunction with the baptism of the Spirit. And this promised sending of the Spirit "the Father had promised, 'Which,' He said, 'you heard of from Me'" (1:4; cf., 2:33). Jesus is referring to the prophecy recorded in the Gospel of John, where He said, "And I will ask the Father, and He will give you another Helper, that He may be with you forever. . . . But the Helper, the Holy Spirit, whom the Father will send in My name, He will teach you all things" (John 14:16, 26).

Joel 2

One of the most important prophecies in the book of Acts is the quotation from Joel 2:28–32, cited by Peter in Acts 2:14–21. This quotation, and how Peter uses it, really begins the book of Acts. But Joel 2 can be taken in any of several ways. Even among premillennialists and dispensationalists there are differences in interpretation and differing ideas about Peter's intent. For more on this prophecy and Peter's quotation, see pp. 145–150.

The Suffering Messiah

The new covenant promises forgiveness of sins because of the substitution of Christ for sins. The Messiah, Isaiah predicted, would be a sacrificial

Lamb (Isa. 53). The apostle Peter recognized this and other related prophecies: "But the things which God announced beforehand by the mouth of all the prophets, that His Christ should suffer, He has thus fulfilled" (3:18). The Ethiopian was reading the Isaiah prophecy when he invited Philip to come up in his chariot and explain it to him (8:31–33). Beginning with Isaiah 53, Philip "preached Jesus to him" (8:35).

Before the high priests, Peter continues his indictment against the Jews by pointing out the prophecy of Psalm 118:22 concerning the suffering Messiah. "He is the stone which was rejected by you, the builders, but which became the very corner stone" (4:11). Part of His suffering was through the betrayal of Judas. In Acts 1:16–20, quoting Psalm 69, which is known for its strong messianic implications, Peter applies 69:25 to Judas: "Let his homestead be made desolate." Peter then quotes Psalm 109, an imprecatory psalm of David, and applies verse 8 to Judas: "His office let another man take." From these verses, Peter argues that the disciples should pick a substitute for Judas. The apostles agree, and the lot falls to Matthias (1:26).

Prophecies of Judgment

Besides the various prophecies of the covenants quoted in Acts, there are also other prophetic subjects the apostles draw upon.

For example, in Acts 13:40–41, Paul quotes Habakkuk 1:5 to warn the Jews that as scoffers they may perish because they refused to believe what was happening in their day. The context of Habakkuk is that the Jews of that day did not believe the Babylonian invasion was imminent. Peter uses Habakkuk as an "illustrative" prophecy applicable to the Jews before him. Habakkuk writes: "Behold, you scoffers, and marvel, and perish; for I am accomplishing a work in your days, a work which you will never believe, though someone should describe it to you." In the context of his speech Peter speaks of the resurrection of Christ, through which forgiveness of sins is proclaimed (13:38). Knowing the Jews of Pisidian Antioch were rejecting what he was saying, Peter quoted this powerful passage.

The apostle Paul does the same in his stinging words against the Jews of Rome, when he was under house arrest (28:26–27). For those who would not believe in Jesus, Paul quotes Isaiah 6:9–10 as a direct reference as to the spiritual state of the Jews he was addressing: "And they have closed their eyes; lest they should see with their eyes, and hear with their ears, and understand with their heart and return, and I should heal them." But as the Jews were departing his dwelling, Paul throws at them one final prophecy of justification. Though they will not accept Jesus as their Savior, God will now send to the Gentiles the truth of salvation: "Let it be known to you therefore, that this salvation of God has been sent to the Gentiles; they will also listen" (v. 28). Paul is quoting the great prophetic song of Jehovah's salvation, Psalm 98. In that psalm God urges His readers to sing a new song (v. 1) of His salvation "made known" (v. 2). By that salvation "He has revealed His righteousness in the sight of the nations" and "remembered . . . His faithfulness to the house of Israel; all the ends of the earth have seen the salvation of our God" (vv. 2–3).

The Prophets Quoted

Acts is replete with Old Testament references, both prophetic fulfillments of promises and illustrations of theological points. We now will address only passages that refer specifically to a given prophet or the prophets collectively. Because 2:14–21 makes such extensive use of Joel 2, it is discussed elsewhere (see pp. 114–116, 145–150).

With great enthusiasm, Peter proclaims in his temple discourse that all the prophets had anticipated Christ's suffering. All of these prophecies Christ has fulfilled, he announces (3:18). Whether Christ's suffering is somehow alluded to by *all* the prophets, it is pervasive enough to justify some literary hyperbole. Paul uses the writings of the prophets and Moses to convict Agrippa (26:22). He refers to Christ's suffering, the resurrection, and the fact that Jesus is "light both to the Jewish people and to the Gentiles" (v. 23). Paul authenticates the power of the prophetic Word with his final question to Agrippa: "Do you believe the Prophets? I know that you do" (v. 27).

Previously, the apostle Paul reiterated before Felix how he served "the God of our fathers, believing everything that is in accordance with the Law, and that is written in the Prophets" (24:14). He then focused on the fact that the prophets hoped in God "which these men [the prophets] cherish themselves, that there shall certainly be a resurrection of both the righteous and the wicked" (v. 15).

The power of the message of the ancient prophets is illustrated in Peter's message in Acts 3. He points out that every soul shall be "utterly destroyed from among the people" who deny the words of Moses the prophet (v. 23). And likewise, "all the prophets who have spoken, from Samuel and his successors onward, also announced these days" (v. 24). Samuel prophesied the covenant with David (2 Samuel 7) by which the descendant of David, the Messiah, would someday reign on the throne in Jerusalem. Referring to this, James says the prophets agree that "after these things [the church age] I will return, and I will rebuild the tabernacle of David which has fallen" (Acts 15:15–16a). James then quotes Amos, Jeremiah, Moses, and Isaiah. The tabernacle of David is a colorful description of the authoritative kingdom reign of Christ, the Son of David.

The prophecies of Isaiah present both a blessing and a curse. The Ethiopian is reading Isaiah 53, from which Philip shows that Christ is the Lamb who would be substituted for sins (Acts 8:26–37). Acts closes with Paul using Isaiah to condemn the Jews for rejecting their own Messiah (28:25–28). Paul quotes Isaiah 6:9–10, which predicts that "the heart of this people has become dull." Now, Paul adds, "This salvation of God has been sent to the Gentiles; they will also listen" (v. 28).

Chapter 5

DEMONOLOGY
AND THE BOOK OF ACTS

Eleven passages in the book of Acts bear directly on the activity of Satan, demons, sorcery, magic, and the worship of the demon-like goddess Diana. Some are historical references that require less comment, whereas others are doctrinal and deserve greater attention.

Satan

Ananias and Sapphira's Deception

Acts 5:1–11 is the first of four passages that use the title *Satan* or *Devil*. When Peter confronts Ananias about withholding money by deception, he said, "Ananias, why has Satan filled your heart to lie to the Holy Spirit?" (5:3a). Some commentaries center attention on the question of whether Ananias and Sapphira were really saved and whether they could have lost their salvation as a result of their sin.

Dr. Homer A. Kent Jr. effectively answers this question:

There are a number of factors which suggest that they may have been Christians who were disciplined by God. (1) Acts 4:32 indicates that all who engaged in the community of goods were believers. . . . (2) Satan can energize saved people (David, 1 Chron. 21:1; Peter, Matt. 16:21–23; Christians in general, 1 Peter 5:8–9). (3) Physical death is a discipline applied to some Christians (1 Cor. 11:30–32). (4) The fact of lying to the Holy Spirit is more easily understood of Christians indwelled by the Spirit than of unbelievers who have no relation to God and specially no relation to the Holy Spirit.[1]

A second doctrinal aspect centers on the question, "Why has Satan filled your heart?" Since the verb *plēroō* is used here and in Ephesians 5:18, where Paul commands Christians to be "filled with the Spirit," it might seem incongruous that Ananias could also experience Satan filling his heart, if indeed he was a Christian. The answer is found in the definition and use of the verb *plēroō*. In the second chapter of this volume the filling of the Holy Spirit was discussed and it was shown that *plēroō* is defined as control. Luke 1:15 describes John the Baptist as having been "filled" with the Holy Spirit "from his mother's womb." The same verb *plēroō* is used, indicating that filling is not synonymous with regeneration or indwelling. Therefore, John the Baptist was not saved from his mother's womb but was controlled by the Holy Spirit and watched over until he came to recognize Jesus as Messiah.

In like manner, Satan can work outside of a believer without indwelling him. He "sifted" Peter (Luke 22:31), tempts believers (2 Cor. 11:3), deceives by his wiles (Eph. 6:11), ensnares (2 Tim. 2:26), and gains advantage over us (2 Cor. 2:11). But all of these are from the outside, that is, apart from the soul. These attempts can be resisted and defeated successfully (James 4:7; 1 Peter 5:9; 1 John 2:13).

Paul's Testimony

Acts 26:18 is the only other passage in Acts that mentions the title *Satan*. Before King Agrippa Paul recounts his vision of the Lord on the road to Damascus. Paul said God had commissioned him to go to the Gentiles, "to open their eyes, so that they may turn from darkness to light and from the dominion [or authority or power] of Satan to God." The word *dominion* or *power* is most precisely translated "authority" (from *exousia*). When Satan tempted Jesus, he claimed to have authority: "And the devil, taking him up into an high mountain, showed him all the kingdoms of the world in a moment of time. And the devil said unto him, All this authority (*exousia*) will I give thee, and the glory of them; for that is delivered unto me, and to whomsoever I will I give it." (Luke 4:5–6 KJV). Even Paul called Satan "the prince of the power (*exousia*) of the air" (Eph. 2:2).

The authority of Satan is no match for that of the gospel, as indicated in the latter part of Acts 26:18: "That they may receive forgiveness of sins, and an inheritance among those who have been sanctified by faith in me."

Christ's Ministry

Acts 10:38 is the first of two passages using the title *Devil (diabolos)*. Peter encapsulates the ministry of Jesus, that "God anointed Jesus of Nazareth with the Holy Spirit and with power, who went about doing good, and healing all that were oppressed of the devil" (KJV). The word *oppressed* translates *katadynateuō*, which is defined by Thayer as "to exercise harsh control over one, to use one's power against one; to oppress."[2] It does not mean indwell, and thus could be used of Satan's attacks on believers or unbelievers.

Elymas the Sorcerer's Deceit

Acts 13:10 uses *diabolos* in describing Elymas the sorcerer as a "son of the devil" *(diabolos)*. By that Paul stresses the meaning of *diabolos* as "slanderer or false accuser." Elymas is described as "full of deceit and fraud," an "enemy of all righteousness" who perverted truth.

Passages Dealing with Demons or Evil Spirits

A second group of passages presents the activities of demons, or evil spirits, including Acts 5:16 and 8:6–7.

Healings of Demon-Caused Ailments

Acts 5:16: "And also the people from the cities in the vicinity of Jerusalem were coming together, bringing people who were sick or afflicted (*ochloumenous*) with unclean spirits; and they were all being healed."

An interesting definition is given for *vexed* from *ochleō*. The root word is ochlos, "crowd, mob;" thus the verb means "to excite a mob against one; to be in confusion or in an uproar; to be vexed, molested, troubled."[3] Though these vexed ones are not included with the sick, they also had to be healed. Demon influence and inhabitation are not to be confused with physical or mental illness as such, but they can produce similar effects on the body or mind. For example, Christ healed a man possessed with a demon which caused him to be mute (Matt. 9:32–33). Yet, He differentiated between healing the sick, cleansing the lepers, raising the dead, and casting out demons in Matthew 10:8.

Acts 8:6–7: "And the multitudes with one accord were giving attention to what was said by Philip, as they heard and saw the signs which he was performing. For in the case of many who had [*echontōn*, "having"] unclean spirits, they were coming out [*exērcheto*] of them shouting with a loud voice; and many who had been paralyzed [*paralelymenoi*, "being paralyzed ones"] and lame were healed."

Significantly, the word that might be translated "possessed" here in Acts 8:7 is simply the participle of *echō*, "to have." The same is true elsewhere. In Acts 16:16 a young woman was possessed with (*echousan*, "having") a spirit of divination. In Acts 19:13 Jewish exorcists tried to help those who "had the [*tous echontas*, "them having"] evil spirits" and in Acts 19:16, "And the man in whom was [*en hō ēn*, "in whom it was"] the evil spirit . . ." Yet, in the Gospels, of the thirteen occurrences of the Greek *daimonidzomai* ("demonize," for example, Matt. 4:24; 8:16; Mark 5:15), translators have tended to use the terms "possessed" or "vexed." This has given rise to the idea that actual demon possession never occurred; rather, people were merely "demonized."

Passages in Acts show that demon possession—the inhabiting of the body of the one afflicted—was a reality. This is proven further by repeated use in the Gospels and Acts of such words as "Unclean spirits . . . came out" (*exercheto*) in Acts 8:7; "And he came out [*exelthein*] the same hour" in Acts 16:18; and in Acts 19:11–12: "And the evil spirits went out of them" (*apollassesthai ap autōn*).

Two other questions are directly related to the fact of demon possession. The first is whether Christians can now confront demons and command them in the name of Christ. The second is whether a Christian can be possessed by demons.

Christians and Demons Today

Can Christians confront demons and command them in the name of Christ to come out of a person? The textual evidence is that exorcism is never meant for Christians today:

1. Acts 14:1–3 shows that *"signs and wonders"* were given to the apostles from the Lord "who was bearing witness to the word of his grace, granting that signs and wonders be done by their hands." This original authority was given to the Twelve in Matthew 10:8, including authority to cast out demons.
2. Acts 8:5–8 relates how Philip was given authority to cast out demons.
3. Acts 16:18; 19:4–12 records two occasions on which Paul used his apostolic authority and commanded evil spirits to depart. Paul was given special powers (*dynameis*) from God to accomplish these miracles.
4. This authority was for one generation only, because the apostles were part of the foundation of the church (Eph. 2:20). Our task today is not to lay foundations on foundations (as though we have the same apostolic authority and apostolic sign gifts), but to build "living stones" (1 Peter 2:5) upon that foundation, as the superstructure, by winning souls to Christ.

5. There are many misconceptions concerning so-called "spiritual warfare" today. Exorcism is never included as part of the spiritual armor. Ephesians 6:11–18 describes the whole armor of God and not the ability to perform exorcism. Further, the spiritual warfare does not include confronting demons directly, as in exorcism. Second Corinthians 10:1–6 clearly states that obedience and submission of our thoughts to the obedience of Christ are our two resources. Our spiritual authority is to submit to God and to resist the Devil, but even this is not in our own power; it is to be "strong in the Lord and in the strength of His might" by putting on the whole armor of God (Eph. 6:10–11).

6. Our authority comes through our "effectual fervent prayer" (Heb. 4:14–16; James 5:16). We go directly to God and ask Him to heal the demon possessed. Those who claim to confront and expel demons in the name of Christ may only be dealing with psychological and mental problems, or, they may be part of that group of whom Jesus warned in Matthew 7:22–23: "Many will say to me on that day, Lord, Lord, did we not prophesy in Your name, and in Your name cast out demons, and in Your name perform many miracles? And then I will declare to them, 'I never knew you; depart from Me, you who practice lawlessness.'"

Demon Possession of a Christian

Can a Christian be possessed, that is, inhabited by demons, or Satan? To answer this we must go to the words of our Lord in Matthew 12:29–30, where he gives several principles, the third being the principle of the "strong man." This illustration tells of a strong man who occupies his house full of his goods.

The problem posed by Christ is this: If anyone wants to enter the man's house and spoil his goods, he must first bind the strong man, which means that there must be one who is stronger than the strong man. In the context, the strong man is Satan (v. 25) or his demons (v. 27). The stronger man must therefore be Christ. The "house" is the body of the demon-possessed man: When the unclean spirit is gone out of a man, he says, "I will return to my house from which I came" (Matt. 12:44). The word for "spoil" (Matt. 12:29) is from *diarpadzō*, "to snatch away or carry away by force," and has to do with the house as well as the goods. Alan H. McNeile says that *skēnē*, the word for "house," refers to human bodies and souls.[4] Since the context deals with Christ casting out demons, He, the stronger man (1 John 4:4), forcibly thwarts Satan and delivers the demon-possessed man.

But what if this principle is applied to the Christian? His "house," or body, is indwelled—"Christ in you, the hope of glory" (Col. 1:27). Any attempt of Satan or his demons to enter into this strong man's house, the body of a

Christian, would immediately be thwarted because the Father, the Son (John 14:23), and the Holy Spirit (1 Cor. 6:19–20) dwell there permanently. Thus, a truly born again Christian can never be possessed or indwelled by Satan or demons.

Passages That Deal with Exorcism

A third group of passages in Acts include two that deal directly with exorcism, Acts 16:16–18 and 19:11–20. Both are from the ministry of the apostle Paul.

Exorcism of a Slave Girl (Acts 16:16–18)

"And it happened that as we were going to the place of prayer, a certain slave-girl having [echousa] a spirit of divination [pythōnos] met us, who was bringing her masters [kyrioi, "lords"] much profit by fortunetelling" (16:16). The word for fortunetelling or soothsaying (KJV) is *manteuomenē* from *manteuomai*, "to act as a seer or deliver an oracle." The noun form is *mantis*, referring to a seer. We derive the English words *mania* and *madness* from this word.

This girl was possessed by a spirit of divination; demons were once considered to have divine connections, thus the idea behind the term *"divination."* Even Paul said in 1 Corinthians 8:5–6 that "there are many gods and many lords, yet for us there is but one God, the Father; . . . and one Lord Jesus Christ."

The specific "god" occupying the body of this slave girl was Python, a Greek god at the oracle of Delphi. The city of Delphi was often referred to as Pytho, because mythology said that the serpent-god dwelling in Pytho guarded the oracle at Delphi until the Greek god Apollo slew it. Eventually the words "spirit of Python" came to refer to those "seers" who claimed to reveal future events. So it was that this particular maiden became possessed with such a demon and was able to bring "much gain" to her masters by "divining" or predicting the future. It is not that demons know the future, except perhaps the plans of Satan, since they are his messengers, but because, then and now, most people are gullible and will believe satanic "lying wonders" (2 Thess. 2:9). As a result, she was used by her slave masters to produce much profit.

The fact that she followed Paul and his companions, shouting that they were "servants of the Most High God who show unto us the way of salvation" (16:17) was not because she believed this for herself. However, it proved to be spoken by the demon within her (16:18), attempting to arouse the anger of the rulers and disrupt the ministry of Paul. This is why Paul became distressed and commanded the demon to "come out [exelthein] of her." As an apostle, Paul had the gift of exorcism. As stated before, apostolic authority was given for one generation only as part of the foundation of the body of Christ (Eph. 2:20).

Exorcism at Ephesus (Acts 19:11–20)
The Power of God over Diseases and Evil Spirits (19:11–12)

"And God was performing extraordinary miracles by the hand of Paul." This clause literally means, "And God was doing powers not common (*dynameis te ou tas tyxousas ho Theos epoie*)." Probably the usual way was for Paul to command evil spirits, as in Acts 16:18, or perhaps healing people with a touch or simply a word. In verse 12, however, we learn that pieces of cloth that had touched his body (*soudaria*, "sweat-rags," or *simikinthia*, "aprons") could convey his authority: "The pieces of material which had been in contact with Paul were those which he used as sweat-rags and aprons while engaged in his leather-working, the sweat-rags being used for tying round his head and the aprons for tying round his waist."[5] As a result of these special miracles, the diseases departed from them and the evil spirits "went out of (*exerchesthai*) them."

The Power of Evil Spirits over the Sons of Sceva (19:13–16)

The identity of Sceva as a "high priest" in verse 14 is not corroborated anywhere else; he may have used this title without warrant. Even harder to identify is the matter of Jewish exorcism rites.

Before Pentecost Jesus identified at least three groups of exorcists using His name. One man is mentioned by His disciples in Mark 9:38–40; and Luke 9:49–50 as specifically "casting out demons in thy name" who was not following with the apostles. Jesus said, "Forbid him not, for he that is not against us is for us." However, Jesus strongly condemns what might be called a second group, though the context is his prophetic interpretation of what the judgment of the lost would be like. Those who say they followed him, even if they go so far as to cast out demons in his name, will find no place if they were not actually under the lordship of Christ. He will say to them "I never knew you" when He judges the lost (Matt. 7:22–23). They are lawless.

A third group is referred to as "sons" of the Pharisees when Jesus said, "And if I by Beelzebub cast out demons, by whom do your sons cast them out? Therefore, they shall be your judges" (Matt. 12:27). Christ could hardly be referring to His apostles; they had not yet aroused the opposition of the Pharisees, and the apostles were well known enough not to be associated with the Pharisees. Who, then, were these "sons of the Pharisees" who cast out demons yet were not condemned by Christ?

The seven sons of Sceva appear to be part of yet another group that we can easily classify as charlatans. Folk Judaism of the first century and later was filled with superstitions and those who preyed on the superstitious. Likely these itinerant vagabonds are fakes, though like Simon the sorcerer in Acts 8 they desire the profits real power might earn. They are probably not truly relying on occultic power in the satanic sense because the evil spirit overcomes and wounds them. Satan's house cannot be divided against itself. In Acts 19:13

these itinerant "exorcists" (from *orkizo*, "adjure, implore, or force someone to take an oath") implored the evil spirit in the name of Jesus to leave. They quickly learn this name is no magical incantation. The evil spirit replies, "Jesus I know [*ginōskō*, "by experience"] and Paul I know [*epistamai*, "by acquaintance"], but who are you?" (v. 15). Then, by the strength of the demon within him, the man leaped upon them and tore off their clothes so that they fled, naked and traumatized.

The Power of God over the Users of Magical Arts (19:17–20)

Acts 19:17–18 indicates that in the whole city of Ephesus, both Jews and Gentiles, were beset with fear, and the name of Jesus was magnified. This is not to infer that the whole city is saved but that many believe. This awakening is so extensive that a grand fortune's worth of occultic books were destroyed (v. 19). These books were related to the *periergo*, "magical arts." *Periergo* literally means "to work around," but it was used in composition to describe those who would not mind their own business and were "busybodies" as in 2 Thessalonians 3:11 and 1 Timothy 5:13. It also was used of those who practiced magic, based on the idea that someone dabbling in the occult was being curious about others' affairs. Thus magical arts delved into "curious" things using herbs, incantations, oaths, and inscriptions to idols.[6] The value of these books is noted to be "fifty thousand pieces of silver" in verse 19. People were willing to pay high prices to have their fortunes told or because they hoped to be cured of diseases or demonism. It is impractical to guess the value of fifty thousand pieces of silver in today's financial market. At the turn of the century, R. B. Rackham estimated it at 1700 pounds sterling, or approximately $8500 in U.S. funds at *that* time.[7] A century later, the equivalent value would be many times that figure.

The Power of God and the Goddess Diana (19:23–35)

There were two goddesses named Diana. Diana of the hunt was a Roman goddess, sister of Apollo. *Artemis*, in the Greek text of the New Testament is the *"Diana of the Ephesians."* She was represented as a woman's figure with many breasts, the goddess of fertility. The image of Diana purportedly "fell down from God (lit. 'Zeus')" (v. 35). Silver shrines for Diana were made and sold by the Ephesian silversmiths; such a business made them wealthy (vv. 23–26).

The great temple of Diana and her magnificence were in danger of declining due to Paul's preaching of Christ as the only One to be worshiped (v. 27a). The temple of Diana has been variously described. So far as can be ascertained, it was 400–425 feet long and 200–239 feet wide, with 100 to 127 columns, each fifty-six to sixty feet tall. It was a major religious attraction in Ephesus and one of the wonders of the world at that time.

Diana was worshiped throughout "Asia" (see p. 341–342, 348–349) and over the inhabited earth (v. 27b). This is not simply hyperbole. The worship of Diana had spread through Greco-Roman culture, and Ephesus was widely known as the temple-keeper of Diana. Thus, the town clerk can feel confident that her worship is secure (v. 36).

The Power of God and Sorcery

Simon the Sorcerer (Acts 8:9–25)

Two passages should be taken together because they both deal with sorcerers: 8:9–25 and 13:6–12.

Acts 8 tells the story of Simon, whom Peter, Philip, and John encountered in Samaria. The words *"used sorcery"* (KJV) or "was practicing magic" (NASB) translate *mageuōn*, the root of which appears and contributes to a noun in verse 11 translated *"sorceries"* (KJV) or "magic arts" (NASB). R. C. H. Lenski gives a good summary of this practice: "The range of their arts extended from the conjuring of demons, dealing with the dead, influencing the gods, to charms for healing, divination, stargazing and the like."[8]

Simon was so successful that he was described by the people as "the great power of God." The Samaritans were amazed or astonished (v. 11, from *existōn*). The King James Bible uses "bewitched," and this interpretation does seem appropriate since Simon successfully keeps the Samaritans under his influence for a long time. But now comes a reversal; many "believe" and are "baptized." Now it is Simon's turn to be amazed at Philip's power (v. 13).

After Peter and John are summoned from Jerusalem to lay hands on the Samaritans, Simon offers them money for the power he sees Philip, and possibly them, using. Peter's reply effectively answers the first theological question involved: "Was Simon the sorcerer really born again?" The answer would seem to be that Simon was still unsaved. First, he thought that "the gift of God could be purchased with money" (v. 20). No true Christian could believe this. Thus, Peter said that Simon's money would perish (from *apolyō*) with him. The noun form *apoleian* is used of the perdition of the unbeliever and signifies eternal death.

Second, his heart is not right in the sight of God (v. 21). This is in direct contrast to those whose hearts the Lord has changed. Third, Simon needed to repent and be forgiven (v. 22), since he was still in the bond of iniquity (v. 23).

That Simon believes and is baptized must be categorized as mere profession. James 2:19 reminds that even the demons believe and tremble.

Does Simon eventually repent? He requests prayer lest those judgments would come upon him (v. 24). As Homer A. Kent Jr. reminds us, however, church writings, some of them quite ancient, universally associate Simon Magus with heresy. Justin Martyr, who lived about 100 years later in Samaria, said Simon had become a gnostic.[9]

A third theological observation has to do with the necessity of the coming of Peter and John from Jerusalem before the Samaritans could receive the Holy Spirit. If the words of Christ in Matthew 16:19 are recalled, Peter was the apostle designated to use the keys of the kingdom (see pp. 52–53, 54–55). In Acts 2 he opened the door of faith to the Jews, and here in Acts 8 he opens the door of faith to the Samaritans. In Acts 10–11 he does the same for the Gentiles. These occasions were necessary to affect the transition from law to grace. By the time Paul writes 1 Corinthians, the Spirit of God has not only come and indwelled each believer at the moment of faith (1 Cor. 6:19–20) but has also *placed* each believer into the body of Christ (1 Cor. 12:13).

Elymas the Sorcerer (Acts 13:6–12)

Even if there is some question about the true conversion of Simon the Sorcerer, there can be no doubt about Elymas. He was never changed. The apostle Paul in Acts 13:10 deems him as full of all deceit and all mischief, a child of the Devil, an enemy of all righteousness, and a perverter of the right way of the Lord.

Elymas was a magus, a sorcerer, and withstood Paul and Barnabas, *"seeking to turn the deputy from the faith"* (13:8). Any speculation concerning the conversion of Elymas while he was blinded for a season or even afterward cannot be answered with evidence. Where Scripture is so definite concerning his spiritual degradation, we have no cause to lift him out of it!

Chapter 6

PAUL IN THE BOOK OF ACTS

The apostle Paul is one of the most dynamic persons in Scripture. "Except for the Lord Himself, no other single figure has done so much for the Christian faith,"[1] says Robert E. Picirilli. "His mission makes up at least half of Acts, and his epistles dominate our New Testament."[2]

Paul is versatile, an apostle, a preacher, a debater, a spiritual father and brother—and always a servant. We see a man whose weakness is far surpassed by the all-sufficient grace of God that powerfully worked in his life.

His life story is a jigsaw puzzle which can be assembled and recounted by collaborating various passages of the New Testament. This exercise is worth undertaking, since upon the chronology of the life of Paul rests the history, the setting, and the general makeup of the New Testament church.

Paul wrote thirteen New Testament books, and without understanding the man it is more difficult to understand the writings themselves.

The Names of Saul and Paul

Paul is identified in the New Testament by two names, Saul and Paul (Acts 13:9). Merrill F. Unger says:

The usual theory is that the apostle had a Jewish name, Saul, and a Roman name, Paul.... But it is best to understand that Saul's name was changed as a matter of course when he became a Christian, that the word Paul means "little," and that Paul wanted to be known as the "Little One" in Christ's service; such changes in the cases of Abram, Gideon, Naomi, etc., are to be noted.[3]

We are uncertain of Paul's date of birth, but tradition suggests that he was born in the second year after the birth of Christ. Picirilli cites a tradition, based on an inference in a sermon attributed to Chrysostom, that Paul died in the year 66 at the age of sixty-eight. That would place his birth in 2 B.C.[4]

He possessed a very respectable heritage. He was the son of a Pharisee of the tribe of Benjamin, a Hebrew of the dispersion (Phil. 3:5). He had the privilege and responsibility to study the Law from his youth, as was common among the Hebrews. He was born at Tarsus (Acts 22:3), the capital of Cilicia, a city founded by the Assyrians and an important crossroads during the first century. In this ideal location, Paul in his youth would have had access to men of all walks of life—Hellenistic philosophers as well as Jews. Not only did he have unlimited access to the Hebrew and Greek cultures but also he was born a Roman citizen (Acts 22:25–28). That his parents had been able to afford a citizenship before his birth implies that they were well off. Citizenship normally cost a great deal of money. This citizenship afforded Paul some impressive audiences.

As all Hebrew boys, Paul learned a trade. After becoming a skilled tentmaker (Acts 18:3) at Tarsus, Paul came of age and was sent to Jerusalem for further study of the Law under the renowned teacher, Gamaliel (Acts 22:3). Paul's heritage, coupled with his study under such an authority made him a Pharisee of importance, a leader of his people. He took leadership in opposing the Christian church, which taught that the Messiah had already come. "He was a strict Pharisee," Tim Dowley notes, "outstanding in his orthodox beliefs and in his hatred of Christians."[5] Paul saw this teaching as unacceptable in light of all he had learned, and as a leader in his sect, he led many persecutions against the Christians.

It is in this frame of mind that we find Paul in his first mention in Scripture, where he is seen approving the murder of Stephen (Acts 7:58; 8:1). Later we see Paul zealously searching out records of Christians residing in Damascus for the purpose of their capture (Acts 9:1–3). He obtained the records and set out to Damascus. But little did he know that this journey would end his life as he knew it.

The Call

Eusebius very appropriately described the events that followed:

> The next stage began when Paul, the chosen vessel—neither from men nor through men, but through revelation of Jesus Christ Himself and God the Father who raised Him from the dead—was appointed an apostle, receiving his call through a vision and the heavenly voice that accompanied the revelation.[6]

On the road to Damascus, Paul met the Lord Jesus Christ face to face, and his misdirected zeal for God was refocused as he came to the personal knowledge of Christ as his Messiah—even this One he had viciously persecuted (Acts 9:3–9). After speaking with and seeing the resurrected Lord, Paul was left blind and had to be led to Damascus. There Paul spent time alone in prayer until Ananias arrived to restore Paul to health and encourage his spirit (Acts 9:10–19). Paul began to teach in the synagogue of Damascus (Acts 9:20–22). He also went to Arabia for solitude and study (Gal. 1:17–18). His sojourn to Arabia is enigmatic, yet significant. John R. W. Stott tells us, "Paul spent a little while in Damascus preaching, which suggests that his gospel was already clearly enough defined for him to announce it."[7] Paul's purpose in going to Arabia must not have been foremost to refine his theology, but rather to commune quietly with God. As J. B. Lightfoot explains,

> A veil of thick darkness hangs over St. Paul's visit to Arabia. Of the scenes among which he moved, of the thoughts and occupations which engaged him while there, of all the circumstances of a crisis which must have shaped the whole tenour of his after life, absolutely nothing is known. . . . It is a mysterious pause, a moment of suspense in the Apostle's history, a breathless calm which ushers in the tumultuous storm of his active missionary life. . . . What was the length of this sojourn we can only conjecture. The interval between his conversion and his first visit to Jerusalem, St. Paul here states to have been three years. . . . For can we doubt that by this journey he sought seclusion from the outer world, that his desire was to commune with God and his own soul amid these hallowed scenes, and thus to gather strength in solitude for his active labours?[8]

The Unique Apostle

Paul emphasizes in Galatians 1 that neither his apostleship nor his teaching came from any man, but rather from God. And that new teaching, which he announced, was that Jesus was indeed the Messiah. Upon returning to Damascus from Arabia, the Jews in the city plotted to kill him, but he fled and made his first post-conversion trip to Jerusalem (Acts 9:23–26). There he tried to associate with the disciples, but they feared him because of his past. Barnabas befriended him, however, and introduced him to the young church community. Paul shared his conversion account and gained their confidence. Paul also met with Peter for the first time. He spent fifteen days in Jerusalem, where he fellowshipped and taught (Acts 9:26–28; Galatians 1:18). His life was again threatened, this time by the Hellenistic Jewish community of Jerusalem of which he had been part. He was forced to flee home to Tarsus, where he spent the next ten years.

Paul then traveled with Barnabas to Antioch, where they taught together for about a year (Acts 11:26). During this time, a famine was prophesied by Agabus, so Paul and Barnabas returned to Jerusalem with provisions for the needy there (vv. 27–30). With a believer named John Mark, Paul and Barnabas came again to Antioch, where they were set apart and commissioned by the Holy Spirit to begin the work for which He had prepared them (13:1–3). Paul's first missionary journey began (A.D. 47–48).

Paul's First Journey

They first journeyed to Seleucia and then Cyprus. They continued to Salamis and taught in the synagogue. At Paphos, they were opposed by Bar-Jesus, the false prophet. From Paphos, Paul and Barnabas set out for Perga, while John Mark returned to Jerusalem. From Perga, the duo traveled to Pisidian Antioch, where they taught for several Sabbaths at the synagogue. Here their message was widely received, but opposition did arise from the Jews. Paul announced their intention to go to the Gentiles. Paul and Barnabas journeyed on to the region of Lystra, where Paul healed a lame man. As a result, he and Barnabas were worshiped as gods.

After Paul corrected the Lystrans, Jews from Antioch and Iconium stirred up a mob, who stoned Paul and left him for dead. His life was spared, and he and Barnabas continued to Derbe, making many disciples there. The two retraced their journey to Lystra, Iconium, and Pisidian Antioch. At Antioch, they stayed for a time to minister to the church and appoint elders. From Pisidian Antioch, they continued on to Pamphylia to Perga to Attalia and back to home base in Antioch (Acts 13–14).

A controversy arose regarding Jewish legalism, which had infected several churches. The Council at Jerusalem was called, in which both Paul and Barnabas participated (Acts 15:1–35).

Paul's Second Journey

Shortly thereafter, Paul and Barnabas determined to return to each city where they had preached in order to follow up on the newborn churches. A sharp disagreement split the two, however, when Barnabas wanted John Mark to accompany them. Paul strongly opposed Mark's presence after the young man had deserted them on their first journey. Barnabas and John Mark journeyed to Cyprus, while Paul chose Silas as his companion and headed through Syria and Cilicia on his second missionary journey (Acts 15:36–41).

Paul and Silas strengthened churches as they went on to Derbe and Lystra. At Lystra, Paul met Timothy, who joined the travelers. They passed through Phrygia and Galatia but were forbidden by the Holy Spirit to teach in Asia. Instead, they came to Mysia and attempted to enter Bithynia, but they were again restrained by the Spirit of God. At Troas, Luke the physician joined the entourage. Paul was then told in a vision to go to the Macedonian region, and did. There they preached the gospel for some time. It was there that Lydia, a seller of purple, became a believer. Then while at Philippi, Paul cast out a spirit of divination from a slave girl. A tumult resulted, leading to the imprisonment of Paul and Silas.

A great earthquake opened the prison doors. This gave Paul and Silas opportunity to minister to the jailer, who became a believer with all his family. The following day, the two were released, upon which time they visited and encouraged Lydia and the brethren at Philippi. Departing for Thessalonica, they went through Amphypolis and Apollonia.

While at Thessalonica, Paul taught for several Sabbaths at the synagogue, and many believed. One of the brethren there, Jason, gave the apostle lodging until more opposition broke out. Paul, Timothy, and Silas journeyed to Berea, where many eagerly searched the Scriptures and believed the message. But Jews from Thessalonica arrived to once again counter the ministry. Paul set out by sea for Athens, while Timothy and Silas remained at Berea. Paul there summoned Timothy and Silas to join him. While waiting, Paul reasoned in the synagogues with Jews, Gentiles, and various philosophers, and as he presented the gospel to them, some believed.

From Athens, Paul journeyed to Corinth, where he was rejoined by Timothy and Silas. He stayed some time in Corinth, working in his trade of tentmaking while fellowshipping with various believers, including Aquila and Priscilla, who were also tentmakers. From Corinth, Paul wrote the two letters to the Thessalonian church, based on the report given him by Timothy, who had spent some time there. Both of these letters were written around A.D. 51.

Paul remained in Corinth for about a year and one-half and afterward journeyed to Syria with Aquila and Priscilla. They came to Ephesus, and Paul taught in the synagogue. While Aqua and Priscilla remained at Ephesus, Paul set out for Caesarea, where he greeted the church and then journeyed on to Antioch. Here his second journey came to a close, approximately A.D. 52 (Acts 15:36–18:22).

Paul's Third Journey

After some time in Antioch, Paul began his third missionary journey as he and his company passed through Galatia and Phrygia, encouraging the brethren—one of whom was Apollos. And from there he came to Ephesus where he instructed the brethren regarding the Holy Spirit, of whom they had not heard. Here he spoke for three months in the synagogue, after which time he spoke for two years at the school of Tyrannus. As a result of his involvement with this school, all in Asia heard the gospel. How incredible is God's timing. Only now did God allow Paul to introduce the gospel into Asia.

While at Ephesus, Paul was also being used of God to perform various miracles. As a result, the church grew rapidly. After some time in Ephesus, Paul and his company traveled to Corinth and then returned to Ephesus once again, from where Paul wrote his first letter to the Corinthians and possibly also his letter to the Galatians (no later than 55; Galatians may have been written as early as 49). Paul then spent three months in Greece, after which he returned to Philippi and was joined by Timothy and Titus. From Philippi, Paul wrote his second letter to Corinth (55–56) and sent it with Titus.

He came again to Corinth, from which he wrote his letter to the Romans (56). From there, he began his journey back to Jerusalem through Assos, Miletus, Cos, Rhodes, Patara, Tyre, Ptolemais, and Caesarea. At Caesarea, he was warned by Agabus and Philip of impending danger at Jerusalem. Nonetheless, Paul pressed on. He was gladly received at Jerusalem (his fifth visit since his conversion). With the elders he recounted the events of his third missionary journey.

Nearing the End

While in Jerusalem Paul was charged by the Jews with teaching heresy and placed under house arrest. He made his defense before the people in a stirring narrative of the gospel and his ministry and was afterward returned to the barracks, where he was being detained, after he almost was illegally scourged (Acts 21:27–22:29).

He later made defenses before the Sanhedrin (Acts 22:30–23:10), Felix of Caesarea (Acts 24), and Festus, in whose presence Paul appealed to Caesar (Acts 25:1–12), and while awaiting the journey to Rome to stand trial he made his defense before King Agrippa (Acts 25:13–26:29).

Paul journeyed to Rome in 58 to make his defense before Nero, the reigning Caesar. Paul passed through Sidon, Myra, and Fair Havens and was shipwrecked off Malta and bitten by a viper when he reached shore. He continued to Puteoli, and finally arrived at Rome (27:1–28:29). He spent nearly two years awaiting trial in Rome, as he spent this time under house arrest (A.D. 59–60), but he did retain considerable freedoms (Acts 28:30).

While imprisoned at Rome, Paul wrote his letters to the churches of Colossae, Ephesus, and Philippi, as well as the personal letter to Philemon. These were written around 60.

Tradition tells us that after two years, Paul was granted a trial before Nero and was then released, upon which time he engaged in further travels, which included visiting such places as Macedonia, Ephesus, Colossae,

Laodicea, Spain, Asia Minor, Macedonia again, from where he wrote his first letter to Timothy and also his letter to Titus at Crete, circa 62. At Nicopolis, he was arrested and sent to Rome for his second trial. This second imprisonment was severe. From there he wrote his second letter to Timothy, which was his last writing (64). The letter expressed his satisfaction with his work, the roughness of his conditions, and his loneliness; only Luke was with him. The letter also expresses that Paul expected his death to come quickly.

Eusebius explains the evidence for the two imprisonments of Paul:

> There is evidence that, having then been brought to trial, the apostle again set out on the ministry of preaching, and having appeared a second time in the same city found fulfillment in his martyrdom. In the course of this imprisonment he composed the second epistle to Timothy, referring both to his earlier trial and to his impending fulfillment. Listen to his testimony on this point: "At my first trial nobody supported me: they all left me to my fate—may God forgive them! But the Lord stood by me and gave me strength, that through me the message might fully be proclaimed in the hearing of the whole pagan world. Thus I was rescued out of the lion's mouth." This passage proves beyond question that on the first occasion . . . he was rescued . . . it was not during the stay in Rome described by Luke that Paul's martyrdom was accomplished. The probability is that since at first Nero's disposition was milder, it was easier for Paul's defense of the Faith to be received, but that when he had gone on to commit abominable crimes, above all else he launched his attack on the apostles.[9]

Paul's expectation of death became a reality in 64 or 65, although some place the death as late as 67 or 68 during the severe persecution by Nero:

> Paul, the apostle, who before was called Saul, after his great travail and unspeakable labours in promoting the gospel of Christ, suffered also in this first persecution of Nero. Abdias, declareth that unto his execution Nero sent two of his esquires, Ferega and Parthemius, to bring word of his death. They coming to Paul instructing the people, desired him to pray for them, that they might believe; who told them that shortly after they should believe and be baptised at his sepulchre. This done, the soldiers came and led him out of the city to the place of execution, where he after his prayers made, gave his neck to the sword.[10]

While it appeared that a great light had been extinguished, Paul had accomplished the work that was set before him.

Chapter 7

THE TEMPLE IN THE BOOK OF ACTS

One of the arguments made against dispensational interpretation, which understands the rebuilding of a literal future temple in a millennial Jerusalem, has been the supposed abandonment of the Jewish temple by the early church. This has been assumed to be a deliberate move away from, and even a symbolic rejection of, Israel as the former heir of the divine promises. Under this argument, these covenant promises have been transferred to the new Israel, the church.

At the center of this view has been the alleged supercession of the physical temple (in Jerusalem) by a spiritual temple (the church), a replacement that has been often argued from the treatment of the temple in the book of Acts. Hans Conzelmann sees this as the reason for the destruction of the temple: "The anti-Temple charges of Acts 7:48 and 17:24 blend together with the view that, since Jesus' occupation of the Temple, the Jews are improper tenants whose possession of the Temple profanes it; thus it falls under judgment."[1]

This chapter will consider the treatment of the temple in Acts and determine if the Lukan theology of the temple supports the view of a replacement of national Israel and its ritual institutions by the church and its "spiritual" form of worship, or permits a future restoration of national Israel and its temple, apart from the church (dispensationalism).[2]

The First-Century Christian Attitude

It has become a common practice in scholarship to distinguish between the attitudes of the different gospel writers concerning the temple. It is argued that Mark, negatively conceiving of the temple's destruction because of the rejection of Jesus, radically reinterprets Jewish expectation so that the end-time significance of the temple is transferred to Jesus and the church, whereas Matthew and John were aware of Jewish eschatological expectations concerning the temple, yet also attempted a similar reformulation of the temple. It is then posited that Luke-Acts, in contrast to the other gospel writers, sees the temple in positive terms and was true to the widespread Jewish expectation that the literal temple in Jerusalem would play an important role in the eschatological age.[3]

These distinctions have been made generally in view of the monolithic interpretation of the conflict in the first century as that of "normative Judaism" versus "apostolic Christianity." However, David Tiede has argued, "It is no longer credible to disregard the complexity of late-first-century Jewish history by reading Luke-Acts simply as a story of "Christianity" versus "Judaism."[4]

Researchers must now take into account the record of tensions that existed within Judaism as to who represented the "true Israel," between the messianist, the Qumran covenanteers, the Pharisees, as well as the diverse social, economic, and political factors that defined the various Jewish groups beyond their competing orthodoxies. In this direction, Marilyn Salmon has argued that the intra-Jewish controversy accounts for Luke's treatment of the Law and the Pharisees.[5]

While theological norms for the temple are difficult to find for this period, the record of dissenters, such as those at Qumran, testify to the importance the temple played in their eschatological formulation and their very existence. There seems to be little doubt that, whether positively or negatively, the Jerusalem temple remained a central part of Judaism in the first century.[6]

The Attitude in Acts

However one dates the book of Acts, it is universally recognized that the events recorded represent a pre-70 viewpoint.[7] In Acts, the temple is still standing and the narratives containing references to the cult are presented in the context of a normative and acceptable ritual function. For example, we find in the opening chapters of Acts the disciples of Jesus in the temple precincts (Acts 2:46; 3:1; 5:21). Not only were the disciples, as observant Jews, keeping the *Shavuot* (Pentecost) feast (Acts 2:1), but they habitually congregated in the temple in the *Stoa* (portico) of Solomon (2:46). This apparently was their favored meeting place (3:11; 5:12).[8] This assembly at the temple for prayer came at the prescribed time of the daily sacrifices.

Acts 2:46 notes that they assembled together "with one accord" (homothymadon), which may simply mean that they were without discord (in comparison with other Jewish sects) or that they enjoyed their exceptional spiritual unity in worship.[9] Various explanations have been offered as justification for their meeting at the temple.

First, the temple was the place designated for public teaching, which is why Jesus frequented the site. Second, the temple was a place where there were crowds [of worshipers], thus, a ready audience for their witness and message. Third, the temple was the place designated for proper Jewish prayer at prescribed times of the daily sacrifices; hence, as good Jews, they were following custom.

In support of the third option, Acts 3:1 specifically finds Peter and John going to the temple at the hour of prayer. The text does not indicate that they were going for any reason other than to pray (and 2:46 expects the reader to understand the reason). This is supported by Peter's later recorded ritual in prayer (Acts 10:9). If Peter and John are among those at the temple in Acts 2:46, and as leaders it would seem probable, and if they are all in "one accord," then this text may indirectly imply their unity of devotion to the temple.[10] If they as followers of Jesus (later to be called Christians) had theological objections to the temple, its priesthood, or even its sacrifices, it is not apparent from these statements in Acts. Based on this evidence, W. O. E. Oesterley concluded that "in Jerusalem the temple was more important for Christian worship, and the synagogue elsewhere."[11] Indeed, as Daniel Falk observes, "It was probably this factor [their regular meeting at the temple] which enabled the Christian Community to maintain a distinctive presence"[12]

The Temple in Early Acts

That the temple was in fact regarded by Peter and John[13] as the legitimate cultic institution is seen in Acts 3:1 (cf. v. 3). It is stated that they pray at the temple specifically at the "ninth hour," the time of prayer associated with the evening sacrifice. Acts 5:12–13 indicates that the regularity of this group's worship, and especially their remarkable demonstrations of spiritual ability, set them apart from other observant Jews and brought them acclaim for their piety.[14]

When members of this group are arrested by order of the Sanhedrin, it is not because their views of the temple and cult are in question but because of their messianic claims concerning Jesus, and apparently the political consequences resulting from the Sanhedrin's complicity in his death (5:26–40). While the accusation against Stephen was that he spoke "against this holy place [the temple]" (6:13), the text, as will be shown, parallels the same accusation made against Jesus at his trial, which was considered a false testimony.

The loyalty of this early Christian leadership to Jerusalem and the temple area is remarkable, in as much as they were Galileans, and most of their ministry with Jesus had centered in regions outside Jerusalem. That Jerusalem should become the center of early Jewish Christianity (cf. Gal. 1:18–2:2) attests to the particular sanctity this group held for the city and the temple. To be sure, Jesus' *modus operandi* upon his arrival in Jerusalem was to teach in the temple (Luke 19:47; 21:37), and Acts 1:8 recorded Jesus' own command to begin their proclamation of the gospel from Jerusalem, a command that when reiterated by an angel (Acts 5:19–20), directs them to the temple.

Furthermore, in view of Jesus' condemnation by the Sanhedrin, his death in that city, and his own predictions of the temple's imminent destruction, it would seem that the disciples might corporately reject temple worship in favor of their own community as a new temple. That the opposite is observed implies that they did not view the literal temple as conflicting with their concept of Jesus' atonement or with the church. In fact, Hegesippus, who was a member of the Christian leadership a generation after the apostles, recorded that James, the head of the Jerusalem church, was renown for his temple worship: "He alone was allowed to enter the Sanctuary, for he did not wear wool but linen, and he used to enter alone into the Temple and be found kneeling and praying for forgiveness for the people, so that his knees grew hard like a camel's because of his constant worship of God, kneeling and asking forgiveness for the people."[15]

Jerusalem in Early Acts

Another reason may be suggested for the establishment and continued presence of the early Jewish-Christian community in Jerusalem. This reason is eschatological and centers on the temple and the city as having a significant role in the coming age of redemption. This hope was drawn from Jesus' apocalyptic discourse on the Mount of Olives (Matt. 24:3–31; Mark 13:3–37; Luke 21:5–38), in which he places the desecration of the temple as the signal event (cf. Dan. 9:27) preceding the Messiah's coming. This hope was voiced in Acts 1:6, where the disciples are told to wait for the promise of the Holy Spirit, which was, according to the prophets, essential to the establishment of this time of restoration (Joel 2:28–29, cited in Acts 2:16–21; cf. Isa. 32:15; 44:3; Jer. 31:33; see also Ezek. 36:27; 37:14; 39:29).

Jesus' interpretation of the time of restoration was consistent with the prophets and non-canonical Jewish apocalyptic writers.[16] Thus, E. P. Sanders, after surveying Jewish literature relevant to this period, concluded: "The hope that seems to have been most often repeated was that the restoration of the people of Israel ... the kingdom expected by Jesus ... is like the present world—it has a king, leaders, a temple, and twelve tribes."[17]

That this hope was a controlling factor in the disciples' presence in Jerusalem may be implied by the central place this hope occupies in their proclamation of repentance to the Jerusalemites (Acts 3:19–21). In this passage, the very terms used to express the promise are drawn from the prophetic message concerning Israel's future restored kingdom, which almost certainly derived its source directly from Jesus' own teaching in Matthew 19:28 (cf. Luke 22:30) and Acts 1:6.[18] In Matthew 19:28 in particular, we have use of the term Robert H. Gundry correctly ascribes to "Israel's renewal when God fully establishes his kingdom on earth."[19] This term complements the prophetic concept of eschatological renewal in the restoration seen in Ezekiel 36:24–38. It figured in the prophetic message of Isaiah (for example 49:5–13; 56:1–8; 60:1–22; 66:18–24).[20]

The Temple Speech of Peter

In Acts 3, the temple is the setting for Peter's second speech during the Pentecost feast (see 3:1). Peter and John are accosted by a lame beggar at "the Beautiful Gate," probably the Shushan or Eastern Gate[21] on the eastern side of the outer temple court, the Court of the Gentiles (vv. 2, 11). The result of this encounter was the healing of the lame man in the "name of Jesus the Messiah, the Nazarene" (vv. 6–8). This miracle drew a large crowd, described as all the people (v. 11). Peter had won an audience to which he could proclaim a witness as he explained what had transpired (vv. 12–26).

The setting for the miracle is perhaps not incidental to the explanation Peter gives, but may in fact be what directs his message toward the eschatological theme. In the evangelistic speech which follows, Peter attributes the miracle to Jesus, whom he refers to in prophetic terms as "the Righteous One" (vv. 13–14, 26; cf. 7:52) and "the Prophet" (vv. 22–23), thereby linking their thoughts especially to the promised Isaianic "Servant" (Isa. 53) and Mosaic "Prophet" (Deut. 18:15–19), although the entire prophetic corpus is offered as support (vv. 18, 21).

It is notable that Peter begins and ends his speech with reference to the patriarchal covenants and promises to Abraham (vv. 13, 25–26) and the eschatological blessing to the Gentile nations (v. 26; cf. Gen. 12:13). This reference may have been prompted by the speech's setting in the Court of the Gentiles. In this location at the eastern entrance of the temple, the sight that presented itself to Peter and his audience was the monumental entrance leading into the Holy of Holies. Behind them was the Mount of Olives, the last visible place to which the *shekinah* glory of God had disappeared during its departure from the temple in the days of Ezekiel (10:18; 11:22–23).

It was this prophet who had uniquely predicted the return of the Shekinah to a restored future temple (Ezek. 40–48) in the millennial kingdom (Ezek. 43:1–7) and, with Isaiah, promised eschatological blessings would flow from this site as a witness to the Gentile nations (Ezek. 37:25–28; see Isa. 2:2–4; 56:6–7). Peter apparently builds on these prophetic promises in a chronological progression of Messiah's redemptive work, first detailing the predicted soteriological redemption that accompanied His first coming (Acts 3:13–18) and then the eschatological restoration that will attend His second coming (vv. 19–21).[22] In this climactic appeal, the temple is again drawn into focus. In verses 19 and 21, the eschatological temple of Ezekiel appears to be in view in Peter's unique use of the expressions *kairoi anapsyxeōs* ("times of refreshing," v. 19) and *chronōn apokatastaseōs pantōn* ("the period of restoration of all things," v. 21).

"The period of restoration" locates the time referenced as the prophetic period of the national restoration of Israel (cf. Matt. 17:11), that is, in the millennial kingdom. The former term suggests the universal blessings that will flow from the eschatological temple. In Ezekiel 47:1–12, a river of water was predicted to flow from beneath the threshold of the temple facing east (vv. 1–2), refreshing the eastern region of the land of Israel, an area known as the Arabah which formerly was barren and inhospitable. The magnitude of this restorative work is exemplified in that even the salty waters of the Dead Sea will become fresh and host life (vv. 8–10).

It should be noted that in these verses the coming of the Messiah and the period of prophetically predicted restoration both depend on Israel's repentance. This ties the passage to the eschatological context of Jesus' Olivet Discourse, which expects Israelite regathering and repentance in a time of tribulation prior to the revelation of the Messiah (Matt. 24:29–31; Mark 13:24–27). This stands in contrast to texts written concerning the imminent expectation of the church for the rapture before the advent of divine wrath (1 Thess. 1:10; Titus 2:13; Rev. 3:10).

The proximity of Peter to the Court of the Gentiles may have in view the fulfillment of Israel's destiny to be both a witness to and a spiritual blessing for the Gentile nations. In this regard the temple played a pivotal role, for the nations are predicted to assist in its construction (Hag. 2:7; Zech. 6:15), worship there (Isa. 2:2–3; 11:10; 56:6–7; Zech. 14:16–19), and even serve selectively as priests (Isa. 66:20–21). If such prophetic temple texts are informing Peter's speech, prompted by his immediate setting, then we have in Acts 3 another indication of the temple's esteemed position as here represented by the apostles.

The Temple Speech of Stephen

The most extensive speech in the book of Acts is Stephen's discourse delivered before the Sanhedrin (7:2–53). In a style uncharacteristic of Luke, the Gentile compiler of the account,[23] the speech repeatedly appeals to the Old Testament, citing some forty passages in its interpretive details of Israel's early history.[24] Assuming, in the light of this extensive use of the Old Testament, that Stephen's speech reflects Christian doctrine,[25] it is debated as to why this sermon appears polemically inclined against the temple and cultic offerings in view of Luke's generally pro-temple position. Such debate presupposes that Stephen here attacks the institution of the temple.

Many have thought this a foregone conclusion simply because speaking "against this holy place" (Acts 6:13) is part of the accusation against Stephen.

Marcel Simon, for instance, maintains that "its main characteristic is a strongly antiritualistic trend, and a fierce hostility towards the temple, which he considers almost as a place of idolatry."[26]

The justification for this argument is drawn from the use of the term *cheiropoiēton* ("made with [human] hands") in 7:48. The contention is that Stephen rejects the Jerusalem temple (first and second) "made with [human] hands," in favor of the tabernacle "made according to the [heavenly] pattern" (v. 44).[27] Further, since the term is used by the *LXX* of the manufacture of idols,[28] it is argued that Stephen identified the temple and its sacrifices with idolatry in verses 42–43. Despite this evidence, it is doubtful that Stephen's speech attacks the temple at all.[29] Several arguments may be offered in defense of this position.

From this theological premise of rejection, it has been then assumed that the only acceptable replacement for the temple is the new spiritual edifice of the church. The opinion that the sanctuary into which Christ enters is the souls or hearts of God's people is an explanation that is to be found as early as the fourth century in Ambrose (cf. his comments on Heb. 8:2), and in Gregory of Nazianzus (cf. *Ad Julianum*, alluding to Heb. 8:2). It has received the approval of F. F. Bruce, who writes on Hebrews 9:11: "What then is the nature of the spiritual temple in which God dwells? . . . Our author stands right in this prophetic tradition when he affirms that the people of God are the house of God: 'whose house are we, if we hold fast our boldness and the glorying of our hope'" (Heb. 3:6).[30] In support of their premise the following arguments are given:

First, while the charge against Stephen is that he spoke against the temple, Luke takes pains to show that this accusation comes from *false* witnesses.[31] Their claim is that Stephen said that Jesus would destroy the temple and its altar (Acts 6:14), an allegation made at Jesus' trial and already shown by the gospel writers to be false (Matt. 26:60–61; Mark 14:56–59).

Second, the claim that *cheiropoiēton* distinguishes tabernacle from temple, and that Stephen thereby views the temple as an idolatrous institution, is erroneous. *Cheiropoiēton* is used in Hebrew 9:11 and 24, also for the tabernacle. Stephen's argument is not against the Davidic/Solomonic temple in favor of the Mosaic tabernacle, but simply to state that God is not to be defined or confined by reference to a human creation, such as a temple.[32] This is the same argument used by Paul in Acts 17:24 concerning the localization of the deity in a pagan, or any such structure "made with [human] hands" (*cheiropoiētois naois*). Both speeches have in view the transcendence of God, who as solitary Creator is undetermined by His creation. The focus of Stephen's historical review is not idolatry in the sense of worshiping images, but rather human self-assertion[33] that refuses to recognize divine revelation and thus leads to idolatry (cf. Rom. 1:18–23).

Third, the argument of Stephen is part of a developed cycle between acts of divine mercy and human rebellion. In this structure, David's desire for a temple is presented as a positive sign of God's favor. Both temple and tabernacle were given according to the divinely revealed "blueprint" of the heavenly tabernacle/temple (Exod. 25:8–9; 1 Chron. 28:19). In this context, Stephen employs the wording of Psalm 132:5 to claim that the original purpose for David's construction of the temple was to serve as a *skēnōma* ("dwelling") for God's presence and that Solomon actually completed the process.

Fourth, the problem for Stephen in Acts 7 is not the temple but the *actions of the people* to whom God had given the temple. This, as F. Weinert has observed, is in keeping with Jesus' attitude in Luke, which did not oppose the temple or its cult but the improper and desecrating behavior of those associated with it.[34] On the one hand, Stephen's concern is to demonstrate that God's revelation of Himself was not always confined to the temple. God revealed Himself [as a Savior] to Abraham in Mesopotamia, to Joseph in Egypt, and to Moses in the burning bush, and likewise through Jesus as Messiah (although he is not here mentioned by name).

On the other hand, the rejection of Jesus as a revelation of God, possibly because he did not fulfill the predicted messianic role of temple restoration, compels Stephen to defend the implied thesis that the messianic purpose first involved a restoration of the hearts of the nation to God, a purpose never realized in Israel's history because of its continued rejection of God's prophetic representatives. This rejection had manifested itself in a form of worship in which the existence of the temple was regarded as an indication of divine favor, despite the impropriety of that worship. However, this was the very attitude of the nation prior to the departure of the *shekinah* and the destruction by the Babylonians.

Behind Stephen's thought may be the argument that Messiah would ultimately build the restoration temple, involving the Gentile nations (Isa. 56:7; Zech. 6:12) and the return of the *shekinah* (Ezek. 43:4). Thus, since Jesus was the Messiah, all acts of rebellion against him were acts of rebellion against God and God's purpose to restore Israel as a witness to the nations. Jesus is thus pictured in verse 52 as standing at the end of a long line of prophets who were sent to Israel and subsequently rejected because of their misplaced confidence in the temple as the revelation of divine blessing.

Stephen argues that to seek for God's blessing through the temple while at the same time refusing God's Word, and especially as mediated through the Messiah (who is greater than the temple, cf. Matt. 12:6), is to desecrate the function of the temple, an act of no less defiance than that displayed at the foot of Mount Horeb. For this reason, he can link them in attitude with their ancestors in verses 51–53.

We conclude that Stephen did not target the temple (Solomonic or, by extension, Herodian) nor argue in any way against its sanctity. His comments concerning the temple rather concerned the idea of God's presence being restricted to an earthly building and of the inadequacy of claiming the temple as security while at the same time being in rebellion to the temple's God. His use of Isaiah 66:1–2 confirms that he is thinking in cosmic proportions, like Solomon in 1 Kings 8:27, and fits well within the traditional Jewish perspective that regarded the temple as the place where God's Name dwelt and as the place of prayer. Like the prophets who condemned trusting in the temple while violating the law for which the temple stood, Stephen condemns those who have rejected Jesus, whose purpose was to fulfill the Law (Matt. 5:17–18), and who himself identified with the prophets in their message against lawbreakers (cf. Matt. 12:5–8). Stephen, then, has directed his condemnation against the people (leadership) who have rejected God's revelation of Himself, not the institution that was meant to reveal Him.[35]

The Attitude of Paul

According to Acts, the temple was central for not only the apostles and early church but also Paul.[36] How did Paul as a Jewish-Christian conceive of himself in relation to Judaism? As the book of Acts moves with chapter 8 to focus on the character of Saul/Paul, it includes historical reports of his veneration of the temple. The list of these observant acts include his observance of the feasts regulated by the temple (Acts 20:6);[37] his religious vows (a Nazarite vow, Acts 18:18); purification rites (in one case involving four other proselytes, Acts 21:23–26; 24:18); payment of their ceremonial expenses, which accounted as a *mitzvah*, "a legally obligated good deed" (Acts 21:24); offering of sacrifices at the temple (Acts 21:26; 24:17); prayers and worship at the temple (Acts 22:17; 24:11); regard for the priesthood (Acts 23:5); and payment of the temple tax (Acts 24:17).

It is true that Acts presents Paul as being accused of temple desecration, but it equally presents the defense that he was guiltless of such charges. The events unfold as follows. After a riot at the temple due to a false rumor that Paul attempted to desecrate the temple (21:29; cf. 24:6) by bringing a Gentile (Trophimus)[38] beyond the forbidden barricade known as the *Soreg*[39] into the Israelite Court, he was rescued from the rabble by Roman guards.[40] Thereupon he addressed his accusers and the crowd in Hebrew and declared himself a Jew (Acts 22:1–3). When his case was finally tried, Paul defended himself against the anti-temple charges by affirming his Jewish heritage and professing his ceremonial purity (24:18).

As we come to the end of the book of Acts, despite the rejection of Jewish opponents, he is depicted as one who can address the leaders of the Jews in Rome as "brothers" and declare to them that he had "done nothing against our people or the customs of our fathers [which included all the temple ritual]," 28:17, and bore no malice against his nation (28:19). These references depict a Paul as devout toward the temple as any Jew, as one who assisted others in performing their temple obligations, and as one who insisted on regulating his life by the temple calendar (the feast days), even to interrupting his own missionary work. All of these actions seem to be strange coming from one who was commissioned as "the Apostle to the Gentiles" (Rom. 1:5; cf. Gal. 2:7–9), if indeed he held a replacement theology and had taught the Gentiles that there was no future for ethnic Israel or its ritual institutions.

Such texts must place Paul in the camp of normative Judaism with respect to his attitude toward the temple, for, as John Townsend has correctly observed, "there is little reason to suppose that Paul, after becoming a Christian, radically changed his attitude toward the Jerusalem temple or that he was opposed to any Christian, Jew or Gentile, taking part in its cult."[41] Such statements caution us to read Paul's disputations with Jewish legalizers and his harsh comments concerning the Law in light of his lifelong adherence to Judaism.

Further, these indications of Paul's temple reverence should suffice to reappraise his use of temple and cultic metaphors in his epistles.[42] When Paul later uses the analogy of the temple with respect to the believer's body (1 Cor. 3:16–17; 2 Cor. 6:16–17) or the body of Christ (Eph. 2:21–22), he is not seeking to replace the physical temple with the spiritual church but arguing for the sanctity of the one by analogy to the other. The presence of God the Holy Spirit indwelled the temple and indwells believers individually and collectively. Therefore, no dispensational distinctive is compromised by the Pauline correspondence.

Part 2

THE THEOLOGY AND WORK OF THE HOLY SPIRIT IN ACTS

M any believe the title of Luke's book should be the Acts of the Holy Spirit. The Spirit's activity overshadows the events surrounding the apostles. As well, new works and happenings are taking place dispensationally by the guidance of the Spirit. The Spirit baptizes, fills, indwells, gives gifts, leads, and speaks to the disciples directly or makes God's will explicit in visions and dreams. All of this forges a new dynamic and direction that energizes the new revelation of the church.

The Spirit of God also leads the apostles out of Palestine to Europe and Asia. This is clearly reflected in the approaching judgment on Israel and the movement of the gospel, by the power of the Spirit, to the Gentile world. The new spiritual body of Christ is formed and molded as Acts progresses. This transition from the dispensation of law to the dispensation of the church is so important that a section of this study is given over to this new work of God's Spirit.

Chapter 1

THE THEOLOGY OF THE HOLY SPIRIT IN ACTS

The major role of the Holy Spirit in Acts is commonly acknowledged by interpreters, regardless of how they interpret that role. Luke's second volume is often retitled "The Gospel of the Holy Spirit,"[1] "The Acts of God," or "The Acts of the Holy Spirit."[2]

Luke uses the word *pneuma* ("spirit") seventy times in Acts,[3] the most of any New Testament book. In Luke's gospel *pneuma* appears thirty-six times, seventeen times referring to the Holy Spirit. Of the seventy occurrences in Acts, fifty-five clearly refer to the third person of the Trinity. Two references speak of "the Spirit of the Lord" (5:9; 8:39) and one of "the Spirit of Jesus" (16:7). The other fifty-two occurrences are unambiguous and clearly refer to the Holy Spirit.[4] *Pneuma* is otherwise used in Acts in reference to the human spirit (three times), and evil spirits (eight times), and spirit beings in a generic sense, presumably angelic or good (two times). It is twice used ambiguously, referring either to the *human* spirit or the *Holy* Spirit.

But Luke reminds the reader that the acts Jesus did while on earth were done in the power of the Holy Spirit (Acts 1:2) and that these acts of the apostles are *the continuing acts* of Jesus—performed through the apostles and members of the church as the body of Christ, *but still facilitated by the Holy Spirit.*[5] As Howard Clark Kee says, "The effective agent in the accomplishment of God's purpose in the epoch of preparation through the prophets, the epoch of Jesus' ministry, and the epoch of the Church's mission is the Holy Spirit."[6]

The "New" Work

The Holy Spirit not only continues as the divine agent in the work of God among the people of God but also is given higher profile. The book of Acts introduces a dispensational change. The key player in this dispensational change is the Holy Spirit. "Acts indeed is not narrowly pneumatological," writes N. B. Stonehouse, who properly notes that

> The distinctive approach of Luke to the history of the Christian church which he records may be summed up in terms of an interpretation of its origin and development as being basically and conspicuously the work of the Holy Spirit. Pentecost is viewed as the foundation of all that follows. The age depicted in Acts is the age of the Spirit, an age that stands apart as "the last days" of prophecy (Acts 2:17) which have been decisively introduced by the divine action in "pouring out" the Spirit.[7]

Thomas Bernard considers Pentecost the opening of a new age: "the dispensation of the Spirit."[8] When a new dispensation is begun, or a new economy of God's rule initiated, unusual transitional events may occur that are common to neither dispensation.

The deaths of Ananias and Sapphira for lying to the Spirit is an example (Acts 5:1–11). As a result of this judgment, "great fear came upon the whole church." Thereafter, however, we do not know of Christians being struck dead for lying. This exceptional judgment impresses upon the church at its beginning that this new work of God must be taken quite seriously and reverently. Similar events can be found at Old Testament junctions in the dispensational development of biblical history.

What Is the New "Normal"?

Since the events recorded in the book of Acts mark a new dispensation, we must guard that we do not make extraordinary occurrences into norms for subsequent church history. Luke does not write with didactic intent about "normal Christian experience." He recounts the unusual, paranormal historical events wrought by the Holy Spirit in that dispensational time-warp. The New Testament concept of the church was so far removed from the mind-set of messianic Judaism that some explanation was needed to show how the church got from messianism to its open-armed worship of Jesus in Spirit and in truth (John 4:23). Apart from the extraordinary events wrought by the Holy Spirit in Acts, the church would never have become what it was.

Luke is saying in effect, "It took a number of miracles, but God did it. Here's how." The *acts* are surely acts of the Holy Spirit. Acts is historically, dispensationally, and theologically transitional in that it records the early events in the new age, this "dispensation of the Spirit."

The Promise of the Holy Spirit

The theology of the Holy Spirit in the Gospels and the Old Testament extends beyond the scope of this work. But a theology of the Holy Spirit in Acts would certainly be incomplete without some consideration of the relationship between the actual *outpouring* of the Spirit on Pentecost and the *anticipation* and *promise* of this outpouring found elsewhere in Scripture.

Luke presents the Pentecost outpouring (Acts 2) as fulfillment of the Old Testament anticipation. This is confirmed by John the Baptist's pronouncement in all three of the other Gospels (Matt. 3:11; Mark 1:8; John 1:33). Promises were made by the Father and by the Son concerning the coming, outpouring, or gift of the Holy Spirit. Though scholars disagree as to the exact nature of *how* the outpouring of the Spirit in Acts fulfills these promises, most agree that in some way they do. In order to understand what occurred on Pentecost and the events subsequent, and to see how these events constitute fulfillment of earlier promises, we must explain the nature of the promises. Prior to His ascension, Jesus gathered His disciples and commanded them "not to leave Jerusalem, but to wait for what the Father had promised, 'Which,' He said, 'you heard of from Me'" (Acts 1:4). He goes on to tell them they shall soon be baptized and empowered by the Holy Spirit (1:5, 8; cf. Luke 24:49). Thus, the promise of the Holy Spirit is made by both the Father and the Son.[9]

The Promise of the Father

Twice, the apostle Paul refers to the "promise of the Spirit" (Gal. 3:14; Eph. 1:13). In Galatians 3:14 this promise of the Spirit is related, in context, to the Abrahamic covenant and its extended blessings for Jews and Gentiles. Paul clearly sees a relationship between the Pentecostal gift of the Spirit to the church and the promised blessing of the nations in the Abrahamic covenant (Gen. 12:1–3).[10]

In the early development of God's covenant program with Israel, the anticipation of the outpouring of the Holy Spirit is implicit. When Israel received the law of God through Moses, they said they would "hear and do it" God commended them. But He lamented their lack of a genuine heart needed to keep all His commandments (Deut. 5:27–29). Chosen as a holy people for God's own possession, Israel, in covenant relationship with Yahweh, was to obey God's commandments (Deut. 7:6, 9, 11). But Israel would not; indeed, they *could not*. God foretells Israel's disobedience and announces his consequent discipline (Deut. 28–30; 31:14–22). Following Israel's repentance, God promises, he would "circumcise" their hearts in order to enable them to obey Him (Deut. 30:6–8). This circumcision of the heart anticipates the teaching of the prophets in regard to the regenerating work of the Holy Spirit.

The promise of the Father concerning the outpouring of the Holy Spirit is *not* an obscure teaching in the Old Testament. It is recurrent and it is clear. But it is contextually and particularly associated with Israel's national repentance, conversion, and restoration. What is *not* clear in the Old Testament is that the outpouring of God's Spirit will be upon *all* mankind and will extend beyond the nation Israel.

So Nicodemus is without excuse when he fails to understand Jesus' teaching that one must be born of the Spirit or "born again" (John 3:5–7, 10) to enter the kingdom of God. The Father had made many promises in the Old Testament to pour out His Spirit; Israel's national conversion and restoration were contingent upon this outpouring. No wonder Jesus said, "Are you the teacher in Israel, and do not understand these things?" (John 3:10).

As a teacher in Israel, Nicodemus should have known that spiritual regeneration was necessary for entrance into the kingdom. He should also have known that God intended to bring this same blessing to the Gentiles. What Nicodemus *could not have known,* and what the Old Testament did not disclose, was that the outpouring of the Holy Spirit would result in a spiritual baptism by which Jews and Gentiles alike would be united in one church, the body of Christ (1 Cor. 12:13; Eph. 3:6). Even on Pentecost, when the Spirit is "outpoured," this mystery remains hidden. Neither Israel, the disciples, nor Peter who quotes Joel 2 to explain the events, understood the full scope of the work. Particularly Peter did not comprehend Spirit baptism and its inclusion of Gentiles into one body with Jews on equal footing.

Expectations and Fulfillment

What the Jews Expected

Within intertestamental Judaism several significant factors shaped the concept of the "Holy Spirit" that would be operative during the ministries of John the Baptist and Jesus.

> Intertestamental literature was conscious of the loss of the Spirit. In the apocryphal and pseudepigraphical writings there is an awareness that the period of prophetic inspiration is over. Prophecy is defunct. Prophetic inspiration departed from Israel with the last prophets. In rabbinical literature it is expressly stated that the Holy Spirit departed from Israel after the last prophets. It is even accepted

that the Spirit was no longer present in the second temple. There was no longer any inspired revelation.[11]

In light of the Old Testament prophecies which proclaimed the coming outpouring of God's Spirit, a new messianic hope increasingly identified "God's Holy Spirit" with "the Spirit of prophecy." T. S. Caulley notes:

> Thus, the messianic expectation of Judaism, which included the eschatological outpouring of God's spirit . . . was bound up with the conviction that the Spirit had ceased in Israel with the last of the prophets; the Holy Spirit was understood as God's spirit of prophecy, which would be given again in the new age to a purified Israel in conjunction with the advent of a messiah.[12]

New Testament Judaism's concept of the Holy Spirit is rooted in the Old Testament's teaching of the withdrawal of the Holy Spirit from Israel and the promise of an eschatological outpouring of God's Spirit. It also shows the intertestamental understanding that prophecy ceased with the Spirit's departure and that the coming outpouring of God's Spirit would bring with it the manifestation of God's power and the Spirit of prophecy.

As a forerunner of Messiah, John the Baptist stands on the dividing line between the age of promise and the age of fulfillment. More accurately, he belongs to the age of promise, though at its end, and presages the age of fulfillment. In his preparatory role, John the Baptist calls Israel to repentance and baptizes with water. And he speaks of Messiah, who will come after him and is mightier than he. Messiah will baptize with the Holy Spirit and with fire (Matt. 3:11; Mark 1:8; Luke 3:16; John 1:33). From John's viewpoint, according to David Ewett,

> Spirit baptism is something that Messiah will do which is yet future. Moreover, in the fourth Gospel the Baptist's promise that the one upon whom the Spirit had descended would baptize with the Holy Spirit (John 1:33), is bordered by the identification of Jesus as the Lamb of God (John 1:29, 37). The evangelist evidently wanted to underscore that the baptism with the Spirit lay beyond the cross and resurrection, when God's lamb would take away the sin of the world. And that, in fact, is what happened.[13]

Jesus told His disciples just before His ascension, "John baptized with water, but you shall be baptized with the Holy Spirit not many days from now" (Acts 1:5). Jesus clearly points to the outpouring of the Spirit on Pentecost as fulfillment of John's prediction that the One coming after him would baptize with the Holy Spirit.

The Promise of the Son

Jesus, of course, understood the promises of the Father in the Old Testament concerning the outpouring of His Spirit. He often used them as the backdrop for what He said and did. On the last day of the Feast of Booths (Tabernacles), Jesus cried out, "If any man is thirsty, let him come to Me and drink. He who believes in Me, as the Scripture said, 'From his innermost being shall flow rivers of living water'" (John 7:37–38). John then tells his readers that Jesus "spoke of the Spirit, whom those who believed in Him were to receive" (John 7:39a). Two things drive home the significance of Christ's words. First, the language and imagery of His words reflect the Old Testament conception of the outpouring of God's Spirit.[14] Second, these words were spoken in the context of water ceremonies at the observance of the Feast of Booths. Each of the seven days of the feast a priest drew water from the Pool of Siloam in a golden flagon. A procession brought it to the temple with the joyful sounding of the trumpet. The water was poured into a bowl beside the altar from which a tube took it to the base of the altar. Simultaneously wine was poured through a similar bowl on the other side of the altar.[15]

After a week of this daily ritual, on the last day Jesus spoke these dramatic words. His listeners must have understood the significance because their response was equally dramatic (John 7:40–44).

The promise of the Son is predicated on the promise of the Father. In the upper room discourse, Jesus told His disciples, "I will ask the father, and He will give you another Helper . . . the Holy Spirit, whom the Father will send in My name" (John 14:16, 26). In Luke 11:13, Jesus speaks of the Holy Spirit as a gift from the Father.

The unfolding of events in Luke's second volume is thus meant to be viewed against the background of Old Testament expectations and Jesus' own predictions.[16]

The Person of the Holy Spirit

The book of Acts confirms that the Holy Spirit is not merely "a force" or "an influence," but a person. He is the third person of the triune Godhead, consubstantial and equal in deity to the Father and the Son, though subject to and sent by both.

The Relationship of the Spirit to the Church

The Holy Spirit in a very real sense is the *sine qua non* of the church, the body of Christ. The Holy Spirit is responsible for and essential to the formation and subsistence of the church; He guides and directs; He advances. Even a cursory reading of Acts shows that the life, ministry, and continuance of the church is contingent upon the personal coming and the abiding presence of the Holy Spirit.

The gifts the Spirit distributes to the church (1 Cor. 12:7, 11) are personal and reflect the personality of the Giver. Could the Giver be any less than those to whom the gifts are given? The church has fellowship and unity to the extent that the Spirit's presence is active (Acts 4:31; 8:14; 9:31). Only a person who is God could establish unity in community. The advance and direction of the church is the work of divine personality (Acts 2:14; 6:10; 8:29). Only a person could be sinned against (Acts 5:3, 9; 8:18–20). The promise of His coming as "another comforter" (John 14:16) is meaningless if the other Comforter is any less a person than the One He replaces.[17] H. D. McDonald stresses that this divine personality is no "sweet influence," as Christians sometimes identify it:

> The Spirit speaks of Himself and is spoken of in personal terms. Very specifically the Spirit comes before us in Acts as a Divine "I" [Acts 10:19–20; 13:2]. Paul and Barnabas are said to be separated by the Spirit "for Me" [Acts 13:2]. The various activities stated above, are one and all personal activities. He speaks, He separates, He sends, and so forth; all of which show the rightness of the prefixed pronoun "He—the Holy Spirit."[18]

The Holy Spirit's relationship to the church is not only fundamental and personal but also is peculiar, primarily because of the nature of Spirit baptism. That the work of Spirit baptism places Jew and Gentile into one body was not revealed in the Old Testament, nor did it become immediately clear once the Spirit was outpoured. The promise of the Father in the Old Testament is always addressed to Israel in the context of eschatological national repentance, conversion, and restoration. This baptism and its implications regarding the Gentiles are still future in John the Baptist's day (Matt. 3:11; Mark 1:8; Luke 3:16; John 1:33) and still future when Christ ascends (Acts 1:4–5).[19] Spirit baptism never occurred prior to Pentecost and its unique role in the formation of the church.

The Relationship of the Spirit to the Godhead

Not only is the Holy Spirit a distinct person, but also He is the third person of the Godhead, distinct from but equal to the Father and the Son. Peter's words to Ananias clearly attribute deity to the Holy Spirit. "Peter said, 'Ananias, why has Satan filled your heart to lie to the Holy Spirit. . . . You have not lied to men, but to God'" (Acts 5:3–4). Luke calls it "the Spirit of the Lord" (8:39) and "the Spirit of Jesus" (16:7).[20] His attributes, actions, and associations with the other persons of the Godhead all demonstrate deity (for example, 1:16; 4:25; 5:3–4, 32; 7:51, 55; 8:29; 28:25). Certainly, Acts testifies that the Holy Spirit is a person distinct from but equal to the Father and the Son. He is a person, and He is God.

His role in the Godhead, or His relationship to the other persons of the Godhead, is conceptually difficult, however. The Holy Spirit is a person and God, but He is not the Father, and He is not the Son. There is only one Holy Spirit (Eph. 4:3–4), yet He is at once the Father's Spirit and the Son's Spirit. Neither Acts nor the rest of Scripture tells *how* this can be, it simply affirms that it *is*. Harry L. Poe finds that the apostles understood this unity very well, as Paul described it in Ephesians 4:3–4, yet they referred to the Spirit in various ways (Gal. 4:6; Phil. 1:19; 1 Peter 1:11; 1 John 3:24; 4:13): "The interrelationship of Father, Son, and Holy Spirit appears regularly in the apostolic writings without any attempt to resolve how the Spirit of the Father and the Spirit of the Son can be the same Spirit."[21]

It has been pointed out that the Holy Spirit is sent by both the Father and the Son. As conspicuous as the Holy Spirit is in Acts, His purpose is to draw attention to the Lord Jesus Christ. The Holy Spirit, while equal to the Father and the Son in deity, is, in respect to His office or function, subordinate to both. This "role" subordination is voluntary, not necessary.[22] In respect to the Father, the Holy Spirit serves as the Executor of the Father's will. He is the administrator and executive of the whole divine purpose from beginning to end.[23] In respect to the Son, the Spirit empowered the incarnate Christ and continues the Son's "acts" in His absence (Acts 1:1). Regarding these different subordinate functions of the nevertheless equal persons of the Trinity, Wayne Grudem says:

> In general, the work of the Holy Spirit seems to be to bring to completion the work that has been planned by God the Father and begun by God the Son. . . . So we may say that the role of the Father in creation and redemption has been to plan and direct and send the Son and Holy Spirit. This is not surprising, for it shows that the Father and the Son relate to one another as a father and son relate to one another in a human family: the father directs and has authority over the son, and the son obeys and is responsive to the directions of the father. The Holy Spirit is obedient to the directives of both the Father and the Son. Thus, while the persons of the Trinity are equal in all their attributes, they nonetheless differ in their relationships to the creation. The Son and Holy Spirit are equal in deity to God the Father, but they are subordinate in their roles.[24]

The Prominence of the Holy Spirit in Acts

The Spirit as Narrative Character

It is difficult to pinpoint the role of the Holy Spirit in Acts, though the Spirit is patently visible in the narrative. As Griffith Thomas says, the Holy

Spirit is given remarkable prominence in this book.[25] William H. Shepherd Jr. suggests that to understand the place of the Holy Spirit in Luke-Acts, we must understand the text as narrative.[26] Using literary or narrative critical categories, Shepherd argues that the Holy Spirit in Acts should be understood as a "character."[27] In literary criticism terms the function of a character is to signal narrative reliability.[28] Luke presents the Holy Spirit as "the Spirit of prophecy," the guarantor of the prophetic word. This attestor is more "indirectly presented" than "directly defined."[29] Because the Spirit is portrayed as a character in the narrative, acting, speaking, and doing, the Spirit must be not merely the activity of God, but God Himself.

Acts itself bears testimony to the Spirit as the Spirit of prophecy (1:2, 16; 2:4, 17, 33; 4:25; 7:49–51; 8:29; 10:19; 11:12; 13:2; 15:8, 28; 19:6; 20:23; 21:4, 11; 28:25). Sometimes it is the Holy Spirit who speaks directly, and sometimes the Spirit speaks through an apostle or a prophet. Moreover, Luke's narrative itself is to be taken as the prophetic word of the Spirit (Acts 1:1–2). "The Spirit can be referred to as speaking even when an unmentioned prophet was doubtless the revelatory medium (Acts 15:28; 20:23). Prophecy, however, is but one of the many manifestations of the Spirit."[30]

L. T. Johnson notes that something more than a literary device is at work here:

> Luke has grasped the Pauline principle that the Spirit's essential work is not extrinsic but intrinsic, the transformation of human identity. The work of the Holy Spirit is not revealed only in the spectacular manifestations of "speaking in tongues and prophesying," although Acts has plenty of those activities (2:4; 10:44–46; 13:2; 19:5–6; 21:7–11); it is not found only in the ability of missionaries to proclaim and work wonders "in the name of Jesus"; it is found above all in their ability also to imitate the suffering of the Messiah (5:41; 7:59; 9:16; 12:4; 14:22; 16:23; 20:19, 22–24, 35; 21:11–14). By establishing a narrative role for the Holy Spirit, Luke has taken a significant step toward the eventual theological recognition of the Holy Spirit as a "person."[31]

The Spirit as Divine Agent

From beginning to end, the Holy Spirit is the operative agent in the outworking of God's will, the communication of God's Word, and the accomplishment of God's purpose. (No single passage of Scripture is sufficient to establish this, but Zechariah 4:6 comes close.) In Acts this role is more prominent and multifaceted, but the Spirit is still the Agent of the Father and the Son.

Luke's language is both retrospective and prospective. It looks backward and forward. As the prophets before (David, Acts 4:25) and after Him (Agabus, 11:28; disciples at Tyre, 21:4), Jesus speaks "through the Holy Spirit" (dia pneumatos hagiou). Jesus is the subject of the Spirit's work in Acts; indeed, in history.

The role of the Holy Spirit in the book of Acts, then, is the effective divine Agent through whom is accomplished the divine purpose. The Spirit serves, first, as the Spirit of prophecy, a character in the narrative, guaranteeing the reliability of both the *events* and their *record*. Second, the Spirit's ministry complements that of Christ. It is not a substitute for Christ's ministry, nor are those ministries analogous. Rather the Spirit continues Christ's ministry. Third, the Spirit is God's conferment of Himself and His gift *(dōrea)* on the church (Acts 2:38; cf. Luke 11:13; Acts 11:17). Fourth, in Acts the Spirit is the divine Controller of persons and events throughout history. The Spirit directs the actors as the events are played out on the stage of history.

The Pentecostal Outpouring

What happened on Pentecost was of critical importance to Luke. He alone recorded the words of Jesus that the heavenly Father will "give the Holy Spirit to those who ask Him" (Luke 11:13). But the Spirit was not given during the earthly ministry of Christ. John explains that this was because "Jesus was not yet glorified" (John 7:39b). This gift of the Spirit that believers were to receive (7:39a) apparently could not be given in the way God intended[32] until Christ ascended to the Father. Jesus Himself told His disciples, "If I do not go away, the Paraclete shall not come to you; but if I go, I will send Him to you (John 16:7b). The coming of the Paraclete was contingent upon Christ "going away." Peter reflects this same chronological understanding in his Pentecost address to Israel. "Therefore having been exalted to the right hand of God, and having received from the Father the promise of the Holy Spirit, He has poured forth this which you both see and hear" (Acts 2:33).

Thus, the outpouring of the Spirit on Pentecost, anticipated in Luke's "first account," his gospel (Acts 1:1), not only confirms and completes that account but also constitutes the *raison d'être* for his second account, the book of Acts.

To understand better the Pentecost outpouring of the Holy Spirit, it will help to discuss (1) the nature of the event itself and (2) its evidence, (3) explanation, (4) results, and (5) significance. For a fuller discussion of Spirit baptism, indwelling, and filling, see chapter 9, "The work of the of the Holy Spirit in Acts."

The Nature of the Event

Bible-believing Christians do not dispute the *fact* that the Holy Spirit was poured out on the day of Pentecost as recorded in Acts 2. What *is* disputed is the nature of this event and whether it is a repeatable experience to be sought today. The question concerns both Pentecost itself (Acts 2) and subsequent events that appear to be repetitions of the Pentecostal event (8:14–17; 10:44–48; 19:1–7).

Acts 2:1–4 describes the outpouring of the Holy Spirit. The coming of the Spirit on this day was indisputably the fulfillment of Christ's promise: "You shall be baptized with the Holy Spirit not many days from now" (Acts 1:5b). This, says William Kelly,

> ... was the baptism of the Spirit, though neither the mighty cause is here unfolded, nor are the effects as yet traced out. But the promise of the Father was now accomplished. The Holy Spirit was sent down from heaven according to the word of the Lord to abide with His own for ever, that other Advocate Who answers on earth to Christ in heaven, the Divine manager of all our affairs according to the will of God. As being a wholly new thing, there were accompanying signs, and these of a twofold character; not only the violent blowing which filled all the house, but the tongues as of fire which sat upon each. Thus was manifested the presence of the Spirit in a general way for all the house, in a special way as power of testimony for each: a distinction of importance also found in other forms elsewhere.[33]

Significantly, the apostles are commanded only to remain in Jerusalem. No other prerequisites are given to receiving the Holy Spirit. They are not told to pray, earnestly seek, desire, or strive for the gift or baptism. No contingencies are given regarding their readiness. They are not told to "renounce self," confess their sins, or prostrate themselves. Nor is the waiting or "tarrying" stressed, only the *place* of waiting.

It is, in fact, difficult to see *any* condition in Christ's instructions to the apostles. He did not say, "If you remain in Jerusalem. ..." He simply tells them to stay in Jerusalem and promises the Holy Spirit. The baptism of the Holy Spirit in Acts is not called the opportunity, responsibility, or even privilege of the believer. It is the promise of the Father (1:4), which is also promised by the Son. Never in Acts is the Spirit achieved or obtained. He is rather the promise or gift of the Father from on high (Luke 24:49), which certainly puts it out of human reach. It is given freely, not to some, but to all. Grammatical form enriches Jesus' statement. Christ's promise is:

- inclusive of all believers.
- passive, not done *by* the believer but *to* the believer.
- not in the verbal subjunctive, but the indicative. Jesus does not say, "You may or might be baptized with the Holy Spirit." He says, "You will be baptized," removing any uncertainty.
- simple future. It is not long in coming and without precondition.[34]

The peculiar thing about the Spirit's coming was the work of baptism. Though the word *baptism* is not used in Acts 2 to describe this event, this is clearly Peter's interpretation of it (Acts 11:15–17). Paul concurs with this understanding (1 Cor. 12:13).

The Behavior of the Disciples

Another aspect of the nature of the Spirit baptism is what happened to the personalities, life principles, and thought patterns of the men and women who experienced it.

Spirit baptism may be defined as *that work whereby the Spirit places the believer into union with Christ and into union with other believers in the body of Christ.*[35] Since Spirit baptism did not occur until Pentecost, the church did not begin until Pentecost. From that day until now, every person who believes in Jesus Christ is, at the moment of conversion and regeneration, baptized into the body of Christ.

This is not a repetition of the Pentecostal experience of Acts 2. That day the Spirit was "outpoured" into a new and empty receptacle, the church. That outpouring since has become unnecessary, for the Spirit fills the church by its members. Spirit baptism that unites the person into this filling is unique to the church age. It affects the baptized person's union with Christ and with others of the one body everywhere.

Given this meaning of Spirit baptism, how are the subsequent "conferrals" of the Holy Spirit to be explained: the Samaritans (Acts 8:14–17), Cornelius and his household (Acts 10:44–48), and the Ephesian disciples (Acts 19)? Peter likens the experience of Cornelius and his household to what had occurred on Pentecost (Acts 10:44–48).

Pentecostal and charismatic renewal groups usually find exegetical basis for their theology of the "second blessing" in these subsequent "conferrals" in Acts 2, 8, 9, 10, and 19.[36] The argument goes something like this:

1. Before the events of Acts 2:1–4, the apostles and other disciples were Christians. Their reception of the Spirit (Spirit baptism) at Pentecost was due to their "tarrying" and prayer and was evidenced by tongues speaking—all subsequent to salvation.

2. In Acts 2:38, Peter's words indicate a paradigmatic moral sequence—"Repent" (conversion), "be baptized" (water baptism), and "you shall receive the gift of the Holy Spirit" (Spirit baptism).

3. The Samaritans in Acts 8:4–25 were believers who had not yet experienced Spirit baptism. Their reception of the Spirit, subsequent as it was to their becoming believers, establishes a pattern.

4. Acts 9:1–19 indicates that Paul's reception of the Spirit was subsequent to his salvation on the road to Damascus.
5. The experience of Cornelius and his household in Acts 10 and 11 is an ideal. Ideally, everyone should receive the baptism of the Spirit when they first believe, as did Cornelius and his household. Even here, though, where all seems to occur at once, there is succession; it's just an *immediate* succession.
6. The ones who receive the Spirit in Acts 19:1–7 were believers or disciples. They simply hadn't heard of the Holy Spirit or known to seek Him. Why else would Paul ask these disciples if they had received the Holy Spirit? He was wanting to point to the need for a second blessing—to "go all the way," to partake of all God wants for every Christian.

Bible readers should immediately be wary of these arguments, for the doctrine of the "second blessing" is based almost entirely on the book of Acts and texts elsewhere contradict the notion. Such exegesis does not take into account adequately the paranormal nature of this singular moment in history. Further, close examination shows that these passages do not support the view that Spirit baptism is a work subsequent to conversion (e.g., 1 Cor. 12:13).

The Place of Miracles

Miracles, so far as the biblical and historical evidence suggests, were not scattered willy-nilly through biblical history. Depending on whether the miracles of Christ are considered to be in a separate time frame from those of the apostles, there are four or five critical periods of Israel's history around which miracles cluster.[37] These time junctures have to do primarily with Israel and Israel's covenant relationship with Yahweh. In each case they involve a paramount message to Israel through extraordinary prophets whose authority is attested to by "signs and wonders."

Spirit baptism passages in Acts (chaps. 2, 8, 9, 10, and 19) are peculiar to the infancy stage of the church. All occurred within approximately the first twenty years. All have to do with geographic and ethnic advancement of the church. And all occur in the very early stages of the inauguration of a new dispensation.[38]

It is true that some conferrals of the Holy Spirit are upon those who are already believers. To some this is proof that Spirit baptism is a blessing subsequent to salvation, which, though not every Christian's experience, can and should be.

However, examined in the light of the transitional nature of the book of Acts and the teaching of the rest of Scripture, especially the Epistles, these passages *cannot* teach a "second blessing" view of Spirit baptism as the norm for Christians today. Since Scripture is internally consistent and other texts are clearly prescriptive and normative while these are merely descriptive, the Acts experiences must be exceptions to the rule and not paradigmatic.

Acts 2:1–4

On Pentecost and in Jerusalem, the Holy Spirit was indeed poured out on a group of people who already were believers. But this can hardly be evidence of a pattern for Christians today. Spirit baptism did not occur prior to Pentecost. Spirit baptism was inaugurated on this day and was to be a phenomenon peculiar to the church age then dawning. In the Old Testament it was a *future* hope ("I will put My Spirit within you," Ezek. 36:27). Prior to Christ's ascension it was still a future hope, only much nearer ("not many days from now," Acts 1:5). Jesus said something that had never happened before was about to occur.

This forces us to look deeply because the Old Testament and Gospels, especially Luke, have referred to others who were filled with the Spirit. Thus, Pentecostals argue from Acts 2:4 that when the disciples were all "filled with the Holy Spirit and began to speak in tongues" what they were doing was similar to the charismatic activity of the Spirit in the Old Testament and the Gospels, especially Luke.

Filling was a precedented work of God. On rare occasions, as recorded in Scripture, people were filled with the Holy Spirit so that they could perform a special task of God in a supernatural way. The craftsmen were Spirit filled for their work on the Tabernacle, but Scripture (e.g., Exod. 31:3) is clear that Bezalel, son of Uri, was filled only in regard to his special calling. It would not extend to all his future work as long as he lived. The same was true of the judges, and the prophets. But Peter and the others refer to the experience of this day as something that had been prophesied (most clearly by Joel but also by others) that never before had happened. We can only see from how the Pentecost experience is described elsewhere that the unprecedented action of which Peter speaks can be called "Spirit baptism." This means that a distinction is properly drawn between Spirit baptism and the filling of the Spirit—both of which occurred on Pentecost.

Yet Luke calls attention to the precedented filling rather than the unprecedented baptism. Probably this is because Acts 2 is narrative, describing what happened visibly in Jerusalem that day. But what was totally new was what was happening *invisibly*, for Spirit baptism is an invisible non-experiential work. It lay hidden, underlying what was sensationally apparent. Luke assumed his readers would understand that the Spirit baptism promised in chapter one was now occurring in Acts 2 in conjunction with the filling. The sensational outward actions signified an inner miraculous work. This accords well with Paul's statement to the Corinthians that "we were all baptized into one body" (1 Cor. 12:13). Often it is assumed that "Spirit baptism" and "filling" are synonymous. This is Roger Stronstad's conclusion:

The inaugural gift of the Holy Spirit on the day of Pentecost is a pivotal event in Luke's history-of-salvation theology. Therefore, it is not surprising to observe that Luke gives a multiplex description to this transfer of the Spirit. Because of the charismatic-prophetic dimension of Pentecost, Luke's favorite phrase, "filled with the Holy Spirit," best approximates the full meaning of the gift of the Spirit. No single term, however, is sufficiently comprehensive to adequately convey the full meaning of this event. Therefore, in Luke's narrative it is at once a clothing, a baptizing, an empowering, a filling, and an outpouring of the Spirit. As Luke uses these terms, they are essentially synonymous. Each term, however, also contributes distinctive and important nuances to the meaning of this complex phenomenon.[39]

In spite of Stronstad's wish to see Spirit baptism and filling as synonymous, he is sensitive to the "distinctive and important nuances" between the two. As we shall see below, this is precisely the point. There *are* distinctions between Spirit baptism and filling as well as other works of the Holy Spirit peculiar to this age that also began on Pentecost.

Spirit Baptism a Collective Experience

The Spirit's permanent indwelling; regeneration; sealing: These works are related, and they all occur on Pentecost, but they are not synonymous. Only the terms *the gift of the Spirit* and *the outpouring of the Spirit* describe the same work of the Spirit on Pentecost. This "gift" may be equated with the "outpouring" of the Spirit on Pentecost, but neither term is synonymous with Spirit baptism. Spirit baptism is that work which places believers into the church and into Christ. But Spirit baptism is only *one* consequence of the "gift/outpouring" of the Spirit on Pentecost. W. Graham Scroggie mentions the filling and baptism of the Holy Spirit along with several other ministries of the Spirit in this age and wisely says, "It cannot for a moment be imagined that these words are used interchangeably or indiscriminately throughout the New Testament; but rather, with the utmost precision."[40]

On Pentecost the Holy Spirit was given in a way never known before; given in fulfillment of the promises of both the Father and the Son. This was the "circumcision of the heart" (Deut. 30:6) and God's Spirit "within" (Ezek. 36:26), of which the Old Testament spoke. This was also the Spirit baptism promised in the Gospels and by our Lord just before His ascension (Acts 1:5). Too, this is the power (filling) which Christ said they would receive "when the Holy Spirit has come upon you" (Acts 1:8).

These promises involve one gift, one outpouring, but separate and distinct works. "Circumcision of the heart" (Deut. 30:6; cf. Ezek. 36:26) anticipates the unprecedented work of spiritual and personal regeneration. Spirit baptism marks the birth of the church when all believers were placed into union with

Christ and His body. "Filling" with the Spirit is that divine enablement for prophetic ministry. Under Old Testament economy,

> the fact of belonging to God was marked by circumcision of the flesh; in the New by the circumcision of the heart, that is to say, the regeneration brought about by the Spirit. "Neither is that circumcision [which counts before God] which is outward in the flesh; [but] . . . that of the heart, in the Spirit, not the letter [the law]" (Rom. 2:28–29). "For we are the circumcision, who worship by the Spirit of God and the glory in Christ Jesus" (Phil. 3:3).[41]

It is true that the disciples were already "Christians" when they received the gift of the Spirit. This reception of the Spirit is, of course, subsequent to their having believed in Christ. But when it is understood that on Pentecost, the Holy Spirit began an entirely new work in hearts—regenerating, permanently indwelling, sealing, baptizing *all* believers into the church—it is *expected* that this should be subsequent to their belief. After all, it had to begin sometime. The church was still future when Christ said to His disciples, who *already* believed in Him, "I *will* build My church" (Matt. 16:18). Christ began to build His church on the day of Pentecost, when He sent the promise of the Father (Acts 1:4) and poured forth (Acts 2:33) the Holy Spirit. This is the significance of Acts 2:1–4.

The Spirit Given to All

The repetitive use of *all* in this passage indicates the Spirit was given to *all* without discrimination. The coming of the Spirit upon believers in this passage is neither selective nor conditional. It might also be noted that the text gives no suggestion that the disciples were asking for the gift of tongues. There is no precedent nor pattern here for the second-blessing view, which urges earnest seeking of a baptism of the Spirit, evidenced by tongues speaking.

Peter's identification of the events of Pentecost with the prophecy of Joel (Acts 2:16) indicates a fulfillment (see pp. 147, 152) of Joel's prophecy. It also signals the beginning of the *eschaton* ("the last days," Acts 2:17). As such, the outpouring of the Spirit on Pentecost is the foundation of all that follows, and gives perspective to ensuing events.

> Pentecost itself is not repeated. It stands apart from what follows as an event that occurred once for all when the ascended Christ decisively sent forth the Spirit to inaugurate the new order. Indicative of this fact is the consideration that the phenomena of the day of Pentecost were not repeated. In what follows there is nothing comparable to the "tongues as of fire" or the "sound as of a mighty wind being borne along."[42]

Some may say, "Yes, but tongues speaking accompanied each subsequent outpouring or reception of the Spirit." Not for certain. There is no mention of tongues in Acts 8 when the Samaritans received the Spirit. Nor is the tongues speaking of 1 Corinthians said to be especially related to, or indicative of, Spirit baptism. In fact, to the Corinthians Paul expressly says that they "were all baptized into one body" (1 Cor. 12:13), but not all speak with tongues (1 Cor. 12:30). Moreover, the experiences of tongues speaking that *did* accompany subsequent receptions of the Spirit (Acts 10, 19) are easily understood in light of the transitional nature of the book of Acts. They are justified exceptions that might be expected.

Acts 2:38

Peter's call to "repent" is especially pertinent to his Jewish audience. He is addressing Israelites. The nation had just rejected and crucified their Messiah (2:33). "Therefore let all the house of Israel know for certain that God has made Him both Lord and Christ—this Jesus whom you crucified" (2:36). Israel's national restoration was (and is) dependent upon repentance (Deut. 30:1–10). Unrepentant Israel lay under sentence of judgment. Peter's call for repentance may be taken as a plea for the nation to repent (the verb is plural), or for individuals to come out from that nation, to *dis*-identify with Israel and to identify with Christ.

The clause *and be baptized, every one of you, in the name of Jesus Christ* is best understood as parenthetical.[43] Luke simply means that repentance results in remission of sins and the gift of the Spirit. By "the gift of the Holy Spirit" Peter means not a subsequent "second blessing" but a consequent attending blessing to forgiveness of sins. The gift *of* the Spirit is not a gift *from* the Spirit. The Spirit Himself *is* the gift. Luke "is not promoting some necessary second experience. He consistently presents both forgiveness and the Spirit as gifts of grace (3:19; 5:31; 13:38; 11:17; 15:8). The gift of the Spirit is the Spirit Himself, who regenerates, indwells, unites, and transforms lives. All the fruit and gifts of the Spirit flow from this one great gift."[44]

Acts 8:4–25

Beginning with the stoning of Stephen, "a great persecution arose against the Church in Jerusalem; and they were all scattered throughout the region of Judea and Samaria, except the apostles" (Acts 8:1b). Luke's exception of the apostles is no accident. It is Philip, not an apostle, who brings the gospel of Christ to the Samaritans. The Samaritans believed and were being baptized (water baptism, 8:12). When the apostles in Jerusalem heard of it, they sent Peter and John, "who came down and prayed for them, that they might receive the Holy Spirit. For He had not yet fallen upon any of them; they had simply ["only," *monon*] been baptized in the name of the Lord Jesus. Then [Peter and John] began laying their hands on them, and they were receiving the Holy Spirit" (8:15b–17).

To this point in the narrative the church has not spread beyond Judea. It begins in Jerusalem. The disciples there experienced the initial outpouring of the Spirit of God. The church then moves into all Judea (Acts 2:9, 14; 8:1; 9:31; 10:37; 26:20). Only *then* is all Samaria covered (1:8). It is this geographic advancement that raises an ethnic issue of major proportions. Until now the church had been strictly Jewish.

The Samaritans claimed that they possessed the "place chosen by Yahweh," Mount Gerizim, where they built a temple.[45] The mutual bitterness, distrust, and hostility between the Jews and the Samaritans was so great that hatred could turn violent. To the Jew, Samaritans were worse than foreigners; they were mixed-heritage heretics, excommunicated schismatics, and "more unclean than swine's flesh."[46]

The apostolic presence of Peter and John authenticated the Samaritan church and prevented schism in the newly emerging church. It is significant that in the Gospels, Luke alone tells us of John's earlier hostility toward the Samaritans (Luke 9:52–54). Here in Acts it is John, along with Peter, who witnesses the *faith* of the Samaritans and their reception of the Holy Spirit. Indeed, he and Peter are the apostolic instrument by which the Holy Spirit is conferred on the Samaritans. By apostolic prayer and laying-on-of-hands the Holy Spirit now becomes the possession of the Samaritans, the Samaritans become the possession of the Spirit, and believing Jews and Samaritans are now one in Christ. There is one church, "one body and one Spirit . . . one Lord, one faith, one baptism" (Eph. 4:4–5).

That unity was connected at its beginning, in the wisdom of God, with the apostles' coming, prayer, and laying on of hands and given a heightened visibility by a dramatic giving of the Holy Spirit. God wanted the first church outside Jerusalem to have apostolic contact. The history, growing tradition, and, above all, the organic unity of the church that had begun in Jerusalem were preserved through the apostolic visitation. The Samaritans were not left to be an isolated sect. Without taking away the ancient hostilities at the level of ultimate authority, the young church would have been split immediately. Instead, God shows the world something new, a body of Jews and Samaritans without the wall of enmity.[47]

The delay in Acts 8, therefore, was necessary and multipurposed. First, it authenticated the experience and legitimacy of the Samaritan believers. Second, it confirmed Philip's ministry among them to the Jerusalem apostles. Third, it confirmed Philip's ministry to those Samaritans who would think connections with Jerusalem impossible. Fourth, it prevented schism in the critical infancy stage of the church. As Robert G. Gromacki observes:

> There is no mention of wind, fiery tongues, or tongues-speaking. There is no indication that the Samaritans prayed or laid hands on each other nor that Philip shared the apostolic power. This time

interval between faith and the reception of the Holy Spirit demonstrated to the Samaritan converts that they had to be under the spiritual authority of Jewish apostles, appointed by Christ and stationed in Jerusalem.[48]

In no sense does this extraordinary situation establish a norm regarding Spirit baptism. Rather, it highlights the abnormality of separation between regeneration and Spirit baptism. The Samaritans became the bridge to span the chasm between Jews and the Gentiles. In Samaria, the gospel and Christianity began its way out to the nations.

Acts 9:1–19

The account of Saul's conversion in Acts 9 brings together two motifs: prophetic vocation and the gift of the Spirit. Luke's use of *pimplēmi* for "filled" always accompanies a description of divine enablement for prophetic ministry. Moreover, in describing Saul's encounter with the risen Lord on the road to Damascus, Luke emphasizes his calling, not his conversion. In fact, Luke does not mention Saul's conversion. Saul is told little more than to "enter the city, and it shall be told you what you must do" (9:6). Paul's use of *kyrios* ("Lord") may imply no more than "Sir." Indeed his question, "Who are you, Lord?" indicates Paul does not know enough to have saving faith.

It was only after he had been blind three days that Ananias came and spoke to him the Word of God and said, "And now why do you delay? Arise and be baptized, and wash away your sins, calling on His name" (22:16). This is an unnecessary exhortation if Paul was converted on the Damascus road (cf. Acts 22:4–21). His conversion may well have taken place in the house of Judas (9:11). Saul's conversion may have been concurrent with his "filling."

But even if it could be established that Saul received saving faith on the road to Damascus, there is no proof that he did not at that time *also* receive the Holy Spirit in regeneration, indwelling, and Spirit baptism. The "filling" of Acts 9:17 would then be understood as a special filling, which did occur repeatedly in the lives of both Peter (Acts 2:4; 4:31) and Paul (Acts 9:17; 13:9). This is consistent with Luke's use of *pimplēmi* for Spirit filling throughout. There certainly is no proof of a spiritual pattern here for *normal* Christian experience.

Acts 10:44–48; 11:1–17

Luke's narrative is freighted with subtle (and not so subtle) indications of how Spirit develops the understanding of the apostles regarding the nature and mission of the church. The inclusion of the Samaritans (half-caste Jews) in Acts 8 is the first step in bridging the separation between Jew and Gentile. Logically, Luke follows the Samaritan account in chapter 8 with Saul's dramatic conversion and commission to go to the Gentiles (9:15), and 9:36–43 describes

Peter's visit to Joppa where he resurrects a dead woman. The result was that "it became known all over Joppa, and many believed in the Lord" (9:42). Peter has established a beachhead for the gospel in a seaport with major Gentile significance. If the gospel is carried from the shores of Joppa, Peter himself was the cause. Between Paul's commission and Peter's Joppa ministry is Luke's statement: "So the Church throughout all Judea and Galilee and Samaria enjoyed peace, being built up; and going on in the fear of the Lord and the comfort of the Holy Spirit, it continued to increase" (9:31). Joppa is Luke's literary hinge to the events of chapter 10.

It is in Joppa, on the rooftop of Simon the Tanner (9:43), that Peter has his vision and command not to reject what God calls clean. Piece by piece, God was building a church large enough to include Gentiles on an equal footing with Jews. Gradually, the Jewish apostles are becoming aware of God's foreign policy (10:1–35).

Peter's vision leads him to the household of Cornelius, an ideal first Gentile convert. Cornelius fears God, is generous toward his Jewish neighbors, and prays continually (10:2). It is of interest that many Gentiles did serve the true and living God.[49] Cornelius was one of these, along with his household (10:2). But was Cornelius saved? Some conclude, on the basis of Acts 11:14, that he was not. The angel tells Cornelius to send for Peter, who "shall speak words to you by which you will be saved, you and your household" (11:14). But Luke has described the piety of Cornelius as unmistakably a God-fearer. His praying about the "ninth hour" (10:3) suggests he was keeping the three traditional Jewish times of prayer, though he evidently was not a Jewish proselyte. This, and the conversation between Cornelius and the angel in Cornelius's vision make it difficult to believe Cornelius was not a believer.

Raymond Saxe holds that Cornelius was a Gentile with "Old Testament salvation."[50] He lacked salvation in the New Testament sense (see Acts 10:2; 11:14).[51] Saxe does not explain what he means by "Old/New Testament salvation" but presumably he means the difference between the Spirit's work of regeneration and indwelling, and the new baptism into the body of Christ. If the Old Testament knew nothing of regeneration, then Acts 11:14 might well mean "saved in a New Testament sense" as opposed to the Old Testament sense.

Of course, many believe that Old Testament saints *were* regenerated. It is true that regeneration is necessary to salvation. Unless one is born-again "he cannot enter into the kingdom of God" (John 3:5). This is true of anyone since Pentecost. But is it true *prior* to Pentecost? Were Old Testament saints "born-again?" Lewis Sperry Chafer cautiously says, "With respect to regeneration, the Old testament saints were evidently renewed; but as there is no definite doctrinal teaching relative to the extent and character of that renewal, no positive declaration can be made."[52] Actually, Chafer's use of *evidently* is more optimistic than Scripture warrants. Chafer seems to sense this, for further on in his discussion he says,

> The silence of God must be respected relative to what constituted one a *just man* according to the Mosaic demands. . . . The Old Testament will be searched in vain for a record of Jews passing from an unsaved state to a saved state, or for any declaration about the terms upon which such a change would be secured. In other words, their national covenant standing was a tremendous spiritual advantage; but it cannot rightfully be compared with the estate of the believer today who is justified and perfected forever, having received the *plērōma* of the Godhead through vital union with Christ (emphasis his).[53]

But it seems the fundamental difference between Old Testament and New Testament saints is the work of the Holy Spirit *since* and *as a result of the Pentecostal outpouring*. In the Old Testament, the promise was "I will circumcise your hearts." But this promise is inseparably linked to the gift of the Spirit in the new covenant. This covenant was not ratified until Christ's death. By His death, Christ ratified the new covenant. Upon His ascension He "sent" the Holy Spirit to the people of God (Acts 2:33) in a way they had never known.

A New Testament saint dies and goes directly to be with Christ (Phil 1:21–23). Not so the Old Testament saint. Is this not because the former is *already* regenerate; already quickened with the divine life, and the latter awaits regeneration? In any case, much of the work of the Holy Spirit in Acts is unprecedented and unexampled.

Visions to both Cornelius and Peter bring about Peter's visit (10:1–34). These events are related in detail by Luke because of the significance of the event in the development of the emerging church. Peter's speech to Cornelius and company was interrupted when the "Holy Spirit fell upon all those who were listening to the message" (10:44). Peter's Jewish companions were amazed when Gentiles received the gift of the Holy Spirit (10:45), yet they heard it confirmed by the audible witness of tongues speaking and "exalting God" (10:46).

This is not merely a private experience of Peter's but a major step in geographic and ethnic expansion of the emerging church. It further illustrates the transitional nature of Acts. The problem at this point was how to convince the Jewish church that Gentiles are to have an equal share in the church—as Gentiles. That this was a problem of major proportions is evidenced by the following:

> First, Luke's allotment of so much space to a second recital of the account "indicates that Luke considered this event one of the most important in the life of the early church."[54]

Second, tongues at Caesarea were a sign to the Jews that the gift of the Spirit poured out on these Gentiles was in every respect equivalent to the gift poured out on them at Pentecost.

Third, Peter is obliged to justify his involvement in the episode at Caesarea by explanation and appeal to the evidence when the Jewish church in Judea took issue with him (11:1–4).

Fourth, the problem is still a "live issue" four chapters later. In Acts 15 the Jewish leaders of the Church are still disputing the question of Gentiles. The question is not "are Gentiles to be included?" but "must the Gentiles become Jews to be accepted in the Church?" They correctly concluded of course, that Gentiles need *not* become Jews. But this already was apparent after the events at Cornelius's house.

Indeed, it is the *absence* of any direct involvement on Peter's part that is his justification before the other apostles when they later take issue with him. Peter says, "As I began to speak, the Holy Spirit fell upon them, just as He did upon us at the beginning" (11:15). The "just as" points to the sovereignty of the Spirit's coming. "The wind blows where it wishes," says John 3:8. Peter then says, "If God therefore gave to them the same gift . . . who was I that I could stand in God's way?" (11:17). M. R. De Haan makes a pertinent observation about the first three baptismal experiences of the Holy Spirit:

> In none of the three incidents of the Gospel going to Jews, Samaritans and Gentiles, was the experience the same. At Pentecost the Spirit was manifested by a mighty wind and tongues like as of fire. In Samaria the Holy Spirit was received by the laying on of the hands of the apostles. There is no baptism mentioned and no speaking in tongues. However, in the case of the Gentiles the Spirit came in response to the hearing of the Word. There was no laying on of hands, no wind or fire, but here speaking in tongues did follow. Here are three different circumstances where Jews, Samaritans and Gentiles received the Holy Spirit, and they were all different. Which shall we follow, if these are meant for today?[55]

The essential difference between the Samaritans (Acts 8) and the Gentiles (Acts 10), and why in Samaria there was the laying on of hands and not in Caesarea, was that Samaria had *rejected* the authority of Jerusalem and was postured in opposition to the Jews. Cornelius had *embraced* Judaism. He was already postured *toward* Jerusalem. Laying on of hands was necessary in Samaria in order to remove the schism and show the Samaritans that they must not continue in rejection and opposition to Jerusalem and the apostles. Conversely, it was necessary that there be *no* laying of hands on the Gentiles so that the apostles would not assume that Gentiles must become Jews to belong to the church of Christ.

Acts 19:1–7

This passage continues to show the church in transition. It is the fourth and final conferral of the Holy Spirit to a distinguishable group. This time Paul, not Peter, is the agent of transfer. Near the beginning of his third missionary journey, Paul encounters about twelve disciples (19:1, 7). This passage, however, cannot be taken to teach a post-conversion Spirit baptism as the norm. These men were disciples, not of Christ, but of John the Baptist. Hence, they were no doubt Jews.[56] Anthony Hoekema says, "It is quite obvious that these disciples were not full-fledged Christian believers when Paul met them."[57] In spite of the statement made in 19:3, Stonehouse rejects the view that these were in fact disciples of John the Baptist rather than Jesus.[58] His reason:

> These men were believers; but in *John's* baptism and *John's* message of a *coming* Christ. Apparently they did not know that Jesus who came, died, and rose again, was the Christ, for Paul had to tell them this (19:4–5). Upon learning it, they are promptly baptized (in water) in Jesus' name and receive the Spirit through the laying on of Paul's hands. Gerhard Hasel seems almost subconsciously aware of this fine distinction when he says, "Luke usually uses the term 'disciple' in the book of Acts as a designation for Christian believers. Inasmuch as Paul asked whether they had received the Holy Spirit when they 'believed,' he seems to consider them as believers. Surely they were believers with partial knowledge."[59]

Gromacki correctly identifies these men as Old Testament saints in the New Testament dispensation:

> These twelve disciples knew that they were supposed to believe in one who would come after John. When Paul explained that that one was Christ, they believed in Him and manifested their belief in Christian baptism. They became New Testament believers and members of the true church. Had they died after Calvary and before this explanation, they would have been classified as Old Testament saints. Christian baptism was necessary because the baptism of John was oriented to Israel and the Jewish hope of the Messianic kingdom (Matt. 3:2; 10:5–7; John 1:31). After Paul laid his hands upon them, they received the Holy Spirit and spoke with tongues. There is no indication that Paul prayed for them or that they prayed for themselves in order to gain this experience.[60]

It may be concluded that the Pentecostal outpouring of the Spirit consists of one outpouring with several subsequent transfers, or conferrals, always with an apostle present. These are not repetitions of Pentecost, nor are they parts of a series that continues, nor are they paradigmatic for Christian experience. They are elements in the initial foundation of the church and so correlate with the events of Acts 2 as part of a unique nonrepeatable complex of events.

Evidence of the Spirit's Outpouring

To anyone who reads the prophets, the coming of the Holy Spirit was serious evidence of the truth claims of the gospel. However, the phenomena which accompanied the coming and bestowal of the Spirit (both visible and invisible) also needed some authentication for those upon whom the Spirit came and for those who merely observed.

The Nature of the Evidence

There were two types of undeniable manifestations. The visible manifestations were spectacular but of secondary importance. At the initial outpouring on Pentecost, both visible and audible spectacular events occurred. The noise of a violent, rushing wind, apparently without force, filled the house. Tongues as of fire rested on each one of them. They began to speak with other languages (2:2–4).

Undeniable Visible Manifestations

All of the manifestations of the Spirit's outpouring are undeniable. No one present at any of these occurrences questions the validity of the manifestations, nor of the reality behind them. On the day of Pentecost some cynical onlookers first mocked, "They are full of sweet wine" (2:13). But in the end they could not deny that "each" (2:7) of the foreign Jews "from every nation under heaven," (2:5) heard the disciples speaking in his or her own language.

Subsequent conferrals of the Spirit lack these manifestations because they are transitional *expansions* of what the Spirit, who is already come, has already done. But it should be carefully noted that tongues speaking is always a sign to Jews (1 Cor. 14:22; cf. Isa. 28:11; Mark 16:17; Acts 2, 10, 19; 1 Cor. 14:21).

Each of the three times tongues speaking is mentioned in connection with the reception of the Spirit unbelieving Jews are present. These spectacular manifestations may be considered of secondary importance because they are not an end in themselves, but are a means to an end. Once the apostolic authority of the Jerusalem church is established and ethnic barriers are breached, sensational manifestations wane.

Primary Invisible Manifestations

Invisible, nonspectacular manifestations of the now-outpoured Spirit of God were more primary. Following Peter's sermon on the day of Pentecost, about three thousand "received his word" and "were baptized" (2:41). Certainly they, too, received the Spirit and were Spirit baptized into the body, yet we do not read of wind, fire, or tongues speaking. What is far more indicative of the Spirit's presence is that they devoted themselves to teaching, fellowship, and prayer. "And everyone kept feeling a sense of awe" (2:42–43a). Luke tells that "many wonders and signs were taking place," but this was through the apostles (2:43).[61] Among the three thousand, the principle manifestation of the Spirit is that they were unified and shared with all. They were single-minded and sincere, praising God and helping others (2:44–47). Joy (8:39; 16:34), comfort (9:31), boldness (4:8, 13, 29, 31), unity, cooperation, and community seem to be principle manifestations of the Holy Spirit in the church in the book of Acts.

Unpredictable and Sovereign Manifestations

As noted above, no two "outpourings" or Spirit baptisms are the same. Either the order or sequence of events differs or attending phenomena differ. Luke presents the gift of the Spirit as sovereignly bestowed rather than "achieved." So also, the evidential manifestations which accompany the gift of the Spirit, which are themselves gifts *from* the Spirit, and given as He wills (cf. 1 Cor. 12:11).

Transitional Manifestations

The evidence of the Spirit's outpouring and subsequent conferrals accompanied events that were transitional. There was always an apostle present, or it concerned an apostle (Acts 9:17). Each instance signaled the beginning of a new and unusual work. Serious ethnic barriers had to be breached. Once the church was born, these barriers breached, and the nature and mission of the church clearly understood, the spectacular evidences stopped or were infrequent. Eventually they appear to have died out completely. Pentecostals, especially the more charismatic, strongly deny this. But that is the evidence of Scripture and church history.[62]

The Need for the Evidence

The primary purpose of the more spectacular evidence was authentication, affirmation, and confirmation and was directed primarily at the Jews. It is not accidental that Scripture tells us "indeed Jews ask for signs" (1 Cor. 1:22; cf. Matt. 12:38; 16:1–4; Mark 8:11; Luke 11:16, 20: John 2:18, 48; Acts 2:22). The wind and fire and other signs and wonders (e.g., Acts 8:13) served at least a threefold purpose.

First, they confirmed to the early disciples that the outpouring of the Spirit on Pentecost was the beginning of a new work of God—the dispensation of the Spirit.

Second, these spectacular evidences attracted the attention of and showed unbelieving Jews that this was the work of God and that the apostles spoke His Word. Spectacular evidences authenticated the apostles as God's messengers, bearing God's message.

Third, these signs confirm *to the Jewish apostles* the validity of the Gentile experience as equal to that of the Jews. The unity, integrity, and expansion of the early Jewish church, was due in part to their absolute conviction that the Spirit of God had been poured out. Spectacular evidences helped authenticate this, especially to the Jew. For more on this issue, see pp. 157–176.

The Spirit's Outpouring and Joel

On the Day of Pentecost, the response of the onlookers was dramatic. Visiting Jews from many other lands and languages each heard the disciples speaking in their own tongue. Luke says "they continued in amazement and great perplexity, saying to one another, 'What does this mean?'" But others (Palestinian Jews?) "were mocking and saying, 'They are full of sweet wine'" (2:12, 13). Peter, taking his stand with the eleven, explains what is happening.

Peter's message is apparently addressed to the entire crowd of Jews, both local and foreign, hence his address, *Men of Israel* (2:22). It begins, however, primarily addressed to the local Jews who may have been mocking. Peter begins, "Men of Judea, and all you who live in Jerusalem" (2:14). To these, he denies the charge of drunkenness. There was no need to explain this to the foreign Jews, for they heard the disciples speaking their own languages— languages which would have sounded foreign to the Palestinian Jews. This may have drawn the charge of drunkenness. Peter explains these events by referring to the prophecy of Joel.

The Issue

Peter's quotation of Joel 2:28–32 closely follows the *LXX*,[63] with minor but significant differences. Peter says, "This is that which was spoken through the prophet Joel" (2:16). What did Peter mean by "this is that"? Though answers to this question vary widely, they reduce essentially to three basic views.[64]

1. The events of Pentecost are the entire fulfillment of Joel's prophecy.[65]
2. There is no fulfillment at all. Peter means only that these events are analogous to or illustrative of Joel's prophecy ("This is *like* that").[66]

3. Events of Pentecost are a partial, or initial, fulfillment of Joel's prophecy. Pentecost *fulfills* Joel's prophecy but does not *exhaust* it. There will be a future fulfillment in connection with Israel's conversion and restoration to the land ("this is that, but *not all* of that").[67]

The first view is common to Covenant theology. Amillennialists, postmillennialists, and covenant premillennialists consider Peter's reference to Joel as proof that this prophecy was fulfilled on Pentecost. On the basis of this and other texts, they conclude that there will be no fulfillment to the nation Israel. The church is considered the "new Israel," and Israel's promises are now fulfilled in the church. Some Covenant premillennialists are an exception in that they see a future for national Israel. George E. Ladd, for example, says:

> It is important to note that a prophecy which in Joel was addressed to the nation Israel now had its fulfillment in the Christian church. However, in God's redemptive purpose, Israel is also to be included in the fulfillment of this prophecy (Rom. 11:26).[68]

The fundamental weakness of this first view is its assumption of a nonliteral hermeneutic. The national promises to Israel are reduced to spiritual fulfillment in the church. And the cosmic signs and wonders predicted by Joel (2:30–31) and quoted by Peter (Acts 2:19–20) must be allegorized. They did not occur at Pentecost, so they must be taken figuratively. This is the approach of Dan McCartney and Charles Clayton. Discussing these cosmic signs, they state: "Sometimes they were literally manifested, as at Jesus' crucifixion, but sometimes they are only figurative, as in Acts 2:19–20, where Peter by inspiration says that the prophecy of Joel 2 was fulfilled at the coming of the Spirit (Acts 2:16)."[69]

By what principle do we determine what is to be taken literally and what is to be taken nonliterally? View one must be rejected on hermeneutic grounds. Consistent application of a literal hermeneutic necessarily leads to a distinction between Israel and the church.

Presumably in an effort to guard this distinction, some dispensationalists have embraced the second view, which denies any fulfillment of Joel's prophecy in Acts 2:16–21. Because Joel's prophecy is addressed to Israel, and because any fulfillment in the church is thought to threaten the distinction between the two, some dispensationalists have insisted that Peter's "this is that" is best understood as "this is *like* that." After all, there is no evidence of fulfillment of the cosmic signs mentioned in Acts 2:19–20. Though held in the main by earlier dispensationalists, this view was recently defended by Clifford Rapp Jr., with this reasoning:

First, Joel speaks of an outpouring of the Spirit on Judah (see Joel 2:28 with the repeated use of the "your" to describe the "all flesh" which will receive the outpouring of the Spirit). Joel 2:32 speaks of Mount Zion and Jerusalem as the recipients of deliverance. Judah and Jerusalem are mentioned in Joel 3:1. *Second,* the events spoken of in Joel 2 that precede the outpouring of the Spirit have not been fulfilled. The heavenly wonders of Joel 2:30, 31 did not take place on Pentecost. The judgment of the Gentiles and the restoration of the land of Israel that follow the outpouring of the Spirit (Joel 3) have not been fulfilled. *Third,* Peter does not specifically say that Pentecost fulfills that which was spoken by the prophet Joel. The experience of Pentecost does not touch upon all that Joel predicted. *Fourth,* the outpouring of the Spirit on Pentecost was for the formation of the Church, the body of Christ. It is similar to but distinct from the outpouring of the Spirit upon repentant Judah. The outpouring of the Spirit on Pentecost is viewed as the fulfillment of the baptism of the Spirit and the beginning of the Church (Acts 1:5; 11:15–17). The Scripture makes careful distinctions and the interpreter should observe them at all times. . . . Over all it seems most satisfactory to understand Peter's words as "This is like that which was spoken by the prophet Joel."[70]

This second view ("this is *like* that") has appeal. It recognizes the need to take literally the promises to Israel and does not ignore the context of Joel's prophecy. It avoids ascribing figurative fulfillment to Joel's prophecies. Nor does it blur the distinction between Israel and the church.

Yet it is hard to negate the force of Peter's "this is that" statement in 2:16. It seems to beg the question to say, "Peter didn't *specifically* say that Pentecost fulfills Joel's prophecy." Taken at face value, Peter's words seem to mean just that.

The third view takes Peter's words at face value, provides for future fulfillment in regard to Israel, maintains the distinction between Israel and the church, and best explains the events of Pentecost. Holding this view does not necessarily make one a "progressive" dispensationalist. This view best explains the biblical data and accords well with classical dispensationalism.

The Interpretation

When Peter cited Joel 2:28–32, saying, "This is that which was spoken through the prophet Joel," he was not speaking of analogy, allusion, illustration, or making homiletic use of Joel's prophecy. The Spirit's outpouring at Pentecost was *partial* fulfillment, or was one *referent* of the prophecy of Joel. The Old Testament promise of the outpouring of the Spirit of God is contextually and theologically linked to the new covenant. There is no reason to dissociate Joel's prophecy of the Spirit's outpouring from those of Isaiah, Ezekiel, Jeremiah, and Zechariah, nor to dissociate any of these from the new covenant.

In the Abrahamic covenant, provision was made for salvation "blessings" to come to the Gentiles (Gen. 12:3). The new covenant, which is the outworking and amplification of the "blessings" aspect of the Abrahamic covenant, promised the outpouring of the Holy Spirit. The gift of the Holy Spirit is the divine enablement at the heart of the new covenant. In an attempt to avoid equating Joel's prophecy with the new covenant in Jeremiah 31:31–34, Zane Hodges states that

> the new covenant promise (whether in Jeremiah 31:31–34 or in Hebrews 8:7–12) does not even mention the Holy Spirit. Much less does it promise the widespread prophetic enablement that Joel revealed.... Of all the passages in the Old Testament which speak of the Spirit's outpouring, Joel 2:28–32 is the one best suited to explain the events of Pentecost. The Pentecostal outpouring was soon to spread to Gentiles. Joel's use of "all flesh" *(kol basar)* opens the door to the Gentile application of this prophecy.[71]

Yet the usage of the phrase "all flesh" *(kol basar)* in the Old Testament not only *allows* for reference to Gentiles in Joel's prophecy but also *suggests* it. Outside of Joel, the phrase occurs thirty-two times. In twenty-three occurrences the expression refers to Gentiles alone. Seldom if ever is "all flesh" reserved or restricted to all Israel. According to Walter Kaiser, "the preponderance of usage favors the meaning of 'all mankind' . . . without distinction of race, sex, or age."[72] Moreover, Joel's reference to "bondslaves" or "servants" (2:29, cf. Acts 2:18) would in some cases, at least, involve Gentiles.

Israel's reception of the Holy Spirit is yet future. Not until Israel repents and calls Him whom they have pierced (Hos. 5:15; Zech. 13:9; Matt. 23:39) will Messiah come and deliver Israel. At this time Israel will be born again; it will be regenerated, filled with the Holy Spirit, and indwelled. In this respect, Joel's prophecy awaits future fulfillment. Whether there will be *another* outpouring of the Spirit, or whether Israel will simply receive the *already-outpoured* Spirit is perhaps another question. In any case, the effect will be the same. Israel will at that time be eligible to receive the blessings of the new covenant and will be restored to their land in messianic blessing.

We conclude that Peter intends, by his citation of Joel, to say that the events of Pentecost are to be understood as *a* fulfillment of Joel's prophecy, but not *the complete* fulfillment. As Walter Price puts it, "Pentecost *fulfills* Joel's prediction about the coming of the Spirit. It does not *exhaust* it, however."[73] I do not see this as "double fulfillment" or "multiple fulfillment." Rather, these are multiple referents of *one* fulfillment.

W. J. Beecher spoke of what he called "generic prediction."

A generic prediction is one which regards an event as occurring in a series of parts, separated by intervals, and expresses itself in language that may apply indifferently to the nearest part, or to the whole—in other words, a prediction which, in applying to the whole of a complex event, also applies to some of the parts.[74]

Walter C. Kaiser cites this passage of Beecher with approval and adds:

The fundamental idea here is that many prophecies begin with a word that ushers in not just a climactic fulfillment but a series of events, all of which participate in and lead up to that climactic or ultimate event in a protracted series that belong together as a unit because of their corporate solidarity. In this way, the whole set of events makes up one collective totality and constitutes only one idea even though the events may be spread over a large segment of history by the deliberate plan of God. The important point to observe, however, is that all of the parts belong to a single whole. They are generically related to each other by some identifiable wholeness.[75]

Dispensationalists should have no problem with this approach to Peter's use of Joel. They generally recognize that the prophecies concerning the *day of the Lord* have multiple referents. In fact, this is the usual approach to Joel's own prophecies concerning the day of the Lord. Israel's return from Babylonian captivity, however one dates the seventy years, is usually understood as *one* of the referents to prophecies that speak of Israel's return to the land. Dispensationalists do not consider this "prophecy" exhausted, however, but look for a future fulfillment when Israel will be restored to the land permanently, in belief and in messianic blessing.

Presumably, dispensationalists have been reluctant to apply this principle of prophetic interpretation to Acts 2:16 because the prophecy in Joel was given to Israel, not the church. To admit fulfillment in Acts 2:16, then, is to admit that at least one referent of the prophecy applies to the church. Does this blur the distinction between Israel and the church? I think not. We have already said that the Abrahamic covenant made provision for Gentiles. Paul D. Feinberg says:

The promise of the outpouring of the Spirit in Joel is an *amplification* of the promise given to Abraham (Gen. 12:1–3). God's promise to Abraham included promises to Abraham personally, to his descendants, and to *all* the peoples of the earth. Thus, when a part of the referent (fulfillment) of these promises turns out to be the church, we should not be surprised. Furthermore, Paul says that these promises were spoken to Abraham and his seed, namely Christ. That is, the Abrahamic promises find their *fulfillment* in Christ. Since the church is related to Christ, we should not be surprised that Paul can call its members "children of Abraham" (Gal. 3:7) and "Abraham's seed" (Gal. 3:29) and make them "heirs according to the promise" (Gal. 3:29). Having established the church's relationship to the Abrahamic promises, it would be wrong to think that this in any way invalidated the right of those who are Abraham's physical seed to these promises, or to think that both Israel and the church have the same relationship to these promises. The church has *direct* access to the promises of spiritual blessing because the spiritual blessings are said to be universal in their application, while its access to the national blessings promised to Israel is only *indirect* through the church's relationship to Israel's Messiah, our Lord Jesus Christ.[76]

The birth, nature, and even the concept of the church were not revealed in the Old Testament (Eph. 3:5; Col. 1:26). In the sovereign plan of God, however, prophecies concerning the new covenant and the outpouring of the Spirit were to apply to the church. In the outworking of Joel's prophecy there is both near and far fulfillment. Joel focuses on the far view or the end point of the process. Peter, by divine insight, recognizes the events of Pentecost as marking the inception of this process. It is doubtful, however, that Peter understood that there would be centuries between Pentecost and Israel's reception of the outpoured Holy Spirit.

In Peter's first two speeches to Israel, the kingdom is again offered to Israel. He calls on Israel to repent (in keeping with the demands of the Palestinian covenant) that their sins might be wiped away, "in order that the times of refreshing may come from the presence of the Lord" (Acts 3:19). The "times of refreshing" refer to the eschatological messianic blessings promised to Israel and which were (and are) contingent upon Israel's repentance. Peter no doubt saw the coming of the Spirit as the inauguration of the messianic age, and considered Israel's salvation to be imminent. What Peter did not anticipate was that Israel's conversion and restoration to the land in millennial blessing would be delayed many centuries by Israel's unbelief. This part of Joel's prophecy is now hindered only by Israel's unbelief.

The Significance of the Outpouring

Who could comprehend, much less encompass, the significance of the outpouring of the Holy Spirit on Pentecost in the explanation of a few pages? It is almost impossible in any amount of space to describe the significance of what God has done, yet we are given the biblical data by which to meditate on these implications.

The Result of the Death of Jesus

The outpouring of the Spirit was the necessary result of the death, resurrection, and ascension of Jesus, for the resurrection declared Him Lord (Rom. 1:4; cf. Acts 2:31–32; Phil. 2:6–11), and His ascension placed Him at "the right hand of God," where He received "from the Father the promise of the Holy Spirit" and from which He "poured forth" this gift on Pentecost (Acts 2:33).

Nevertheless, the outpouring of the Spirit is inseparably linked to the death of Jesus Christ. The death of Christ and the outpouring of the Spirit are the two sides of the coin of the new covenant. By the shedding of His blood, Jesus *ratified* the new covenant, a *blood* covenant. The outpouring of the Holy Spirit *inaugurated* the new covenant. The pouring out of the Holy Spirit is the central element of the new covenant, the inauguration of that which Christ ratified (Luke 22:20).

It is commonly agreed that the outpouring of the Holy Spirit on Pentecost was the dawning of the last days, in which God would complete His plan of salvation.[77] But there is disagreement on the nature of this new age and on how we are to understand the term, *the last days*. Views range from extreme *discontinuity* to extreme *continuity*.

We have met the dispensationalists who so stress discontinuity that they deny any fulfillment of Joel's prophecy on Pentecost and reject any idea that the new covenant promised to Israel was inaugurated then. Some covenant theologians, on the other hand, so stress continuity that Joel's prophecy is completely fulfilled in the church, which they consider to be the "new Israel." Still other Bible students find the truth somewhere in-between. The issue is not simple. Answers to seemingly trivial questions have far-reaching ramifications. Progressive dispensationalists are aggressively reexamining traditional answers to the questions and even reexamining the questions themselves. Nor is it necessarily easy to pigeonhole commentators as "classic dispensationalist" or "progressive dispensationalist." This depends both upon where the *commentator* stands and where the *viewer* stands in the spectrum of continuity versus discontinuity.

Using the following scale to represent the spectrum of continuity versus discontinuity, those at each point along the spectrum likely consider themselves at the "normative" position. Those toward the "continuity end" from them are "progressive"; those in the discontinuity direction are "classical." A person at point five might consider the person at point six to be "progressive" and someone at point eight to be "very progressive." The one at point two, however, would see those at five, six, and eight all to be "progressive" or "very progressive." To the person at point one, even a Bible student at point two seems "progressive." To a person at point eight, the person at two is "traditional," "classical," or just "not progressive enough," while nine and ten are progressive. It all depends on where one stands in the spectrum.

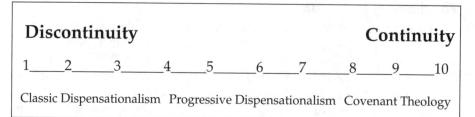

The allowance of continuity between Israel and the church at one place does not necessarily negate discontinuity in another. Continuity and discontinuity can coexist. Paul D. Feinberg concludes his excellent essay on "The Hermeneutics of Discontinuity" with these words:

> The *unity* of the two Testaments does not require the *uniformity* of the two Testaments. Unity does not preclude *diversity*. The two Testaments may be unified just as certainly through discontinuity as through continuity. Both continuity and discontinuity are a part of the unity of the biblical revelation. There is both continuity and discontinuity between Israel and the church; and, if I understand Scripture correctly, there will be both continuity and discontinuity in the future between the church and Israel.[78]

Based on this assumption, some suggestions can be made concerning the significance of the Spirit's outpouring on Pentecost.

The New Covenant Was Inaugurated

The coming of the Holy Spirit marks the inauguration of the new covenant. Though the new covenant in the Old Testament is promised to Israel, with no mention of the church, the church inherits the Abrahamic promise of universal blessings by its relationship to the Mediator of the new covenant. In Christ are amplified the blessings aspect of the Abrahamic covenant. In this sense, the church is the "seed" of Abraham. In no way does this entitle the church to the national blessings promised to the nation of Israel. Nor does this make the church the "new Israel" as in what is sometimes called "replacement theology."

The Eschaton Was Initiated

The "eschaton" or "last-days era" was initiated with the outpouring of the Spirit. This period will culminate in the millennial kingdom as the threshold of the new heaven and the new earth. The kingdom has, in some sense, been instituted. This is not to deny a future millennial kingdom in which Christ will rule on earth over the nations from David's throne and David's kingdom. Israel's messianic promises are not fulfilled in the church. At the conclusion of the tribulation period, Israel will repent, will experience the outpouring of the (or the now-outpoured) Spirit, and will be restored to the land in eschatological fulfillment of Old Testament promises. Nor is this to say that the present form of the kingdom is in any sense the millennial or messianic kingdom. It is "messianic" in that Christ, the Messiah, inaugurated it. It is not messianic in the sense of that messianic kingdom in which Christ will rule from the throne of David over David's kingdom. Christ is not ruling over David's kingdom Israel from David's throne in Jerusalem in fulfillment of the promises of the Davidic Covenant. The restoration of the "fallen tabernacle of David . . . as in the days of old" (Amos 9:11) remains to be fulfilled.

To admit *some* sort of application of the new covenant to the church and the presence now, in *some* sense, of the kingdom does not vitiate complete, literal future fulfillment in regard to Israel. Some extreme views are unnecessary, such as the exegesis that finds the Sermon on the Mount relevant only to the millennial kingdom and thus not for today. So is the view that there must be two new covenants, one for the church and one for Israel. Feinberg considers these to be "inaccurate applications" of proper foundational hermeneutic principles:

> As to the Sermon on the Mount, one need not deny the kingdom's presence in some sense in this age to safeguard a special expression of it later for national Israel. The spiritual dimension of it can be operative now for all people (which allows the Sermon on the Mount to be relevant today) without precluding a future earthly 1000–year social, political, and spiritual expression of the kingdom with special emphasis on Israel. As to the New Covenant, why can it not have one application to the church now plus a further application to national Israel in the future?[79]

While some argue over terms and other semantic matters, most dispensationalists are not that far apart in their understanding. Progressive dispensationalism, however, is showing an alarming tendency to drift from the moorings of dispensational grammatical-historical interpretation.[80] Whatever conclusions one draws, the grammatical-historical interpretation of Scripture must not be abandoned.

Peter's use of *last days* in Acts 2:17 refers to the *initiation* of end times, not their *consummation*. The writers of the New Testament speak of an "age to come" (Heb. 6:5) yet clearly indicate that present day believers have now "tasted" of the powers of that age (Heb. 6:14). This refers to the work of the Holy Spirit in the life of the New Testament or new covenant believer. The outpouring of the Holy Spirit on Pentecost is the initiation of the eschaton in that the Old Testament inseparably associates the new covenant, the gift of the Spirit, and the latter days. Though there are latter days to come and latter days that are here, Peter speaks not just of the beginning of a *new* age but also the beginning of the *latter* age.

The Church Was Born

That Jews and Gentiles could be on an equal footing in one organic body was a mystery until the time of the "apostles and prophets" (Eph. 3:5–6). The church, which is the body of Christ, could not exist until Christ had ascended. Paul clearly identifies the resurrection and ascension as necessary to Christ's headship over the church (Eph. 1:20–23; cf. 5:23). The gifts necessary for the church to operate could not be given until Christ was seated at the right hand of the Father (Eph. 4:7–12).

Nor can a case be made for an Old Testament church, either linguistically or theologically. Israel is called "the people of God," as is the church. Both are part of the kingdom of God. But they are not one and the same. In addition to arguments already made, there is other evidence that the church was born on Pentecost. First, the church was still future when Jesus said to Peter, "You are Peter, and upon this rock I will build My church" (Matt. 16:18). Second, a comparison of passages makes it clear that it is Spirit baptism that places believers into the body of Christ. In Acts 1:5, the ministry of Spirit baptism is still *future*. According to Acts 11:15–16, Spirit baptism took place on Pentecost in Acts 2. The apostle Paul tells us what Spirit baptism does. According to 1 Corinthians 12:13, Spirit baptism places *all* believers into the body of Christ. It is important to remember that Paul was addressing Christians in Corinth who were what he calls "carnal" or "men of flesh"—babes in Christ (1 Cor. 3:1). These weren't spiritual giants who had achieved a higher level of sanctification or a "second blessing." These were carnal Christians who were in need of rebuke and discipline. Yet Paul says they "were *all* baptized into one body." They were "*all* made to drink of one Spirit" (1 Cor. 12:13). Since Spirit baptism first occurred on Pentecost, we can conclude that the church began on Pentecost.

The Messiah Was Attested

According to Acts 2:33, when Jesus was exalted He received from the Father the promise of the Holy Spirit. What is meant is not that Jesus received a promise concerning the Holy Spirit, but that He received the promised Holy Spirit in fulfillment of the promise of the Father. Jesus now has lordship over the gift of the Spirit to the church. The Spirit of prophecy inherent in the new covenant has become the Spirit of Jesus (Acts 16:7). He can give to the church the Spirit (2:33), who in turn distributes His individual and varied *gifts (charismata)*. By the Holy Spirit's presence in the church, the Lord Jesus Christ directs and empowers the church. In consequence, the church worshiped Jesus as both Lord and Christ (Messiah). The now-outpoured Holy Spirit evidenced at Pentecost is the basis for Peter's claim, "Therefore let all the house of Israel know for certain that God has made Him both Lord and Christ—this Jesus whom you crucified" (Acts 2:36).

The Work of Jesus Was Continued

Luke opens the book of Acts with the announcement that his second volume is the record of the continuing acts of "all that Jesus began to do and teach" (1:1).

Paul informs us "that a partial hardening happened to Israel until the fullness of the Gentiles has come in" (Rom. 11:25). This hardening, of course, is not unrelated to Israel's unbelief (Rom. 11:20, 23). Israel habitually resisted the Spirit of God in Old Testament times (Acts 28:25–28). They resisted the Spirit during our Lord's earthly ministry (Matt. 12:31–32; Acts 2:22), and continued nationally to resist the Spirit even after Pentecost and the preaching of Peter and the other apostles (Acts 13:44–48; Rom. 11:16–25). Peter's Pentecostal address was to the "men of Israel" (2:22). Though about three thousand souls repented and believed (Acts 2:37–41), the nation as a whole continued to resist the Spirit (Acts 7:51; 28:24–28; cf. 4:1–4).

As a result, Israel has been set aside (Rom. 11:17, "broken off"). The covenant promises as they relate to Israel are in abeyance. F. B. Hole notes that Christ's death closed God's dealings with Israel as a nation. His resurrection and the descent of the Holy Spirit on Pentecost inaugurated this dispensation."[81]

Speaking of the ministry of the outpoured Holy Spirit in the world, Jesus said that the Spirit would "convict the world of sin, and righteousness, and judgment" (John 16:8). Acts shows us the global consequences of this ministry in the ethnic and geographic spread of the gospel and growth of the body of Christ. Empowered and emboldened by the Holy Spirit, the church carries the witness of the gospel first "in Jerusalem, and in all Judea and Samaria, and even to the remotest part of the earth" (Acts 1:8).

The various ministries of the Holy Spirit in the church are described in chapter 9, 164–168. It is important here to note, however, that the Gift of the Spirit was, to the church, the awareness of Christ's unseen presence.

The Life of Jesus Was Imparted

The outpouring of the Holy Spirit on Pentecost not only made present the ascended Christ, so that fellowship with Christ was again a vital reality. The very life of Christ was and is imparted to those who believe in Him. Harry Poe notes:

> When Peter preached the first gospel sermon on the Day of Pentecost, he did not offer his audience eternal life. Instead, he offered them "the promise" that God had made to Israel by the prophets of old, announcing that those who turned to Jesus would "receive the gift of the Holy Spirit" (Acts 2:38–39). Jesus Christ makes possible the genuine, positive experience with God that people everywhere long to have. By the Holy Spirit, the exalted Lord Jesus maintains immediate relationship with those who have faith in him and dispenses the benefits of salvation available

through him. The Holy Spirit takes possession of and occupies those who submit their lives to the Lord. Through the Spirit they then share his life, and he begins to change them.[82]

The Conclusion

The outpouring of the Holy Spirit on Pentecost has manifold significance. It marked the beginning of a new age, the dispensation of the Spirit. The gift of the Holy Spirit is unique to this age, is universal in this age, and is continuous in this age. The Spirit is permanent in the church, but certain ministries of the Spirit are occasional, repeatable, and increasingly appropriated. As Christ's death was the ratification of the new covenant, the Spirit's outpouring was its inauguration.

Typologically, geographically, and theologically, the promise of both the Father and the Lord Jesus concerning the new covenant gift of the Spirit was fulfilled. It came on time, in Jerusalem as prescribed, fifty days after the resurrection of "Christ the first fruits," and in proper sequence to Passover.

Further, the now-outpoured Holy Spirit facilitates the continuation of the work of Jesus Christ in respect to Israel, the world, and especially to the church that is His body (Eph. 5:30; Col. 1:24). Over the church Christ is Head (Eph. 4:15; 5:23), imparting His life to the church and nourishing it (Eph. 5:29).

Chapter 2

THE WORK OF THE HOLY SPIRIT IN ACTS

In regard to the work of the Holy Spirit, the book of Acts is given almost entirely to the Spirit's work in the church. There are a few references to the work of the Spirit in the earthly life of Jesus and a few (by implication) to the ascended and exalted position of Christ. Passages in Acts speak of the Spirit's work in the Old Testament or, more particularly, to the inspiration of the prophetic Word of Scripture. Fewer refer to the Spirit's work in the world, and most of these relate to national Israel. Thus, the bulk of our discussion here is given to the work of the Spirit in the church, both in the lives of individuals and in the community. This division is somewhat artificial, for the two overlap. We shall consider the work of the Holy Spirit first in the life of Christ, second in the inspiration of the Old Testament Scripture, third in the life of the church, and fourth, in the world.

The Spirit in the Life of Christ

The Spirit in Christ's earthly ministry is mentioned twice, in Acts 1:2 and 10:38. Three other texts relate by implication to the Spirit's work in the ascended and exalted Christ (1:5, 8; 2:33).

Anointer of the Earthly Christ

The Old Testament predicted that the Spirit of God would be upon and would anoint the Messiah (Isa. 42:1; 61:1–2). Isaiah 11:2 says the Spirit of the Lord "will rest on Him." The language which immediately follows describes the Messiah's ministry as performed by the power and wisdom of the Holy Spirit. Jewish literature of the intertestamental period entertained this hope. *The Psalms of Solomon,* for example, say that "God will make Him mighty in the Holy Spirit" (17:37), and His subjects shall share in this gift (18:8).[1] The suffering servant who brings redemption to the world does so by the enabling of God's Spirit. His theme in Isaiah 61:1–2 ("The Spirit of the Lord God is upon me, because the LORD has anointed me to bring good tidings to the afflicted") is applied by Jesus to Himself in His early pronouncement in Nazareth, when He said, "The Spirit of the Lord is upon me, because he has anointed me" (Luke 4:18).

In Acts, Luke records Peter's summary of the role of the Spirit in Jesus' ministry. Peter speaks of "how God anointed Him with the Holy Spirit and with power, and how He went about doing good, and healing all who were oppressed by the devil; for God was with Him" (Acts 10:38). The Spirit was upon Jesus at all times. His entire ministry was the result of the presence and power of the Spirit. Luke notes that even at the end of Jesus' earthly ministry, just before His ascension, Jesus gave orders to the apostles by the Holy Spirit (Acts 1:2).

Agent of the Ascended Christ

It follows that the Holy Spirit is more than a *means* or instrument by which Christ accomplishes His work. The Holy Spirit is the *acting Agent.* The Holy Spirit acts in Christ's stead and as sent by Christ. This is sometimes obscured in discussions of Spirit baptism. It is true that John the Baptist's pronouncement, recorded in all four Gospels, makes clear that the Christ will act as Agent of Spirit baptism. "He Himself [the Greek form is emphatic] will baptize you with *[en]* the Holy Spirit" (Luke 3:16; see also Matt. 3:11; Mark 1:8; John 1:33). The Greek preposition *en* is thus taken as indicating *locus* or sphere, or an instrument of means. Thus, grammatically speaking, Christ is the *Agent* of Spirit baptism, and the Holy Spirit offers the *sphere* into which, or the *means* by which, we are baptized. Indeed both aspects are true.

At the same time, it is not improper to speak of the Holy Spirit as Agent of Spirit baptism. John Walvoord writes:

> The entire ministry of the Spirit is being accomplished for the believer at the will of Christ. The Spirit is His agent and doing His work. It can be said, therefore, that we are baptized by Christ in the sense that Christ sent the Spirit. Accordingly, references to baptism of the Spirit as performed by Christ can be interpreted in this light. As the act of the sword in the hands of a disciple (Luke 22:49)

is at once the act of the sword and the act of the disciple, so the work of baptism while accomplished by the Holy Spirit is also a work of Christ.[2]

In as much as the Spirit is sent by Christ (Acts 2:33) and is the Instrument or Means[3] by which Christ accomplishes His will, it is not improper to think of the Spirit as the Agent of Spirit baptism. We simply must understand that the Holy Spirit is directed by the Lord Jesus Christ, the working Agent of Spirit baptism. As Warren Vanhetloo puts it, "Christ is the author, the Holy Spirit the accomplishing agent."[4]

Legacy of the Exalted Christ

The Holy Spirit is Christ's gift to the church in fulfillment of the promise of the Father (Luke 24:49; Acts 2:33). In association with their Spirit baptism (Acts 1:5), the disciples were to "receive power when the Holy Spirit has come upon you; and you shall be My witnesses . . . " (Acts 1:8). As the Father had endowed Christ with the Holy Spirit, enabling and empowering Him for ministry, so Christ endowed His disciples with the Holy Spirit, enabling and empowering them for ministry ("you shall be My witnesses"). As Jesus said in His high priestly prayer to His Father, "As Thou didst send Me into the world, I also have sent them into the world" (John 17:18). The Holy Spirit is Christ's living legacy to the church.

The importance of this "legacy" to the church can hardly be overstated. If Jesus Himself was dependent upon the Spirit for enabling to execute His earthly ministry—even for teaching—how much more are those He commissioned to continue His witnesses. Recognizing Jesus as the example in this respect, R. Kent Hughes says,

> His preaching came after the Holy Spirit's descent upon Him and in full Spirit-dependence. The sequence is unmistakable. The heavens were "torn open" (Mark 1:10; cf. Luke 3:21), and then, with all eyes focused on the sundered sky, the Holy Spirit circled downward, fluttering on the bodily wings of a dove, and lighted on Jesus. A palpable descent for all to see. And then the Father spoke: "You are my Son, whom I love; with you I am well pleased" (Luke 3:22). Following this, Jesus, "full of the Holy Spirit" (4:1), returned from the Jordan and was then led into the wilderness and tempted. Emerging victorious, Jesus returned to Galilee and ultimately stood in the synagogue in Nazareth and began His preaching ministry by announcing "The Spirit of the Lord is upon me" (Luke 4:18; cf. Isa. 61:1–2). Jesus preached only in the power of the Holy Spirit!

All apostolic preaching was in the power of the Holy Spirit, as Paul explained to the Corinthians: "My message and my preaching were not with wise and persuasive words, but with a demonstration of the Spirit's power" (1 Cor. 2:4–5).[5]

The Spirit in the Believer

The Spirit works in the life of the church through individual believers, and He works in the life of every believer through the corporate life of the entire church, as it constitutes the "body of Christ." Some of the Spirit's works are both individual *and* corporate. Spirit baptism, for example, happens to every believer and becomes corporate as it results in organic union with Christ and with all other believers who are in union with Christ. Therefore, categorizing the Spirit's work as either individual or communal (as follows) is somewhat artificial, but it can facilitate our thinking.

Writing as a historian, Luke offers factual descriptions rather than theological analyses. J. I. Packer correctly states that Luke's interest in the Spirit is historical and eschatological rather than subjective and charismatic:

> It focuses, that is, on the coming of the kingdom of God rather than on the supernaturalizing of individual experience. Norms for experience are no part of Luke's concern, a fact to be remembered when we study the variety of Pentecostal happenings that he records (2:1–13; 8:14–17; 10:44–48; 19:1–6).[6]

An understanding of this is imperative to a proper interpretation of the book of Acts. Luke simply does not define or develop in a systematic way the theology of the Holy Spirit or any of the Spirit's works. Spirit baptism is a case in point.

Spirit Baptism

Peter identifies the outpouring of the Spirit on the Gentiles as the same as that which occurred on Pentecost and explains it by referring to "the word of the Lord, how He used to say, 'John baptized with water, but you shall be baptized with the Holy Spirit'" (11:15–18). Peter's final appeal is to God. "If God therefore gave to them the same gift as He gave to us also after believing in the Lord Jesus Christ, who was I that I could stand in God's way?" (11:17).

Unquestionably then, Spirit baptism occurred on Pentecost, and it occurred again at Cornelius' house in Caesarea (10:44–48; 11:15–18). Luke does not say what Spirit baptism is. We are dependent upon Paul for a definition. To the church at Corinth, Paul bemoans the fact that he cannot speak to them as spiritual "but as to men of flesh, as to babes in Christ" (1 Cor. 3:1). Yet it is to these same people that he also says, "For by one Spirit we were all baptized into one body, whether Jews or Greeks, whether slaves or free, and we were all made to drink of one Spirit" (1 Cor. 12:13). This "one body" is defined in context as the body of Christ (1 Cor. 12:12, 27).

From this may be deduced that Spirit baptism also occurred when the Samaritans "were receiving the Holy Spirit" (Acts 8:17), and again in Acts 19 when the Ephesian disciples of John the Baptist embraced the gospel of Jesus Christ and received the Holy Spirit. Indeed, it may be deduced that Paul was Spirit baptized when he believed (whether on the road to Damascus or on the street called Straight). The same must be true of the Ethiopian eunuch (Acts 8:25–39) and others who were being saved (Acts 2:47; cf. 2:41; 4:4; 5:14; 17:12). Luke, of course, does not say so directly.

But when the pieces are assembled (Acts 1:5, 8; 2:4; 10:44–48; 11:15–18; 1 Cor. 12:13), it becomes clear that Spirit baptism occurs every time someone believes in Jesus Christ and is saved. Through Spirit baptism one is placed into the body of Christ, placed into organic union with Christ, and is actually identified with Christ in His death, burial, and resurrection (Rom. 6:1–11). Moreover, that person is identified with every other believer who is in Christ. He, or she, becomes a member of the body of Christ.

This is not to say that the manifestation of the Spirit at Pentecost is repeated every time a person believes. Nor is the Spirit again outpoured in the all-encompassing way it was in the beginning. The Holy Spirit was once outpoured on the day of Pentecost. The subsequent experiences recorded in Acts of the Samaritans (8:14–17), the Gentiles (10–11), and the Ephesian disciples (19) are not new outpourings of the Spirit. They are necessarily delayed conferrals of the already-outpoured Spirit. Their delay may be explained by the transitional nature of the era covered in the book of Acts and the dispensational changes of which Acts is the historical record.

As Paul describes it, the essence of Spirit baptism is identification, not empowerment, though this may simultaneously occur. Spirit baptism is also nonexperiential and nonemotional, though this work of the Spirit may be accompanied by experiential works of the Spirit. Moreover, though Spirit baptism occurs each time someone is converted, it occurs only once in a person's spiritual life. In this sense, it is nonrepeatable. Luke's record in Acts of the events subsequent to Pentecost and the delay in giving the Holy Spirit to certain groups is best understood as Luke's intent to describe, not the usual or expected pattern of Christian experience, but the unusual, unexpected, and abnormal.

For Luke, these events are remarkably unusual and extraordinary. He reports them as stupendous and assumes his readers already know something of the chasm that must be bridged between Old Testament Judaism and the New Testament church. How else could one explain the unity of Jews, Samaritans, and Gentiles on equal footing in one body? Luke wants to report how we got from there to here. The fact that these events are extremely unusual should caution us not to quickly accept them as paradigmatic.

Filling

Opinions differ concerning the doctrine of the filling of the Spirit.[7] In the New Testament, outside of the one reference in Ephesians 5:18, in which Paul exhorts his readers to be filled with the Spirit, only Luke speaks of the Spirit's ministry of filling. For Luke, the Spirit's primary activity is to fill believers[8] (see pp. 121–122).

The filling of the Spirit appears four times in Luke and ten times in Acts. In Luke, it is said of John the Baptist that he would "be filled with the Holy Spirit, while yet in his mother's womb" (Luke 1:15). The implication is that John was filled with the Spirit throughout his life and even before his birth. His mother Elizabeth and father Zecharias (1:41, 67) are also said to have been filled with the Holy Spirit.[9] In both cases, the immediate result and apparent purpose of this filling was prophetic utterance. Certainly this was the purpose of John's filling (cf. 1:15–17, 76). Finally, Jesus was said to have been full of the Holy Spirit (Luke 4:1). We have already observed that Christ's ministry was performed in the power of the Holy Spirit. Whatever else His ministry was, it was primarily prophetic.

One-half of the ten occurrences in Acts refer to repeatable fillings or empowerment, using the verb *pimplēmi* (Acts 2:4; 4:8, 31; 9:17; 13:9). The other five refer to the *state* or *condition* of being full (Acts 6:3, 5; 7:55; 11:24; 13:52). The adjective *plērēs* is used four times, and in one instance the verb *plēroō* appears. Concerning the first five mentioned, the *act* of filling (*pimplēmi*), the result and apparent purpose was prophetic utterance, whether immediate (2:4; 4:8, 31; 13:9) or prospective (9:17).

In every instance where Luke speaks of the act of the filling of the Holy Spirit, certain significant factors remain constant. First, Luke consistently uses the verb *pimplēmi* to describe the *act* of filling. When it is remembered that Luke quotes the *LXX*,[10] this becomes a signal factor. The act of the filling of the Spirit is mentioned five times in the Septuagint (Exod. 28:3; 31:3; 35:31; Deut. 34:9; Mic. 3:8). Always it is the verb *pimplēmi* that is used, rather than *plēroō*.[11] In each Old Testament case, the filling of the Holy Spirit is associated with divine enablement for the accomplishment of a divine directive.

A second constant in Luke's use of *pimplēmi* to describe the act of filling is that of the eight occurrences, all are passive. This is significant because the passive voice indicates that the filling is not done *by* human beings but *to* them. Thus it is a sovereign work of God. This filling cannot be achieved by our efforts.

A third constant in Luke's description of the act of filling is that all except one of the eight occurrences use the aorist tense of the verb. The one exception is the prediction concerning John the Baptist's filling, which is, of course, future tense. If Luke wanted to indicate that Peter (4:8) or Paul (13:9) were experiencing an ongoing state of filling, rather than a onetime original act of filling, the perfect or imperfect tenses would have been the grammatical choices. He uses instead the aorist tense, which strongly suggests a once-but-no-more past experience.

The two exceptions are the aorist participles in Acts 4:8 and 13:9. Aorist participles usually suggest *antecedent* time to that of the main verb, that is, past time in a *relative* sense.[12] This could mean that 4:8 and 13:9 are not indicating a *new* infilling but an earlier infilling that still is effective.

Some insight can be drawn from the *LXX* descriptions of infillings of the Spirit in the Old Testament. These were special, sovereign works of God to enable individuals to do a certain work. Most commonly this infilling enabled prophetic utterance. The *LXX* consistently uses *pimplēmi* to describe the *act* of filling, and favors *plērēs* or its cognate *plēroō* to describe the *state* or *condition* of being full of the Spirit. This probably explains Luke's like preferences in Luke-Acts.

Luke's use of the terms is in complete conformity to the *LXX* usage. Luke seems to distinguish between two kinds of filling. The first, distinguishable by the consistent use of *pimplēmi* to describe the act, is a special, sovereign work whereby the Spirit "fills" a believer for a specific task. Without fail in Luke and Acts, the primary result of the filling is prophetic utterance. For Luke, the duration of the filling seems to have been only long enough to complete the given task.[13] Luke gives no hint that sin terminated the filling. Nor does Luke lay down conditions for the filling or command anyone to seek it. This is precisely like the "in-fillings" of the Spirit in the Old Testament. Probably such activity was becoming infrequent. If this special filling was given for the purpose of prophetic utterance, as seems apparent, it probably ceased when prophecy ceased.

The second kind of filling of which Luke speaks might be called a "normal filling," or a "requisite filling."[14] As Gerhard Delling says, Luke "is acquainted with a normal Christian endowment with the Spirit which is to be differentiated from his intensive and concentrated work in, for example, preaching, tongues, or the apostolate."[15] Luke's "acquaintance" with this normal filling of the Spirit was on occasion no doubt firsthand. But his theological understanding of it may be attributed (in large measure) to his close association with the apostle Paul. Indeed it is Paul who (alone outside of Luke) speaks of a filling by the Spirit which is incumbent upon all believers and to which all believers should aspire (Eph. 5:18). This normal filling, which Luke identifies by the consistent use of *plērēs* or *plēroō*, indicates a state or condition of fullness in respect to the control of the Holy Spirit over a person's life. It denotes *not a method* toward spiritual maturity or Spirit control but the *condition* of spiritual maturity or Spirit control.

Thus, Luke describes Jesus (Luke 4:1); the seven in Acts (6:3), including Stephen (cf. also 6:5; 7:55); Barnabas (11:24); and the disciples (13:52) as "full" of the Spirit. That is, they are men who are notably submissive to the leadership and control of the Holy Spirit over their thinking and actions. They are men in whom the fruit of the Spirit is abundantly produced. Their lives exhibit a high degree of spiritual maturity. This is not a sovereign *event* that happens suddenly but a state or condition of maturity achieved through progressive spiritual growth.

This fullness or normal filling of the Spirit is associated by Luke with good men (Acts 11:24) or men of good reputation who are full of wisdom (Acts 6:3), faith (6:5; 11:24), grace (7:55–60), and joy (13:52). Such "normal filling" is potentially real for all believers. Paul commands all believers to be "filled by the Spirit" (Eph. 5:18). But while Luke attributes a certain measure of fullness to "the disciples" in general, he does seem to use the phrase of exceptional men in Acts 6:3. This may indicate that not all believers in any given time or place reach such a condition. Perhaps the phrase "full of the Spirit" should be reserved for mature, spiritual Christians who manifest in abundance the fruit of the Spirit (Gal. 5:22–26).

Regeneration and Indwelling

That the Holy Spirit is the source of the believer's life is supported by Luke but not expressly stated. Luke neither develops nor directly addresses the connection between regeneration and the indwelling of the Spirit. Indwelling and regeneration are probably part and parcel of passages like Acts 2:38; 5:32; and 8:16–17, where the Spirit is spoken of as a gift that all believers receive. But Luke does not expressly say that everyone who trusts in Christ will be "permanently indwelled" and "born again" or "regenerated" or, for that matter, "sealed."

Luke regards the outpouring of the Spirit on Pentecost as the (initial) fulfillment of the new covenant. Apart from its application to national Israel and her restoration to the land, the heart of the new covenant is the permanent indwelling of the Spirit and spiritual regeneration (Jer. 31:31–34; Ezek. 11:19–20; 36:25–27). Forgiveness of sin (Jer. 31:34) and cleansing (Ezek. 36:25) are, of course, part of it. But does not one require the other? Again, it is not Luke's purpose to develop the doctrine of the Holy Spirit but to reveal His involvement in the birth and the ethnic and geographic expansion of the church.

The Internal Witness

In his farewell speech to the elders of the Ephesian church, Paul stated: "The Holy Spirit solemnly testifies to me in every city, saying that bonds and afflictions await me" (Acts 20:23). That Paul understood and intended by this an inner, subjective witness of the Holy Spirit to his spirit is made certain by Paul's legacy to the church in the form of written revelation (Rom. 8:16; 1 Cor. 2:4, 10; Gal 4:6; Eph. 6:17; 1 Thess 1:5). John also spoke of this internal witness of the Spirit (John 14:26; 1 John 3:24; 5:7).

It has been said that the Spirit is, before all other things, a *witness*.[16] How the Holy Spirit persuades and illuminates is a mystery. Jesus taught as much (John 3:8). There is no uniform procedure by which the Spirit bears His witness. Nor does He avoid earthly instruments or circumstances. As Paraclete, He illumines hearts and minds to the truth (John 14:26). The illumination is persuasive; it is not a revelation nor impartation of knowledge.

The object of the internal witness is the divine revelation of the Scriptures. Scripture is the product of the Spirit—and the objective truth to which He bears inner witness.

The Spirit in the Body of Christ

While Luke speaks of the work of the Spirit in individuals, his emphasis is on the work of the Spirit in the community of believers. Luke emphasizes that the church is by nature a Spirit-indwelled community. True, every believer is indwelled, but every indwelled believer is an organic member of one body in union with Christ and each other. This constitutes the Spirit-indwelled community, the result of Spirit baptism. It places the believer in Christ and Christ in the believer. Luke does not develop the intricacies of the doctrine of the many in one. This is the particular concern of Paul (cf. Rom. 5).

The filling, empowering, gifting, guiding, even *healing* of individuals was not an end in itself, but a means to an end. That is, while the Spirit works in individuals to their individual benefit, this work is ultimately for the sake of the community and its mission as the church, the body of Christ. For example, Saul is healed of blindness and filled with the Holy Spirit (Acts 9:17–18). Certainly this is an individual work of the Holy Spirit and is of vast individual importance to Saul. But no one can read the book of Acts, let alone the rest of the New Testament, and fail to see the corporate significance of this work of the Spirit. It was of paramount importance individually and communally. Immediately following his healing and filling, Paul is baptized (9:18) and immediately begins to proclaim Jesus (9:20). The immediate results of Paul's personal experience with the Holy Spirit were identity, unity, and fellowship with other believers and ministry, both *for* and *to* the church, as a witness and apostle of Jesus Christ.

So it is in Acts, that the Spirit's work is both individual and communal. When the Spirit guides or directs certain individuals (for example, Acts 8:29; 16:9–10) it is for the good of the church, the growing community of believers. A review of the book of Acts reveals the Holy Spirit guarding and guiding the church. The Spirit brings unity and blessing on the community through His gifts and wise rule.

Guarding the Church

The Holy Spirit guarded and protected the church from problems which arose both from within the community and from without. When the moral integrity of the church was threatened by the hypocrisy of Ananias and Sapphira (Acts 5:3–11), the Spirit acted swiftly and decisively. Notes Darrell Bock, "In executing judgment in the community, the spirit jealously guarded the church's integrity. He sees what happens in the church."[17] As a result, both within and without the church, God's holiness is held in reverence (Acts 5:11).

The Spirit also guarded the *unity* of the church. We have seen on pages 18–20 how the early church was threatened with disunity and schisms when the gospel spread to the Samaritans and then to the Gentiles. The Spirit was at first withheld from the Samaritans and received only by apostolic conferral in order to prevent the possibility of a Samaritan church emerging as a Christian community independent of the mother church.[18]

The Gentiles, on the other hand, received the Spirit *apart* from apostolic conferral so as to prevent inequality. Acts makes very clear that Gentiles are to be received into the church as Gentiles. The early Jewish church was slow to comprehend this distinction (Acts 10:32–11:18; 15:1–29). The sporadic outpouring of the Spirit on these (and other) groups in Acts is due to the various and variable social, ethnic, religious, and geographic barriers that the church was not only born with but also called upon to bridge.

Bridging the barrier from Jews to Samaritans was not the first test of unity which the church faced. The potential for disunity already existed in the Judean-Jerusalem church. Luke reports that "a complaint arose on the part of the Hellenistic Jews against the native Hebrews because their widows were being overlooked in the daily serving of food" (Acts 6:1). At the direction of the apostles, seven men "full of the Spirit" are selected by the congregation to devote themselves to the administration of relief for the poor. It is interesting to note that the seven chosen have Hellenistic names; "it may be that the Hebraists graciously relinquished their leadership in this ministry to offset a division along cultural and linguistic lines."[19] Thus, the Spirit guards the unity of the church by placing over it men "full of the Spirit."

The Spirit also guarded the church against the onslaught of spiritual powers and evil spirits. People were healed of unclean spirits (5:16; 8:7; 16:18; 19:12). Both Peter (8:14–20) and Paul (13:4–12) have confrontations with magicians or sorcerers. "Filled with the Spirit" (4:8, 31; 13:9), they withstand both spiritual and earthly evil powers. The guarding and protection of the church must be balanced by the martyrdom and persecution suffered. To say that the Spirit guards and protects the church is not to say life will run smoothly. The Spirit not only permits persecution He also *uses* persecution (Acts 8:1–4). Persecution drove the church beyond the confines of Jerusalem "throughout the regions of Judea and Samaria" (8:1). As the gospel "spread" (13:49), persecution arose (13:50). As persecution arose, the gospel spread (13:51; 14:6–7). Eventually, the gospel reached Rome, and the apostle Paul carried Christ's name "before the Gentiles and kings and the sons of Israel" (Acts 9:15). This all came through suffering for Christ's name's sake (9:16).

Guiding the Church

The church received instruction and direction, indeed, revelation, not only as the Spirit spoke through the prophets of the Old Testament (Acts 1:16; 4:24–25; 28:25) but also as the Spirit spoke through the prophets of the apostolic era (Acts 11:28; 13:1; 21:4, 10–11). At times the Spirit gave personal instruction to certain individuals (Philip, 8:29; Ananias, 9:10–16 [with Ananias, it is the Lord who speaks]; Peter, 10:19; 11:12; Paul, 20:23; Agabus, 21:11). Other times the Spirit's guidance was communal in that He spoke to a group (the church at Antioch, 13:2; the Jerusalem council, 15:28; Paul and his companions, 16:6).

Summarily, it may be said that the Holy Spirit guided the church, in part, through circumstances (Acts 16:10). By closing certain doors and opening others, the Spirit guided those who were sensitive to His leading. There is no reason to believe He does not still do so today. Then, too, the Spirit used other believers to guide His people (Acts 6 and 13). Again, it may be certain that God uses other believers (through teaching, counseling, etc.) to guide Christians today. Chiefly, however, the Spirit guided the early church through the Old Testament Scriptures (Acts 1:16, 20; 2:16–21, 25–28, 34; 4:25; 28:25) and by the gift of prophecy and the development of New Testament Scriptures (Acts 8:29; 10:19; 11:12; 13:2; 21:11; 2 Tim. 3:16; 2 Peter 3:15–16). If the gift of prophecy has ceased from the church, then the Christian today must look to the Word of God, the Scripture, for guidance. God still opens and closes doors, and so guides through circumstances. But the Spirit primarily guides believers through the Scriptures.

Gladdening the Church

Comfort and gladness were a result of the Spirit's presence and grace to the church. Immediately following Pentecost and the conversion of *"about three thousand souls"* (Acts 2:41), Luke notes that "all those who had believed were together" (2:44) and "taking their meals together with gladness and sincerity of heart" (2:46). After Paul's conversion and commencement of his ministry (9:19–30), "the church throughout all Judea and Galilee and Samaria enjoyed peace, being built up; and, going on in the fear of the Lord and in the comfort of the Holy Spirit, it continued to increase" (9:31). Barnabas, "full of the Holy Spirit" rejoiced at the grace of God (11:23–24). "And the disciples were continually filled with joy and with the Holy Spirit" (13:52).

While the world seeks gladness and comfort in drink, drugs, and other dubious dangers, Luke tells us that true joy, gladness, and comfort are to be found in intimate communion with the Spirit of the Lord (8:39). It is Luke, recording Peter quoting David, who said, "Thou wilt make me full of gladness with Thy presence" (Acts 2:28).

Giving Gifts to the Church

The Spirit protects, guides, and comforts the early church by His gifts to the church. These gifts consisted of unusually able leaders and the special abilities for ministry in the *charismata* (spiritual gifts) that go to each true member. While Paul develops this more fully (Rom. 12:3–8; 1 Cor. 12–14;

Eph. 4:8–16), Luke speaks clearly of the Holy Spirit's gift of leadership to the church. He records the words of Paul to the elders of the Ephesian church, "Be on guard for yourselves and for all the flock, among which the Holy Spirit has made you overseers, to shepherd the church of God which He purchased with His own blood" (Acts 20:28).

The leadership of the church is not self-appointed but Spirit-appointed. Luke speaks of the apostolic replacement of Judas Iscariot by Matthias, who was chosen by the Lord as "the lot fell" (Acts 1:15–26). The apostles, among whom was Paul, were chosen and commissioned by the risen Christ (Acts 1:2–8, 21–26) and were invested with the authority of Christ. Through the apostles the Spirit jealously guarded the integrity of the church. Apostolic authority is displayed on Pentecost when "Peter, taking his stand with the eleven, raised his voice and declared...." (2:14) and a lame man at the temple gate is healed by Peter and John (3:4–8). In effect, Peter places himself in the line of prophets when he speaks of Israel's eschatological hopes and then says "all the prophets who have spoken, from Samuel and his successors onward, also announced these days" (3:24).

Miracles attest to their apostolic authority (4:16, 22, 30). It was the apostles' teaching to which the Christians "were continually devoting themselves" (2:42). It is by apostolic authority that the Holy Spirit is conferred upon the Samaritans (8:14–17) and the Ephesian disciples (Acts 19:6). It is the apostle Peter who is there to witness the outpouring of the Spirit on the Gentiles and who, along with the rest of the apostles (15:28), issues a letter (15:23) confirming the inclusion of Gentiles, as Gentiles (chap. 15), into the body of Christ.

Governing the Church

According to Acts 15:28, the Holy Spirit presided at the first church council. It is the Holy Spirit in 20:28 who is said to appoint the leadership of the church. If 20:22 is a reference to the Holy Spirit, then He is here governing the movement and development of Paul's ministry. On another unusual occasion the Spirit simply "snatched Philip away" (8:39).

If the Spirit truly rules the church, then to wrong the church is to wrong the Holy Spirit. The Spirit takes jealous ownership and possession of the church. It is His, and it is His habitation. We do more when we sin against the church than sin against the church.

Another implication is that the leaders of the church should be carefully Spirit guided. They must be in submission to the Spirit of God. Every Christian—and especially every Christian leader—should be sensitive to the direction and presiding government of the Holy Spirit, lest doors are closed that He opens and doors are opened that He closes.

The Gifts of the Holy Spirit

When speaking of the gifts of the Spirit, one must distinguish between the *charismata* or spiritual gifts to individual believers listed in Romans 12:6–8, 1 Corinthians 12:8–10, and 1 Peter 4:11 and the leader gifts, such as apostles , prophets, evangelists, and pastor-teachers. The latter are given to the church also for the benefit of the church and are mentioned in Ephesians 4:11 and portrayed prominently in Acts. In Ephesians 4:11, certain men are gifts to the church for the equipping of the saints for the work of service, to the building up of the body of Christ. Paul pictures the church as having been built on "the foundation of the apostles and prophets, Christ Jesus Himself being the corner stone" (Eph. 2:20). Acts vividly illustrates the office of apostles and prophets, evangelists, and teachers in the infancy stage of the church. For a discussion on the leadership gifts and how they are presented in Acts, see pp. 42–51.

Before addressing the *charismata*, we must reiterate several things about the leadership given to the early church, for the *charismata* are closely related. The book of Acts implies, and Ephesians 4:11 clearly states, that many of the gifted leaders were given to the early church as *foundational* to the building of the body of Christ. Thus, we should not expect these offices or specially gifted leaders to continue in the church. This must be admitted unless we are willing to admit apostolic succession (see p. 45). Apostles and prophets were given in the infancy stage of the church. Apostolic authority and leadership were absolutely essential for bridging the ethnic, social, religious, and geographic barriers the church faced. Prophets were essential to the navigation of uncharted territories. Once the new revelation was recorded in written form and the way of God was charted fully in the Word of God, prophets were no longer necessary. (See Append. 2, beginning on p. 393, for a discussion of the sign gifts.)

The Charismata Today

Finally, it is interesting to note that few (if any) of those who claim that the Spirit's working in the book of Acts is to be understood as the "norm" for today speak of being miraculously transported, as Philip was, from one place (or town) to another (Acts 8:39–40). We are urged to receive "the baptism of the Spirit" (the evidence of which, to most, is tongues speaking), urged and often *coached* "to speak in tongues," to perform miracles of healing, and to utter prophetically. But no one speaks of being miraculously transported from, say, Portland to Dallas.

Jack Deere, an evangelical who was teaching at Dallas Seminary when he moved to a Pentecostal theology, speaks of a time when he "didn't have a clue about bringing a revelation, a tongue, or an interpretation."[20] Nor, he says, "did I understand how the other supernatural gifts functioned—gifts like words of wisdom, words of knowledge, the gift of faith, the gift of healing or miracles, or the gift of distinguishing spirits, and so on."[21] He then states:

"I found out that the process of learning the language of the Holy Spirit is similar to the process of learning any foreign language."[22] He then goes on to describe what amounts to a "trial and error" *practice* method of learning the supernatural gifts. But the book of Acts gives no evidence that supernatural gifts were "learned" by "practice" or by trial and error.

On Pentecost, the disciples *miraculously* spoke in *unlearned* languages. What is miraculous about a gift that must be learned? If Acts is describing normal Christian experience with the Holy Spirit, then at least *occasionally* (admittedly, apostles and prophets normally traveled by normal means) we should see a "prophet" miraculously snatched away by the Holy Spirit to a signs-and-wonders conference apart from trains, planes, cars, and boats. Or is the Holy Spirit not doing that kind of thing today? And when is the last time the Holy Spirit struck dead a believer for lying? Luke is not describing "normal Christian life" but abnormal and unusual to the extreme.

The early church understood that the Holy Spirit did not manifest the same gifts, powers, and abilities in all Christians; rather, God provided these gifts—sovereignly bestowed as the Spirit willed (1 Cor. 12:11)—in given times and places to accomplish His ministry through the church (Rom. 12:1–8; 1 Cor. 12:1–31; Eph 4:1–16). The sign gifts, at least as far as Acts is concerned, are discussed below, along with reasons why they should not be considered the "norm" for today.

The Gift of Tongues

The gift of tongues was the supernatural ability to speak an unlearned language. It was not an unintelligible ecstatic utterance.[171] Nor were there two kinds of the gift of tongues: one the supernatural ability to speak an unlearned language, as is clearly the case in Acts 2, and the unintelligible ecstatic utterance alleged of 1 Corinthians 12–14. This is often the view held by charismatic believers. Faced with the weight of evidence that the tongues of Acts 2 were unlearned languages, yet seeking to justify their experience of "unintelligible ecstatic utterance," the tongues of 1 Corinthians are explained as unintelligible ecstatic utterance, a different type of tongues speaking than that of Acts 2.

The Nature of Tongues

It is outside the scope of this guide to interact with all of the pros and cons offered in this debate or to give a full-blown defense of the authors' view that tongues speaking was the supernatural ability to speak in unlearned languages. Some general observations can be made in support of the view that this supernatural ability involved spontaneously speaking, without prompting or practice, an unlearned language.

1. The ecstatic utterance view came with higher criticism, which attributed tongues speaking in Corinth to the *glossolalia* of the mystery religions, attempting thereby to remove the supernatural from the Bible. This in itself does not invalidate an "ecstatic utterance" view of tongues, but it connects tongues to a dubious source.[23]

2. The normal sense of *glōssa*, "tongue," is "language." We even use it today as such when we speak of our "mother tongue." *Glōssa* occurs thirty times in the LXX Old Testament. Each time it refers to a known language. It is improbable, therefore, that in 1 Corinthians it means anything else.

3. It is unlikely that ecstatic utterances spoken for personal edification (1 Cor. 14:4) would constitute a sign for unbelievers (1 Cor. 14:22). Moreover, Paul's statement that speaking in tongues is personally edifying is not an endorsement but a reproach. His teaching and instruction concerning gifts is that they are *not* given for personal edification but the "common good" (1 Cor. 12:7; cf. 12:12–13:13).

4. Speaking an unlearned language would best serve as a sign to unbelievers.

5. If the tongues of 1 Corinthians were different than the tongues of Acts 2, it seems Paul would have clarified this or been more explicit in his use of terms. There is no basis for assuming that he was thinking something else unless he specifically says so. He does not. Furthermore, when Luke wrote Acts (after 1 Corinthians was written) he did not redefine or distinguish between the tongues in Acts and those referred to by Paul.

6. Clearly 1 Corinthians 14:21, a citation of Isaiah 28:11ff., refers to known languages. Paul says the tongues of 1 Corinthians 14 are an application of the prediction of Gentile languages (Assyrian) and these in judgment. No distinction is made between Isaiah's reference to tongues as known languages and any other kind of tongues.

7. In Matthew 6:7, Jesus condemns the repetition of meaningless sounds as prayer. Would Paul condone what Christ did not? *Battalogēsēte*, translated "meaningless repetition" (NASB) in Matthew 6:7, is a compound from *batta*, which is not a word but a sound (unintelligible utterance), and *logeō*, "to speak." The compound word means "to babble or speak unintelligible utterances or speak without thinking."

8. *Diermēneuē*, in 1 Corinthians 14:13, *can* refer to the explaining of mysterious utterance, but its consistent biblical usage argues

against this. The word is best taken to refer to translation of a language.

9. The terms *in the world* and *foreigner* in 1 Corinthians 14:10–11 indicate references to foreign languages spoken on earth. Foreigner *(barbaros)* is one who speaks a foreign language known on earth.

10. In 1 Corinthians 14:7–10, Paul's comparison between tongues and the sounds of musical instruments like harps and flutes implies that, whatever their source, sounds must be distinct and intelligible. He is not suggesting that tongues are non-languages like musical sounds. Rather, to be effective and meaningful, tongues, as disciplined musical notation, must be distinct and intelligible.

11. The clearest reference, Acts 2:8–11, defines the phenomenon as speech in foreign languages.

12. Acts 10:44–48 refers to foreign languages because (1) Luke uses the same words to describe the phenomenon as in Acts 2:4, 11; (2) the listeners could not have understood that Cornelius and his household were magnifying God unless they understood them; (3) in Peter's subsequent report to the Jerusalem church, he said that the Gentiles had received the "like gift" (11:17) and that "the Holy Spirit fell upon them, just as upon us at the beginning" (11:15). This refers to the experience at Pentecost. This likeness of experience extends not only to the Spirit but also to the nature of tongues speaking in foreign languages.

13. In Acts 19:1–7, the same basic words are used to describe the phenomenon as the earlier two cases.

14. The phrase "kinds of tongues" (1 Cor. 12:10) indicates languages. The word "kinds" *(genē)* refers to a family, offspring, race, nation, kind, sort, and class in NT usage. It always depicts that which is related to each other.

15. Since foreign languages are definitely referred to in 1 Corinthians 14:21 *(heteroglōssois)*, then the usage of "tongues" *(ai glōssai)* in verse 22 (which immediately follows) must also refer to foreign languages. This is confirmed by the usage of the article of previous reference *(ai)* and the function of the inferential conjunction "so then" *(hōste)*.

16. Speaking in an unlearned human language constitutes a miracle, whereas unintelligible utterance can be (and is) done by Christians or non-Christians. It seems unlikely that God would institute a miracle which could be duplicated by man for which there is no objective standard by which such speaking could be evaluated. It should be remembered that

tongues was a sign gift. Its source, then, must be above question.

17. At Babel (Gen. 11:1–9), God changed the one language of the world into many languages. This was not only a "sign" of judgment; it *was* a judgment. Paul identifies tongues in Corinthians as a sign of judgment (1 Cor. 14:22), connects them with Isaiah's tongues (v. 21), which were human languages (Assyrian) and also a sign of judgment to Israel. Precedence makes it reasonable to believe that God repeated the basic nature of this miracle at Pentecost, especially because Israel was at that point under sentence of judgment.

Thus, it seems best to understand the nature of the biblical gift of tongues to be the miraculous ability to speak in an unlearned language. The tongues of Acts are clearly seen to be languages. Cumulative evidence indicates that the tongues in Corinth were also languages, though in the Corinthian church there may have been some who were reverting to the heathen form of *glossalalia* to which they had been accustomed before conversion. That tongues were human languages is further attested to by a consideration of the purpose of tongues.

The Purpose of Tongues

The purpose of sign gifts, of which tongues is one, is addressed on pp. 64–65. As has been argued, tongues were *not* for personal edification, though they may have been personally edifying. Neither were they for evangelism, edifying the church (though this may have been a secondary result), or evidence of Spirit baptism. *Every* believer is Spirit baptized (1 Cor. 12:13); *not* every believer speaks in tongues nor, according to Paul, should all Christians expect to (1 Cor. 12:30).

The Cessation of Tongues

There is evidence that tongues ceased between 56 and 70. First, there is a deafening argument from silence in the historical record of the church, biblical and extrabiblical, which indicates that tongues did not become a lasting institution. Prophecy passed (Eph. 2:20), healings passed (Acts 5:16; Phil. 2:25–28; 1 Tim 5:23; 2 Tim 4:20), sudden judgments ceased (compare Acts 5:1–11 with 12:20–25; 1 Cor. 5:1–5; 1 Tim 1:19–20; 2 Tim 4:14–15). Other kinds of miraculous interventions on behalf of Christian leaders ceased (compare Acts 5:19–20; 12:6–10; 16:25ff.; 28:16–31; Phil. 1:12–26; 2 Tim. 4:9–21; 2 Peter 1:12–15).

If tongues and prophecy are part of the norm for Christian believers today, why not miraculous prison escapes, sudden lethal judgments (Acts 5:1–11), and miraculous transport (Acts 8:39)? Why not the certain healings of Acts? Why are today's "prophets" sometimes wrong and have to learn by a sort of "trial-and-error" method?[24] Though there is infrequent mention of *glossolalia* in the church fathers, all of these appear to be unintelligible ecstatic utterances. There is simply no evidence of the biblical gift of tongues.

Second, even at the start, sign gifts were integrally related to the apostles and were used for apostolic accreditation. B. B. Warfield states that the sign gifts "were distinctively the authentication of the Apostles. They were part of the credentials of the Apostles as the authoritative agents of God in founding the church. Their function thus confined them to distinctively the Apostolic church, and they necessarily passed away with it."[25]

Third, as tongues was a judicial sign against the unbelieving nation Israel and an attestation to the apostolic message in the founding of the church, it was uniquely useful to the infant church. When the infancy period ended at about the time of the judgment of Israel in 70, there was no further need to authenticate the church *via* the apostles or to judge Israel.

Fourth, the biblical pattern of signs and wonders demands their cessation. Only at three points in biblical history has there been an outburst of signs and wonders (four if we consider the eschatological outburst during the tribulation of Revelation 11). These are always connected with God's covenant relationship with Israel. The signs and wonders accompanied God's messengers who brought God's message to the nation with a view to bringing the nation into the obedience of belief. When the nation rejected this revelation, signs and wonders ceased.

Concerning the miracles performed in the era of Christ and the apostles, Custance writes, "So long as such signs and wonders were being performed, God was actively demonstrating the reality of His covenant relationship with Israel. Once, however, that active covenant relationship began to be undermined because of their rejection of Him as the Lord's Messiah, then signs and wonders became less and less frequent."[26]

Fifth, tongues were an inferior method of communication (1 Cor. 14:1–12) and an inferior method of "approaching" God (Matt. 6:7; 1 Cor. 14:20); an inferior method of prayer, worship, and praise (1 Cor. 14:14–19); and an inferior method of evangelism (1 Cor. 14:20–25). If tongues were inferior in the infancy stage of the church with its apostles, prophets, and evangelists with such supernatural abilities as Philip, it is unlikely that tongues would continue.

Sixth, the writer of Hebrews already speaks of the sign gifts in the "past tense" (2:3). The phrase "was confirmed" indicates a completed event or activity (in context this would indicate a *past* event) emphasizing that this is an unrecurring event. The word *testified* is a present participle which describes action contemporaneous with that of the main verb ("was confirmed"). This means that not only the confirmation is past tense but also the corroborative witness God provided in the form of signs and wonders. The gift of tongues was one of these signs. As Hebrews was apparently written before the destruction of Jerusalem in 70, it appears that tongues had ceased by this time. Actually, the last known references to tongues speaking was in the Epistle of 1 Corinthians, written about 56.

Seventh, tongues ceased with the founding of the church and the closing of the canon. From a logical standpoint, the closing of the canon rendered tongues obsolete.

For more on the cessation of the charismatic gifts, see pp. 168–175. The argument for the cessation of tongues does not stand on the interpretation of 1 Corinthians 13:8–13 or any other single text. Nevertheless, this passage indicates there will come a time when tongues will cease. It is said that when "the perfect" comes, tongues, knowledge, and prophecy will pass away. The interpretive question revolves around the meaning of "the perfect." Various interpretations boil down to two basic views: Either "perfect" refers to the second coming of Christ or the coming of the eternal state, which is virtually the same thing, or "perfect" refers to the reaching of maturity, whether absolute or relative, by the church. This would mean passing from the foundation stage to the superstructure stage, or from infancy to maturity, to completion of special revelation and the closing of the canon of Scripture.

However one interprets "the perfect," Paul sees the gifts of tongues, prophecy, and knowledge as temporary. And the evidence that the gift of tongues has indeed ceased is compelling. The closing of the canon and the cessation of prophecy simply adds another reason. As J. Lanier Burns says, "If the sign gifts were for authentication of new revelation for Jewish unbelievers, then there is no possibility for their existence today unless the Canon is open for new revelation for the same audience."[27]

The Spirit in the World and Israel

Luke does not teach that Israel is permanently rejected or replaced by the church. He nowhere suggests that the church is the "new Israel." Rather, he is concerned with explaining that portion of the Abrahamic covenant which made provision for blessing to "all the families of the earth" (Gen. 12:3), that is, the Gentiles (see Stephen's speech in Acts 7). With the death of Christ, the new covenant, promised to the covenant people Israel, was ratified. At the pouring out of the Spirit on Pentecost, the new covenant was inaugurated. When Israel should have been enjoying the fruits of this harvest (Pentecost), they were unrepentant and therefore ineligible to receive the blessing (Deut. 30:1–10; 2 Chron. 7:14). Luke's purpose is to explain why, then, the gospel has gone to the Gentiles and how in the doing of it a church unrevealed in the Old Testament was born. Jews and Gentiles on equal footing constitute this new body of Christ. This church will continue, Paul tells us, until the fullness of the Gentiles has come in (Rom. 11:25). After this is accomplished, "all Israel will be saved" (Rom. 11:26).

The Holy Spirit is therefore at work in blinding Israel (2 Cor 3–4), for the Spirit administers life or death depending upon our response to the ministry of the Word. The Spirit is convicting the world of sin and making the way for righteous judgment (John 16:8). But God is also giving the Holy Spirit "to those who obey Him" (Acts 5:32), and the Gentiles upon hearing the gospel "began rejoicing and glorifying the Word of the Lord; and as many as had been appointed to eternal life believed" (Acts 13:48).

Conclusion

The Holy Spirit is the lead Actor in the book of Acts. His prominence must be understood in light of the Old Testament eschatological promise that God would one day pour out His Spirit on all humankind. The promise was to Israel, but it was not limited to Israel in its application. The Abrahamic covenant and subsequent covenant framework made with Israel also made provision for the redemption and blessing of Gentiles. The outpouring of the Spirit on Pentecost was the fulfillment of the promise of God, as connected to the new covenant.

On Pentecost, Christ sent forth the Holy Spirit. On that day, the Spirit was given to all believers in Christ and from that day forward made available to all who believe in Christ. On that day, the church was born. On that day, Spirit baptism occurred, which is the work whereby the Holy Spirit places every believer into union with Christ and with each other. At the moment of saving faith, every Christian believer is placed into the body of Christ, His church, and is therefore fully identified with Christ in His death, burial, and resurrection. This is Spirit baptism. The sporadic nature of Spirit baptism in Acts is not intended by Luke to be programmatic or paradigmatic for Christian experience. Rather, it was unusual but necessary because of the socioreligious and ethnic barriers the early church faced. Gifted and guided by the apostles, whose authority was attested to by signs and wonders, the church successfully crossed these barriers.

Part 3

A VERSE-BY-VERSE BACKGROUND GUIDE TO THE BOOK OF ACTS

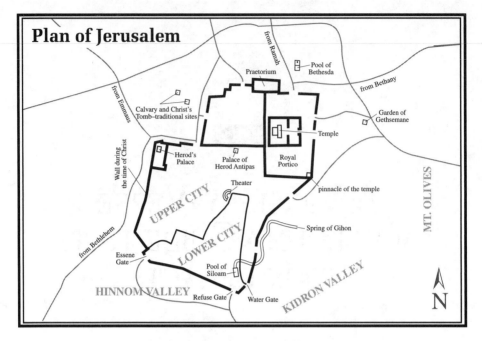

Plan of Jerusalem

- from Ramah
- Praetorium
- Pool of Bethesda
- from Bethany
- from Emmaus
- Calvary and Christ's Tomb–traditional sites
- Garden of Gethsemane
- Temple
- Wall during the time of Christ
- Herod's Palace
- Palace of Herod Antipas
- Royal Portico
- pinnacle of the temple
- MT OLIVES
- Theater
- UPPER CITY
- LOWER CITY
- Spring of Gihon
- from Bethlehem
- Essene Gate
- Pool of Siloam
- HINNOM VALLEY
- Refuse Gate
- Water Gate
- KIDRON VALLEY
- N

Chapter 1

A.D. 30 (Pentecost)

THE WAIT FOR THE COMING OF THE HOLY SPIRIT

Synopsis

(1–5) Luke addresses his history to Theophilus (1). He describes the period of Christ's teaching following His resurrection (2) and tells how Jesus presented Himself alive to His apostles, giving "convincing proof" for forty days (3). The Lord told His disciples to wait for the coming of the promised Holy Spirit by whom they would be "baptized," though not with water (4–5).

(6–11) On the Mount of Olives, the disciples asked about the restoration of the promised kingdom (6), but Jesus said it was not for them to know the Father's kingdom plans (7). Rather, they were to wait for the giving of the Spirit by whom they would be empowered to witness even "to the remotest part of the earth" (8). The Lord then ascended into heaven (10–11).

(12–26) The disciples return to Jerusalem and gather for prayer with more than 100 other followers of the Lord (12–15). It is determined necessary to replace Judas as one of the twelve so that the witness to the resurrection might be complete (16–22). Matthias is chosen by lot (23–25) and is added to the eleven apostles (26).

1:1 The first account I composed, Theophilus, about all that
Jesus began to do and teach,

Theophilus. See page 15.

Jesus. The Greek version of the Hebrew name *Ieshua*, or *Joshua* ("Jehovah
saves"). Related linguistically is the name Isaiah, in Hebrew *Yeshaiah* ("the
salvation of Jehovah"). The Hebrew noun *yashay* is translated "deliverance,
aid, salvation." Psalm 18:46 reads, "the God of my salvation." By New
Testament times, *Jesus* or *Ieesous* was a common name. With the addition of
the title *Christ* ("Anointed One"), it gives to the name of Jesus of Nazareth a
definite messianic connotation. He is identified as the Deliverer anticipated
by the ancient prophets. See also p. 72.

1:2b He had by the Holy Spirit given orders to the apostles
whom He had chosen.

Holy Spirit. In Acts, the Holy Spirit is regarded as active in the inspiration
of the Old Testament Scriptures and directly or indirectly orchestrates the
movements and ministries of the apostles. The Lord is said to have given
orders to the apostles through the Holy Spirit following his ascension. The
Spirit led them by voice or vision or providential direction of their minds.
The Spirit is clearly seen in Acts as a personality who acts, decides, and
motivates. The Spirit speaks (1:16), can be resisted (7:51), encourages (9:31),
and compels (20:22).

Concerning inspiration of the Old Testament, Luke writes that the Spirit
of God spoke "through the mouth of our father David" (4:25). His message
was the great psalm of the coming Christ, Psalm 2. In Acts 28:25–27, Paul
makes it clear to the resisting Jews of Rome that the Spirit also inspired the
prophet Isaiah and "rightly spoke" against his own Jewish generation the
great Judgment passage of Isaiah 6:9–10. Peter pointed out in Acts 1:16 that
the Spirit inspired David the prophet when he predicted the betrayal of Christ
by Judas: "Even my close friend, in whom I trusted, who ate my bread, has
lifted up his heel against me" (Ps. 41:9).

The Spirit could be lied to, as in the case of Ananias, who was filled
(controlled) by Satan to hold back part of a promised gift (Acts 5:3). Peter
and other apostles reminded the Jews that the Spirit gave witness to the work
of Jesus (5:32). Stephen tells his Jewish critics that their fathers had always
resisted the Holy Spirit and so were they (7:51).

To lead the church, the Spirit of God encouraged (9:31), directed ministry
(13:4; 16:6), approved the acceptance of Gentile believers (15:28), and warned
(20:23; 21:11). See chaps. 8, 9.

Apostles. See p. 42.

> **1:3** To these he also presented Himself alive, after His
> suffering, by many convincing proofs, appearing to them
> over a period of forty days, and speaking of the things
> concerning the kingdom of God.

He also presented Himself alive. See under 2:24, 25, 31; see also p. 73.

Kingdom of God. See under 1:6; see pp. 22, 52.

> **1:4** And gathering them together, He commanded them not
> to leave Jerusalem, but to wait for what the Father had
> promised, . . .

Jerusalem. See under 1:8.

To wait for [the Holy Spirit]. See pp. 34, 125.

Father had promised. Through Jesus, the disciples heard of the Father's promise of the Holy Spirit in the upper room discourse (John 13–17). There Christ said, "When the Helper comes, whom I will send to you from the Father, that is the Spirit of truth, who proceeds from the Father, He will bear witness of Me" (15:26). At Pentecost, Peter reminds the Jews of that promise, explaining that after Christ's ascension to the right hand of God, the Father poured forth the spirit "which you both see and hear" (2:33).

> **1:5** "for John baptized with water, but you shall be baptized
> with the Holy Spirit not many days from now."

Baptized with the Holy Spirit. See next entry; see also p. 160.

John the Baptist. John the Baptist is mentioned eight times in the book of Acts (1:5; 1:22; 10:37; 11:16; 13:24–25; 19:3–4), each time in the context of his baptism of water and repentance. John's baptism is contrasted in Acts with the baptism of the Holy Spirit.

Joel 2:28–29 relates: "And it will come about after this, that I will pour out My Spirit upon all mankind; and your sons and daughters will prophecy and your old men will dream dreams, your young men will see visions. And even on the male and female servants I will pour out My Spirit in those days." Jesus expounded on this outpouring in John 14–16. Its fulfillment began at Pentecost (Acts 1:5; chap. 2).

The reference to "the baptism of John" in Acts 1:22, regarding the replacement of Judas, is unique for Acts, as it refers not to John's baptism in general but to John's baptism of Jesus. As A. T. Robertson clearly states, "The ministry of Jesus began with the baptism of John and lasted until the Ascension."[1] F. F. Bruce links this reference also to the general work of John in noting that an acceptable successor to Judas must have been associated with the Lord "from the time of John the Baptist's activity to the day of the Lord's ascension."[2]

In 10:37, Peter sets John's baptism in its salvation context as he presents the good news to the Gentiles at Caesarea and again in 11:16, as he reports to the church at Jerusalem how God had given His Holy Spirit to the Gentiles.

In 13:24, Paul calls it "a baptism of repentance to all the people of Israel." In 19:3–4, in which Paul announces to the Ephesians the reality of the Holy Spirit, the Ephesians, having been baptized only in John's baptism, had not received the Holy Spirit.

To understand the theology of Acts, it is imperative to distinguish between these two baptisms. John's baptism, as Paul points out in Acts 19, was a baptism of repentance and of association. As Charles Ryrie explains:

> Theologically, baptism may be defined as an act of association or identification with someone, some group, some message, or some event. Baptism into the Greek mystery religions associated the initiates with that religion. Jewish proselyte baptism associated the proselyte with Judaism. John the Baptist's baptism associated His followers with His message of righteousness (he had no group for them to join). . . . Observe how impoverished we would be without a proper understanding of the meaning and ramifications of baptism.[3]

John's baptism of repentance depended on the righteousness of the coming Messiah John proclaimed. In this regard, it was a national ordinance. All of Israel should have welcomed her Messiah, but the nation rejected both John's baptism and the Messiah. Only those who had accepted the Messiah could later be initiated into the body of Christ by the baptism of the Holy Spirit. After the transitional events of the early church, this baptism occurred at the moment of belief. John Walvoord explains that the baptism of the Holy Spirit "is the one work of the Holy Spirit which is found only in this present dispensation, . . . [and] is therefore of great significance."[4] Walvoord adds that "the Scriptures make it very plain that every Christian is baptized by the Holy Spirit at the moment of salvation. Salvation and baptism by the Holy Spirit are therefore coextensive, and it is impossible to be saved without the work of the Holy Spirit."[5]

John's baptism was a baptism of water. As commanded by our Lord, believers today are also baptized by water, but clearly this is distinct from the baptism of John: John's baptism looked forward; ours looks backward on redemption accomplished and applied by the Holy Spirit. John's baptism was a baptism of repentance for the Jews as they prepared to receive their King. The baptism depicted in Acts symbolizes the joining of believers into the spiritual body of Christ. Paul will explain this further in 1 Corinthians 12.

> **1:6b** "Lord, is it at this time You are restoring the kingdom
> to Israel?"

Restoring the kingdom to Israel. The Greek *kathistanō* and means "to establish," or "set up." With the preposition *apo* on the front of the word, it has the idea of "completeness," "restitution."[6] In the present tense, the word is generally used in reference to matters of prophecy, with the idea of fixed determination. The disciples were expecting the promised kingdom fulfillments, with the Messiah reigning as clearly prophesied in the Old Testament. Jesus does not conflict with their anticipation but lets them know that a postponement is going to take place. See p. 86.

> **1:7** He said to them, "It is not for you to know times or
> epochs which the Father has fixed by His own authority;"

The Father has fixed by his own authority. More precisely the Greek translates: "has appointed by His own power." God has the epochs in His foreknowledge, and, while He announces the events, He conceals the times.[7] Concerning the coming millennial King and kingdom, Jesus refers to His Olivet Discourse, where He prophesied, "But of that day and hour no one knows, not even the angels of heaven, nor the Son, but the Father alone" (Matt. 24:36). Though this verse has puzzled many, it seems Christ is saying that the authority for bringing in the kingdom lies completely with the Father's will. "Know" in this sense means to have exclusive authority. The passage is not teaching that the Son of God does not have awareness of when the millennium begins. As the second person of the Trinity, He has full cognizance as God the Father and His plans and purposes. But rarely the Greek *oida* ("know") means "respect," "take an interest in," or "honor."[8] Jesus may be saying in Matthew that the one who has responsibility for that aspect of the kingdom is God the Father. It is not the affair of the Son until it is time for Him to come to earth to bring in the kingdom.

> **1:8b** "and you shall be My witnesses both in Jerusalem, and
> in all Judea and Samaria, and even to the remotest part of
> the earth."

Witnesses. *Witness* (verb, *martyreō*; noun, *martys*) and related words draw on legal imagery. The verb form can mean "testify, bear witness, prove, declare, or confirm."[9] In the New Testament the word can carry the idea of being a "martyr" and giving up life for faith. The word is used about 200 times in the New Testament, twenty-one times in Acts.

Jesus told the apostles that they would bear witness from Jerusalem, ultimately "to the remotest part of the earth" (1:8). Specifically, their message would be that "God raised up again" Jesus, "to which we are all witnesses" (2:32), the "One who is the Prince of life" (3:15). Further, the apostles witnessed to the resurrection "with great power" (4:33), and an abundance of grace was "upon them all." Peter tells Cornelius that he and the other apostles were witnesses to more than just the resurrection. They saw "all the things He did both in the land of the Jews and in Jerusalem" including His death on the cross (10:39). The apostles' testimony confirmed that God had brought something new to the Jewish people—and to the Gentiles.

Peter adds that all the prophets first witnessed God's plan for forgiveness of sins (10:43). As more Gentiles came to the Lord, Barnabas was sent to Antioch to investigate and bring his witness back to the Jerusalem church (11:23).

In Acts, witnessing is always to people (13:31) about God's word of grace in Christ (14:3). Paul was told he would be a witness "to all men of what you have seen and heard" (22:15). Though other apostles, and especially Peter, have a witnessing ministry in Acts, the last of the book is dominated by the testimony of Paul. Clearly, Paul was to be the most important witness to the gospel as it spread beyond Israel to Greece and Rome.

Jerusalem. At the time of Acts, Jerusalem was at least in its third millennia of occupation. The city had been under the rule of Canaanites, Egypt, Israel, Babylon, Persia, Greece, Syria, and Rome. The first written reference to Jerusalem is in a text dating back to 2500 B.C. There is some evidence of prehistoric settlement. Jerusalem is never mentioned under that name in the first five books of the Bible. However, Salem, which was ruled by King Melchizedek (Gen. 14:18), may well be the same place.

Although Joshua and his army defeated the Jebusites who inhabited Jerusalem and their allies (Josh. 15:63), the city remained under Jebusite rule until David captured it shortly before 1000 B.C. (2 Sam. 5). Under the Jebusites it was already known as "Zion," a word whose meaning is obscure but has remained synonymous with God's identification with Jerusalem. It also acquired the title "City of David."

God's approval of David bringing the ark of the covenant to Zion meant that He had chosen Jerusalem for His habitation (Ps. 132:13). David's son Solomon built the first temple on Mount Zion, the highest point surrounding Jerusalem. The ark of the covenant rested in the inner sanctuary, the "holy of holies" (1 Kings 5–8). Once the temple was complete, the city became a religious center where people gathered to celebrate festivals and holy days. It soon acquired symbolic significance as a holy city. The Psalms are full of references to the city and its place in the kingdom of God, with such exhortations as "Pray for the peace of Jerusalem" (Ps. 122:6) and "If I forget thee, O Jerusalem, let my right hand forget her cunning" (Ps. 137:5).

Around 930 B.C. the kingdom was divided and, as capital of the smaller southern kingdom, Jerusalem declined in importance. The city frequently came under attack, by the Egyptians in 922, the Philistines in 850, the northern kingdom in 786, and the Assyrians in 701. More than once the palaces and temple were sacked. In 586, Jerusalem was besieged and captured by the Babylonians under the king Nebuchadnezzar; the entire city and the temple were destroyed, and the people were taken into captivity in Babylon (2 Kings 25).

In 538, Cyrus II of Persia overcame Babylon and allowed the exiles to return to Jerusalem. The temple was rebuilt and later, under Nehemiah, the city walls were restored. Two centuries later, the city came under the rule of Alexander the Great and subsequently, Ptolemy. In 198 B.C. it fell to the Syrians. Again the temple was desecrated, but after a Jewish revolt under Judas Maccabeus, it was rededicated in 165.

Jerusalem remained under Jewish rule until it was taken by the Roman general Pompeii in 63 B.C. However, Roman influence was countered by the power of the Herodian dynasty; Herod the Great repaired the ravages of the various plundering armies and began rebuilding the temple on a grand scale, among many ambitious building projects. Under Herod, Jerusalem became great again, but his successors were less competent, and Jerusalem became part of a minor Roman province under the rule of a procurator. So it was when the city was the scene of Jesus' trial, crucifixion, and resurrection.

At the time of Acts, Rome is the center of power economically, and Jerusalem is the center of the religious world. It is also the first center for the church (Acts 1–7) until persecution scatters Christians into other regions (Acts 8:1). Paul keeps returning to Jerusalem to report to the elders. The city symbolizes God's glory for Christians as well as Jews, and in the last book of the Bible, John describes his vision of Heaven as "the holy city, new Jerusalem" (Rev. 21:2).

In A.D. 66, the Jews rebelled against their Roman rulers, and four years later Roman forces under Titus besieged and destroyed Jerusalem. There was never to be another temple, but the Emperor Hadrian built Aelia Capitolina on the city site in 130. Aelia Capitolina, laid out on a typical Roman grid plan but smaller than before 70, became the basis for the modern city center.

Jerusalem from its very beginning has been in the center of God's plan and remains in the center of world attention. Soon, Jesus Christ will return, and the Bible says,

> Behold a day is coming for the Lord when the spoil taken from you will be divided among you. For I will gather all the nations against Jerusalem to battle, and the city will be captured, the houses

plundered, the women ravished, and half of the city exiled, but the rest of the people will not be cut off from the city. Then the Lord will go forth and fight against those nations, as when He fights on a day of battle. And in that day His feet will stand on the Mount of Olives, which is in front of Jerusalem on the east, and the Mount of Olives will be split in its middle from east to west by a very large valley, so that half of the mountain will move toward the north and the other half toward the south. . . . And it will come about in that day that living waters will flow out of Jerusalem, half of them toward the eastern sea and the other half toward the western sea; it will be summer as well as in the winter. And the Lord will be king over all the earth; in that day the Lord will be the only one, and His name the only one. (Zech. 14:1–4, 8–9)

Judea. When Canaan was portioned out in about 1400 B.C. (Josh. 14:6–15:63), the tribe of Judah was given the central core of the nation—geographically the high ground. Judah/Judea became the most southern of the three large regions of Israel, with Galilee and Samaria. The most important element in Judea, of course, was the capital city of Jerusalem, which is about 2400 feet above sea level. When the Romans occupied Palestine, they sensed the strategic importance of Judea by covering the territory with roads.

At the time of the New Testament, Judah is comprised largely of descendants of the southern kingdom families who returned from the Babylonian captivity to reoccupy the old kingdom. Judeans had come to be called "Jews," until the word encompassed all the children of Abraham.

In the book of Acts, the gospel begins in Jerusalem, Judea. Jesus commissions his disciples to be His witnesses "both in Jerusalem, and in all Judea and Samaria, and even to the remotest part of the earth" (Acts 1:8). Since Judea is the heart of both the land and the majority of the population, Jesus emphasizes "all Judea."

The regional name Judea and its inhabitants play an important role in Acts. Peter addresses the citizens of Judea and Jerusalem in his Pentecost sermon: "Men of Judea, and all you who live in Jerusalem, let this be known to you, and give heed to my words" (2:14). Persecution first scatters believers throughout Judea and Samaria (8:1). After chief persecutor Saul's conversion, Luke notes that peace came to Judea, Galilee, and Samaria (9:31). As the gospel moves outward, "the apostles and the brethren who were throughout Judea heard that the Gentiles also had received the word of God" (11:1).

Much of the early church is comprised of Judeans, including the prophet Agabus (21:10) and the legalists who spread the heresy that Christians must be circumcised (15:1).

Though Paul knows it is dangerous, he desires to return to minister in Jerusalem (2 Cor. 1:16). Though the churches of Judea cannot recognize him by sight, Paul said, they are glad that "he who once persecuted us is now preaching the faith which he once tried to destroy." The Judeans "were glorifying God because of me" (Gal. 1:23–24).

Samaria. The geographical progression of the gospel in Acts 1:8 is from Jerusalem to Judea and then to Samaria and the rest of the earth. The most unlikely of these locations in the native Jewish mind is Samaria.

First Kings 16:24 tells us how Omri purchased from Shemer a hill called Samaria, on which he built the capitol of the Northern Kingdom of Israel. As the capitol city, Samaria also became the term used to identify the entire territory of the ten tribes of the Northern Kingdom, all the tribes over which Jeroboam made himself king.[10] Since the Northern Kingdom did not want its citizens traveling to the temple in Jerusalem, capital of the Southern Kingdom, they established Samaria as a competing religious as well as political center. All sorts of idolatrous worship evolved there.

In 722 B.C., the Northern Kingdom was defeated and exiled by the Assyrians. Foreigners from Babylon and other subjugated lands were settled in the cities of Samaria (2 Kings 17:24). Gradually, Jews began to return to these northern cities, intermarrying with the foreigners. The resulting Samaritans were half Jew, half foreigner, and they worshiped God with a syncretistic form of Judaism. They were looked upon with disdain by the "purer" Jews of the south. Martin Gilbert catches the irony that "the New Testament story of the 'Good Samaritan' clearly illustrates the contempt in which the Jews held even the Samaritans, despite the fact that these people were closest to them in religion and custom."[11]

While this hatred of the Samaritans was seemingly undeserved, the Jewish historian Josephus explains that the Samaritans did not aid their cause, for

> when they see Jews in prosperity, they pretend that they are changed, and allied to them, and call them kinsmen, as though they were derived from Joseph, and had by that means an original alliance with them: but when they see them falling into a low condition, they say they are in no way related to them, and that the Jews have no right to expect any kindness from them, but they declare that they are sojourners that come from other countries.[12]

Under these conditions it took the prodding of persecution to get early Christians from Jerusalem to Samaria (Acts 8:1). Perhaps if the church had been quicker to obey the Lord's command in 1:8, the persecutions might not have been so severe. Once the church stepped into Samaria with the gospel (8:25), she "enjoyed peace, being built up" (9:31). In Acts 15:3, Paul and Barnabas pass through Phoenicia and Samaria, "describing in detail the conversion of the Gentiles, and were bringing great joy to all the brethren."

1:10b behold, two men in white clothing stood beside them;

Two "men" (angels). Hebrews tell us that angels are "ministering spirits, sent to render service for the sake of those who will inherit salvation" (Heb. 1:14). Angels ministered to the Son of God also, while He was on earth. They predicted His birth (Matt. 1:20; Luke 1:26–38) and ministered to Him after his temptation (Matt. 4:11) and in the garden (Luke 22:43). They heralded his resurrection (Matt. 28:2–8; John 20:12).

Not surprisingly, they attend His ascension as well. Their message to the disciples is that His return at the second coming will be in the same way as they have seen him go. This could only mean that Christ's return will be visible and bodily. The angels probably meant that he would return to the same spot (Zech. 14:4). The presence of the angels and their message emphasize that Christ is entering heaven only for the next stage of salvation history. This message comes on the heels of Christ's commission to carry out the missionary enterprise. The church's missionary zeal is thus encouraged by the fact that Christ reigns in heaven, and His return is imminent.

Angels are also seen in the book of Acts carrying out their ministering duties toward believers. They rescue (5:17–20; 12:7–11), encourage, and strengthen (27:23–25). They performed similar services in Old Testament times (for example, Dan. 6:22). Angels in Acts also carry out God's divine judgment, striking down Herod for accepting worship as a god (12:22–23). This also is seen in other portions of Scripture (for example, Genesis 18; 2 Sam. 24:16; 2 Kings 19:35).

Stephen's sermon refers at least three times to the Old Testament angel of the Lord, usually regarded as the preincarnate Christ (Acts 7:30, 35, 38). In 7:30, 31, Stephen ascribes to the angel at the burning bush "the voice of the Lord" (cf. 7:35, 37–38) and applies the Old Testament "angel of the Lord" to the New Testament Christ.

In the Old Testament, there is no indication that angels were involved in the ordaining of the Mosaic Law, but Stephen reveals that there were (7:53). Paul confirms this as he infers the inferiority of the Mosaic Covenant to the Abrahamic Covenant (Gal. 3:19–20).

One of the clearest ways that the angelic host figures in the theology of Acts is by *directing* the strategic missionary efforts of the early missionary force. It was an angel that directed Philip to share the gospel with the Ethiopian eunuch (8:26), who would take it south into Africa. An angel directed Peter to share the gospel with the Gentile Cornelius (10:3, 7), and directed Cornelius to send for Peter (10:22; 11:13).

1:11 "Men of Galilee, . . . This Jesus, who has been taken up from you into heaven, . . ."

Men of Galilee. See under 2:7.

This Jesus, who has been taken up. The doctrine of the ascension is one of the most important truths of Acts. The ascension of Christ to the right hand of the Father is predicted in Psalm 110:1: "Jehovah says to my *Adonai*: 'Sit at My right [hand] until I make Your enemies a footstool for Your feet' (literal translation). In this passage, the Messiah is called *Adonai*, the Master who is seen even as the Master or Lord over king David. Before His arrest and trials, Jesus reminded His disciples, "I go [to My Father] and prepare a place for you" (John 14:3), and "I go to the Father" (v. 12). As Christ is lifted "out of their sight" (Acts 1:9), the angels reminded the disciples that He "will come in just the same way you have watched Him go into heaven" (v. 11).

Referring to the resurrection and ascension, Peter in Acts 2:34 reminds the Jews that the Psalm 110 prophecy was not speaking of David, "for it was not David who ascended into heaven," but Jesus! Because of the ascension, Christ was declared Lord (v. 36). Stephen was given a view of the exalted Christ, "the Son of Man standing at the right hand of God" (7:56). But probably the most important statement in regard to the reason for the ascension is given by Peter when he says Jesus "is the one whom God exalted to His right hand as a Prince and a Savior, to grant repentance to Israel, and forgiveness of sins (5:31).

> **1:12** Then they returned to Jerusalem from the mount called Olivet, . . . a Sabbath day's journey away.

Mount Olivet. The beautiful hill that dominates the east side of the city of Jerusalem. In Jesus' day, there were many garden sites and olive groves, thus the name. There is a magnificent view overlooking the city from the western side, with the deep Kidron Valley running between. Christ went up from this place (Acts 1:12) and will return here, as prophesied by Zechariah. When His feet touch the ground, the hill will "split in its middle from east to west by a very large valley" (Zech. 14:4). From this spot, He will enter the city of Jerusalem and take charge as King of kings. The hillside is dotted with the graves of the orthodox Jews who wished to be buried near where the Messiah returns in order to be first in the resurrection.

Sabbath Day's Journey. See p. 60.

> **1:13** And when they had entered [Jerusalem], they went up to the upper room, where they were staying; that is, Peter and John and James and Andrew, Philip and Thomas, Bartholomew and Matthew, James the son of Alphaeus, and Simon the Zealot, and Judas the son of James.

Peter. See pp. 51–56.

John (the Apostle). John the apostle is mentioned in the Synoptic Gospels as one of the first of Jesus' disciples. John's name is recorded nearly equally among the three Synoptics and Acts. In his gospel, John refers to himself but not by name.

Luke describes in detail John's call to be a disciple (Luke 5:8–11). John's father, Zebedee, was a fisherman and a Galilean wealthy enough to have hired servants in the boat (Mark 1:20). John is often mentioned with Peter and James as present at the most important events, such as the transfiguration (Luke 9:28) and during Jesus' agony in Gethsemane. John and his other brother James must have had a strong and judgmental temperament; they desired to call down fire on the Samaritan village that refused them shelter (Luke 9:54). John and his brother were called "sons of thunder" (Mark 3:17) for their zeal and vehemence.

Known as "the disciple whom Jesus loved," John demonstrated his closeness and loyalty by being at the foot of Christ's cross. There Jesus charges him with the duties of a son to take care of the Lord's mother (John 19:26). John and Peter are together at Jesus' resurrection (20:2; 21:2). John closes his gospel account with a most poetic description of the life and ministry of Christ: "And there are also many other things which Jesus did, which if they were written in detail, I suppose that even the world itself would not contain the books which were written" (John 21:25).

In Acts, Peter and John are entering the temple at the time of prayer (3:1) when they meet the lame man (v. 2). Peter spoke for both apostles as he uttered those famous words: "I do not possess silver and gold, but what I do have I give to you: In the name of Jesus Christ the Nazarene—walk!" (v. 6).

After the healing, both apostles are singled out to be questioned by the Sadducees, certain priests, Annas, and Caiaphas about their proclamation of Christ (4:1–7). Everyone recognizes their courage, even though they appear to be uneducated men (v.17). When told not to speak in the name of Jesus, the two fellow disciples answer: "Whether it is right in the sight of God to give heed to you rather than to God, you be the judge; for we cannot stop speaking what we have seen and heard" (vv. 19–20).

John is not seen again in Acts until the apostles in Jerusalem send him and Peter to Samaria to see if the conversions there are genuine and led by the power of the Holy Spirit. Both men lay hands on the Samaritans, who then received the Spirit (8:14–17). Though Peter is mentioned most often as doing the majority of the speaking, verse 25 indicates that "they" solemnly testified of Christ and spoke of the Lord.

John is no longer mentioned after Acts 8. Church history indicates that perhaps John early took residence in Ephesus. Tertullian says he came to Rome and suffered by being placed in a cauldron of boiling oil, yet he survived by a miracle. Eusebius says John was banished to Patmos under the persecution of Domitian and then returned to Ephesus under Caesar Nerva. Polycrates notes that he was made an Ephesian bishop and even wore a priestly headdress when officiating. He died and was buried in that city.

James (Son of Zebedee). James the apostle was the brother of John (Matt. 4:21; 10:2). His name always precedes John's in the Gospels, probably indicating that he was the elder of the two brothers.

Their father, Zebedee (Matt. 4:21), a successful fisherman, owned several boats and had hired servants (Mark 1:20; Luke 5:11). James and John would have been part of their father's business, along with Peter (Luke 5:10) and possibly Andrew, Peter's brother (Mark 1:16). James's immediate response to Jesus' call (Matt. 4:22) was probably the result of previous knowledge of Jesus. He apparently was not with Andrew, Peter, and even possibly his brother John when they first met Jesus in Judea and received their call to discipleship (John 1:35–51). If John was the other disciple of John the Baptist who followed Christ (John 1:35–40), James may have been back in Galilee taking care of the fishing business. But he became convinced that Jesus was the Messiah and immediately responded to His call. James was in Jesus' "inner circle" with Peter and John. He was with them at the house of Peter's mother-in-law (Mark 1:29–31), the house of Jairus (Mark 5:37; Luke 8:51), and the transfiguration (Matt. 17:1). He was with Jesus in Gethsemane (Matt. 26:37; Mark 14:33).

James and John were referred to by Jesus as the "sons of thunder." Their impetuous personalities compelled them to want to call down fire on Samaritans who would not allow Jesus to stay in their village (Luke 9:51–56). Another time, they asked for the seats on the right hand and on the left hand of Christ when He came into His glory (Mark 10: 35–45). James fulfills the prophecy that he would drink from the same cup as his Master (Mark 10:39). When King Herod Agrippa I starts his persecution against the church, he puts James to death by the sword (Acts 12:2) and then arrests Peter (12:3). James is the only one of Christ's apostles whose martyrdom is recorded in the New Testament.

Andrew. The first apostle called and the brother of Peter. Traditionally, their mother was named Joanna and their father Jonas or John. In the Gospels, both men are called together while they are fishing (Matt. 4:18–22). John records that Andrew was a disciple of John the Baptist who heard the Baptist's testimony, "Behold the Lamb of God." After a day with Jesus, he leads his brother Peter to the Lord. Andrew tells Christ of the youth with the loaves and fish (John 6:5–13) and with Philip introduced a group of Greeks to Jesus (John 12:20–22). Andrew may spend most of his ministry in Jerusalem. He is not mentioned in reference to the growth of the church in Acts nor after Acts 1.

Philip. One of the first apostles directly called by the Lord (John 1:43) and the fourth of those selected early in the ministry of Jesus. Philip appears only three times in the gospel narratives. Acts revolves around the successful preaching of Philip in Samaria, followed by his command to go to the Jerusalem-Gaza road where he explained the gospel to, and baptized, the Ethiopian Eunuch. Acts 8:39 makes the remarkable statement that the Spirit then "snatched Philip away," and he found himself at Azotus. He continued his preaching at least as far as Caesarea. The church father Polycrates, quoting Eusebius, says Philip was one of the great lights of Asia and was buried in Hierapolis.

Thomas. Generally listed sixth or seventh in the order of the apostles. In the book of John, he has a noted position. When the other apostles would have tried to dissuade Jesus from going up to Bethany, where Lazarus lay dead, Thomas said, "Let us also go that we may die with Him" (John 11:16). After the Lord's resurrection, Thomas refused to believe until he, too, had seen and touched Jesus (John 20:25). But after encountering the risen Christ, he shouted, "My Lord and my God" (John 20:28). A gnostic writing, *The Acts of Thomas,* says that Jesus urged Thomas in a vision of Himself to go to India as a missionary. There is no historical evidence for the claim.

Bartholomew. Probably the Nathanael of the book of John, for Bartholomew is never mentioned in John and the name *Nathanael* is never recorded in the Synoptic Gospels. Though Bartholomew means "son of Talmai" and Nathanael means "God has given it," neither name gives much of a clue as to the background or the family of this apostle. There is no other mention of Bartholomew after this verse in Acts. Little credit is given to the tradition that he too traveled to India and was martyred there.

Matthew. Listed seventh or eighth in the three lists of the apostles. He may have been the most influential and educated of them all. As a tax-collector assigned to the area of Capernaum, Matthew must have been a very influential official. He was originally called Levi, the son of Alphaeus, but became better known as Matthew. Though he appears to have suddenly followed Jesus when invited (Matt. 9:9), he must have already been familiar with the words and works of Christ as the rumors spread all around the Galilee area. Though this verse is the last mention of Matthew in the New Testament, his reputation as a soulwinner must have been well known because he is called, by tradition, Matthew the Evangelist.

James (Son of Alphaeus). Nothing more is known about this James. He is usually identified with James the Less, the brother of Joses and son of Mary (Matt. 27:56; Mark 15:40). It is possible that he was the brother of Matthew since Matthew also is called the son of Alphaeus (Mark 2:14).

Simon the Zealot. The Zealots or Cananeans were a sect founded by Judas of Gamala who resisted the Romans and opposed the census of Quirinius (A.D. 6 or 7). The Zealots were "not a religious sect in the same class with the Pharisees or the Essenes. They were a group of fanatical nationalists who advocated violence as a means of liberation from Rome."[13]

The founding of this sect is described by Gamaliel in Acts 5:37, which describes its founder as Judas of Galilee and the eventual scattering of this group. Josephus refers to Judas as a Gaulonite, while in all other instances he refers to him, like Luke, as of Galilee. Josephus tells of these events:

> Yet there was one Judas, a Gaulonite, of a city whose name was Gamala, who, taking with him Sadduc, a Pharisee, became zealous to draw them to a revolt, who both said that this taxation was no better than an introduction to slavery, and exhorted the nation to assert their liberty. . . . All sorts of misfortunes also sprang from these men, and the nation was infected with this doctrine to an incredible degree. . . . But of the fourth sect of Jewish philosophy, Judas the Galilean was the author. These men agree in all other things with the Pharisaic notions; but they have an inviolable attachment to liberty; and say that God is to be their only Ruler and Lord.[14]

As Merrill Tenney explained, the Zealots were not by nature a new religious sect, yet we see clearly that their impact was heavily felt, and not just in the political arena. Cecil Roth explains that they "cut down without scruple any person who appeared too friendly towards the Roman oppressor."[15] The Zealots came to be known as Sicarii, "after the short daggers they plunged into their victims."[16]

The fact that Simon was still called a Zealot after his conversion is evidence that, while the group as a whole was often fanatical and violent, some of its members were not involved in that aspect. Rather, they simply held strong views regarding the rule of God and the independence of Israel. It is doubtful that, having walked with Jesus, he remained a convinced insurrectionist. He now knew the heart must first be changed.

Simon is mentioned in Matthew 10:4; Mark 3:18, and Luke 6:15; 1:13 is his only mention in Acts.

Judas (Son of James). Called in Luke also "Judas of James" (6:16), he is identified with the disciple named Lebbaeus (Matt. 10:3) and Thaddaeus (Matt. 10:3; Mark 3:18). It is also surmised that he replaced Thaddaeus when he died during Christ's ministry. Judas is not to be confused with Judas or Jude the brother of Jesus. Nothing is known of his career, nor what happened to him at the end of his life.

1:14b along with the women, and Mary the mother of Jesus, and with His brothers.

The Women. Though not all named, this is probably the group of faithful women who often were among the disciples of Jesus. Some of them may have been those healed of evil spirits and sicknesses by Jesus, including Mary Magdalene, "from whom seven demons had gone out." Those who met might also have included "Joanna the wife of Chuza," who was Herod's steward, Susanna, and others who helped support the Twelve disciples out of their private means (Luke 8:2–3). Some of these were likely the same women who went to the place of burial of Jesus "and saw the tomb and how His body was laid" (Luke 23:55). These were the women at the crucifixion "who accompanied Him from Galilee, [and] were standing at a distance, seeing these things" (23:49).

Some of these women played a key role in the resurrection story. Since they knew the actual tomb where Christ was laid (Luke 23:55), three days later they returned "early in the morning" to anoint His corpse (Luke 24:22; Mark 16:1). They reported to the disciples that the body was gone and that angels had told them Jesus was alive (Luke 24:23). Cleopas and the other disciple recounted this to Jesus on the Emmaus road before they had recognized Him: "And some of those [disciples] who were with us went to the tomb and found it just exactly as the women also had said; but Him they did not see" (Luke 24:24). Though not mentioned again in the book of Acts, these brave women may have been significant enablers in the early church.

Mary the mother of Jesus, and with His brothers. Though born of Mary by the working of the Holy Spirit, Jesus had at least two half-brothers, Jude and James, and two or more sisters through the union of Mary and Joseph (Mark 6:3). Jude and James were the authors of the two short epistles named after them.

When Jesus began His ministry, His mother Mary was at the marriage in Cana when the water was turned to wine (John 2:1). As the Lord traveled in His ministry he made at least occasional contact with His family. At Nain they tried to see Him but "were unable to get to Him because of the crowd" (Luke 8:19). Mary stood "by the cross" with her sister, also named Mary. When Jesus saw her He committed her care to John. Turning to John the disciple, Christ committed His mother to John's care. "And from that hour the disciple took her into his own household" (John 19:25–27).

Of the siblings of Jesus, the most is known of James and Jude. James was probably with the family when they sought to see the Lord somewhere in Galilee (Matt. 12:46); as well, he went with Jesus to Capernaum (John 2:12), and later joined in the attempt to persuade Him to go to Judea for the Feast of Tabernacles, though he did not believe in him (John 7:3, 5, 10). When Jesus appeared to him alone after his resurrection (1 Cor. 15:7), James may first have believed in Him as Savior.

Jude was possibly here in Acts 1:14 in the upper room following Christ's ascension. He was married and apparently traveled a lot, taking his wife along (1 Cor. 9:5). Most believe he remained in Israel and carried out the agreement of the Jerusalem Council (Gal. 2:9). Henry C. Thiessen adds:

> Hegesippus tells us that near the end of Domitian's reign (c. A.D. 95), two grandsons of Jude, farmers, were brought before the emperor on the charge that they were descendants of David and were Christians. When Domitian learned that they were poor and saw their horny hands, he dismissed them as harmless Jews.[17]

1:15a Peter stood up in the midst of the brethren

Brethren. The Greek *adelphos* describes the larger core of 120 disciples. In Acts, the word is used most often to delineate the Christian fellowship of believers, such as the far-off brothers who were being taught in Antioch (15:1). But the word could be used in a restrictive way, as when James addressed the Jerusalem Council (15:23). Peter and Paul addressed fellow Jews as brothers, using the word as a term of endearment (2:37; 23:1). The compliment was not often returned.

1:16 "Brethren, the Scripture had to be fulfilled, which the Holy Spirit foretold by the mouth of David concerning Judas, who became a guide to those who arrested Jesus."

David. Spoken of with great affection in Acts. He is respected as the servant of the Lord, and a father, great grandfather, or patriarch (2:29; 4:25). As well as king of Israel, he is recognized as an Old Testament prophet (1:16; 2:25, 34; 13:22, 34). At Pisidian Antioch, Paul cites David as a central figure of God's plan. Paul points out that it is through David's offspring, "according to promise," that "God has brought to Israel a Savior, Jesus" (13:23). Paul also quotes 1 Samuel 13:14: "I have found David the son of Jesse, a man after My heart, who will do all My will." And finally: "For David, after he had served the purpose of God in his own generation, fell asleep, and was laid among his fathers, and underwent decay" (13:36).

Judas Iscariot. At every mention in the Gospels, Judas is stigmatized for his treacherous betrayal of Jesus (Matt. 10:4; Mark 3:19; Luke 6:16; John 6:71). The epithet "Iscariot" probably refers to Judas's home town, Kerioth, in south Palestine. The other disciples were from the north. It seems clear from all the Gospels that Judas from the beginning was not a true disciple of Christ. It was after he had left the Upper Room to betray the Lord, that Jesus said to the other men, "You did not choose Me, but I chose you, and appointed you, that you should go and bear fruit" (John 15:16). Moments before, at the Passover meal, Judas had a prime position near Jesus and next to the feasting bowl where the bread was dipped into the gravy-covered meat (John 13:26). As Satan entered Judas to cause him to perform his evil act, Jesus told him, "What you do, do quickly" (13:27). Judas "went out immediately; and it was night" (13:30).

Judas must have been selected to keep the finances for the disciples (John 13:29), yet he was all along pilfering the funds (John 12:4–6). Despite his evil, Peter notes that Judas was "counted among us, and received his portion in this ministry" (Acts 1:17). Peter argues that he must be replaced for the sake of the full witness "with us" of the resurrection (v. 22). The Lord's betrayal by Judas was prophesied (Zech. 11:12–13), and Peter quotes Psalm 69:25 to show that Judas's birthplace would be cursed. "Let his homestead be made desolate, and let no man dwell in it" (Acts 1:20).

> **1:19b** that field was called Hakeldama, that is, Field of Blood.

Field of Blood. According to this verse, the entire city knew this was the place of Judas's death. Most commentators believe this verse is an addition by Luke and not part of what Peter said.

> **1:22** "beginning with the baptism of John, until that day he was taken up from us—one of these should become a witness with us of His resurrection."

Baptism of John. See under 1:5.

Resurrection. See p. 73.

> **1:23** And they put forward two men, Joseph called Barsabbas (who was also called Justus), and Matthias.

Joseph (Barsabbas). Joseph was the unsuccessful candidate for the position of apostle. His name is a common Hebrew name, *Iōsēp*, meaning "May He (God) add (sons)."[18] Luke notes his other two names, Barsabbas (son of Sabbas) and Justus. He is not mentioned again in the New Testament passage.

He was put forward before the disciples as one who would replace Judas Iscariot as part of the "twelve" (Acts 1:21–26). As proposed by Peter, it was necessary to replace Judas as a witness to the life and resurrection of Jesus (vv. 21, 22). The disciples responded by putting forth two candidates, Joseph and Matthias (v. 23). The disciples then prayed: "Thou, Lord, who knowest the hearts of all men, show which one of these two Thou hast chosen to occupy this ministry and apostleship from which Judas turned aside to go to his own place" (vv. 24–25).

Lots were drawn and Matthias chosen (1:26). Though not mentioned again in Scripture, Joseph Barsabbas more than likely continued as an effective witness for the Lord. The church father Eusebius says he was one of "the Seventy," the larger body of followers of Christ, mentioned in Luke 10:1. There is no reason to doubt this report.

Matthias. Matthias was a Jew whose Hebrew name means "gift of God." Many believe he was part of the larger following of the seventy disciples (Luke 10:1). After Peter calls for a substitute apostolic witness to take the place of Judas Iscariot who had betrayed the Christ and then hanged himself (Matt. 27:3–10), the prerequisites were that the new apostle was associated with Jesus throughout his ministry and was a witness to the resurrected Lord (Acts 1:21–22). Lots were cast between Joseph called Barsabbas and Matthias, with Matthias being selected. It is surmised that their names were written on small pieces of tablet, shaken in a vessel with one drawn out.[19]

Many believe the apostles were carrying out the harsh command of Psalm 109 that addresses the demotion of a wicked man: "Let his days be few; let another take his office" (v. 8). The question has been raised as to whether this substitution was necessary. Was it simply a fleshly attempt to maintain the number twelve for the apostolic leadership? R. C. H. Lenski argues that the selection was from the Lord:

> The choice between the two was entrusted to Jesus by means of prayer. . . . Peter no doubt spoke the prayer in which all joined silently. . . . Jesus is asked in contrast to any selection the assembly might make. And the reason for the appeal to him is that he is the "heart-knower" and thus able to choose with unerring insight.[20]

John Gill notes the disciples demonstrate a desire to "be certain of the mind and will of God, and act according to it."[21] Simon J. Kistemaker concludes:

> The decision, therefore, is made not by the apostles but by the Lord himself. . . . the apostles resort to the Old Testament custom of casting lots to learn the will of God. The lot is cast into the lap, but its every decision is from the Lord [Prov. 16:33]. The practice of casting the lot was common in Old Testament times; . . . After the outpouring of the Holy Spirit on Pentecost, the practice ceases. In the period between Jesus' ascension and Pentecost, the apostles

determine the conditions for apostleship, pray for divine guidance, and cast the lot to ascertain God's choice.[22]

Thus, what Peter and the apostles did seems clearly to be led of the Lord. They asked for guidance and the Lord answered.

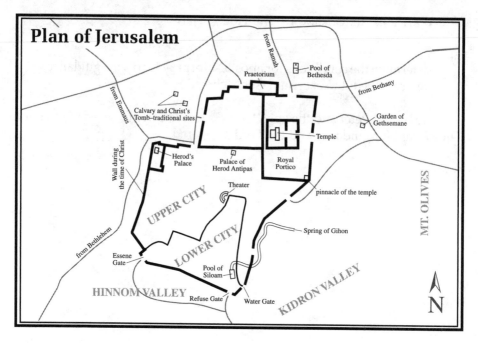

Plan of Jerusalem

from Ramah

from Bethany

from Emmaus

from Bethlehem

Praetorium

Pool of Bethesda

Calvary and Christ's Tomb–traditional sites

Garden of Gethsemane

Temple

Herod's Palace

Palace of Herod Antipas

Royal Portico

Wall during the time of Christ

Theater

pinnacle of the temple

UPPER CITY

LOWER CITY

Spring of Gihon

Essene Gate

Pool of Siloam

HINNOM VALLEY

Refuse Gate

Water Gate

KIDRON VALLEY

MT. OLIVES

N

Chapter 2

A.D. 30 (Pentecost)

THE OUTPOURING AND EMPOWERMENT OF THE HOLY SPIRIT

Synopsis

(1–13) On the Day of Pentecost, the Holy Spirit fills the disciples and they begin to speak with other languages (1–4). By this miracle of tongues, many Jews and Gentile proselytes on pilgrimage to Jerusalem heard the gospel of Christ and "the mighty deeds of God" (5–13).

(14–36) Emboldened, Peter delivers his first sermon on what this outpouring of the Spirit means (14–21). In the second part of his message, Peter proves Christ's resurrection was prophesied (22–32) and declares that Christ is at the right hand of God (33–35). Jesus is thus established as Messiah and Lord (36).

2:1a And when the day of Pentecost had come,

Day of Pentecost. See pp. 34–36.

2:4 And they were all filled with the Holy Spirit and began to speak with other tongues, as the Spirit was giving them utterance.

Filled with the Holy Spirit. See pp. 36–37, 133, 162–64.

Began to speak with other tongues. See pp. 37–42.

2:6b they were each one hearing them speak in his own language.

Language. See pp. 37–39.

2:7 And they were amazed and marveled, saying, "Why, are not all these who are speaking Galileans?"

Galileans. The word *Galilee* means "circuit," or "district." Apparently, everyone from the northern region known as Galilee spoke with a marked accent. They were looked down upon as well because Galilee was far from the metropolitan capital of Jerusalem. There was a well-known phrase among southern Jews: "Can anything good come out of Galilee?" Nathanael/Bartholomew made a similar statement about Nazareth in particular (John 1:46). Galilee was also the region of the Decapolis, the ten cities most occupied by Gentiles (Matt. 4:25). It was called "Galilee of the Gentiles" or "The District of the Gentiles." Some thought certainly no prophet would come from Galilee (John 7:52).

Possibly also the uprising by the rebel Jew Judas of Galilee had stirred more dislike for the region. When Gamaliel warns the Jewish leadership not to be too hasty in persecuting the disciples, he reminds the Sanhedrin that this particular Galilean rebellion by Judas came to nothing because God was not in it (5:34–39).

Despite what some said, Jesus was called "the prophet from Nazareth in Galilee" (Matt. 21:11). From this district both John the Baptist and the Lord began their ministries. Jesus was known as the Galilean (Matt. 26:69). He evidently loved this area and continually returned there. Though His home town of Nazareth rejected Him, the region overall accepted Him and His message (John 4:45).

As the miracle of tongues is activated at Pentecost, the crowd has distinguished the Galilean accent. Perhaps they have already heard Peter and the others speak (Acts 2:7). But now disciples begin to speak in tongues. The crowd asks, "How is it that we each hear them in our own language to which we were born?" (v. 8). The crowd cannot believe Galileans are sophisticated enough to speak all of these languages.

The final reference to Galilee in Acts is positive. At Pisidian Antioch, Paul reminds the Jews of all the living witnesses to the resurrection. The risen Christ "appeared to those who came up with Him from Galilee to Jerusalem, the very ones who are now His witnesses to the people" (13:31).

2:9 "Parthians and Medes and Elamites, and residents of Mesopotamia, Judea and Cappadocia, Pontus and Asia,"

Parthians. Modern Iran. The Romans had never conquered this territory and the peoples were bitter enemies.[23] Parthia was part of the ancient Persian Empire that was conquered by Alexander the Great in the third century B.C. In ancient times, their exclusive use of cavalry-bowmen made them a formidable enemy, as the Romans discovered.[24] Josephus notes that deported Jews were settled there and continued to speak an Aramaic dialect and to worship Jehovah. They also sent tribute funds to the temple in Jerusalem.

Medes. The ancient Indo-European peoples of northwestern Iran. The Median people were absorbed into the Persian Empire around the seventh century B.C. None of the language of the Medes came down to the time of the New Testament, except possibly a few loan words that found their way into other languages. Generally speaking, as a people, they melted into other cultures over the course of wars and shifting rule. Acts 2:9 is the only New Testament reference to them, and their presence on this day shows how far the Jews had spread in their early dispersions.[25]

Elamites. Elamite Jews were part of the semiautonomous country of Elymaîs, a district of Elam. After Assyria collapsed, Elam was joined to the Indo-Europeans who had gained power in Iran following their invasion around 1000 B.C. The Jews had spread throughout this region as early as the Babylonian Captivity, from which many did not return to Jerusalem. The Jews of Elam spoke the Hebrew-related Aramaic. This is the only New Testament reference to this country.

Residents of Mesopotamia. The area of modern Iraq. *Mesopotamia* comes from the Greek *mesos* ("middle") and *potamos* ("river"), thus it literally means "the middle of the river." This is an appropriate name for an area located between the Tigris and the Euphrates rivers. It was referred to by the Hebrews as Aram, Aram-Naharaim, Padan-Aram, or any of several other names. The residents of this region in Jerusalem during the feast of Pentecost were probably from the area near Babylon where they had lived since the time of the captivity. Carl E. DeVries notes:

Stephen's allusion to the fact that the call of God came to Abraham, "while he was in Mesopotamia, before he lived in Haran" (Acts 7:2), definitely puts southern Iraq in Mesopotamia, for Abraham was then in the city of Ur (Gen. 11:31). The southern part of Mesopotamia, including Ur and a number of other city-states, was known as Sumer; the central section was called Addad and later was named Babylonia, after the city of Babylon gained its ascendancy; the northern division, along the Tigris, was Assyria, the land of Asshur.[26]

Cappadocia. A large region of Asia Minor which apparently received its name from the Persians, though its people were called Syrians by the Greeks. In the later Persian Empire, it was divided into two regions and maintained this division under the Romans. *Pontus* was the northern part along the Black Sea. The southern part maintained the name *Cappadocia*. In New Testament times it was bordered on the north by Polemon, on the south by Cilicia and Syria, on the west by Galatia and Lycaonia, and on the east by Armenia and Syria. There was apparently a significant population of Jews there. Those who believed in Christ at Pentecost probably took the gospel back and proclaimed it in their native land. Peter directed his first epistle partly to churches in this region as among the elect (1 Peter 1:1).

Pontus. The northern region of Cappadocia, bordering the Black Sea, divided in the time of the late Persian Empire. In the New Testament Pontus was bordered to the west by Bithynia and on the west by Galatia. Aquila, husband of Priscilla and Paul's tent-making companion, was from Pontus (Acts 18:2). Paul was forbidden to evangelize this northern area of Asia Minor by the Holy Spirit just before his "Macedonian call" (Acts 16:7). Peter addressed his first epistle to "those who reside as aliens, scattered throughout Pontus." This lends support to the tradition that Peter preached in northern Asia Minor rather than Rome after Pentecost.

Asia. Not until the fourth century was the term *Asia* used of the continent which today bears that name. In the first century, *Asia* typically referred to Asia Minor or the proconsular province of Asia, which contained the seven churches of Revelation. Merrill F. Unger explains that in addition to the two typical uses, "Luke appears to have used the term *Asia* in a still more restricted sense, counting Phrygia and Mysia as provinces distinct from Asia (Acts 2:9–10; 16:6–7)."[27] The book of Acts contains fifteen references to Asia (2:9; 6:9; 16:6; 19:10; 19:22; 19:26; 19:27; 19:31; 20:4 (twice); 20:16; 20:18; 21:27; 24:18, and 27:2). J. Strong thinks *Asia* denotes Asia Minor in 19:26–27; 21:27; 24:18, and 27:2. He believes proconsular Asia is referred to in 2:9; 6:9; 16:6; 19:10, 22; and 20:4, 16, and 18.[28]

Politically, Asia was governed by Rome, as was the rest of the civilized world. Merrill Tenney observes that at the time of the New Testament the entire civilized world, except for little-known kingdoms of the Far East, were under Rome:

> From the Atlantic Ocean on the west to the Euphrates River and the Red Sea on the east, and from the Rhone, the Danube, the Black Sea, and the Caucasus mountains on the north to the Sahara on the south, stretched one vast empire under the headship and virtual dictatorship of the emperor, called both "king" (1 Peter 2:17) and "Augustus" (Luke 2:1) in the New Testament.[29]

Josephus tells us that Rome ruled 500 cities in Asia.[30] Robert Young has studied the significant role Asia played in the dissemination of the gospel. He says it was "intimately connected with the early history of Christianity, and the first Christian churches were planted here."[31]

While the gospel had great impact in Asia, persecution came both from Rome and natives. Eusebius explains that the Christians of Asia were "laboring under injuries of every kind at the hands of the local population."[32] Also note Paul's statement in 2 Timothy 1:15, "You are aware of the fact that all who are in Asia turned away from me."

2:10 "Phrygia and Pamphylia, Egypt and the districts of Libya around Cyrene, and visitors from Rome, both Jews and proselytes,"

Phrygia. A large region in Asia Minor on the western watershed of the great Anatolian Plateau. It reaches north into the upper Sangarius Valley, southwest down the valley of the Maeander, and southeast to perhaps as far as Iconium.[33]

The Phrygians developed their own simple cloth headcovering, and this cap was eventually adopted by freed Roman slaves. The original inhabitants of Phrygia are believed to have been Indo-Europeans who entered Asia Minor from Thrace about 1200 B.C. According to Diodorus, they were for a time the masters of the sea. Other Thracian tribes entered into Phrygia and it divided into two parts. Greater Phrygia was a high, barren plateau. Farther east, the land was known for its grapes and marble mines. The most fertile region was the valley of the Sangarius. Lesser Phrygia stretched along the shores of the Sea of Marmara and the Hellespont to Troas, which later was to become a part of Mysia.

The Phrygian religion was centered around the worship of nature and was very sensual and erotic. The Great Mother of the Gods, Rhea or Cybele, and a male deity, Sabazius, were the most prominent deities. Later, this religion was to have a great effect upon the religions of Greece and Rome.

Phrygia was ruled by a succession of kings, who alternately bore the names Gordius and Midas, until the seventh century B.C. The Cimmerians held power until the sixth century, when Croesus, king of Lydia, marched in. Phrygia, as most of Asia Minor, was ruled by the Persians, then the Greeks, then the Romans.

The mention of Phrygians in the Pentecost crowd is not surprising. The province had a large number of Jewish inhabitants. Paul passed through the region on his second missionary journey (Acts 16:6). Horatio Hackett sums up Paul's travels through these lands:

> The travelers, having passed through the eastern section of Phrygia into Galatia, proposed next to preach the word in Proconsul Asia. With that view, they turned their steps to the south-west, and, crossing the north part of Phrygia, came down to the frontier of Mysia, the first province in Asia which they would reach in that direction. Being informed here that they were not to execute this design, they turned again toward the north and attempted to go into Bithynia, which was adjacent to Mysia. Restrained from that purpose, they passed by Mysia—i.e., did not remain there to preach—and proceeded to Troas. This portion of the apostle's travels, though they embrace so wide a circuit, admits of very little geographical illustration. Phrygia and Galatia are parts of Asia Minor of which the ancient writers have left but few notices, and which remain comparatively unknown to the present day. We must infer from 18:23 that Paul gained disciples in Phrygia at this time, but in what places is uncertain. Colosse was a Phrygian city, and may have received the gospel on this journey, unless it be forbidden by Col. 2:1.[34]

Phrygia also opened Paul's third missionary journey. Many of these converts that are present to hear Paul could be from the surrounding cities, wanting to hear his message. These converts would be the ones to carry on when he left and strengthen their own brethren. Though some commentators argue that Paul was the sole instigator of Christianity wherever he went, we must remember that on the Day of Pentecost more than five thousand were added to the church. These people would have gone home and spread the Word and let people know what had happened to them. Paul's ministry in many respects was teaching, not preaching. In many areas, he simply taught those who already believed. In Acts 18:23 we read, "And having spent some time there, he departed and passed successively through the Galatian region and Phrygia, strengthening all the disciples." Obviously, someone had come through before, or maybe people had come back, believing and teaching faith in Christ.

Pamphylia. A southern coastal country in Asia Minor, bordered on the west by Lycia and by Cilicia Tracheia to the east. Pamphylia was in some places fifteen to twenty miles broad and extended eighty miles long east to west. Mount Taurus dominated the coast.

The original inhabitants of Pamphylia were of a strange mixture of aborigines, Cilicians, and Greek colonists. Cities within Pamphylia never were successfully Hellenized after the conquest by Alexander the Great. Some coins and inscriptions are written in a form of Greek that is almost unintelligible. Pamphylia served primarily as a trading post. As a result, the people never attained great prosperity. After the death of Alexander the Great, Pamphylia was ruled by the Seleucid dynasty. It was bequeathed in 133 B.C. by Attalus III to the Roman kingdom.

There are several references to Pamphylia in the book of Acts. The next reference to Pamphylia (13:13) records John Mark's defection on the first missionary journey. In the region of Pamphylia, John Mark left Paul and his company and returned home. Theories abound as to why he left: (1) He feared the area's many bandits; (2) he feared contracting one of the rampant diseases; (3) he was just overwhelmed. Whatever the case, his leaving had serious ramifications when Barnabas wanted to bring him along on the second journey (Acts 15:36–40). Paul refused, and the team divided.

Why Paul was so hard on Mark is not known. Possibly he was not patient with young people, or he expected his own high zeal and enthusiasm in Mark. God used the division to create two missionary teams from the one. On their way to the Council at Jerusalem, Paul and company again passed through Pamphylia (Acts 14:24, 25). On their first trip, it is not revealed if they taught or preached; however, on the return trip they spent some time there in Perga, the capitol. Perga provided excellent ground. Artemis was worshiped in this town. However, the preaching of Paul did not stir up Artemis worshipers in Perga as it did in Ephesus (Acts 19:24–41).

The last reference to Pamphylia is in relation to Paul's sea voyage to Rome (Acts 27:5). Luke records this as one of the coasts followed to circumvent the strong westerly winds of the early autumn. By clinging to the coast, Paul's vessel was kept safer than if it had attempted an open sea crossing.

Egypt. Josephus tells us that during the time of the New Testament the Jewish population in Egypt was around 1 million. These were Jews who had fled to Egypt for protection after the invasion by Nebuchadnezzar. The majority of these Jews lived in the coastal city of Alexandria. The Septuagint (LXX) Greek Old Testament was translated over a period of many years in Alexandria in the second century B.C. The translation had become quite popular with New Testament writers.

Libya. Libya is the ancient Greek name (Heb. *Put*) for the territory encompassing northern Africa west of Egypt. Its people were referred to as *Lubim*. Most of the Jews that lived in the country lived in the capital city of Cyrene. Simon, who bore the cross of Jesus, was a Cyrenian.

Cyrene. The capital of Libya (see Libya above).

Rome. Rome is believed to have been founded in 735 B.C. It was built on seven hills east of a large south bend in the River Tiber some fifteen miles upstream from its mouth. First-century Rome was a sprawling metropolis of about 1 million people, one of the most splendid cities of its day. It was the very center of the Roman Empire with all major roads leading to it. Romans celebrated about 159 official holidays, and freedmen had plenty of leisure. There were a multitude of theaters and coliseums for sport and pagan ritual. The city was full of gods and goddesses, including the temple of Apollo and the temple to the Magna Mater or Chebele.

The Jews in Rome were divided into a number of district synagogues, rather than gathered as a single community. The earliest, and certainly the largest, Jewish community was in the area called Transtiberium on the bank of Tiber. By the time of the early empire, there were probably 40,000 to 50,000 Jews resident in Rome. Many had arrived as slaves after Pompey invaded Palestine in 63 B.C. These Jewish people had considerable freedom and legal protection within Rome. Julius Caesar granted them freedom to worship and to raise money for communal purposes. They had exemption from military duty, and Jewish legal cases could be heard in Jewish courts.

Likely the church of Rome was founded by Jewish Christians from among the "visitors from Rome, both Jews and proselytes" at Pentecost (Acts 2:10). Although they were a dedicated group living in the strategic heart of the Roman Empire, Rome's believers had not had the benefit of apostolic teaching when Paul wrote the Epistle of Romans in about 56. Paul wanted to remedy that deficiency by visiting with them, as well as "to preach the gospel to you also who are in Rome" (Rom. 1:15). Paul had a great desire to get to know the believers in Rome and to have them get to know and to pray for him. He implored near the end of his letter, "Now I urge you, brethren, by our Lord Jesus Christ and by the love of the Spirit, to strive together with me in your prayers to God for me so that I may come to you in joy by the will of God and find refreshing rest in your company" (15:30, 32).

Paul finally reached Rome at the expense of the Roman government. Paul was a Roman citizen and had demanded as a Roman citizen that he be tried before Caesar concerning the charges brought against him by the chief priests and other Jewish leaders in Jerusalem (Acts 25:2, 11). When he wasn't under arrest, Paul's Roman citizenship allowed him great freedom to travel throughout the known world. He crossed borders without being challenged.

God used a pagan culture to accomplish His purposes of making the world a relatively safe environment in which the gospel of Jesus Christ could spread to every corner of the world.[35]

Proselytes, God-fearing Gentiles, God worshipers. The phrase *those who fear* accurately describes such Gentiles as Cornelius (Acts 10:1–48). But what is meant by the description that Cornelius is "a devout man, and one who feared God with all his household, and gave many alms to the Jewish people, and prayed to God continually" (10:2)?

Some scholars have held that God-fearers and God-worshipers (Acts 18:7) are the same as proselytes in Acts. The term *proselyte* is used only three times in the book. There are proselytes on the day of Pentecost from every nation (Acts 2:10). At least Nicolas, one of the seven chosen to minister to the needs of the Hellenistic widows, is described as a proselyte (Acts 6:1–6), and the term is used in Acts 13:43 to describe some "God-fearing proselytes" in the Pisidian Antioch synagogue.

As he discusses the Ethiopian eunuch in Acts 8:27, R. C. H. Lenski explains differences even among those who can be called proselytes:

> When Luke adds that the eunuch had come to Jerusalem to worship (future participle, denoting purpose, Robertson, 1128) he informs us that this Gentile was a proselyte of the gate. In 2:10 we read about proselytes of righteousness; these had become completely Jewish and had really been absorbed into Judaism and had lost their character as Gentiles. No eunuch could be more than a proselyte of the gate, since because of his mutilation he was debarred from entering the inner temple courts (Deut. 23:1). These second-class proselytes [proselytes of the gate], who were exceedingly numerous in the Jewish diaspora, did not submit to circumcision and were bound only to the so-called Noachian commandments (Gen. 9:4–6) against idolatry, blasphemy, disobedience to magistrates, murder, fornication or incest, robbery or theft, and eating of blood. They were quite generally open to the gospel and received it with great readiness; in the New Testament they are designated as *sebomenoi* or *phoboumenoi ton theon* [the ones who worship, or the ones who fear God]."[36]

Charles Feinberg likewise argues that *proselytes, God-fearers,* and *worshipers of God* were not synonymous terms:

> It is undoubtedly true that for every full convert to Judaism there were many partial converts who accepted almost all of Judaism in the realm of belief and practice with the exception of circumcision.

They were referred to in the 1st century as "those who fear (worship) God," an expression from the Hebrew phrase *yir'ê Yahweh*, which appears often in the OT. It was the usual terminology for godly Israelites (Ps. 15:4; Mal. 3:16; cf. also Ecclus. 34:13–15). On the ground of Acts 13:16, 24, 43, some have equated "God-fearer" with "proselyte." This cannot hold, because, when Paul (Acts 18:7) left the Corinthian Jews to go to the Gentiles, he proceeded to the home of Titius Justus, who was called a "worshiper of God," though evidently an uncircumcised Gentile. According to the strict Jewish view, no one was considered a proselyte if he did not keep all the law, and this was impossible without circumcision.[37]

It appears from this evidence that the term *proselyte* is used in the book of Acts to denote someone who fully conforms to Jewish faith, including circumcision (Acts 2:10; 6:5; 13:43). Conversely, such phrases as "those who fear God" or "God-fearer(s)" and "worshiper(s) of God" are used to describe those who are not full participants: the Ethiopian eunuch (9:27); Cornelius (10:2); Lydia, a woman from Thyatira (16:14); and Titius Justus, a Corinthian Gentile (18:7). This would seem to mean that Feinberg and Lenski are correct; "God-fearers" had a belief in the God of the Jews and observed many of the standards of the Mosaic Law but had not submitted fully. To the Jews they were still considered Gentiles and not full proselytes. The exception seems to be Acts 13:43, in which both terms are used, but the context clarifies (cf. 13:16, 26).

It is perhaps easier for a Hellenistic Jew (probably a proselyte) such as Philip to carry the gospel outside the realm of Jerusalem (Acts 8). He is not encumbered by the legalistic mind-set that restricted native Hebrews (for example, Peter, Acts 10:9–20). God must use persecution to expel Jewish Christians from the comforts of Jerusalem into other areas of Judea and Samaria. Philip, as a legate of the apostle, possessed the sign gifts to validate his message as he proclaimed the gospel (8:6). He had probably also learned much from the theology of Stephen, as he proclaimed the message of grace in his address to the Sanhedrin (see pp. 66, 114–116). Philip reached the Samaritans, who were looking for the Messiah (4:25), and then took the gospel to the first of the Gentiles, the Ethiopian eunuch (8:27). We concur with Lenski that he was a near proselyte or a proselyte of the gate. Possibly his only barrier to becoming a full proselyte was circumcision. This would explain Luke's placement of this episode in Acts. Luke would probably not have considered the eunuch a true Gentile but would have placed him with the Samaritans in the Jewish milieu.

The first use of the phrase *God-fearer* as the description of an individual and group or, more accurately, *one who feared God* is the episode of Cornelius in Acts 10. It is uncertain how much of Judaism to which Cornelius and his household adhered. Here, the phrase is probably used in a more loose sense. Luke's expanded description of Cornelius seems to indicate that he does not mean here a near proselyte, which he would have probably indicated by simply using the phrase *one who worships God* (i.e., Acts 16:14; 18:7). Richard Longenecker states:

> Here in Acts 10, however, we should probably understand *phoboumenos ton theon* not as a technical term for this special class associated loosely with Judaism [as it is used in Acts 13:16, 26, 43], but more broadly as meaning something like "a religious man" (NEB, TEV) or "a deeply religious man" (Ph). The fact that Luke adds *eusebes* ("devout," "pious") to his assessment of Cornelius here and *dikaios* ("righteous") in repeating his spiritual qualities in v. 22 suggests that he meant *phoboumenos ton theon* to be taken not technically but generally. [Thus, Cornelius was probably] a Gentile who, having realized the bankruptcy of paganism, sought to worship a monotheistic God, practice a form of prayer, and lead a moral life, apart from any necessary association with Judaism.[38]

This explains why Luke places this episode where he does. This was the first conversion of a true Gentile. Not a proselyte' or a near proselyte, but a Gentile who had turned his allegiance to God and sought to serve him in his limited knowledge. This would open the way to the tremendous outpouring of missionary activity that follows with the apostle Paul at the helm (9:15). It is significant, though, that God gave Peter an attitude adjustment (10:9–20) and sent him first to the Gentiles. With Peter's authority, his understanding of the fact that "God is not one to show partiality" guaranteed the fact that the Jerusalem church would be mentally and spiritually prepared for the tremendous growth in the church through Gentile converts. In fact, Luke later recounts Peter's defense of his preaching the gospel and their valid conversions in 11:1–18.

2:11 "Cretans and Arabs—we hear them in our own tongues"

Cretans. Crete is an island located 60 miles southeast of the mainland of Greece. Crete is oblong in shape, extending about 160 miles from east to west, from 6 to 35 miles north to south. The island covers an area approximately 3218 square miles. Crete is a very mountainous island, of which some peaks reach upwards of 7500 feet. The northern coast has many good harbors, whereas the south is inaccessible to shipping.

One of our earliest references to Crete is found in Homer's *Odyssey*. The island was a mix of peoples including Achaeans, Dorians, and Pelasgians. Crete had ninety (some sources say one hundred) independent cities, of which Knossos was the greatest. Knossos became the capital of the realm of the legendary king Minos (though some sources maintain that he was an actual person around which legends were built). Other important cities included Gortyna, Cydonia, and Lyctus. The inhabitants of the island were very warlike, due to their environment of independent cities.

The Cretans had very little to do with the affairs of ancient Greece. At this time they were composed primarily of Dorian stock, and their concerns were elsewhere. In 67 B.C., the island was taken by Metellus of the Romans. The island was joined to Siren and made a Roman province. Later, under Augustus, Creta-Cyrene was made a senatorial province. The Romans maintained control of the island until 395, when it passed on to the Byzantine Empire.

Several references are made to Crete and the Cretans throughout the Scripture. Their first mention here is on Pentecost. They are numbered among the many nations present when the Holy Spirit descends upon the people. When the Holy Spirit descends and the people speak in tongues, the Cretans are among the many who heard their language spoken. While it cannot be ascertained who planted Christianity in Crete, it is assumed that some who heard on this day believed and took it back to their fellow Cretans.

Crete is later mentioned in Acts 27, where Paul is on a ship bound for his first visit to Rome to stand trial under Caesar. As with other islands in the Mediterranean, Crete was to provide a shelter for Paul's journey (27:7). The dangerous winds of the Mediterranean forced the boat to creep along the coasts of provinces and islands. This provided an excellent block and gave safety to the crew and passengers.

Paul makes two references to Crete in his letter to Titus. Titus had been left behind in Crete to make sure all went well. Paul, in his letter, gives him practical advice as well as doctrinal teaching (Titus 1:5). Titus was given a big job. The appointing of elders was of the utmost importance for they gave the church the spiritual guidance and teaching that was necessary. Obviously, Paul felt that Titus himself was mature enough to see such a job to its completion.

The second reference was more practical advice to Titus. Paul writes, "One of themselves, a prophet of their own, said, 'Cretans are always liars, evil beasts, lazy gluttons'" (Titus 1:12). Did Paul disagree with this statement? No, he states of the Cretans, "This testimony is true. For this cause reprove them severely that they may be sound in the faith" (Titus 1:13). The prophet spoken of in verse 12 was a Greek poet by the name of Epimenides, who was known for his exaggerations. However, it was a popular saying, "To Cretanize is to lie." A. Duane Litfin comments:

> To emphasize his point Paul quoted from Epimenides, a Cretan poet and philosopher from the sixth century B.C. who was widely believed to be a religious prophet. Though the quotation may originally have referred to a particular lie (viz., that Zeus was buried in Crete, which was especially offensive to those who believed that

Zeus was still alive), by Paul's day the saying had become a proverb which merely emphasized the low reputations of Cretans generally. So little did others think of the Cretans that the verb *kretizo* was invented to mean "to lie." Of course many noble Christians were in the congregations in Crete, but Paul was frontal in his assertion that the false teachers possessed these baser Cretan tendencies.[39]

Arabs. These were residents of Arabia, but what area was referred to as Arabia? Simon Kistemaker writes:

> The Arabs who came to Jerusalem for the feast of Pentecost presumably were Jews who resided in Nabatea. The Nabateans were desert dwellers who lived in an area that stretched in a southwesterly direction from Damascus to Egypt. Petra, situated to the southeast of Palestine, was its capital. Paul spent time in the Nabatean kingdom of Arabia (Gal. 1:17).[40]

2:14 But Peter, taking his stand with the eleven, . . .

Peter. See pp. 52–53.

2:16 "but this is what was spoken of through the prophet Joel:"

What was spoken. See pp. 145–150.

2:22 "Jesus the Nazarene, a man attested to you by God with miracles and wonders and signs"

The Nazarene. See p. 72.

Miracles and wonders and signs. See pp. 64–69.

2:23 "this Man, delivered up by the predetermined plan and foreknowledge of God, you nailed to a cross"

Delivered up. God's own purposes, by the delivering up of His Son, would make salvation possible for those He chose. This delivering up came about by a predetermined plan that came only from the mind of God.

Predetermined plan. The Greek word *orizō* is the word from which we get "destined" or "predestined." The word is used of the election or predestination of the saints (Rom. 8:29), but here in Acts it is applied to God's plan concerning the death of His Son for the salvation of men.

Foreknowledge. See p. 182.

You nailed to a cross. The death and resurrection of Jesus are two "non-negotiable" truths in Acts. There would be no gospel and no salvation without these historic facts! At least seven times in the book the death of Christ is mentioned. Besides the reference to His death here, Peter brings it up in 2:23 by pointing out that it was not David who "died and was buried," as referred to in Psalm 16, but it was the Messiah prophesied in that passage. The human factor is brought up in 3:13, where Peter remarks that God glorified Jesus, "the one whom you delivered up" (3:13). In God's providence, He may manipulate the evil designs of men for His purposes, in this case, the salvation of the world.

Peter brings this up again in 3:15 and 4:10, where he notes that the Jews put the Prince of life to death. Peter mentions God's providence again in 3:18, where he says that "God announced beforehand by the mouth of all the prophets, that His Christ should suffer, He has thus fulfilled." Finally, Peter quotes the well-known Psalm 118:22 passage that prophesies the Stone the builders reject would become the cornerstone. But because of this, ". . . there is salvation in no one else; for there is no other name under heaven that has been given among men, by which we must be saved" (4:12).

2:24 "And God raised Him up again,"

Raised up. See pp. 73–74.

2:25 "For David says of Him,"

David said. See under 1:16, p. 194.

2:30 "[David] knew that God had sworn to him with an oath to seat one of his descendants upon his throne,"

Upon his throne. See pp. 87–88.

2:31 "he . . . spoke of the resurrection of the Christ,"

Christ. See pp. 74–75.

2:33 "Therefore having been exalted to the right hand of God,"

Having been exalted. See p. 81.

2:34 "For it was not David who ascended into heaven,"

Ascended. See p. 188.

2:36 "Therefore let all the house of Israel know for certain that God has made Him [Jesus] both Lord and Christ—this Jesus whom you crucified."

Both Lord and Christ. See pp. 74–75.

2:38 And Peter said to them, "Repent, and let each of you be baptized in the name of Jesus Christ, for the forgiveness of your sins; and you shall receive the gift of the Holy Spirit.

Repent. *Metanoeō* in Greek means "to change the mind." John the Baptist came proclaiming, "Repent, for the kingdom of heaven is at hand" (Matt. 3:2). This was a cleansing for the nation of Israel in preparation for the coming of their promised Messiah and Lord. It brought salvation to the Jewish people under the dispensation of the Law, during the period of the Old Testament.

But here in Acts, the new object of faith is now proclaimed, which is the death, burial, and resurrection of Christ in order to receive permanent forgiveness of sins and the gift of eternal life. Though this expression "repentance that leads to life" was uttered by Peter, it seems as if it is repeated by Paul in 2 Corinthians 7:10. There the apostle writes, "For the sorrow that is according to the will of God produces a repentance without regret, leading to salvation."

The first reference given in the New Testament about repentance has to do with the message of John the Baptist to the nation of Israel when he called out, "Repent for the kingdom of heaven is at hand" (Matt. 3:2). Since the king was being presented to the Jewish people, they were to "change the mind" (*metanoeō*) in regard to their sin and way of life. Jesus was the herald of the same message when He began His ministry (4:17). But in the new dispensation of the church and the context of Acts, the word repent goes beyond simply a confession and a change of attitude. The word will encompass the issues of salvation and a belief of Christ as Savior.

Though the Gospels mention John's baptism unto repentance, in most references the wider theological and dispensational use is given. Here in 2:38, each individual Jew was to be baptized in the name of Jesus. And this repentance leads to the receiving of the Holy Spirit. This repentance could bring about a "conversion" (*epistrephō*) for Israel that could herald the coming of Christ to reign (Acts 3:19). After the Lord's ascension, whereby He is seated at God's right hand, the Jews should turn to Him as Savior, through repentance, and thus receive forgiveness of sins (5:31).

At Mars Hill, Paul taught that God desired that men "everywhere should repent" (17:30), and he later added that he had testified "to both Jews and Greeks of repentance toward God and faith in our Lord Jesus Christ" (20:21). Finally, Paul related to Agrippa how his duty was to tell the Gentiles "they should repent and turn to God, performing deeds" that would show forth their sincere repentance" (26:20). Since Paul mentions repentance only five times in his epistles, the word was more vivid in meaning to a Jewish audience rather than a Gentile one, though the fact of changing one's mind away from sin and toward Christ is certainly part of the process of salvation for both Jew and Gentile.

The forgiveness of sins. Forgiveness is the Greek word *aphesis* that is related to the verb *aphiēmi*, which means to "dismiss." It is used here and four other times in Acts. By repentance, the Jews receive forgiveness of sins (5:31; 13:38), but also "everyone who believes in [Jesus] receives forgiveness of sins" (10:43). In 26:18, Paul tells how the Lord, when He struck him to the ground, revealed his coming mission. He would someday turn Jew and Gentile "from the dominion of Satan to God, in order that they may receive forgiveness of sins and an inheritance among those who have been sanctified by faith in Me."

Be baptized. See p. 136.

Gift of the Holy Spirit. See pp. 135–43.

2:40 "Be saved from this perverse generation!"

Saved. *Sōzō* is the most common Greek word for salvation, but within that theological meaning it can be translated "rescued," "delivered," "made whole," or "healed." Calling upon the name of the Lord brings salvation (2:21), and that salvation given can mean "to be rescued" from a cursed generation, as implied in this verse here. The doctrine of election is clearly implied in the salvation process in 2:47: "And the Lord was adding to their number day by day those who were being saved." In Acts, salvation has a narrow sense in that only through Christ are men redeemed. "And there is salvation in no one else; for there is no other name under heaven that has been given among men, by which we must be saved."

2:42 And they were continually devoting themselves to the apostles' teaching and to fellowship, to the breaking of bread and to prayer.

Apostles' teaching. The apostles would have the authority over the message of salvation and all the doctrines of the church that follow. They would confirm or deny whether God was with or against words or certain miraculous events as Acts unfolds. This would be the "binding and loosing" spoken about to Peter and the disciples by Jesus (Matt. 16:18–19).

Fellowship. In time, the church would develop into a spiritual haven and a place of warm fellowship. Surprisingly, the word fellowship (*koinōnia*) would be used but this one time in the book of Acts. However, it is used fourteen times in Paul's epistles and three times in John's first epistle (1:3, 6, 7). Though the word is used only once in Acts, there are indicators of communal blessing flowing through the churches, as illustrated in what was happening in Antioch. There, the people "rejoiced" when the Jerusalem letter was read to them (15:31) and were "encouraged and strengthened" by its message (v. 32). And finally, those who brought them the letter, Judas and Silas, were sent away in peace by that local congregation (v. 33). (See p. 167.)

Breaking of bread. In Acts, the Lord's Table is called the "breaking of bread" and was apparently done daily (2:46–47). It was a condensed version of the ceremony of Passover that pointed to the Messiah as the substitutionary sacrificial Lamb. Jesus refers to it this way (Luke 22:19) but also says that the wine cup "poured out for you is the new covenant in My blood" (v. 20). The breaking of bread is also mentioned in Acts 20:7, 11, and 27:35, though 27:35 is probably simply referring to the eating of a meal.

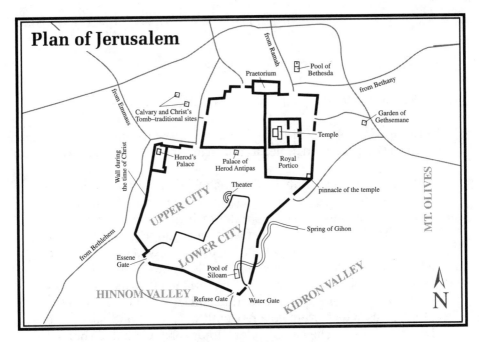

Plan of Jerusalem

from Ramah
Praetorium
Pool of Bethesda
from Bethany
from Emmaus
Calvary and Christ's Tomb–traditional sites
Garden of Gethsemane
Temple
Wall during the time of Christ
Herod's Palace
Palace of Herod Antipas
Royal Portico
pinnacle of the temple
MT. OLIVES
Theater
UPPER CITY
LOWER CITY
Spring of Gihon
from Bethlehem
Essene Gate
Pool of Siloam
HINNOM VALLEY
Refuse Gate
Water Gate
KIDRON VALLEY
N

Chapter 3

A.D. 30

THE HEALING OF THE LAME MAN AND ITS RESULTS

Synopsis

(1–11) Though many healings and miracles were taking place, Luke focuses on the raising of the man born lame because it would somehow more forcefully lead into the power of Jesus to perform miracles.

(12–26) Peter reminds the Jews it was not because of the disciples that the man was healed (12–13) but by the power of the Righteous One whom they had killed and God has raised from the dead (14–15), and it is in His name that health is restored (16–17). The prophets "announced beforehand" Christ should suffer (18). The nation should therefore repent (19) and wait for the restoration "of all things" (20–21). Jesus is both the great Prophet prophesied by Moses and God's Servant (22–26).

3:1 Now Peter and John were going up to the temple at the ninth hour, the hour of prayer.

John. See under 1:13.

Temple. See pp. 109–18.

> **3:2** the gate of the temple which is called Beautiful,

Beautiful Gate. A gate of Herod's temple renowned for its splendor and before which Peter and John healed a lame man (Acts 3:2, 10). Anderson writes:

> There is some uncertainty concerning the identification of the gate but the evidence seems to favor its being taken as the Nicanor Gate (mentioned in the *Mishna*, e.g., Middoth, ii, 3, 6) which led from the court of the Gentiles into the women's court. Judging by the ossuary inscription discovered on Mt. Olivet, the gate owed its existence to a Jew from Alexandria named Nicanor. Josephus refers to this gate as the Corinthian Gate (*Wars*, 5.5.3). It was larger than the other gates of the temple being fifty cubits in height. Also, in contrast to the other gates which were covered with only gold and silver, the Beautiful Gate excelled in splendor because of its Corinthian brass.[41]

> **3:11** all the people ran together to them at the so-called portico of Solomon,

Portico of Solomon. The "portico of Solomon" bordered on the east side of the outer court of the temple, resting on a massive Herodian retaining wall (still largely visible as the lower courses of the present temple-area wall) built out over the Kidron Valley. It may have been so named because of a tradition that Solomon had once constructed a similar east wall and cloister (Josephus, *Jewish War* 5.5.1; cf. *Antiquities* 8.3.9). It was here that Christ walked and talked (John 10:23) and that His disciples seem later to have regularly to have gathered (Acts 5:12, cf. 3:11).[42]

> **3:13** "The God of Abraham, Isaac, and Jacob, the God of our fathers, has glorified His servant Jesus, the one whom you delivered up, and disowned in the presence of Pilate,"

Abraham, Isaac, and Jacob. Acts 3:13 gives the first reference in Acts to "the God of Abraham, Isaac, and Jacob, the God of our fathers." Peter in his sermon at the portico of Solomon uses this phrase to relate the healing of a lame beggar to the covenants of the Old Testament. By his mention of Abraham, Isaac, and Jacob, Peter not only uses a common reference to God as he related to His covenants but also found it necessary to relate the act of God of healing they had witnessed. The cripple had been cured because Jesus was glorified.[43]

But who was it that glorified Jesus? The God of their fathers—Abraham, Isaac, and Jacob. The Jews took great pride in calling these men their fathers, and for Peter to say that the Covenant God Himself glorified Jesus, whom the Jews put to death, would have been to say that the Jews had wandered far from the God of their fathers. This was a powerful indictment indeed.

Peter sought to demonstrate that the Covenant God of the Jews—Jehovah Himself—was accessible only through faith in Jesus Christ, whom the Jews had murdered. Peter could not have insulted Israel any more than he did by making this statement, truthful though it was.

The only other use in Acts of this phrase is found in 7:32, where Stephen, in his great sermon, quotes the words of God to Moses.

Has glorified his servant Jesus. See pp. 72–81.

Servant Jesus. See p. 79.

Pilate. All four Gospels mention Pontius Pilate. The gospel of John gives the most insight as to his character and philosophy. Other information comes from Josephus (*Antiquities Ad Gaium*) and Philo of Alexandria (*Legtio ad Gaium*). Of these, Josephus is the more reliable, for Philo is strongly prejudiced against him. In 1961, a stone tablet was discovered at Caesarea bearing the Latin names of Pontius Pilate and Tiberius, affording archeological proof of Pilate's existence.

Pilate was a Roman citizen, born in Italy. His wife is mentioned in Scripture (Matt. 27:19), but it is unknown if he had children. He was a member of the equestrian or middle class of Romans. His career prior to becoming procurator of Judea is unknown, but he certainly held a series of civil or military appointments before he could become procurator of a province. Pilate was the fifth Roman procurator of Judea, appointed in A.D. 26 by the Emperor Tiberius to replace Valerius Gratus. Pilate's authority over all persons, except Roman citizens, in his area was virtually absolute. However, he allowed the Jews a degree of liberty and self-government. The Sanhedrin retained judicial prerogatives, but death sentences could not be carried out until confirmed by the procurator.

Pilate's political ruin came about through his own folly. A Samaritan fanatic claimed that he knew where, on top of Mount Gerizim, Moses had hidden golden objects pertaining to the Tabernacle. This claim proceeded from ignorance, for Moses had never crossed the Jordan and could not have visited Mount Gerizim. A large number of Samaritans, however, gathered at the base of the mountain, intending to climb to the summit to search for the alleged treasure. Foolishly they were armed, which Pilate interpreted as a threatened insurrection. Many of the Samaritans were killed by Pilate's soldiers. There was never any threat to Rome, and the incident was considered minor. The Samaritans, however, filed a complaint with Vitellius, the governor of Syria and Pilate's immediate superior. Vitellius deposed Pilate and ordered him to Rome for the judgment of the emperor on his poor handling of the affair. So ended Pilate's ten years as procurator.

In Acts 3:13, Peter charges his audience with complicity in the death of Jesus, for although the Sanhedrin had delivered Him to Pilate, the representatives of the people supported the demand for His death. They bore special responsibility for having put pressure on Pilate when he had been inclined to release the prisoner (Luke 23:4, 15–16, 20, 22). God used Pilate, a weak leader, to hand Jesus over to the executioner.

> **3:14a** "But you disowned the Holy and Righteous One,"

Holy One. See p. 76.

Righteous One. See pp. 76–77.

> **3:15a** "But [you] put to death the Prince of life,"

Prince of Life. See p. 77.

> **3:18** "But the things which God announced beforehand by the mouth of all the prophets, that His Christ should suffer, He has thus fulfilled."

Prophets. See p. 91.

Christ should suffer. See pp. 73, 89–90.

> **3:19** "Repent, therefore and return, that your sins may be wiped away, in order that times of refreshing may come from the presence of the Lord;"

Repent. See under 2:38.

Your sins may be wiped away. Some have tried to associate this verse with baptism, but the force of the clause begins with the work of repenting (changing of the mind) and not with the issue of water. J. A. Alexander notes:

> Instead of remission, we have here the stronger figure of . . . obliteration. The Greek verb (*exaleiphō*) is applied by Xenophon to the erasure of a name from a catalogue or roll. It may here denote the canceling of charges against any one, and thus amounts to the same thing with the remission of [sins] 2:38. The metaphor of blotting out occurs several times elsewhere (e.g., Pss. 51:9; 109:14; Isa. 43:25; Jer. 18:23; Col. 2:14).[44]

Times of refreshing may come. See pp. 55, 114.

> **3:20** "and that he may send Jesus, the Christ appointed for you,"

Appointed for you. "Appointed" *(procheirizō)* with the perfect tense could read: "The One who through a process has been chosen, destined before hand" for you, or "The perfect passive participle here bears the sense, "one who stands chosen by God"[45] (see under 2:23).

> **3:21** "whom heaven must receive until the period of restoration of all things about which God spoke by the mouth of His holy prophets from *ancient time.*"

Heaven must receive. See under 1:11.

Period of restoration of all things. See p. 182.

God spoke by the mouth of His holy prophets. See p. 82.

> **3:22a** "Moses said, 'The Lord God shall raise up for you a prophet like me from your brethren;"

Moses. Moses is mentioned some twenty-three times in Acts. In this passage, Peter quotes Deuteronomy 18:15 and the prediction, by Moses, that the Lord had another great prophet in view, the Messiah Jesus. There are important implications in verses 22 and 23 for the Jews of Peter's day:

1. this future prophet would be like Moses,
2. He would be a brother Jew,
3. the nation must give heed to Him in everything,
4. He would speak directly to them, and
5. the soul of anyone who does not pay attention to what He says "shall be utterly destroyed from among the people" (v. 23).

In Acts 6, the name of Moses is used against Stephen and his ministry of "wonders and signs among the people" (vv. 8–10). The testimony of false witnesses is introduced that said he spoke blasphemous words "against Moses and against God" (v. 11) and further, that he said Jesus "will destroy this place and alter the customs which Moses handed down to us" (v. 14). In Stephen's long discourse before the high priest in chapter 7, he refers to Moses thirteen times in his rehearsal of the history of God's dealing with Israel.

At Pisidian Antioch, Paul and Barnabas set forth how God raised up Jesus (13:37), gave through Him forgiveness of sins (v. 38), and "through Him everyone who believes is freed from all things, from which you could not be freed through the Law of Moses" (v. 39). These are powerful and startling words that at first seem to unfairly destroy the Law and the revelation that came through Moses. Instead, Paul is showing the victory over sin, by faith, because of the work of Christ.

The Council at Jerusalem mentions Moses. Some taught, "Unless you are circumcised according to the custom of Moses, you cannot be saved" (15:1), and some Pharisees were also teaching, "It is necessary to circumcise [the Gentiles], and to direct them to observe the Law of Moses" (v. 5). But after much discussion the disciples came to the conclusion that God was setting aside the Mosaic code, giving the Gentiles the Holy Spirit, "just as He also did" to the Jews (v. 8), cleansing the hearts of Gentiles by faith (v. 9), saving Jews and Gentiles by "the grace of the Lord Jesus, in the same way as they also are" (v. 11).

But no matter what the Jerusalem Council and Paul proclaimed, the Jewish leadership would not hear of it. Jewish critics were saying Paul was urging Jews living among the Gentiles to forsake Moses, "telling them not to circumcise their children nor to walk according to the customs" (21:21). In some of Paul's final testimonials, though still honoring Moses, he points out that he taught nothing "but what the Prophets and Moses said was going to take place; that the Christ was to suffer, and by reason of His resurrection from the dead He should be the first to proclaim light both to the Jewish people and to the Gentiles" (26:23). As Acts records Paul's final debate with his Jewish brothers in Rome, he uses the same persuasions concerning Jesus, "from both the Law of Moses and from the Prophets, from morning until evening" (28:23). From what Paul said, "some were being persuaded by the things spoken, but others would not believe" (v. 24).

With the new dispensation of grace, clearly the law of Moses is being set aside in the book of Acts. But in the process, Paul and others used the writings of Moses and other prophets to prove and demonstrate the new dispensation of grace. In this, Paul in no way was destroying the work of Moses, as claimed by his enemies. Yet Paul could see the law was being set aside. In Galatians, he makes it clear that "the Law [of Moses] has become our tutor to lead us to Christ, that we may be justified by faith" (3:24). Thus, the Law of Moses could never make one righteous, for "by the works of the Law shall no flesh be justified" (2:16).

Prophet. See p. 78.

> **3:24a** "All the prophets who have spoken, from Samuel and his successors onward,

Samuel. Mentioned because he is one of the most respected of the Old Testament prophets. R. C. H. Lenski writes: "The prophets after Moses are reckoned from the time of Samuel and his school of prophets. Samuel was not only himself great, he also founded a school of prophets, for which reason the Talmud calls him *magister prophetarum.*"[46]

> **3:25a** "It is you who are the sons of the prophets, and of the covenant which God made with your fathers,"

Covenant which God made with your fathers. In Acts 3:22–36, Peter reminds the Jews that, through the Abrahamic covenant, they are the chosen people of God. God made certain promises through the Old Testament prophets. In Deuteronomy 18:15, Moses prophesied, "The LORD your God will raise up for you a prophet like me from among you, from your countrymen, you shall listen to him." The point is not that Jesus was a prophet but that He was *the prophet* for whom many were looking. He was the One who would appear and set up the Kingdom.

The Jewish people were descendants of the prophets and should have taken seriously their predictions. They were also the beneficiaries of the covenant God had made with Abraham. As his posterity, they could enter into the blessing of the covenant for themselves and receive forgiveness of their sins. God had raised up His Servant Jesus "first" to Israel. This was expected, for God could not ignore His covenant (Rom. 1:16; note in Matt. 15:24 how Jesus restricted His ministry to Israel); yet His responsiveness to their faith (Matt. 8:13) demonstrated that there was room for Gentiles in the divine plan. Scripture presents the prospect that through a believing Israel "all the families of the earth" can and will be blessed (Gen. 12:3). This is what the book of Acts is all about, a transition of the gospel message being passed on to the Gentiles through the Jewish remnant. The covenant God made with Abraham will be fulfilled.

The Abrahamic covenant has four major features. First, God promised to make a great nation of Abraham; this means the Jews as a whole. The Jews are a nation because of their origin in Abraham, Isaac, and Jacob. Second, to this nation God promised a land, Canaan or Palestine. It is irrelevant whether the Jews are in the land or outside the land or whether anyone else may control it. The land of Israel belongs to the Jews by divine decree. Third, those that bless this nation will be blessed and those that curse it will be cursed. This is God's foreign policy to the Gentiles in their relationship to the Jewish people. Fourth, the sign of the covenant for the members of this nation was circumcision, to be performed on the eighth day after birth.[47]

The Jewish leaders knew these promises, but they were so concerned for their positions and the power that they had that they missed the offer of the kingdom by Jesus their Messiah. Peter is prompted by the Holy Spirit to warn the leaders that they are without excuse. They had the Old Testament Prophets and Moses, who had spoken of a Great One who would come. The Messiah had come, just as the Old Testament had prophesied. Peter tells them that the message would now go out to the heathen. Peter was not aware at the time that the gospel would be preached to the Gentiles. It was not until later that God revealed to Peter that His providential plan would include the Gentiles (Acts 10).

Now the kingdom would be put on hold and a period of grace would begin, giving the Gentiles an opportunity to put their faith in Jesus Christ and gain eternal life. Salvation was always by grace through faith in the Messiah, plus nothing.

> **3:26** "For you first, God raised up His Servant, and sent Him to bless you"

For you first. See under 13:46.

Servant. See p. 79.

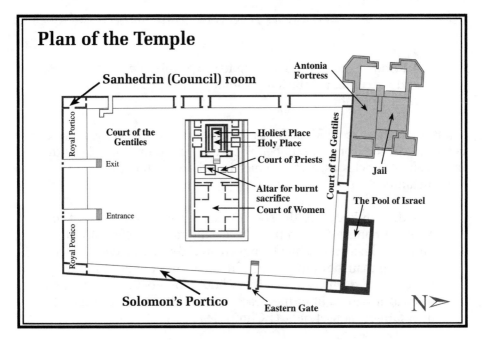

Plan of the Temple

- Sanhedrin (Council) room
- Antonia Fortress
- Royal Portico
- Court of the Gentiles
- Holiest Place
- Holy Place
- Exit
- Court of Priests
- Court of the Gentiles
- Jail
- Altar for burnt sacrifice
- Court of Women
- The Pool of Israel
- Entrance
- Royal Portico
- Solomon's Portico
- Eastern Gate
- N

Chapter 4

A.D. 31

THE FIRST ORGANIZED, OFFICIAL PERSECUTION

Synopsis

(1–22) The temple leaders and rulers react against the preaching of Jesus and the resurrection (1–4). John and Peter are interrogated before the Sanhedrin (4:5–7). Boldly Peter answers that there is no salvation but in the name of Jesus, the one God raised from the dead (8–12). They are threatened and released (13–18). Yet they answer that they cannot stop speaking what they have seen and heard (19–22).

(23–31) Upon seeing Peter and John released, the other disciples praise God and give a unified sermon of thanks for what the Lord was doing in their midst (23–30). They were all filled by the Spirit and "began to speak the word of God with boldness" (31).

(32–37) Because the new Christian community is in physical need, believers share what they have to help one another (32–36). Some even sold land, and the apostles distributed the money (37).

4:1 And as they were speaking to the people, the priests
and the captain of the temple guard, and the Sadducees,
came upon them,

Priests. These are evidently the priests who were officiating in the temple at the time, or some of their number. The active temple priesthood was divided into twenty-four classes, each of which had charge of the temple service for a week at a time.[48]

> David, with Zadok of the sons of Eleazar and Ahimelech of the sons of Ithamar, divided them according to their offices for their ministry. Since more chief men were found from the descendants of Eleazar than the descendants of Ithamar, they divided them thus; there were sixteen heads of fathers' households of the descendants of Eleazar and eight of the descendants of Ithamar, according to their fathers' households. (1 Chronicles 24:3–4)

Ryrie writes that dividing the priests into twenty-four groups meant that each group would serve two weeks in each year. The way the Jewish year was divided meant that their service would gradually move around the calendar. This arrangement was reinstituted after the exile and continued until the Jewish War.[49]

Day-to-day duties were assigned by lot. This is how Zacharias came to enter the temple to burn incense before the Lord in Luke 1:9. During the observance of festivals, the number of priests was increased, as the labors to be performed were greater. It is possible that the feast of Pentecost had not yet terminated at the time the priests accosted Peter and John.[50] The priestly work changed little. The duties prescribed in the Pentateuch are mentioned by Scripture writers of centuries later. Duties included:

In the Holy Place: to burn incense on the golden altar, morning and evening; to clean and trim lamps and light them every evening; to put the bread of the Presence on the table every Sabbath.

In the Court: to keep the fire continually burning on the altar of burnt offering, to clear away ashes from the altar, to offer the morning and evening sacrifices, to bless the people after the daily sacrifice, to wave different portions of the sacrifice, to sprinkle the blood and put various parts of the animal upon the altar and see to their burning, to blow the silver trumpets and the Jubilee horn in festival seasons.

Generally: to inspect unclean persons, especially lepers and, when so warranted, to declare them clean; to administer the oath of purgation to a woman accused of adultery; to appraise things dedicated to the sanctuary; to instruct the people in the law; to act as a high court of appeals in any difficult case; in war to address the troops before battle.[51]

Captain of the temple guard. This officer of the temple was second in authority only to the high priest. Responsibilities included keeping order in the temple and making sure sentries were on watch at night. The captain had a body of levitical temple police under his command, effectively making him a sort of police chief. Josephus mentions this office several times. For example:

> (294) Now, those that kept watch in the temple came hereupon running to the captain of the temple, and told him of it; who then came up thither, and not without great difficulty, was able to shut the gate again. (*War of the Jews*, 6.5.3)

> (409) At the same time Eleazar, the sons of Ananias the high priest, a very bold youth, who was at that time governor of the temple, persuaded those that officiated in the divine service to receive no gift or sacrifice for any foreigner. . . . (410) and when many of the high priests and principal men besought them not to omit the sacrifice which it was customary for them to offer their princes, they were not prevailed upon. These relied much upon their multitude, for the most flourishing part of the innovators assisted them, but they had the chief regard to Eleazar, the governor of the temple." (*War of the Jews*, 2.17.2)

> (131) whom Quadratus ordered to be put to death: but still he sent away Ananias the high priest, and Ananus the commander [of the temple], in bonds to Rome, to give account of what they had done to Claudius Caesar." (*The Antiquities of the Jews*, 20.6.2)

In Luke 22:52 we read that "Jesus said to the chief priests and officers of the temple and elders who had come against him, 'Have you come out with swords and clubs as you would against a robber?'" The best explanation for this text is that the temple guard was divided into companies. Each company had a commander. Yet there was one captain who was chief in command.[52]

Sadducees. Sadducees, from the Hebrew *Tsaddaqim*, traced their lineage to Zadok, the high priest during the reign of David. Shortly after the captivity, the sect arose within the priesthood, while the Pharisee sect had its beginnings among the scribes. The Sadducees were fewer in number and held less spiritual authority than did the Pharisees, but they held the political power. Cecil Roth explains that the Sadducees were "recruited especially from the priesthood, backed up by the aristocracy and landowners."[53] The Sadducees did not survive the destruction of Jerusalem in 70, since their power was political. Once the power structure was destroyed, so was the sect.

Doctrinally, they held only to the canonicity of the Torah, discarding the oral tradition as nonauthoritative. They were stricter legalists even than the Pharisees and harsher in their judgments. They struggled to keep the temple system in the forefront. They did not believe in spirits nor in an afterlife. These doctrines put the Sadducees strongly at odds with the Pharisees.[54] Undoubtedly, had the Sadducees been greater in number than the Pharisees, the Pharisees would not have been allowed to continue, but as it remained, the struggle for power continued until the nation was destroyed. While the Pharisees and the Sadducees sparred with Jesus, they sought not only to destroy Him but also to destroy the credibility of the other sect among the people.

The Sadducees' disbelief in the resurrection and their legalistic righteousness were major points of contention with Christ and with the early church later. They, like the Pharisees, sought to keep the Jewish house in order so as not to incur the wrath of Rome. Christ's claims as Messiah and King greatly disturbed them. The Sadducees and Pharisees felt so threatened by Christ and His message that in the end they united long enough to destroy Him. In Acts, the Sadducees grow jealous of the apostles' power and charisma (5:17). As leaders in the Sanhedrin they presided over the trial of Paul (23:1–10).

> **4:2** being greatly disturbed because they were proclaiming in Jesus the resurrection from the dead.

Resurrection. See pp. 73–74.

> **4:5** And it came about on the next day, that their rulers and elders and scribes were gathered together in Jerusalem;

Rulers. Normally members of the Sanhedrin are referred to as "the high priests, the elders, and the scribes," but here Luke uses the more impressive term *rulers*. R. C. H. Lenski says Luke has in mind the group normally called the "high or chief priests." *Rulers* fits them in a special way since they had the leadership in the Sanhedrin, Caiaphas being the presiding officer who had the executive power in his hands. There is no reason for including lay rulers who were not priests in this first group."[55]

Elders. Jewish elders were heads of family and tribe who were leaders in the synagogues. Some of them were among the seventy members of the Sanhedrin. They were closely associated with the priestly hierarchy and were guardians of tradition. Generally they stood with the Pharisees, Sadducees, scribes, and chief priests against Christ and His church.

These elders were present at the questioning of Peter and John (Acts 4:5, 8, 23). They participated in the mob indignation at the stoning of Stephen (6:12) and were accomplices in the plot to take Paul's life (23:14). Later, they brought formal charges against Paul and sought his condemnation (24:1; 25:15). The Jewish elders are not to be confused with the elders of the church, even though the same Greek word *presbyteros* is often used to identify both. Context dictates the distinction.

Josephus observes that it was "forbidden to slay any man, even though he were a wicked man, unless he had been first condemned to suffer death by the Sanhedrin."[56] And thus the elders were valuable allies to any who would seek to bring condemnation to the church. It is also worthy of note that it was not simply imprisonment of Christians that the elders and the others sought. They sought to stamp out the new church's leaders through the death penalty.

Scribes. The Scribes (Heb. *sopherim;* Gk. *grammateus*) appear in Acts 4:5, along with the rulers, elders, and those of high priestly descent, at the questioning of Peter and John. In 6:12 they are stirred up against the message of Stephen; however, in 23:9 they defend Paul against the Sadducees because of their belief in the resurrection of the dead.

The scribal heritage can be traced to the renewal of emphasis on the law during the time of Ezra, shortly after the Babylonian captivity. Many scribes were Pharisees and lawyers as well. They were scholastics who worked in government and as experts on texts. They were repositories of tradition.[57] With their level of knowledge of the Scriptures, they, if anyone, should have recognized Messiah when He came. But, on the contrary, they opposed the Christ because His message trampled their hermeneutic of righteousness and threw down their traditions. They supported Paul in Acts 23 because Paul appealed to the resurrection, and that drew the ire of the Sadducees.

> **4:6** and Annas the high priest was there, and Caiaphas and John and Alexander, and all who were of high-priestly descent.

Annas. F. F. Bruce identifies Annas as "the senior ex-high priest,"[58] and Matthew Henry calls him "president of the Sanhedrin."[59] It is interesting that Annas is referred to in Acts 4:6 as "high priest," for he held that power in all but title. Annas came to power as a high priest in A.D. 7, appointed by Quirinius, the governor of Syria. A master at playing power politics, he was forced to resign the high priesthood in 14 and was no longer recognized by the Roman government. However, his family held the position off and on over subsequent decades, and Annas was always a controlling influence. The nation regarded him as high priest, whatever Rome said.[60] Just weeks after questioning Jesus,

Annas faces Peter and John in Acts 4:6. Ironically, Jesus had suggested that Annas question His disciples to learn His teachings (John 18:21).

Luke 3:2 identifies both Annas and Caiaphas as high priests at the beginning of the ministry of John the Baptist. John 18:13–24 explains that Annas is the father-in-law of Caiaphas. Jesus is first taken to his house upon His arrest. It was Annas who questioned Jesus and sent Him bound to Caiaphas.

Technically, only one person at a time held the position of high priest, so the references to Annas as high priest in conjunction with Caiaphas can be confusing. Caiaphas was high priest by Roman law, Annas by popular opinion of the Jews."[61] Merrill Unger observes that "his great age, abilities, and influence, and his being the father-in-law of Caiaphas made him practically the high priest, although his son-in-law held the office."[62]

Caiaphas. Caiaphas, the son-in-law of Annas, became high priest shortly after Annas' resignation in A.D. 14, and he held this position until he was deposed in about 38. Josephus unfolds the procession of the high priesthood from Annas to Caiaphas:

> This man [Valerius Gratus] deprived Ananus of the high priesthood, and appointed Ismael, the son of Phabi, to be high priest. He also deprived him in a little time, and ordained Eleazer, the son of Ananus, who had been high priest before, to be high priest: which office, when he held it for a year, Gratus deprived him of it, and gave the high priesthood to Simon, the son of Camithus; and when he had possessed that dignity no longer than a year, Joseph Caiaphas was made his successor.[63]

Acts 4:6 presents Caiaphas in the high priestly line, but as noted above (see "Annas" under 4:6), Luke identifies both Annas and Caiaphas as high priest in Luke 3:2. While Annas was recognized generally as the high priest, Caiaphas officially was given that role by the Roman authorities. Thus, Annas and Caiaphas, with John and Alexander, pressed the case against Peter and John.[64]

Caiaphas was earliest identified in Luke 3:2 as high priest during the beginning of John the Baptist's ministry. Next, he is seen conspiring to kill Jesus in John 11:49 (cf. Matt. 26:3). John records Caiaphas's prophecy that Christ would die for the nation. Finally, in Matthew 26:57 and John 18, Caiaphas is present and active at the trial of Jesus.

John. There is no way to be certain, but this may be the Jonathan who was the son of Annas, the high priest after Caiaphas. Little is known with certainty about John.

Alexander. The identity of Alexander is uncertain. Horatio Hackett writes, "It is improbable that he was the 'Alexander' mentioned in Josephus (*Antiquities*, 18.8.1), who was a brother of Philo and Alabarch of the Jews in Alexander."[65] If this was the same man, he might have been present in the Sanhedrin as a guest.

> **4:8** Then Peter, filled with the Holy Spirit, said to them: "Rulers and elders of the people,"

Filled with the Holy Spirit. See pp. 162–64.

> **4:10b** "by the name of Jesus Christ the Nazarene, whom you crucified, whom God raised from the *dead*."

The Nazarene. See p. 72.

Whom you crucified. See under 2:23.

Whom God raised from the dead. See pp. 73–74.

> **4:11** "He is the stone which was rejected by you, the builders, but which became the very corner stone."

The stone. The imagery of Christ as the stone of stumbling and the cornerstone is important to New Testament soteriology. It originates in Psalm 118, of which verse 22 is quoted here. The final verses of this song are particularly messianic: "O LORD, do save, we beseech Thee" (v. 25a); "Blessed is the one who comes in the name of the LORD" (v. 26a), and "The LORD is God, and He has given us light" (v. 27a). New Testament passages with this motif include Matt. 21:42; Mark 12:10; Rom. 9:32; Eph. 2:20; 1 Peter 2:6, 8.

> **4:12** "And there is salvation in no one else; for there is no other name under heaven that has been given among men, by which we must be saved."

Saved. See under 2:40.

> **4:15** they had ordered them to go aside out of the Council,

Council. The Sanhedrin (Gk. *synedrion*) was the Jewish supreme court. Most often referred to as "the council," the Sanhedrin was composed of seventy elders, scribes, and high priests, both Pharisee and Sadducee. They had jurisdiction over both legal and spiritual matters throughout Israel.

During Roman rule, the Sanhedrin lost its absolute authority, though Rome allowed a generous home-rule jurisdiction by the council. Only in certain cases would Rome intervene. The Sanhedrin could not execute the condemned but had to appeal for judgment to the procurator in the case of Jesus (John 18:31). This was a dramatic reversal from the past, when even the powerful Herodian kings were "forbidden to slay any man, even though he were a wicked man, unless he had first been condemned to suffer death by the Sanhedrin."[66]

Despite its loss of prestige and power as the council for a subject people, the Sanhedrin retained the power to play a large part in the persecution of the early church. This authority lasted until the destruction of Jerusalem, when all the Sanhedrin was deposed. In the book of Acts, the Sanhedrin, time after time, hears cases regarding the various apostles as the Jewish leaders seek to silence their message to the extent of killing the messengers. Evidently Roman authorities looked the other way at the killing of Stephen, which was technically by mob violence rather than judicial action, and perhaps others. Herod, under prerogatives granted to him as king, did have the power to kill James (Acts 12:2) and seek the life of Peter (Acts 12:3–4).

The Sanhedrin presented the most accurate picture of the aristocratic sentiments toward the church. The Jewish leadership sought to maintain not only their traditions but also their political stability under Rome. They foresaw that the gospel message endangered their rabbinic traditions, and they recognized that the gospel message would have political impact.

Since the membership of the council was so varied, one could have expected less unity in its opposition to the church; however, it is rather amazing to the extent that Jewish leaders could set aside bitter divisions among themselves in their common quest to destroy the gospel.

> 4:23 And when they had been released, they went to their own companions and reported all that the chief priests and the elders had said to them.

Chief priests. See under 4:6, 15.

Elders. See under 4:5.

> 4:25 "who by the Holy Spirit, through the mouth of our father David Thy servant, didst say,"

By the Holy Spirit. See under 1:2.

Our Father David. See under 1:16.

4:27 "For truly in this city there were gathered together against Thy holy servant Jesus, whom thou didst anoint, both Herod and Pontius Pilate, along with the Gentiles and the peoples of Israel."

Holy Servant Jesus. See p. 79.

Whom thou didst anoint. See under 10:38.

Pontius Pilate. See under 3:13.

4:28 "to do whatever Thy hand and Thy purpose predestined to occur."

Thy Purpose. The Greek *boula* can be translated "will" or, especially when used of God, "decree." In Acts 20:27, *boula* describes the whole decree of God concerning the gospel. He told the Ephesian elders, "I did not shrink from declaring to you the whole purpose *(boula)* of God." Describing this new message of the gospel, even Gamaliel advised, "if this plan *(boula)* or action should be of men, it will be overthrown" (5:38).

Predestined to occur. See under 2:23.

Herod. The reference is to Herod Antipas, who was a younger son of Herod the Great (Matt. 2:1; Luke 1:5). Upon his father's death, Antipas, the younger son, became tetrarch of Galilee and Perea. He is the Herod who put to death John the Baptist (Matt. 14:1–12; Mark 6:14–29). Lenski well notes:

> Note that the verb "there were gathered" is repeated and put into the emphatic forward position. For the striking feature of the killing of Jesus was this very coalition of his foes, notably Herod and Pilate, who actually again became friends in this strange way. Who would have thought it possible? But it occurred "of a truth"—it actually did. And "in this city," the last place in the world where one would have thought it possible for Jews and pagans, a Jewish king and a pagan ruler, to combine against Jehovah and his Messiah.[67]

4:30 "the name of Thy holy servant Jesus."

Thy holy servant Jesus. See p. 79.

4:31 they were all filled with the Holy Spirit.

Filled with the Holy Spirit. See pp. 17, 162.

4:33 giving witness to the resurrection.

Giving witness. See under 1:8.

Resurrection. See p. 73.

4:36 And Joseph, a Levite of Cyprian birth, who was also called Barnabas by the apostles (which translated means, Son of Encouragement),

Barnabas. Acts tells us only that Joseph was a Levite born in Cyprus. The apostles changed his name to Barnabas, which means "son of exhortation or encouragement" (4:36). Tradition says he was one of the larger body of seventy disciples sent out by Jesus (Luke 10:1–12).

During the explosive growth in the early church, there is great need for members with both spiritual maturity and financial substance. Barnabas has both, and a willing heart to use them. Historically, Levites had no share in the land (Num. 18:20–21; Deut. 18:1–2), but the ancient tribal land laws disintegrated in the Assyrian and Babylonian captivities. Barnabas owns a plot of land, sells it, and gives all of the profit to the apostles for the care of those in need (4:34–37).

Barnabas had enough influence among the Jerusalem disciples to overcome the natural fears of the Christian community toward their former enemy Saul. Barnabas sponsors Saul to the apostles (9:27). He explains how Saul has been speaking "out boldly in the name of Jesus" at Damascus (v. 27) and now is witnessing in Jerusalem (v. 28).

Approximately twelve years later, the gospel has spread in a roundabout way from Phoenicia, to the island of Cyprus, and back to the mainland to Antioch. A large number believe. When the Jerusalem church hears what is happening, they dispatch Barnabas to Antioch to see if the conversions are genuine. Barnabas confirms the work of the grace of God and stays to urge the new converts to "remain true to the Lord" (11:19–23).

Since there was a large Gentile population at Antioch, Barnabas knew Saul was the right man for the city. Saul could speak the language of the non-Jews. Barnabas journeyed to Tarsus, found Saul, and brought him to Antioch. Together, they stayed for a year and met with the church and "taught considerable numbers" (v. 26).

With Saul, Barnabas took a contribution from the Antioch elders to relieve famine-stricken believers in Judea (v. 30). Several years later, he and Paul are set apart by the Antioch congregation as a church-planting mission team (13:2). This commissioning launches Paul's first missionary journey along with his companions Barnabas and John (Mark), their helper (v. 5). From this time on, both men hold the title of apostle, though they are not numbered with the Twelve (14:14).

On this first mission trip, the two apostles make a profound impression, especially among the citizens of Lystra. Barnabas is called by the superstitious crowds "Zeus," maybe because of his imposing height. Saul (now Paul) is called "Hermes" (the messenger of the gods) because "he was the chief speaker" (v. 12).

Paul and Barnabas's first missionary journey is a relatively short circuit that begins and ends in Antioch. Both men then appear at the Jerusalem council of the apostles to argue "what signs and wonders God had done through them among the Gentiles" (15:12). With Peter's help, they convince the rest that the Lord is indeed reaching toward the nations. Both men are commissioned by the apostles and the whole Jerusalem church to return to Antioch (v. 22). The disciples Judas and Silas are their companions.

The second missionary journey is launched but no longer with Paul and Barnabas as a team. Barnabas characteristically argues to give John Mark a second try after he abandoned them on their first trip. Paul refuses and departs with Silas for Syria and Cilicia (13:39–41). Barnabas and John Mark go to Cyprus, and Paul and Silas departed for Syria and Cilicia (vv. 39–41). On this separation, Ryrie notes that Barnabas's continued interest in John Mark rescued the young man from possible uselessness.[68] Horatio Hackett concludes:

> It deserves to be remarked that this variance did not estrange these brethren from their work or occasion any permanent diminution of their regard for each other. In 1 Cor. 9:6, which was written after this occurrence, Paul alludes to Barnabas as a Christian teacher who possessed and deserved the fullest confidence of the churches.[69]

As far as is known, Paul and Barnabas never minister together again, but their mutual friendship and spiritual purpose remains unbroken. Barnabas is continually mentioned in Paul's letters (1 Cor. 9:6; Gal. 2:13; Col. 4:10).

Tertullian (c. 160–c. 215) believed that Barnabas wrote the Epistle to the Hebrews. Though this cannot be substantiated, the view has some merit. G. B. Stevens writes:

> As a prominent member of the Jerusalem Church and a disciple of the primitive apostles (cf. ii. 3), Barnabas might naturally write to his fellow-believers in Palestine to warn them against lapsing back into Judaism. Moreover, as a Hellenist from Cyprus, Barnabas might be supposed to possess the requisite literary qualifications for writing such an epistle, and as a Levite he might, not unnaturally, have the familiarity with the details of the Levitical worship and the keen interest in it which the epistle so frequently displays.[70]

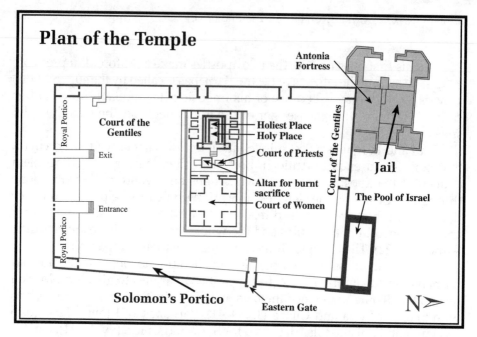

Plan of the Temple

Antonia Fortress

Royal Portico

Court of the Gentiles

Exit

Entrance

Royal Portico

Holiest Place
Holy Place

Court of Priests

Altar for burnt sacrifice

Court of Women

Court of the Gentiles

Jail

The Pool of Israel

Solomon's Portico

Eastern Gate

N

Chapter 5

A.D. 31

PROBLEMS IN THE CHURCH; PERSECUTION OUTSIDE

Synopsis

(1–11) The sharing of goods and income naturally brought some disciples into the limelight. The couple Ananias and Sapphira wanted the praise but were unwilling totally to commit proceeds from the sale of their land to the Lord. So they lie about giving the whole amount (1–3) and are struck dead for lying to the Holy Spirit (4–10). Great reverence for God comes on the church as a result (11).

(12–42) With "signs and wonders" multiplying, thousands are healed through the instrumentality of the apostles (12–16). Disciples are again placed in prison by the high priest (17–18), but they are released by an angel that instructed them to speak "the whole message of this Life" to the people (19–20). Instead finding the prisoners escaping, the officers of the prison found them teaching (21–26). Taken before the Sanhedrin, Peter and the apostles proclaim the gospel and argue, "We must obey God rather than men" (28–33). Though not a disciple, Gamaliel, the respected teacher of the law, counsels the Sanhedrin to leave the disciples alone, or

"you may even be found fighting against God" (34–39). The disciples were flogged and ordered to stop teaching in the name of Jesus. However, the apostles "kept right on teaching and preaching Jesus as the Christ" (40–42).

5:1 But a certain man named Ananias, with his wife Sapphira, sold a piece of property,

Ananias and Sapphira. Ananias ("Jehovah is gracious") and Sapphira ("beautiful, pleasant") were a husband and wife in the Jerusalem church. They, along with many others, sold possessions or property and gave it to the disciples to help support the growing church.

Their deception about holding back some of the money while saying they had given it all had dire consequences. Benevolence ministry grew as fast as did the baby church. This was not a form of Christian communism, and no one was required to sell and turn over all things to the church, but many did so to meet the needs of those who lacked the basic necessities of life. These donations were made on a strictly voluntary basis. If they had simply given the amount they wished, they would not have sinned. Their sin lay in their deceptive display of self-glorification. They wanted to give the appearance of a self-denying lifestyle to be highly esteemed. In so doing, they lied to God in the person of the Holy Spirit. Their lie and hypocrisy led to divine judgment. Merrill Unger comments:

> The offense of Ananias and Sapphira, according to the average standard of human morality, was not a heinous one. They had devoted a large sum to charity; they had defrauded no one but had simply retained their own and then denied the fact. The following considerations are offered in explanation by Whedon (*Com.*, ad loc.): "1. The divine Spirit being present with unparalleled power in the church, the sin, as Peter says (vv. 3, 4) is *directly against Him.* 2. The reason for this selection was to present and record at the *beginning* of the Christian church a representative and memorial instance of the just doom of the *hypocrite.* This couple were deliberate, positive, conceited, and intentionally *permanent hypocrites.* Their death was God's declaration to all future ages of the true deserts of all deliberate *hypocrites* in the church of Christ."[71]

Firmly displayed in this passage is an affirmation of the Trinity. Peter charges Ananias with lying to the Holy Spirit (v. 3) and totally equates that act with lying to God (v. 4). Lying to the Holy Spirit is identical is lying to God, for the Holy Spirit is God.

> **5:12** And at the hands of the apostles many signs and wonders were taking place among the people; and they were all with one accord on Solomon's portico.

Signs and wonders. See pp. 64–69.

Solomon's portico. See under 3:11.

> **5:17a** But the high priest rose up, along with all his associates (that is the sect of the Sadducees)

Sadducees. See under 4:1.

> **5:19a** But an angel of the Lord during the night opened the gates of the prison

An angel of the Lord. With twenty references to angels, the book of Acts has a defined teaching on the subject. An angel of the Lord releases Peter and others from the prison in Jerusalem. Stephen refers to revelations of the angel of the Lord to Moses (7:30, 38). An angel speaks to Philip (8:26), to Cornelius (10:3) and again, an angel unchains Peter when he is thrown into prison for the second time (12:7, 8). An angel was directly involved in the death of Herod because he allowed the crowd to ascribe to him godlike qualities (12:22–23). Paul witnesses to his sailing companions how an angel spoke to him in a vision and promised they would all be spared from the terrible storm they were in (27:23).

> **5:20** "Go your way, stand and speak to the people in the temple the whole message of this Life."

The temple. See p. 109.

This life. By the time referred to in Acts 5, the gospel was exploding in its impact throughout the region of Jerusalem and especially in the city. Were the conversions and changed lives so dramatic that no one could deny the reality of the confessions of faith?

The test of this would come as the apostles continued to minister "many signs and wonders" that "were taking place among the people" (Acts 5:12). These signs were apparently healings performed around the colonnade on the east side of the outer court of the temple. With all this dramatic evidence of the Lord's presence, and because the conversions were so explosive, some people dared not associate with the disciples (5:13).

Nevertheless, multitudes of men and women were coming (5:14), to such an extent that many sick were laid out in the streets so that Peter's mere passing shadow falling on them would heal (5:15). Thousands poured into the temple area.

The high priest and the Sadducees could stand this religious outpouring no longer, and they arrested Peter and the other disciples. However, during the night an angel (5:19–20), released Peter and the others and spoke these words: "Go your way, stand and speak to the people in the temple the whole message of this *Life*" (Gk. *zōa*). Correctly, the New American Standard Bible capitalizes *Life*. The sense seems to be, "this new way of Life." E. H. Plumptre writes, "The use of the demonstrative pronoun *(tautas)* is significant. The 'life in Christ' which the apostles preach is that eternal life which consists in knowing God (John xvii.1), and in which the angels are sharers."[72] *Stand* is an aorist passive participle *(stathēntēs)* and can mean "hold your ground, or stand firm." It suggests a dogged steadfastness in the face of opposition.[73] Simon J. Kistemaker summarizes:

> When crowds of people forsook Jesus during his ministry, Jesus asked the twelve apostles, "You do not wish to leave too, do you?" Then Peter ... said, "Lord, to whom shall we go? You have the words of eternal life" (John 6:67–68 NIV). These words, then, convey the message of salvation—eternal life through the resurrection of Christ. ... The Sadducees rejected the doctrine of the resurrection, yet the apostles publicly proclaim it as "the full message of this new life." (NIV)[74]

For example, Peter comes down hard on the "men of Israel" and accuses them of murder and adds that they disowned (denied) the Holy and Righteous One (3:14), even putting "to death the Prince of life, the one whom God raised from the dead, a fact to which we are witnesses" (3:15). Jewish believers are shocked to hear of Gentile conversions. But Peter assures them that the Gentile believers are receiving the "same gift" of the Holy Spirit upon belief (11:17). The apostles and other brothers accepted Peter's words and added, "Well then, God has granted to the Gentiles also the repentance that leads to life" (11:18). At Pisidian Antioch, Paul pronounces judgment upon his synagogue hearers with the fact that Israel should hear the gospel first. But he points out that in repudiating the gospel his Jewish hearers are being judged unworthy "of eternal life." So he will go to the Gentiles (13:46). "When the Gentiles [in the synagogue] heard this, they began rejoicing and glorifying the word of the Lord; and as many as had been appointed to eternal life believed" (13:48). R. C. H. Lenski notes:

> Not all of those who had come to the synagogue on that Sabbath but only those "who were such as had been ranged in order for life eternal" believed. *Tassō* is a military term that means to draw

up in rank and file and is then used generally for placing in an
orderly arrangement and then to appoint. . . . By their own fault
the Jews are out of the [rank]; by God's grace these Gentiles are in
it. Again the contrast: the Jews regard themselves unworthy of
eternal life; these Gentiles are in line for eternal life.[75]

> **5:21b** Now when the high priest and his associates had
> come, they called the Council together, even all the Senate
> of the sons of Israel,

The senate. This is the Sanhedrin. The word *Sanhedrin* refers to the
function of the body sitting together and taking counsel; while *gerousia* [senate]
indicates its dignity as being composed of the presbytery. "Sons of Israel" is
a dignified version of "of the people."[76] See also under 4:15.

> **5:22** But the officers who came did not find them in prison;
> and they returned, and reported back.

Officers. This definition does not rightly describe the word *yparetai*, which
is better translated "underlings." These club-carrying temple police were
Levites who moved about in large groups, keeping order in the crowds that
would flood into the area on ceremonial and feast days.

> **5:24** Now when the captain of the temple guard and the
> chief priests heard these words, they were greatly
> perplexed about them as to what would come of this.

Captain of the temple guard. See under 4:1.

Chief priests. See under 4:6, 15.

> **5:30** "The God of our fathers raised up Jesus, whom you
> had put to death by hanging Him on a cross."

Raised up Jesus. See pp. 73–74, under 2:7.

Jesus, whom you had put to death. See under 2:23.

> **5:31.** "He is the one whom God exalted to His right hand as
> a Prince and a Savior, to grant repentance to Israel, and
> forgiveness of sins."

He is the one whom God exalted to His right hand. See p. 75.

Prince. See p. 77.

Savior. See p. 73.

Repentance. See under 2:38.

Forgiveness of sins. See under 2:38.

> **5:32** "And we are witnesses of these things; and so is the
> Holy Spirit, whom God has given to those who obey Him."

We are witnesses. See under 1:8.

So is the Holy Spirit. See pp. 125–26.

[Holy Spirit] given to those who obey Him. See p. 135.

> **5:34a** But a certain Pharisee named Gamaliel, a teacher of
> the Law,

Pharisee. The Pharisees, from the Hebrew *Perushim* ("seceders or separatists"), were the dominant Jewish sect during the time of the New Testament and essentially the only major sect to survive through their relationship to rabbinic Judaism. Their origin can be traced back to shortly after the captivity. At a time in which the scribes and priests were essentially one and the same, there arose strong disagreements between the two. The scribes leaned to strict keeping of all of the Old Testament and the oral tradition. The priests based their theology only upon the Torah, not considering the Writings and the Prophets to be canonical. The divisions were so deep that two new groups were born from the scribes and priests. The Pharisees drew followers from among the scribes, while the Sadducees drew from among the priests. Merrill Tenney describes the Pharisees as "the separatists, or Puritans of Judaism, who withdrew from all evil associations and sought to give complete obedience to every precept of the oral and written law."[77]

The primary opposition to pharisaic philosophy came from the Sadducees.

Two parties had thus developed, Sadducees looked to the temple for instruction and sacrificial worship; Pharisees sought enlightenment wherever it might be found. Sadducees were essentially conservative, recruited from the priesthood and aristocracy; Pharisees were more eclectic in thought and the backgrounds of its members. Sadducees supported the absolute monarchy and the hereditary high priesthood; Sadducees tended to be democratic. Gradually, the one party came to be known after the priestly house of Zadok, ancestors of the Hasmonaeans, as *Zadokim,* or Sadducees, while the others were given the name of *Perushim* (Pharisees), or Seceders.[78]

To deepen further the division between Pharisee and Sadducee, the Pharisee believed in a spiritual world of angels and resurrection whereas the Sadducee did not. This point of dissension became supremely prominent during Jesus' earthly ministry and the time of Acts.

The Pharisees had depended upon their oral traditions, along with an intense legalism, as a means of righteousness. They also sought to maintain the *status quo* politically, respecting the authority of Rome. These issues became major points of contention between Christ and the Pharisees, as Christ dethroned their traditions and preached a righteousness that was simply through belief in Him. He proclaimed Himself King. All of this enraged the Pharisees to the extent that they had Jesus killed. This controversy continued into the book of Acts and even heightened as Paul elaborated on the nature of righteousness as a gift of God and as coming from the same Jesus Christ, whom the Jews, including the Pharisees, had murdered.

However, Christians could appeal to the Pharisees for support in one area, the hope of the resurrection. Paul's use of this appeal in Acts 23 demonstrates the intensity of the Pharisee-Sadducee disagreement.

Gamaliel. His name means "reward of God." He was a grandson of the famous doctor of the law Hillel. Representing a liberal wing of the Pharisees, he opposed the more orthodox interpretation taught by the lawyer Shammai. Here in 5:33–40, he warns the Sanhedrin not to persecute the disciples lest they find themselves to be fighting against God (v. 39). If the new message of the resurrected Messiah is not from the Lord, "it will be overthrown" (v. 38). Paul acknowledged Gamaliel as his early teacher (22:3). Since Gamaliel was so respected, he was called "Rabban, our teacher." *The Mishnah* says of him: "Since Rabban Gamaliel the Elder died there has been no more reverence for the Law, and purity and abstinence died out at the same time" (Sota 9.15).

> **5:36a** "For some time ago Theudas rose up, claiming to be somebody;"

Theudas. The name means "false teacher." He was an insurgent mentioned along with Judas of Galilee by Gamaliel at the arraignment of Peter and the apostles before the Sanhedrin. Josephus records an incident centered on an insurgent by the name of Theudas. Gamaliel's comment *"claiming to be somebody"* is in line with Josephus's account. This "Theudas" was an alias, his true name being *Simon*, a slave of Herod's who claimed to be king. By assuming the name Theudas, he was better able to conceal his servile origins.[79]

Josephus records the following concerning Theudas:

(97) Now it came to pass, while Fadus was procurator of Judea, that a certain magician, whose name was Theudas, persuaded a great part of the people to take their effects with them, and follow him to the river Jordan; for he told them he was a prophet, and that he would, by his own command, divide the river, and afford them an easy passage over it; (98) and many were deluded by his words. However, Fadus did not permit them to make any advantage of his wild attempt, but sent a troop of horsemen out against them; who, falling upon them unexpectedly, slew many of them and took many of them alive. They also took Theudas alive, and cut off his head, and carried it to Jerusalem. (99) This was what befell the Jews in the time of Cuspius Fadus's government.[80]

However, the Theudas of Josephus's account and the Theudas mentioned in Acts 5:36 are probably not the same man. The Theudas that Josephus records acted at least ten years after the delivery of Gamaliel's speech whereas the Theudas of Acts is mentioned as being before Judas of Galilee, whose revolt occurred in A.D. 6. The name *Theudas* was not uncommon, even among insurgents. One Theudas led a rebellion in the time of Augustus, another fifty years later during the reign of Claudius.

In one mode of thought reconciling Luke's account with Josephus, Hackett accords, somewhat illogically, the truth to both accounts. He contends that Luke's Theudas must be Simon, the slave of Herod:

First, this Simon, as he was the most noted among those who disturbed the public peace at that time, would be apt to occur to Gamaliel as an illustration of his point; secondly, he is described as a man of the same lofty pretensions . . . ; thirdly, he died a violent death, which Josephus does not mention as true of the other two insurgents; fourthly, he appears to have had comparatively few adherents, in conformity with Luke's about four hundred; and lastly, his having been originally a slave accounts for the twofold appellation, since it was very common among the Jews to assume a different name on changing their occupation or mode of life. It is very possible, therefore, that Gamaliel speaks of him as Theudas, because, having borne that name so long at Jerusalem, he was best known by it to the members of the Sanhedrin; and that Josephus, on the contrary, who wrote for Romans and Greeks, speaks of him as Simon, because it was under that name that he set himself up as king, and in that way acquired his foreign notoriety.[81]

5:37a "After this man Judas of Galilee rose up in the days of the census,"

Judas of Galilee. He is the second insurgent mentioned by Gamaliel at the arraignment of Peter and the disciples before the Sanhedrin. Josephus records the events of his rebellion. Judas was born in Gamala in Lower Gaulonitis. The title *of Galilee* means either that he subsequently lived in Galilee or because the province of Gamala was included in Gaulonitis. His seditious acts were committed in A.D. 6, shortly after the birth of Christ. Judas of Galilee must be distinguished from another insurrectionist named Judas who appeared ten years earlier.

The "census" Gamaliel mentions included a tax levied on the Jews from Emperor Augustus. Judas led a revolt against paying this tax.

> (118) Under [Archelaus's] administration it was that a certain Galilean, who name was Judas, prevailed with his countrymen to revolt; and said they were cowards if they would endure to pay a tax to the Romans, and would, after God, submit to mortal men as their lords. This man was a teacher of a peculiar sect of his own, and was not at all like the rest of those their leaders.[82]

Eventually this rebellion was squashed and many who followed Judas were captured and crucified. The fate of Judas was never revealed. Those not captured were scattered by Coponius, procurator of Judea, and Quirinius, proconsul of Syria.

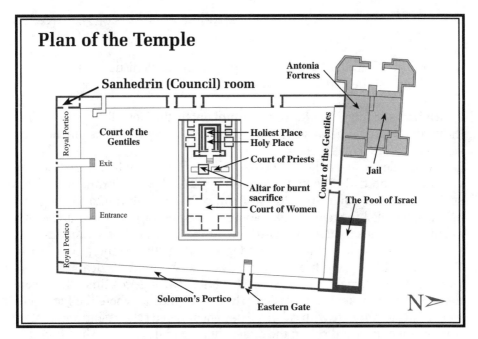

Plan of the Temple

Antonia Fortress

Sanhedrin (Council) room

Royal Portico

Court of the Gentiles

Exit

Entrance

Royal Portico

Holiest Place
Holy Place
Court of Priests

Court of the Gentiles

Jail

Altar for burnt sacrifice
Court of Women

The Pool of Israel

Solomon's Portico

Eastern Gate

N

Chapter 6

A.D. 31 (Exact time uncertain)

THE SELECTION OF DEACONS; STEPHEN BEFORE THE SANHEDRIN

Synopsis

(1–7) Problems of charity, especially for poor Christian widows, began to develop in the community of believers (1). The disciples urged a selection of seven men, full of the Holy Spirit and wisdom, who would take care of the problem, in order that the apostles could continue teaching the word of God (2–4). The congregation accepted the idea and put forth seven men (5) who were then prayed over and approved by the apostles (6). The disciples were then free to continue to teach, "and the word of God kept on spreading" with many being saved, including "a great many of the priests [who] were becoming obedient to the faith" (7).

(8–15) Though not of the twelve apostles, Stephen was a key disciple who was "performing great wonders and signs" (8). He met tremendous opposition from Jewish immigrants (9–10), so much so, that false accusers said that he had blasphemed Moses and God (11). Taken before the elders, scribes, and the Sanhedrin, he was further accused of religious treason (12–14). Stephen held his ground and stood with supreme confidence before these men with "his face like the face of an angel" (15).

6:1b a complaint arose on the part of the Hellenistic Jews
against the native Hebrews,

Hellenistic Jews. There arose "a complaint by the Hellenistic Jews against the native Hebrews, because their widows were being overlooked in the daily serving of food" (Acts 6:1).

The Hellenists were Jews who had been influenced when Alexander the Great conquered the Persian empire in 332/331 B.C. Alexander and his successor broke down the old national, political, cultural, and religious barriers, establishing new Greek colonies and cities, rapidly spreading Koine or common Greek by the intermarriages of the Greek with the Asiatics.

According to Josephus, Alexander's relationship to the Jews both in Palestine and in Alexandria was friendly. After Alexander's death, the Jews were under Ptolemaic influence until 198 B.C. During this time, they were treated with consideration, particularly in Alexandria, where the Ptolemies were trying to compete with Athens. They encouraged scholarship and writers from every nation and set up the largest library in the world. They founded learned societies and established schools to teach the Greek culture and language. It was this influence that led the Alexandrine Jews in the third century to translate the Bible into Greek.

The Ptolemaic influence over Palestine ended with their defeat by the Seleucids in 198 B.C. The Seleucids gained control of the selection of the high priesthood, which allowed some Hellenistic influence to penetrate. However, when the Seleucids tried to force their way of life, the Jews resisted and the Maccabean War was begun in 168 B.C.

The entrenchment of Hellenism can be seen more readily among the Alexandrine Jews, especially among some of their philosophers such as Philo, who adopted the allegorical interpretation, which led to the sacrificing of the truth in the Old Testament on the altar of pagan philosophy.

There is a theory that the Hellenists referred to in Acts 5 are Gentile Greeks, not Jews. This is not likely because (1) the context of Acts 1–5 is the spread of the church among Jews in Judea; (2) the Gentiles being admitted into the church marked a new phase that begins in Acts 10–11; (3) the later conflict of the church regarding the admission of the Gentiles without circumcision (Acts 15) would have been pointless if the Gentiles were admitted in the church at its inception."[83]

The Hebrews spoken of in Acts 6:1 refer to the Israelites. The name *Hebrew* is a constant reminder of their pilgrimage across the desert to the Promised Land. A Hebrew was of pure Hebrew stock and had retained the language and traditions of his ancestors. Unlike Jews who had become Hellenized, the Hebrews considered themselves to be special and did not want to associate with anyone outside their society.

Even though there were great differences between Hellenists and Hebrew Jews, God in His sovereignty brought these two groups together in the first body of believing Christians. It was now up to the disciples to ensure that equality was established and maintained. The walls of division must come down. The disciples moved with great speed in choosing seven men to make sure everyone was treated equally. The disciples knew that if the church was going to grow there must be equality among members of all backgrounds.

> **6:2** And the twelve summoned the congregation of the disciples and said, "It is not desirable for us to neglect the word of God in order to serve tables."

Congregation of the disciples. Congregation *(plēthos)* simply means a crowd or company. This crowd is comprised of the disciples *(mathētēs)*. The definition of *mathētēs* usually has in view a learner, pupil, or apprentice,[84] though in a broad sense it could simply mean an adherent or follower. More in line with what the Bible usually means by *mathētēs* would be to imply that this "crowd" was not only listening to the Word but also studying and analyzing it. They may have attended lectures about Christ, His death and resurrection, and what it all meant.

To serve tables. See p. 50.

> **6:3** "But select from among you, brethren, seven men of good reputation, full of the Holy Spirit and of wisdom, whom we may put in charge of this task."

Select. The Greek *episkeptomai* can mean "to look at, examine, or inspect."[85] This is not a vote, but an examination of the most able candidates to do the work.

Full of the Holy Spirit. See pp. 28, 62.

> **6:4** "But we will devote ourselves to prayer, and to the ministry of the word."

The ministry of the word. *Ministry* in Greek is the noun *diakonia* that is related to the verb *diakoneō*, "to serve."

> **6:5b** and they chose Stephen, a man full of faith and of the Holy Spirit, and Philip, Prochorus, Nicanor, Timon, Parmenas and Nicolas, a proselyte from Antioch.

Stephen. (Acts 6:5) Stephen first arrives on the scene of Scripture during a disturbance in the infant church. By this time, the church would have easily been more than 8000 (cf. Acts 2:41; 4:4) and probably much larger. Coordinating the care for the widows has become an overwhelming job. Some Hellenistic Jews' widows were being neglected each day in the food rations (Acts 6:1). The apostles realized that their main ministry should be study, teaching, and prayer (Acts 6:2, 4). Therefore, the solution was to have the congregation choose seven administrators who were wise, of good reputation, and Spirit controlled (Acts 6:3).

Stephen is distinguished as "a man full of faith and of the Holy Spirit" (Acts 6:5). Stephen and the other men were Hellenistic Jews whose native language was Greek. He had lived with Gentiles in other parts of the Roman Empire. Many scholars believe that this was the birth of the office of deacon (Phil. 1:1; 1 Tim. 3:8). The men were approved by the apostles, and the ceremony of "laying on of hands" was conducted (see pp. 386–92).

As a legate of the apostles, Stephen showed miraculous sign gifts to validate his message among the people (Act 6:8). Since the problem with the widows is never again mentioned, the seven must have successfully worked out the logistics and delegated the work. Stephen almost immediately became an outspoken apologist (Acts 6:7).

His evangelism put him into conflict with members of the Synagogue of the Freedmen, Hellenistic Jews from Alexandria and Cyrenia [in North Africa], Cilicia, and Asia. They took offense and argued with him (Acts 6:9), but Stephen's spirit and wisdom in the Scriptures were too much for them. So they brought a false accusation of blasphemy against him (Acts 6:11), and Stephen was brought before the Sanhedrin. In Stephen's defense we see Stephen's incredible insight into God's plan.

Stephen was accused of speaking incessantly against the holy place and the law (Acts 6:13) and of saying that Jesus the Nazarene would destroy this place and alter the customs Moses had handed down (6:14). These accusations, although false, probably had a grain of truth. Stephen, a Hellenistic Jew, had probably not grown up under the stringent legalism of native Judaism. This made him more objective, better able to discern the message of Christ without the mental grip of tradition. W. T. Dayton observes that Hellenists also brought the charges against Stephen. These Jews may have been hungry for the traditional faith they believed he was attacking.

> They would be bitter in their opposition against anything that seemed to undermine their traditional faith. It is probably not necessary to believe that Stephen had gone as far as Paul in concluding that the law was no longer the final, binding code that he had formerly thought it to be. He had, no doubt discovered the inadequacy of a mere formalism and ceremonialism in the temple

worship. Perhaps Christ's own words regarding the temple (John 4:20–24; Mark 13:2) had shown him that true worship of God is not confined to the temple. He may also have seen in the words of Jesus the transitory nature of the law. Jesus had defended laxity in matters of tradition and had observed a freer attitude toward Sabbath observance (Mark 2:15f.; 7:1–27; Luke 15:1f.). He had even superseded the law on rare occasions (Matt. 5:33–37; Mark 10:2–12). Stephen, with his broad background in the Dispersion, maintained this important aspect of Jesus and held open the way for the future advance into Gentile evangelism.[86]

Both native Hebrews and some Hellenists would see such an attitude and teaching as a threat to the Jewish religion and to them as a distinct people. Stephen, having a vital relationship with the living Lord, realized the types and shadows involved in the temple ceremony and that the law was a poor substitute to a relationship with the Righteous One they had crucified. This was nothing new since, throughout Jewish history, prophets had been killed by the "stiff-necked" Jewish leaders (7:32).

The latter part of Stephen's defense directly addressed the charges against him. Using the words of the prophets, he pointed out that God and his true worship were much too big to be confined to the temple (7:48–49). His hearers could not keep the law they so tenaciously clutched (v. 53). "The fundamental difference between Stephen and his opponents," Tenney wrote, "lay in that he judged the OT history from the prophetic viewpoint while they represented the legalistic view."[87] Stephen was not against the law and Moses; he simply saw how Christ fit into the progressive revelation of Jewish history. On the other hand, the leaders of Israel were so locked into their legalistic observance of the law and self-righteousness that they were blinded to the truth. They could not see how the prophets had foreseen Christ the Righteous One (v. 52).

Stephen charged them with betraying and murdering the Righteous One their own prophets had said would come and with not keeping the law they so strongly defended. That was all their consciences could take. They "cried out with a loud voice, and covered their ears, and they rushed upon him with one impulse" (v. 57). They then drove him from the city and stoned him. Stephen's response was very similar to that of Christ. He asked the Lord Jesus to receive his Spirit and to forgive his attackers (vv. 58–60). Before his stoning, Stephen was given divine grace to see Christ in all his glory at the right hand of God (v. 55).

Stephen's witness and stoning had two significant effects on the early church. His martyrdom initiated a persecution that scattered believers. Wherever they went, they shared their faith (as Philip in Acts 8).

These saints, after hearing Stephen's message, would understand more clearly how the gospel fit into God's overall plan. And Saul, later the apostle Paul, witnessed the tremendous wisdom and conviction of Stephen. He stood and watched the grace of this great saint of God as he prayed for those who stoned him. This must have had a tremendous impact on Paul. It prepared him for his miraculous conversion on the road to Damascus and future ministry to the Gentiles.

Philip. Also called "the evangelist" (Acts 21:8), Philip is first mentioned in Acts 6 as one of the seven administrators of care to the widows. Though the personal noun *deacon* is not used, the general noun *diakonia* ("ministry, service, office") is in the passage, along with the verb *diakoneō* ("to administer, serve"). Therefore, this is often regarded as the first appointment of deacons.

Under one of the first periods of persecution, Philip and some of the disciples scatter and go forth preaching the word (8:4–5). Philip chooses to go to Samaria and proclaim Christ. Earlier, Jesus had made followers in Samaria (John 4). Though the Samaritans were a mixture of other races and Jewish blood and did not worship in Jerusalem, they believed in the coming of Israel's Messiah (John 4:25). Because of Christ's visit to the area, it was softened for Philip's witness.

Philip performs miracles (v. 6) that caused people to attend to his message. Demons are driven out of those possessed, and the paralyzed and lame are healed (v. 7). So "there was much rejoicing in that city" (v. 8) as Philip preaches the good news about the kingdom of God and the name of Jesus Christ (v. 12).

Though a multitude receives the Lord under Philip's preaching, the Holy Spirit is withheld. Peter and John arrive to ascertain the truthfulness of the conversions and help them receive the Holy Spirit (v. 15). In certain cases, the apostles had to confirm that those making professions of faith were genuine. The apostles were given the earthly authority to signify what was happening to be real. Charles Ryrie explains in his study notes:

> Though the Samaritans had been baptized in water (v. 12), the gift of the Holy Spirit was delayed until Peter and John came and laid their hands on them. Normally the Spirit is given at the moment of faith (10:44; 19:2; Eph. 1:13). In this instance, however, it was imperative that the Samaritans be identified with the apostles and the Jerusalem church so that there would be no rival Samaritan Christian church.[88]

Philip also encounters in Samaria the magician Simon, who claims to be "someone great" (v. 9). By his illusions he amazes the crowds, who shout that he has the power of God (v. 10). Simon professes belief in Christ and is baptized. He asks for power to do the miracles taking place (v. 13). Peter rebukes him: "Your heart is not right before God. Therefore repent of this wickedness of yours, and pray the Lord that if possible, the intention of your heart may be forgiven you" (vv. 21–22). Simon asks the apostles to "pray for me yourselves, so that nothing of what you have said may come upon me" (v. 24). There came to be a heretic named Simon Magus, who troubled the church. It cannot be known whether this Simon became the heretic, but it is a strong possibility.[89]

Philip is most well-known for bringing to the Lord the Ethiopian on the Gaza road (8:26–40). Finding the man reading the prophet Isaiah, Philip explains the prophecy about the Messiah being the Lamb of God (vv. 32–33). The Scriptures say Philip "preached Jesus to him" (v. 35). This passage is important because it shows that, early on, the disciples recognized the substitutionary work of Christ as predicted by the prophets. When Philip had finished explaining the Isaiah text, the eunuch believed (v. 37). After baptizing the eunuch, who was a court official of Candace, queen of Ethiopia (v. 27), Philip was "snatched" away by the Spirit. But his dynamic work continued: Philip found himself at Azotus, site of the Philistine city of Ashdod. As he passed through, he kept preaching the gospel to all the cities, until he came to Caesarea" (v. 40), which was his traditional birthplace. Approximately twenty-two years later in 53, Luke records staying with Philip in his home (21:8).

Interestingly, Luke notes that Philip has four daughters who become prophetesses (21:9). However, it is Agabus, not these women, who prophesy Paul's coming arrest in Jerusalem (v. 10). The answer to why the Lord sent Agabus from Judea instead of giving the warning to these prophetesses (vv. 11–14) seems to come in Paul's later epistles. The apostle says that women can prophesy (1 Cor. 11:5). But prophesying in the early church context was more exhortation and teaching, "that all may learn and all may be exhorted" (14:31). But he adds that women are to keep silent in the church setting and are not to speak (nor prophesy, 14:34–35). Likely the apostle encouraged older women to teach younger women, as he sets forth in Titus 2:3–4.

Though not mentioned by name, Philip is probably included with Paul's friends who ministered to him while he was imprisoned in Caesarea, awaiting his hearing. The Roman commander Lysias keeps the apostle "in custody and yet hav[ing] some freedom" (24:22–23). Merrill Unger theorizes that Luke ministered to Paul during his imprisonment at Caesarea (Acts 27:2), so details of Philip's early evangelistic ministry could have come from Philip himself. Tradition says that Philip fled with other Jewish Christians in 65, when the Jewish revolt broke out in Caesarea.

Prochorus, Nicanor, Timon, Parmenas, and Nicolas. These men, with Philip and Stephen, take care of the logistics of feeding the widows. They fade into obscurity after apparently successfully completing the task given to them. They are never spoken of again.

[Syrian] Antioch. Located on the Orontes River and near the Mediterranean Sea, Antioch was founded around 300 B.C. by Seleucus I as one of sixteen cities so named. The name celebrates his victory over Antigonus at Issus (310 B.C.). The city fell to the Roman general Pompey in 64 B.C. and was declared a free city. It was the capital of the Roman province in Syria and became the third largest city in the empire.

In Acts the city plays a major role as the place where followers of Christ are first called "Christians" (11:26). Nicolas, one of the first seven deacons, was from here (6:5), as was Barnabas. At the death of Stephen in Jerusalem, many disciples flee to this city (11:19). Here a concentrated effort first is made to reach the Greeks for Christ (11:20). The city becomes a vital launching point for trips of the disciples. Paul is brought here from Tarsus to begin his teaching ministry because of the large population of Greeks, with whom he related well (11:25–26).

Because the Gentiles receive Jesus as Savior in large numbers, Jews visiting Antioch are offended and proclaim the requirement of circumcision for salvation. The church at Antioch sent leaders to Jerusalem, including Paul and Barnabas, to settle the issue (15:1–2). James the Elder concluded, "Therefore it is my judgment that we do not trouble those who are turning to God from among the Gentiles" (15:19). A letter was sent from the Jerusalem leadership freeing the Gentiles from keeping the Jewish ceremonial law and urging them to abstain from eating food served to idols, from fornication, from what is strangled, and from blood (v. 20). When the letter arrived in Antioch, "they rejoiced because of its encouragement" (v. 31).

Antioch maintained a long-standing Christian witness. Fourth-century archaeological excavations have uncovered ruins from some twenty churches.

> **6:6b** and after praying, [the apostles] laid their hands on them.

Laid their hands on them. See pp. 402–8.

> **6:8** And Stephen, full of grace and power, was performing great wonders and signs among the people.

Great wonders and signs. See pp. 64–69.

> **6:9** But some men from what was called the Synagogue of the Freedmen, including both Cyrenians and Alexandrians, and some from Cilicia and Asia, rose up and argued with Stephen.

Synagogue of the Freedmen. The Freedmen, or Libertines (KJV), were probably descendants of Jews taken captive by Rome during Pompey's conquest of Jerusalem in 63 B.C. In this battle the Jews held the nearly impregnable temple mount for three months, until one Sabbath (or, according to another account, the Day of Atonement), their fortifications were stormed and its defenders massacred.[90] Those not killed were taken captive. Some of them gained their freedom. As freedmen, they continued to live in Rome, but they built at their own expense a synagogue at Jerusalem, which they frequented when in that city.[91]

Here we read that "some men from what was called the Synagogue of the Freedmen, *including* both Cyrenians and Alexandrians, and some from Cilicia and Asia, rose up and argued with Stephen." A. T. Robertson clarifies the references to these various geographical areas as to synagogues of Jerusalem. There were synagogues of the Cyrenians and the Alexandrians, for example. Philip would have been appearing as a Hellenist preaching Christ in all of them. There is a grammatical question because of the Greek construction as to whether there are five synagogues in view here or two made up of persons from multiple city backgrounds.[92]

In any case, the freedmen, being Jews, were opposed to the message of Stephen and, unable to cope with the Spirit with whom Stephen was speaking, they incited false witnesses against Stephen, leading ultimately to his martyrdom.

Synagogue. The word is a compound of two words, *syn*, "together," and *agō*, "to lead or to bring together." Some see synagogues as places of meeting and prayer in various Old Testament passages. But probably the first-century meeting house concepts arose in the Babylonian captivity. There, away from the destroyed temple site in Jerusalem, the rabbis met for study, worship, and socialization. With the return under Ezra, synagogues were formed throughout Palestine. With a certain dispersion of the Jews from the Maccabean times until the Roman period, synagogues could be found from Israel to Africa, Babylon, Greece, and Rome. The synagogue became the place where tradition was preserved, where new religious ideas were shared, and where social customs were scrupulously guarded.

This is why in the book of Acts Paul found such resistance to the gospel because the local Jewish communities were strongly linked by a fear of innovation. Also, the legalistic system of salvation through keeping the law of Moses blinded many. Yet many Jews heard Paul speak in the synagogue and responded to the gospel.

The synagogue plays a key role in Acts. The synagogue is mentioned more often in Acts than in the rest of the New Testament combined. In the synagogues children were taught and the Jews found a certain community and a place of social protection. Ideas were discussed, Pharisaism was kept alive, legalism was made religion, and resistance to change was nurtured.

Paul went first to the synagogues when he arrived in a city to bring the gospel to the Jews (Acts 14:1). On the Sabbath, guests at synagogue customarily were invited to speak (13:14; 18:4). Paul preached, debated, and even argued (18:4). He devoted "himself completely to the word, solemnly testifying to the Jews that Jesus was the Christ" (v. 5).

At Corinth, the Jews in the synagogue "resisted and blasphemed" his message (18:6). Paul answered, "Your blood be upon your own heads! I am clean. From now on I shall go the Gentiles." When he departed, a man named Titius Justus, who lived next door to the synagogue, took Paul in. The leader of the synagogue, Crispus, also became a believer. Paul stayed there, next to the synagogue, and taught for a year and a half. At Achaia, more Jews turned on Paul. The local governor Gallio refused to hear the charges of the Jews and turned them away from the place of indictment, the judgment seat (v. 16). Here too, the leader of the synagogue, Sosthenes, became a believer in Christ (v. 17).

Despite opposition, Paul felt compelled to go to the synagogues first and witness to the Jews. This was not done meekly. As was his pattern, Paul spoke with authority and argued logically and biblically for the gospel, by historical account, and by prophecy. Luke notes that Paul customarily attended synagogue (14:1; 17:2), where he reasoned (17:17) and "began to speak boldly" (18:19, 26).

Cyrenians. See under 2:10.

Alexandrians. Jews from Alexandria, Egypt, tended to be intellectual, liberal, and cosmopolitan. Some suggest that the Alexandrine Jews were so sophisticated they philosophized away the messianic hope. If true, this would partly explain their antagonism to the gospel. It is not impossible that the allegorical method of studying Scripture, developed in Alexandria by Philo and others, blunted Old Testament truth and destroyed any concept of messianic prophecy or literal fulfillment of promises. If this was their philosophy, no wonder they could not cope with Stephen's arguments (v. 10).

Cilicia. Cilicia was a country in the southeast corner of Asia Minor, on the Mediterranean coast adjoining Syria. Cilicia lay with Pamphylia on the west, the Amanus Mountains on the east, Lycaonia and Cappadocia on the north, and the Mediterranean on the south. The coastline of Cilicia ran approximately 430 miles. Cilicia was more closely connected with Syria than with Asia Minor. The area was best known for its goat hair industry. The goat hair was used extensively in tents.

From the sixth to the fourth centuries B.C., when most of Asia Minor was under the Persians, Cilicia was an independent kingdom paying tribute to Persia. For a time, it was part of a Persian satrapy. After the conquests of Alexander the Great, through the second century B.C., most of Cilicia was part of the Seleucid Empire. Cilicia was conquered by the Romans in 103 B.C., and all of Cilicia became a Roman province in about 67 B.C. The province was later in the Byzantine Empire and was captured in the eighth century by Arabs. In the eleventh century, it became part of Lesser Armenia. In the fifteenth and sixteenth centuries, Cilicia was in the Ottoman Empire.[93] Major cities of Cilicia during the Roman occupation were Tarsus, Seleucia, and Issus.

Whether the Freedmen included those from Cilicia (Acts 6:9) is debated, but they agreed with the other Jews about the threat posed by Stephen. Stephen's wisdom and understanding confused them. They were unable to counter his witness. So, instead of studying harder or more wisely, accepting what Stephen said, the Cilicians joined the conspiracy to accuse him unjustly.

Christians from Cilica are among recipients of the pastoral letter sent out by the Council of Jerusalem (Acts 15:23). When Paul and Silas visited the churches that they had evidently helped found, Cilician churches were on the itinerary (15:36, 41).

Tarsus, one of the leading cities of Cilicia, was Paul's birthplace. Paul's comments lend evidence to the size and reputation of Tarsus (Acts 21:39). It was "no insignificant city," a common phrase used by orators and writers when referring to major cities. Paul seemed to take a patriotic pride in his home city. Tarsus was famous for its commercial enterprises. It was a land and sea highway hub.

Ryrie notes the precision with which Luke presents references to Cilicia when Paul appeared before the Roman governor of Caesarea. Paul first was asked what province he was from (Acts 23:34–35).

> Roman law required that this question be asked at the opening of a hearing, for Paul had the right to be tried in his home province or in the province where the alleged crime was committed. Tarsus was in Cilicia. Felix was a deputy of the legate of Syria and Cilicia, and so claimed the right to conduct the hearing, whichever choice Paul made. Such a detail is strong proof that Luke was with Paul at the hearing.[94]

The last reference to Cilicia in the book of Acts is found in Acts 27:5, where the coastline is along the path of Paul's voyage toward Rome. It is not long after this that the storms emerge that will eventually shipwreck Paul and his companions on Malta. Mediterranean winds were well known for their ferocity, and knowledgeable sailors hugged the Cilician shoreline for safety and recognizable landmarks.

Asia. See under 2:9.

Nazarene. See p. 72.

> **6:11b** "We have heard him speak blasphemous words against Moses and against God."

Moses. See under 3:22.

> **6:13b** "This man incessantly speaks against this holy place,
> and the Law"

This holy place. See p. 114.

The Law. The Law is respected in the Acts narrative, but it represents the legalistic oppression wielded by Judaism to keep the nation "under the yoke." The Law *(nomos)* is spoken of as "the law of our fathers" (22:3) and as being ordained through Moses by angels (7:53). It is with honor called the Law of Moses (13:39; 15:5) our own law (24:6), and Gamaliel is called a teacher of the Law (5:34). Paul was accused of advocating worship to God contrary to the Law (18:13). The religious discipline of keeping the Law and the new dispensation of grace clashed at the Jerusalem Council and later. Certain believing Pharisees said of the Gentiles, "It is necessary to circumcise them, and to direct them to observe the Law of Moses" (15:5). But Peter argues that God has given Gentiles the same gifts of the Spirit (v. 8), and he adds that Gentile disciples must not be put under a yoke that even the Jews have never been able to bear (v. 10). He reminds the gathering that "we are saved through the grace of the Lord Jesus, in the same way as they also are" (v. 11). With these words, the issue is settled: Jew and Gentile are saved by faith in Christ and not by law keeping!

> **6:14** "for we have heard him say that this Nazarene, Jesus,
> will destroy this place and alter the customs which Moses
> handed down to us."

Nazarene. See p. 72.

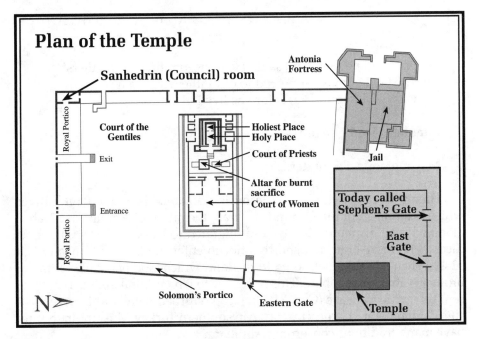

Plan of the Temple

Antonia Fortress

Sanhedrin (Council) room

Royal Portico

Court of the Gentiles

Holiest Place
Holy Place

Exit

Court of Priests

Jail

Altar for burnt sacrifice

Court of Women

Entrance

Royal Portico

Today called Stephen's Gate

East Gate

Solomon's Portico

Eastern Gate

Temple

N

Chapter 7

A.D. 32 (Exact time uncertain)

STEPHEN'S SERMON AND MARTYRDOM

Synopsis

(1–53) Asked by the high priest if he was guilty of plotting the destruction of the temple and the altering of the customs of Moses (1), Stephen begins a lengthy discourse on the spiritual history of the Jewish people through construction of Solomon's temple (2–50). Since he was asked about the temple, he used this occasion to call the men before him "stiff-necked and uncircumcised" and "always resisting the Holy Spirit" as the ancient fathers did (51). He said that this present generation slew the prophesied Righteous One and that they now were "betrayers and murderers" who "did not keep" the Law (52–53).

(54–60) The entire religious leadership in the assembly began gnashing their teeth at him (54). At that moment, Stephen saw Jesus as Lord and as the Son of Man, standing at the right hand of God in glory (55–56). Having stated what he saw to the crowd, they rushed forward and, seizing him, drove him out of the city where they stoned him to death (57–59). His last words were, "Lord, do not hold this sin against them!" (60).

7:2 "And he [Stephen] said, 'Hear me, brethren and fathers! The God of glory appeared to our father Abraham when he was in Mesopotamia, before he lived in Haran,'"

[Stephen] Said. See p. 114.

Mesopotamia. See under 2:9.

Haran. Haran, a city in northern Mesopotamia, is on the Balikh River, which is a branch of the Euphrates. Terah, the father of Abram, and Nahor, along with all his family, left Ur and migrated to Haran (Gen. 11:31). Terah died there and Abram left shortly after to enter the land of Canaan (Acts 12:4). When Abraham left to go to the land which God had called him, his brother Nahor stayed there. This is the city to which Abraham's servant was sent for a wife for Isaac (Gen. 24:40). Jacob returned there for his wives. The site is still inhabited in nearby Haran in southern Turkey. Muslims in the area have many traditions concerning Abraham.[95]

7:4a "Then he departed from the land of the Chaldeans,"

Chaldeans. The name for the land and inhabitants in southern Babylonia is later used to denote Babylonia as a whole. This ancient name is used in Genesis 11:28 to locate the homeland of Abraham. In the tenth century B.C., some Assyrian documents call the land Kaldu and designated it the "Sea-land." The name *Chaldea* in Acts probably simply designates all of Mesopotamia. This is the only New Testament mention. By using the older word, Stephen was possibly reminding his audience more vividly of the origins of Abraham.

7:8 "And He gave him the covenant of circumcision; and so Abraham became the father of Isaac, and circumcised him on the eighth day; and Isaac became the father of Jacob, and Jacob of the twelve patriarchs."

Circumcision. The sign of the Abrahamic covenant (Gen. 17:10), circumcision also had hygienic benefits. It kept the Jews free of many of the genital diseases of the Middle East. More importantly, it became a spiritual symbol for a people set aside and made special.

Abraham. See p. 82; see also under 3:13, 25.

Isaac. Since Ishmael through Hagar was not God's intended son for Abraham, Isaac, born of Sarah, was the link through which the Lord created the Jewish nation. In fact, Jehovah told Abraham that Isaac is "your son, your only son, whom you love" (Gen. 22:2). Stephen reminds the Jews that they are descended from Isaac, not Ishmael.

Jacob. Isaac's son, who will have the twelve sons through which the nation of the Jews will develop (Gen. 25:19–24). At a spiritually low moment in his life, Jacob called upon the "God of my father Abraham" and confessed his unworthiness to the Lord (Gen. 32:9–10). In the form of a man, the Lord comes to him and wrestles with him until daybreak. His name is changed to Israel, meaning "to strive with God" (32:25–32). He is important to the Jews as the father of the twelve tribal founders, whose new name became the nation's. See also under 3:13.

Twelve patriarchs. The tribes of Israel come from these men and their descendants. Jacob prophesies about each son in Genesis 49. The most striking is that through the tribe of Judah the king's scepter will come and not depart (49:10). In this cryptic verse Messiah is called "Shiloh" or "peace-giver." The Jews took great pride in their relationship to these patriarchs.

> 7:9 "And the patriarchs became jealous of Joseph and sold him into Egypt. And yet God was with him,"

Joseph. By being sold into slavery in Egypt by his jealous brothers, Joseph becomes the link of salvation for the tribes because of the famine that swept the Middle East (Gen. 46). Joseph truly learned of God. Toward the end of his life, his brothers begged his forgiveness (50:15–18). Joseph comforts them by saying, "Do not be afraid, for am I in God's place?" (50:19; cf. v. 21). Joseph is frequently depicted as a type of Christ for His royal mercy to His enemies.

Stephen presents Joseph in a light his listeners will not appreciate. Joseph, as mentioned in verse 9, was sold into Egypt by the "jealous" patriarchs. His point is that, even in antiquity, the Jewish nation did not have any problem raising its hand against the Lord's chosen. And even though he was younger than they, God had already testified to the brothers that Joseph was chosen— yet they rejected him. Stephen is showing that repeatedly, Israel has missed God's message and rejected his anointed messengers, until finally they rejected even their Messiah, Jesus. But just as Joseph was rejected by his brothers and later saved their lives, so Jesus can still be Israel's Savior.

This message strikes a cacophonic chord in the hearts of his listeners with the result that these Israelites reject once again both their chance at repentance and salvation and the one who speaks it.

Egypt. Often in Scripture this land is a type for the sinful world. The children of Israel will be released from Egypt by the strong hand of the Lord. Egypt pictures spiritual slavery, moral darkness, and painful servitude. See also p. 203.

7:10b "Pharaoh, king of Egypt;"

King of Egypt. This could be Sesostris II, who could be the one who named a Nile canal (Bahr Yusef) after Joseph in honor and testimony to Joseph's contribution to important public works projects.[96]

7:11a "Now a famine came over all Egypt and Canaan,"

Canaan. At the time of the Exodus, besides the mixture of peoples that are generically called "Canaanites," Palestine was home to the Sidonians, Hivites, Amorites, Hittites, and Jebusites. These peoples looked to a pantheon of gods. *El*, a name that simply means "god," was the head of this hierarchy of gods. His wife, *Asherah*, was the mother goddess.

> **7:14a** "And Joseph sent word and invited Jacob his father
> and all his relatives to come to him,"

Jacob. See under 3:13; 7:8.

> **7:16** "And from there they were removed to Shechem, and
> laid [Jacob] in the tomb which Abraham had purchased for
> a sum of money from the sons of Hamor in Shechem."

Shechem. Shechem is one of the most important sites in Old Testament history and theology. When Abraham entered the land, he went all the way north to this area and encamped at the "oak of Moreh" (Gen. 12:6). Here God renewed His covenant with him, and, in response, Abraham built an altar to the Lord (v. 7). Jacob also raised an altar at Shechem (33:20), and Joseph sought his brothers here (37:12). Here Joshua called for a renewal of the covenant (Josh. 8:30–35). Later, Canaanite worship moved back into this area, though it was holy to the Israelites (Judg. 9:4).

Shechem is one of the most mentioned names in the Old Testament, but in the New Testament it is referred to only here in Acts. But this reference is significant in that it alludes to the fact that, for a price, Abraham now owns a part of the promised land. Piece by piece, his children will be given Palestine as their eternal possession. In the original statement of the Abrahamic covenant, God promised to give "the land which I will show you; and I will make you a great nation" (Gen. 12:1). Stephen refers to this in 7:16 and in verse 45 when he points out that God dispossessed the peoples of Canaan and, through Joshua, drove them out "before our fathers."

Son of Hamor. Though Hamor was the Canaanite ruler of Shechem during the days of Jacob, Stephen in his sermon makes reference to the fact that the family of Hamor goes all the way back to the days of Abraham when he had purchased the plot for the burial of Sarah. A burial site indicated a partial possession of territory for a family that up to that moment had been strangers. The Genesis 23 account is detailed because it outlines how God providentially gave the patriarch a national toehold in the promised land. Stephen reminded his Jewish audience of the land blessing granted them.

> **7:18** "until there arose another king over Egypt who knew nothing about Joseph."

Another king over Egypt. Much debate continues to consider the identity of this new pharaoh. The implication seems to be a major shift in dynasty, of which there are a few during these centuries. This could possibly be Amosis of the Egyptian eighteenth dynasty.[97]

> **7:29** "And at this remark Moses fled, and became an alien in the land of Midian,"

Land of Midian. After the death of Sarah, Abraham took another wife, Keturah, by whom he fathered six children (Gen. 25:1–2). One of them was a son named Midian. His descendants, the Midianites, ranged over an immense arid region lying mostly east of the Jordan and south along the Gulf of Arabah. In Genesis 37 Joseph was sold to a caravan of traders called "Ishmaelites" as children of Ishmael (vv. 25, 28) and "Midianites" as inhabitants of the land of Midian (vv. 28, 36).

Moses fled from Pharaoh to Midian forty years before the Exodus. There, he met the daughters of a "priest" of Midian. One of these daughters of Jethro, Zipporah, later became his wife. Jethro recognized the God of Israel (Jehovah) as supreme and gave Moses sound advice on leadership (Exod. 18, esp. v. 11).[98]

> **7:30a** "And after forty years had passed, an angel appeared to him in the wilderness of Mount Sinai,"

Angel. This is likely the preincarnate Son of God, making a voice appearance as the Angel of Jehovah. The voice speaking from the burning bush identifies Himself as "I AM WHO I AM" (Exod. 3:14). Jesus virtually repeats this before the Jews when He said, "I say to you, before Abraham was born, I am" (John 8:58). With this, He is clearly referring to the Exodus reference.

> **7:36a** "This man led them out, performing wonders and signs in the land of Egypt"

Led them out. The date of the exodus as calculated by conservatives is the reign of Amenhotep II, c.1445–46 B.C.[99]

7:38 "the angel who was speaking to him on Mount Sinai,"

Mount Sinai. This mountain was also referred to as Horeb (Exod. 3:1, 12; 18:5) and is the same mountain where Moses first met with God (via the angel or preincarnate Christ) at the burning bush. Later Moses returned here as he led the children of Israel through the Sinai Peninsula. Here he received the Law from God (Exod. 19:3). Scholars are divided as to the location of Mount Sinai. Tradition and scholarship offer at least four possibilities: (1) Mount Serbal, on Wadi Feiran, (2) Jebel Musa (Mountain of Moses), (3) Jebel Hellal, and (4) Mount Seir in southern Palestine. See *Unger's Bible Dictionary* for a summary of the evidence for each site.

7:40a "[Our fathers] saying to Aaron, 'Make for us gods who will go before us;'"

Aaron. Aaron was the brother of Moses and Miriam. He was born during the captivity but apparently before the death sentence was issued on all the male Israelites born. He was three years older than Moses (Exod. 7:7). When God called Moses to be the deliverer of Israel from the Egyptians, Moses objected that he could not speak well. In response, God designated Aaron as Moses' mouthpiece to the people (Exod. 4:14–16). A good description of what can be discerned about the man was compiled by Steven Barabas:

> In character he was weak and occasionally jealous. He and Miriam criticized Moses for having married an Ethiopian (Cushite) woman, outside the nation of Israel, and complained that Moses was not God's sole spokesman (Num. 12:1, 2). When Moses went up on to Mt. Sinai to receive the tables of the law from God, Aaron acceded to the people's demands for a visible god they could worship. Taking their personal jewelry, he melted it in a furnace and made a golden calf similar to the familiar bull-god of Egypt. Aaron did not remonstrate with them, but built an altar and proclaimed a feast to Jehovah on the morrow, which the people celebrated with revelry and debauchery (Exod. 32:1–6). When Moses returned from the mountain and rebuked Aaron for aiding this abuse, he made the naive answer: "They gave it (the gold) to me, and I threw it into the fire, and there came out this calf" (Exod. 32:24). It may be that Aaron meant to restrain the people by a compromise, but he was wholly unsuccessful.[100]

7:43a "You also took along the tabernacle of Moloch and the star of the God Rompha"

Tabernacle of Moloch. Moloch is an English form for Molech. Molech was a Semitic deity who was particularly delighted in the sacrifice of children. The Jews brought this worship with them and it revived at different times in Jewish history. The levitical law strictly forbade such worship (Lev. 18:21; 20:1–5), but that did not stop the idolatry. Several Jewish kings, including Solomon, encouraged worship of this deity. Josiah attempted to destroy this religion, but it returned under Jehoiakim. The prophets sternly denounced this form of worship. The worship of Molech was the most abhorrent idol worship in Semitic history.

Star of the God Rompha. A star god worshiped by the Israelites during the sojourn in the desert after being released from Egyptian bondage. Stephen uses this idol and Molech to compare the Jews of that time with the Jews who had killed their Messiah. Either generation had God's presence flatly before them; either generation had a multitude of miracles performed before their eyes. Yet both generations turned to another god, the Egyptian Jews to idols, the Jews of Stephen's day to legalism and tradition.

The quotation in Acts is from a version of Amos 5:26, where the star is referred to as *Kiyyun*.[101] Archaeology frequently uncovers zodiac-related images in ancient Jewish buildings and literature, and forms of astrology and horoscopes remained a recurring interest among the people. Kiyyun or Rompha was one of the planets and was one of numerous heavenly beings that drew worship.

7:44a "Our fathers had the tabernacle of testimony in the wilderness,"

Tabernacle of testimony. The tabernacle that Moses had constructed for the wilderness journey testified of the nature of God and of the righteous demands placed upon His people. It showed the judgment of the Lord and His mercy. Its central function was as a setting for the offering of sacrifices.

7:45b "our fathers brought [the tabernacle] in with Joshua"

Joshua. This is the Old Testament Hebrew word translated into Greek, "Jesus." See pp. 72, 179.

7:47 "But it was Solomon who built a house for Him."

Solomon. Solomon's role in building a house for God presents an incredible view of God's sovereignty. Stephen's mention of Solomon as king is ironic, for Solomon should not have been king by human reckoning. He was not the first born of David, but God set him apart to be king (1 Chron. 22:6–10); thus, by the word of the Lord, the improbable came to be. It was improbable that David would not build the temple, but, in God's divine choosing, this task went to Solomon. It was improbable that after having so much evidence of the presence of God in their midst, that Israel would reject Him, yet they did, and this not apart from the sovereignty of God (Rom. 11).

Solomon's building of a temple, rather than leading to a more true worship of God, led to arrogance that God was with Israel alone. As F. F. Bruce observes, "It was rather the state of mind to which the temple gave rise . . . that Stephen reprobated."[102]

This mention of Solomon was one of many indictments Stephen pronounced against the nation—all indicative of the same symptoms: spiritual arrogance. Stephen beseeched them to repent, but rather than repent of their spiritual arrogance, they grew more proud and would not tolerate the words of Stephen any longer.

> **7:52b** "And they killed those who had previously announced the coming of the Righteous One, whose betrayers and murders you have now become."

Righteous One. See pp. 76–77.

> **7:55a** But being full of the Holy Spirit,

Full of the Holy Spirit. See pp. 162–64.

> **7:56** "Behold, I see the heavens opened up and the Son of Man standing at the right hand of God."

Son of man. See p. 81.

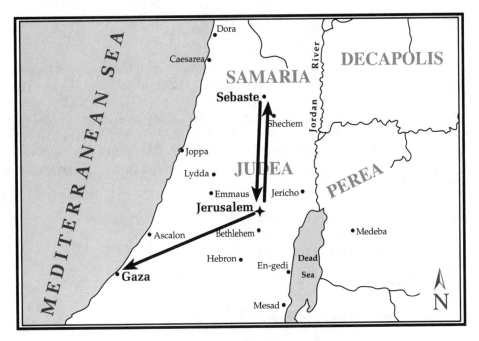

Chapter 8

A.D. 32 (Exact time uncertain)

THE GOSPEL IN SAMARIA;
THE ETHIOPIAN EUNUCH

Synopsis

(1–3) The religious zealot Saul is part of the "great persecution" that now begins against the church in Jerusalem. Thousands scatter through Judea and Samaria.

(4–8) Since Samaria lies north of Judea, it is a natural area for the gospel to spread, including the city of Samaria itself (4–6). The crowds are attentive and marvel at the signs Philip performs (7–8).

(9–25) Simon, who formerly practiced magic, has heard Philip preach the gospel, believes, and is baptized (9–13). Being "amazed" with the miracles, Simon desires the same authority to give the Holy Spirit (14–19). Peter rebukes him for thinking he could obtain "the gift of God with money" (20) and commands that he repent of his wickedness and pray for forgiveness (21–23). Simon appears to repent and asks that Peter pray for him (24). Many villages in Samaria seem to have responded openly to the gospel (25).

(26–40) An angel directs Philip toward the seacoast city of Gaza. On the way, he encounters an official of the court of Candace, queen of Ethiopia (26–28). The Spirit urges Philip to speak to the man, who is sitting in his chariot reading Isaiah 53 and its verses prophesying of Christ as the Lamb who is led to slaughter (29–33). Philip preaches Christ as the Lamb of Isaiah 53, and the man believes (34–37). Philip baptizes the man and is then "snatched" away. The eunuch goes on his way rejoicing before God (38–39). Philip then travels north on the coastal road until he arrives at Caesarea (40).

> **8:1** And Saul was in hearty agreement with putting him to death. . . . And they [believers] were all scattered throughout the regions of Judea and Samaria,

Saul/Paul. See pp. 67–68, 102–3.

Judea and Samaria. See under 1:8.

> **8:5** And Philip went down to the city of Samaria and began proclaiming Christ to them.

Philip. See under 6:5.

City of Samaria. Some scholars believe this was a small town in the territory of Samaria, or the city called Sebaste. The territory of Samaria runs through the heart of ancient Canaan. In 721 B.C., after the fall of the Northern Kingdom, the Assyrian king placed in Palestine colonists from Assyria who, in time, intermixed with some of the remaining Jews. This mixture of races infuriated later generations of pious Jews.

In the city of Samaria, Philip "began proclaiming Christ to them. And the multitudes with one accord were giving attention to what was said by Philip, as they heard and saw the signs which he performed" (vv. 5–6). Many men and women were being baptized (v. 12). Peter and John came from Jerusalem to confirm that what was happening was really of God. As they returned to the capital, they "were preaching the gospel to many villages of the Samaritans" (v. 25). See also pp. 185–86.

> **8:7a** For in the case of many who had unclean spirits,

Unclean spirits. See pp. 94–95.

> **8:9a** Now there was a certain man named Simon, who formerly was practicing magic in the city

Simon. Simon is a Samaritan magician. Church tradition indicates that he may have become a notorious heretic who called himself "Simon Magus." Simon's abilities at performing are so good that many believed his claim to greatness. So he takes a professional and personal interest regarding the impressive new power that has entered the town. This man, who for a long time has practiced fakery, now finds a different art form. The signs and miracles of Philip far exceed anything Simon has accomplished.

Philip, meanwhile, has sent for Peter and John. When the two apostles arrive, they pray for the people, who then receive the Holy Spirit. Simon sees what they are doing and reverts back to paganism and his craft; he asks, "Give this authority to me as well, so that everyone on whom I lay my hands may receive the Holy Spirit" (v. 19). Simon's objective is to add this spiritual power to his inventory of magic tricks. Peter swiftly denounces both his proposition and the man himself. He included not only a denial of the idea but also condemnation of the spiritual state of Simon, from which the idea, had come. Simon probably believes he has done all the outward requirements, so he is "in" with the apostles. Yet, on the inside, he was still in his sins. His answer to Peter reveals not a spirit of sorrow and need, but rather one of terror. Simon realizes the futility of his prayers and asks Peter to intercede for him. Whether Simon truly realizes he is separated from God, or his magic background tells him that Peter is more powerful and his prayers more effective, is not revealed.

Justin Martyr records that Simon was "born at Gitton, a village of Samaria, identified with modern Kuryet Jit, near Nablus. He probably was educated at Alexandria and there became acquainted with the various tenets of the gnostic school. Either then or subsequently he was a pupil of Dositheus, who preceded him as a teacher of gnosticism in Samaria and whom he supplanted with the aid of Cleobius."[103]

8:10b "This man is what is called the Great Power of God."

Great Power of God. Literally the text reads, "This one [is] the power being called great of God." R. C. H. Lenski explains:

> This Simon belonged to a class of charlatans that were rather common at this period, who practiced occult arts in order to impress the people and to gain a following. Much was plain sorcery which was at times combined with a shrewd use of natural laws that were otherwise unknown. The range of their arts extended from the conjuring of demons, dealing with the dead, influencing the gods, to charms for healing, divination, stargazing, and the like. . . . He was certainly successful, for he astonished not only the city but [also the] . . . "nation of Samaria." It is this power of the man among the people as a whole that shows us what the gospel really accomplished through Philip's activity.[104]

8:11 And they were giving him attention because he had for a long time astonished them with his magic arts.

Magic arts. See p. 99

8:12 when they believed Philip preaching the good news about the kingdom of God, . . . they were being baptized,

Kingdom of God. See pp. 51–60, 85–88.

They were being baptized. See under 1:5.

8:13 [Simon] observed signs and great miracles taking place,

Signs and great miracles. See pp. 64–65.

8:14b [The apostles in Jerusalem] sent them Peter and John.

Peter and John. See under 1:13.

8:17 Then they began laying their hands on them, and they were receiving the Holy Spirit.

Laying their hands on them. See pp. 69–71, 402–8.

Receiving the Holy Spirit. See pp. 133–43.

8:25b and they were preaching the gospel to many villages of the Samaritans.

Samaritans. See under 1:8.

8:26 But an angel of the Lord spoke to Philip saying, "Arise and go south to the road that descends from Jerusalem to Gaza."

Angel of the Lord. See under 5:19.

Gaza. Gaza was one of the oldest cities in the world, existing as a Canaanite city before the time of Abraham (Gen. 10:19). In the Old Testament, it was on a hill above a fertile plain about fifty miles southwest of Jerusalem and about three miles south of Ashkelon. It was only a short distance inland from the Mediterranean Sea. Its strategic position along the major coastal trade route connected it to Egypt. It was blessed with fifteen freshwater wells, enough to provide water for fields and flocks as well as for a large populace. It was a Philistine city from the time of Joshua (Josh. 13:3, 4). In fact, it was one of the border cities and the capital of the Philistine confederacy.

Several Old Testament events took place in Gaza. Samson lifted off the doors of the city and carried them to Hebron (Judg. 16:1–3). It was at Gaza that Samson eventually was taken to be imprisoned and humiliated (Judg. 16:21).

In the middle of the eighth century, the prophet Amos proclaimed the Lord's condemnation against Gaza because "they deported an entire population to deliver it up to Edom" (Amos 1:6–7). Nebuchadnezzar (605–562 B.C.) later conquered Gaza and Ashdod (another Philistine city) and transported their kings to Babylon.

The only New Testament reference to Gaza is here in Acts 8:26. Philip is directed by an angel to travel south to the road that led from Jerusalem to Gaza. The Ethiopian proselyte was the first Gentile convert to the Christian faith. The trade route through Gaza was still the normal route from North Africa through Palestine. This Ethiopian eunuch, already a convert to Judaism, is ready for the witness of Philip. After Philip explains that Jesus Christ was the person spoken of in Isaiah 53:7–8, which the eunuch has been reading, he immediately believes and requests to be baptized (Acts 8:36). He would not only take the gospel back to the African continent but also, more importantly, he would take it to the interior of Africa, where the Alexandrine Jews would probably never have reached.

> **8:27b** behold, there was an Ethiopian eunuch, a court
> official of Candace, queen of the Ethiopians,

Ethiopian eunuch. Verse 27 introduces us to "an Ethiopian eunuch, a court official of Candace the queen of all Ethiopians, who was in charge of all her treasure; and he had come to Jerusalem to worship." Bruce writes, "The Ethiopian treasurer was probably a Gentile worshiper of the God of Israel. He is referred to by a term which may have the more general sense of 'chamberlain' or the stricter sense of 'eunuch.'"[105] This man was not only a court official of the queen of Ethiopia (*Candace* was a dynastic title), but he was over all her treasure. This was indeed an influential man.

He probably had just completed a pilgrimage to Jerusalem to worship God when God sovereignly introduced him to the way of salvation. God directed Philip to the southern road descending from Jerusalem to Gaza. Here Philip met the Ethiopian (vv. 26–27). In the sovereignty of God, the Ethiopian was reading Isaiah 53:7, which reads, "He was led as a sheep to slaughter; and as a lamb before its shearer is silent, so he does not open his mouth. In humiliation his judgment was taken away; who shall relate to his generation? For his life is removed from the earth." This gave Philip the perfect opportunity to "preach Jesus" to him, and the Ethiopian, having believed, was baptized. Eusebius understood the historical significance of this event:

> While every day the saving message spread farther afield, some providence brought from Ethiopia, a country traditionally ruled by a woman, one of the queen's principal officers. The first Gentile to receive from Philip by revelation the mysteries of the divine word, and the first-fruits of the faithful throughout the world, he is believed to have been the first to go back to his native land and preach the gospel of the knowledge of the God of the universe and the life-giving sojourn of our Saviour among men. Through him came the actual fulfillment of the prophecy: "Ethiopia shall stretch out her hand to God." (Psalm 68:31)[106]

His baptism in 8:38–39 is the Ethiopian's last appearance in Scripture. The narrative of Luke regarding him breaks off as abruptly as it began. This event beautifully demonstrates the loving sovereignty of God, who reached out to an entire nation through the salvation of one influential leader.

Candace. The name means "Queen or Ruler of Children." *Candace* is not a proper name. It is a title once assumed by the dynasty of the royal family of the Ethiopians, much as *pharaoh* was the title of the Egyptian king and *caesar* was the title of Roman emperors.

The ancient kingdom of Ethiopia lay between Aswan and Khartoum and corresponds to modern Nubia. It was ruled by a queen mother who had the dynastic title Candace and ruled on behalf of her son the king, since the king was regarded as the child of the sun and therefore too holy to become involved in the secular functions of the state.[107]

George Reisner has identified pyramid tombs of the Candaces of Ethiopia constructed from c. 300 B.C. to A.D. 300.[108]

> **8:36b** and the eunuch said, "Look! Water! What prevents me from being baptized?"

Being baptized. In the Gospels the baptism of John was a sign of repentance in anticipation of the coming earthly kingdom. But in Acts the rite is a symbol of the spiritual baptism of the Holy Spirit. See p. 134; see also under 1:5; 11:16.

> **8:40** But Philip found himself at Azotus; and as he passed through he kept preaching the gospel to all the cities, until he came to Caesarea.

Azotus (Ashdod). Ashdod was one of the principal cities of the Philistines. It was located between Ashkelon, which was a seaport, and Ekron along the caravan route between Lydda and Joppa. Today, this would be just south of modern Tel Aviv. The ark of God was carried by the Philistines into the temple of Dagon at Ashdod following their victory at Ebenezer (1 Samuel 5).

Ashdod is the Hebrew name related to a noun meaning "foundation, bottom."[109] The "As" part of the word means fire. In New Testament times, the Greek name of the same city was *Azotus*. Today, Ashdod is a port in Israel through which potash is transported and shipped worldwide from the area of the Dead Sea.

On the coastal Gaza road, Philip witnessed to the Ethiopian eunuch. Following the eunuch's conversion and baptism, Philip "was found" in Azotus (v. 40) after he was miraculously carried away by the Spirit of the Lord (v. 39). Philip did not stay in the region but passed through Azotus, traveling north on the coastal road. He preached in all the seacoast villages until he came to Caesarea (v. 40).

Caesarea. Known as *Caesarea Palaesinae,* the city was on the northern Mediterranean coast on the road from Tyre to Egypt. Its first mention in Acts is here in chapter 8, though the city will play a major role in the drama unfolding later in the book. Named for the Roman caesars, the city was the chief naval base for the Romans. Paul embarked from here to go to his home town of Tarsus (9:30). At Caesarea, Peter proclaimed the gospel to the Roman centurion Cornelius (10:1–48).

After Peter's miraculous release from the Jerusalem jail (12:3–11), he came to Caesarea to escape Herod (v. 19). Paul came to Caesarea several times (18:22; 21:8, 16). He was sent here by the Jerusalem Roman commander for his hearing before Felix and later before Festus and Agrippa (23:23; 26:32). The city was used as a regional headquarters for the authorities ruling over the northern territories. It is from here that Paul began his journey to Rome for his hearing before Caesar (27:1).

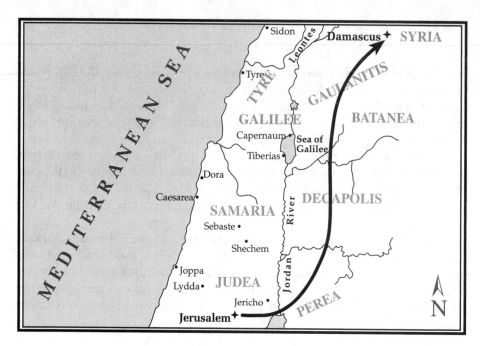

Chapter 9

A.D. 32–35

THE CONVERSION OF SAUL; SAUL'S JOURNEY TO JERUSALEM

Synopsis

(1–19) Saul continues his threats and murder against the disciples of the Lord (1), receiving letters of authority from the high priest to capture men and women who are following Christ and belong "to the Way" (2). On the Damascus road, Jesus appears to Saul, who falls to the ground as he hears the words, "Saul, Saul, why are you persecuting Me?" (3–4). Blinded, Saul is led to Damascus where the Lord in a vision speaks to the disciple Ananias (5–12). The Lord commands him to lay hands on Saul that he may regain sight, though the man is frightened by Saul's reputation for persecuting Christians (13–14). In the vision God assures Ananias that this work is of God and that Saul may be a "chosen instrument of Mine" to reach Gentiles, kings, and the sons of Israel. Saul also learns that he will suffer much for the name of the Lord (15–16). Saul is filled by the Spirit, baptized, and remains with the disciples for several days (17–19).

(20–31) Saul begins almost immediately preaching "Jesus" in Damascus, proving that this One is the Christ (20–22). At Jerusalem, the believers are afraid of him (23–26). Barnabas calms the fears of the apostles, and Saul continues to witness

of Jesus in Jerusalem. However, he is led out of the city down to the seaport of Caesarea and sent home to Tarsus before the Jews can kill him for being a turncoat (27–30). For a brief period the church will enjoy peace, during which it will be strengthened and will continue to increase (31).

(32–43) Peter travels through the Mediterranean coastal area around Lydda and Sharon (32–35) south to Joppa. In this seacoast town, Peter performs one of the most spectacular of apostolic miracles, raising Dorcas (or Tabitha) from the dead (36–37). Kneeling by the dead woman, Peter prays and orders, "Tabitha, arise" (39–40). Tabitha opens her eyes and arises, with the result that many in Joppa believe in the Lord (41–43).

9:1 "Now Saul, still breathing threats and murder against the disciples of the Lord, went to the high priest."

Saul. See pp. 67–68, 102–3.

High priest. See under 4:6.

9:2 [Saul] asked for letters from [the high priest] to the synagogues at Damascus, so that if he found any belonging to the Way, both men and women, he might bring them bound to Jerusalem.

Damascus. Damascus is first mentioned in the book of Acts in 9:3 as Saul, the persecutor of the Way, travels there to arrest certain individuals belonging to what he believes is a heretical sect. The city is located on a plain surrounded on three sides by mountains. The climate is arid, and the city depends heavily on irrigation from the streams running off the Anti-Lebanon and Mount Hermon.

The city of Damascus has a rich biblical history. Archaeological findings indicate that it has been controlled by the Egyptians, Hittites, Arameans, Hebrews, Syrians, Assyrians, Babylonians, and Persians. King Saul fought the Arameans, and David incorporated much of Aram, including Damascus, into his empire (1 Sam. 14:47; 2 Sam. 8:5, 6). Under Rezon, Syria resisted Israel's domination, and Damascus gained independence in about 940 B.C. (1 Kings 11:23–25). After Judah called for Assyrian help against Pekah of Israel and Rezon of Damascus, Tiglath-pileser III (also known as Pul [745–727]) annexed both regions. Never again would Damascus head an independent Aramean state.[110]

At the time of Paul's conversion, the city was probably under Nabatean rule since "the ethnarch under Aretas the king was guarding the city of the Damascenes" (2 Cor. 11:32). It is possible that at this time Damascus was a "free" member of the Decapolis, a chain of ten autonomous cities that coined their own money. Aretas IV, who hated the Romans, would have acceded to the high priest's favor to grant to Saul (Paul) official letters to the heads of the synagogues in Damascus, giving him some authority to arrest the Christians and bring them back to Jerusalem for trial (9:2).

Paul's mission was drastically altered when Christ himself appeared to him and he was temporarily blinded by the glory of the Lord (9:3–6). Because Paul's blindness continued, he entered Damascus by the help of the men traveling with him and did not eat or drink for three days until Ananias laid hands on him (v. 9–17). After his initial conversion, Saul left Damascus and went into the Arabian desert (Gal. 1:17). This incident is not mentioned in Luke's account, but it would fit here between verses 21 and 22 of chapter nine. Paul returned to Damascus (Gal. 1:17) with fuller knowledge and was "proving that this Jesus is the Christ." Christianity took root in Damascus and spread to the surrounding regions.

The Way. Simply as a descriptive noun, the expression *the Way* is used a remarkable number of times in the New Testament. "Way" is the Greek word *hodos* and can be translated "road, highway, path, or journey." But as used in this descriptive fashion, it is pointing to a path, a way of life related to accepting Jesus as the Messiah, thus a commitment, a journey, and a living expression of personal dedication.

The theological concept of the Way begins in Christ's statement in John 14:6: "I am the way, and the truth, and the life; no one comes to the Father, but through Me." Jesus is the only Way; His is the only path to eternal life. The book of Acts, more than any other New Testament writing, focuses on this concept.

The Way is first mentioned in 9:2. It is used as an expression of derision, as Saul enthusiastically sets out to capture and even kill all those trusting in Christ. Saul was "breathing threats and murder against the disciples of the Lord" (9:1) and was asking for letters from the high priest to seek out in Damascus "if he might discover any being 'of the Way.'" And before his Jewish brothers in Jerusalem Paul adds: "I persecuted this Way to the death, binding and putting both men and women into prisons" (22:4).

The expression *the Way* is used in various other contexts in Acts. In one case, a witch with a "spirit of divination" met Paul and Luke. She cried out, "These men are bond-servants of the Most High God, who are proclaiming to you *the way* of salvation" (16:17). Apollos is said to have known "*the way* of the Lord" (18:25) but was taught more accurately by Priscilla and Aquila "*the way* of God" (18:26).

But in the synagogue of Ephesus, "some were becoming hardened and disobedient, speaking evil of *the Way* before the multitude" (19:9). Because of this reaction, Paul "withdrew from them" but continued to teach in the city for two years at the house school of a philosopher or rhetorician named

Tyrannus. From here, the gospel was spreading throughout Asia with such force that the trade in the silver shrines of Artemis was diminishing. Luke tells us, "About that time there arose no small disturbance concerning *the Way*" (19:23). Thousands in the silver trade who made the idols to Artemis, with a single outcry, forced Paul to leave the city for Macedonia. Among those in Ephesus, the Way was despised and hated even more.

Facing Felix, who was the deputy legate of Syria and Cilicia, the apostle Paul pleaded his case, but he also gave his testimony as to how he previously had persecuted those trusting in Christ. With great boldness Paul said, "This I admit to you, that according to *the Way* which they call a sect I do serve the God of our fathers, believing everything that is in accordance with the Law, and that is written in the Prophets" (24:14). Paul called this the "hope in God" (v. 15) with a certainty of "a resurrection of both the righteous and the wicked." Luke says that Felix put off a judgment about the apostle but he was now more informed "about *the Way*" (v. 22). Paul was placed in a loose military confinement there in Caesarea until Festus could hear his case two years later (24:27).

Though not in the same definite sense as used in the book of Acts, the expression "the way" is also mentioned in other epistles. For example, Peter speaks of "*the way* of truth" that is evil spoken of (2 Peter 2:2), and writes about those who have forsaken "*the right way*" (2:15), not having known "*the way*" of righteousness (v. 21).

The expression *the Way* clearly divides the world into three camps—the Jews, the pagans, and those following "*the way* of the Lord" (John 1:23). The Christians were thus marked as those who were out of step with the rest in the Roman culture.

> **9:10a** Now there was a certain disciple at Damascus, named Ananias;

Ananias. Ananias means "protected by Jehovah." He was a Jew of Damascus called upon by the Lord (Acts 9:10) to find a man named Saul from the city of Tarsus. After hearing that he was to lay his hands on this Saul so that he would regain his sight, Ananias remonstrated that Saul was infamous for committing atrocities against Christians (Acts 9:13–14).

In the next verses, we read of the long-suffering patience of God. God explained to Ananias what was to happen to this Saul and what he would accomplish (vv. 15–16). By the obedience of Ananias the world would be given a messenger who would turn it upside down. Obedient, but most likely scared out of his wits, Ananias obeyed. We read in verse 17, "And Ananias departed and entered the house, and after laying his hands on him said, 'Brother Saul, the Lord Jesus, who appeared to you on the road by which you were coming, has sent me so that you may regain your sight, and be filled with the Holy Spirit.'" This man, having gone to Saul with fear and trembling, is the first to acknowledge him as a brother.

Later, when Paul had been chained in Jerusalem (21:33), he asked to speak to the people before being taken off (21:39). To these Jews with whom he was speaking, he began to recount his conversion. His memories of Ananias are both complimentary and truthful (v. 12).

Tradition reports that Ananias became the bishop of Damascus and suffered martyrdom.

> **9:11** And the Lord said to him, "Arise and go to the street called Straight, and inquire at the house of Judas for a man from Tarsus named Saul, *for behold, he is praying.*

Judas. This is the only mention made of Judas of Damascus in Scripture. For his part, where he lived would prove to become more remembered than himself. It was at his house on Straight Street that Paul was lodged after his encounter with the Lord on the Damascus road (9:2–6). "The Street called Straight" ran east and west. It is still one of the main thoroughfares of Damascus, the *Derb el-Mustaqim.* In Roman times, it had colonnaded halls on either side and imposing gates at each end. Presumably it was as well known in antiquity as Regent Street in London or Michigan Avenue in Chicago is today.[111] It was about one English mile long and about 100 feet wide. According to Merrill Unger, "It is not quite straight now, nor is its architecture imposing."[112]

Tarsus. For Paul to claim Tarsus as his birthplace impressed both Jew and Gentile. The city has a rich antiquity that goes all the way back to Genesis. "And the sons of Javan were Elishah and Tarshish" (10:4). The Jewish scholar Josephus believes that ancient Tarshish became Tarsus.

Tarsus appears sporadically throughout history. The Assyrians ruled here in the ninth century B.C. The Medes and Persians followed. Before Christ's time, the Greeks and then the Romans controlled the region. Around 171 B.C., Jewish settlers made their way to the city. Tarsus was visited by Mark Antony. The Emperor Augustus granted it special consideration because it was the home town of Athenororus, his teacher and lifelong friend. Some Tarsian Jews had been Roman citizens since Pompey's settlement in 65 or 64 B.C.[113]

Located sixteen miles inland from the coast, Tarsus was the capital of the Cilician region, an influential center of wealth and commerce. In Paul's time, the city had a population of about half a million citizens. Paul could well boast of being from Tarsus. There was even a Cilician synagogue in Jerusalem at which the young Saul might have fellowshipped and studied.

After Paul returns to Jerusalem following his conversion, the Jews plot his death (9:24). The disciples accompany him to Caesarea and send him by ship home to Tarsus (v. 30). There it is likely that Saul pours himself into the study of the Old Testament. Under the inspiration of the Holy Spirit, the Lord reveals to him new truth about the new dispensation of the church.

Years later, when a large number of Greeks come to the Lord in Antioch (11:19–24), the question seems to arise, "Who could speak more clearly to these people about salvation?" Barnabas leaves for Tarsus for Saul, who spends a year in Antioch, teaching large numbers about Christ (v. 26).

Paul appeals to his Tarsus background for credibility in his defense in Jerusalem (21:27–22:29). Speaking in Aramaic and pleading with the commander of the Jerusalem garrison, he tells him, "I am a Jew of Tarsus in Cilicia, a citizen of no insignificant city; and I beg you, allow me to speak to the people" (21:39). To the mob he adds, "I am a Jew, born in Tarsus of Cilicia, but brought up in this city, educated under Gamaliel, strictly according to the law of our fathers, being zealous for God, just as you all are today" (22:3).

> **9:20** immediately [Saul] began to proclaim Jesus in the synagogues, saying, "He is the Son of God."

Son of God. See p. 80.

> **9:22** Saul . . . [was] proving that this Jesus is the Christ.

Jesus is the Christ. See pp. 74–75.

> **9:27a** But Barnabas took hold of him

Barnabas. See under 4:36.

> **9:31a** So the church throughout all Judea and Galilee enjoyed peace

Judea. See 1:8.

Samaria. See under 1:8.

Galilee. Judea, Samaria, and Galilee made up the three provinces of Palestine west of the Jordan River. Galilee was the farthest north. During the time of Christ on earth, this area covered more than a third of western Palestine. It extended from the base of Mount Hermon on the north to the ridges of mounts Carmel and Gilboa on the south. The width was from the Jordan to the Mediterranean Sea, so the district covered about fifty miles by seventy-five miles. The word *Galilee* means "ring, circle," thus a district or region.

Christ ministered extensively in Galilee. The Synoptics—Matthew, Mark, and Luke—record mostly His Galilean ministry. Many of Jesus' parables were given in Galilee, and many of His miracles were performed there. During the life of Christ on earth, Herod Antipas was tetrarch of Galilee. The major cities of the province were Nazareth, Tiberias, and Capernaum. Jesus considered Capernaum a kind of home base.

At Christ's ascension back to the Father, two angels addressed the disciples who had seen him go as "men of Galilee." It was in this context that they heard the promise that the same Jesus who had disappeared would come again to the earth (1:11). The angels may have used the identification to stress the lowly and personal backgrounds of the disciples. For those in Jerusalem or Galilee or anywhere else, the second coming to the Mount of Olives (Zech. 14:4) will be both personal and visible.

The reference to Galilee in Acts 9:31 is in a summary statement of the state of the church at the end of the first campaign of persecution. Without the leadership of Saul/Paul, the enemies of the Way were in disarray. Their anger was directed more at finding and killing the turncoat than in rooting out and arresting other believers. With Paul sent on his way home to Tarsus (v. 30), the church, which was primarily an organization localized in Galilee and Judea, knew peace and was built up.

Galilee is mentioned by Peter in his sermon to the household of Cornelius as the epicenter of Christ's work (Acts 10:37–39). Paul makes a final reference when speaking of Christ's ministry after His resurrection. It was in this beautiful region, probably around the lake, that the risen Jesus spent teaching His disciples. In the synagogue at Pisidian Antioch, Paul notes that many of the witnesses to the resurrection were Galileans (13:31).

> **9:32b** [Peter] came down also to the saints who lived at
> Lydda.

Lydda. In 1 Chronicles 8:12, the area of Lydda is referred to as Lod. Lydda was a Benjaminite town near the Plain of Sharon. The community was north of Joppa on the main caravan routes to Egypt and Babylon and on the roads to Joppa and to Jerusalem. Ezra 2:33 states that it was resettled after the Exile, and it became the district capital of Samaria. Peter travels to this city and heals Aeneas, a man bedridden for eight years (see below). This man is well known, and those who saw him healed turned to the Lord (9:35). The revelation of Gentile salvation given to Paul had not yet gone everywhere, so it is assumed that the "all who lived at Lydda and Sharon" were Jewish Samaritans connected with the local synagogue. Many migrant herdsman wandered through the area. If they were evangelized, the gospel may have also migrated with them. God throughout this portion of the book of Acts is continually overcoming the physical limits of human frailty.

This is the only mention of Lydda in the New Testament. In modern times, the town is once again called Lod and is located just south of Israel's international airport.

9:33 And there he found a certain man named Aeneas,

Aeneas. *Aeneas* means "praise," and the Aeneas healed by Peter was evidently a fairly well-known resident of Lydda and the Plain of Sharon. He was a believer. How Aeneas had become paralyzed eight years before is not told. The text does confirm that this was not a disability from birth. Many probably knew him when he could still walk and knew that his bedridden state was genuine.

Peter's statement, "Jesus Christ heals you," is written in the aorist present. Christ is healing him at that moment. It is not a future event, nor something that has occurred in the past that Aeneas must simply recognize. Peter's command, "Make your bed," is most appropriate; what others for years have done for him, now he can do for himself.

Because of his healing, the text says that "all who lived at Lydda and Sharon" believed. Certainly the number must have been significant to warrant such language (9:35). For a description of Sharon, see below. The healing of Aeneas and the resurrection of Dorcas give special confirmation of Peter's ministry. Peter's next step will be the open door to the house of Cornelius and the Gentile world. The name *Aeneas* indicates that he may have been a Hellenistic Jew. His being a Greek is highly doubtful, since Cornelius and his household were the first Gentile converts.

9:35 And all who lived at Lydda and Sharon—

Sharon. An area of coastal plains, marsh land, forests, and dunes, Sharon extends from Joppa to just south of Mount Carmel. It is approximately fifty miles long. Very few settlements were in the area during the first century. It was mainly used by migrant herdsman. This area was not susceptible to floods and was highly fertile. Isaiah refers to this area as excellent for flocks and a place of peace for God's people (65:10). In response to the healing of Aeneas at Lydda (see above), many in this region turned to the Lord. The evangelized shepherds may have carried the gospel in all directions.

**9:36a Now at Joppa there was a certain disciple named
Tabitha (which translated in Greek is called Dorcas);**

Joppa. *Joppa, Japho, Jaffe,* or *Yafo* means "beautiful." The Phoenician form of the word is used in mythology to denote *Jafe,* the daughter of Aeolus, god of the winds. Joppa lies between the Plain of Sharon and the Plain of Philistia on the Mediterranean coast, approximately thirty-five miles north of Jerusalem. Occupation dates to 1650 B.C. Joppa was known in ancient times for its skilled workman of leather, wood, and metal. Its natural harbor was nearly impossible to navigate, either from the north or the south.

During the time of Joshua, Joppa was captured and given to the tribe of Dan. The Philistines took the city, only to be defeated by King David. Solomon used the harbor to receive cedar logs for the temple that had been floated in from Lebanon. By the time of Jonah, Joppa had been captured by the Phoenicians. Successive waves of upheaval brought Assyrian, Babylonian, and Persian governments to the city. After the exile, the port again was used to receive logs from Lebanon for the second temple. In 164 B.C., Judas Maccabeus raided the city after more than 200 Jews were drowned there by Gentiles. Joppa was conquered by Pompeii in 63 B.C. and joined to the Province of Syria. Cleopatra received the city as a gift from Antony, and it was later given by Caesar Augustus to Herod the Great.

Peter traveled to Joppa from Lydda at the request of several brethren upon the death of Tabitha (or Dorcas). When Peter raised her from the dead, news of the miracle spread throughout the region. This first miracle resurrection by the apostles caused many to believe in the Lord. Peter stayed in Joppa for some time with Simon the tanner. While on Simon's roof one afternoon, he received the vision preparing him to go to the Gentiles. See below. Peter leaves Joppa to go to Caesarea and the home of Cornelius.

The miracle of raising Dorcas from the dead was the first of its kind by any of the apostles, and it launched the early church in this region. God showed that even the humanness of death could be overcome by His Spirit and might. God's vision to Peter also cleared the way for the revelation of Gentile salvation and Paul's subsequent mission journeys. One of the largest gaps between the Jews and the pagan cultures of the area was due to the fact that other ethnic groups did not adhere to the dietary guidelines of Mosaic Law, which rendered them unclean. Even in the spread of the gospel, God used the miraculous nature of visions to restructure the mind-set of Peter and the rest of the disciples. This restructuring lead to a quicker acceptance of the Gentiles in the early church, which helped to spread Christianity throughout the first-century world.

Tabitha (Dorcas). *Tabitha* is the Hebrew form of the Greek *Dorcas*, who was the recipient of the second great miracle of Peter before the conversion of Cornelius and his household. Both forms are given, perhaps because she frequented both Greek and Hebrew circles in Joppa, and *Dorcas* may have been used by her Greek friends. Both translations of her name mean "gazelle."

She is recorded as a woman of outstanding deeds. This is the only instance in the New Testament where the word *disciple* is used in the feminine form. Tabitha apparently spent much of her time and energy helping destitute widows. Verse 39 indicates the effect she had upon widows and reveals that Dorcas was a seamstress.

The disease of which she fell sick and died is not revealed. Her body was washed but not anointed. Because of the warm climate of Joppa the burial of her body would have to take place quickly. In most cases, bodies were buried the same day. But upon hearing that Peter was in Lydda, two men were sent to entreat him on Dorcas' behalf. The distance between the two towns is about twelve miles. Scripture does not reveal the motivation of the people in sending for Peter. There had not been a person yet raised from the dead in the book of Acts. J. W. McGarvey comments:

> We are left by the historian entirely to conjecture as to the purpose for which Peter's presence in Joppa was desired, whether to minister comfort to the distressed little band of believers, in the way which is the only one left to modern preachers under the circumstances, or with the hope that he would raise the sleeping saint from the dead. It is more probable that the former was their thought; for it was not the custom of the apostles to bring back to life their deceased brethren and sisters merely because they had been useful in their lives; otherwise Stephen and others who had been cruelly slain in the midst of their usefulness would have been resuscitated.[114]

Whatever the motivation, Peter is urged to come to Joppa. Upon entering the upper room he encounters a mourning scene similar to one he had seen at Jairus's house, before Jesus raised a child to life (Luke 8:49–56). Peter allows no one to stay in the room (9:40a). He kneels and prays. Reminiscent of his Messiah, Peter tells the woman to rise and she does (9:40b). No recorded words pass between them. Peter raises her to her feet. The once insecure Peter, who denied Christ three times, performs the greatest miracle for his Lord. Word spreads, with results similar to those in Lydda (9:42).

There is no further mention of Tabitha in Scripture, though one is left to wonder what witness and ministry she had afterward.

9:43 And it came about that [Peter] stayed many days in Joppa with a certain tanner, Simon.

Simon. By staying with Simon the Tanner, Peter takes a step toward understanding the vision of clean and unclean animals he sees on Simon's rooftop. As a tanner who worked with the skins of dead animals Simon was continually unclean ceremonially; he was an outcast in Jewish eyes. He likely lived by the sea because the smells from his occupation made him unwelcome to close neighbors. It is interesting to note that the two Simons, a fisherman and a tanner, stayed under the same roof. In his vision on the rooftop of this unclean home, Peter is told to take the next step and reach out to the Gentiles he thought unclean. This is a double blow. He already lives under the roof of a tanner; now he learns that both Jews and Gentiles are also his mission field. It is at Simon's house that Cornelius's men soon call, looking for Simon Peter. Peter's stay at Simon's house prepares him for his future mission to the Gentiles and gives to us an insight into his character and Christian liberty.

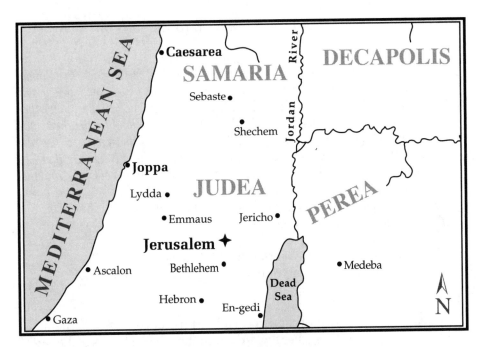

Chapter 10

A.D. 35 (Exact time uncertain)

PETER AND THE
FIRST GENTILE CONVERSIONS

Synopsis

(1–8) While Peter stays in Joppa, up the coast at Caesarea, a God-fearing Roman centurion named Cornelius sees an angel of the God in a vision (1–3). The angel instructs him to send some men to Joppa and call for the man Peter (4–8).

(9–22) Meanwhile in Joppa, Peter in a trance is shown a large sheet coming down from heaven that held a number of unclean animals (9–12). Peter is instructed to kill and eat, but he replies that he has never eaten any unholy or unclean thing (13–14). But a voice explains that what God has cleansed is no longer considered unholy, and immediately the sheet is taken up into the sky (15–16). Almost instantly the men sent by Cornelius arrive and inquire about Peter (17–18). The Spirit of God alerts Peter that the three are looking for him and that he should accompany them because they have been sent by the Lord (19–20). The men then explain that an angel directed Cornelius in order that he might "hear a message from" the apostle (21–22).

(23–48) Arriving in Caesarea at the house of Cornelius, Peter finds the Roman centurion anxiously waiting for him. In fact, the man bows down to worship Peter. The apostle tells him, "Stand up; I too am just a man" (23–26). Peter then shares with Cornelius and his household how God had shown him that he should call no man unholy or unclean (27–29). Cornelius tells that an angel has also appeared to him (30–33). Peter explains the gospel of Jesus of Nazareth, that God anointed Jesus with the Holy Spirit. He tells of the resurrection of Christ and that he and other witnesses of these things have been ordered to preach to the people (34–43). The Holy Spirit falls on all who are listening (44–45). Cornelius and others are baptized in the name of Jesus (46–48).

> **10:1** Now there was a certain man at Caesarea named
> Cornelius, a centurion of what was called the Italian
> cohort,

Cornelius. As salvation and the Holy Spirit encompass Cornelius, a Gentile, the gospel truly reaches toward "even the remotest parts of the earth" (1:8). God was propelling the message toward the world.

If there was a rift between the Samaritans and Jews, a practically unbridgeable chasm separated Gentiles and Jews. A Jew returning from a Gentile country would shake the dust off his feet and his clothes because he did not want to carry Gentile dirt into Judea. A Jew could not enter the house of a Gentile or eat a meal prepared by Gentile hands. Some Jews would not buy meat that had been cut by Gentile knives. This was a hatred that only God could heal.

Nevertheless, the Lord gave Peter a vision that taught him God was no respecter of persons. Right after Peter had the vision, three men came to the house, explaining that they had been sent by Cornelius, who wanted to see Peter and hear about God.

As a centurion, Cornelius commanded 100 soldiers of the Italian Cohort. This was an elite unit recruited in Italy. Unusual for a hardened soldier in the difficult Palestine occupation force, Cornelius was a devout God-fearer who apparently felt special compassion for the Jewish people (Acts 26:17). His gifts to the Jewish people evidently expressed thanks for what he had received in the synagogue. He was much like the kind centurion whose servant Jesus healed, who expressed strong faith (Luke 7:5; for more on the Italian Cohort, see under 27:1).[115]

Peter swallows his Jewish pride to accompany the Gentiles back to Cornelius. There, all who hear the gospel believe. What is perhaps more amazing to Peter and the Jews with him is that the gift of the Holy Spirit is poured out upon the Gentiles, just as on the believing Jews at Pentecost (10:45–46). Peter concludes that water baptism is the next logical step, symbolically uniting these Gentiles to the heretofore Jewish church (10:47).

By the visible evidence of the Holy Spirit, God heads off any attempt to make the Gentile church a separate institution. These men and women have shown themselves to be full members in the body of Christ. Peter equates receiving the Holy Spirit with salvation. Peter knew beyond doubt that Cornelius and the others in his household were saved and should be baptized.

> **10:3a** About the ninth hour of the day [Cornelius] clearly saw in a vision an angel of God

Angel of God. See under 1:10.

> **10:11** [Peter] beheld the sky opened up, and a certain object like a great sheet coming down, lowered by four corners to the ground.

Great sheet. R. C. H. Lenski observes that God himself abrogates the Mosaic dietary commands. This, then, becomes a far-reaching command that does away with "cleanness" and "uncleanness." Only the Lord could bring about this revolutionary break, which had to be made. Lenski wrote, "Even they needed much time to recognize that all the ceremonial laws were only temporary, intended only for the old covenant, in force only until the Messiah should come, and not the divine will for all time."[116]

> **10:22** "Cornelius, . . . was divinely directed by a holy angel to send for you to come to his house and hear a message from you."

Holy Angel. See under 1:10.

> **10:38** "You know of Jesus of Nazareth, how God anointed Him with the Holy Spirit and with power, and how He went about doing good, and healing all who were oppressed by the devil; for God was with Him."

Nazareth. See p. 72.

God anointed Him with the Holy Spirit. There is a slight play on words here. Jesus is the *Christos*, the "Anointed One," and the word "to anoint" is *Chriō*. Isaiah 61:1 speaks for the Messiah that "the Spirit of the Lord God is upon me, because the Lord has anointed me to bring good news to the afflicted." The author of Hebrews quotes this Isaiah passage in his long list of verses concerning the deity of Jesus as the Son of God (1:9). Following the temptation of Jesus by the devil, Luke relates in his gospel how Christ was led back to Galilee "in the power of the Spirit" (4:14). Teaching in the synagogue in His home town of Nazareth, at the morning reading, He opened the scroll for the congregational reading to Isaiah 61:1. He said, "Today this Scripture has been fulfilled in your hearing" (Luke 4:21). This anointing of the Lord is mentioned earlier in 4:27. The fact of this work by the Holy Spirit relates to the ministry of the Son of God in His coming in human form. Though deity, He came as a man, and in a mysterious sense He was obedient to the Lord and dependent upon the Spirit's power to accomplish His earthly mission. Again, the paradox is that, as God's Son, He had His own innate divine power to do as He pleased. See p. 80.

> **10:39** "And we are witnesses of all the things He did both
> in the land of the Jews and in Jerusalem. And they also put
> Him to death by hanging Him on a cross."

Witnesses. See under 1:8.

Put Him to death. See p. 73.

> **10:40** "God raised Him up on the third day, . . ."

Raised Him up. See pp. 73–74.

> **10:41** "[He became visible] not to all the people, but to
> witnesses who were chosen beforehand by God, that is, to us,
> who ate and drank with Him after He arose from the dead."

Witnesses. See under 1:8.

> **10:42b** "this is the One who has been appointed by God as
> Judge of the living and the dead."

Judge. By proclaiming Christ as the "Judge of the living and the dead" Peter was assuring these Gentiles that all will stand before Christ some day. There are no alternatives to this judgment, no plea that humans can make. For the believer, that judgment will involve rewards obtained in this life. Believers will never face Christ for a judgment that will jeopardize their salvation. This salvation judgment was made on the cross. However, those in Christ face a judgment concerning their actions as his people.

The unbeliever will face Jesus as a Judge for the sins of their lives. After the millennial reign of Christ, all unbelievers will be brought before His throne for judgment:

Then I saw a great white throne and Him who sat upon it, from whose presence earth and heaven fled away, and no place was found for them. And I saw the dead, the great and the small, standing before the throne, and books were opened; and another book was opened, which is the book of life; and the dead were judged from the things which were written in the books, according to their deeds. (Rev. 20:11–12)

These will be judged for their destiny according to their deeds. No one is saved by deeds and all who stand before this judgment will be sentenced to the second death, the lake of fire. This is the ultimate judgment by the Great Judge on the unbelievers.

10:43b "every one who believes in Him receives forgiveness of sins."

Forgiveness of sins. See under 2:38.

10:44 While Peter was still speaking these words, the Holy Spirit fell upon all those who were listening to the message.

Holy Spirit fell upon. See pp. 36–37.

10:45 And all the circumcised believers who had come with Peter were amazed, because the gift of the Holy Spirit had been poured out upon the Gentiles also.

Circumcised. If the circumcised Jews accompanying Peter were amazed, what would it be like for those who were not there to see God pour out his Spirit on the Gentiles? Knowing what crisis is to come over the Gentile converts, Luke points out that it wasn't easy for any of the Jews involved. As soon as Peter reached Jerusalem, those who wanted to reserve Christ for the Jews "began to contend with him." Lenski explains that this verb is an inchoative imperfect. That means the end of the action is not in view at the moment it starts. Luke is saying that the contending would go on for some time.[117]

In this regard, the term *circumcision* is used in two ways. In 10:45 it simply means that Peter's companions were Jews. They had undergone the rite of circumcision. In Acts 11:3, the term is more narrowly defined by those who would make circumcision necessary for membership in the church. In Galatians 2:12, it may be even more strictly defined as a schismatic party of Jewish legalists that had developed around the issue. See also under 7:8.

The Holy Spirit . . . poured out upon the Gentiles. See pp. 138–42.

> **10:46a** For they were hearing them speaking with tongues and exalting God.

Tongues. See pp. 37–42.

> **10:47** "Surely no one can refuse the water for these to be baptized—

Baptized. See p. 160; see also under 1:5; 8:36; 11:16.

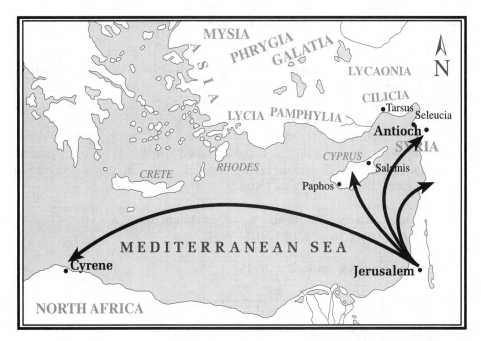

Chapter 11

A.D. 35 (Exact time uncertain)

THE GENTILE WITNESS CONTROVERSY; SAUL AND THE ANTIOCH CHURCH

Synopsis

(1–18) The Christian Jews of Judea receive the news that Gentiles have also received the word of God (1). Going up to Jerusalem, Peter gives a special report to the so-called "circumcised party" of Christian Jews who still felt Gentiles unworthy of the gospel unless they performed certain Jewish rituals. Peter tells of the vision of clean and unclean and how God had spoken to Cornelius (2–14). He tells these zealous Jewish Christians that God had given these Gentiles the same Spirit that had fallen at Pentecost (15–16). Peter asks the pointed question, "Who was I that I could stand in God's way?" (17–18).

(19–30) Even as Cornelius comes to Christ, the gospel moves toward the Gentiles through the persecution-scattered Christians. After Stephen's death, believers make their way to Phoenicia, Cyprus, and Antioch. They witness to Jewish communities (19), but at Antioch some have more contact with the Greeks, and many believe (20). When word of this Gentile awakening filters back to Jerusalem, Barnabas is

287

sent to Antioch to supervise (21–24). Since he is dealing with a large body of Greeks, Barnabas reasons that a Hellenized Jew such as Saul can best teach the converts. Saul comes from Tarsus to Antioch for a year, and many disciples are added to the assembly. Here they are first called Christians (25–26). Coming from Jerusalem to Antioch, the prophet Agabus, foretells the coming of a worldwide drop in food production. When the region of Judea is struck by the predicted famine, disciples of Antioch contribute to their relief (27–29). The gift is delivered to Jerusalem by Barnabas and Saul (30).

11:2 And when Peter came up to Jerusalem, those who were circumcised took issue with [Peter],

Circumcised. See under 7:8; 10:45.

11:5 "I was in the city of Joppa praying;"

Joppa. See under 9:36.

11:16 "John baptized with water, but you shall be baptized with the Holy Spirit."

Baptized with water . . . with the Holy Spirit. This is what Jesus said in 1:5. The "real" baptism is by the Spirit; the water ritual is but an outward sign of the inward spiritual reality done in operation by God's Spirit whereby believers are united with Christ (1 Cor. 12:12–13). See p. 160; see also under 1:5; 8:36.

11:15 "And as I began to speak, the Holy Spirit fell upon them, just as He did upon us at the beginning."

Holy Spirit Fell upon them. See pp. 36–37.

11:18b "God has granted to the Gentiles also the repentance that leads to life."

Repentance that leads to life. See under 2:38.

11:19 So then those who were scattered because of the persecution that arose in connection with Stephen made their way to Phoenicia and Cyprus and Antioch, speaking the word to no one except to Jews alone.

Phoenicia. Luke again picks up the account of the persecution and the scattering of believers after it (Acts 11:19). It took time before many Jewish followers were ready to take the gospel outside Judaism (1:8). Jesus, of course, had told them to take the message first to the Jews (Matt. 10:5–6). Thus, some felt they should witness only to Jews in their areas of refuge. One of those, Phoenicia, was 200 miles of narrow coast along the northeast side of the Mediterranean Sea. To the east were the mountains of Lebanon, and to the south were the Galilean hills. Phoenicia included the well-known Tyre and Sidon. In the Old Testament, the area held by the Phoenicians was called in Hebrew "Canaan" (Isa. 23:11).

Paul and Barnabas passed through Phoenicia on their way to the Jerusalem council (15:3). Later, the apostle and his party sailed to Phoenicia as they left Miletus and headed toward Tyre (21:2–3). During the ministry of Jesus, Phoenicia was referred to as the seacoast and the district of Tyre and Sidon (Matt. 15:21; Luke 6:17). Its citizens, including Greeks, were considered "Syro-Phoenicians."

Cyprus. Cyprus is a Mediterranean island between the coasts of Cilicia and Syria. Its greatest breadth is sixty miles; its length is 145 miles. Its 3707 square miles is larger than Corsica and Crete yet smaller than Sicily or Sardinia. Cyprus is noted for its two mountain ranges. The northern range is called the Kyrenia Mountains, which reach to 3343 feet. The southern Troodos Mountains reach 6406 feet. The two mountain masses are separated by a broad, low-lying plain.

Abundant copper and timber on Cyprus gave the island an early commercial bonanza. Around 1450 B.C., Thutmose III invaded and occupied the island. As people of the Mediterranean began to trade, settlements sprouted along the coast. Evidence of Greek civilization dates back to about 1400 B.C. and of Phoenician civilization to about 800 B.C. Control of Cyprus was traded to each of the empires that dominated the eastern Mediterranean: Assyrian, Egyptian, and Persian. Avagoras I, ruler of Salamis, tried to unify the island to break from the Persian empire and temporarily broke away in 391 B.C. with the aid of Athens.[118] After the passing of Alexander the Great, the Ptolemies controlled the island from about 323 B.C. until about 58 B.C., when it became part of the Roman Empire.

Cyprus figures several times in the book of Acts. Barnabas was a Cypriote Christian (4:36), as was Mnason (21:15). Mnason was apparently wealthy, as his house was able to accommodate Paul and his large traveling party. The phrase *disciple of long standing* infers that Mnason was either a convert from Pentecost or even a disciple of Jesus.

Cyprus was a safe haven from the persecution of Jerusalem, yet it had a large Jewish population. It was to these that the Word was spoken. These believers were not content to hide on their island for long, for Cypriote Christians were among those who were soon evangelizing the Greeks at

Antioch (11:20–21) and at Siren in North Africa.[119] While alive, Stephen influenced many, and with his death more were converted to Jesus.

Cyprus was the second stop for Barnabas and Paul on their first missionary journey (Acts 13:4). Why they went here first is not known. The fact that it was Barnabas's homeland may have been one reason they stopped there. The Scriptures do not record whether they preached or taught in Cyprus, but most commentators assume they did. Paul and Barnabas intended to begin their second missionary journey there, but when they argued over whether to take John Mark along, Barnabas took Mark and went to Cyprus (15:39). Charles Ryrie comments: "God brought good out of it in that two missionary teams were sent out, and Barnabas's continued interest in John Mark rescued him from possible uselessness."[120]

The last two references to Cyprus in Acts involve Paul's travels once more. In 21:3, he sailed around it enroute to Tyre at the end of the third missionary journey. And Paul is on his way to Rome when Cyprus provides shelter from the stormy seas (27:4). Early autumn winds were so severe that only the hardiest of vessels would attempt to make a crossing on the open seas. Paul's vessel, being a coastal vessel, wisely chose to avoid the open sea route. Instead, they went to the east end of Cyprus, where the force of the winds was blocked. Hugging the coast of the island, they were able to come around safely and head for the coast of Cilicia.

Antioch. See under 6:5.

> **11:20a** But there were some of them, men of Cyprus and Cyrene, who came to Antioch

Cyrene. See Libya under 2:10.

> **11:22b** and they sent Barnabas off to Antioch.

Barnabas. See under 4:36.

> **11:24a** [Barnabas] was a good man, and full of the Holy Spirit and of faith.

Full of the Holy Spirit. See pp. 36–37.

> **11:26c** and the disciples were first called Christians in Antioch.

Christians. It is no wonder that the title *Christians (Christianos)* began to be used in Antioch (11:26). The Holy Spirit began working early in this city, and thousands came to Christ. Antioch was an important metropolis on the Mediterranean coast, 300 miles from Jerusalem. It was the gateway into the Middle East. The ripple effect of the conversions there was felt in Jerusalem and in Rome.

Antioch has been called the third most influential city in the Roman Empire of this time. It was the capital of the Roman province of Syria and the third largest city in the empire, with a population of about one-half million.

Jews first heard the gospel at Antioch (11:19), but disciples from Cyprus and Cyrene came to the city and began preaching to Greeks as well (11:20). "And the hand of the Lord was with them, and a large number who believed turned to the Lord" (11:21). The news reached Jerusalem, from which Barnabas was dispatched to Antioch, where he witnessed the grace of God at work in the citizens. Finding a considerable number coming to the Lord, Barnabas went to Tarsus and brought back Paul to Antioch. This happened around 45. Both men ministered for one year with the established church (11:26).

King Herod Agrippa II knew of the term *Christian*. Twelve years later, he said to Paul, "In a short time you will persuade me to become a Christian" (26:28). The word is used only one other time in the New Testament. Referring to martyrdom, Peter wrote, "but if anyone suffers as a Christian, let him not feel ashamed, but in that name let him glorify God" (1 Peter 4:16).

The disciples never used the term *Christian* to describe themselves; they used instead *brethren* and *saints* The hostile Jews used the scornful expression *Nazarenes*. E. H. Plumptre records that tradition ascribes the term *Christian* to Euodius, the first Bishop of Antioch, and his successor, Ignatius, uses it frequently. Ignatius also forms from it *Christianismos,* as opposed to *Judaismos,* calling the whole system of faith and life *Christianity.*[121]

> **11:27** Now at this time some prophets came down from Jerusalem to Antioch.

Prophets. See pp. 82–91.

> **11:28** And one of them named Agabus stood up and began to indicate by the Spirit that there would certainly be a great famine all over the world. And this took place in the reign of Claudius.

Agabus. The name *Agabus* means "a locust." Prophets of the first-century church, such as Agabus, possessed, along with other sign gifts, a supernatural gift of revealing the Word of God that was helpful for the edification of the church before the canon was completed.[122] While this is the first mention of the gift of prophecy among the disciples, it obviously had a history. Those who heard at Antioch immediately took action, certain that the words of Agabus were from the Lord (11:29, 30).

Agabus is again mentioned in 21:10–11. As Paul prepares to enter Jerusalem, Agabus delivers a dire warning (21:11) of what will happen to him at Jerusalem. Like the prophets of the Old Testament (cf. 1 Kings 11:29–31; Jer. 13:1–7; Ezek. 4), Agabus uses actions to illustrate his prediction. By binding his own feet and hands (21:11), he illustrates what the Jews will do to Paul.

Agabus seemingly appears out of nowhere and delivers news that no one wants to hear. Yet all listen to and heed him, for they know the Lord God speaks through him.

Many who hear the word *prophet* assume the person is able simply to foretell the future. *Vine's Expository Dictionary* comments on this:

> Though much of OT prophecy was purely predictive, see Micah 5:2, e.g., and cf. John 11:51, prophecy is not necessarily, nor even primarily, fore-telling. It is the declaration of that which cannot be known by natural means. Matt. 26:68, it is the forth-telling of the will of God, whether the reference is to the past, the present, or the future. . . .
>
> In such passages as 1 Cor. 12:28; Eph. 2:20; the "prophets" are placed after the "Apostles," since not the prophets of Israel are intended, but the "gifts" of the ascended Lord, Eph. 4:8, 11; cf. Acts 13:1; . . . the purpose of their ministry was to edify, to comfort, and to encourage the believers, 1 Cor. 14:3, while its effect upon unbelievers was to show that the secrets of a man's heart are known to God, to convict of sin, and to constrain to worship, vv. 24, 25.
>
> With the completion of the canon of Scripture prophecy apparently passed away, 1 Cor. 13:8, 9. In his measure the teacher has taken the place of the prophet, cf. the significant change in 2 Peter 2:1. The difference is that, whereas the message of the prophet was a direct revelation of the mind of God for the occasion, the message of the teacher is gathered from the completed revelation contained in the Scriptures.[123]

Nothing is recorded on the early life of Agabus. He is assumed by some commentators to have been one of the seventy disciples sent out by Christ. In the New Testament, other than Christ and the apostles, his are the only prophecies actually recorded (see also Acts 21:10–11). Other prophets (Acts 13:1; 15:32) and prophetesses (21:9; 1 Cor. 11:5) are mentioned.

Claudius. Claudius (10 B.C.–A.D. 54) was the first emperor chosen by the army. Following the assassination of Caligula, he was proclaimed emperor by the Praetorian Guard. The reign of Claudius was from A.D. 41 to 54. Claudius was the son of Nero Claudius Drusus, the younger brother of emperor Tiberius. Until age forty-seven, when he was named consul and shortly thereafter emperor, he held no important public offices. Claudius is responsible for the banishment of all Jews from Rome about the middle of his reign (about 49; see under 18:2).[124] He is not otherwise mentioned in Scripture, but his peaceful reign was an important factor in the spread of Christianity.

Roman history records several bad harvests and famines during his reign. Josephus writes of a severe famine in Palestine that lasted from A.D. 45–47:

> (51) Now her coming was of very great advantage to the people of Jerusalem; for whereas a famine did oppress them at that time, and many people died for want of what was necessary to procure food withal, queen Helena sent some of her servants to Alexandria with money to buy a great quantity of corn, and other of them to Cyprus, to bring a cargo of dried figs; (52) and as soon as they were come back, and brought those provisions, which was done very quickly, she distributed food to those that were in want of it, and left a most excellent memorial behind her of this benefaction, which she bestowed on our whole nation; (53) and when her son Izates was informed of this famine, he sent great sums of money to the principal men in Jerusalem. However, what favors this queen and king conferred upon our city Jerusalem, shall be further related hereafter. . . ."[125]

> Thus this legislation, which appeared to be divine, made this man to be esteemed as one superior to his own nature. Nay, further, a little before the beginning of this war, when Claudius was emperor of the Romans, and Ismael was our high priest, and when so great a famine was come upon us, that one-tenth deal [of wheat] was sold for four drachmae, (321) and when no less than seventy cori of flour were brought into the temple, at the feast of unleavened bread (these cori are thirty-one Sicilian, but forty-one Athenian medimni), not one of the priests were so hardy as to eat one crumb of it, even while so great a distress was upon the land."[126]

When outside forces did not interfere, Claudius's reign was mild and in many ways beneficial. He was an able administrator in civil and military affairs and chose qualified advisors. During his reign, Judea was officially made a Roman province, as was Mauritania and Thrace. Britain was invaded, and successful campaigns were made against the Germanic tribes.[127] After a plot on his life was uncovered, he went into semi-seclusion, and his wife Messalina, who was cruel and violent, became the true leader.[128]

Claudius's attitude toward the Jews was generally favorable. The Jews in Asia and Egypt seem to have received preferential treatment as recorded by Josephus (*Ant.* 19.5.2.3; 20.1.2), though the Jews of Palestine would at times suffer under the hands of governors he appointed. Claudius's administration started the decline in the power of the nobility and the granting of wealth and responsibility to personal followers of the emperor, including former slaves.

> In 48 Claudius ordered the execution of Messalina, who had indicated her contempt for him by publicly staging a mock marriage with her lover. He then defied widespread disapproval by marrying his niece, Agrippina the Younger, under whose influence he deprived his son by Messalina, Britannicus, of his heritage, adopting instead Agrippina's son by a former marriage, Nero, later emperor of Rome.[129]

Claudius's reign ended in 54 when he was poisoned. Much about this assassination is unknown, but there is speculation that Agrippina was involved.

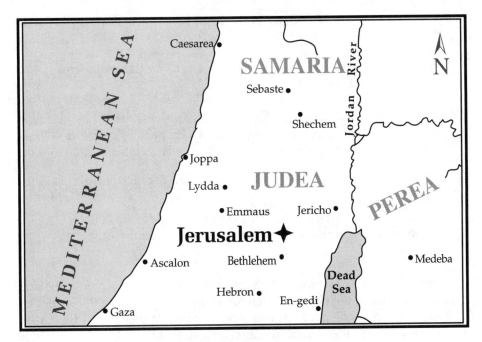

Chapter 12

A.D. 44 (Passover)

INCREASING PERSECUTION AND THE DEATH OF HEROD

Synopsis

(1–2) Administering the government in Judea in the name of the Romans, Herod Agrippa I is probably coerced by the Jews to execute a Christian leader. James, the son of Zebedee, one of the twelve disciples, is beheaded.

(3–11) Next, Herod arrests Peter during the days of Unleavened Bread. Putting him in prison, he intends to bring him before the Jewish mob and execute him (3–4). With the apostle securely guarded in prison, an angel appears to Peter and "his chains fell off his hands" (5–7). Not certain whether he is seeing a vision, Peter follows the angel all the way out of the prison. "When Peter came to himself," he realizes the Lord has rescued him from Herod and the people (8–11).

(12–19) After Peter makes his way to the house of Mary, the mother of John Mark, the servant girl Rhoda refuses to let Peter in. Those inside the dwelling think that she is out of her mind or that she is seeing Peter's spirit (angel) (12–15). Peter reports what happened and tells them to share these events with James (the son of

Alphaeus) and the other disciples. Peter then departs for Caesarea. Herod has his guards executed for losing the prisoner (16–19).

(20–23) The drama ends concerning king Herod at the sea coast area of Tyre and Sidon. Hearing cries from the people who wish to gain his favor that he is a god, he is struck by an angel of the Lord. Luke adds that he was eaten by worms and died (20–23).

(24–25) Going back to Antioch from Jerusalem, Barnabas and Saul take John Mark.

> **12:1** Now about that time Herod the king laid hands on some who belonged to the church, in order to mistreat them.

Herod [Agrippa I]. Herod Agrippa I, was the son of Aristobulus and grandson of Herod the Great. The Herod of this story was the third ruler by that name to cross the pages of the New Testament: first Herod the Great, Herod Antipas, and then Herod Agrippa I. He spent his youth in Rome where he was a friend of Gaius, who became the emperor Caligula. As a result, Gaius granted him in 37 the tetrarchies of Philip, the brother of Antipas (including districts North and East of Galilee), and of Lysanias in southern Syria (Luke 3:1). In 39, Galilee and Perea were added to his realm, and in 41 he was made king of Judea. At that point he ruled a territory about as large as his grandfather's kingdom. He made it plain that he would do all in his power to be agreeable to the Jewish people, who responded by according him widespread popularity.

Everett F. Harrison writes in *The Expanding Church:*

> Because of his position as King he felt able to do what no Roman procurator in previous years would have dared to do, attack the church. Luke speaks of "some" who were his targets, but names only two, both of them Apostles. James the brother of John, and Peter may have been the only members of the twelve in Jerusalem at the time. Jesus had prophesied the martyrdom of both men (Mark 10:39; John 21:18–19). But it important to notice that with reference to Peter, Jesus explicitly stated that he would lose his life only when he was old. His time had not yet come. James died by "the sword" probably beheaded like John the Baptist. This pleased the Jews, encouraging Agrippa to arrest Peter. This direct action against the church met with great approval. It shows how little Judaism had become reconciled to the existence of Christian beliefs in Judea.[130]

In events leading up to those described in Acts 12:20, Agrippa had had a quarrel with the inhabitants of Tyre and Sidon, prominent cities on the coast of Phoenicia, although the cause is unknown. Upset by his failure to kill Peter, his fighting-mad mood was worse than usual. Agrippa was treacherous, superficial, cruel, and extravagant, although not as bad as his grandfather Herod the Great. Suing for "peace" does not in this case imply the existence of armed conflict, but only the termination of the quarrel. The cities had to make terms with Agrippa because they relied on northern Palestine for much of their food. The suppliants made an adroit move by contacting "Blastus the king's chamberlain," since he presumably had a closer relationship with Agrippa than any others of his official household. His cooperation was doubtless gained at a price.

Herod's willingness to settle differences was in line with his policy of cultivating leaders and governments in his general area, a policy that made Rome look askance at him. The government suspected he was seeking more power. It is significant that at his death the emperor Claudius did not appoint his son to succeed him, but restored Roman rule through procurators.

"On the appointed day," when Herod met with the envoys from the Phoenician cities, the king made a state occasion by donning "royal apparel" and dignifying the concord by making an "address" to the visitors from the north. To the obsequious people of Caesarea, largely Gentiles, it presented an opportunity to hail their monarch as "a god" (the Jews, of course, would not take part in any such acclaim). Josephus, in describing this event, locates it during a festival in honor of Claudius (*Ant.* 19, 8. 2).

Harrison writes:

> The two accounts agree that Herod did nothing to resist or refuse the plaudits of the throng, and that from this very time he was smitten with an incurable illness that speedily brought death. Josephus credits the monarch with a speech in which he recognized that the sentence of death was on him, fate providing thereby an immediate refutation of the lying words of the multitude. Scripture does not use any such pagan terminology, but attributes death to angelic action because of unwillingness to "give God the glory."[131]

Josephus speaks only of intense pain in the bowels, while Luke says he was devoured by worms. Luke's professional exactness as a physician brings out the horror of his death. God knows how to bring to nothing the proud.

12:2 And he had James the brother of John put to death with a sword.

James the brother of John. See under 1:13.

12:3b Now it was during the days of Unleavened Bread.

Unleavened Bread. This feast began with Passover on the fourteenth of Nisan and continued for seven days (Exod. 12:3–19). Through the seven days, one goat daily was offered to make atonement for the people. By eating unleavened bread, the Jews were reminded of their own leavened condition. Thus, the goat had to be presented daily for the cleansing of their sins. Peter possibly was arrested during this holiday because the authorities thought the people would be preoccupied.

> **12:4b** [Herod intended] after the Passover to bring [Peter] out before the people.

Passover. In Exodus 12:21–27, Moses calls the elders of the people together and instructs them about this ceremony. Using hyssop, the Jews were to stain the lintel of the doorway with blood. When Jehovah passed through, He would smite the Egyptians but pass by the sons of Israel because He would see the blood on the doorway. God did not allow the destroyer to enter. This same ceremony takes place annually as a memorial of God's providential care of the nation. The animal sacrificed for the blood pictures the substitution of Christ for sins. Specifically, Jesus is said to be the Passover of believers (1 Cor. 5:7).

> **12:12** And when he realized this, he went to the house of Mary, the mother of John who was also called Mark, where many were gathered together and were praying.

Mary, the mother of John. Little is known of this woman, except that she clearly is a believer in Christ. Barnabas was related to her because he was cousin to John Mark (Col. 4:10). Possibly it was at her home that the Last Supper was held. Acts pictures her house as a stop for believers and a meeting place for the Jerusalem church. It is also probable that Mary was a widow, since her husband likely would have been mentioned if he were alive. Too, she surely was well off economically since her dwelling accommodated many guests.

John who was also called Mark. John was a Jew, for his mother holds the Jewish name of Mary and the family participates prominently in the church when it was a totally Jewish institution (12:12). The family must have been wealthy, having a large house. They also had servants (v. 13). The home probably became a place of refuge for "the brothers in Jerusalem." Peter must have come here regularly (v. 14).

John was a cousin of Barnabas (Col. 4:10), who was a Levite of means from Cyprus and a leader in the early church (Acts 4:36–37). John, too, may have been part of the Cyprus colony.

John Mark is first mentioned here. In verse 25, he returns with Saul (Paul) and Barnabas to Syrian Antioch. When Paul and Barnabas are directed to

Cyprus to proclaim the word of God (13:2–5), John is their helper. But then suddenly John leaves the group and heads back to Jerusalem (13:13). One speculation is that until now, Barnabas has held a leadership position, but Paul is taking leadership, which might have made Mark jealous, or it may have been fear or an inability to withstand the rigors of an arduous journey.

Paul labeled John's return to Jerusalem desertion (15:38). Thus, when Barnabas wanted to take John Mark along on the second missionary journey, a sharp disagreement arose with Paul. In the end, Barnabas took his cousin John to Cyprus. Paul chose Silas as his traveling companion (15:39–40). The differences fade with time. Twelve years later, Paul looks at John as an encouragement (Col. 4:10–11; Philem. 24) and useful in the apostle's service (2 Tim. 4:11). It was John Mark for whom Paul asked when he was a prisoner in Rome.

Though John Mark is mentioned in various places in Acts and in Paul's letters, not enough is known to appreciate his full and valuable ministry. As with many servants of Christ, from the account in the written record, he labored more or less unnoticed.

While Mark was a common surname, church fathers ascribed authorship of the gospel to John Mark. Papias (c. 140) believed John was Peter's interpreter and wrote the essentials of his recollections of Jesus after Peter was martyred (65–70). On the other hand, there is reason to set the writing of the gospel as early as the 40s. On the assumption that John Mark did write the gospel, it is interesting to speculate that he may have been the young follower of Jesus who eluded capture and fled naked on the night of Jesus' arrest (Mark 14:51–52).

> **12:13** And when he knocked at the door of the gate, a
> servant-girl named Rhoda came to answer.

Rhoda. Servants of wealthy Jews were commonly female. The Greek name *Rhodē* means "rose." Despite only her Greek name being given, she could have been of Jewish origins. Though she is mentioned only in 12:13–15, her actions must have led to chuckles for years afterward as the early believers recalled it.

Peter, who had escaped Herod's prison by angelic intervention, has come to Mary's house seeking shelter (12:13). When Rhoda approaches to see who is knocking on the door, she hears Peter's voice. In her excitement, she leaves him outside and runs to tell the others gathered in the house (12:14). She is immediately rebuked, even to the point of being called insane (12:15a). However, she was not one to be put off (12:15b). Like Mary and others who testified of the risen Christ, Rhoda knew the truth and attempted to communicate it, even if they failed to listen to her (12:15c–16). Finally, the others decide to see for themselves.

12:17b "Report these things to James and the brethren."

James [son of Alphaeus]. See under 1:13.

12:20 Now [Herod] was very angry with the people of Tyre and Sidon; and with one accord they came to him, and having won over Blastus the king's chamberlain, they were asking for peace, because their country was fed by the king's country.

Tyre and Sidon. These Phoenician seaport trade centers date back to about 2000 B.C. Both are mentioned in the Old Testament as early as Genesis 10:15. They were located between the Lebanon mountains and the Mediterranean Sea. Tyre had two harbors and extended offshore to an island. The Phoenicians who inhabited much of this area were descendants of the Canaanites and Philistines.

The ancient Semitic alphabet of this region figured in development of the Greek alphabet, in which most of the New Testament was written. Sidon seems first to have been the dominant city, but Tyre dominated the region's later history. Tyre and Sidon were known for blown glass and for production of a precious purple dye from seashells.

Joshua was unable to conquer this area. Israel had relations with these cities, especially Tyre. For his royal palace, David (c. 1000 B.C.) employed Tyrian stone masons and carpenters and used cedar logs from the area. Solomon also relied heavily on materials and manpower from the region of Tyre. Ahab, the king of Israel (r. 874–853 B.C.), married Jezebel the daughter of the king of Tyre. In Ezekiel 28, Tyre is depicted as the ultimate example of pride. Assyria besieged the city five years without capturing it in about 700. Nebuchadnezzar failed despite a thirteen-year siege in the late sixth century. Alexander the Great conquered Tyre with siege ramps to the island in the late 330s B.C. Alexander devastated the city and killed its inhabitants. Under Roman occupation, Sidon and Tyre became important stops on trade routes but never regained prominence. The area is dependent on imports of food.

Jesus spent time in both Sidon and Tyre and, in response to the prophets' description of the two cities, contrasted them with the Jews as examples of faith (Luke 10:13). In Acts 12:20–23, emissaries of Tyre and Sidon come to Caesarea to beg mercy of Herod (see Herod Agrippa I under 12:1).

Returning from his third missionary trip (21:3), Paul spends seven days in Tyre and sails on to Ptolemais. Disciples in Tyre warn Paul not to set foot in the city of Jerusalem. It is evident that the gospel has been received in Tyre and Sidon and that there is a Christian community. In 27:3, after Paul has appealed to Caesar, he is allowed by his guard Julius to receive care in Sidon.

Although nothing is specifically stated in the book of Acts of the importance of these cities to the spread of early Christianity, the fact that there were a group of Christians there with a heart after God would lead Bible teachers to believe that the port cities of Sidon and Tyre helped send the gospel across the sea. Certainly these cities were embarking points for the first-century church.

Blastus. A chamberlain was a secretary-advisor who might have as much authority and responsibility as a diplomat or foreign minister. Extremely trusted, Blastus held the keys for anyone wanting a hearing before his master. The people of Tyre and Sidon were able to do just that through begging or bribery. Nothing more is known of this man nor is he mentioned again in the New Testament.

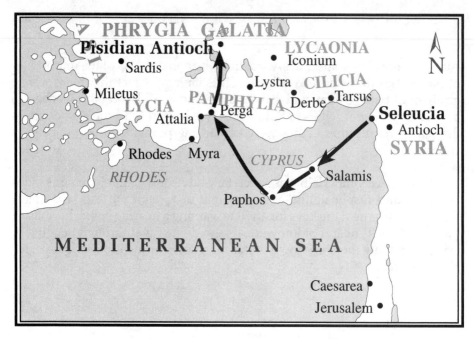

Chapter 13

A.D. 47

FIRST MISSIONARY JOURNEY;
PAUL AT PISIDIAN ANTIOCH

Synopsis

(1–3) Back in Antioch, Barnabas and Saul are surrounded by some of the most able of prophets and teachers of the church at that time (1). To this prepared group the Holy Spirit ordered that Barnabas and Saul be set apart as world evangelists (2). Together, the two men depart on the first missionary journey (3).

(4–12) On the island of Cyprus the two are hindered by a magician named Elymas (Bar-Jesus). He tries to prevent the local proconsul, Sergius Paulus, from hearing the word of God (4–8). But Saul, now known as Paul, filled with the Holy Spirit, places a curse of blindness upon the man (9–11). Sergius Paulus believes in Jesus (12).

(13–52) Paul next journeys to Pisidian Antioch in Phrygia where he gives one of his most powerful messages to his Jewish brothers. In this sermon Paul focuses on Abraham, King David, and the resurrection of the Messiah. (13–41). When Paul and Barnabas are finished, many Jews and God-fearing proselytes beg them to stay

another Sabbath and speak more about the Lord. The next Sabbath nearly the whole city, pious Jews and Gentiles, gather to hear the gospel. Many Gentiles believe (42–49). Hardened Jews arouse others against the apostles and starts a persecution. Paul and Barnabas leave, shaking the dust from their feet in protest (50–52).

> **13:1** Now there were at Antioch, in the church that was there, prophets and teachers: Barnabas, and Simeon who was called Niger, and Lucius of Cyrene, and Manaen who had been brought up with Herod the tetrarch, and Saul.

Prophets and teachers. In Acts, a few godly disciples are called prophets (21:9). Paul will later be recognized as an apostle as "eminent" as the Twelve who perform signs and wonders (2 Cor. 12:11–12) and who reveal God's message. But as far as can be ascertained, prophets seldom foretold the future, with the notable exception of Agabus (11:28; 21:10). It is mentioned that other prophets journeyed with him from Jerusalem to Antioch (11:27), and concerning Agabus that he spoke by the Holy Spirit (v. 28). The others apparently were teaching prophets. These had a most important gift of imparting truth before the canon of Scripture was complete and doctrinal truth could be seen codified in the New Testament documents. Paul seems to have in mind the ministry and gift of teaching in his references to prophets in 1 Corinthians 12–14. There seems to be little doubt that this gift, along with the gifts of knowledge and tongues, would someday no longer be needed (1 Cor. 13:8–10). See pp. 90–91; see also Agabus under 11:28.

Simeon who was called Niger. Simeon was a prominent prophet and teacher of the church at Antioch. He was also called Niger, a Latin form of his name. He was a Jew by birth but used the name Niger when dealing with foreigners. Charles Ryrie comments that the name *Niger* indicates that Simeon was from Africa. It is possible that this is Simon of Cyrene, who carried Christ's cross (Matt. 27:32; Mark 15:21), but this is speculation with no factual evidence behind it.[132]

Lucius of Cyrene. *Lucius* means "of the light or luminous." He was one of the prophets and teachers at the church of Antioch. "Of Cyrene" indicates that he was from Cyrene, the capital city of Libya in northern Africa (See 2:10). Some have speculated that this is Luke. Yet it is inconsistent with the rest of Acts, where Luke continually uses the first-person plural "we or us" when describing his journeys with Paul. Also, the name Luke was very common.

One reference to Lucius is made by Paul in the closing greetings of Romans. "Timothy my fellow worker greets you, and so do Lucius and Jason and Sosipater, my kinsmen" (16:21). Whether this is the same Lucius is debatable.

Manaen. The name means "consoler, or comforter." This is the only occurrence of this name in Scriptures. He was one of the prophets and teachers residing at the church of Antioch. He is recorded as being a foster-brother or someone brought up with Herod the tetrarch. This Herod was the one who had put John the Baptist to death and who treated the Lord shamefully. It is obvious that they grew up together and were educated together. It is interesting to note that in such an atmosphere one man would be brought up to become a disciple of Jesus (Manaen) and the other an antagonist of the Lord (Herod).

> **13:2b** the Holy Spirit said, "Set apart for Me Barnabas and
> Saul for the work to which I have called them."

The Holy Spirit said. See comments on the personality of the Spirit, pp. 125–127.

> **13:3** Then, when they had laid their hands on them,

Laid their hands. See pp. 402–8.

> **13:4** So, being sent out by the Holy Spirit, they went down
> to Seleucia and from there they sailed to Cyprus.

Sent out by the Holy Spirit. See pp. 166–67.

Seleucia. Seleucia, the port of Syrian Antioch, located five miles north of the mouth of the Orontes River and sixteen miles from Antioch. At the time of the New Testament, Seleucia was on a fertile plain still noted for its beauty. The city was founded in 301 B.C. by Seleucus I Nicator, one of Alexander's generals, who founded the Seleucid Empire and wanted Seleucia as an impregnable western capital. It fell to Antiochus Epiphanes in 219 B.C., who beautified it, but it was beginning to fade in importance by the time of the early church.

Only Acts 13:4 names Seleucia (13:4). This city was Paul and Barnabas's first stop on their first missionary journey. Seleucia was a wealthy port city and an ideal place for them to stop over as they began their trip. From Seleucia, they set sail for Cyprus, beginning in earnest the first missionary journey.

> **13:5** And when they reached Salamis, they began to
> proclaim the word of God in the synagogues of the Jews;
> and they also had John as their helper.

Salamis. Salamis was the chief city on the island of Cyprus, located in the Gulf of Saronikos. It is the chief city on the isle of Cyprus. Excavations have uncovered a large first-century theater that would hold approximately 15,000 people. At the south end of the city stood a temple of Zeus on a high podium. Wheat, olive oil, and wine have been major production items of the city, and fishing an important industry. Salamis was said by Homer to be the home of the legendary Greek heroes Ajax and Teucer.

Salamis was conquered by Athens in the sixth century B.C. Salamis fell to Macedonia in 318 B.C. but returned to Athenian control in the following century. Unfortunately, the region has been plagued by earthquakes that have destroyed much of the archaeological record. It is difficult to learn much about Salamis during the time of Paul's ministry.

Salamis was the first place visited by Saul and Barnabas after leaving the mainland of Seleucia. Though the city was chiefly made up of Greeks, the use of the plural *synagogues* confirms the large Jewish presence on Cyprus from the fourth century B.C. The effectiveness of their proclamation is not given, but persecution evidently did not break out there as at many other synagogues in which they preached.

John. "John" mentioned in this verse is John Mark. See under 12:4. As their helper, John Mark might aid Paul and Barnabas with baptisms and teaching converts. See 12:12.[134]

> **13:6** And when they had gone through the whole island as far as Paphos, they found a certain magician, a Jewish false prophet whose name was Bar-Jesus.

Paphos. Paphos, also called "New Paphos," was the Roman provincial capital of Cyprus. It was ten miles northwest of the old Phoenician city of Paphos and 100 miles southwest of Salamis.

Paphos was famous for the worship of Venus, whose great temple was at Old Paphos. Excavations have uncovered a theater and two rather luxurious villas, one believed to have been the governor's palace. Old Paphos was settled by Greek or Phoenician colonists late in the second millennium B.C. New Paphos was the port of the old city and gradually became the more important town.[134]

Acts mentions Paphos in 13:6, 13. A road from Salamis to Paphos enables Paul and company to travel at a rapid pace. At Paphos they are summoned by the Roman proconsul, Sergius Paulus, who is curious as to what Paul is teaching. Withstanding Barnabas and Saul is a Jewish magician named Bar-Jesus (or Elymas). In the presence of Paulus, Bar-Jesus is struck blind in judgment. This so impresses Paulus that he becomes a believer.

The second reference to Paphos relates to the company departing.

Bar-Jesus. Bar-Jesus, meaning "son of Joshua," is identified in 13:6 by Luke as a certain "maggot," magician, or sorcerer. His Aramaic name was Elymas. He also is called a Jewish false prophet who had gained the favor of the proconsul Sergius Paulus. Luke describes the proconsul as an intelligent man, despite his association with Bar-Jesus. Bar-Jesus opposed Paul and Barnabas as the two proclaimed the gospel to Sergius Paulus. Paul ordered that he be temporarily blinded, an action reminiscent of his own experience on the Damascus Road (13:10–11).

> **13:7a** [Bar-Jesus] was with the proconsul, Sergius Paulus, a man of intelligence.

Sergius Paulus. The Roman proconsul of Cyprus is described by Luke as an intelligent man who was seeking to hear the Word of God (13:7). Until Paul and Barnabas encountered him on their first missionary journey, he had been under the influence of Elymas Bar-Jesus (see under 13:6). As a result of his opposition to the gospel, Bar-Jesus was temporarily blinded, giving Sergius Paulus the evidence of the truth he needed. Stanley D. Toussaint comments on the significance of Paul's first recorded miracle being formed in conflict with a Jew over the evangelizing of a Gentile.[135]

> **13:8** But Elymas the magician . . . was opposing them, seeking to turn the proconsul away from the faith.

Elymas. See under 13:6.

> **13:9a** But Saul, who was also known as Paul,

Paul. At Paphos Saul is first called Paul. Saul was his Jewish name and Paul his Roman or Gentile name. Both were given at his birth, but he begins to use his Gentile name in this Roman environment.[136] See also p. 102.

> **13:13a** Now Paul and his companions put out to sea from Paphos and came to Perga in Pamphylia;

Perga. A city on the river Cestus, Perga lies twelve miles east of Attalia in Pamphylia. Perga was so large that many referred to it as a metropolis. The city of Perga was quadrangular. It contained very broad streets, which divided the city into quarters.

Modern archeology is uncertain as to how old Perga truly is. Alexander the Great made Perga a base for his conquest of Asia Minor in the 330s B.C. Ancient walls have been uncovered that seem to come from the Seleucid period (third century B.C.). Coinage has been uncovered from 200 B.C. to A.D. 286.

Perga was the seat of local worship of the Asiatic goddess Leto (better known as Artemis and Diana). She is depicted on coins as having a bow in hand and sphinxes and stags at her side. A yearly festival was held in honor of Leto.

Two references are made in Scripture to the town of Perga. Acts 13:14 names it as the debarkation point for Paul, Barnabas, and John Mark. It was here that John Mark abandoned the mission and returned to Jerusalem. This part of Paul's first missionary journey undoubtedly was very disheartening. This coastline was heavily infected with malaria, and some believe Paul may have contracted it here. Paul's illness of Galatians 4:13 could have been a result of the malaria. Fears for his health may have persuaded John Mark to leave.

Another plausible theory was that John Mark feared to continue on the road to Pisidian Antioch. The trip was 100 miles long and infested with robbers. William Ramsay has translated a number of inscriptions from the Pisidian area referring to the lawlessness of this region and the armed soldiery needed to guard the peace of the country.[137] This mountainous region also was renowned for the dangers flash floods posed after rain.

Perga is also mentioned in 14:25 as Paul and Barnabas return through the city. On his first pass through the city, it is not recorded if Paul preached or taught. However, Luke assures us that on his way back he speaks the Word. His results are not recorded, so success may have been minimal.

Pamphylia. See under 2:10.

13:14 But going on from Perga, they arrived at Pisidian Antioch, and on the Sabbath day they went into the synagogue and sat down.

Pisidian Antioch. Pisidia was a highland area in Asia Minor. It was bordered by Lycaonia to the east and north, by Pamphylia to the south, and by the province of Asia to the north and west. As with other areas of ancient times, it is difficult to determine the amount of land possessed at various times. Wars continually changed borders.

Pisidia was noted for its lawless mountain tribes. These tenacious tribes were never subdued by the Persians or the Greeks.

Pisidian Antioch was in reality not in Pisidia but in Phrygia near the Pisidian border. To distinguish it from the other Antioch in Phrygia, it was popularly called "Antioch of Pisidia." It was founded by Seleucus I Nicator about 281 B.C., one of the sixteen cities he named for either his father or his son, both named Antiochus. Antioch occupied a high plateau on the Via Sebaste, the Roman road from Ephesus to the Euphrates. Augustus incorporated Antioch into the expanded Roman province of Galatia in 25 B.C. and imported three thousand army veterans and their families from Italy. It became *Colonia Caesarea*. Antioch was the most important city of southern Galatia and included Greek, Roman, Oriental, and Phrygian traditions. Acts speaks of a sizable Jewish population.[138]

Only two references are made in the book of Acts to Pisidian Antioch. Paul makes a rest stop there and teaches in the synagogue on his first missionary journey (13:14). Here Paul gives what has been called the first of three missionary sermons. When Paul entered the synagogue with Barnabas, he may have been dressed as a Pharisee. This would have given him the right to speak to the gathering and appropriated for him some respect. In Paul's audience were both Jews and "God-fearing" Gentiles.

Paul begins his sermon by informing the Jews of what God has done for them, and what God has promised to do. Throughout their history they can see the hand of God upon them, how God has kept all His promises. Then he points out that God has sent the promised Messiah in the person of Jesus Christ of the line of David.

Paul explains the three important points regarding the Christ: (1) The Romans crucified Him, but God raised Him from the dead. (2) Jesus fulfilled the Messianic promises from the Old Testament. (3) Forgiveness is available to those who believe on the Messiah.

Many of the Jews and God-fearing Gentiles follow Paul and Barnabas so they can learn more. They stay and speak at the synagogue the next week, and many come (13:44). Their popularity makes unbelieving Jews so furious that they heckle and blaspheme him. Paul and Barnabas then deliver a shocking retort (13:46). The joy of the Gentiles could not be contained, and they praise and glorify God. Many of them believe and spread the message around the area. Soon the Word had gone throughout the entire area.

However, the Jews are not finished. They arouse city leaders, who expel Paul and Barnabas from the city. But they cannot stop those who had been touched.

The next reference is a brief note on Paul's return for the Council of Jerusalem (14:24). No mention is made of Paul's preaching or teaching on this return trip. There is the possibility he wanted to remain nondescript after the trouble he had on his first time through. Or maybe he saw the growth of the church there and realized his teachings were not necessary.

Synagogue. See under 6:8.

> **13:19** "And when He had destroyed seven nations in the
> land of Canaan, He distributed their land as an inheritance—
> all of which took about four hundred and fifty years.

Seven nations. The Hittites, Girgashites, Amorites, Canaanites, Perizzites, Hivites, Jebusites. See Deuteronomy 7:1.

Took about four hundred and fifty years. "By adding together all the periods mentioned in the book of Judges, given that some judges worked concurrently in different parts of the land, the periods of foreign domination and the intervals of rest under the Judges, the 450 years cited here can be closely accounted for.[139]

> **13:20** And after these things He gave them judges until Samuel the prophet.

Samuel. Paul may have a specific point in mentioning Samuel. Few are seen as more godly and law keeping. This had to bring a strong conviction to a Jew who listened with any openness of heart. Merrill Unger writes that it is impossible not to be impressed with Samuel's piety: "God was the center around which he, as well as heaven, turned. In all his difficulties he repaired to God for counsel. In all his acts and decisions he was guided by the word of Jehovah. His advice to the Israelites was the motto of his own life, 'Turn not aside from following the Lord, but serve the Lord with all your heart.'"[140]

> **13:21a** And then they asked for a king, and God gave them Saul the son of Kish,

Saul the Son of Kish. King Saul represents the epitome of arrogance and pride, disobedience and presumption in the Old Testament. When he was rejected as king over Israel, Samuel said to him: "Behold, to obey is better than sacrifice, and to heed than the fat of rams" (1 Sam. 15:22b).

> **13:22a** And after He had removed him, He raised up David to be their king,

David. See p. 79.

> **13:23** From the offspring of this man, according to promise, God has brought to Israel a Savior, Jesus,

Savior, Jesus. See p. 73.

> **13:26b** to us the word of this salvation is sent out.

Salvation. See under 2:40.

> **13:28b** they asked Pilate that He be executed.

Pilate. See under 3:13.

13:30 But God raised Him from the dead;

Raised Him from the dead. See pp. 73–74.

13:31 for many days He appeared to . . . the very ones who are now His witnesses to the people.

His witnesses. See under 1:8.

13:33a God has fulfilled this promise to our children in that He raised up Jesus,

He raised up Jesus. See pp. 73–74.

13:35 Therefore He also says in another Psalm, "Thou wilt not allow Thy Holy One to undergo decay."

Holy One. See p. 76.

13:39 and through Him everyone who believes is freed from all things, from which you could not be freed through the Law of Moses.

You could not be freed through the Law of Moses. See under 15:10–11.

13:43a Now when the meeting of the synagogue had broken up, many of the Jews and of the God-fearing proselytes followed Paul and Barnabas,

God-fearing proselytes. See under 2:10.

13:46 "It was necessary that the word of God should be spoken to you first; since you repudiate it, and judge yourselves unworthy of eternal life, behold, we are turning to the Gentiles.

Word . . . spoken to you first. See under 3:26.

13:48b and as many as were appointed to eternal life believed.

Appointed. In the Greek, this is a perfect, passive participle of *tassō* and can be translated "the ones who have, through a process, *been fixed, ordained,* *or determined* to eternal life." This implies the sovereign work of God in salvation. J. A. Alexander believes it scandalous the "violent attempts which have been made to eliminate the doctrine of election or predestination from this verse."[141]

Eternal life. This expression is used forty-eight times in the New Testament, including six other words and phrases that are almost synonymous in implication. For example: we are to be with Christ in eternal glory (2 Tim. 2:10), Jesus is the source of eternal salvation (Heb. 5:9), we have obtained eternal redemption (Heb. 9:12), and we have the promise of an eternal inheritance (Heb. 9:15) through the blood of an eternal covenant (Heb. 13:20). And, in the book of Revelation, there is to be preached an eternal gospel (14:6).

Believed. This is the result of being sovereignly appointed to salvation. Second Thessalonians 2:13 reads: "God has chosen you from the beginning for salvation through sanctification by the Spirit and faith in the truth." Belief is but the process and the result of being first chosen by God's mysterious providence!

> **13:52** And the disciples were continually filled with joy and with the Holy Spirit.

Filled with the Holy Spirit. See pp. 162–64.

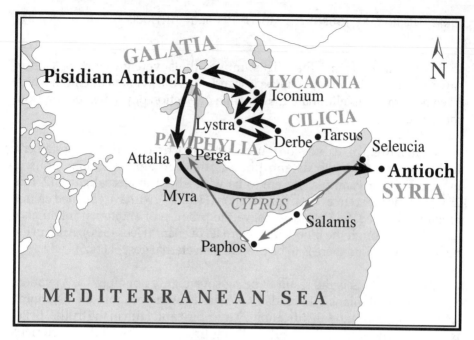

Chapter 14

A.D. 48

Outreach to Iconium, Lystra, and Derbe; Return to Antioch

Synopsis

(1–20) From Pisidian Antioch, Paul and Barnabas flee to Iconium, where they have great success in the local synagogue. A great number of Jews and Gentiles accept the Lord (1–2). But certain Jews who do not believe stir up the Gentiles against the gospel. The city was divided, and Paul and Barnabas are in danger (3–5). They travel to Lycaonia, Lystra, and Derbe and the surrounding area and continue to preach (6). After Paul and Barnabus perform a healing at Lystra, the crowd of onlookers calls Barnabas Zeus and Paul Hermes (7–14). Frustrated that they have missed the point, Paul shouts out that they are mere men. Though Paul explains that the one Creator God has left a witness for Himself in nature, the crowd still tries to offer sacrifices to them (15–18). Later, zealous Jews who have followed Paul and Barnabas from Antioch stir up another mob against Paul. He is stoned and dragged from the city (19). Paul revives and eventually travels on to Derbe with Barnabas (20).

(21–28) Having returned to Syrian Antioch, Paul and Barnabas appoint elders in that city and then journey on to Pamphylia, Perga, and Attalia and then back to Antioch (21–26), where they report to the church all the Lord has done and how "He had opened a door of faith to the Gentiles" (27). Needing to rest, the apostles settle for a period (28).

14:1a And it came about that in Iconium they entered the synagogue of the Jews together,

Iconium. Despite a tremendous response in Antioch of Pisidia (13:42), Paul and Barnabas are ultimately driven from the city and even from the region (13:50). Undiscouraged, the disciples and Paul end up in Iconium and speak in the synagogue to both Jews and Gentiles. A "great multitude" believe in the Lord (14:1). Then disbelieving Jews in the city agitate a Gentile riot against the apostles (v. 2). Paul and his companions flee to Lycaonia, Lystra, and Derbe.

Iconium was the Damascus of Asia Minor, with financial wealth and a rich history. Though strongly Romanized, it was not at this time a Roman colony. Jews, Greeks, and Romans shared the city. In time, Iconium became a major center for the spread of the gospel. It was located on a well-watered plateau that was ideal for agriculture and farming. This entire region of Asia Minor was prosperous; its fame and prestige grew under Roman rule. The city was also famous for its mother goddess worship with a host of eunuch priests. The emperor Claudius honored the city with the title of Claudiconium. In New Testament times, Iconium was an important Hellenistic city with an elite Jewish community and synagogue.

Jews from Iconium followed Paul and Barnabas to Lystra and poisoned the city against them. After the nearly fatal riot and stoning there, the apostles returned to Iconium, strengthened the budding church, and appointed elders (14:21–23). With joy years later, Paul reviews with Timothy the events at Iconium. He wrote of the things that "happened to me at Antioch, at Iconium, and at Lystra, what persecutions I endured, and out of them all the Lord delivered me!" (2 Tim. 3:11).

14:6 [Paul and Barnabas] . . . fled to the cities of Lycaonia, Lystra and Derbe, and the surrounding region;

Lycaonia. Lycaonia occupied the area between the Anatolian foothills. It was bordered on the north by Iconium of Phrygia, east by Cappadocia, and south by Isauria. The region lay along the overland route from western Anatolia to the Cilician Gate and Syria. It was a volatile place that changed political hands often throughout ancient history. It became part of Cilicia under Roman rule and by the time of the New Testament was known as Galatia. In New Testament times this area still had its own separate dialect (see 14:11).

Sheep and warrior archers came from Lycaonia. It also became fertile ground for the gospel. Persecution caused the gospel to spread throughout the region. News of the healing and the message of Paul and Barnabas undoubtedly passed through other regions from this strategic section of the overland highway. The area was fiercely defended by Rome because of its importance to trade and transportation routes to the East and to Africa.

Lystra. Lystra was a south-central Lycaonian center. Like Derbe and the rest of this area, it spoke the Lycaonian dialect. This city was founded by Augustus Caesar as a colony of veteran Roman legion soldiers who would protect Rome's interests. Lystra had its own temple dedicated to Zeus just outside the city gates (14:13).

At Lystra, Paul commands a cripple to stand. Because of this, both he and Barnabas are proclaimed to be gods. Barnabas is considered to be Zeus (father of the gods) and Paul to be Hermes (messenger of the gods). Apparently Barnabas was the more imposing man, who looked like the leader. Paul and Barnabas were at Lystra long enough for word to spread back to the Jews in Iconium and Antioch. Jews came to Lystra and started the riot that left Paul nearly dead outside the gates.

In Acts 16:1–2, Timothy is introduced as being from Lystra. Timothy most certainly was saved as the result of Paul's first mission trip to the city (1 Cor. 4:17; 1 Tim 1:2; 2 Tim 1:2). Already by Paul's second missionary trip Timothy is well spoken of by all the brethren. From this point, Paul devotes much time to grooming Timothy for the ministry. Six New Testament books list both Paul and Timothy as authors (see 2 Cor. 1:1; Phil. 1:1; Col. 1:1; 1 Thess. 1:1; 2 Thess. 1:1; Philem. 1). Timothy was sent on several critical mission trips of his own (Acts 17:14–15; 18:5; 19:22; 20:4; Rom. 16:21; 1 Cor. 16:10; 2 Cor. 1:19; 1 Thess. 3:2, 6). During Paul's later imprisonment, Timothy was sent to Corinth and Philippi. Timothy of Lystra was Paul's only frontline defense for the gospel in his absence.

Derbe. Derbe is a major city of Lycaonia in Galatia. Residents of this city spoke a different dialect from that of the rest of northern Iconium (14:11). Paul and Barnabas arrive here after Paul was left for dead from a stoning in Lystra. Paul preaches in this city very successfully and makes many brethren (14:21). Paul and Barnabas also appoint elders and deacons within the loose structure of the church. Paul encourages them to keep the faith in light of the many tribulations and persecutions that the church will most certainly endure. On his second missionary trip, Paul and Silas return through Derbe on the way to Lystra. Gaius from Derbe traveled with Paul on his third and final missionary trip (20:4). Derbe was strategic for reaching much of the ancient world because it was a popular stopover on the overland road.

14:12 And they began calling Barnabas, Zeus, and Paul,
Hermes, because he was the chief speaker.

Zeus. Zeus (or Jupiter in the Roman pantheon) was considered to be the chief of the Olympian gods. He was ruler of the world and presided over the councils of the gods on Mount Olympus. As George Howe and G. A. Harrer explain, "His mere nod sufficed to enforce his will, and would cause all Olympus to tremble. All things were under his sway. . . . Good or ill fortune for mortals ultimately depended on his attitude."[142]

At Lystra, after Paul healed a man lame from birth, the people declared Barnabas to be Zeus. For whatever reason, the people at Lystra attributed to their gods the power of healing they had witnessed. This gave Paul and Barnabas an excellent opportunity to explain the true Source of Paul's healing authority. F. F. Bruce explains that "Barnabas may have been identified with Zeus because of his more dignified bearing."[143] A. T. Robertson considers that the identification was "because Barnabas was the older and the more imposing in appearance."[144]

Hermes. Acts 14:12 contains the only biblical reference to the deity the Greeks named *Hermes* and the Romans *Mercurius* or *Mercury*. Hermes was generally thought to be the son of Zeus and Maia and was one of the great Olympian gods. His functions were more varied than those of any other god. He ruled over eloquent speech and was the messenger of Zeus.[145] Robertson observes, "Hermes was of beautiful appearance and eloquent in speech, the inventor of speech and legend. Our word hermeneutics, or science of interpretation, comes from this word."[146] *Hermeneō* is the Greek word for "to explain, interpret."[147]

14:16 And in the generations gone by He permitted all the
nations to go their own ways;

To go their own ways. Paul develops this further in his letter to the Romans when he writes, "God gave [men] over in the lusts of their hearts to impurity" (1:24), "God gave [men] over to degrading passions" (v. 26), "God gave [men] over to a depraved mind" (v. 28). He explains that the race "exchanged the glory of the incorruptible God for an image in the form of corruptible man . . ." (v. 23).

14:17a He did not leave Himself without witness,

[Natural] witness. Paul continues to explain in Romans that in the creation of the world God's "invisible attributes, His eternal power and divine nature, have been clearly seen, being understood through what has been made, so that [men] are without excuse" (1:20).

14:19a But Jews came from Antioch and Iconium,

Antioch. See under 13:14.

Iconium. See under 14:1.

14:20b And the next day he went away with Barnabas to Derbe.

Derbe. See under 14:6.

14:23a And when they had appointed elders for them in every church,

Appointed elders. The Greek *cheirotoneō* originally meant "to raise the hand," as in voting. But the idea of voting in a democratic way is probably not in view here, especially sense the decision is made between just two men, Paul and Barnabas. The same may be true of the other place where the word is used, 2 Corinthian 8:19. In that passage, Titus is "appointed" by several churches to travel with Paul in his "gracious work." Since more than one church was involved, many scholars believe this was an approval or agreement, but not voting in the normal sense.

14:24 And they passed through Pisidia and came into Pamphylia.

Pisidia. See under 13:14.

Pamphylia. See under 13:13.

14:25 And when they had spoken the word in Perga, they went down to Attalia;

Perga. See under 13:13.

Attalia. From this seaport in Pamphylia on the south coast of Asia Minor, Paul and Barnabas sail for Antioch, Syria, after evangelizing a few miles away in Perga. There is no record as to how their message is received. Attalia was founded between 165 and 138 B.C. by Attalus II of Pergamum. It had been taken over by the Romans and was an important commercial harbor.

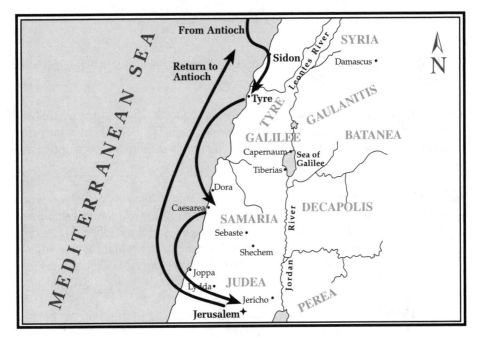

Chapter 15

A.D. 49

THE JERUSALEM COUNCIL; SECOND MISSIONARY JOURNEY

Synopsis

(1–5) At Antioch, challenging Paul and Barnabas, are believing Jews from Judea who teach that Gentile converts must be circumcised to be saved (1). The church rules that Paul and Barnabas should go up to Jerusalem and present the argument before the apostles and other leaders (2). The issue is presented, and certain Pharisees heatedly demand that the Law of Moses must be observed (3–5).

(6–18) A sharp discussion follows. Peter explains how God has giving the Holy Spirit to uncircumcised Gentiles as He did the Jews on Pentecost. Salvation is by grace of the Lord Jesus, Peter argues (6–11). Barnabas and Paul relate how signs and wonders have been done through them among the Gentiles (12).

(13–29) James, the elder of the apostles, ends the argument by quoting from Amos 9, where the Lord speaks of "the Gentiles who are called by My name." James concludes that the church should not lay the burden of the Mosaic law on the Gentiles, beyond the most basic commands for propriety among the Jewish brethren

(19–20). Paul and Barnabas are sent back to Antioch with a letter from the Jerusalem leaders (21–29).

(30–35) The letter brings rejoicing to the Antioch church. The brethren rejoiced and were greatly encouraged by the Jerusalem decision (30–31). The two men then remained in the city for some time, teaching and preaching the word of the Lord (32–35).

(36–41) While planning their second missionary trip, a difference of opinion breaks out between Paul and Barnabas in regard to taking John Mark on the journey. Paul argues that this young man deserted them in Pamphylia when they were on their first trip (36–38). The disagreement became so sharp that the two apostles separate, with Paul taking Silas and Barnabas traveling on to Cyprus with John Mark (39–41).

15:1b "Unless you are circumcised according to the custom of Moses, you cannot be saved."

Moses. See under 3:23.

Cannot be saved. The opposition over law-keeping would not die, but in fact continued to grow in intensity and emotion. See under 2:40.

15:2a And when Paul and Barnabas had great dissension and debate with them,

Dissension and debate. Using two strong Greek words, *stasis* and *zētēsis*, Luke relates the intensity of the quarrel. The issue as to whether Gentiles had to be circumcised in order to be saved had become volatile. In some contexts, *stasis* may be translated "uprising, riot, revolt."[148] *Zētēsis* can mean "to question, be controversial."[149] The issue was so emotional that only a council convened in Jerusalem could settle the matter.

15:3a Therefore, being sent on their way by the church, they were passing through Phoenicia and Samaria,

Phoenicia. See under 11:19.

Samaria. See under 1:8.

15:5 But certain ones of the sect of the Pharisees who had believed, stood up, saying,

Pharisees. See under 5:34.

15:8 "And God, who knows the heart, bore witness to
them, giving them the Holy Spirit, just as He also did to us;

Giving the Holy Spirit. See under 10:47; 11:15. See pp. 160–65.

15:9 and He made no distinction between us and them,
cleansing their hearts by faith.

Cleansing their hearts by faith. Or, "by means of faith." Faith is the
human access that brings on this cleansing process. The same Greek word
katharizō is used in 1 John 1:7, 9: "The blood of Jesus Christ His Son *cleanses*
us from all sin," and "*cleanses* us from all unrighteousness."

15:11 "But we believe that we are saved through the grace
of the Lord Jesus, in the same way as they also are."

Saved through grace. See under 2:40.

15:12—Barnabas and Paul–were relating what signs and
wonders God had done through them among the Gentiles.

Signs and Wonders. See pp. 64–69.

15:13 And after they had stopped speaking, James
answered, saying, "Brethren, listen to me.

James [Jesus' half-brother]. James the brother of Jesus, as his other
brothers, did not believe in Jesus' claims (Mark 6:4; John 7:5). The Lord's
brothers even chided Him that if He were the Messiah He should go to Judea
since the question could not be settled in Galilee (John 7:1–4). Although Jesus'
claims embarrassed James, at times he must have wondered if these claims
were true.

James's conversion must have occurred when Jesus appeared to him in
his postresurrection body as recorded by Paul in 1 Corinthians 15:7. James
quickly became a committed believer in the Jerusalem fellowship. He rose to
prominence, probably in part because he had seen Christ in a postresurrection
appearance—one of the qualifications for an apostle (1 Cor. 9:1). He also was
a witness to Christ's earthly ministry, which Peter believed was essential for
an apostle (Acts 1:21–2).

Whatever his gifts and credentials, James clearly assumed a headship
role of the Jerusalem church. He may have been a logical elder as the apostles

took up missionary ministries and left Jerusalem. Only three years after Paul's conversion on the road to Damascus, Paul met with James in Jerusalem (Gal. 1:9), indicating that already James was a leader there (approx. 37). Several years later, Herod brought persecution on the church by putting James the Apostle to death and throwing Peter into prison. When God miraculously released Peter, he went to John Mark's mother's house, where the brethren were gathered praying and told them to "report these things to James and the brethren" (12:17). While in Antioch, Peter acted hypocritically when "certain men from James" came to visit, indicating that James was the leader of the church.

James appears again as prominent at the Jerusalem council in chapter 15. Peter reminded the gathering that God had called him earlier to preach the gospel to Gentiles and that they had been given the Holy Spirit by simply placing their faith in Christ (15:7–9). It is James who agreed with Peter that they should not put the Gentiles under circumcision and the bondage of the Law (15:12–21). James quoted Amos 9:12 to show that this should not surprise them since even the prophets agreed there would come a day when Gentiles would be called by the name of the Lord. This decision of James came at a critical juncture in the transition of Christianity from Jewish sect to world movement. Justification by faith alone was upheld, and the church spread among Gentiles.

When Paul returned to Jerusalem after his last missionary journey, he again met with James and all the elders of the church (21:18). In almost every instance James is distinguished from the other elders. There had apparently been a vicious rumor going around Jerusalem that Paul was teaching his Jewish converts who lived among Gentiles to forsake the Jewish customs. James showed sensitivity by advising Paul to sponsor four men who had taken a Nazarite vow to show that the rumors were lies, that he still respected and observed customs. This was important since many Jewish believers felt very strongly that all Jewish Christians should continue to observe Jewish customs.

God's sovereign wisdom in choosing James to lead the Jerusalem church is seen in his Jewish mind-set as reflected in his epistle. The book of James is, according to W. T. Dayton, "the most Jewish book in the New Testament. Except for two or three references to Christ, it would fit rather well in the Old Testament. The life to which the epistle exhorts is that of a profoundly pious Jew who is fulfilling the Law in every regard."[150]

> **15:15** "And with this the words of the Prophets agree, just as it is written,

The Prophets agree. See p. 90–91.

15:22 Then it seemed good to the apostles and the elders, . . .
to choose men from among them to send to Antioch with
Paul and Barnabas—Judas called Barsabbas, and Silas,
leading men among the brethren,

Judas [called Barsabbas]. This Judas carries the same surname as Joseph Barsabbas, who was nominated before Pentecost to replace Judas Iscariot among the Twelve (1:21–26). It is suggested by commentators that they were brothers, so likely Judas was also a longtime follower who had walked with Christ.

Silas. The mission of Judas Barsabbas and Silas, also called Silvanus, was both to represent the authority of the Jerusalem church against those who might question the pastoral letter and to minister to the Gentile brothers at Antioch, Cilicia, and Syria (15:22–23). Judas and Silas were to come back to Jerusalem with a verbal report about the Gentile believers (v. 27).

Silas was considered a teaching prophet (v. 32) and gave a lengthy message of encouragement among the brothers in Antioch. There is good evidence that after Judas returned to Jerusalem with his report, Silas stayed on to minister with Paul and Barnabas (vv. 34–35). A Roman citizen, Silas was chosen by Paul, after he broke with Barnabas, to revisit the cities and new converts of Greece (vv. 38–40). Silas went through his baptism of fire at Philippi. He and Paul were dragged into the marketplace, beaten (16:19–23), and jailed, where they sang hymns into the night (v. 25). Silas experienced the providential earthquake that released them (v. 26) and the conversion of the thankful jailer (vv. 30–31).

Paul and Silas also escaped Thessalonica under cover of night when they encountered violent opposition in the synagogue (17:1–10). Silas played such an important role in that city that he co-addressed the two epistles to Thessalonica with Paul and Timothy (1 Thess. 1:1; 2 Thess. 1:1). Later, Silas joined Paul in Athens and is seen with Timothy in Corinth as Paul was "solemnly testifying to the Jews that Jesus was the Christ" (18:5). Silvanus and Timothy, of course, also proclaimed Christ at Corinth (2 Cor. 1:19).

It must be noted that Silas/Silvanus carried political weight as a Roman citizen (Acts 16:37), but his most important asset was spiritual. He was a prophet and leading member of the Jerusalem church (15:22, 32). Peter calls him "our faithful brother." Silvanus apparently ended up with Peter and even acted as this apostle's secretary: "Through Silvanus . . . I have written" (1 Peter 5:12).

15:23b "The apostles and the brethren who are elders, to
the brethren in Antioch and Syria and Cilicia who are from
the Gentiles, greetings.

[Syrian] Antioch. See under 6:5; 11:26.

Syria. The Greek *Syria* is derived from the Hebrew *Aram,* for Aram the son of Shem (Gen. 10:22) and father of the nation of Aram (Num. 23:7). *Syria* has come to be recognized as an abbreviation of *Assyria,* and pertained to a very large territory north of Israel, the borders of which were not well defined. This territory, over the years, was under the prominent influence of the Babylonian, Greek, and Roman empires; thus, the inhabitants had varied backgrounds and heritages. Syria and Israel feuded throughout history. Josephus notes the Syrian enmity against the Jewish nation.[151]

Just as the church did not spread into Samaria until trouble arose in Jerusalem, it took persecution to move the church into Syria (11:19). Only after Stephen's martyrdom did the church grow in Syrian Antioch. Antioch was the leading city of Syria and the staging place for launching Christianity into the world.[152]

At Antioch, the gospel was first preached to the Jews (11:19) but also for the first time was preached to the Greeks (11:20). As a result, a great many Jews and Gentiles were saved. It was at Antioch the believers first were called Christians. Antioch would become one of the most important cities in early church history. The Gentile believers at Antioch and the rest of Syria were recipients of the letter sent from the Council of Jerusalem (15:23).

We see in 15:41 that Syria was one of the first stops by Paul on his second missionary journey, as he traveled with Silas. In 18:18, Paul, with Priscilla and Aquila, left Achaia by sea for Syria, where they finally arrived at Antioch.

Again on his third missionary journey Paul determined to sail from Greece to Syria (20:3). And later, Syrian disciples warn him not to set foot in Jerusalem (21:3–4). While these are the only references to Syria, there are many more of Antioch. Through Antioch, Syria played a large role in the spread of the Word of God. F. F. Bruce called Antioch "the metropolis of Gentile Christianity."[153] Not only was Antioch the center of Syria, but also it became a center for Christianity as it provided a springboard for the gospel to go not only into the rest of Syria but also to the rest of the world.

Cilicia. See under 6:9.

15:37 And Barnabas was desirous of taking John called Mark, along with them also.

John called Mark. See under 12:12.

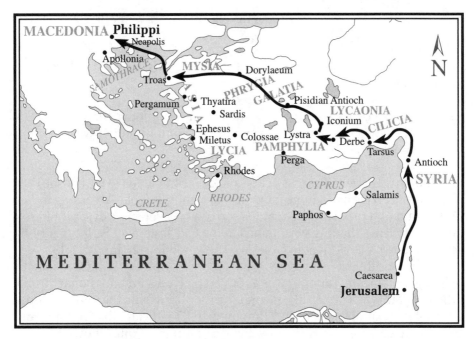

Chapter 16

A.D. 49

THE GOSPEL IN MACEDONIA; THE MINISTRY AT PHILIPPI

Synopsis

(1–5) Paul and Silas pass through Lystra, where they meet young Timothy, who is "well spoken of by the brethren" (1–2). Because Timothy's father is Greek and his mother Jewish, Paul desires that Timothy join them as a witness (3). As Paul travels, he delivers the Jerusalem decrees. The churches are stabilized and strengthened "in the faith, and were increasing in number daily" (4–5).

(6–10) Paul travels to Troas where he received the vision of the call from Macedonia. He concludes that the vision is a call from God to go there and preach the gospel (6–10).

(11–40) Reaching Philippi, Paul encounters Lydia, a seller of purple cloth, whose heart the Lord opens to give hospitality (11–15). Paul also meets a slave-girl with a spirit of divination and finally casts out the spirit (16–18). The girl's masters have Paul and Silas seized, beaten, and dragged off to the prison (19–24). God uses an earthquake to open the prison doors, but no one escapes. The jailer is so touched he takes Paul and Silas home to wash their wounds. His entire household comes to Christ (24–34). Paul is released and returns to the house of

323

Lydia, where he finds more believers. Paul and Silas leave for Thessalonica
encouraged (35–40).

> **16:1b** a certain disciple was there, named Timothy, the son
> of a Jewish woman who was a believer, but his father was a
> Greek,

Timothy. Though Silas was a close and dear companion to the apostle Paul, Timothy may have had a more intimate and significant role. According to Acts and 2 Timothy 1:5–6, Timothy was the son of a believer and a disciple himself. At the very least Timothy was trained in the Old Testament Scriptures by his Jewish mother. Of his Gentile father we know nothing (2 Tim. 1:5; 3:15).

First Corinthians 4:17 suggests that Paul was Timothy's "father" in faith. Whether that means Timothy was a convert on Paul's first missionary trip or whether Paul was a father-like mentor for Timothy's faith, the two developed a close-knit relationship. Second Timothy 3:10–11 indicates that Timothy may have traveled some with Paul on his first journey: "You followed my . . . persecutions, and sufferings, such as happened to me at Antioch, at Iconium and at Lystra; . . . out of them all the Lord delivered me!" (vv. 10–11).

Paul linked up with Timothy at Derbe (16:1), so he may have been a native of that city. He was commended by those at Lystra and Iconium (v. 2).

Timothy is loosely classed with Paul and Silas as an "apostle" (1 Thess. 2:6) and travels extensively with them. He is with Paul at Ephesus on the third missionary journey (19:22), and he is soon sent on his own missions for the apostle. He travels with Erastus and others (1 Cor. 4:17) to Macedonia and then on to Corinth. Timothy returns to Paul with the bad news of problems in the church at Corinth. Titus is sent to deal with the situation. Timothy is sent by Paul to various churches to minister and is with the apostle at different places. Paul ties Timothy with his ministry in saluting the churches at Corinth (2 Cor. 1:1), Philippi (Phil. 1:1), Colossae (Col. 1:1), and Thessalonica (1 Thess. 1:1).

Timothy joins the team as Paul's helper on his second missionary journey (Acts 15:36–41). When Paul starts his last trip to Jerusalem, Timothy is with him (Acts 20:4) and is at his side during the Roman imprisonment. By what Paul writes, the great apostle takes comfort and encouragement from Timothy (Phil. 2:20–22).

From Hebrews 13:23, it seems Timothy was arrested at a fairly early point: "You should understand that our brother Timothy has been released." Since the Hebrews author mentions this man without any explanation, he must have been familiar to the readers. Very likely this then is the same Timothy who was known by the churches, who had walked with Paul, who was imprisoned following Paul's death at Rome, but who also had escaped execution and was set free. Tradition says Timothy died at Ephesus and was buried, like the apostle John, on Mount Prion nearby.[154]

16:3 [Paul] took [Timothy] and circumcised him because of
the Jews who were in those parts, for they all knew that his
father was a Greek.

Circumcised [Timothy]. Since Timothy's mother was Jewish (v. 1), and
he was apparently raised in the Old Testament faith, it would be important
to the Jews that he demonstrate that heritage by circumcision. Otherwise, the
issue could become a stumbling block to the Jews whereby they would not
even begin to consider anything he or Paul had to say. This circumcision for
Timothy would in no way be for salvation nor for any legalistic reasons.

16:6 And they passed through the Phrygian and Galatian
region, having been forbidden by the Holy Spirit to speak
the word in Asia.

Phrygian region. See under 2:10.

Galatian region. The term *Galatia* was used in both an ethnographic
(cultural and geographic) sense and a political sense. Originally, Galatia was
central Asia Minor, where Celtic tribes eventually settled after their conflicts
with the Romans and the Macedonians. In 189 B.C., Galatia came under Roman
domination, and in 25 B.C. Augustus declared it a Roman province. Political or
provincial Galatia included territory not originally part of Galatia (for example,
Pisidian Antioch, Iconium, Lystra, and Derbe).

There are two theories concerning the Galatian territories as referred to
in Acts 16:6. The North Galatian Theory holds that Paul was speaking of
Galatia in its earlier, more restricted sense, so the churches of Galatia were
north of the cities Paul visited on his first missionary journey. This would
mean that Paul visited geographic and cultural Galatia (the smaller region to
the north) for the first time on his second missionary journey, probably enroute
to Troas (16:6). On his third missionary journey, Paul revisited the Galatian
churches he had established (Acts 18:23) and wrote his epistle to them in
either Ephesus (53–56) or Macedonia (56).

This theory is supported by the church fathers, but this may be due to the
exclusive use of the ethnographic sense of Galatia by the second century.
Advocates of this view also point to Luke's apparent use of Galatia in the
northern sense (Acts 16:6; 18:23). Similarities between Galatians and Romans
also help to support this late-date theory for Galatians. But this theory is hurt
by the fact that Acts does not say Paul evangelized in North Galatia. In fact,
he would have had to have taken a radical detour to the northeast on his
second missionary journey to do so, whereas no such detour would have
been necessary if he went to South Galatia.

According to the South Galatian Theory, Paul was referring to Galatia in its wider political sense as a province of Rome. This means that the churches he had in mind in this epistle were the cities he evangelized during his first missionary journey with Barnabas (13:13; 14:23). This was just prior to the Jerusalem Council (15), so the Jerusalem visit (Gal. 2:1–10) must have been the Acts 11:27–30 famine relief visit. Galatians was probably written in Syrian Antioch in 49 just before Paul went to the Council in Jerusalem. The South Galatian cities that Paul visited were more strategic from an evangelistic point of view than those in the north because of their location, population, and commerce. Barnabas would have been more familiar to the South Galatian churches than those to the north because he was not with Paul on his second missionary journey, when the churches in North Galatia were supposedly established.[155]

Forbidden by the Holy Spirit. See under 1:2.

Asia. See under 2:9.

16:7 and when they had come to Mysia, they were trying to go into Bithynia, and the Spirit of Jesus did not permit them;

Mysia. A province in northwest Asia Minor, Mysia is separated from Europe only by the Propontis Sea (modern Sea of Marmara) and the Hellespont Straits (or Dardanelles, connecting the Aegean Sea with the Sea of Marmara). Mysia is considered to be bordered by the Aegean Sea on the west, Bithynia on the north, Phrygia on the south, and an area of Lydia on the southwest. Because of a lack of true borders, it is difficult to ascertain the size of Mysia. It covered northwest branches of the Taurus Mountains, the ancient seaport of Troas, and some ten miles inland the site of ancient Troy.

Because of its location Mysia was traded among conquerors throughout history. The Thracians are believed to have been the original inhabitants, crossing over from Asia. Mysia was at one time part of the empires of Persia and of Alexander the Great. Mysia became important in the third century B.C. as the center of Pergamum, a Hellenistic state that controlled much of western Asia Minor.[156] In 133 B.C., Mysia came under the control of the Roman Empire. Mysia remained a province until the reign of Diocletian (A.D. 284–305), when it was among several provinces that were broken up.

Mysia is mentioned only here in Scripture. Paul and company entered Mysia on the second missionary journey. As Mysia bordered the province of Bithynia, which was north along the Black Sea, Paul attempted to cross Mysia to Bithynia (see below). Roads in this part of the world were well-made Roman highways, so Paul and his companions could travel easily and speedily to spread the gospel. However, for a reason Scripture does not relate beyond that it was the Spirit's doing, Paul could not enter Bithynia. Instead he was directed back to the west. Acts 16:8 suggests that the team did not consider Mysia itself an evangelizing stop but an area to cross on the way elsewhere. *The Expositor's Bible Commentary* comments:

> The participle *parelthontēs* literally means "they passed by" Mysia and at first glance seems somewhat out of place since one could not get to Troas without passing through Mysia. Probably, however, Luke used *parelthontēs* instead of *dielthontēs* ("they passed through") to indicate that they did not stay in Mysia to evangelize.[157]

Bithynia. Is a region of northwest Asia Minor bordered on the Propontis (Sea of Marmara), the Bosporus Thracius (Strait of Bosporus), and the Pontus Euxinus (Black Sea.). Bithynia is a mountainous region, laced with heavy forests and fertile valleys.

Bithynia received its name from the original tribe that settled in the land, the Bithyni, who emigrated from Thrace and settled in the fertile lands. Croesus, king of Lydia, conquered the land in 560 B.C. Four years later, the Persians conquered Lydia, taking control of Bithynia. In 334, Alexander the Great occupied Bithynia. After Alexander's death, Ziobetes, a native prince, led the Bithynians to regain their independence. Ziobetes's son began a ruling dynasty of kings, under which Bithynia flourished. Nicomedes III (r. 91–74 B.C.) became a close ally of the Romans. At his death, he bequeathed Bithynia to the Roman kingdom. It was united with the Roman province of Pontus.

Later, under Byzantine rule, the territory of Bithynia was restricted to an area west of the Sangarius River (now the Sakarya River). It formed a province in the Diocese of Pontus. In 1298, Bithynia was overrun by the Seljuk Turks under Osman and thereafter formed an integral part of the Ottoman Empire. Bithynia is now part of Turkey.[158]

On Paul's second missionary journey, he attempted to enter Bithynia (Acts 16:17). Paul undoubtedly knew of many strategic cities and seaports that were waiting for the gospel. Roman roads had provided an excellent means of transportation throughout the region. But he was prevented by an unspecified obstacle from this goal of evangelization. He attributed the circumstances to the Spirit of Jesus overruling his plans. Scripture attests to the fact that the gospel did reach these people (1 Peter 1:1). There were enough Bithynian Christians by the early second century that Pliny the Younger, governor of Bithynia in 110–12, wrote Emperor Trajan during a time of official persecution asking for policy clarification regarding them.[159]

16:8 and passing by Mysia, they came down to Troas.

Troas. Troas was a port city on the western coast of the Aegean Sea and part of Roman Mysia in Asia Minor. It was founded in 300 B.C. during the

Seleucid dynasty of Syria and drew its name from the ancient city of Troy, whose remains stand about ten miles to the north. Troas was important because it was the nearest Mysian port to Europe. It was a Roman colony in Paul's day.

On Paul's second missionary journey, he and his companions had traveled through Galatia and Phrygia and had decided to head north into Bithynia. When the "Spirit of Jesus" stopped them (Acts 16:7; see above), they traveled west through Mysia to Troas. Paul and his companions here received their "Macedonian call" (16:9). Some scholars speculate that Luke may have been the "man of Macedonia" who appealed to Paul in his dream. It appears that Luke joined him at Troas (cf. 16:11; the narrative begins to use the first-person plural, "we"). Paul and his companions left Troas and traveled across the Aegean to Neapolis, a Macedonian port opposite Troas. They then journeyed to Philippi.

Approximately ten years later, following the great revival in Ephesus that caused a riot led by Demetrius and the silversmiths, Paul traveled again to Troas. This time he preached the gospel, and a church was established (2 Cor. 2:12; 7:5–7).). He also hoped to see Titus and receive a report about the Corinthian church, but Titus was not there. Subsequently, Paul traveled to Macedonia (19:21) and met with Titus, where he composed his second letter to the Corinthian church. Paul's third trip to Troas is recorded in Acts 20:4–12. There he raised from the dead Eutychus, a young man who had fallen asleep listening to him speak (20:9–12). On one of Paul's visits, he left a cloak and some books there (2 Tim. 4:13).

16:9a And a vision appeared to Paul in the night: a certain man of Macedonia

Macedonia. Macedonia in the time of Paul's journeys was a Roman senatorial province covering most of northern Greece. It was bordered on the north by Illyricum, Moesia, and Thrace, on the west by the Adriatic Sea, on the east by the Aegean Sea, and on the south by Achaia. Its history starts around the seventh century B.C., but the first two centuries of Macedonian history is shrouded in obscurity. Macedonia's zenith came in the 340s to 320s B.C. under Philip I and his son, Alexander the Great. They were geniuses at military strategy. At the time of Alexander's death in 323, Macedonia had become the capital of a world empire.

By the middle of the second century B.C., all of the Greek mainland came under Roman rule. From about A.D. 15 to 44, Macedonia was combined with Moesia and Achaia into one large imperial province ruled by a legate from Moesia. It reverted back to the status of a senatorial province in 44.

When Paul visited Neapolis (16:11), Philippi (16:12), Amphipolis (17:1), Apollonia (17:1), Thessalonica (17:1), and Berea (17:10), these cities were all a part of this thriving Roman province. The province was strategically and commercially important because it was crossed by the Egnatian Way (via Egnatia), which extended across its territory from the Adriatic to Thrace. The highway started at the seaports of Dyrracium and Apollonia, opposite southern Italy, extended across the mountains to the port of Thessalonica, and from there to a second Apollonia on the Aegean, to Amphipolis, Philippi, and Neapolis.[160]

Strategically speaking, God's guidance to establish churches in Philippi, Thessalonica, and Berea is logical. Untold thousands of people traveled along the Egnatian Way through these cities. These became two of Paul's healthiest church plants. His epistles to them are full of affection and gratitude for their love and faith.

When Paul left Macedonia for Achaia, he left Silas and Timothy to continue the work there (17:14). Among Paul's converts in Macedonia, several became later traveling companions, including Gaius, Aristarchus (19:29), Sopater, and Secundus (20:4). The churches in Macedonia gave generously to help the famine victims in Jerusalem (Rom. 15:26) and to Paul's ministry (2 Cor. 8:1–5; Phil. 4:15). Paul returned to this area to exhort the believers as recorded in 20:1–6, but no details are given. He possibly returned a third time after his first Roman imprisonment (see Phil. 2:24; 1 Tim. 1:3) and very possibly wrote 1 Timothy from there (1 Tim. 1:3).

16:11b we ran a straight course to Samothrace, and on the day following to Neapolis;

Samothrace. Perhaps meaning the "height of Thrace," Samothrace is a mountainous island in the northern Aegean sea, approximately thirty-eight miles from Thrace. Its peaks rise more than 5,000 feet above the shore. It was settled by the Greeks who intermarried with the Thracian natives in about 700 B.C. It became the main center of the cult religion of the *Cabiri*. Cabiri comes from the Semitic word *kabir*, "lord." These gods or lords varied in number and size and were both male and female deities. At Samothrace, the deities took the form of the patron gods of the smiths, sailors, and fertility. As late as 27 B.C., King Ptolemy of Egypt was a patron of the temple and sent royal money to help fund the site. There was a large theater, and Samothrace was aligned with many political leagues. It was an active naval base. The apostle Paul on his second missionary trip arrived in Samothrace from Troas and went to Neapolis the following day.

Neapolis. Neapolis (modern Kavalla) was a port in the northwest corner of the Aegean Sea about ten miles from Philippi. Merrill Unger writes, "Its remains are remarkable, and its aqueduct still indicates its importance, long since departed." It was the terminus of the Via Egnatia.[161]

16:12—and from there to Philippi,

Philippi. Philippi was a leading city of the Roman province of Macedonia. In ancient times, it was known for fertile plains and the gold mines to the north in the mountains. It was formerly the Thracian city of *Crenodes*, which Philip II of Macedon, father of Alexander the Great, fortified and renamed after himself. He "recognized its importance and sent a large colony there in 356 B.C."[162]

When Paul arrived in Philippi during his second missionary journey, it was a leading district of Macedonia (16:12) and a Roman colony (16:12). M. G. Easton writes that being a "Roman colony" meant that it was a military settlement of Roman soldiers, there planted for controlling the district recently conquered.[163] Being a Roman colony also meant that the citizens enjoyed freedom from beating, from arrest except in extreme cases, and the right to appeal to the emperor. The city was located on the Egnatian Way, the major Roman road through Greece connecting Rome and Asia. The city would have been one of great commerce and trade since it was only ten miles from the port of Neapolis. There was apparently no synagogue in Philippi (16:13) so it probably did not have a large Jewish population. Lenski suggests that when Claudius expelled the Jews from Rome, this colony city followed his example. The population was mostly Greek and Roman. F. F. Bruce comments that the lack of a synagogue means that there were very few Jews, for it took only ten Jewish men to constitute a synagogue. No number of women could compensate for the absence of even one man necessary to complete the quorum of ten.[164]

With no synagogue, the worshipers of God (16:14) meet at the Gangites River on the Sabbath (16:13), a deep and rapid stream about ten miles from the sea. Nonrabbinic sources attest the ancient habit of the Jews to recite prayers near rivers or the seashore.[165] God's divine guidance through the vision was probably for at least two reasons. From an earthly standpoint, it was good strategy for a church to be planted in Philippi. Being a city of great commerce and trade, since it was on the Egnatian Way and close to the port of Neapolis, multitudes of people traveled through. More personally, it was time for God's call on the lives of Lydia, the Philippian jailer, and their families (16:14, 27–31).

Paul and his companions encountered demonic activity (16:16) and were also imprisoned after being beaten (16:23), a violation of their rights as Roman citizens. Roman law prohibited the proselytizing of Roman citizens, thus the persecution that came on Paul and Silas (16:19–24). Their ministry did see success when Lydia and then the Philippian jailer came to Christ (16:14–15, 30–34). The same persecution that Paul and his companions experienced eventually come on the new church. The Epistle of Philippians shows that there were opponents to the gospel (Phil. 1:28) and that believers were suffering (Phil. 2:17–18, 29–30; 3:10; 4:1, 5). They were also hearing false teaching from the Judaizers (Phil. 2:17–19; 3:1–16). There was a unity problem (Phil. 1:27; 2:2; 4:2) that Paul hoped his letter would correct (Phil. 2:3, 25–30).

The Christians of Philippi were special to Paul. They appear to have become one of the most mature of Paul's church plants, and they were missionary minded. Twice they sent a gift to Paul during his stay in Thessalonica to assist him in his work (Phil. 4:15, 16).

16:14a And a certain woman named Lydia, from the city of Thyatira,

Lydia. Paul, Silas, Luke, and probably others sail from Troas to Samothrace and finally to Neapolis, from where they travel inland to Philippi. They spend some days in the city (v. 12), probably looking at the spiritual atmosphere. On the Sabbath they go outside the city to find a group praying (v. 13), since apparently there was no synagogue. The Gentile proselyte Lydia was a worshiper of God (v. 14) in the Old Testament sense. Neither she nor the others had heard of the grace of God through the death and resurrection of the Lord Jesus. But the "Lord opened her heart to respond to the things spoken by Paul."

Originally, *Lydia* meant "a Lydian," one from that city. But because her home was Thyatira, located on the confines of Lydia and Mysia in Asia Minor, her name probably was common in that general area. Thyatira was a city of dye-makers, especially famous for purple from the shellfish *Purpura Murex*. Lydia could have been in Philippi temporarily, selling her wares from her home town.

Apparently Lydia was a widow, because her household is mentioned but not her husband. Some feel her household could have been comprised of slaves and freedwomen. Whoever the family, all were baptized in the Gangites (v. 15). She invites the entire party to stay in her home (v. 15b).

After Paul and Silas are released from the Philippian jail, Lydia takes them in, apparently to recuperate from their beating (v. 40). As Paul and the disciples are leaving her home, they are greeted by a growing gathering of believing brothers. The painful experience must have been worth it all to Paul and his companions, for Luke tells us they were encouraged as they departed the area (v. 40b).

Thyatira. Thyatira is sometimes referred to as "the city of Lydia," Paul's first convert in the district of Macedonia. The city is in Asia Minor near the river Lycus. When the Persian Empire was destroyed by Alexander, this Macedonian colony was established, as were others throughout Asia Minor. Apollo was the major deity of the city around the time of Paul's second journey. He was worshiped as the sun-god with the surname of Tyrimnas. Thyatira came under Roman rule in 133 B.C. and remained an important point in the Roman system of highways. It was an important center for dyeing garments and for pottery and brass manufacturing. Thyatira was the location of one of the seven churches mentioned in Revelation 2 and 3. Lydia could have played an important role in the development of that church.

> **16:23** And when they had inflicted many blows upon them, they threw them into prison, commanding the jailer to guard them securely;

[The Philippian] Jailer. Paul and Silas are arrested, beaten, and jailed after they cast the spirit of divination from the slave-girl who has brought her masters "much profit by fortune-telling" (Acts 16:16). The girl's masters agitate a crowd against the strangers (16:20–22). The chief magistrates are furious and order the men beaten with rods. The charge apparently is illegal proselytizing, since Paul and Silas are Jews and are "proclaiming customs which it is not lawful for us to accept or to observe [since we are] Romans" (v. 21). J. A. Alexander notes:

> *Being Romans,* an obvious antithesis to *Being Jews* in the preceding verse, and intended as a double aggravation of the charge, that Jews should dare to force their own religion upon Romans. The appeal is rather to the pride of race or national connection than to the Roman laws, conversions and innovations without public sanction and authority.[166]

After a vicious beating, the two are cast into the "inner prison" and fastened with stocks (v. 24). The jailer is given a stern reminder to *"guard them securely"* (v. 23). While the men pray and sing hymns to the Lord, with other prisoners and possibly the jailer's family listening, at midnight an earthquake struck the prison, opening doors and unfastening chains (v. 26). Thinking all the prisoners have escaped, the jailer draws his sword to kill himself (v. 27). Guards who allow prisoners to escape received whatever punishment the prisoner would have gotten. Alexander believes the man was probably a Roman soldier or at least subject to Roman discipline. In such a circumstance, suicide was considered a duty by Roman soldiers.[167]

Upon Paul's cry that no one had escaped, the relieved jailer was more than ready to hear the gospel and respond (vv. 28–30). That he asks, "What must I do to be saved?" (v. 30) may mean that Paul and Silas have already made him aware in a general way with the need for salvation in Jesus. Paul answers him with one of the classic invitations of Scripture: "Believe in the Lord Jesus, and you shall be saved, you and your household" (v. 31).

Some have inferred that the "household" included children who would either receive salvation through the parents (Roman Catholics) or be brought under the covenant promise as occurred with circumcision in the Old Testament (Reformed). The text, however, says Paul and Silas spoke the word of the Lord to the jailer, "together with all who were in his house" (v. 32). The gospel was explained to the jailer and all present who could understand the message responded in personal faith. The jailer and his household "believed in God" (v. 34) and were baptized (v. 33).

Possibly because of the earthquake, the chief magistrates the next morning wanted Paul and Silas released. But Paul forced the issue that, as Roman citizens, they had been mistreated without a hearing or trial (v. 37). "Let them come themselves and bring us out," Paul demanded. Hearing the two men were Romans, the magistrates became afraid (v. 38) and begged them to leave the city (v. 39). One can only guess the fate of the jailer and his family. They may have gone the way of martyrdom as many who trusted Christ in the early church.

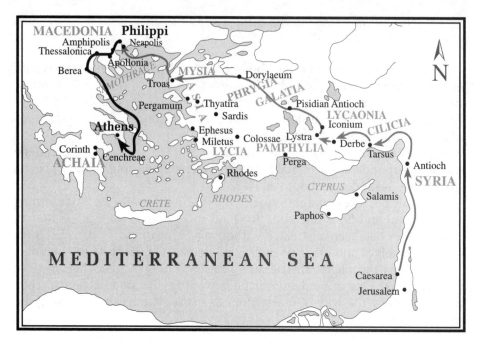

Chapter 17

A.D. 51

THE MINISTRY AT THESSALONICA, BEREA, AND ATHENS

Synopsis

(1–9) At Thessalonica, Paul speaks freely of "Jesus whom I am proclaiming" (1–3). Teaching and reasoning in the synagogue for three Sabbaths, Paul and Silas persuade many God-fearing Gentiles and Jews (4). But zealous Jews stir the mob and set the city in an uproar. They vent their anger against Jason, a believer in Christ who had welcomed the two men into his home. The cry of the crowd is that these men "act contrary to the decrees of Caesar, saying that there is another king, Jesus" (5–9).

(10–34) Paul and those with him leave the city and journey by night to Berea. Timothy and Silas remain there for a few days while Paul travels on to Athens, where he teaches again in the local synagogue. But the intellectual Epicureans and Stoics scoff at his reasonings, and he is called to defend "this new teaching" before the council of philosophers known as the Areopagus. There he begins with what all people know of God from nature, quoting the Greek poets' insights. Paul holds his

listeners until he approaches the resurrection of the dead, when he is cut off. Some do want to hear more and come to believe in Christ.

17:1 Now when they had traveled through Amphipolis and Apollonia, they came to Thessalonica, where there was a synagogue of the Jews.

Amphipolis. Amphipolis is on the Strymon River, which surrounds the city on three sides. The city was captured by Darius during the Persian invasion of 512 B.C. Two successive colonization attempts, one by Persians and the other by Greeks, failed. Amphipolis held a strategic coastal position between northern Greece and the Hellespont (see Mysia under 16:7), and it was a major economic center for the Strymon River Valley. Philip II, Alexander the Great's father, captured it in 357 B.C., and it received favored status for its rich mineral and timber commodities. Alexander made it his chief mint because of the numerous silver and gold reserves found in the area. Under Roman occupation, it became an important link on the Egnatian Way. Paul and Silas passed through on their way to Thessalonica after having been jailed in Philippi.

Apollonia. The name of this city means "belonging to Apollo" in honor of the Greek sun god Apollo. It was located on the Egnatian Way 28 miles west of Amphipolis and 38 miles east of Thessalonica in Macedonia.

Thessalonica. Thessalonica lay on the bay at the end of a winding gulf from the Aegean Sea, so it had the strengths of both a port and an inland crossroads. It was a splendid location for exporting and importing. In addition, Thessalonica controlled the wealthy resources of the area around Mount Olympus and received the waters of the rivers Axius, Lydias, and Haliacmon. The city was possibly named by Cassander (350–297 B.C.), the regent who presided over the breakup of Alexander's empire. Cassander's wife was named Thessalonica, and he was responsible for rebuilding the city in 315 B.C. Following the conquest of Macedonia by the Romans, the city was called "the mother of all Macedonia."[168]

Thessalonica was given free status by the Romans in Paul's day, which meant that no troops were garrisoned within the city limits. When Paul came here on his second missionary journey (A.D. 50) and preached Jesus as Messiah (17:3), the wealthy Jewish population turned on him (v. 5). Possibly they feared the message of a new king might antagonize the Romans and threaten their commercial endeavors. After Paul left, the Christian community was persistently persecuted. Paul sends two letters to comfort and stabilize the beleaguered congregation in about 52. First Thessalonians was written to give special instruction about daily work, answering questions about the rapture of the church and dealing with friction. Second Thessalonians corrected some erroneous notions about how their persecutions related to "the great and terrible Day of the Lord" from which they expected deliverance. They were most anxious for the second coming of Christ to end their troubles.[169]

> **17:4** And some of them were persuaded and joined Paul and Silas, along with a great multitude of the God-fearing Greeks and a number of the leading women.

God-fearing Greeks. The term *God-fearing Greeks* is used only here. These "God-fearing Greeks" make up a part of Paul's audience at the "synagogue of the Jews" (17:1) in Thessalonica. Based on the use of the terms *proselytes, God-fearing Gentiles,* and *worshipers of God* in Acts, it would be expected that these "God-fearing Greeks" are those Gentile followers of Judaism known as "near proselytes" or "proselytes of the gate." They were attending the synagogue service. This is called in question, though, by Paul's later letter to these same believers. In 1 Thessalonians he states: "For they themselves report about us what kind of a reception we had with you, and how you turned to God from idols to serve a living and true God." Robert Thomas believes the mention of idol worship means these Christians hadn't been connected in any way with the Jewish community:

> Normal expectation would be for "God-fearers" to already have separated themselves from idolatrous paganism because of affiliation, though loose, with a Jewish synagogue. Yet their release from past darkness may not have been total till secured by their relationship to God through Jesus Christ. Also probably included were additional Gentile converts who had no previous contact with Judaism.[170]

These Greeks must have feared God and adhered to Judaism to varying degrees, but not all of them had been weaned from pagan influence until they believed in Jesus as the Messiah. The presence of Christ in their lives had given them the power to overcome idolatry's hold (see also under 2:10).

> **17:5b** and coming upon the house of Jason, they were seeking to bring them out to the people.

Jason. *Jason* was a common Jewish name and a possible nickname for Joshua or Jesus. This God-fearing and bold Jew of Thessalonica assisted Paul when the city's Jews rioted over the gospel.

Paul teaches on three Sabbaths from the Scriptures, explaining with evidence that Christ (vv. 2–3) had to suffer and then come forth from the grave. But some of the Jews, "becoming jealous" (v. 5), gather a mob in order to create an uproar. Jason, an influential Jew, rescues Paul and his company (v. 5b) but the mob breaks into his house and drags Paul and his party out, shouting, "These men who have upset the world have come here also" (v. 6). The city authorities fear drawing any attention from Roman troops to their free Greek city. So the city fathers make Jason and other believers responsible for what might happen if the gospel is preached and the crowds revolt (vv. 8–9).

Though the unrest may have subsided for a short time when Paul and Silas left town, the Thessalonian epistles make clear that persecution continued relentlessly.

Jason remains an unsung warrior for Christ in the turmoil with which the gospel spread across Greece and Asia. How he accepted Christ and whether he died for his faith in the end are not recorded. Paul does include a Jason as a traveling companion when he writes Romans from Corinth (Rom. 16:21). When the Roman epistle was penned, his fellow workers and companions were Timothy, Luke, Jason, and Sosipater.

17:10a And the brethren immediately sent Paul and Silas away by night to Berea;

Berea. Berea was a prosperous city with a Jewish colony about 40 miles from Thessalonica. After they had been at the center of the riot in Thessalonica, it seems things go well at first in Berea for Paul and Silas. Luke writes that those at the Berean synagogue "were more noble-minded than those in Thessalonica, for they received the word with great eagerness, examining the Scriptures daily, to see whether these things were so" (17:10b–11). Before long, however, the troublemakers arrive, no doubt the same ones who were so active in Thessalonica.

Paul's approach in Berea is basically the same as it has been—synagogue preaching, personal witnessing, and faith. Then great opposition follows. The one major difference here, however, is that the Bereans were stirred up to enquire.[171] At its root, the word "noble-minded" connotes "good-birthed or wellborn," implying the Bereans were from good families, probably somewhat educated, and ready to study and think for themselves. By contrast with the common people in Thessalonica, the Bereans are willing to listen to Paul's message and test what he says with Scripture.

Paul is forced to leave Berea because the Jews from Thessalonica are stirring up crowds (17:13). Timothy and Silas remain, however. These two later join Paul in Athens (1 Thess. 3:1–2).

17:15a Now those who conducted Paul brought him as far as Athens;

Athens. After the Jews of Thessalonica follow Paul, Silas, and Timothy as far as Berea, "agitating and stirring up the crowds" (Acts 17:13), Paul thinks it well to divide the team and go on alone to Athens (1 Thess. 3:1). Silas and Timothy are "to come to him as soon as possible" (17:15b).

On such a missionary enterprise, it would have been almost impossible for Paul to bypass Athens. The city was one of the most outstanding and wealthy cities of Greece, and yet it was not a commercial center. Around magnificent rolling hills, the city spread stately buildings and promenades, and blocks of statues, many dedicated to "the unknown gods." Writers of the time said the Athenians were "over-religious" and "the most pious of the Greeks."[172] Why did Paul wish to come here alone? Perhaps he expected a hard-fought struggle against a certain intellectualism that only he could combat.

Luke notes that Paul was provoked in his spirit by the idolatry (17:16). He engaged the Jews in the synagogues and changed his city strategy a bit by speaking daily in the market place (v. 17). He debated with the Epicurean and Stoic philosophers who called him an "idle babbler," a "proclaimer of strange deities" because he announced the resurrection of Jesus (v. 18). He mentions an altar in the Areopagus dedicated "TO THE UNKNOWN GOD" (v. 23b). From this, Paul makes a leap to the God of the Scriptures, pointing out His being, which cannot dwell in temples, and His work in creation. This God has declared that all men should repent (vv. 24–30). He concludes with the fact that Christ will someday judge all humankind and that He is the One who is resurrected from the dead (vv. 31–32). A small group of Athenians trust in Jesus. Paul then departs for Corinth (18:1). He must have been content that his witness in Athens was complete, for he never returns to the city.

> **17:18a** And also some of the Epicurean and Stoic philosophers were conversing with him.

Epicureans. The Epicureans gleaned their worldview from Epicurus who advocated pursuing the pleasures that can be enjoyed in moderation, such as friendship, peace, and aesthetic contemplation. Epicureans took Epicurus's teachings a step further into hedonism, so Epicureanism became a way of life based on sensual enjoyment.[173] The philosophy allowed for the existence of gods but did not view them as active in the lives of humanity.

Stoics. The Stoics followed Zeno of Citium, who taught at the stoa or porch (hence the name *Stoics*). Zeno taught an austerity that particularly appealed to the Roman philosophers, a self-mastery and hardness that produced pride in success and looked to suicide in case of failure. It was a selfish and unloving pantheistic philosophy.[174] The Stoics and the Epicureans were the two extreme groups. Among others were the transcendentalists, who looked to a god who was absolutely separate from the concerns of earth. God could not associate with matter, for matter itself was evil. The immanentists identified god with the world in a pantheism.[175]

17:19a And they took him and brought him to the Areopagus,

Areopagus. The Areopagus is another name for Mars Hill, a rocky area that faced the Acropolis itself. It was said that the highest courts of ancient Athens used to meet at this spot. This hill was named after the god of war (*Ares* in the Greek, *Mars* in the Latin) because mythology said he had stood trial there for the murder of Halirrhothius, son of Poseidon, who had violated his daughter Alcippe.[176] Over 450 years before, Socrates was arraigned on this hill for introducing strange gods to the Greeks. Now Paul answered a similar charge concerning Jesus. Thus, he was ostensibly brought to this customary location for public speaking, but it was actually a mock trial, in keeping with the humor of the day of deriding new religious ideas.[177]

Despite the origin of the name of the court, it was not a trial court, as Bruce explains, "Before this body, then, Paul was brought, not to stand trial in a forensic sense, nor yet to be examined with a view to being licensed as a public lecturer, but simply to have an opportunity of expounding his teaching before experts."[178]

17:23b "I also found an altar with this inscription, 'TO AN UNKNOWN GOD.'"

"To an unknown god." Athens overflowed with idols. Realizing the need and opportunity, Paul went into the synagogue and the marketplace daily to reason with both Jew and Gentiles. He also brought attention to himself among two groups of professional philosophers, the Epicureans and the Stoics (see above). Paul's teaching might have intrigued these two groups, for he stood centered philosophically between their extremes with his doctrine of "God the Redeemer."[179]

As he began to explain and defend his teaching before the council of philosophers at the Areopagus, Paul appealed to their own admitted ignorance of God, for among their objects of worship stood an altar with the inscription *"Agnōstō Theō,"* "To an unknown God." The Athenians feared giving praise to the wrong deity, lest the scorned deity grow vengeful. To protect themselves, they inscribed altars to *unknown* gods. Merrill Unger writes that Pausinius (1.1.4) and Philostratus (Vit. Appolon. 6.2) both mention "unknown gods." According to one story, Epimenides built some of the altars to stop a plague in Athens. He turned sheep loose on the Areopagus. Where each lay down, it was sacrificed, so whatever god had sent the disease would be propitiated. The practice began of erecting altars to unknown gods whenever there was a calamity.[180]

Paul had gained the interest of the philosophers, and now he appeals not just to the philosophers but to all the "men of Athens" (v. 22). The philosophers were not concerned with idol worship, yet a vast majority of the common people were, and Paul speaks to a great plurality, offering them enlightenment.

Paul first presents God as Creator and Sovereign, not dwelling in human-made temples, or needing human-made worship, since He is Sovereign. This statement eliminates the need for idols; the Athenian system of worship was unnecessary. Paul goes on to establish the origin of all people from one, thus removing any false superiority from the minds of the listeners. It is from God that they have received their very being, and they have been designed to seek Him. With Paul's clear statement that God is "not far from each one of us" (v. 27), he stresses that the unknown god of the Athenians was in fact the one true God who sought them.

Paul then refers to two Greek poets, Epimenides and Aratus. Paul could not agree with the pantheistic conclusions of these two poets, but he wants his listeners to see that they already have a sense of their relation to this one true God—they are his children by creation. As F. F. Bruce explains: "We are, then, the offspring of God, says Paul, not in any pantheistic sense but in the sense of the biblical doctrine of man, as beings created in His own image."[181]

But what homage is due to such a God? Paul declares (vv. 29–30) that it is not image worship He desires but a true repentance from the ignorance of the past. The motivation for this is not just that God has created humankind, and it is fitting that people should seek Him; there also is coming a day in which Christ will judge the world in righteousness (v. 31). The Athenians did not respond well to Paul's mention of the resurrection of Christ. Bruce writes that the Epicureans would have gone along with a teaching of the immortality of the individual soul. But all endorsed the sentiments attributed to the god Apollo on the very occasion of the founding of the Areopagus: "Once a man dies and the earth drinks up his blood, there is no resurrection." Bruce wrote, "Some of them, therefore, ridiculed a statement which seemed so absurd. Others, more polite if equally skeptical, suggested that there might be an opportunity later for further exposition of his teaching."[182]

Most reject Paul's message, but not all. Of those who believe, two are mentioned by name—Dionysius from the Areopagus, and a woman named Damaris.

> **17:26** "having determined [humanity's] appointed times, and the boundaries of their habitation,"

Determined. See "Predetermined Plan" under 2:23.

Boundaries. This might refer to historical epochs, during which nations rise, decline, and cease to exist; the habitable areas of the planet, or to boundaries erected to separate tribal and national territories. The emphasis seems to be on God's lordship over history. Paul's point is the care and providence of God in his creation.[183]

> **17:28b** "your own poets have said, 'For we also are His offspring.'"

Offspring. Paul apparently quotes the third century b.c. Stoic poet Aratus of Soli who appears to be quoting from a hymn to Zeus by the poet Cleanthes.[184] Paul is substituting the God of Scripture in the place of Zeus. He is setting Jehovah as the true and living deity who is master of all creation. Offspring *(genos)* does not make humans little gods. The word is translated "race, stock, nation, kind."[185] Paul's thought is "we are a race of human beings together who have our physical origins from God."

> **17:34** But some men joined him and believed, among whom also was Dionysius the Areopagite and a woman named Damaris and others with them.

Dionysius. The name *Dionysios* means "divinely touched." The facts that he is specifically mentioned and that he is called an "Areopagite" means that Dionysius was an influential Athenian, an intellectual, and a member of the Council of the Areopagus (see above).[186]

Through the preaching of Paul on Mars Hill, Dionysius became a believer (17:34). It must have encouraged Paul that such a man came to the Lord when his counterparts would not receive the truth (17:32). Nothing more is recorded in Scripture concerning Dionysius. Some early Christian writers assumed that he and the Damaris were husband and wife. However, such a conclusion is based more upon one's personal interpretation than upon the passage. One must ask whether after his conversion he was still able or if he was allowed to stay on the Council of Areopagus. Unger comments that

> Suidas recounts that he was an Athenian by birth and eminent for his literary attainments, that he studied first at Athens and afterward at Heliopolis, in Egypt. The name of Dionysius has become important in church history from certain writings formerly believed to be his but now known to be spurious and designated as the Pseudo-Dionysian writings.[187]

Damaris. *Damaris* means "gentle." She was an Athenian woman converted by the teachings of Paul after his speech to the Areopagus, during his second missionary tour. Though it was unusual for a woman to be present in this audience of philosophers, she demonstrates to the reader the freedom that Greek women exercised during Paul's travels. Some of the early Christian writers, notably Chrysostom, believed her to be the wife of Dionysius since they are mentioned in the same verse. However, a literal reading of the passage does not bear out such a conclusion. It may be inferred that since she is singled out with Dionysius the Areopagite, she was a woman of some personal or social distinction.

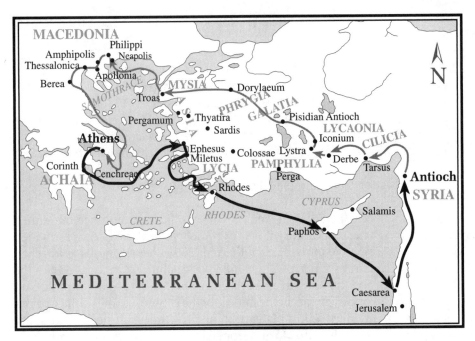

Chapter 18

A.D. 52

THE MINISTRY AT CORINTH; THIRD MISSIONARY JOURNEY

Synopsis

(1–17) Timothy and Silas join Paul in Corinth where he teaches and reasons each Sabbath in the local synagogue. Here in Corinth Paul also meets a couple who will become important team members with Paul, Aquila and Priscilla (1–5). Though the Jews resist his message and blaspheme, Paul moves in next door to the synagogue in the home of the believer Crispus. In a night vision, the Lord assures him he is safe. Paul continues to teach for three and a half years in Corinth (6–11). In resisting the gospel, the local Jews appeal to the proconsul Gallio of Achaia. "This man persuades men to worship God contrary to the law," they cry. But he answers that their dispute is simply over words, names, and their law, and he will not be a judge in these matters. He drives the accusing Jews from the judgment seat (18:12–16). The crowd is so angry over the charge of the Jews that the synagogue leader Sosthenes is beaten (17).

(18–22) Paul eventually returns to Caesarea by sea and goes to Antioch, where he is greeted by the church.

(23–28) After a rest at Antioch, Paul begins his third missionary journey through Galatia and Phrygia. Many of the disciples are strengthened (23). Priscilla and Aquila meet the Alexandrine Jewish orator Apollos and tell him of Jesus. The man is an eloquent speaker and "mighty in the Scriptures [Old Testament]" (24–26). Apollos begins his own ministry in Achaia, where "he powerfully refuted the Jews in public, demonstrating by the Scriptures that Jesus was the Christ" (27–28).

18:1 After these things he left Athens and went to Corinth.

Corinth. Today Corinth is a small town with little significance other than historical. But in the first century it was extremely important. Greece is divided geographically into two parts. The southern part, the Peloponnesus, is attached to the northern part by a narrow, four-mile-wide isthmus. On the west lies the Gulf of Corinth and the port city of Lechacum. On the east lies the Saronic Gulf and the port city of Cenchreae. In the middle of the isthmus, to the south, Corinth is situated on a commanding plateau. In ancient times, all north and south overland traffic, including that to and from Athens, passed through Corinth.

Sea travel around the Peloponnesus was time-consuming and dangerous. It was so treacherous that mariners had a saying, "A sailor never takes a journey around Malea (the cape at the south end of the peninsula) until he first writes his will." Most captains chose to carry their ships overland on skids or rollers across the narrow isthmus, directly past Corinth. The procedure was quicker, more economical, and much safer than sailing 250 miles around the peninsula. In fact, the isthmus came to be known as Dialcas, which means "the place of dragging across." Corinth benefited from traffic in all directions and consequently became a major trade center.

Corinth was also a successful entertainment center. Corinth hosted the Isthmian Games, one of the two great athletic festivals, with the Olympian games. The Isthmian Games were played on the isthmus of Corinth.

Corinth was destroyed by the Romans in 146 B.C. and rebuilt by Julius Caesar 100 years later. At first it was a Roman colony, largely populated by Romans, and eventually became the capital of the Roman province of Achaia. Because of its location, it soon became again a major trade center, with a cosmopolitan population of Greeks, Romans, and Near-Eastern peoples, including many Jews.

Like most Greek cities, Corinth had an acropolis (literally "high city"), called *Acrocorinth,* which was a place of defense and pagan worship. From its top on a clear day, Athens can be seen, some forty-five miles away. Situated on a 2,000-foot-high granite mound, Acrocorinth was large enough to hold all the population of Corinth and its surrounding farm lands in time of siege. It also held a famous temple of Aphrodite, goddess of love. The temple normally housed some 1,000 priestesses—ritual prostitutes who each night would come down to Corinth to ply their trade among foreign travelers and the local men.

Even to the pagan world the city was known for its moral corruption, so that in classical Greek *"corinthiazesthar"* ("to behave like a Corinthian"), came to represent gross immorality and drunken debauchery. The name of the city became synonymous with moral depravity.

Paul's first trip to Corinth was on his second missionary journey. From Philippi, he had gone to Thessalonica, Berea, Athens, and then Corinth (Acts 16:11–18:1).[188] Upon Paul's arrival in Corinth, he met Aquila and Priscilla, Jews who had been driven out of Rome because of the great persecution to the Christians. Paul stayed with them for awhile and began to preach the gospel on a regular basis in the synagogue every Sabbath. Paul preached and ministered in Corinth for one and a half years (18:11). The Jewish opposition became so bad that he was brought before a Roman court. Since the charges were of a religious nature, the proconsul, Gallio, refused to hear the case. After being set free, Paul left Corinth with Priscilla and Aquila and went to Ephesus.

God in His sovereign decree chose to spread the gospel in cities like Corinth. Even though sin was the norm, God's grace was also present. Paul went to the Jewish synagogue first, but once he was rejected he went to the Gentiles. God was breaking down walls between the Jews, Gentiles, and Samaritans. Once the message was preached in Corinth, it became a flame that would not go out.

> **18:2** And he found a certain Jew named Aquila, a native of Pontus, having recently come from Italy with his wife Priscilla, because Claudius had commanded all the Jews to leave Rome.

Aquila and Priscilla. Aquila and Priscilla appear on the scene here in chapter 18 where Paul meets them in Corinth. The husband-wife duo are mentioned six times in Scripture (18:2, 18, 26; Rom. 6:3; 1 Cor. 16:19; 2 Tim. 4:19). Four out of six times Priscilla is named first. "This prominence has been explained as due to her superior ability and zeal, or that she had a higher social standing than Aquila as a member of an old Roman family," according to D. E. Hiebert. Aquila is native of Pontus, a Roman province in northern Asia Minor just north of Mysia. "Since the race of Priscilla is not mentioned," Hiebert adds, "she probably was non-Jewish, but may have become a proselyte before marrying Aquila."[189]

They were in Corinth because the Emperor Claudius had expelled the Jews from Rome (A.D. 49–50; see 18:2). Some scholars believe that this edict came as a result of disturbances among Jews reacting to Christianity's growth in Rome. Paul immediately developed a close friendship with the couple since they were all tentmakers (18:3). Their trade would have involved weaving the tent cloth or cutting and sewing together the tents. In any event,

Paul stayed with them, probably in quarters they had rented in Corinth, and they worked together not only in business but also in ministry. In Paul's letter to the Romans, he indicates that at some point they had risked their lives for him (Rom. 16:4).

Apparently the business they developed together was mutually beneficial enough that Aquila and Priscilla moved to Ephesus to work with Paul there (18:18–19). Certainly in the time of making tents, Paul, Aquila, and Priscilla must have often discussed doctrinal truth, and it appears from their later work that they must have been inclined toward teaching (Acts 18:24–28; 1 Cor. 16:19).

Aquila and Priscilla must have been excellent students. After Paul left for Antioch (18:22), they worked alone to lay the groundwork for the Ephesian church (18:19–21). In fact, later, when Apollos came to Ephesus and began to teach and preach in the synagogue, they were able to take him aside and "explain to him the word of God more accurately" (18:24–26; see Apollos, under 18:24). They were so effective in their teaching that when Apollos wanted to go to Achaia they "encouraged him and wrote to the disciples to welcome him" (Acts 18:27). They would have done this only if they were confident in Apollos' knowledge and teaching ability.

When Paul wrote his first letter to the Corinthians, Aquila and Priscilla, along with the church that was in their home, sent greetings to the Corinthian church (1 Cor. 16:19). Thus, they had been effectively grounding the believers that Paul had evangelized, and they had opened their home to establish a church there. At some point they returned to Rome, as is indicated by Paul in his letter to the church there (Rom. 16:4). As would seem natural, in their stay there they had a church fellowship in their quarters (Rom. 16:4–5). They later returned to Ephesus and would certainly have been of great benefit to young Timothy, whom Paul had sent there to become the pastor-teacher of that congregation.

Aquila and Priscilla's key role in Acts seems to have been their impact on Apollos. Apollos was clearly a man of incredible gifts in teaching and instruction, but because he did not know about the crucifixion of Christ and the coming of the Holy Spirit on Pentecost, he carried with him the potential to cause much confusion at Ephesus and other places he might travel. God strategically place Paul in the path of Aquila and Priscilla to become educated by the master theologian, and then the Lord carried them into the path of Apollos to prepare him for an effective teaching ministry later in Corinth and beyond. In addition, God continued to use this couple in grounding and equipping believers in Rome and Ephesus and probably other places as well.

Pontus. See under 2:9.

Claudius. See under 11:28.

18:5 But when Silas and Timothy came down from
Macedonia,

Silas and Timothy. See under 15:22.

18:7 And [Paul] departed from there and went to the house
of a certain man named Titius Justus, a worshiper of God,
whose house was next to the synagogue.

Titius Justus. Justus (*Ioustos*) was a common name borne by Jews and
proselytes. *Titios* is mentioned only here in 18:7. He is probably a Roman of
the Corinthian colony. When Paul, Silas, and Timothy come to Corinth to
reason with the Jews and Greeks in the synagogue (18:4), the Jews reject the
message that Jesus is the Messiah, with blasphemous outrage (v. 6). The apostle
storms from the synagogue but moves to Justus' house next door. Justus is
called "a worshiper of God" (v. 7). He thus is a godly man in Old Testament
terms, but he seems to have become a Christian shortly.

Staying with Justus for a year and a half, Paul sees the leader of the
synagogue Crispus, his whole house, and many other Corinthians believe in
Jesus and be baptized (v. 8). Justus is brave and apparently not afraid to bring
Paul into his own home, right under the noses of the Jewish community. In a
vision, the Lord tells Paul to continue to speak and not to be frightened, for
"I have many people in this city" (v. 9). Paul did not stop sharing "the word
of God among them" (v. 11).

18:8 And Crispus, the leader of the synagogue, believed in
the Lord.

Crispus. The name *Krispos* means "curled." He was a chief, or leader, of
the synagogue in Corinth. The "Ruler of the Synagogue" (Gk. *archisynagogos*)
conducted public worship and supervised the daily business of the synagogue
in general. Being in such a position gave him great leadership and power in
the community. Merrill Unger writes that the ruler appointed Scripture and
the prayer readers, arranged for preaching, and made sure nothing improper
took place in the synagogue (Luke 13:14); he took care of the building.
Sometimes there were more than one ruler in a synagogue (Acts 13:15).[190]

The conversion of Crispus must have put him in a difficult position, given
the anti-Christian feelings of the town. His conversion so affected his family
that they all believed also (18:8a). Though not recorded, many commentators
theorize that Crispus' position allowed him to be a great example to live
Christ before those under him. More likely, a Christian believer did not retain
his position in the synagogue long. Verse 17 records another leader of the

synagogue who may have been Crispus' successor—Sosthenes. Tradition holds that Crispus became the bishop of Aegina.

> **18:12** But while Gallio was proconsul of Achaia, the Jews with one accord rose up against Paul and brought him before the judgment seat.

Gallio. The son of Marcus Annaeus Seneca, a Spanish rhetorician, and the younger brother of Lucius Annaeus Seneca, a Stoic philosopher, Gallio was born in Cordova at the beginning of the Christian era. When he came to Rome during the reign of Claudius, he was adopted by Roman rhetorician Lucius Junius Gallio and afterward bore the name of his adoptive father.

Gallio was famous for his charm. "No mortal is so pleasant to any person as Gallio is to everyone," his brother reportedly said. In 65 he, along with his brother Melna, fell victim of Nero's paranoia and was killed.

Gallio's actions in the book of Acts will have profound effect on the growth of Christianity in the Roman world by postponing official persecution. Paul has preached for several months before Gallio becomes proconsul of Corinth. When Gallio takes office, the Jews immediately bring Paul before him (18:12). The Jews claim that Paul is preaching a new religion, a forbidden practice under Roman law. Gallio disagrees, ruling that Paul teaches an extension of Judaism. That this "extension" does not suit the Jewish leaders doesn't concern Gallio. He ejects the plaintiffs (18:14,15), angry with the Jews for wasting his time with their bickering. They should decide what is done in their own religion (18:16).

The incident arouses anti-Semitic feelings among the Gentile onlookers. On cue from Gallio's snub of the Jews, a crowd grabs Sosthenes, the synagogue ruler, and beats him in the marketplace (Acts 18:17a). The people are expecting a beating; they want to see blood. When Paul is released, the crowd who normally gathers at the judgment seat is disappointed. But they are allowed, actually encouraged, to beat Sosthenes. By ignoring it, Gallio likely hopes others will be warned not to waste his time (18:17b).

Gallio's refusal to indict Paul has ramifications throughout the Empire. Had he sided with the Jewish leaders and proclaimed Christianity a new religion, it would be illegal under Roman law. A precedent would have been set that could outlaw the church at a time it is still weak and vulnerable. His refusal to indict Paul protects the preaching of Christianity for a time. *Ryrie's Study Bible* comments:

> Judaism was a "licensed religion" under Roman law. Christianity could take advantage of this protection as long as it sheltered itself under the tent of Judaism. The Jews must have complained that these Christians were not a division or sect of Judaism, and Gallio refuses to see it their way. He says, in effect, "Settle your own religious squabbles yourselves."[191]

Achaia. When Greece was free, the term *Achaia* applied to a strip of land bordered by the Corinthian Gulf on the south. By the time of the Romans, Achaia generically was applied to the entire country of Greece. Technically, Achaia still was a small region. Because of its semipermanent borders, no one could calculate how much land it comprised.

The Achaean League had provided most of the resistance to Roman rule. Eventually, Achaia was conquered in 146 B.C. and joined with the province of Macedonia until 27 B.C. Then Achaia was made a separate province, governed by a proconsul appointed by the Senate from among the expraetors. Two periods of time became exceptions to this system in Achaia. From A.D. 15 to 44 the province was under the Caesarean legate of Moesia, and for a period beginning in 67 Nero benevolently suspended Roman supervision. Vespasian returned it to its status as a senatorial province; thereafter, so long as the empire lasted it was governed by a proconsul. Large Jewish settlements and synagogues in Corinth and Athens, the two largest cities of Achaia, are reasons the churches in this area may have grown so fast.

There are only three references to Achaia in the book of Acts but several more in the New Testament. Acts 18:12 tells of the appointment of Gallio as proconsul (in 51) and the confrontation with the Jews over Paul (see above). On the third missionary journey, Paul is warmly welcomed by the brethren in Achaia (Acts 18:27). Obviously, the brethren at Achaia are having a hard time with the Jews. The Jews contend over calling Jesus Messiah. Paul takes up the argument, teaching the believers and defending the gospel from attack through use of Scripture (Acts 18:28).

Paul intends to go back to Jerusalem at the end of his third missionary journey. However, his plans also included revisiting the young groups of believers he had planted. Perhaps his desire to see Achaia once again comes with fear of Jewish opposition. Has he strengthened the believers adequately to prepare them for their trials (Acts 19:21)?

Elsewhere in the Epistles, Paul speaks to and admonishes the believers, including Romans 15:26 and this commendation in 2 Corinthians: "For I know your readiness, of which I boast about you to the Macedonians, namely, that Achaia has been prepared since last year, and your zeal has stirred up most of them" (2 Cor. 9:2).

Paul commends the Greeks for their giving attitude. Not only do they give of themselves spiritually but also materially. Achaia is especially set forth, for they had been preparing for a year for their giving. Paul begins to use them as an example of Christian charity.

First Corinthians 16:15 tells of Paul's first converts in Achaia. Paul greets all of the Achaian believers in his second letter to the Corinthians (2 Cor. 1:1). However well the believers in Achaia were living up to Christian standards, Paul used the trials and tribulations of the Thessalonians to show them what could happen (1 Thess. 1:7). And while the believers in Achaia had material prosperity, they were still developing spiritually. Believers in Thessalonica were held up as examples of Christian living. The word from Thessalonica had penetrated into the land of Achaia (1 Thess. 1:8).

> **18:17a** And they all took hold of Sosthenes, the leader of the synagogue, and began beating him in front of the judgment seat

Sosthenes. The name *Sōsthenēs* means "of safe strength." He was a leader of the synagogue in Corinth. There are differing theories on his association with Crispus since both are mentioned as the leader of the synagogue (18:17b). (1) It is possible he served together with Crispus, though synagogues usually had only one leader. (2) Crispus may have stepped down after his conversion and was succeeded by Sosthenes. A born-again believer would find it very difficult to lead a completely Jewish ceremony without a mention of Christ. (3) Sosthenes and Crispus may have been rulers of separate synagogues in the city.

Sosthenes, a member and possibly the head of the anti-Pauline faction, was among those upset with Paul's teachings (18:12b). With the other Jews, Sosthenes brought Paul before the judgment seat of Gallio, the proconsul of Achaia. They explained how Paul had taught the people that which was contrary to the Law. Gallio was not impressed by their accusations. Before Paul could speak, Gallio dismissed their case (18:14b–15).

Whether Sosthenes was targeted because he was the Jewish spokesman, or whether he was just close at hand, he became the target of anti-Jewish feelings (18:17). Sosthenes' position in the synagogue could not save him from the angry citizens of Corinth. McGarvey comments:

> The judgment seat, the chair of state in which the proconsul sat, was not erected inside of a court room, as with us, but in the open air, and usually in the agora, or forum. Consequently, all trials which excited public interest were witnessed by a crowd of spectators made up largely of the idlers on the streets. . . . With that keen sense of the fitness of things which often characterizes a crowd, they saw that Sosthenes deserved the beating which he had laid up for Paul; and perhaps with a laugh and a yell they gave it to him."[192]

A crowd that may have been thirsty for the blood of Paul satisfied itself on the blood of Sosthenes. Gallio turned his back on the violence committed against this man (18:17). His inaction was obviously intended to be a warning to other Jews. The public beating of a leader of the synagogue would be told and retold many times throughout the city.

In Paul's first letter to the Corinthians, he mentions "Sosthenes our brother" (1 Cor. 1:1). Could this be the same Sosthenes from Acts 18:17? It has been conjectured that he became a Christian as a result of his beating. William Ramsay writes, "Probably two persons at Corinth named Sosthenes were brought into relations with Paul, one a Jew, the other a prominent Christian; or, perhaps the Jew was converted at a later date."[193]

18:18b In Cenchrea he had his hair cut, for he was keeping a vow.

Cenchrea. Cenchrea was the eastern harbor of Corinth, about eight miles away. Archeology and history provide little information on this harbor. It served as the port for Corinth, handling traffic from the Aegean and the Levant. What is known is that it was an important trading city of its time, making it a target for bandits and pirates.

Luke says in Acts 18:18, "And Paul, having remained many days longer, took leave of the brethren and put out to sea for Syria, and with him were Priscilla and Aquila." Cenchrea was only a stopover for Paul. It is not recorded that he preached or taught. It would have been expedient for Paul to get his hair cut and continue to Ephesus.

The other mention of Cenchrea is in the book of Romans: "I commend to you our sister Phoebe, who is a servant of the church which is at Cenchrea" (Rom. 16:1). Obviously a church was founded at Cenchrea. Phoebe was given the honor of bearing Paul's letter to the Romans. A church here would have tremendous benefits for the spreading of the gospel. Sailors would be exposed to the gospel message, maybe even converted. The gospel would spread up and down the coast and to other ports of call.

Hair cut. Paul evidently had kept a Nazarite vow that did not allow the cutting of hair. Now he has his head shaved, signifying the end of a Nazarite vow (Num. 6:18; Acts 21:24). Why he took the vow is not known.[194]

18:19a And they came to Ephesus, and he left them there.

Ephesus. Ephesus was the metropolis of the Roman providence of Asia, sharing with the Syrian Antioch and Egyptian Alexandria designation as one of the three great cities of the eastern Mediterranean. It was three miles from the sea on the Cayster River, at the head of one of the four river valleys traversed by highways that run from the seacoast up into the high plateau that forms Asia Minor. Ephesus was a transportation junction between East and West, between sea lanes and highways (19:21; 20:1, 17). Ephesus became a racial melting pot, a cosmopolitan commercial center of the Empire, and a battlefield of religion. From the days of Croesus (c. 560 B.C.), a Lydian fertility goddess, *Ashtoreth*, had dominated religious life at Ephesus. Ashtoreth was similar to the Phoenician *Astarte* and identified by Greeks with their *Artemis* and by the Romans with their *Diana*. All these versions of the fertility goddess were worshiped with legalized prostitution, commercialized subsidiaries, and a wonderful temple. Ephesus was proud of its designation as "temple warden" for the goddess (Acts 19:35). Ephesus also was a center for occult practice. Magic had its followers and its commercial promoters. Fees were charged by charlatans for consultation (Acts 19:13–16, 19).[195]

Idolatry and immorality were so bad in Ephesus, the city was labeled *arch paganismi*, "the height of paganism." The temple of Artemis spawned a busy idol manufacturing center. Prostitutes and pornography were the next staple fare offered to thousands of pilgrims and tourists. Sailors and travelers flooded in from its seaport docks and from trade plying the Cayster River.

The Romans made the city a regional proconsular headquarters with large army units stationed here. But many nationalities mixed in Ephesus, especially the Jews, who saw that wealth could be made by trade and commerce.

The temple of Artemis was not only the center of a sexual cult but also the bank of Asia Minor. It was one of the seven wonders of the world, an immense, columned building of great beauty. The city also boasted the largest Greek open-air theater, seating fifty thousand spectators. The stadium held races and wild animal fights to please the crowds in the midst of drugs, sorcery, witchcraft, and disease-ridden orgies. The atmosphere was thick with paganism, a stronghold of satanic influence.

Paul spent a year and a half in Ephesus. His later epistle to the Ephesians speaks beautifully about the sovereignty of God, who controls all and is above the filth of mankind. In the misery of pagan sin, God exists only as pure. He sovereignly lifts souls from this crushing death of evil. Paul writes about no longer walking the deadening course of this world's culture. Practically, he writes about love and order in a marriage relationship that is as pure as the relationship of Christ and His Own bride, the church.

> **18:24** Now a certain Jew named Apollos . . . came to
> Ephesus; and he was mighty in the Scriptures.

Apollos. Apollos was a Jew born and presumably educated in Alexandria, Egypt (Acts 18:24). In this educational center of the Hellenistic world, Gentile and Jewish learning interacted.[196] Priscilla and Aquila encounter Apollos in the synagogue. Luke states that he was an eloquent (lit. "learned") man who was "mighty in the [Old Testament] Scriptures" (v. 24). Apollos had received knowledge of "the way of the Lord" and "was speaking and teaching accurately the things concerning Jesus" (v. 25). It is unknown where he received this knowledge. He could have been a disciple of John the Baptist. He knew enough to be convinced that Jesus was the Messiah. Thus, he was "fervent in spirit" about convincing the Jews of this truth in the Ephesian synagogue.

Though knowing of Jesus, the core of Apollos's knowledge seems to have been the message of "John's baptism" of repentance (19:4). The repentance was to prepare for the Messiah and the coming Kingdom (Matt. 3:2). Apollos may have had a limited knowledge of the Messiah's rejection by the Jews, but he did not understand that through His crucifixion He had become the Redeemer of humankind. Nor was he aware of the coming of the Holy Spirit on Pentecost. Therefore, he didn't know about the Christian gospel and baptism "in the name of the Lord Jesus." His "baptism of John" showed repentance in preparation for the coming King and kingdom, whereas "baptism in the name of the Lord" pictures union with Christ in His death, burial, and resurrection by means of Spirit baptism (Rom. 6:3–10; 1 Cor. 12:13; Gal. 3:27; Col. 2:12). As Stanley D. Toussaint writes, "This episode (18:24–28) and the following (19:1–7) underscores the transitional nature of this phase of church history. It may be assumed from 19:1–7 that Apollos had not received Christian baptism and probably had not received the Holy Spirit."[197]

Priscilla and Aquila "took him aside and explained to him the way of God more accurately" (18:26). With this new-found knowledge, Apollos desired to cross the Aegean to Achaia, and in this endeavor he was encouraged. He was even sent on his way with letters of commendation (18:27). His ministry there was very successful, and he was a master at debating the Jews and showing them Jesus was the Christ out of the Prophets (18:28).

Apollos's ministry at Corinth was successful but produced some division (probably mostly due to the immaturity of the believers). A partisan spirit developed. Cliques argued, "I am of Paul," "I of Apollos," "I of Cephas," and "I of Christ" (1 Cor. 1:12). Paul rebuked the Corinthians, not Apollos (1 Cor. 1–4). At the writing of Paul's first letter to the Corinthians, Apollos was with him in Ephesus. And although Paul encouraged him to return to Corinth, Apollos had no desire to go back, possibly because of the factional squabbling that had occurred since his last visit. Hiebert states, "It would seem that Apollos did not feel called to the pioneer work of planting new churches. He apparently devoted his efforts to the strengthening of churches already established."[198]

The last mention of Apollos is in Titus 3:13, where he, along with a lawyer named Zenas, were dropping off Paul's letter as they passed through Crete.

Chapter 19
A.D. 52–55 (27 months in Ephesus)

THE MINISTRY AT EPHESUS

Synopsis

(1–20) Journeying to Ephesus, Paul finds more disciples of John the Baptist who knew nothing of Jesus. After the gospel is fully explained to them, the men are baptized in the name of Jesus. With Paul's laying on of hands, they receive the Holy Spirit and begin to speak with tongues and to prophesy (1–7). For two years, Paul confines his teaching in the house school of a man by the name of Tyrannus. Many miracles followed his ministry (8–12). Following an encounter with one demon possessed, the people became reverently fearful, and "the name of the Lord Jesus was being magnified." In this awakening, many believed in Christ and repented of their own demonic practices. Magic books were burned, and "the word of the Lord was growing mightily and prevailing" (13–20).

(21–41) The most dangerous opposition in Ephesus was led by a silversmith named Demetrius, who alarmed the city that worship of the goddess Artemis was declining. "Our prosperity depends upon this business," he cried (21–25). Paul was nearly killed as the crowds shouted, "Great is Artemis of the Ephesians." Paul and his companions leave the city after calm is restored by the town clerk (26–41).

19:1b Paul having passed through the upper country came
to Ephesus, and found some disciples.

Some disciples. The word *disciple (mathētēs)* is used thirty times in Acts,
including two references to disciples of John the Baptist (19:1, 9). The word
carries the strong implication of one who is a "learner, seeker, or student." In
his gospel, Luke calls the apostles the twelve disciples. The meaning implies
a far broader circle of believers in Acts. For example, in chapter six, the
"disciples were increasing in number" (v. 1) and were called the "congregation
of the disciples" (v. 2). Saul before his conversion was "breathing threats and
murder" against the disciples (9:1–2).

At the Jerusalem Council, new-believer Gentiles are called disciples who
should not have to bear the burden of the Law, which even the Jews could
not keep (15:10). Whenever possible, Paul comforted and taught new
believers, always seeing them as learners or disciples who were completely
giving themselves to the Lord Jesus and to His service. After Paul and
Barnabas preached the gospel at Derbe, they "made many disciples." At
Antioch (14:21), they strengthened and encouraged the disciples (v. 22). To
create mature followers in Antioch "they spent a long time with the disciples"
(v. 28). In this city, the disciples were first called Christians (11:26).

19:6 And when Paul laid his hands upon them, the Holy
Spirit came on them, and they began speaking with
tongues and prophesying.

Laid his hands upon them. See pp. 402–8.

They began speaking with tongues. See pp. 37–42.

Prophesying. See under 13:1.

19:9 But when some were becoming hardened and
disobedient, speaking evil of the Way before the multitude,
he withdrew from them and took away the disciples,
reasoning daily in the school of Tyrannus.

The Way. See under 9:2.

Tyrannus. The name *Tyrannus* means "a tyrant, or an absolute
sovereign." This also was either the given name or the nickname of the
owner of a lecture hall school in Ephesus. By tradition, his academy would
be open to traveling philosophers and teachers. After three months of
preaching in the synagogue, Paul's problems with the unbelieving Jews

were becoming more severe (19:9a). Though Paul's three months in the synagogue is one of his longest recorded stints, he encountered much opposition. Opposition in the past had often turned violent, so Paul wisely chose to withdraw from the synagogue (19:9b).

Scripture reveals nothing about Tyrannus, except he owned a school. It is possible that Tyrannus is a nickname, possibly given by his students. It is hard to believe that a society that placed such importance on the meaning of names would name their child "tyrant." Most likely Tyrannus taught rhetoric. Many such schools were open to traveling philosophers and teachers. Paul would find himself at home in such an atmosphere. So taking those who were following him, Paul began a stint at Tyrannus's school that was to last for two years. The name Tyrannus leads most scholars to believe that he was a Greek.

> **19:11** And God was performing extraordinary miracles by the hands of Paul,

Miracles. See pp. 64–69.

> **19:12b** and the evil spirits went out.

Evil spirits. See pp. 92–101.

> **19:14** And seven sons of one Sceva, a Jewish chief priest, were doing this.

Sons of Sceva. Sceva was a Jewish chief priest at Ephesus. His seven sons attempted to exorcise spirits from a possessed man. By occupation, these seven sons appeared to be professional exorcists. They believed they had hit upon the magical formula for casting out demons. Earlier, Paul had been able to cast out demons by this name, so the sons assumed they could do likewise. Unger comments:

> The narrative of Acts 19:13–19 is valuable in showing the prevalence of itinerating Jewish exorcists, and in illustrating the contrast between their magical methods for casting out demons and the simple employment by the Apostles of the mighty name of Jesus.[199]

The seven brothers confronted a possessed man and the spirits in him by the "name of Jesus." The response was not what they expected. The spirits answered, "I recognize Jesus, and I know about Paul, but who are you?'" (19:15). The man attacked all seven so violently that he tore off their robes, and they left them behind in their terror. (19:16). They were injured by the evil spirit. The name of Jesus, like a weapon misused, exploded in their hands;

and they were taught a lesson about the danger of using the name of Jesus in dabbling in the supernatural.[200]

This event affected the countryside (19:19). The power and glory of the Lord fell upon the inhabitants and they began to call upon the Lord.

> **19:19a** And many of those who practiced magic brought their books together and began burning them in the sight of all;

Magic. See p. 99.

> **19:21b** after [Paul] had passed through Macedonia and Achaia,

Macedonia. See under 16:9.

Achaia. See under 18:12.

> **19:22** And having sent into Macedonia two of those who ministered to him, Timothy and Erastus, he himself stayed in Asia for a while.

Erastus. *Erastos* means "beloved." He was sent by Paul, along with Timothy, into Macedonia (19:22). During this time, Paul composed and sent his first letter to the Corinthians. Possibly either Timothy or Erastus carried it to the church there.

There are two further mentions of Erastus in the New Testament. In 2 Timothy we read that "Erastus remained at Corinth, but Trophimus I left sick at Miletus" (2 Tim. 4:20). Erastus seemed to be dedicated to the church at Corinth. Looking through the Corinthian letters and the sad spiritual shape it was in, Erastus may have felt the need to stay there and be an example. After being taught under Paul, he would be most needed at this location.

In Romans, Paul writes, "Gaius, host to me and to the whole church, greets you. Erastus, the city treasurer, greets you, and Quarus, the brother." (Rom. 16:23). Most critics distinguish him from the Erastus written of in Acts. Unger, however, identifies the two as the same person. Unger comments that "the conversion of such a man to the faith of the gospel was proof of the wonderful success of the apostle's labor in that city (Corinth)." But others believe:

> We have no means of discovering whether one or more than one person is meant in these references. A. C. Headlam thinks it improbable that one who held an office implying residence in one

locality should have been one of Paul's companions in travel. On the other hand, Paul may be designating Erastus (Rom. 16:23) by an office he once held, but which he gave up to engage in mission work.[201]

19:24 For a certain man named Demetrius, a silversmith, who made silver shrines of Artemis, was bringing no little business to the craftsmen;

Demetrius. *Dēmētrios* ("belonging to Demeter") was a silversmith of Ephesus, whose main trade was in manufacture of small silver reproductions of the idol to the Greek goddess Artemis. Through this business, he was very successful. When Paul and other believers began to preach the one true God, Demetrius began to see his business slack off. Demetrius gathered his fellow craftsmen and incited them against Paul and his companions (Acts 19:25–26).

Demetrius has an age-old dilemma that strikes when the Word of God comes to an area where Satan enjoys strength. Under satanic control, witch doctors, psychics, shamanists, and other occult practitioners live the most comfortable lives. People hold them in fear for their perceived powers. And where a people worship or revere statues of gods, saints, or other holy figures, the true gospel becomes a threat to financial well-being, and they respond in a very ugly fashion.

Demetrius gives witness to the power of the gospel and the ministry of Paul, that wherever he has gone people have turned from idols (Acts 19:26b). Pagans could see the power with which Paul taught and preached, though they could not see the truth.

In a sly move, Demetrius appeals to civic pride by proclaiming that Paul is attempting to discredit the great temple of Artemis (19:27). This Artemis was not the huntress of Greek mythology. The Ephesians worshiped a Near Eastern mother-goddess, a grotesque, many-breasted fertility goddess whose image was believed to have been fashioned in heaven and to have fallen from the sky.[202] This temple was the basis for much of the wealth of Ephesus, attracting thousands of pilgrims every year. The temple was also a huge bank, where kings, princes, and the wealthy deposited their money under the protection of the goddess.

The crowd works itself into a frenzy. Demetrius's further actions are not recorded, but the effects of what he started escalate. "The city was filled with confusion, and they rushed with one accord into the theater, dragging along Gaius and Aristarchus, Paul's traveling companions from Macedonia" (19:29). As often is the case in riots, any scapegoat will do.

These associates of Paul are brought before the "town clerk," the chief executive officer of the local government. He works for two hours to quiet the crowds. He must have been quite concerned. Ephesus has prestige in

Roman eyes, and the town clerk is responsible for maintaining peace. When the people finally quiet, the town clerk berates them. The people of Ephesus may meet in a lawful legislative assembly, but this gathering is unlawful.[203] By opening with remarks on how magnificent the temple of Artemis truly was, he allays the fear that he might side with Paul's friends. But he observes that those charged have not directly attacked Artemis or the temple (19:37). They are innocent, and if the silversmiths have definite charges to make, there are courts in which to make them (19:38–39). The blame is put onto Demetrius and those he stirred up.

One other Demetrius is mentioned in 3 John: "Demetrius has received a good testimony from everyone, and from the truth itself" (3 John 12a). Few suggest that this is the one in Acts.

Artemis. While Acts 19 is the only chapter of Scripture in which Artemis/ Diana is mentioned, she appears in verses 24, 27–28, and 34–35. She is referred to in various translations by *Artemis*, her Greek name, or by *Diana*, her Latin name. Her history can be traced to early Greek mythology, though the Ephesians had merged the Greek goddess with ancient fertility goddesses of their own history. Elsewhere she was called Cynthia, Pythia, and Phoebe.

The Greek version was the daughter of Zeus and Leto and twin sister of Apollo. She was a favorite Olympian deity. She was most commonly conceived as the goddess of the hunt and of childbirth. In contrast with the immoral Ephesian worship, the Greek Artemis was chaste and punished whoever violated her laws of virginal chastity. The many-breasted goddess at Ephesus was early identified with Artemis by the Greeks, and came to be known as "the Ephesian Artemis."[204] Although Artemis was born in the Greek pantheon, she took differing forms where Greek, Roman, and other cultures collided and was often vaguely similar to the original.[205] Not only did the merging of the two cultures influence the nature and personality of the various deities, but also the worship of a particular deity would vary from locale to locale, blended with local deities.

At Ephesus, Artemis was transformed into an object of cult worship for at Ephesus she hardly resembled the Greek original and was worshiped in fertility rites as the mother goddess.[206] The worship of Artemis at Ephesus, while cultic, was a prominent way of life. Her temple was a grand monument, destroyed in the mid-fourth century B.C. but now magnificent.[207]

The legend that the Ephesian Artemis had fallen from heaven had brought the city world fame, as the clerk said.[208]

> **19:29** And the city was filled with the confusion, and they rushed with one accord into the theater, dragging along Gaius and Aristarchus, Paul's traveling companions from Macedonia.

Gaius [of Macedonia]. Gaius and Aristarchus, who are Paul's traveling companions and probably have been in Ephesus for at least part of his two years there, are nearly killed by the mob incited by Demetrius. The Gaius of this event is not mentioned again in Scripture.

Aristarchus. Aristarchus is one of Paul's most devoted companions and is mentioned in several epistles as one who continually shared the ministry of suffering. In Acts 20:4 and 27:2, he is identified as a Macedonian citizen of Thessalonica. He is one of a group of companions going through Greece ahead of Luke and Paul to Troas (20:5).

Aristarchus takes the treacherous journey with Paul to his Roman imprisonment and is with him when the apostle writes his Colossian and Philemon letters (Col. 4:10; Philem. 24). It is believed that he and Epaphras voluntarily were imprisoned with Paul. They may "have participated in the apostle's bonds alternately."[209] Tradition says Aristarchus died a martyr's death in Rome under Nero.

> **19:31** And also some of the Asiarchs who were friends of his sent to him and repeatedly urged him not to venture into the theater.

Asiarchs. The Asiarchs, *tōn Asiarchōn,* were ten officers elected by cities in the province who helped finance public games and festivals. Each province had such a group. It was a rich man's position but one with great prestige and eagerly desired.[210] These men in particular were friendly toward Paul and wanted to protect his safety. The evident aristocratic Asian attitude toward Christianity was positive, Bruce explains, reflecting generally amicable relations between Rome and Christianity. Luke's narrative makes the point that it was the superstitious who feared Paul, not the educated.[211]

> **19:33** And some of the crowd concluded it was Alexander,

Alexander. Alexander, whose name means "man-defender,"[212] was a Jewish citizen of Ephesus who represents the Jews, probably as they try to make their own complaints against the Christians. He does not have a chance to make his defense, for when the pro-Artemis riot recognize him as a Jew, they identify him with offenders against Artemis and become all the more frenzied.

Chapter 20

A.D. 55

TRAVELS THROUGH GREECE AND ASIA MINOR

Synopsis

(1–5) Paul travels on from Ephesus to Macedonia, and on to Greece (1–2) But after three months there, more Jewish opposition arises and he must depart again (3–5).

(6–12) At Troas, the young man named Eutychus, in a deep sleep, falls from a window as Paul is speaking. Paul falls upon the boy and revives him.

(13–38) From Miletus, Paul invites the Ephesian elders to a last church conference. Paul reminds them of the plot of the Jews against his life and that he doesn't know what awaits him in Jerusalem. He is prepared to finish the course no matter what (13–26). He rehearses his record among them and warns them to be on guard against perverted teachers and teachings. Finally, he says, "be on the alert" and "admonish each one with tears" (27–31). Paul concludes with prayer, and there is a sad farewell as Paul boards the ship for Caesarea (32–38).

> **20:2** And when he had gone through those districts and had given them much exhortation, he came to Greece.

Greece. The great city-state of Athens developed considerably in the sixth century B.C. The Acropolis changed from being a citadel to a shrine, with a temple devoted to Athena, the goddess of wisdom, who gives her name to the city. Many smaller shrines and temples were erected, and it was decorated with large sculptures representing lions, bulls, and mythical beasts.

In 490 B.C., Greece suffered its first attack from the Persians, who were defeated by the Athenian army at the battle of Marathon. However, attacks continued, and in 480 the city was invaded and destroyed by the Persians. When the Athenians returned to their ruined homes the following year, they began a program of rebuilding under their leader Pericles, creating the beautiful city associated with the golden age of Athens.

Athens became the leading city of Greece, not only in art and architecture, but also in literature and philosophy. Plato (428–348), Aristotle (384–322), Epicurus (341–270), and Zeno of Citium (335–263) started the stoic school. Writers included tragedians Euripides (484–406) and Sophocles (496–406), the comic dramatist Aristophanes (450–388), and the historian Herodotus (484–430?), who wrote an account of the city's wars with Persia. The city was also the birthplace of democracy. All male adult citizens could vote on matters of domestic and foreign policy. The golden age came to an end when Athens lost the Peloponnesian War to the Spartans in 404.

In the Hellenistic period, the 300 years between 323 B.C. and the death of Alexander the Great, Athens benefited from building works undertaken by foreign rulers. The Egyptian Ptolemies built a gymnasium and a sanctuary for the gods Isis and Sarapis in the second century B.C. The Attalid rulers of Pergamum built colonnades, one on the slopes of the Acropolis and the other a long building incorporating a row of shops in the agora.

In 86 B.C., Athens was captured by the Romans. Although there was considerable bloodshed when the city was taken, it was not sacked, and the fine public buildings were generally left intact. The invading Romans apparently respected the city's independence and cultural reputation. They allowed it considerable autonomy and erected new buildings. At the time Paul preached there, the city had lost its former wealth and power but remained a center of learning.

However, the gospel message was too alien to Greek philosophical and religious thinking to appeal to many Athenians. The passage in Acts 17 describing Paul's stay in Athens mentions his disputes with philosophers from the Epicurean and Stoic schools. The Epicureans were devoted to the achievement of serenity and happiness through detachment from the desires of the world. They believed that after death the body's constituent particles were dispersed. The Stoics, who took their name from the Stoa Poikile, where Zeno had taught, believed primarily in universal reason and in the disinterested pursuit of virtue and duty. Paul's message might have had some attraction for these philosophers, but his insistence on the idea of resurrection was unacceptable. Although a small Christian community was established, for five or six centuries pagan religion flourished.

The Romans were affected deeply by Greek thought, even before the Empire. The language, mythology, and literature of Greece had become more or less familiar throughout the region during the golden age of Athens. How early, how widely, and how permanently this Greek influence prevailed among educated Romans we know from their surviving writings and from the biographies of eminent men. Cicero, governor of Cilicia about half a century before the birth of Paul, speaks in strong terms of the universal spread of the Greek tongue among the educated. In the 60s, about the time of Paul's martyrdom, Agricola, the conqueror of Britain, was receiving a Greek education at Marseilles in Gaul.

The arrangement of God for the spread of the gospel included two supreme facts of first-century life: the spread of Greek thought and language and the maturity of the Roman government. When all parts of the civilized world were bound to one empire, with new facilities of traveling and a relatively common tongue, then was the fullness of time when the Messiah came.[213]

> **20:4** And he was accompanied by Sopater of Berea, the son of Pyrrhus; and by Aristarchus and Secundus of the Thessalonians; and Gaius of Derbe, and Timothy; and Tychicus and Trophimus of Asia.

Sopater. Sopater (lit. "savior of the father") is said to be from Berea. This is probably the "Sosipater" mentioned in Romans 16:21. If so, Paul there calls him his kinsman, so he may be a Jewish relative of the apostle.

Secundus. The name *Secundus* is listed with Sosipater on the well-known Thessalonian inscription that lists leaders of the city, those known as the Politarchs. Whether the same man, Thessalonians Secundus and Aristarchus joined this most important trip with the apostle to Europe. Secundus may have been one of the disciples who made the trip from Macedonia to Jerusalem with contributions for the Christians there (Acts 24:17; 2 Cor. 8:23).

Gaius [of Derbe]. It would seem that the Gaius mentioned in Acts 20:4 is the same companion of Paul mentioned in 19:29. But this is generally believed to be a different disciple. From time to time various believers from other regions would join Paul. They may have been both encouragers and also fellow witnesses. They were probably learning from watching how Paul gave the gospel, and they may have contributed financially.

Tychicus. Tychicus was more than simply a traveling companion of Paul. He seems to have been Paul's messenger to various churches. The apostle writes that "Tychicus, the beloved brother and faithful minister in the Lord, will make everything known to you [about my circumstances]. And I have sent him to you for this very purpose, so that you may know about us, and that he may comfort your hearts" (Eph. 6:21–22).

Luke calls Tychicus an Asian *(asianoi)* (Acts 20:4) who traveled from Macedonia to Asia and then on to Troas ahead of Luke and Paul. Tychicus was probably with Paul the seven days he taught and ministered at Troas (20:6). He likely took word of Paul's arrival to the Ephesian elders and heard Paul's parting charge to them (20:17–35). Tychicus carried the Ephesian and Colossian letters to their destinations while Paul was in prison. With the highest of praise, the apostle commends "our beloved brother and faithful servant and fellow bond-servant in the Lord (Col. 4:7).

It seems Tychicus was sent on a second journey to Ephesus (2 Tim. 4:12). Church tradition says he was made the bishop of Chalcedon in Bithynia or that he was the appointed bishop of Colophon following Sosthenes and finally suffered martyrdom.[214]

Trophimus. Most believe Trophimus went on with Paul to Jerusalem and there was the target for the riot that broke out at the temple. Luke reports the people had seen "Trophimus the Ephesian" with Paul and supposed that Paul had brought this Gentile into the temple (Acts 21:29).

Trophimus is mentioned again by Paul who, speaking of their journeys together, writes, "Trophimus I left at Miletus sick" (2 Tim. 4:20). Paul notes also that he sent Trophimus to Ephesus, probably during his first imprisonment (2 Tim. 4:12). He is possibly "the [other] brother" who with Titus carried Paul's second letter to the Corinthians from Ephesus (2 Cor. 8:16–24). Church history says he was killed at Rome under Nero in July 64.

> **20:6a** And we sailed from Philippi after the days of
> Unleavened Bread, and came to them at Troas

Days of Unleavened Bread. See under 12:3.

Troas. See under 16:8.

> **20:9a** And there was a certain young man named Eutychus,
> sitting on the window sill,

Eutychus. *Eutychos* means "fortunate," but the young man was not very fortunate on this night, as he drowsed off in the stifling air of this upper room. At Troas, this could have been an upper apartment of the popular Roman-style tenement dwellings. These apartment buildings were often poorly constructed and could be several stories high. Eutychus may have fallen a considerable distance. Rather than "fortune," God's power was demonstrated. The language of the text indicates that Eutychus was dead rather than just knocked unconscious and that Paul miraculously raised him to life. The act brought great comfort to the church in Troas (20:12).

20:13a But we, going ahead to the ship, set sail for Assos,

Assos. Assos was an impregnable city on the southern coast of the Gulf of Adramyttium (modern Edremit), an inlet into the Aegean Sea. The city was also called South Troas and looked toward the island of Lesbos. A platonic school was started at Assos in the fourth century B.C. by Hermias. Aristotle taught at the school from 348–345. Assos controlled the coast roads and trade of the region. It possessed a large theater and several temples. The apostle Paul on his third missionary trip met up with his traveling companions in Assos.

20:14 And when he met us at Assos, we took [Paul] on board and came to Mitylene.

Mitylene. Mitylene, Mytilene, or Mitilini was the chief city on the island of Lesbos. Its large walls surrounded an area similar in size to Athens. The Greek poetess Sappho lived here in the sixth century B.C. She is widely known for her erotic homosexual verses. Primarily because of Sappho, the word *lesbian* is derived from the name of the island. The society and mystery religions that possessed the island were purely pagan.

Mitylene was a large seaport and a stopping point for most trade. Mitylene was known for its gray terra cotta pottery and a pickled fish called "Garum." A large theater could have seated 18,000–20,000. The island was conquered in 522 B.C. by King Darius of Persia, and Aristotle stayed in Mitylene after the murder of his father-in-law Hermias by the Persians. The city itself was known for inflicting beatings arbitrarily on unsuspecting individuals. Lesbos was given to Rome in 133 B.C. by the king of Pergamum and became a favorite travel spot of the Roman elite.

20:15 And sailing from there, we arrived the following day opposite Chios; and the next day we crossed over to Samos; and the day following we came to Miletus.

Chios. After Paul traveled overland to meet his companions, who had sailed to Assos, they eventually put in opposite the island of Chios (20:15). This body of land constituted one of the largest Aegean islands off the west coast of Asia Minor. It was a free Roman city-state until the time of Vespasian.

Samos. Samos is an island off the southwest coast of Asia Minor below Chios and above Patmos, where John later received his Revelation of Jesus Christ. During Paul's day, Samos was a free city and the seat of the worship of Juno. Her temple, the Heracon, was enriched by some of the finest works of art known to Greece. Its chief manufacture was a fine red-clay pottery, Sumian ware, which was celebrated all over the civilized world. Its wine (Levantine) was also of a high caliber.[215]

Miletus. Miletus, about thirty-six miles south of Ephesus, was once an independent state of some military strength. Between the eighth and sixth centuries B.C., according to E. M. Blaiklock, Miletus colonized all around the Black Sea and had a vigorous metropolitan life. "Miletus must have exercised strong sea power during these active centuries, and her military might is shown by the resistance she offered to the Lydian kings, and the privileged position accorded even by the greatest of those rulers, Croesus."[216] In Paul's day, it was the capital city of Ionia and housed the great temple of Apollo. This is also city the where Paul left Trophimus sick (2 Tim. 4:20).

> **20:28b** the Holy Spirit has made you overseers, to shepherd the church of God which He purchased with His own blood.

Holy Spirit made you overseers. See p. 47.

To shepherd the church of God. See p. 48.

Which he purchased. Used but a few times in the New Testament, *peripoieō* is translated "to acquire, obtain, gain for oneself."[217] In New Testament literature, the verb is always in the middle voice (for oneself). The great love of Jesus is here so graphically explained. His own death and shedding of blood was required to redeem the church as His own. R. C. H. Lenski believes this verse strongly proclaims the deity of Christ. "Let us not forget the great reality here expressed so clearly: We are purchased by means of God's blood. *Dia* ["with"] expresses means. This blood was the price; as being God's blood its value is infinite and could and did effect the purchase."[218]

> **20:29b** savage wolves will come in among you, not sparing the flock;

Savage wolves. This is an amazing "foretelling" prophecy of Paul, not that great maturity would come upon the churches, but that they would be rent by heretical doctrine. Despite this, Paul sees a certain spiritual benefit when troubles brew within the local church body in that it seems to clarify those who are genuine and those who are departing from the faith. He writes in 1 Corinthians, "For there must also be factions among you, in order that those who are approved may have become evident among you" (11:19).

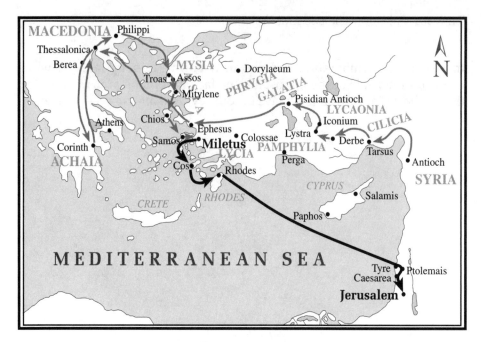

Chapter 21

A.D. 56 (Journey Ends in Jerusalem)

RETURN TO JERUSALEM;
THE ARREST OF PAUL

Synopsis

(1–14) On the way to Caesarea, Paul and his party land at Tyre, where they stay for seven days, and Ptolemais, where they stay for one day. At both places they visit with other Christians. All along, Paul is urged not to go on to Jerusalem because of fierce opposition from the Jews (1–7). At Caesarea, Paul and company visit Philip the Evangelist. The prophet Agabus comes from Judea and warns that Paul will be bound over to the Gentiles. The believers beg him not to go on, but Paul answers that he is ready to die, if necessary, in Jerusalem (8–14).

(15–26) Having been received with joy in Jerusalem, Paul shares what God has done among the Gentiles. When the brothers in the church heard his report, they glorified God (15–20). But some took Paul aside to warn him that his work among the Gentiles had been misrepresented. Jews zealous for the Law had heard that Paul was urging the Gentiles to forsake the Law of Moses, "telling them not to circumcise their children nor to walk according to the customs" (21). The men of the church suggest a visible demonstration that Paul still keeps the Law (22–24). He is advised to go up to the temple with four men who have proclaimed a Nazarite vow. Paul

can join them, pay their temple tax, purify himself along with them, and offer up sacrifice. Paul follows their suggestion (25–26).

(27–40) Seeing him in the temple, a group of Asian Jews cry out to the crowd to seize Paul for "This is the man who preaches to all men everywhere against our people, and the Law" (27–28). Paul is rescued from the mob by the local Roman commander stationed in Jerusalem and is taken bound to the military barracks (29–37). Explaining that he is a Roman citizen and a Jew from Tarsus in Cilicia, Paul begs for permission to speak to the people. He is granted an opportunity before a large, hushed crowd (38–40).

21:1b we ran a straight course to Cos and the next day to Rhodes and from there to Patara;

Cos. A small island located in the Aegean Sea, Cos is long and narrow, oriented east to west. It is approximately twenty-three miles long and sixty-five miles around, with a land mass of about 111 square miles. In the middle of the island stands Mount Ordomedon, traditionally used by navigators as a landmark. Cos was famous for the Asclepion, the sanctuary to Asclepius, god of healing. It was the Roman world's version of a medical clinic. Its ferrous and sulfur springs, combined with a healthy climate, were used extensively by Hippocrates (460–377 B.C.) to cure his patients. The Asclepion boasted a hospital and a medical school.

Cos was an island with a turbulent past. Its use as a beacon made it invaluable for navies. Going from one conqueror to another, the island found enough peace after the conquest of Alexander to become a flourishing center of trade, especially in wine, ointments, and silks. After Alexander's death, Ptolemy Philadelphus took over control of the island, turning it into a literary center (c. 300 B.C.) and eventual birthplace for the poet Philetas.

After 1933, when an earthquake struck the island, archaeological finds were made dating habitation to as early as the Bronze Age Mycean culture (c. 1400 B.C.). Also uncovered were Roman baths, fed by the island's springs, with inscriptions from Nero's reign and thus to the time of Paul's ministry.[219] Luke's record indicates that Cos was used by Paul's party only as a short rest stop.

Rhodes. Rhodes is an island in the Aegean Sea southeast of Greece near Turkey. It has a length of about 45 miles and a breadth of 22 miles. Rhodes has a healthy climate and is known for its fertile soil. It is confusing as to whether references to Rhodes mean the island or the city on the island of the same name.

Rhodes is still a trading port, and near the southern harbor stands the old walled city built by the Knights of Saint John of Jerusalem in the early fourteenth century.

The history of the island of Rhodes can be traced to the second millennium B.C., when it was inhabited by the Dorians. The chief towns—Camirus, Lindus, and Ialysus, were to become wealthy commercial centers. For a short while, the three cities were members of the Delian League, a confederacy of Greek states under Athens. In 408 B.C., the ancient city of Rhodes was constructed. When Alexander came through, the people submitted to his authority. Upon his death, they revolted and expelled the Macedonians. The island of Rhodes became a staunch ally of Rome, especially of Julius Caesar. In 42 B.C., the Roman general Gaius Cassius invaded Rhodes and massacred friends of Caesar, breaking the power of Rhodes.[220]

Rhodes is mentioned only once in Scripture, as a stopover near the end of Paul's third missionary journey (21:1). Paul's hurry to get back to Jerusalem did not allow for many stops along the way.

Patara. A large port in Lycia (Asia Minor), Patara was important for traders and seafarers, and it had the oracle of Apollo. This oracle was second only to the oracle at Delphi. It spoke during the six winter months only, whereas Paul visited during the summer.

As early as the fifth century B.C., Patara had struck its own coins.[221] Because of its excellent harbor, Patara became a wealthy marketplace for merchants from all over the world. To attest to the wealth and luxury of Patara a triumphal arch there read: "Patara the metropolis of the Lycian nation."

Patara is thought to be of Phoenician origin. Like Cos, this location caught the eye of Ptolemy Philadelphus, who enlarged the city in the late fourth century B.C. Ptolemy changed its name to *Arsinoe,* in honor of his wife.

Among ruins excavated have been found a deep circular pit with steps leading down. This could be the location of the oracle of Apollo.

As with Cos, Paul does not appear to preach or teach in this town. At Patara, Paul and his companions transferred to another ship. Various views have been expressed concerning why. One suggestion is that the sailors did not know the coast any farther than Patara and terminated their voyage. Another opinion, equally valid, is that Paul wanted to avoid the time-consuming ports of call on the first vessel's itinerary. Possibly a larger merchant ship would sail in the open sea directly from Patara to Phoenicia and save a considerable amount of time.[222]

> **21:2** and having found a ship crossing over to Phoenicia, we went aboard and set sail.

Phoenicia. See under 11:19.

21:3 And when we had come in sight of Cyprus, . . . we kept sailing to Syria and landed at Tyre; for there the ship was to unload its cargo.

Cyprus. See under 4:36.

Syria. See under 15:23.

21:7a And when we had finished the voyage from Tyre, we arrived at Ptolemais;

Ptolemais. Not to be confused with the more important city of Egypt, Ptolemais, as it was known to the ancient Greeks and Romans, was located on Haifa Bay at a natural dividing line along Israel's coastal plain. It is north of Mount Carmel. By the time of the Crusades, it was called "Acre," from the Hebrew name for the place, *Akko.* A. F. Rainey said the location has been a seaport since far back in Israel's occupation, when there was a small town along the shore. There evidently was a Canaanite site there as well. It is mentioned in Judges 1:31–32: "Asher did not drive out the inhabitants of Acco . . . so the Asherites lived among the Canaanites, the inhabitants of the land: for they did not drive them out." [223]

During the Hellenistic period, the community grew rapidly. Ptolemais acquired its name from Ptolemy, the king of Egypt, who rebuilt it about 100 B.C. Under the Emperor Claudius in A.D. 52–54, it was made a Roman colony, settled by veterans of various legions.

Toward the end of Paul's third missionary journey (A.D. 57), he and his companions visited Ptolemais on their way from Tyre to Caesarea (21:7). There was a fellowship of believers there, probably from the dispersion after Stephen's death (11:19).

21:8a And on the next day we departed and came to Caesarea;

Caesarea. See under 8:40.

21:9 Now this man [Philip] had four virgin daughters who were prophetesses.

Prophetess. See more on prophets under 13:1.

21:10b a certain prophet named Agabus came down from Judea.

Agabus. See under 11:28.

21:11 "This is what the Holy Spirit says . . ."

Holy Spirit says. See under 1:2.

21:16 And some of the disciples from Caesarea also came with us, taking us to Mnason of Cyprus, a disciple of long standing with whom we were to lodge.

Mnason. *Mnasōn* means "reminding." He was an early disciple of Christ, who may have been converted at the time of Pentecost, or possibly he was one of the seventy followers of Christ during his earthly life. Paul and his companions sought shelter in his residence (21:6). Mnason was a native of Cyprus and may have known fellow Cypriote. That Mnason owned a house in Jerusalem in which all of Paul's company could lodge implies that he had wealth.[224]

Though Mnason is given brief mention in Scripture, some things can be inferred about him. He was a man of hospitality. Paul's company at times could be very large and included Gentiles. We do not read of any hesitance toward Gentiles in his household. Being a disciple of long standing would put him in the category of possibly being a witness to Christ. Or his long exposure to the Christian teachings would make him an invaluable preparation for Paul's rough roads, which lay just ahead.

21:27 And when the seven days were almost over, the Jews from Asia, . . . began to stir up all the multitude and laid hands on him.

Asia. See under 16:6.

21:29a For they had previously seen Trophimus, the Ephesian, in the city with him.

Trophimus. See under 20:4.

21:38 "Then you are not the Egyptian who some time ago stirred up a revolt and led the four thousand men of the Assassins out into the wilderness?"

The Egyptian . . . Assassins. Lysias, the Roman captain of Jerusalem who rescues Paul, first believes him to be an Egyptian Jew, whose name was *Assasius*. Around 54, as recorded by Josephus, Assasius appeared in Jerusalem claiming to be a prophet. From the text of Josephus we learn the basic facts that Assasius led a large band of followers, four thousand according to Acts 21:38, into the wilderness. He then led his followers to the Mount of Olives. From there, they prepared for the messianic overthrow of Jerusalem. Felix and his men drove him off, killing or capturing most. Assasius himself escaped and disappeared. Most Jews considered him to be a fake.[225]

The tribune (the Greek has *chiliarch*, i.e., "ruler of a thousand") had reason to be elated in the thought that he had captured the notorious Egyptian who had recently stirred up a revolt.

21:39a But Paul said, "I am a Jew of Tarsus in Cilicia,"

Tarsus. See under 9:11.

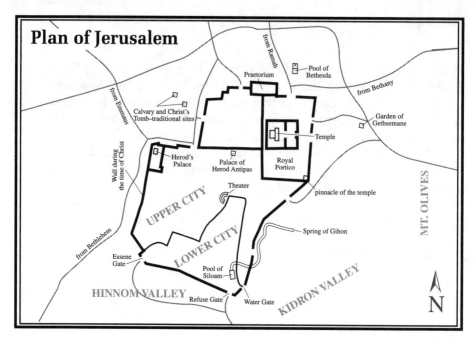

Plan of Jerusalem

Chapter 22

A.D. 56

PAUL'S DEFENSE BEFORE THE JERUSALEM CROWD

Synopsis

(1–21) Paul reviews his life before the quiet crowd. He tells how he met the risen Christ on the Damascus road, how he was blinded, and how Jesus commissioned him to witness of Him before all men (1–15). He also related how the Lord commanded him to be sent far away "to the Gentiles" (16–21).

(22–30) At the mention of Gentiles, the crowd reacts with rage. Paul is taken back into the barracks and is about to be scourged as a troublemaker when he asks the centurion, "Is it lawful for you to scourge a man who is a Roman and uncondemned?" (22–28). The Roman centurion becomes fearful, having put a citizen in chains unlawfully. The next day, Paul is released but is still ordered to appear before the Sanhedrin to be formally accused by the chief priests and other leaders (29–30).

22:3a "I am a Jew, . . . educated under Gamaliel,"

Gamaliel. See under 5:34.

22:4a "And I persecuted this Way to the death,"

This Way. See under 9:2.

22:5a "as also the high priest and all the Council of the elders can testify. From them I also received letters to the brethren and started off for Damascus"

Council. See under 5:21.

Damascus. See under 9:2.

22:8b "'I am Jesus the Nazarene, whom you are persecuting.'"

Nazarene. See p. 72.

22:11b "I was led by the hand by those who were with me, and came into Damascus."

Damascus. See under 9:2.

22:12a "And a certain Ananias,"

Ananias. See under 9:10.

22:16b "'Arise and be baptized, and wash away your sins, calling on His name.'"

Wash away your sins. Baptismal regeneration cannot be found in the New Testament; thus, to the contrary it is denied that any such work of piety can save. Therefore, this passage must be looked at closely to see what Ananias actually is telling Paul. The answer may be found in the fact that the last clause is an aorist participle and can be translated, "Having called yourself upon His name." This controls the entire passage, and R. C. H. Lenski notes that this clause is either simultaneous with the two aorist imperatives ("be baptized" and "wash away") or it precedes them.[226] Thus, the baptism and the being washed was part of calling upon His name. That "washing" was not the outer physical act, connected to the physical water, but the work of the Holy Spirit. (See Titus 3:5.)

22:20a "'And when the blood of Thy witness Stephen was being shed,'"

Witness. See under 1:8.

Stephen. See pp. 246–248; see also under 7:58.

> **22:24a** the commander ordered him to be brought into the
> barracks, stating that he should be examined by scourging

Commander. The fortress of Antonia was joined by two flights of stairs to the court of the Gentiles. In it was stationed a Roman cohort (1000 men). Because of the frequent riots in the temple area, especially during feasts, Roman sentries were stationed around the court. These quickly detected the riot, and soldiers rushed down to bring it under control. Since centurions were dispatched, at least two hundred soldiers were called out to quell the mob.

The Roman commander is later identified (23:26) as Claudias Lysias. In 22:24, 26, 27, 29, 30, and 23:17, 19, and 22 he is referred to as "commander." Bruce writes that he was evidently of Greek birth. His Greek name Lysias became his *"cognomen"* when he gained citizenship. He took for his *"nomen"* the name of Claudius, who was emperor.[227]

Lysias saves Paul's life on at least two occasions. First, he protects him from the mob. And in Acts 23, he takes seriously the words of a young man, the nephew of Paul, who had overheard of a plot to kill Paul. He took great precautions in escorting Paul to the governor, Felix. With Paul, the soldiers delivered a letter from Claudius Lysias to Felix. Protocol required that Lysias send a written statement of the case, called a *elogium.*[228]

Claudius Lysias' shrewdness is demonstrated by his words and actions. He is quite concerned about protecting himself from the consequences of harm coming to someone under his jurisdiction, so he is thorough in his protective action. However, he does not mention in his letter to Felix the orders he had given for Paul to be scourged, since Paul, as a Roman citizen, could not legally have been scourged without first being condemned.

> **22:26** And when the centurion heard this, . . . "What are
> you about to do? For this man is a Roman."

Centurion. See p. 282.

This man is a Roman. By law a Roman citizen not proven guilty of a crime could not be flogged. Paul identified himself as a Roman citizen and at the same time reminded the soldiers of the citizen rules. The commander was incredulous that a citizen could be the object of such hatred by the Jews.[229]

22:28 And the commander answered, "I acquired this
citizenship with a large sum of money." And Paul said,
"But I was actually born a citizen."

I acquired this citizenship with a large sum of money. During the reign
of Emperor Claudius (41–54) it was possible to purchase Roman citizenship.
Those in government who sold this privilege could feather their nests with
the bribery money. In contrast with the commander, Paul was a citizen because
his parents were citizens.[230]

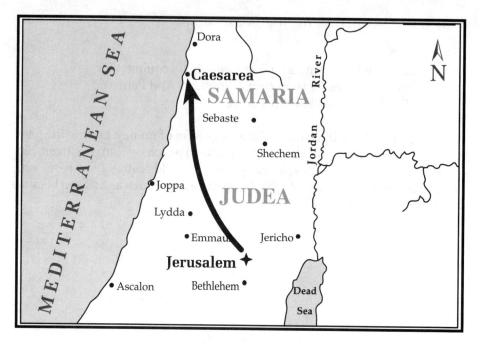

Chapter 23

A.D. 56

PAUL BEFORE THE SANHEDRIN; JOURNEY TO CAESAREA

Synopsis

(1–10) *Before the Sanhedrin Paul pleads his case that he has lived with a good conscious "up to this day" (1). But the high priest Ananias orders that he be struck in the mouth. Paul retaliates by calling him a "whitewashed wall," not realizing that he was the current high priest (2–3). He is informed by a bystander that the man is indeed the high priest, and Paul is reminded from Exodus 22:28 that it is a sin to speak evil "of a ruler of your people" (4–5). Sensing that the assembly is divided between Sadducees (who do not believe in the resurrection) and Pharisees (who do), Paul divides the audience by saying he is a Pharisee who holds to this biblical truth (6–8). When a great uproar and dissension arose, the commander of the guard ordered Paul brought back to the Roman barracks lest he be "torn to pieces" by the crowd (9–10).*

(11–35) *The night following, the Lord comes to Paul and says, "Take courage; for as you have solemnly witnessed to My cause at Jerusalem, so you must witness at Rome also" (11). The next day, a conspiracy was formed against him by the high*

priests and elders that they would not eat nor drink until Paul was dead (12–14).
Paul is warned of the threat by his nephew, who tells the commander of the guard.
Four hundred and seventy soldiers are readied to move Paul secretly from Jerusalem
to Caesarea to present him before the governor, Felix (15–24). A letter is written
to give Felix the facts (25–30). Paul finally arrives in Caesarea for his hearing
before Felix (31–35).

> **23:6** But perceiving that one part were Sadducees and the
> other Pharisees, Paul began crying out, . . . "I am on trial for
> the hope and resurrection of the dead!"

Sadducees. See under 4:1.

Pharisees. See 15:5.

> **23:24** They were also to provide mounts to put Paul on and
> bring him safely to Felix the governor.

Felix. Felix was a freedman and brother of Pollas, perhaps one of the
most influential freedmen under Claudius. Felix's connections at Rome
through his brother Pollas meant that he felt he could act with impunity. In
Tacitus's view, Felix, backed by vast influence, believed himself free to commit
any crime. Pollas himself received his freedom from Antonia, the mother of
Claudius, and it has been suggested that the procurator was thus Antonius
Felix. However, Josephus calls him Claudius Felix.

Felix dealt with the brigand Eleazor and sent him to Rome as punishment;
he crucified his associates and punished the common people who were
perceived as aiding brigands. At the same time, there grew up a band of
assassins, the *sicaru,* whose victims included Jonathan the High Priest. Another
group gathered in the desert; Felix regarded this as preliminary to insurrection,
so he sent a body of cavalry and heavily armed infantry, and put a large
number to the sword. Around 54, Felix had to deal with a revolt by an Egyptian
prophet who planned to storm Jerusalem (see under 21:38). Felix anticipated
the attack and met him with the Roman heavy infantry, the whole population
joining him in the defense. The outcome of the ensuing engagement was that
the Egyptian escaped with a few of his followers; most of his force were killed
or taken prisoner, the remainder dispersed and stealthily escaped to their homes.

It was probably during Paul's imprisonment at Caesarea that a riot there
took place. Toward the end of Felix's procuratorship, the Jews claimed that
Caesarea belonged to them. The Greeks pointed out the statues and temples
which Herod had allowed to be erected there stood as evidence that it was not
to be considered a Jewish city. After the riots and the inability of the local
magistrates to quell the unrest, Felix came forward to the agora and ordered

them to retire. When they refused, he sent his troops upon the Jews, killing many. Their property was subsequently plundered. As a result, Nero summoned Felix to Rome to answer charges regarding his mistreatment of the Jews.

Felix, wanting to keep peace at any cost, kept Paul under confinement. The Jews had an intense hatred for Felix. They knew that he was an ungodly man whose whole life was a reproach to the high office he held.

Felix and his wife, Drusilla, sent for Paul from time to time so that they might discuss Christ and his faith in Him. Felix is interested, as Herod was curious about Jesus and desired to see Him. Felix evidently knew a great deal about what had happened in Palestine, especially in Judea. He knew about Jesus and His crucifixion. He knew that it was common knowledge that He had risen in triumph from the dead. He knew how the gospel was spreading through all that part of the world and how it was reaching out to distant lands.

We read in Acts 24:25, "Felix became frightened, and said, 'Go away for the present and when I find time, I will summon you.'" Given a chance to make a decision for Christ, he loses his opportunity. Felix passes from the pages of Holy Scripture just as he had lived, corrupt and full of wickedness.

> **23:31** So the soldiers, in accordance with their orders, took
> Paul and brought him by night to Antipatris.

Antipatris. To this city Paul was taken as prisoner by night, as Luke tells us in Acts 23:31. The city was built by Herod the Great as a tribute to his father, who was named Antipater. It stood forty miles from Jerusalem on the road to Caesarea, and was therefore quite a distance to travel in one night.

> **23:35** He said, "I will give you a hearing after your accusers
> arrive also," giving orders for [Paul] to be kept in Herod's
> Praetorium.

Herod's Praetorium. Herod the Great built the Praetorium fortress at Caesarea for himself. Now it served as the procurator's headquarters.[231] From the Latin *praetorium,* meaning the place of the magistrate, this was the place where Paul was taken and held in 23:35 while he awaited hearing before Felix. In light of the conspiracy of the Jews to kill Paul (vv. 12–15), this would have been a most secure location for Paul to be held.

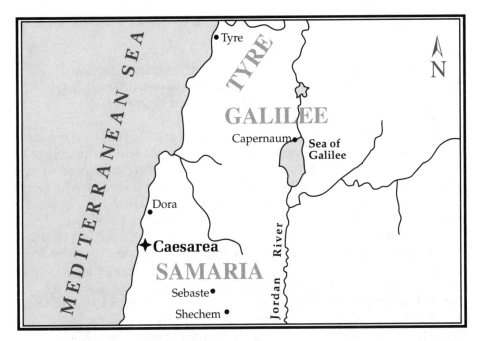

Chapter 24

A.D. 56

PAUL'S ADDRESS BEFORE FELIX

Synopsis

(1–21) Paul is now given a hearing in Herod's Praetorium in Caesarea, with his accusers from Jerusalem present as well. Within five days of his arrival, Ananias the high priest with some other elders, along with an attorney named Tertullus, come and charge, "We have found this man a real pest and a fellow who stirs up dissension among all the Jews." Too, he is "a ringleader of the sect of the Nazarenes" (1–5). Other Jews joined in the attack against Paul (6–9). The apostle admits that he is in the movement known as the Way but insists that he still serves God according to the Law. He adds, "For the resurrection of the dead I am on trial before you today" (10–21).

(22–27) Felix responds to Paul that he will decide the case when Lysias, the commander, arrives (22). Some days later, Paul comes before Felix and his Jewish wife, Drusilla. The apostle then speaks of his faith in Christ Jesus, of "righteousness, self-control, and the judgment to come." Felix comes under great conviction and orders that Paul "go away for the present, and when I find time, I will summon you" (23–25). Felix hopes that Paul or others will offer a bribe. Two years pass, and Felix is succeeded by Porcius Festus. Meanwhile, wishing to placate the Jews and in the absence of a bribe, Felix leaves Paul imprisoned" (26–27).

> **24:1** And after five days the high priest Ananias came down with some elders, with a certain attorney named Tertullus; and they brought charges to the governor against Paul.

Tertullus. Though the Jews did employ pagan lawyers, it is not clear whether Tertullus was Roman, Greek, or Jew. *Tertullus* is the diminutive of *Tertius*. Tertullus uses the smooth, flattering speech of an experienced lawyer. The Jewish leaders hire the best lawyer to ensure that Paul will be found guilty and condemned. These men are envious of Paul's success and feel a murderous rage against Paul. They will go to any length to kill him.

The charges against Paul are political and religious: Paul is a "pest," a creator of dissension among Jews throughout the world, and a ringleader of the sect of the Nazarenes (v. 5). It is further charged that he attempted to profane the temple. The former charge that he actually took Greeks into the temple has been modified for lack of evidence. The charges imply sedition, which is the most serious that could be submitted to a Roman court. The desire to see Paul condemned makes it necessary to stress the political, rather than the theological, case. Christianity has not been given independent status in the Roman Empire, so Judaism could claim the right to judge it as a disloyal sect within its own ranks.

Probably Tertullus is very much aware that Paul is innocent, but it makes no difference. He charges ahead to do his best to convict Paul. His reputation is on the line. He has an opportunity to make a real name for himself. Little did Tertullus know that nothing will stand in the way of God's plan for Paul to go to Rome.

> **24:5c** "[Paul] a ringleader of the sect of the Nazarenes."

Nazarenes. See p. 72.

> **24:7** "But Lysias the commander came along, and with much violence took him out of our hands,"

Lysias. See under 24:22.

> **24:18b** "But there were certain Jews from Asia"

Asia. See under 21:27.

> **24:24** But some days later, Felix arrived with Drusilla, his wife who was a Jewess, and sent for Paul, and heard him speak about faith in Christ Jesus.

Drusilla. Not a lot is known about Drusilla. She was the daughter of Herod Agrippa I (see under 12:1) and the sister of Herod Agrippa II (see under 25:13). According to Josephus, Drusilla was given in marriage by her brother to the King of Emesa, a small domain on the Orontes River. Drusilla soon was lured away from her husband and persuaded to marry Felix, who was attracted by her great beauty. When Drusilla left her legal husband for Felix, she was about sixteen years of age. Her decision was totally against Jewish law. Drusilla had not obtained a legal divorce from her husband, so she was not free to marry. Additionally, Felix had not agreed to become a Jew.

Felix, now the governor of Judea, had the responsibility to preside over the trial of Paul. Both sides had presented their cases, and now all eyes were on Felix. What would the governor decide? His decision is to put off both sides. He suspends the trial until he can confer with Lysias, the commander who saved Paul from the crowd in Jerusalem.

The next contact between the governor and Paul occurs a few days later, when Felix arrives with his wife, Drusilla. Drusilla, being well versed in Jewish laws, can provide another reason why Felix might have had a more accurate knowledge of "the Way" (Acts 24:22). Felix, desiring to please Drusilla, sends for Paul. What is so remarkable is that Drusilla is moved to hear Paul and his message of Jesus Christ. It may be that, because she knows the Law, she realizes that no one can live up to the Law. She wants to hear Paul and the message of faith alone.

Notice that God draws special attention to Drusilla's presence with Felix. Her father was of Edomite and Jewish extraction. She was schooled in the religion of Israel, but she had married a pagan. Drusilla had rebelled against all of Jewish tradition. She knew of the high standards set forth in the law of God and she was very much aware that she was living a life opposed to all that she had been taught.

Even though Felix and Drusilla had several meetings with Paul in private, they never came to a saving faith in Jesus Christ.

> **24:27** But after two years had passed, Felix was succeeded by Porcius Festus; and wishing to do the Jews a favor, Felix left Paul imprisoned.

Porcius Festus. Porcius Festus seems to have taken over for Felix in 60 after the riots in Caesarea. Because of all the trouble under Felix, Festus is eager to get along with the Jews and leaves Paul in prison. Paul must now take his appeal to Caesar and be sent to Rome. One of the first acts of Festus is to travel from Caesarea to Jerusalem, where he meets the chief priests and leading members of the Jewish community. Festus wants peace with the Jewish leadership.

Festus is probably to be credited with an attempt at fairness to all. He is at a disadvantage as a Roman, puzzled by the strange interests and laws of the Jews. He is convinced that Paul is innocent of all criminal charges, yet Jewish leaders could hardly be ignored by a new procurator. He acts as did Pilate in Jesus' case. Pilate knew Jesus was innocent, but he would not stand; he let the Jewish leaders make up his mind. In this case, Festus lacked the courage to act decisively and let Paul go free. Festus probably purposed to appease the Jews by conducting a trial in Jerusalem, as they requested, but to protect Paul by keeping the Jerusalem trial under his own control. It is important to observe that Festus did not propose to turn Paul over to the Sanhedrin but only to move the trial to Jerusalem. "Before me" is emphatic in the proposal of Festus. No doubt, Festus is relieved to turn Paul over to a higher court in Rome and thus avoid the dilemma of either sacrificing an innocent man or offending the Jewish rulers.

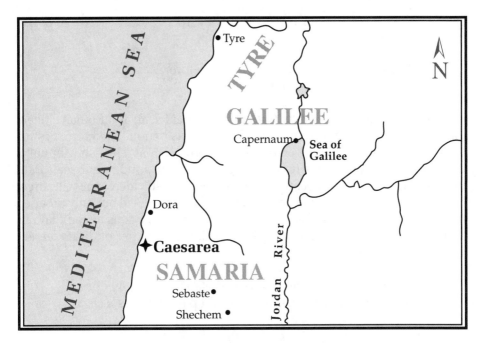

Chapter 25

A.D. 58

PAUL'S TESTIMONY BEFORE FESTUS

Synopsis

(1–5) Shortly after Festus arrives in Caesarea, he travels up to Jerusalem and meets with the leading men who had brought charges against Paul. After hearing their arguments, he urges that some of the most influential men accompany him back to his court in Caesarea, "and if there is any thing wrong against the man, let them prosecute him."

(6–12) Back in Caesarea, Festus orders Paul to be brought before his tribunal and the Jews from Jerusalem. They bring many charges against him they cannot prove (6–7). Paul proceeds to argue that he is willing to stand before Caesar's tribunal. "I appeal to Caesar," he answers (8–12).

(13–27) Herod Agrippa II, whose territories he ruled under Roman jurisdiction, arrives for a visit in Caesarea. Though Paul does not have to answer before Agrippa, he takes this opportunity to witness to him. Festus admits to Agrippa that he can find nothing against Paul (13–26). Festus adds, "It seems absurd to me in sending a prisoner [to Rome], not to indicate also the charges against him" (27).

25:10 But Paul said, "I am standing before Caesar's tribunal, where I ought to be tried."

Caesar's tribunal. Literally Caesar's judgment seat; as a Roman citizen, Paul has a right to stand trial under Roman jurisdiction. Therefore, Festus' request that Paul stand trial before him in Jerusalem at a Jewish tribunal is unreasonable. Paul insists he stand before Caesar's judgment seat. Paul understands that to stand before a Jewish tribunal is suicide, for he will surely be condemned to death, whereas to stand before Rome will not only broaden his audience, but also give a more objective outcome. Festus already knows that Paul's so-called offense to the Jews is simply a matter of disagreement regarding religious matters (vv. 18–19).

25:13 Now when several days had elapsed, King Agrippa and Bernice arrived at Caesarea, and paid their respects to Festus.

King Agrippa II. Marcus Julius Agrippa, or Agrippa II, succeeded his uncle in 48 as Herod, at first ruling Lebanon and later the regions of Iturea, Trachonitis, Abilene, and numerous other villages. He eventually ruled about one-third of Palestine. Eusebius explains that Claudius made Agrippa "king of the Jews."[232] It seems that, due to Agrippa's young age of seventeen, Claudius did not fully follow through with this empowerment. In any case, Agrippa II exercised his authority to change the high priests frequently, this "making him quite unpopular with the Jews."[233] In general, he did not enjoy the popularity of his subjects.

In Acts 25:13, he arrives at Caesarea with his sister Bernice, and after speaking to Festus, Paul is provided a hearing before Agrippa and Bernice. Paul's statement in 26:2–3 can clearly be understood in the light of Agrippa's deep involvement with the workings of Judaism. Paul is not simply flattering him; rather, he understands Agrippa's background. This background makes Agrippa an interested listener. Whether Agrippa ever believes the gospel message is unknown, but his statement in 26:28 at least introduces the possibility.

Bernice. On inscriptions, Bernice is called "queen" or "great queen."[251] She was born in 28, the daughter of Herod Agrippa I. She was sister to Agrippa II. Josephus tells us that "[Marcus] married Bernice, the daughter of Agrippa. But when Marcus, Alexander's son was dead, who had married her when she was a virgin, Agrippa gave her in marriage to his brother Herod, her uncle."[234] After Herod's death, Josephus said she lived as a widow, but was accused with having a sexual relationship with her brother. To stop the reports, she persuaded Polemo, king of Cilicia, to be circumcised and to marry her, which he did because of her money.

After a brief marriage to Polemo, she returned to Agrippa and continued what was probably an incestuous relationship. She afterward became mistress of Vespasian and his son Titus.[235]

If not of high moral fiber, Bernice was at least for a time sympathetic to the Jewish plight, and she was in general agreement with Agrippa and Festus that Paul was not worthy of death or imprisonment.

> **25:25b** "since [Paul] himself appealed to the Emperor, I
> decided to send him."

Emperor. Festus, in Acts 25:25, refers to Caesar, the one to whom Paul appealed, as the *Sebaston,* "the venerable one." This term of reverence was commonly used for the caesars, Nero being the caesar at this time. Why Festus chose to call him Emperor at this time is uncertain. He may have been referring to caesar as the highest judge in religious matters, or he may have been emphasizing caesar's superiority over himself, thus abdicating his own responsibility.

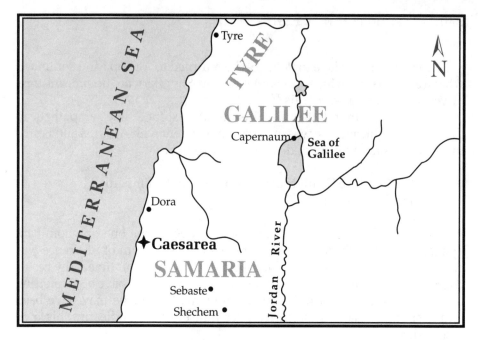

Chapter 26

A.D. 58

PAUL'S DEFENSE BEFORE AGRIPPA

Synopsis

(1–23) Given the chance to speak, Paul points out that all Jews have known his manner of life and how he lived as a strict Pharisee (1–5). But now he stands trial for "the hope of the promise made by God to our fathers" (6). He tells the king how he pursued the saints in Christ and locked them up, how he punished them, and how he chased them even to foreign cities (7–11). He then describes seeing Jesus on the Damascus road and his conversion (12–15). He adds how Christ spoke to him of going to the Gentiles "to open their eyes." Paul tells how he kept telling of the Lord from Damascus, Jerusalem, all the region of Judea, and even among the Gentiles. His final point is that from the Prophets and Moses it was told the Messiah must suffer but that He would come forth from the dead by the resurrection (16–23).

(24–32) Festus cries out, "Paul, you are out of your mind! Your great learning is driving you mad" (24). Paul with great conviction says, "King Agrippa, do you believe the Prophets? I know that you do." Agrippa replies, "In a short time you will persuade me to become a Christian" (25–28). Paul gives his great answer, "I would to God, that whether in a short or long time, not only you, but also all who hear me this day, might become such as I am, except for these chains" (29). The king then

arises and confers with Festus. They agree that Paul is guilty of no crime. Agrippa adds, "This man might have been set free if he had not appealed to Caesar" (30–32).

26:1 And Agrippa said to Paul . . .

[King] Agrippa [II]. See under 25:13.

26:5 ". . . I lived as a Pharisee . . ."

Pharisee. See under 5:34.

26:9 "So then, I thought to myself that I had to do many things hostile to the name of Jesus of Nazareth."

Nazareth. See p. 72.

26:18b in order that [the Jewish people] may receive forgiveness of sins

Forgiveness. See 2:38.

26:22b "I stand to this day . . . stating nothing but what the Prophets and Moses said."

Prophets. See under 3:18.

Moses. See p. 219.

26:28 And Agrippa replied to Paul, "In a short time you will persuade me to become a Christian."

Christian. Agrippa chides Paul that he is trying to persuade him to Christianity by his belief in the prophets. With an air of lofty superiority to impress the company, he lets Paul know that he sees through his plan of operation. Here we see the man's evasion. He turns from the prophets and their plain, compelling utterances about the Christ. He looks only at Paul and Paul's purpose."[236]

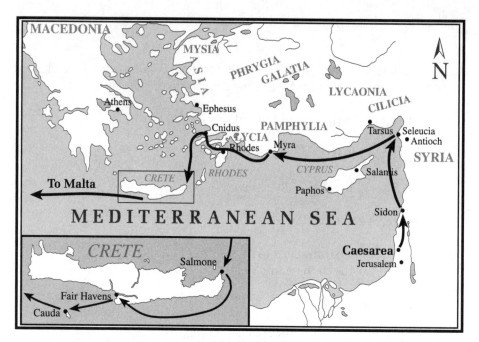

Chapter 27

A.D. 58

PAUL'S JOURNEY TO ROME

Synopsis

(1–24) Within a few days, Paul is on his way to Rome by ship. And almost immediately they run into terrible weather at sea. As the journey becomes more fearful, an angel appears to Paul to tell him that they will all survive because he must appear before Caesar.

(25–41) Because of the heavy seas, the boat runs aground and strikes a reef.

(42–44) The soldiers plan to kill all the prisoners on board, fearing they will try to escape once they wade ashore (42). But the centurion in charge, wanting "to bring Paul safely through, kept them from their intention" (43). Everyone was brought safely to land by holding on to planks or swimming (44).

27:1b they proceeded to deliver Paul and some other
prisoners to a centurion of the Augustan cohort named Julius.

Augustan cohort. Several legions in the Roman army, certainly the second, third, and eighth, bore the designation *Augustan Band,* or *Augustan Cohort.* Nowhere is it recorded that any one of these units was stationed in the East.

Most historians hold that the Augustan Band was an independent cohort assigned to that particular service. It was known as the "imperial" because of its relationship to the procurator in that it corresponded in some sense to the emperor's life guard at Rome.

It may have taken the place of the Italian Cohort mentioned in Acts 10:1, or very possibly may have been the honorary appellation of the Cohort. The "Italian" Cohort actually was comprised mostly of Caesareans, who were called "Italians" as a nickname by the people.

Another view says that Nero organized a bodyguard, which he denominated Augustanic. It is believed that Julius may have been a centurion in the cohort, whose station was at Rome and, having been sent to the East for the execution of some service, he was now returning to Italy with these prisoners under his charge. But that guard was organized in the year 60, and according to the chronology of Acts that was the very year Paul was sent from Caesarea to Rome.[237]

Even though Paul was not a threat to Rome itself, it is significant that the Romans felt they needed to assign a large number of troops to guard Paul, along with the other prisoners accompanying him. Rome had conquered the entire known world, but the Empire always had problems with the Jews. The Jewish religious leaders wanted Paul dead, and some Zealots had sworn to kill him. Paul, being a citizen of Rome, was afforded the protection of the Roman army.

Julius. Julius, a centurion of the Augustan cohort, was assigned to escort Paul to Rome (Acts 27:1). Luke emphasizes his consideration of Paul throughout the journey. In Sidon, Julius allows Paul to be comforted by his friends (v. 3). And during the Euraquilo storm, Julius listens to Paul's counsel and spares his life, as well as the lives of all the other prisoners. This is contrary to the common practice to kill all prisoners and so avoid their escape. Rather, Julius seeks to bring Paul to land safely (v. 43).

> **27:2** And embarking in an Adramyttian ship, which was about to sail to the regions along the coast of Asia, we put out to sea, accompanied by Aristarchus, a Macedonian of Thessalonica.

Adramyttian ship. Adramyttium was located in Mysia (see Assos under 20:13 for identification of the Adramyttian Gulf). This region was active in virtually every period of Persian history. This port is located on the northwest shore of modern Turkey and was considered part of the Roman province of Asia. The entire area of Mysia included Assos, Pergamum, and Troas and was a crossroads for travel, trade, and conquest. From the Trojan wars to Medo-Persia and the Roman Empire, this region was important to the strength and stability of defenders and conquerors. Paul boarded a ship in Caesarea bound for Rome from Adramyttium and sailed to Myra.

Aristarchus. See under 19:29.

27:5b we landed at Myra in Lycia.

Myra. Was one of the six most important and largest cities of Lycia. It is situated about two miles inland from the coast of the Mediterranean on the river Andracus. Its history dates back to the fourth century B.C. Myra was so influential in Lycia that it held three votes in the federal government and was referred to as a "metropolis." Myra ran a shuttle to nearby Limyra, and its greatest asset was the harbor at Andrice. Myra was home to the pagan cult that worshiped Artemis. It had a large Roman theater. This site of ancient ruins is called Dembre today.

> **27:7** And when we had sailed slowly for a good many days,
> and with difficulty had arrived off Cnidus, . . . we sailed
> under the shelter of Crete, off Salmone;

Cnidus. Cnidus, or Cindos, was a city in the country of Caria in Asia Minor. Cnidus was on the Aegean Sea in what is now southwestern Turkey, built partly on Cape Krio, the peninsula that extends between the islands of Cos and Rhodes, and partly on Triopion Island. A bridge and causeway connected the water-divided parts of the town, each of which was walled. The entire length of this community was about one mile.[238]

The Greek goddess Aphrodite was said to favor Cnidus. A statue of her by the Greek sculptor Praxiteles stood in her temple. The modern political difficulty of gaining access to the ruins of this city has made it hard to collect information on its early history. Cnidus was founded by the Spartans and became an important commercial center. The Dorian settlements can be traced back to approximately the eighth century B.C. In 394 B.C., the Athenian admiral Conon defeated a Spartan fleet. This defeat brought about the downfall of Spartan power in Asia Minor.

In Roman times, Cnidus was a free city, with a Jewish community dating back at least to the second century B.C. Its one mention in Scripture appears to be more a landmark reference. The waters off Cnidus were among the most treacherous known to Mediterranean sailors, and Cnidus was the last port of call for most ships sailing across the open sea to Greece. The winds and sea conditions make an open sea voyage impracticable on this voyage; instead, they sail under the shelter of Crete.

Salmone. Salmone (now Cape Sidero) is a promontory or high point of land and rock projecting into the water on the coast of Crete, a prominent mass hardly suited for human habitation. Paul and other prisoners were enroute to Rome on an Alexandrian ship sailing for Italy (Acts 27:6), which was most likely loaded with wheat from Egypt (v. 38). Suddenly they encountered strong winds and storms that caused them to sail slowly for a number of days. They made little progress because of the fierce winds and could not maintain a direct course. Making no progress toward their destination they "sailed under the shelter of Crete, off Salmone" (27:7). Scarcely escaping shipwreck, they came to Fair Havens (v. 8). By now the seas were extremely rough because of the winter storms. It was unsafe to go on.

> **27:8** and with difficulty sailing past it we came to a certain
> place called Fair Havens, near which was the city of Lasea.

Fair Havens. The Greek *Kaloi Limenes* literally means "good harbors." Fair Havens is a harbor on Crete serving the nearby city of Lasea. Archaeologists have identified the site as a small bay east of Cape Matala. It still bears the name *Limeonas Kalois* in modern Greek.[239]

Lasea. The Crete city of Lasea was about five miles from the harbor town of Fair Havens at approximately the halfway point on the island. Lasea has not been extensively examined. What few archeological expeditions have penetrated have found their discoveries to be much in question. Lasea seems to have served more as a fortress than a harbor. This lack of accommodations would account for the captain's reluctance to stay in the area for the winter.

The different spellings of Lasea suggest that the place was not well known, and (why) it was not mentioned by ancient geographers. This need not be surprising, since even in Homer's time there were ninety (or even 100) cities on Crete (*Odyssey* 19.174). In 1853, T. A. B. Spratt, directing a Mediterranean survey, found ancient ruins on the shore near Fair Havens that may be identified with Lasea.[240] Lasea is possibly the same as *Lasos*, mentioned by Pliny as one of the island cities in *Natural History* 4.12.20.[241]

Luke's casual mention of this city seems to be given more as a landmark. Since Luke does not elaborate on the place, it may have been very plain indeed.

> **27:12b** the majority reached a decision to put out to sea
> from there, if somehow they could reach Phoenix, a harbor
> of Crete,

Phoenix. At Fair Havens the shipboard passengers hold a fast, probably related to the Day of Atonement (27:9). It is October, and soon the Mediterranean will be completely closed to winter navigation. Paul warned the captain that if they went on, the ship and all the lives on board could be lost at sea (27:10). But the centurion in charge, Julius (see above), commands that the party must leave Fair Haven, since it is not suitable for wintering.

The ship arrives at the harbor of Phoenix on the safe side of the island of Crete (v. 12). But thinking all the heavy storms were for a time over, the ship weighed anchor and sailed away from Phoenix and along the shore of Crete. Then they are caught by the Euraquilo.

> **27:14** But before very long there rushed down from the land a violent wind, called Euraquilo—

Euraquilo. The *Euraquilo,* or "nor'easter," reaches typhoon strength on the Mediterranean Sea, and its gales sink modern merchant ships of some tonnage. The small wooden cargo vessel of the first century was not made to withstand anything approaching this level of storm. *Euraquilo,* translated, simply refers to the direction of the wind. It is a bilingual compound of the Greek *euros* ("east wind") and the Latin *aquilo* (northeast). It is a wind generally blowing from the east northeast.[242]

> **27:17b** and fearing that they might run aground on the shallows of Syrtis, they let down the sea anchor,

Syrtis. It soon became obvious that the ship will not even make it to Phoenix (Acts 27:7–44). As they sail along the island of Crete, the wind becomes so violent that eventually all the cargo is thrown overboard, and all hope of being saved fades. After Paul hears from an angel (27:23–24), he encourages the crew and passengers to keep up courage. God has promised that no lives will be lost, and that they will run aground (27:26).

The crew do all they can to save the ship. They lash the vessel more firmly together and rerig for more stability. The sea anchor provides drag against the current without having to touch bottom. They fear running aground on the shallows of Syrtis (27:17) because those shallows are banks of quicksand just off the African coast. This place has always been feared by Mediterranean sailors. It was called "Syrtis Major" and was located near Cyrenaica. In modern times, it is the Gulf of Sidia.

> **27:27a** But when the fourteenth night had come, as we were being driven about in the Adriatic Sea,

Adriatic Sea. The Adriatic Sea (Gr. *Adria*) of Paul's day included the expanse between Italy and Malta on the west and Greece and Crete on the east. Therefore, the Adriatic Sea included the waters of the Mediterranean where the ship that Paul was on encountered the severe storm. The ship eventually wrecked on the shallows of the island of Malta.

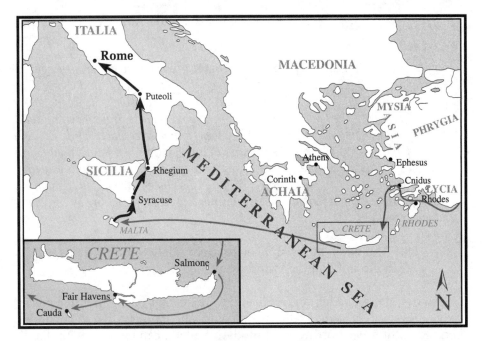

Chapter 28

A.D. 59 (Roman Imprisonment)

PAUL'S ARRIVAL AT ROME;
MEETINGS WITH THE ROMAN JEWS

Synopsis

(1–16) The party reaches land on the island of Malta, where they are treated well by the local people (1–2). While Paul and others gather wood for a fire, the apostle is bitten by a snake. The local natives reason that Paul must be a murderer (3–4), but they think better of him when the poison doesn't harm him. They finally decide he must be a god (5–6). Staying on Malta for three months because of the weather, Paul begins ministering to the people. Many are healed, and Paul and his party are honored and respected (7–11). The boatload of prisoners and soldiers finally arrive on Italian soil at the seaport of Puteoli and walk overland to Rome. Paul is placed under house arrest with soldiers guarding him (12–16).

(17–31) Paul is allowed visitors. He summons leading Jews of Rome (17). He explains why he is there and that he was forced as a citizen to appeal to Caesar. He assures them that he will not make accusations against the Jewish people (18–19). The men answer that they have received no information from Jerusalem about Paul,

*but they want to hear more about Christianity because it is "spoken against
everywhere" (20–22). A large crowd gathers to hear Paul in his lodging. The
apostle speaks about the kingdom of God and attempts to persuade them concerning
Jesus, "from both the Law of Moses and from the Prophets, from morning until
evening" (23). Some are persuaded. When they cannot agree and when some begin
to leave, Paul quotes the prophesied curse of Isaiah 6 (25–27). Paul's final words
to the Jews as they leave are, "Let it be known to you therefore, that this salvation
of God has been sent to the Gentiles; they will also listen" (28). Paul remains in
Rome for two years in rented quarters, openly and freely preaching and teaching
all who come (29–31).*

28:1 And when they had been brought safely through, then
we found out that the island was called Malta.

Malta. Malta or Melita is an island at the center of the Mediterranean,
sixty miles south of Sicily. Malta encompasses about ninety-five square miles.
Located eight miles northwest of modern Valletta can be found "St. Paul's
Bay." This site is believed to be where Paul landed when he and his company
where shipwrecked.

Malta was colonized by about 1000 B.C. by Phoenicians, and the vernacular
language in Paul's day was a Punic (Carthaginian) dialect. But in 218 B.C. it
was captured by Rome at the start of the Second Punic War against Carthage.
Malta was granted the status of *municipium*, which maximized local autonomy.
Augustus sent a Roman governor to be "chief man over all in the municipality
of Malta." Augustus settled a number of army veterans and their families
there. In Paul's day, the island was prosperous with distinctive architecture.
Natives probably spoke Phoenician and some Latin and Greek.[243]

The Maltans show great kindness to the shipwrecked soldiers, sailors,
and prisoners. They kindle small fires to warm the castaways. This is when
Paul is bitten by a viper (Acts 28:3) the natives know to be deadly poisonous.
They reason that Paul may have escaped the judgment of the seas, but he will
not escape the justice of the snake. Instead, they witnessed a miracle (vv. 5–6).
For the second time in his career, Paul is considered a god (see Acts 14:15–18).
This time he is gentler in rebuking the people, maybe because they were not
so intent on sacrificing to him as had been the Lystrans.

Today, there are no poisonous snakes on Malta. They may have been
eradicated as more people came and most land was cultivated. A small island
with a growing population does not leave much room for animal life,
especially poisonous life.

For three days, the leading man, Publius, entertained them. His father
lay sick. Paul displayed the healing power of God on him and others of the
island (28:8–9). This is the only incident recorded of the three months they
were on the island. The natives, being impressed by Paul and his ministry to

them, gave the travelers many honors. They supplied the ship with all that was needed for their journey. *The Expositor's Bible Commentary* notes that Luke's description seems to make the Malta visit

> "a high point in his ministry—a time of blessing when God worked in marvelous ways, despite the shipwreck and his being still a prisoner. God seems, through the experiences at Malta, to have been refreshing Paul's spirit after the two relatively bleak years at Caesarea and the disastrous time at sea and preparing him for his witness in Rome."[244]

28:7a Now in the neighborhood of that place were lands belonging to the leading man of the island, named Publius,

Publius. *Publius* (Lat. "common") was the Roman governor of the island of Malta. When Paul and his party are shipwrecked, he allows them to stay at his home for three days while their respective situations are taken care of. Being governor, he was in charge of keeping peace on the island and sending taxes back to Rome. Publius's father probably was sick with what is now known as "Malta fever," for which a vaccine has been discovered. Paul prays and lays his hands on him and heals him. Results of the healing are immediate. Paul and his company have both a physical and a spiritual witness of God. Use by Luke of Publius's first name indicates that this is the name he heard the islanders use for their governor, or Publius, Paul, and Luke became close friends.

It can be assumed, given the miracles he saw, their miraculous journey, and the gospel presentation he no doubt heard, that Publius most likely believed. Church tradition asserts that he was the first bishop of the island and afterward succeeded Dionysius as bishop of Athens. Jerome records that he was killed for his faith.[245]

28:12 And after we put in at Syracuse, we stayed there for three days.

Syracuse. The island of Sicily and the city of Syracuse were founded by the Corinthians in 734 B.C. Its earliest form of government was aristocratic, and the elite ruling party of the "Gamoroi" employed the natives in the construction and the maintenance of the city. In 480 B.C., the Gamoroi were expelled in a democratic revolution, and the natives of the island governed themselves. The city was strong enough to defeat an Athenian attack in 413 B.C. but was conquered by the Romans in 212 B.C. There is a large theater that dates back to the fifth century B.C. and several temples to Apollo, Jupiter, and Zeus. Syracuse became the capital of the island during the Roman occupation and throughout its turbulent history enjoyed economic prosperity.

It was a formidable fortress with more than seventeen miles of fortified walls around the city. It was decreed a colony by Caesar Augustus and was required to pay a tithe to Rome. Paul boards a ship in Malta and goes to Syracuse. No doubt the shipwreck, his snakebite, and the healing of the residents of Malta were common knowledge to the crew and passengers. It is easy to conclude that because of the importance of the port at Syracuse that God through Paul, the eager teacher of the gospel, witnessed to the crew as well as the others in Syracuse.

> **28:13** And from there we sailed around and arrived at Rhegium, and a day later a south wind sprang up, and on the second day we came to Puteoli.

Rhegium. On the very toe of Italy's boot was the city of Rhegium, where Paul's ship stopped as it neared Rome (Acts 28:13). *Rhegium* means "breach" and refers, according to some, to the tradition that Sicily was torn from the continent by an earthquake. Others believe the name is a corruption of the Latin *regium,* which means "royal." The master of the ship Paul was on took the vessel by a south wind near the whirlpool of Charybdis and passed the rock of Scylla. Because of its strategic location, the place has had an important role in history. Rhegium was an old Greek colony but became very important to the Roman Empire because of its role in navigation. Today, Rhegium is called Reggio, the capital of Calabria.

Puteoli. After Rhegium, Paul's ship arrived at the seaport of Puteoli, a harbor on the Bay of Naples and the southwest entrance to the main part of the boot of Italy. Puteoli was for hundreds of years an early Greek settlement, but it was taken over by the Romans in 338 B.C. Puteoli was famous as a trading center, and a large number of Jews lived there. The apostle found believers and perhaps even a local church. Luke writes, "There we found some brethren, and were invited to stay with them for seven days; and thus we came to Rome" (Acts 28:14). To this very day it is believed a visible part of the pier of the city is where Paul's ship landed. After the week, Paul and his party began walking toward Rome.

> **28:14b** and thus we came to Rome.

Rome. See under 2:10.

> **28:15a** And the brethren, when they heard about us, came from there as far as the Market of Appius and Three Inns to meet us;

Market of Appius. The *Appiou Forou*, literally the Forum of Appius, was a hub on the Appian Way *(Via Appia)*, approximately forty miles outside Rome and ten miles farther from Rome than Three Inns. To this station a group of Roman brethren traveled to meet Paul on his journey to Rome (Acts 28:15).

Three Inns. From *Trion Tabernon*, this was literally Three Taverns, a small village most probably specializing in lodging travelers. The village stood on the Appian Way approximately thirty miles outside Rome. More Rome Christians joined the procession of Paul toward Rome, bringing Paul courage and thankfulness (Acts 28:15).

> **28:17** he called together those who were the leading men of the Jews.

Leading men. Earlier, emperor Claudius had banned the Jews from Rome. His decree either had lapsed or was rescinded. These leaders may have been living in the old Jewish quarter of Rome. The leaders were the rulers (*archohtes*) of the synagogue. The synagogue in Rome had a special inscription, *the Archisynagogus*. This title is found today in the Jewish cemetery in Rome. Paul called these men together hoping to lead them to accept Jesus as their risen Messiah. He was bitter as to their response. See also 4:5.

> **28:19** I was forced to appeal to Caesar.

Caesar. See pp. 386–87.

> **28:31** preaching the kingdom of God, and teaching concerning the Lord Jesus Christ with all openness, unhindered.

Kingdom of God. See pp. 52–60.

With all openness, unhindered. While Paul was in Rome during his first incarceration, he was allowed open visitation and the opportunity to preach and teach boldly. The last word in the Greek text of Acts is the adverb *akōlytōs*, which means "without binding or without hindrance." Noticing this, *The Bible Knowledge Commentary* makes the comment, "Men may bind the preachers, but the gospel cannot be chained!"[246]

Appendixes

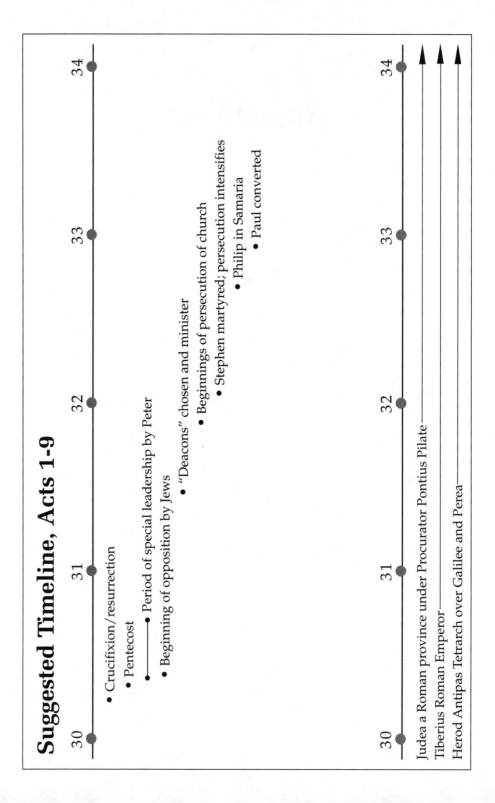

Suggested Timeline, Acts 1-9

30   31   32   33   34

• Crucifixion/resurrection
• Pentecost
• Period of special leadership by Peter
• Beginning of opposition by Jews
• "Deacons" chosen and minister
• Beginnings of persecution of church
• Stephen martyred; persecution intensifies
• Philip in Samaria
• Paul converted

30   31   32   33   34

Judea a Roman province under Procurator Pontius Pilate
Tiberius Roman Emperor
Herod Antipas Tetrarch over Galilee and Perea

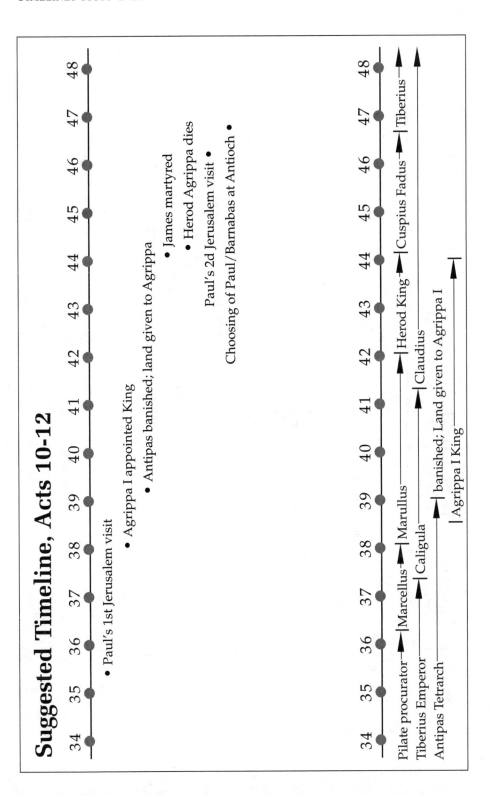

Suggested Timeline, Acts 10-12

34 35 36 37 38 39 40 41 42 43 44 45 46 47 48

- Paul's 1st Jerusalem visit
- Agrippa I appointed King
- Antipas banished; land given to Agrippa
- James martyred
- Herod Agrippa dies
- Paul's 2d Jerusalem visit
- Choosing of Paul/Barnabas at Antioch

34 35 36 37 38 39 40 41 42 43 44 45 46 47 48

Pilate procurator → |Marcellus → |Marullus → |Herod King → |Cuspius Fadus → |Tiberius →
Tiberius Emperor → |Caligula → |Claudius →
Antipas Tetrarch → |banished; Land given to Agrippa I
|Agrippa I King →

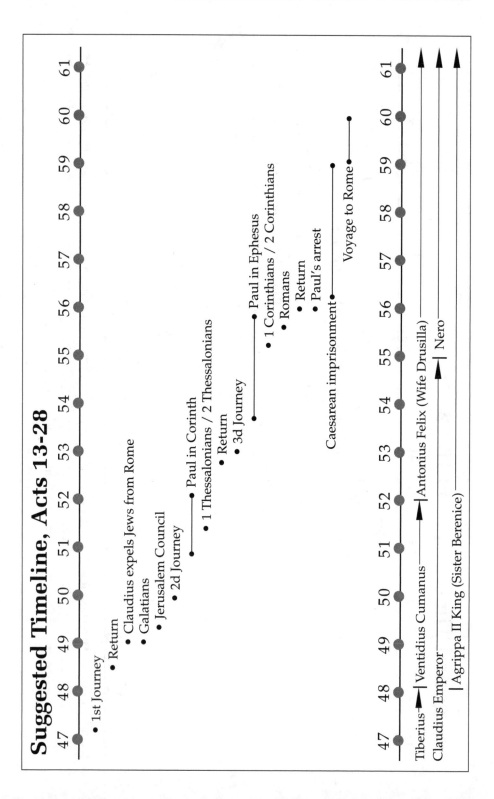

Suggested Timeline, Acts 13–28

THE LAYING ON OF HANDS IN THE OLD TESTAMENT AND THE GOSPELS

Laying on of Hands in the Old Testament

The ceremonial laying on of hands was most commonly used in levitical sacrifices in Old Testament times. A person presenting a burnt offering (Lev. 1:4), a peace offering (Lev. 3:1, 8, 13), or a sin offering (Lev. 4:4, 24, 29, 33; Num. 8:12) placed hands upon the head of the animal that was to die. The object was not to transfer guilt from the sinner to the animal. Rather, the laying on of hands upon the head of the animal seems to have identified symbolically the individual with the propitiatory sacrifice. By the substitution of the animal's innocent, unblemished life, the offerer propitiated God in the burnt offering. And the offering looked forward to the time when atonement would be made for the sins of the offerer (Lev. 1:4). As Roland de Vaux says, "The rite of laying hands on the victim does not symbolize the transference of the life or the sins of man to the victim; it merely testifies that this victim comes from this particular individual, and that it is being presented on his behalf and that the fruits of this sacrifice shall be his."[1]

When the whole congregation of Israel became guilty of a sin, the leaders of the congregation were to lay their hands on the head of the animal to be sacrificed (Lev. 4:15). Again, it should not be assumed in these sacrifices that the symbolic act of laying on of hands involved a transference of guilt from the sinner/offerer to the animal sacrificed. However, transference of guilt from the worshiper to the victim *did* apparently occur in the laying on of hands on the scapegoat on the day of Atonement. The high priest laid his hands on the head of the goat, conferring the sins of the congregation of Israel. The goat was then driven away into the wilderness, bearing the sins of the people (Lev. 16:21). The laying on of hands in the sacrificial rite then, can signal "identification with," "transferal to," and perhaps even "separation from."

A second ceremonial use of the laying on of hands was in the ordination or consecration of someone to office. Beginning with the laying of hands on an animal sacrifice for the ordination of the Aaronic priesthood (29:10, 15, 19; Lev. 8:14, 18, 22) and the laying of hands on the heads of the Levites to consecrate them (Num. 8:10, 12, 22), the laying on of hands set apart persons for spiritual office. Moses officially commissioned Joshua to be leader of Israel, transferring his role and authority to Joshua by laying his hands upon him (Num. 27:18; Deut. 34:9). It seems in this instance that neither the Holy Spirit nor special gifts were conferred in the laying on of hands. Joshua is said to already have been in possession of the Spirit (Num. 27:18). Moses merely invested Joshua with his office and authority. Here the basic ideas seem to be ordination, separation, and perhaps transfer.

A third and most ancient recorded use of the laying on of hands is in patriarchal blessing. Though there is no record of divine institution of this practice, the custom was practiced in Eastern society and had a special place in Israel in the passing on of covenant privileges. In the pronouncement of a blessing, the hands were sometimes merely raised (Lev. 9:22). Usually, hands were placed on the head of the one blessed (Gen. 48:14, 17). This is used figuratively of the hand of God in blessing (Ps. 139:5, 10) and in judgment (Exod. 7:4; Ezek. 39:21). Divine blessing always underlies human blessing.[2] The basic idea in this blessing seems to be transfer.

A fourth use of the laying on of hands was in the judgment and execution of a blasphemer. At the trial of a blasphemer, all witnesses to the blaspheming were to place their hands on the blasphemer's head. The blasphemer was then stoned by the whole congregation (Lev. 24:14). D. W. Wead suggests that the purpose here of laying on of hands was "to show acceptance of the verdict of judgment."[3] The apocryphal book *Susanna* (v. 34) speaks of "elders" bearing a false charge of adultery against Susanna. Here, the laying on of hands seems to be the means of swearing to, or affirming, their testimony as to her guilt. Perhaps the idea behind this use of the laying on of hands is confirmation, identification, and setting apart the person for judgment and execution.

The laying on of hands also was used by the prophets. Ardel B. Caneday calls this usage "prophetico-dynamic."[4] In 2 Kings 4:34, Elisha laid his hands upon the hands of a dead child, the son of a Shunamite woman, then laid his body upon the boy. Thus, while the laying on of hands is part of the ritual performed by Elisha in raising this boy from the dead, there is little correspondence between this case and the New Testament practice of healing.

On another occasion, Naaman the leper is disappointed that Elisha does not lay his hands on him to heal him (2 Kings 5:11). Naaman's healing occurs without any laying on of hands. On another occasion, Elisha lays his hand upon the hands of King Joash, as Joash holds a bow (2 Kings 13:16). The purpose here, though, is not healing but prophetic communication, perhaps illustration. The laying on of hands seems to be little more than a visual aid. The basic idea behind this laying on of hands may be authentication or identification; that is, the identification of the prophetic Word with the authority of God.

Laying on of Hands in the Gospels

In the manner of patriarchal blessing, Jesus laid hands on children to bless them (Matt. 19:13–15; Mark 10:13–16; Luke 18:15). We are not told what this blessing was. However, Henry Barclay Swete observes that the children were brought for that purpose, so it must have been a custom.[5]

Jesus performed many miracles, especially of healing, by laying on of hands.[6] But He seems to have followed no particular pattern. Sometimes He laid (epitithēmi) His hands upon someone (it may or may not have been their head). Sometimes He merely touched them or took them by the hand. Eleven times the verb epitithēmi occurs with "hand(s)" in connection with Jesus' healing or blessing someone. Another eleven times, reference is made to Jesus' hands healing or blessing without the use of epitithēmi. And once (again, without epitithēmi) reference is made to the "miracles performed by His hands" (dia tōn cheirōn, Mark 6:2). Moreover, Jesus performs many miracles without the laying on of hands or even a touch. Caneday states that

> the more the Jews became imbued with the idea that the miraculous effects were connected with the physical laying on of hands, the more Jesus operated without this visual symbol (Mark 5:23, 41; 7:32). He sometimes healed by simply a word and at other times demonstrated His transcendence even over space as He healed individuals from a great distance (John 4:46–54). At times the healing was vitally connected with the physical touch. However, the relationship between the laying on of hands and healing did not appear to be established as the only means of healing by Christ.[7]

Surely, the miraculous power was inherent in the *person* of Christ, and not especially connected to the hands.

Just before His ascension, Jesus, after the manner of Aaron (Lev. 9:22), "lifted up His hands and blessed" His disciples (Luke 24:50). Frank Thielman is probably correct to suggest that Christ is "acting as the great high priest" in this passage.[8] Quite possibly He has in mind Leviticus 9:22. So far as we know, this is the first and only time that Jesus lifted up His hand to bless them (Luke 24:50). At least it is only recorded once. In the light of their knowledge of the covenant and of Christ, the natural place to look for the significance of this act would be the Old Testament. As good Jews who knew their Old Testament, they probably recognized immediately the significance of Christ's lifting His hands and blessing them and its similarity with the blessing of Israel by Aaron the high priest (Lev. 9:22).

It is likewise recorded only once that "Aaron lifted up his hands toward the people and blessed them" (Lev. 9:22). This is not to say that Aaron never repeated this action. But the fact that the Old Testament records it only once, in the context of atonement for the sins of the people as well as Aaron's consecration to the office of high priest, is suggestive. Aaron's blessing comes *after* his appointment to be high priest (Num. 17:1–18:7, cf. Heb. 5:4), his consecration (Lev. 8:12), his ordination (Lev. 8:22–36), and his completion of atonement for himself and the people. Lifting his hands toward the people and blessing them is the last thing Aaron did before "he stepped down after making the sin offering and the burnt offering and the peace offerings" (9:22).

Jesus, our great high priest (Heb. 4:14), was also appointed (John 1:15, 29–34; Heb. 5:1). He was then anointed, consecrated, and ordained (Matt. 3:16–17; 11:3; Luke 3:21–22; 4:18–21). He then, as high priest, offered Himself as the Lamb of God (John 1:29), thereby making atonement for sin "once and for all" (Heb. 7:27). *After completing His work as high priest,* He "lifted His hands and blessed" his people (Luke 24:50). It is interesting to note that when Christ had finished atonement and blessed the disciples, He *"sat down"* (Heb. 1:3; 10:12). Aaron *"stepped down"* (Lev. 9:22). Both phrases show finished work, Aaron's only for the day (Heb. 7:27) but Christ's forever (Heb. 7:27). Might not the similarities have struck the disciples' minds when they saw the wounded, risen Christ raise His nail-scarred hands and bless them before he "stepped down"?

It is intriguing to speculate about further parallels between the two contexts. After Aaron had finished the work of atonement, blessed the people, and stepped down from the altar, he and Moses "went into the tent of meeting." "When they came out and blessed the people, the glory of the Lord appeared to all the people. Then fire came out from before the Lord and consumed the burnt offering and the portion of fat on the altar; and when all the people saw it, they shouted and fell on their faces" (Lev. 9:23–24). Are we to think of Christ's ascension as having entered the "tent of meeting" as Aaron did after making atonement and giving the blessing? Is there a parallel between Aaron's return from the tent of meeting along with the appearance of the glory of the Lord and Christ's return when He shall appear in all His glory? Will not all the Lord's people fall on their faces at Christ's return? Aaron is first said to be a prophet before he is said to be priest. Christ also is revealed to us as "the greater prophet" and then as high priest. One would not want to push this too far. But perhaps there is some connection to be seen between Aaron's act and that of Christ.

It is probable that during the time of Christ, the Sanhedrin practiced the laying on of hands in the appointment and admission of new members. In

Palestine, education in religious law and rabbinic discipleship was tied to the *semikhah*—ordination—which bestowed the right to the title of *rabbi*.[9] According to H. L. Strack and G. Stemberger, "The rabbinic *semikhah* (from Hebr. 'leaning against,' hence 'laying on of hands' as a gesture of transferring an office) entitled the recipient to the authentic transmission of tradition. It assured the unbroken chain of tradition from Moses down to one's own time."[10] According to the *Mishnah*, the appointment of judges in the Sanhedrin was to be done according to a certain procedure or ceremony called *semikhah*, which, of course, has *samak* as its basal root. As we have already seen, *samak* ("to lean, lay") seems to take on a technical sense when used with *yad* ("hand"). So also, its counterparts in Greek, *epitithēmi* ("lean, lay") and *cheir* ("hand").

There is disagreement, however, whether this rite was still practiced by the Sanhedrin in the first century, the time of Christ and the apostles. Strack and Stemberger say that the laying on of hands at the *semikhah* was replaced by an oral formula.[11] The question is, *when* was it abandoned? The evidence suggests that it was sometime *after* the time of Christ and the apostles that the laying on of hands was omitted from the *semikhah*.

John Lightfoot thinks it was abandoned before the time of Christ. Commenting on the laying on of hands in Acts 13:3, he quotes the following from the Talmud: *"The ordaining of the elders and beheading the heifer is by three"* (Sanhedr I.3) and then states: "In this thing, therefore, this present action agreeth with the common usage of the synagogue, that three persons, Simeon, Lucius, and Manaen, lay their hands on two that were to be sent out, viz. Paul and Barnabas. But in that they lay on their hands, they do also recede from the usual custom."[12]

Lightfoot enforces this statement with another quotation (*Maimon. Sanhedr. cap.* 4): "After what manner is the ordaining of elders for ever? Not that they should lay their hands upon the head of the elder, but only should call him 'rabbi,' and say to him, 'Behold, thou art ordained, and thou hast power of judging.'"[13]

But Lightfoot's citations are problematic. First, it is difficult to know for sure which documents he is citing. His references are abbreviated, and he offers no table or index of abbreviations that clearly identifies his sources.[14] Second, since his abbreviations and the title of his work make it safe to assume he is quoting the talmudic literature, his sources postdate the first century. At the earliest, the *Mishnah* was not compiled until late second century.[15] The first of the above quotations by Lightfoot appears to be from the "Sanhedrin," the fourth tractate in the *Mishnah*, order of Nezikin (fourth order). But this text actually *affirms* the laying on of hands in the ordination of elders. And the *Talmud*, of which the *Mishnah* is part, was not completed until c. A.D. 500.[16] If Lightfoot's reference to *"Maimon. Sanhedr.* cap. 4" is a reference to Maimonides' commentary on the Mishnah, then we are looking at a source dated as late as the twelfth century and a commentary at that.[17]

Possibly certain tractates that make up the *Mishnah* were circulating in written form before they were compiled. But when they were written and how long they circulated is very uncertain. We don't even know that they *did* circulate in written form. There is reason to believe that from the time of the Babylonian captivity (586 B.C.) to the destruction of the temple by Titus in A.D. 70, Jewish tradition existed primarily in oral form.[18] Indeed, the term *Mishnah* is from the Hebrew, *šana*, "to repeat," a word for "the oral tradition which developed around the law."[19] The *Tannaim* who were Jewish teachers, or rabbis of the first and second centuries A.D., from the time of Hillel to the compilation of the *Mishnah*,[20] continued this oral tradition.

Our point here is not to prove that no Jewish writings existed prior to the Mishnah. Of course they did. Our purpose is simply to point out that Lightfoot's references to Maimonides' commentary on the *Talmud* (completed in 1168) or to the *Talmud* itself (there are two versions: the *Babylonian Talmud*, completed by the end of the fifth century, and the *Jerusalem* or *Palestinian Talmud*, completed probably a century earlier) to demonstrate that the laying on of hands was no longer practiced in the first century are invalid. It is anachronistic to ascribe second- or third-century customs to the first century from second- or third-century (or later) literature.

Moreover, it seems there is evidence that the laying on of hands was still part of the *semikhah*, or ordination of rabbis, during the time of Christ. Joachim Jeremias cites a post-tannaitic reference to the practice of *semikhah*, or ordination of scribes, by the laying on of hands.[21] This, at least, is his assumption, for he adds in a footnote, "The corresponding custom in primitive Christianity (Acts 6:6, *et passim*) is a guarantee of the antiquity of this rite."[22] "This rite" in Acts 6:6 is, of course, the laying on of hands. According to Dan Cohn-Sherbok, the *Talmud* traces the origin of this institution (*semikhah*) to Moses, "who conveyed leadership to Joshua by placing his hands on Joshua's head."[23] Cohn-Sherbok goes on to say:

> In modern times a candidate for the rabbinate undergoes a lengthy period of study in a seminary, at the end of which he is given the certificate of Hattarat Horaah; this usually includes the phrase *"yoreh yoreh, yadin yadin"* (he may surely give a decision and may surely judge). In some seminaries the graduation ceremony is described as "ordination" and may involve the laying on of hands.[24]

J. Coppens also concludes that the rite of laying on of hands was practiced during the time of Christ:

> At the time of Christ, the documents of Judaism relate two additional applications of the old rite that are very important for understanding the rite in the NT. First, the rite was used for healing [see the Qumran

document: N. Avigod and Y. Yadin, *A Genesis Apocryphon* (Jerusalem 1956) 20.22.29]. Second, it was employed also in the installation of rabbinic teachers. . . . According to the latest research [H. Mantel, "Ordination and Appointment on the Period of the Temple," *Harvard Theological Review* 57 (1964) 325–46], one must distinguish between the appointment of judges "to judge cases involving fines" (an appointment called *minnui* and not involving the laying on of hands) and the giving of permission (*rᵉsut*) to teach, involving in Palestine, even at the time of the temple and of Christ, the *sᵉmika*, or imposition of hands.[25]

While the *Encyclopedia Judaica* notes the eventual discontinuance of the rite of laying on of hands in ordination (14:1140), it states that *śemikhah* was still granted during the talmudic period.[26]

Addressing the issue of the laying on of hands, David Daube asserts that the rabbinic tradition of *śemikhah* originally involved the laying on of hands and states that it was not altered during New Testament times.

When we come to the rabbinic position in New Testament times, there is one change: The occasions on which the rite is performed have become fewer. It is practically restricted to the sacrificial cult and the ordination of a rabbi.[27] Daube continues:

in the case of ordination, it can be clearly shown that, at least up to the first half of the 2nd cent. A.D., the rite is executed in the original manner and with the original intent: it involves a real "leaning on" as opposed to a gentle "placing," and its object is the pouring of the ordaining scholar's personality into the scholar to be ordained.[28]

While we cannot say for sure how widely the laying on of hands was practiced during the time of Christ, it does appear that this rite was still performed by, and found significance in, the Judaism of the New Testament era. The evidence indicates that the Sanhedrin, the religious and judicial body of rulers of the Jews, still practiced the ceremonial rite of laying on of hands.[29]

We know with certainty that it was practiced in the Old Testament and that tradition carried on this rite into the intertestamental period and on into the first-century Diaspora. The rite of laying on of hands was not uncommon in the time of Christ or the apostles. Moreover, the rite served various purposes.

THE SIGN GIFTS

Nature and Purpose of the Gifts

Generally speaking, the sign gifts are spectacular, easily observable, obviously supernatural, and impossible to ignore. The sign gifts specifically listed (cf., Rom. 12:6; 1 Cor. 12:8–10; Eph. 4:11, and 1 Peter 4:11) are "word of wisdom," "word of knowledge," "faith," "healings," "miracles," "prophecy," "distinguishing of spirits," "tongues," and "interpretation of tongues."

What distinguishes the sign gifts from the nonsign gifts is that their purpose is to signal something (1 Cor. 14:22). They are generically related to *"signs and wonders"* (Heb. 2:4). Just because they are intended to signal something does not mean the sign gifts are not personally edifying or useful. But these gifts primarily are attention-getters, signposts toward something other than the gift itself. On one hand, sign gifts demonstrate and vindicate the glory of God. On another, they indicate that God is at work, inaugurating a new era for His people or judging His people. All of these times of inaugurating and judging have to do with the salvation history of Israel. Sign gifts also stimulate faith. Sign gifts do not *produce* faith; but for those inclined to believe, sign gifts encourage faith (Isa. 28:16; John 20:30–31; Rom. 11:7). For those disinclined to believe, sign gifts further harden the heart (Isa. 28:16ff.; Mark 6:52; Rom. 11:7, 25). Foremost, they authenticate God's messengers (Matt. 11:2–6) and God's message (Heb. 2:1–4). Sign gifts are particularly associated with the apostles, or with those upon whom the apostles laid hands. Stephen and Philip are prime examples of the latter. So closely were the sign gifts associated with the apostles and apostolic authority as confirmation, attestation, or authentication of apostolic authority that when the apostles passed from the scene, so also did the sign gifts.

Sign gifts are primarily related to, and occur in conjunction with, God's covenant program with Israel. They authenticated God's messengers and message at the eruption of new eras in His theocratic dealings with the covenant nation. The biblical pattern of signs and wonders and miracles reveals a concentration of these miracles during four periods of time. Consider these comments by Bible scholars representing differing theological schools of thought:

> We do not find the miracles sown broadcast over the whole Old Testament history, but they all cluster round a very few eminent persons and have reference to certain great epochs and crises of the kingdom of God.[1]

> God does not shake miracles into nature at random as if from a pepper-caster. They come on great occasions: they are found at the great ganglions of history—not of political or social history, but of spiritual history which cannot be fully known by men.[2]

> Although miracles cluster around the Lord Jesus Christ like steel shavings to a magnet, they are found throughout the Bible. However, even a casual reading of Scripture reveals that miracles occur with greater frequency at special times. Israel's deliverance from Egypt and entrance into Canaan provided one great concentration of miracles. So did the ministries of Elijah and Elisha when God sought to stem the tide of apostasy among His people. Related to the earthly life and miracles of Jesus are the miracles of the apostolic church.[3]

> Many people get the idea that the Bible is an account of continuous miracles from Genesis to Revelation. Actually, miracles in the Bible are the exception, and always are connected with God fulfilling His promise to the Jews.[4]

The three periods in history when sign gifts definitely were in action were the nation-founding years of Moses and Joshua, the national turning-point years of Elijah and Elisha, and the time of Christ and the apostles. Each period lasted perhaps seventy years.[5] A fourth outbreak of miracles mentioned in the Bible is still future. In Revelation 11, the "two witnesses" will be granted authority and they will prophesy (11:3). To authenticate this ministry, the prophets will do many signs and wonders (11:5–6, 11). It is during Daniel's seventieth week (Daniel 9), the tribulation period, that this occurs. Inasmuch as this period is the "time of *Jacob's* trouble" (Jer. 30:7), it has to do with Israel. The outbreak of signs and wonders also will directly relate to Israel as a covenant people.

These periods are always (1) nationally related to Israel, (2) kingdom oriented to Israel, and (3) covenant oriented to Israel. Even the period of Christ and the apostles was related primarily to the nation Israel. Christ came first to Israel (Matt. 10:6; John 1:11). His miracles primarily addressed Israel. So also did those of the disciples in the Gospels, and even later as apostles, in Acts. The church experienced most of its signs and wonders when it was all or mostly Jewish. The signs and wonders which served to encourage faith in believers, also served as a sign of judgment against unbelieving Israel (1 Cor. 14:22; cf. Acts 2–4; 7:49; 28:25–28).

Signs and wonders were performed to authenticate God's messengers, whether prophets, Messiah, or apostles, and His message through them to Israel. This is contrary to Jack Deere, who says that God used miracles to authenticate Jesus and the message of Jesus but not to authenticate the apostles.[6] This simply does not accord with the facts. What does fit the evidence is that signs and wonders are always associated with Israel and always address either their belief or their lack of it. Miracles do not cause or create faith. The fact that God's signs and wonders were performed within Israel, and primarily for Israel's benefit, does not mean they were not directed secondarily toward Gentiles (Ps. 65:8). The frequency of signs and wonders came only at those times when God's kingdom burst into human history—times that directly addressed the nation Israel and His covenant program with Israel.

In Acts, the signs of the apostles validated the apostles and their message to Israel (Acts 2:14, 22; 3:12). They were continually addressed to Israel throughout the entire book of Acts, and Acts closes with a rebuke to Israel for unbelief. The sign gifts, therefore, did three things: They (1) encouraged belief during the infancy stage of the church; (2) they removed any excuse for Israel's unbelief, and (3) they vindicated God's judgment of Israel in 66–71, especially the judgment on Jerusalem in 70.

For signs and wonders to happen willy-nilly today would require

1. that God is again directly addressing national Israel concerning the commencement of a new era,
2. that God has sent prophets whose message is directed toward Israel,
3. that the signs and wonders authenticate the messengers and the message, and
4. that this message concern an intrusion of the kingdom into this world that is inherent to God's covenant program.

All this will be the situation during the tribulation period (Rev. 11). Until then, signs and wonders have ceased.

The Cessation of Signs and Wonders

The sign gifts were directly related to the infancy of the church (1 Cor. 13:8–11; Eph. 2:20; Heb. 2:3–4; Jude 3; Rev. 22:18). Paul pictures the church growing through progressive stages of development and gradually coming to maturity at the second coming of Christ, or at the completion of the canon, which Paul probably saw as happening at the same time (1 Cor. 13:8–13; Eph. 4:1–6). Paul seems to have in view three different stages of church growth. First, the foundational or infancy period provides shelter under the umbrella of institutional Judaism, when direct revelation was being given prior to the completion of the canon of the New Testament. Second, there is the entire interadvent period, during which faith, hope, and love remain but not the temporary gifts (1 Cor. 13:13). Third, there is the period following the second coming when the church moves into full maturity (1 Cor. 13:12). Dillow seems to be correct that the "perfection" of 1 Corinthians 13:10 is the "maturity" of Ephesians 4:13:

> Paul didn't know whether that maturity would reach its absolute state at the second coming of Christ in his lifetime or whether it would be only a relative maturity characterized by the completion of knowledge and prophecy and independence from Judaism in the temporal state. As it turned out, relative maturity was in view, because Christ did not return in Paul's lifetime.[7]

Isaiah warned Israel that continued disobedience would bring judgment in the form of an invading Assyrian army: "Indeed, He will speak to this people through stammering lips and a foreign tongue" (Isa. 28:11). Paul cites this passage of Isaiah in his discussion of the gift of tongues, explaining that tongues are a sign for those who do not believe. He says, "In the law it is written, 'By men of strange tongues and by the lips of strangers I will speak to this people, and even then they will not listen to me,' says the Lord. So then tongues are for a sign, not to those who believe, but to unbelievers" (1 Cor. 14:21–22). Though the original mention of foreign tongues had reference to the Assyrian invasion of Judah, Paul applies it to his day. Tongues are for a sign—a sign of impending judgment!

This text does apply to the Israel of Paul's day. The first sign gift to be manifested in the book of Acts was the gift of tongues. On the day of Pentecost, when the Spirit of God whom God had promised to pour out on Israel was poured out, Israel was in unbelief and guilty of rejecting and crucifying Messiah. Accompanying the outpouring is the manifestation of the gift of tongues. Peter stands and addresses not the church, but Israel, concerning Jesus "whom you [Israel] crucified" (2:36). Hearing this, many were "pierced to the heart" and said "what shall we do?" (2:37). Peter's advice was to "repent and be baptized in the name of Jesus Christ," a message covenantally suited to Israel (cf. Deut. 30:1–10; 2 Chron. 7:14). He exhorts, "Be saved from this perverse generation" (2:40). Why "this generation"? The generation Peter addressed was under sentence of judgment, a judgment which took temporal form in the destruction of Jerusalem in 70. This is also implied in Peter's second sermon, also to Israel (3:11–26). It is the unstated implication of Paul's scathing rebuke of Israel at the close of the book of Acts (28:24–28).

PROGRESSIVE DISPENSATIONALISM AND THE BOOK OF ACTS

The theology of progressive dispensationalism has taught, among other things, that Christ is now seated on the royal throne of David in heaven, dispensing Davidic covenant blessings. Having been inaugurated, the Davidic kingdom will come to full manifestation in the earthly millennium. In the following critique, only connections to the book of Acts will be considered.

Acts 1:4–8; 2:2–36

There is no argument among dispensationalists that the disciples' question in Acts 1:6 concerned the future earthly messianic kingdom promised to David in 1 Samuel 7:14–16. The disagreement comes when progressive dispensationalists attempt to show that this kingdom was *inaugurated* by Jesus at His ascension and that one of His first Davidic promises (from Acts 1:8) to be fulfilled was the sending of the Holy Spirit on Pentecost (Acts 2). Two leading spokespersons for the arguments, Craig A. Blaising and Darrell S. Bock, write:

> As the divine, Davidic king, He is the one who gives the Spirit to His people, recreating their hearts, and binding them in submission to Himself. It was said of Him that He would baptize people with the Holy Spirit (Matt. 3:11; Mark 1:8; Luke 3:16; John 1:33) a testimony which He began to fulfill on the Pentecost following His ascension (Acts 1:5, 8; 2:4, 33, 38–39).[1]

An earlier reference to Acts occurs with reference to one of their hermeneutic principles:

> A second characteristic of terms is that the same idea can be said in different ways. Biblical concepts or themes often involve more than one term. So to limit looking for a concept by looking for the presence of a specific term can often result in underdeveloping the theme in Scripture. An example is that Jesus as Lord (Acts 2:30–36) and Jesus as Head (Eph. 1:19–23) are two ways to portray Jesus' ruling over the church. Both titles are associated with imagery from Psalm 110:1, which is a regal (or royal) psalm. Note how, in this example, the presence of imagery about being exalted and seated at God's right hand (Ps. 110:1) helps to fill out the portrait of a "head" (a regal, ruling image). To talk about Jesus' kingship or lordship includes discussing His headship.[2]

Bock proposes that the *headship* and *lordship* of Jesus over the church should be extended to include His *kingship*. But the mere fact that there is a certain similarity of leadership function in all three words does not therefore mean that the terms are synonymous. Further, Christ is never called king of the church. The specific term *"head"* is related to the concept of His *body* over and over again in 1 Corinthians 12:12–27 and Ephesians 1:18–23.

Psalm 110:1–2 definitely states that He is not yet ruling over His enemies; He is to remain seated at the right hand of Jehovah "until I make thine enemies thy footstool." Then (v. 2) "the LORD shall send (future) the rod of thy strength out of Zion; rule thou in the midst of thine enemies." It is quite significant that in the Scripture index totaling over 1,000 quotations, Bock and Blaising do not quote Hebrews 2:8 or 10:13 even once. Hebrews 2:8 states, "But now we see not yet all things put under him," and 10:13 says, "From henceforth expecting till his enemies be made his footstool."

It is just as significant that Ephesians 1:20–23, in describing the ascension of Christ, tells us that God set Jesus at His right hand in the heavenly places, far above all principality, power, might, and dominion," not only in this age but also in the one to come. And He put (past tense) all things in subjection under His feet and gave Him as head over all things to the church, which is His body, the fulness of Him who fills all in all." The only way to reconcile Hebrews 2:8; 10:13, and Ephesians 1:20–23 is that Christ is *not now* ruling in His *kingly* function but that He is ruling in His *headship* position over the church. Lordship and headship over the church are in no way political positions, nor do they have anything to do with earthly rulers today.

In chapter six of the same book, Blaising returns to Acts 2:22–36 to prove that the resurrection and ascension of Christ are in fulfillment of the Davidic covenant:

The promise to raise up a descendant in 2 Sam. 7:12 is connected with the promise to establish his kingdom, or putting it another way, to establish his throne. Peter argues in Acts 2:22–36 that David predicted in Psalm 16 that this descendant would be raised up from the dead incorruptible, and *in this way* He would be seated upon his throne (Acts 2:30–31). He then argues that this enthronement has taken place upon the entrance of Jesus into heaven in keeping with the language of Ps. 110:1 that describes the seating of David's son at God's right hand. Peter declares (Acts 2:36) that Jesus has been made Lord over Israel (Ps. 110:1 uses the title Lord of the enthroned king) and Christ (the anointed king) by virtue of the fact that He has acted (or been allowed to act) from that heavenly position on behalf of His people to bless them with the gift of the Holy Spirit.[3]

To summarize the points made by Blaising, the words "raised up Christ to sit on his throne" (2:30) means not just human descent but also resurrection from the dead. This seating at God's right hand is part of the Davidic promise. Christ is now Lord over Israel. Christ sends the Holy Spirit, not merely at Pentecost but also as part of the gospel.

The best response to this is to note what Peter actually says. In Acts 2:22–23, Peter recounts the death of Christ and the resurrection of Christ in 2:24–29 using Psalm 16:8–10. In Acts 2:30, Peter says that David prophesied first that God had sworn that He would *raise up* a descendant according to the flesh, to sit on David's throne. This cannot be stretched to mean anything more than it says. This same word is used in the same way in Acts 3:22, "The Lord God shall raise up for you a prophet like me from your brethren" (cf. 7:37), and in 3:26, "For you first God raised up His Servant, and sent him to bless you."

Thus, in Acts 2:30 Christ is spoken of as *incarnated* ("raised up") as a descendant of David who would eventually sit upon David's throne. Then, in Acts 2:31 David, "seeing what was ahead" (NIV), that the Messiah would have to become incarnate, live, present Himself to Israel, only to be rejected as Messiah/King, die, be buried, be raised from the dead, ascend into heaven to sit at God's right hand, and wait until God makes His enemies His footstool. Only then will He begin to fulfill the Davidic covenant when His enemies are defeated and He sits on David's throne and judges them.

It is interesting that the only reference to Revelation 3:21 in progressive dispensationalism is where Bock attempts to show that "my Father's throne" is David's throne simply because Christ, as the "Root of David" (Rev. 5:5), is sitting there. Yet, Christ Himself makes the great distinction: "He who overcomes, I will grant to him to sit down with Me on My throne, as I also overcame and sat down with My Father on His throne" (Rev. 3:21).

Acts 2:31–36 rehearses Psalm 16:10–11, showing that Christ saw no corruption, that God raised Him from the dead, and that God exalted Him to

His right hand. The conclusion in verse 36 is that Jesus, the crucified One, is indeed Lord and Messiah. However, Peter does not say that the Messiah is now King; he does not say that the Pentecost experience in any way inaugurates the Davidic covenant. Rather, it is the fulfillment of John 14:16–17.

Blaising assumes that Jesus has been made Lord over Israel, but Acts 2:36 merely says that Israel is to know that Jesus is made Lord and Christ, not with reference to the nation Israel but simply as a proof of His claims as the One sent from God. Further, in John 14:16–17 the sending of the Holy Spirit is to be an act of the *Father* in the name of the Son (cf. John 14:26). At most, it can be said that the Holy Spirit is sent by the Father *and* the Son (14:26, cf. 16:7) Even Christ Himself said, "When the Helper comes, whom I will send to you from the Father, that is the Spirit of truth, who proceeds from the Father, He will bear witness of Me" (John 15:26). The only proper conclusion to be drawn from these passages is that the sending of the Holy Spirit at Pentecost was a *divine* act, not a Davidic act. The three definitive continuing ministries of the ascended Christ are as our Advocate (1 John 2:2), our Intercessor (Heb. 7:25), and our Mediator (1 Tim. 2:5). None of these is related to the Davidic covenant.

Acts 3:19–21

In Peter's second sermon to Israel, he repeated the facts about their denial of Christ and his subsequent crucifixion and resurrection, saying that this was in fulfillment of the prophets. Peter told them to "Repent, therefore and return, that your sins may be wiped away in order that times of refreshing may come from the presence of the Lord; and that He may send Jesus, the Christ appointed for you, whom heaven must receive, until the period of restoration of all things, about which God spoke by the mouth of His holy prophets from ancient time." This translation more accurately portrays the basic purpose of God for the future of Israel. Some writers have called this a reoffer of the kingdom; others have seen it as a reaffirmation that there must be national repentance of Israel before these things can be fulfilled. In any event, the response of these men of Israel was to put the apostles in custody and the next day to command them not to speak nor to teach in the name of Jesus. The Davidic covenant was *not* fulfilled, but some five thousand were added to the *church* according to Acts 4:4.

Acts 5:30–31

"The God of our fathers raised up Jesus, whom you had put to death by hanging Him on a cross. He is the one whom God exalted to his right hand as a Prince and a Savior, to grant repentance to Israel, and forgiveness of sins." Because the words *Prince and a Savior* are mentioned, Blaising uses this passage in connection with Psalm 110:1 and Acts 2:33–36 to support his premise that

Christ is now fulfilling the Davidic covenant.[4] But since he does not quote the entire passage, the emphasis is distorted. Peter is still preaching to the *Jews*. Just as he did in 3:19–21, so here he refers this to the repentance of Israel and their forgiveness, the same requirement as in 3:21 for the return of Christ some time in the *future*. There is *no* indication of this being fulfilled now and certainly *no* reference to the church and her blessings.

Acts 15:13–17

"And after they had stopped speaking, James answered, saying, 'Brethren, listen to me; Simeon has related how God first concerned Himself about taking from among the Gentiles a people for His name. And with this the words of the Prophets agree, just as it is written: "After these things I will return, and I will rebuild the tabernacle of David which has fallen; and I will rebuild its ruins, and I will restore it, in order that the rest of mankind may seek the Lord, and all the Gentiles who are called by My name, says the Lord, who makes these things known from of old."'"

Few dispensationalists would doubt that this quotation from Amos 9:11–12 refers to the future fulfillment of the Davidic covenant. But just why did James use it in the controversy concerning Gentile salvation within the church? Is there any sense in which Amos 9:11–12 is fulfilled today?

Remember that the controversy in Acts 15 is not *whether* Gentiles can be saved; that was settled in Acts 10–11. Here the controversy concerns *how* Gentiles are to be saved, that is, must they first become proselyte Jews, be circumcised, and keep the Law? Peter had already given his answer in 15:11: Gentiles are saved by grace. What James says is that there will be Gentile believers as well as Jewish believers at the time of the restoration of the line of David in the messianic kingdom. Gentiles will not be required to become proselyte Jews. Why, then, should Gentiles be required to observe Jewish rites and commandments *now* in order to be saved? There is nothing in James's statements that even hints that the tabernacle of David has been inaugurated by the exaltation of Jesus to the right hand of the Father.

The New Covenant

Through the years there have been several interpretations of the new covenant by dispensationalists. Three major views include those of J. N. Darby, C. I. Scofield, and Lewis Sperry Chafer. Darby taught that the new covenant directly concerns Israel and not the church. The church has a covenant also, but "not specifically a new covenant but rather the only covenant."[5] Scofield's view was that the one new covenant has two aspects, one for Israel and one for the church. Chafer's position was that there are two new covenants, one for Israel and one for the church. The consensus among many dispensationalists today seems to be that there is one new covenant, made in the blood of Christ (Luke 22:20) with a present aspect for the church, the means of all spiritual blessings (2 Cor. 3:6; Eph. 1:3), and a future aspect for the nation Israel, which will someday fulfill the promises of Jeremiah 31:31–34 when Christ returns to the earth. There are distinct sets of promises in the new covenant for the church and for Israel, not contradictory yet not overlapping.

While the new covenant is not specifically mentioned in Acts, several passages relate to it directly. When Jesus established the new covenant at the last Passover, "And He took a cup and gave thanks, and gave it to them, saying, 'Drink from it all of you; for this is My blood of the covenant, which is to be shed on behalf of many for forgiveness of sins'" (Matt. 26:27–28).

This theme of the remission of sins occurs in Acts 2:38a, "Repent and let each one of you be baptized in the name of Jesus Christ for the forgiveness of your sins." In Acts 3:19a, Peter says, "Repent, therefore and return, that your sins may be wiped away." As stated previously, this message of Peter was directed to Israel with the promise that the new covenant blessings would come to the nation at the second advent of Christ. Acts 5:31 also calls attention to this future fulfillment as Peter refers to Christ: "He is the one whom God exalted to his right hand as a Prince and a Savior, to grant repentance to Israel, and forgiveness of sins." In each of these passages the promise is given to the Jews, and yet this same forgiveness of sins is offered "for all who are far off" (Acts 2:39).

The apostle Paul continued this offer to both Jews and Gentiles in Acts 13:38–43, contrasting it with the old covenant, the Law of Moses, and referring to this forgiveness as "the grace of God." His statement was, "Therefore let it be known to you, brethren, that through Him forgiveness of sins is proclaimed to you, and through Him everyone who believes is freed from all things, from which you could not be freed through the Law of Moses" (13:38–39). Then, in 13:43, "Now when the meeting of the synagogue had broken up, many of the Jews and of the God-fearing proselytes followed Paul and Barnabas, who, speaking to them, were urging them to continue in the grace of God." This angered the Jews and was the occasion for Paul and Barnabas to announce that they were "turning to the Gentiles" (13:46).

Finally, in Acts 20:24–28, in giving his farewell to the Ephesian elders, Paul mentions his ministry "to testify solemnly of the gospel of the grace of God" (v. 24), "preaching the kingdom" (v. 25), and then he commands the elders to "shepherd the church of God which he purchased with his own blood" (v. 28).

In Acts, therefore, the new covenant was first offered to the Jews by Peter as well as Paul, and though some Jews believed, Paul had to say, "It was necessary that the word of God should be spoken to you first; since you repudiate it and judge yourselves unworthy of eternal life, behold, we are turning to the Gentiles" (13:46). As a nation, therefore, the Jews will have to wait until Christ returns for the blessings of the new covenant to be poured out upon them.

Meanwhile, any individual, Jew or Gentile, may receive the blessings of the new covenant to the church by faith in His sacrifice of blood on the cross, thereby becoming a member of this new organism, the body of Christ. To confuse the blessings of the new covenant with Israel as somehow being partially fulfilled today by Christ as the Davidic mediator is to confuse Israel and the church. This is not dispensationalism; it is covenant theology.

ENDNOTES

Chapter 1

1. James Hastings, ed., *A Dictionary of the Bible* (Peabody, Mass: Hendrickson, 1988), 3:161.
2. Ibid., 162.
3. Harold Hoehner, *The Chronological Aspects of the Life of Christ* (Grand Rapids: Zondervan, 1975), 182.
4. W. J. Conybeare and J. S. Howson, *The Life and Epistles of St. Paul* (Grand Rapids: Eerdmans, 1980), 832–38.
5. James L. Boyer, *New Testament Chronological Chart* (Chicago: Moody, 1968). John C. Whitcomb, *Chart of Old Testament Patriarchs and Judges,* 3d rev. ed. (Chicago: Moody, 1968).
6. Albert Barnes, "Acts," in *Notes on the New Testament* (Grand Rapids: Baker, 1983), iii.
7. Ibid., iv.
8. Richard H. Longenecker, "Acts," in *The Expositor's Bible Commentary,* ed. Frank E. Gaebelein (Grand Rapids: Zondervan, 1981), 9:236–37.
9. Ibid., 238.
10. R. C. H. Lenski, *The Interpretation of St. Luke's Gospel* (Minneapolis: Augsburg, 1946), 17.
11. Ibid., 33.
12. Geoffrey W. Bromiley, gen. ed., *The International Standard Bible Encyclopedia* (Grand Rapids: Eerdmans, 1993), 4:831–32.
13. Robertson Nicoll, ed., *The Expositor's Greek Testament* (Grand Rapids: Eerdmans, 1988), 2:11–12.
14. R. C. H. Lenski, *The Interpretation of the Acts of the Apostles* (Minneapolis: Augsburg, 1946), 5.
15. John Walvoord, *The Holy Spirit* (Wheaton, Ill.: Van Kampen, 1954), 192–93.
16. Stanley Toussaint and Charles Dyer, *Pentecost Essays* (Chicago: Moody, 1986), 24.
17. Ibid., 27.

18. Ibid., 22.
19. Ibid., 69.
20. Ibid., 70.
21. Ibid., 69.
22. William Gesenius, *Hebrew and Chaldee Lexicon* (Grand Rapids: Eerdmans, 1974), 112.
23. Franz Delitzsch, *Biblical Commentary on the Prophecies of Isaiah* (Grand Rapids: Eerdmans, 1960), 2:53.
24. *Holy Bible, The Berkeley Version* (Grand Rapids: Zondervan, 1959), 711.
25. Joseph Henry Thayer, *Greek-English Lexicon of the New Testament* (New York: American Book Co., 1889), 590.
26. Ibid., 517.
27. Gerhard Delling, *"plēroō,"* in *Theological Dictionary of the New Testament,* ed. G. W. Bromiley (Grand Rapids: Eerdmans, 1971), 6:291.
28. *Analytical Greek Lexicon* (New York: Harper and Brothers, n.d.), 308.
29. William Hendriksen, *New Testament Commentary: The Gospel of Luke* (Grand Rapids: Baker, 1981), 31.
30. Ibid., 33.
31. William F. Arndt and F. Wilbur Gingrich, *A Greek-English Lexicon of the New Testament* (Chicago: University of Chicago Press, 1959), 238.
32. Ibid., 196.
33. Colin Brown, ed., *The New International Dictionary of New Testament Theology* (Grand Rapids: Zondervan, 1978), 3:96.
34. Henry Alford, *The Greek Testament* (Chicago: Moody, 1958), 1:636.
35. Albert Barnes, "Luke and John," in *Notes on the New Testament* (Grand Rapids: Baker, 1983), 142.
36. Lenski, *Interpretation of St. Luke's Gospel,* 1020.
37. Ibid.

Chapter 2

1. Robert Gromacki, *The Modern Tongues Movement* (Philadelphia: Presbyterian and Reformed, 1967), 59.
2. Edward J. Young, *The Book of Isaiah* (Grand Rapids: Eerdmans), 2:277–78.
3. Ibid., 279.
4. J. B. Lightfoot, *The Epistle of Paul to the Galatians* (Grand Rapids: Zondervan, 1967), 92–94.
5. Robert Culver, "Apostles and the Apostalate in the New Testament," *Bibliotheca Sacra* 134, no. 534 (April 1977): 131–34.
6. Gene Getz, *The Measure of a Man* (Venture: Regal, 1974); Paul Benware and Brian Harris, *Leaders in the Making* (Chicago: Moody, 1991), 45–55; and Robert Saucy, *The Church in God's Program* (Chicago: Moody, 1972), 146–48.

7. William Hendriksen, *New Testament Commentary: The Gospel of Matthew* (Grand Rapids: Baker, 1982), 651. The question is raised whether Jesus means the same thing by *kingdom* that He does by *church* in verse 18. A. T. Robertson, *Word Pictures in the New Testament*, 6 vols. (Nashville: Broadman, 1930), 1:133–34.

8. R. C. H. Lenski, *The Interpretation of Matthew* (Minneapolis: Augsburg, 1961), 628–29.

9. D. A. Carson, "Matthew," in *The Expositor's Bible Commentary*, ed. Frank E. Gaebelein (Grand Rapids: Zondervan, 1984), 8:369.

10. Hendriksen, *Matthew*, 646.

11. Edward Denny, *Papalism* (London: Rivingtons, 1912), 11.

12. Ibid., 13, 15, 17.

13. Carson, "Matthew," 8:370–71.

14. Denny, *Papalism*, 30.

15. Ibid., 41.

16. Joseph Deharbe, *A Complete Catechism of the Catholic Religion* (New York: Schwartz, Kirwin and Fauss, 1912), 134.

17. Ibid.

18. Ibid., 135–36.

19. Ibid., 139.

20. Ibid., 141.

21. Ibid., 141–42.

22. Ibid., 142.

23. Ibid., 145.

24. Ibid., 146.

25. Ibid., 148–49.

26. Ibid., 149.

27. Ibid., 148.

28. Richard P. McBrien, *Catholicism*, rev. ed. (New York: Harper Collins, 1994), 673.

29. Ibid., 692.

30. Ibid., 694.

31. Ibid.

32. Ibid., 730.

33. Ibid., 1180.

34. Ibid.

35. Ibid., 1181.

36. Merrill F. Unger, *Unger's Bible Dictionary* (Chicago: Moody, 1961), 941.

37. M. Max B. Turner, "The Sabbath, Sunday, and the Law in Luke/Acts," in D. A. Carson, *From Sabbath to Lord's Day* (Grand Rapids: Zondervan, 1982), 135–36.

38. Silva New says, "The 'laying on of hands' is not only a well-known Jewish custom, but frequent in all ages and in all countries." See F. J. Foakes Jackson and Kirsopp Lake, eds., *The Beginnings of Christianity*,

Part I: The Acts of the Apostles, Additional Notes to the Commentary, ed. K. Lake and H. J. Cadbury (reprint, Grand Rapids: Baker, 1979), 5:137.

39. The count is seventeen if Revelation 1:17 is included. I *exclude* it because (1) it uses the verb *tithēmi* instead of *epitithēmi* and (2) it appears not to involve the ceremonial use of the laying on of hands. There is some similarity to the ceremonial laying-on-of-hands for healing, if such a practice can be said to be ceremonial.

40. John B. Polhill, "Acts," in *The New American Commentary,* vol. 26 (Nashville: Broadman, 1992), 182; Henry Barclay Swete, *The Holy Spirit in the New Testament* (London: Macmillan, 1910; reprint, Grand Rapids: Baker, 1964), 90–91; F. F. Bruce, *Commentary on the Book of Acts, New International Commentary on the New Testament* (Grand Rapids: Eerdmans, 1954), 130; David John Williams, *Acts, A Good News Commentary* (San Francisco: Harper & Row, 1985), 108; William J. Larkin, *Acts, InterVarsity Press New Testament Commentary* (Downers Grove, Ill.: InterVarsity, 1995), 101–2; George E. Ladd, "The Acts of the Apostles," in *The Wycliffe Bible Commentary,* ed. Charles F. Pfeiffer and Everett F. Harrison (Chicago: Moody, 1962), 1134–35.

Chapter 3

1. J. W. McGarvey, *New Commentary on Acts of Apostles* (Delight, Ark.: Gospel Light, n.d.), 2:17.
2. R. C. H. Lenski, *The Interpretation of the Acts of the Apostles* (Minneapolis: Augsburg, 1946), 370–71.
3. Robert Baker Girdlestone, *Synonyms of the Old Testament* (Grand Rapids: Eerdmans, 1897), 175.
4. Horst Balz and Gerhard Schneider, eds., *Exegetical Dictionary of the New Testament* (Grand Rapids: Eerdmans, 1994), 1:327.
5. Lenski, *Interpretation of the Acts of the Apostles,* 135.
6. Albert Barnes, *Notes on the New Testament* (Grand Rapids: Baker, 1983), 179.
7. Lenski, *Interpretation of the Acts of the Apostles,* 523.
8. John B. Polhill, "Acts," in *The New American Commentary* (Nashville: Broadman, 1992), 26:304.

Chapter 4

1. Paul Enns, *The Moody Handbook of Theology* (Chicago: Moody, 1989), 52.
2. Ibid., 36.
3. J. W. McGarvey, *Commentary on Acts* (Delight, Ark.: Gospel Light, n.d.), 288.
4. A. T. Robertson, *Word Pictures in the New Testament* (Nashville: Broadman, 1930), 3:216.
5. R. C. H. Lenski, *The Interpretation of the Acts of the Apostles* (Minneapolis: Augsburg, 1961), 585.

6. Richard H. Longenecker, "Acts," in *The Expositor's Bible Commentary*, ed. Frank E. Gaebelein (Grand Rapids: Zondervan, 1981), 9:446.
7. Enns, *Moody Handbook of Theology*, 67.

Chapter 5

1. Homer A. Kent Jr., *Jerusalem to Rome* (Grand Rapids: Baker, 1972), 53.
2. Joseph Henry Thayer, *Greek-English Lexicon of the New Testament* (New York: American Book, 1889), 331.
3. Ibid., 410.
4. Alan H. McNeile, *The Gospel According to Matthew* (Grand Rapids: Baker, 1980), 177.
5. F. F. Bruce, *The Book of Acts, The New International Commentary on the New Testament* (Grand Rapids: Eerdmans, 1975), 389.
6. W. F. Moulton and Milligan, *The Vocabulary of the Greek New Testament* (Grand Rapids: Eerdmans, 1957), 505.
7. Richard B. Rackham, *The Acts of the Apostles* (London: Methuen, 1901), 356.
8. R. C. H. Lenski, *Interpretation of the Acts of the Apostles* (Columbus, Ohio: Wartburg, 1944), 319.
9. Kent, *Jerusalem to Rome*, 86.

Chapter 6

1. Robert E. Picirilli, *Paul the Apostle* (Chicago: Moody, 1986), vii.
2. Ibid., 1.
3. Merrill F. Unger, *The New Unger's Bible Dictionary* (Chicago: Moody, 1988), 968.
4. Picirilli, *Paul the Apostle*, 7.
5. Tim Dowley, *The History of Christianity* (Oxford, England: Lion, 1977), 62.
6. Eusebius, *The History of the Church from Christ to Constantine*, trans. G. A. Williamson (New York: Barnes and Noble, 1965), 74.
7. John R.W. Stott, *The Message of Galatians* (Downers Grove, Ill.: InterVarsity, 1968), 34.
8. J. B. Lightfoot, *St. Paul's Epistle to the Galatians* (Peabody, Mass.: Hendrickson, 1995), 87, 89–90.
9. Eusebius, *History of the Church*, 97–99.
10. John Foxe, *Foxe's Book of Martyrs* (Old Tappan, N.J.: Revell, n.d.), 13.

Chapter 7

1. Hans Conzelmann, *The Theology of St. Luke* (London: SCM, 1982), 165.
2. Dispensationalism holds that this restoration will be the result of a national Jewish turning to Jesus as the Messiah at the end of days. The temple to be rebuilt will be for the glory of Messiah. Salvation for the

Jew is the same as for the Gentile—by grace, through faith in Jesus, the Messiah and Lord (Acts 15:11).

3. Bradley Chance, *Jerusalem, the Temple, and the New Age in Luke-Acts* (Macon, Ga.: Mercer University Press, 1988); James M. Dawsey, "The Origin of Luke's Positive Perception of the Temple," *Perspectives in Religious Studies* 18, no. 1 (spring 1991): 5–21.

4. David L. Tiede, *Prophecy and History in Luke-Acts* (Philadelphia: Fortress, 1980), 328.

5. Marilyn Salmon, "Hypotheses About First-Century Judaism and the Study of Luke-Acts" (Ph.D. dissertation, Hebrew Union College, 1985). See also, David Flusser, *Judaism and the Origins of Christianity* (Jerusalem: Magnes, 1988), 617–44; and Jacob Neusner, "Parallel Histories of Early Christianity and Judaism," *Bible Review* (spring 1987), 42–55.

6. Those who argue that the temple was of secondary importance argue that the synagogue replaced the temple as the center of worship. See George Foot Moore, *Judaism in the First Centuries of the Christian Era* (Cambridge: Harvard University Press, 1930), 2:13ff.; and R. T. Herford, *Pharisaism* (New York: Putman, 1912), 27ff. However, the two institutions were never in conflict. The synagogue arose during Second Temple times for those outside Jerusalem who could only infrequently go to the temple. Synagogue services corresponded to the temple liturgy and were a constant reminder of the prominence of the temple. In later Jewish thinking, the synagogue, as well as the home, were a microcosm of and a supplement to the temple in theology and worship.

7. Scholarly consensus is that Luke-Acts, if written by the same author, was composed by a Gentile writing outside of Palestine after A.D. 70. Dawsey, "The Origin of Luke's Positive Perception of the Temple," points out that it is ridiculous to posit that a Gentile, writing after 70, presumably to a Gentile audience (note address to "Theophilus," Luke 1:3; Acts 1:1), would borrow and incorporate a positive view of the temple from Judaism into both the gospel and the history of Christianity.

8. Based on the description of the site from the ancient sources, and especially Josephus, *Ant.* 20.221, the Stoa of Solomon was a colonaded nave 667 feet long situated on the eastern side of the temple complex at the deepest descent from Mount Moriah into the Kidron Valley.

9. The word *homothymadon* occurs thirty-six times in the *LXX* and was used as a technical term to denote the exceptional unity of thought and character of Christian conduct (cf. Acts 1:14; 2:46; 4:24; 5:12; 8:6). Acts 7:57 and 19:29 employ the term to depict united hatred of mobs.

10. The early disciples of Jesus were all observant Jews, Peter in particular (cf. Acts 10:14; Gal. 2:7, 11–14). Even at the Jerusalem Council, still years away, the laws against eating blood are still applied through the Noahic covenant to the Gentile converts (Acts 15:19–21, 28–29), a proviso agreed

to by even the most observant among the group (Acts 15:5 with v. 22). These Jewish believers continued to revere the temple as the place designated by God for daily prayers. Just as Jesus' condemnation of the Jewish nation had not led them to abandon their country, so Jesus' announcement of the temple's destruction had not caused them to reject its validity.

11. W. O. E. Oesterley, *The Jewish Background of the Christian Liturgy* (Oxford: Clarendon, 1925), 96.

12. Daniel K. Falk, "Jewish Prayer Literature and the Jerusalem Church in Acts," in *The Book of Acts in Its First Century Setting: Paul in Roman Custody*, ed. Brian Rapske (Grand Rapids: Eerdmans, 1995), 299.

13. Later, in Acts 10:14, Peter's adherence to dietary laws is presented in his denial: "I have never eaten anything unholy ('profane, ceremonially unclean') and unclean ('ceremonially impure')." This observation should also balance the thinking of those who regard John as the most anti-Semitic of the Gospels.

14. Such specificity of purpose must indicate the high esteem held by these for the temple. This argues against John Calvin, who supposed the reason for going to the temple was that it offered the best opportunity for missionary work. He incorrectly infers this from the angel's command in Acts 5:20 to preach at the temple. That prayer, not missionary endeavor, was the purpose of the assembly is made clear by Acts 5:13, which relates that unbelievers were fearful and hesitated to join gatherings at the temple, though the disciples were admired for their piety and miracles. Luke in Acts 5:13–14 clarifies the non-Christian Jews' reserve by stating that some joined their ranks.

15. Eusebius, *Ecclesiastical History, Loeb Classical Library*, trans. Kirsopp Lake (New York: G. Putnam's Sons, 1926–1932), 2.xxiii.

16. This concept was of an earthly messianic reign preceding the eternal state, sometimes of a thousand-year duration (as Rev. 20:4). See J. W. Bailey, "The Temporary Messianic Reign in the Literature of Early Judaism," *Journal of Biblical Literature* 53 (July 1934): 170–87. This hope of literal restoration was shared by Philo. Though accustomed to allegorizing Scripture, he nevertheless could write: "The cities that now lay in ruins will be cities once more," *De Praemiis et Poenis*, 168. For the documentation of this view at Qumran, see Shemaryahu Talmon, *The World of Qumran from Within: Collected Studies* (Jerusalem: Magnes, 1989), 300ff.

17. E. P. Sanders, *Jesus and Judaism* (Philadelphia: Fortress, 1985), 87, 103.

18. Terms in Acts 3:19–21 are drawn from the language of prophetic discourse. The phrase *times or moments of refreshing, kairoi; anapsyxeōs*, is parallel with *period of restoration chronōn apokatastaseōs* in verse 21. The former use of *anapsyxis* is attested in the *LXX* only in Exodus 8:15, where it must have the sense of "respite." The idea, then, is of a "respite" from

Gentile oppression through deliverance from Gentile domination by the Messiah (cf. Zech. 12–14). This domination was considered a judgment from God for past apostasy (cf. Deut. 28:36, 47–50) that would be reversed in Israel's restoration (cf. Isa. 11:11–12; cf. Luke 21:24; Rom. 11:25). The latter use of *apokatastaseōs* is identical to Acts 1:6 of the "restoration" or "establishment" of Israel's kingdom, and parallel in sense to *pallingenēsia* ("renewal, regeneration") in Matthew 19:28. The prophetic hope is that Israel would repent and be restored, which in turn would bring the Messiah to fulfill the promise of the messianic age. Note also that Acts 3:19–21 qualifies this eschatological age with restoration motifs: "times of refreshing" and "the period of time of the restoration of all things." Luke is clear that this period yet to come is predicted in the Prophets.

19. Robert H. Gundry, *Matthew: A Commentary on His Literary and Theological Arts,* 392.

20. The term in context clearly indicates an era yet future, cf. Friedrich Buschel, s.v. *"palliggenēsia," TDNT* (Grand Rapids: Eerdmans, 1976) 1:686–689; and F. W. Burnett, *"Palingenesia* in Matt. 19:28: A Window on the Matthean Community?" *Journal for the Study of the New Testament* 17 (February 1983): 60–72.

21. Some have conjectured that this was the bronze Nicanor Gate, since this was alledgedly the most beautiful of the gates. However, the Nicanor Gate opened into the Israelite Court and would not have been an acceptable place for a man defiled by disease. It was guarded by priests and Levites, who could not risk contamination by one ritually impure. The best evidence identifies this as the Eastern Gate, also called the "Susa or Shushan Gate" because it had a relief of the Shushan palace (*Mishnah* tractate *Middot* 1:3). This gate has incorrectly been called the "Golden Gate." For a recent discussion of the problem of identification, see Martin Hengel, "The Geography of Palestine in Acts," in Brian Rapske, ed., *The Book of Acts in Its First Century Setting: Paul in Roman Custody* (Grand Rapids: Eerdmans, 1995), 37–45.

22. By giving the Abrahamic covenant a present application through Messiah (vv. 25–26), Peter implies that, just as the messianic redemptive blessings are presently enjoyed, so will the fullness of eschatological redemption be enjoyed when national Israel embraces her Messiah.

23. Luke as a historian reports Stephen's trial, likely based on details from Paul (Acts 7:58; 8:1–2) or other members of the Sanhedrin who later became Christians, cf. J. J. Scott Jr., "Stephen's Speech: A Possible Model for Luke's Historical Method?" *Journal of the Evangelical Theological Society* 17 (1974): 93; M. H. Scharlemann, "Stephen's Speech: A Lucan Creation?" *Concordia Journal* 4 (1978): 57. The speech probably was preserved in a fixed oral or written tradition, since it is not thought to be a verbatim account. In word choice, at least twenty-three words of Stephen's speech appear nowhere else in Acts or any other New

Testament book. Several literary forms peculiar to Luke-Acts are absent. See J. Kilgallen, *The Stephen Speech: A Literary and Redactional Study of Acts 7, 2–53, Analecta Biblica* 67 (Rome: Pontifical Biblical Institute, 1976), 113; and Simon J. Kistemaker, "The Speeches in Acts," *Criswell Theological Review* 5, no. 1 (1990): 34–35.

24. A partial listing of Stephen's Old Testament allusions is Acts 7:3, Gen. 12:1; v. 5, Gen. 48:4; vv. 6–7, Gen. 15:13–15; v. 7, Exod. 3:12; v. 14, Gen. 46:27 *(LXX)*; v. 18, Exod. 1:8; vv. 27–28, Exod. 2:14; v. 30, Exod. 3:2; v. 32, Exod. 3:6; v. 33, Exod. 3:5; v. 34, Exod. 3:7–8, 10; v. 35, Exod. 2:14; v. 37, Deut. 18:15; v. 40, Exod. 32:1, 23; vv. 42–43, Amos 5:25–27 *(LXX)*; vv. 49–50, Isa. 66:1–2.

25. The question of Luke's sources for Stephen's sermon as well as Paul's at the Areopagus (Acts 17) is hotly debated. Because the literary style of the sermon appears to be non-Lukan, C. C. Torrey early argued for a single Aramaic source, "The Translations Made from the Original Aramaic Gospels," *Studies in the History of Religions Presented to Crawford Howell Toy by Pupils, Colleagues, and Friends,* ed. D. G. Lyon and G. F. Moore (New York, 1912), 269–317. C. K. Barrett revised Torrey's argument and posited instead that the sources were Hellenistic Jewish. "Attitudes to the Temple in the Acts of the Apostles," *Templum Amicitiae: Essays on the Second Temple presented to Ernst Bammel, JSNT* 48, ed. William Horbury (Sheffield, 1991), 365–67; and *New Testament Christianity for Africa and the World. Essays in Honor of H. Sawyer,* ed. E. W. Fashole, *Luke* (London: SPCK, 1974), 69–77. Barrett discovered that the Aramaisms in the speech can also be found in other Hellenistic writings not based on Aramaic or Semitic sources. See also H. J. Cadbury, "Luke—Translator or Author?" *American Journal of Theology* 24 (1920): 436–55. F. J. Foakes Jackson in his Moffatt New Testament Commentary, *The Acts of the Apostles* (New York: Harper & Row, 1931), 65, cited the apparent lack of references to Jesus and other Christian symbols. Others argue that it lacks affinity with other speeches in Acts and does not seem to fit well in the narrative (Acts 6:8–7:60). However, affinities can be drawn between Stephen's speech and, for example, Peter's sermon in Acts 3, which also uses Deuteronomy 18:15f. J. Dupont, *"L'utilisation apologetique de l'Ancien Testament dans les discours des Acts," Eph. Theol. Lov.* 29 (1953): 292–94; and John Townsend, "The Jerusalem Temple in New Testament Thought" (Ph.D. dissertation: Harvard University, 1958), 141–43. That the Stephen speech contains little Christian theology is answered by the reference in verse 52 to "the Righteous One," certainly an epithet of Jesus. Peter already expounded the Christian position in his sermon. Luke may have felt no need to include a restatement here, cf. H. J. Cadbury, "The Speeches in Acts," F. J. Foakes Jackson and Kirsopp Lake, eds., *The Beginnings of Christianity, Part I: The Acts of the Apostles, Additional Notes to the*

Commentary, ed. K. Lake and H. J. Cadbury (reprint, Grand Rapids: Baker, 1979), 5:402–27, esp. 409.

26. Marcel Simon, "Saint Stephen and the Jerusalem Temple," in *The Journal of Ecclesiastical History* 2 (1951): 127.

27. Simon also argues by reference to exploited Hellenistic Diaspora Jews who, carrying the opposition at Qumran from simply the present priesthood to the temple itself, would see the very construction of a man-made building for worship as a violation of God's will. See Marcel Simon, *Saint Stephen and the Hellenists* (London: Longmans, 1958), 84–94.

28. It is not accurate to say that the *LXX* uses *cheiropoiētōn* only of the making of idols, for in *LXX* Isaiah 16:12 it is used to refer to the Moabite "holy place."

29. Cf. J. R. Brown, *Temple and Sacrifice in Rabbinic Judaism*, The Winslow Lectures 1963 (Ill.: Seabury-Western Theological Seminary, 1963), 13–14. Brown says Stephen's speech "is surely not a polemic against the temple. In fact, the accusation that he was against the Holy Place is very carefully ascribed by the author to false witnesses." Rather, Brown says, Stephen argues that the rejection of Jesus is just one more episode in a long series of disobedient actions, some of which relate to the temple.

30. F. F. Bruce, *The Epistle to the Hebrews, The New International Commentary on the New Testament* (Grand Rapids: Eerdmans, 1964), 199–200.

31. Cf. J. Jervell, "The Acts of the Apostles and the History of Early Christianity," *Studia Theologica* 37 (1983): 24.

32. See the statement of Joseph Alexander: "The error here denied is that of Heathenism and corrupted Judaism, namely, that Deity could be confined or unchangeably attached to any earthly residence, not the genuine Old Testament doctrine of Jehovah's real and continued dwelling in the tabernacle and temple," in *Commentary on the Acts of the Apostles* (Grand Rapids: Baker, 1983), 616.

33. The term *cheiropoiētois* has the meaning in secular Greek of "human-made as opposed to natural," and while Philo uses it of idolatry, he also uses it to denote "calamities artificially provoked by man's destructive energy," cf. *Spec. Leg.* 1.184; 3.203; *Flacc.* 62.

34. F. Weinert, *"The Meaning of the Temple in the Gospel of Luke"* (Ph.D. dissertation, Fordham University, 1979), 27, 84, 127.

35. By contrast is the typical approach of a writer who, while acknowledging Stephen's acceptance of the temple as a divine institution, does so only for the past age: "Stephen is far from denying that the law and the temple were of God, but like the Lord Himself he was aware that a new dispensation had come which outmoded the old" ("The Attitude of the Primitive Church toward Judaism," *Bibliothecra Sacra* 113, no. 450 [April 1956]: 136).

36. On the historical reliability of Paul in Acts, see F. F. Bruce, "Is the Paul of Acts the Real Paul?" *Bulletin of the John Rylands Library* 58 (1976): 282–305.

37. Paul was so intent on observing the feasts, that at the end of his third journey he avoided the province of Asia in order to reach Jerusalem by Pentecost (Acts 20:16).
38. The Ephesian Jews had apparently seen Trophimus in Jerusalem with Paul. Believing the rumors that Paul taught the Gentiles to forsake the Law, they assumed Paul had no regard for temple sanctity and would violate the prohibition against bringing his companion into the restricted area.
39. The *Soreg* was a protective barrier that separated the inclusive Court of the Gentiles from the exclusive Court of Israel. Posted at regular intervals along this balistrade—in plain sight—was a Greek inscription warning of the death penalty for a Gentile to enter the Court of Israel. The remains of one of these "warning placards" was found in Temple Mount excavations under Benjamin Mazar and is displayed in the Israel Museum, Jerusalem.
40. For more discussion of Paul's "offense" see Brian Rapske, "Paul on Trial in Acts," in *The Book of Acts in Its First Century Setting: Palestinian Setting,* ed. Richard Bauckham (Grand Rapids: Eerdmans, 1994), 135–49, 160–67.
41. John Townsend, *"The Jerusalem Temple in New Testament Thought" (Ph.D. dissertation: Harvard University, 1958).*
42. Such an understanding must be applied to the interpretation of a passage such as Galatians 6:16, where reference is made to the "Israel of God." This could not have reference to the church *per se* but only to a division within the church (i.e., Jewish-Christians). While a part of the body of Christ, Jewish Christians are nevertheless uniquely related to the chosen people whose calling preceded the formation of the church.

Chapter 8

1. Mark Allan Powell, *What Are They Saying About Acts?* (New York: Paulist, 1991), 50, cited by William H. Shepperd Jr., *The Narrative Function of the Holy Spirit as a Character in Luke-Acts* (Atlanta: Scholars, 1994), 1; H. D. McDonald, *Living Doctrines of the New Testament* (Grand Rapids: Zondervan, 1972), 137; and William G. Moorehead, *Outline Studies in Acts, Romans, First and Second Corinthians, Galatians and Ephesians* (Pittsburgh: United Presbyterian Board of Publication, 1902), 25.
2. George Sweeting and Donald W. Sweeting, *The Acts of God* (Chicago: Moody, 1986); Arthur T. Pierson, *The Acts of the Holy Spirit* (London: Morgan and Scott, n.d.); Arno Clemens Gaebelein, *The Holy Spirit in the New Testament* (New York: Our Hope, n.d.), 31; and W. H. Griffith Thomas, *The Holy Spirit of God* (Grand Rapids: Eerdmans, 1972), 39.
3. W. F. Moulton and A. S. Geden, *A Concordance to the Greek Testament,* 5th ed., rev. by H. K. Moulton (Edinburgh: T & T Clark, 1978), 820–21; Alfred Schmoller, *Handkonkordanz zum griechischen Neuen Testament,* 8th ed.

(Stuttgart: Wurttembergische Bielanstalt, 1949), 418, 421; and Leon Morris, *New Testament Theology* (Grand Rapids: Zondervan, 1986), 191.

4. The Greek word *hagio*, "holy," is used with *pneuma*, "Spirit," forty times (out of fifty-two). In the remaining twelve occurrences, it is clearly implied.

5. Norman Perrin, *The New Testament: An Introduction* (New York: Harcourt Brace Jovanovich, 1974), 205. Perrin refers to Luke's gospel as "Book One: The Ministry of the Spirit Through Jesus" and to Acts as "Book Two: The Ministry of the Holy Spirit Through the Church." The Holy Spirit figures prominently throughout the Luke-Acts narrative. See Michael Green, *I Believe in the Holy Spirit* (Grand Rapids: Eerdmans, 1975), 37.

6. Howard Clark Kee, *Understanding the New Testament*, 4th ed. (Englewood Cliffs, N.J.: Prentice-Hall, 1957), 186.

7. N. B. Stonehouse, *Paul Before the Areopagus: And Other New Testament Studies* (Grand Rapids: Eerdmans, 1957), 70.

8. Thomas Dehaney Bernard, *Progress of Doctrine*, 107. It is interesting to note the number of nondispensationalists who use the word *dispensation* to refer to this age of the Spirit. See for example, Richard Belward Rackham, *The Acts of the Apostles*, 7th ed., Westminster Commentaries (London: Methuen, 1901), xxxviii; John R. W. Stott, *The Baptism and Fullness of the Holy Spirit* (Downers Grove, Ill.: InterVarsity, 1964), 11 (Stott is quoting 2 Cor. 3:8). Others are listed under footnote 50.

9. David Ewert, *The Holy Spirit in the New Testament* (Scottdale, Pa.: Herald, 1983), 22, properly observes: "To wait for the 'promise of the Father' does not mean to wait for the Father to promise something, but to wait for the Father's promise (of the Spirit) to be fulfilled."

10. The Holy Spirit, of course, is not mentioned in any of the Old Testament covenants. It is in connection with the new covenant that God promises to "give" His Spirit. But inasmuch as the new covenant is the outworking of the Abrahamic covenant, Paul (with the benefit of Spirit-guided hindsight) could speak of the "promise of the Spirit " in connection with the Abrahamic covenant. See Ibid., 22.

11. George Eldon Ladd, *A Theology of the New Testament* (Grand Rapids: Eerdmans, 1974), 343.

12. T. S. Caulley, "Holy Spirit," in *Evangelical Dictionary of Theology*, ed. Walter A. Elwell (Grand Rapids: Baker, 1984), 522; see also M. M. B. Turner, "Holy Spirit," in *Dictionary of Jesus and the Gospels*, ed. Joel B. Green, Scot McKnight, and I. Howard Marshall (Downers Grove, Ill.: InterVarsity, 1992), 342.

13. Ewert, *The Holy Spirit in the New Testament*, 42.

14. There is no agreement as to what specific text Christ is citing. But the language of the OT likens and compares the outpouring of God's Spirit to the outpouring of water on thirsty ground (cf. Isa. 44:3). Perhaps the ambiguity is intended so as to bring any number of passages to mind. For a good discussion of this question, see Zane C. Hodges, "Rivers of

Living Water—John 7:37–39," *Bibliotheca Sacra* 136 (July–September 1979): 239–48. Hodges suggests that Ezekiel 47:1–11 is the passage behind the citation.

15. Leon Morris, *The Gospel According to John* (Grand Rapids: Eerdmans, 1971), 420, cited in Hodges, "Rivers of Living Water," 244–45. See also the discussion by J. Carl Laney in "John," *Moody Gospel Commentary* (Chicago: Moody, 1992), 145–47.

16. David Peterson, "The Motif of Fulfillment and the Purpose of Luke-Acts," in *The Book of Acts in Its First Century Setting*, vol. 1, *The Book of Acts in Its Ancient Literary Setting*, ed. Bruce W. Winter and Andrew D. Clarke (Grand Rapids: Eerdmans, 1993), 94.

17. John uses *allos* for "another" (14:16), which probably means another of "like kind." The distinction between *allos* and *heteros* is disputed. Some deny that these two words differ from each other in any substantial way. See, for example, William F. Arndt and F. Wilbur Gingrich, *A Greek-English Lexicon of the New Testament* (Chicago: University of Chicago Press, 1957), 39, 315; Friedrich Buchsel, "*allos*," in *Theological Dictionary of the New Testament*, vol. 1, trans. and ed. G. W. Bromiley, ed. Gerhard Kittel (Grand Rapids: Eerdmans, 1964), 264; and D. A. Carson, *The Gospel According to John* (Grand Rapids: Eerdmans, 1991), 499–500.

Others maintain a distinction. For example, see W. Robert Cook, *The Theology of John* (Chicago: Moody, 1979), 63–64; Henry Barclay Swete, *The Holy Spirit in the New Testament* (London: Macmillan, 1910; reprint, Grand Rapids: Baker, 1964), 300; William Hendriksen, *Exposition of the Gospel According to John*, New Testament Commentary (Grand Rapids: Baker, 1953), 275; Leon Morris and Richard Chenevix Trench, *Synonyms of the New Testament* (Grand Rapids: Eerdmans, 1953), 357–61; W. E. Vine, *An Expository Dictionary of New Testament Words* (London: Oliphants, 1966), 60; Joseph Henry Thayer, *Greek-English Lexicon of the New Testament* (New York: American Book Company, 1889), 29; *The Complete Biblical Library*, vol. 11, *The New Testament Greek-English Dictionary: Alpha-Gamma*, ed. Denis W. Vinyard and Donald D. Wimer (Springfield: World Library, 1990), 172; and Turner, "Holy Spirit," 349.

18. McDonald, *Living Doctrines*, 137.

19. On this issue I am indebted to Zane C. Hodges, "A Dispensational Understanding of Acts 2," in *Issues in Dispensationalism*, ed. Wesley R. Willis, John R. Master, and Charles C. Ryrie (Chicago: Moody, 1994), 167–80.

20. Charles C. Ryrie, *The Holy Spirit* (Chicago: Moody, 1965), 21–22, points out that "the Spirit of Jesus" (Acts 16:7), and the "Spirit of Christ" are simply designations for the Holy Spirit. The same is true for "the Spirit of the Lord" (Acts 8:39). There is one Spirit (1 Cor. 12:11, 13; Eph. 4:4). These references no more refer to different spirits than the grace of God (Gal. 2:21) and the grace of Christ (Gal. 1:6) refer to two different graces."

21. Harry L. Poe, *The Gospel and Its Meaning* (Grand Rapids: Zondervan, 1996), 229.

22. Henry C. Thiessen, *Lectures in Systematic Theology,* rev. by V. D. Doerksen (Grand Rapids: Eerdmans, 1979), 98; Floyd H. Barackman, *Practical Christian Theology* (Old Tappan: Revell, 1984), 44–45; and Wayne Grudem, *Systematic Theology* (Grand Rapids: Zondervan, 1994), 248–252.

23. Lewis Sperry Chafer, *Systematic Theology,* vol. 1, *Prolegomena, Bibliology, Theology Proper* (Dallas: Dallas Seminary Press, 1947), 411, 413.

24. Grudem, *Systematic Theology,* 249; cf. Edwin H. Palmer, *The Holy Spirit* (Grand Rapids: Baker, 1958), 15–18; and John F. Walvoord, *The Holy Spirit,* 3d ed. (Grand Rapids: Zondervan, 1965), 30–31.

25. Thomas, *The Holy Spirit of God,* 39.

26. Shepherd, *Narrative Function,* 26.

27. Ibid., 41.

28. Ibid., 247.

29. Ibid., 40–41, 247–248.

30. David E. Aune, *Prophecy in Early Christianity and the Ancient Mediterranean World* (Grand Rapids: Eerdmans, 1983), 191–92.

31. Luke Timothy Johnson, *The Acts of the Apostles, Sacra Pagina* Series, vol. 5 (Collegeville, Minn.: Liturgical, 1992), 14–15.

32. Before Christ's ascension, the Spirit did come *upon* or "fill" select individuals for particular purposes, and for indefinite (but limited) duration. John the Baptist was to be filled with the Holy Spirit while yet in his mother's womb (Luke 1:15); Elizabeth was filled with the Holy Spirit (Luke 1:41); Zacharias also (Luke 1:67); the Holy Spirit was "upon" Simeon (Luke 2:25). But this special filling seems to be distinct from the "gift" which was to come to *all* believers and which was poured out on Pentecost.

33. William Kelly, *An Exposition of the Acts of the Apostles,* 3rd ed. (Denver, Col.: Wilson Foundation, 1952), 17.

34. Ibid., 157–59.

35. Paul Enns, *The Moody Handbook of Theology* (Chicago: Moody, 1989), 266.

36. Mark 16:17 is also marshaled as evidence that Spirit baptism is a work subsequent to salvation accompanied by tongues speaking. Though Mark 16:17 is outside the scope of this study, it may be noted that this passage is textually suspect.

37. Taking the period of Christ and the apostles as one period, these periods are: (1) Moses and Joshua, (2) Elijah and Elisha, (3) Christ and the apostles, and (4) the two witnesses of Revelation 11:1–13, whose ministry and miracles will occur during the tribulation, and this, again, in connection with Israel. The tribulation is the time of "*Jacob's* trouble" (Jer. 30:7) and is primarily (though not exclusively) Jewish in nature and purpose.

38. It is not at all uncommon for nondispensationalists to refer to the Church era as "the dispensation of the Spirit." See for example: Julius Robert Mantey, *Depth Explorations in the New Testament* (New York: Vantage, 1980), 81; Richard B. Gaffin Jr., *Perspectives on Pentecost* (Phillipsburg, N.J.: Presbyterian and Reformed, 1979), 25; Stonehouse, *Paul Before the Areopagus*, 81; and Bernard, *Progress of Doctrine*, 107.

39. Roger Stronstad, *The Charismatic Theology of St. Luke* (Peabody, Mass.: Hendrickson, 1984), 49–50.

40. W. Graham Scroggie, *The Baptism of the Spirit: What Is It?* and *Speaking in Tongues: What Saith the Scripture?* (London: Pickering and Inglis, n.d.), 8.

41. Rene Pache, *The Person and Work of the Holy Spirit*, trans. J. D. Emerson (Chicago: Moody, 1954), 54.

42. Stonehouse, *Paul Before the Areopagus*, 75.

43. Stanley D. Toussaint, "Acts," in *The Bible Knowledge Commentary*, New Testament ed. (Wheaton, Ill.: Victor, 1983), 359.

44. William J. Larkin Jr., "Acts," in *The IVP New Testament Commentary* (Downers Grove, Ill.: InterVarsity, 1995), 59.

45. Roland de Vaux, *Ancient Israel*, vol. 2, *Religious Institutions* (New York: McGraw, 1965), 342.

46. Daniel-Rops, *Daily Life in Palestine at the Time of Christ*, trans. Patrick O'Brian (London: Weidenfeld and Nicolson, 1962), 39–41.

47. Frank Pack, *Tongues and the Holy Spirit* (Abilene: Biblical Research, 1972), 21–22, suggests that the Samaritans had already received the Spirit when they believed and that this is a special filling relating to spiritual gifts. But the phrase *elambanon pneuma hagion*, "they received [imperf.] the Holy Spirit," makes this reading incorrect.

48. Robert G. Gromacki, *New Testament Survey* (Des Plaines: Regular Baptist, 1974), 157.

49. William Kelly, *Lectures Introductory to the Study of the Acts, the Catholic Epistles, and the Revelation* (reprint, Sunbury: Believers Bookshelf, 1970), 65. See also R. S. Sugirtharajah, "Luke's Second Volume and the Gentiles," *Expository Times* 100 (February 1989): 179. Sugirtharajah states that most commentators attribute Cornelius's piety to his association as a God-fearer with the Jewish synagogues, scriptures, and religious practices. M. Wilcox, though, questions that the term *God-fearer* refers to a fringe group of Gentiles who gathered around synagogues. Wilcox points out that *phoboumenoi* indicates personal piety. According to Wilcox, "the very strength of this description suggests that it is his personal quality of devotion and not his being a synagogue adherent (if in fact he was) which Luke was seeking to stress." See M. Wilcox, "The 'God-Fearers' in Acts—A Reconstruction," *JSNT* 13 (1981): 105. So piety means more than simply affiliation. The virtues were not the monopoly of one religious group. Both Cornelius and his household had these virtues. Luke is showing his readers that Gentile piety was

as faultless as that of any Jew or Christian and that there is little to choose between them.

Sugirtharajah continues, "What emerges from the Cornelius narrative is that it was God and not Peter who pictures a people of God which included the Gentiles on equal footing with the Christians. It dawns slowly on Peter that God does not play favorites. The Cornelius incident is often dubbed as Peter's Damascus road. In reality, it was his Nineveh. It was a bitter reminder to Peter, just as it was to Jonah at Nineveh, that it is God who has the last say and that Peter had no right to determine what God had already cleansed. Unlike Jonah, Peter reluctantly accepts the fact and reports back to the circumcision party at Jerusalem that if God has given the Spirit to the Gentiles as He has done to the believers, 'who was I that I could withstand God?'"

50. Raymond H. Saxe, *The Battle for Your Bible: A Study of Experience Versus Scripture* (Ann Arbor, Mich.: Grace Bible, 1975), 50.

51. Ibid., 52. Compare, Charles C. Ryrie, *The Acts of the Apostles* (Chicago: Moody, 1961), 61; Robert Glenn Gromacki, *The Modern Tongues Movement* (Philadelphia: Presbyterian and Reformed, 1967), 91; and Anthony A. Hoekema, *Holy Spirit Baptism* (Grand Rapids: Eerdmans, 1972), 39.

52. Lewis Sperry Chafer, *Systematic Theology*, vol. 6, *Pneumatology* (Dallas: Dallas Seminary Press, 1948), 73.

53. Ibid., 73–74. Arthur H. Lewis, "The New Birth Under the Old Covenant," *The Evangelical Quarterly* 56 (January 1984): 35–44. Lewis argues for regeneration of Old Testament saints, but his arguments are not convincing.

54. George Eldon Ladd, "The Acts of the Apostles," in *The Wycliffe Bible Commentary*, ed. Charles F. Pfeiffer and Everett F. Harrison (Chicago: Moody, 1962), 1143.

55. M. R. De Haan, *Pentecost and After* (Grand Rapids: Zondervan, 1964), 99.

56. M. Baumgarten, *The Acts of the Apostles: The History of the Church in the Apostolic Age*, vol. 2, trans. A. J. W. Morrison. (Edinburgh: T & T Clark, 1854), 271.

57. Hoekema, *Holy Spirit Baptism*, 41.

58. Stonehouse, *Paul Before the Areopagus*, 80.

59. Gerhard F. Hasel, *Speaking in Tongues* (Berrien Springs, Mich.: Adventist Theological Society, 1991), 98–99.

60. Gromacki, *Modern Tongues Movement*, 93. See also Merril F. Unger, *New Testament Teaching on Tongues* (Grand Rapids: Kregel, 1971), 65.

61. There is some textual uncertainty here. A variant reading adds "in Jerusalem; and great fear was upon all." The shorter reading is to be preferred. See C. K. Barrett, *A Critical and Exegetical Commentary on the Acts of the Apostles*, vol. 1, *Preliminary Introduction and Commentary on Acts I–XIV*, The International Critical Commentary (Edinburgh: T & T

Clark, 1994),167; Bruce M. Metzger, *A Textual Commentary on the Greek New Testament* (New York: United Bible Societies, 1971), 302; and Zane C. Hodges and Arthur L. Farstad, eds., *The Greek New Testament According to the Majority Text* (Nashville: Nelson, 1982), 379.

62. Gromacki, *Modern Tongues Movement,* 1–29; Pack, *Tongues,* 135–48; George W. Dollar, "Church History and the Tongues Movement," *Bibliotheca Sacra* 120 (October–December 1963): 316–21; Gilbert B. Weaver, "Tongues Shall Cease," *Grace Theological Journal* 14 (winter 1973): 12–23; and Cleon L. Rogers Jr., "The Gift of Tongues in the Post Apostolic Church," *Bibliotheca Sacra* 122 (April–June 1965): 134–43.

63. Alfred Rahlfs, ed., *Septuaginta, id est, Vetus Testamentum Graece iuxta LXX interpretes,* vol. 2 (Stuttgart: Privileg. Wuertt. Bibelanstalt, 1959), 522. This volume follows the Hebrew division of the Massoretic Text (Joel 3:1–5) in contrast to *The Septuagint Version of the Old Testament with an English Translation and with Various Readings and Critical Notes* (London: Samuel Bagster & Sons, n.d.; reprint, Grand Rapids: Zondervan, 1975), 1083 (which has Joel 2:28–32); and Henry Barclay Swete, ed., *The Old Testament in Greek According to the Septuagint,* vol. 3, *Hosea–4 Maccabees,* 2d ed. (Cambridge: Cambridge University Press, 1899), 42 (which also has Joel 2:28–32).

64. Some views are difficult to categorize. Views range from "complete fulfillment" to "no fulfillment" of Joel's prophecy. The truth probably is to be found somewhere between the two extremes. Partisans cling to the extremes because it is believed they best serve the theological system by which they are embraced.

65. Anthony A. Hoekema, *The Bible and the Future* (Grand Rapids: Eerdmans, 1979), 57; Oswald T. Allis, *Prophecy and the Church* (Philadelphia: Presbyterian and Reformed, 1945), 136; Simon J. Kistemaker, *Exposition of the Acts of the Apostles, New Testament Commentary* (Grand Rapids: Baker, 1990), 89; French L. Arrington, *The Acts of the Apostles* (Peabody, Mass.: Hendrickson, 1988), 28; and Barrett, *Critical and Exegetical Commentary on the Acts of the Apostles,* 135.

66. John Nelson Darby, *Miscellaneous Writings of J. N. D.,* vol. 4 (Oak Park, Ill.: Bible Truth, n.d.), 91; E. W. Bullinger, ed., "Appendixes to *The Companion Bible*" [bound with and appended to] *The Companion Bible* (reprint, Grand Rapids: Kregel, 1990), 205–6; Paul Lee Tan, *The Interpretation of Prophecy* (Winona Lake, Ind.: BMH, 1974), 184–85; Charles C. Ryrie, *The Acts of the Apostles* (Chicago: Moody, 1961), 20–21; H. A. Ironside, *Notes on the Minor Prophets* (New York: Loizeaux Brothers, 1909), 130–31; and F. W. Grant, *The Numerical Bible,* vol. 6, *Acts to 2 Corinthians* (New York: Loizeaux Brothers, 1901), 20.

67. August Van Ryn, *Acts of the Apostles* (New York: Loizeaux Brothers, 1961), 38; John F. Walvoord, *The Holy Spirit,* 3d ed. (Grand Rapids: Zondervan, 1958), 52; Lehman Strauss, *The Third Person* (New York:

Loizeaux Brothers, 1954), 25–26; Kenneth L. Barker, "False Dichotomies Between the Testaments," *Journal of the Evangelical Theological Society* 25 (March 1982): 3–16, esp. 4, n. 5; J. Dwight Pentecost, *Thy Kingdom Come* (Wheaton, Ill.: Victor, 1990), 270–72; Paul D. Feinberg, "Hermeneutics of Discontinuity," in *Continuity and Discontinuity: Essays in Honor of S. Lewis Johnson, Jr.*, ed. John S. Feinberg (Westchester, Ill.: Crossway, 1988), 126–27; Robert L. Saucy, *The Case for Progressive Dispensationalism* (Grand Rapids: Zondervan, 1993), 178–80; Homer Heater Jr., "Evidence from Joel and Amos," in *A Case for Premillennialism*, ed. Donald K. Campbell and Jeffrey L. Townsend (Chicago: Moody, 1992), 162–63; Darrell L. Bock, "The Reign of the Lord Christ," in *Dispensationalism, Israel and the Church*, ed. Craig A. Blaising and Darrell L. Bock (Grand Rapids: Zondervan, 1992), 47–49; and Mal Couch, *The Biblical Doctrine of the Holy Spirit* (Ft. Worth: Tyndale Biblical Institute, 1995), 70–72.

68. Ladd, "Acts of the Apostles," 1127.

69. Dan McCartney and Charles Clayton, *Let the Reader Understand* (Wheaton, Ill.: Victor, 1994), 220.

70. Clifford Rapp Jr., "Acts 2:16—'This Is That,'" *Chafer Theological Seminary Update* (spring 1995): 4–7. To my knowledge, Rapp's discussion is the best defense of the "This is *like* that" view.

71. Hodges, "Dispensational Understanding of Acts 2," 178.

72. Walter C. Kaiser Jr., "The Promise of God and the Outpouring of the Holy Spirit: Joel 2:28–32 and 2:16–21" in *The Living and Active Word of God*, ed. Morris Inch and Ronald Youngblood (Winona Lake, Ind.: Eisenbrauns, 1983), 119.

73. Walter K. Price, *The Prophet Joel and the Day of the Lord* (Chicago: Moody, 1976), 66.

74. Willis Judson Beecher, *The Prophets and the Promise* (New York: Thomas Y. Crowell, 1905; reprint, Grand Rapids: Baker, 1975), 130.

75. Kaiser, "*Promise*," 110.

76. Feinberg, "*Hermeneutics of Discontinuity*," 127.

77. Warren W. Wiersbe, *The Bible Exposition Commentary*, vol. 1 (Wheaton, Ill.: Victor, 1989), 409.

78. Feinberg, "Hermeneutics of Discontinuity," 128.

79. John S. Feinberg, "Systems of Discontinuity," in *Continuity and Discontinuity*, 68.

80. See Robert L. Thomas, "The Hermeneutics of Progressive Dispensationalism," *The Master's Seminary Journal* 6 (spring 1995): 79–95; idem, "A Critique of Progressive Dispensational Hermeneutics," in *When the Trumpet Sounds*, ed. Thomas Ice and Timothy Demy (Eugene, Ore.: Harvest House Publishers, 1995), 413–25 and 469–71; and Thomas D. Ice, "Dispensational Hermeneutics," in *Issues in Dispensationalism*, 29–49.

81. F. B. Hole, *Outlines of Truth*, 3d ed. (London: The Central Bible Truth Depot, n.d.), 113.

82. Poe, *Gospel and Its Meaning*, 220.

Chapter 9

1. David Ewert, *The Holy Spirit in the New Testament* (Scottdale, Pa.: Herald, 1983), 28.

2. John F. Walvoord, *The Holy Spirit*, 3d ed. (Grand Rapids: Zondervan, 1965), 147–48.

3. To refer to the Holy Spirit as "instrumental" or "means" does not deny the personality of the Holy Spirit. See Daniel Wallace, *Greek Grammar Beyond the Basics* (Grand Rapids: Zondervan, 1996), 374.

4. Warren Vanhetloo, "Spirit Baptism," *Calvary Baptist Theological Journal* 3 (spring 1987): 54.

5. R. Kent Hughes, "Preaching: God's Word to the Church Today," in *The Coming Evangelical Crisis* (Chicago: Moody, 1996), 96.

6. James I. Packer, "The Holy Spirit and His Work," in *Applying the Scriptures*, ed. Kenneth S. Kantzer (Grand Rapids: Zondervan, 1987), 66.

7. Though not agreeing on all points, the following works are helpful discussions of the filling of the Spirit: Thomas Ice, "The Filling of the Holy Spirit: A Quality of Life," *Chafer Theological Seminary Journal* (spring/summer 1996): 9–11; Clifford Rapp Jr., "Ephesians 5:18, Holy Spirit or Human Spirit?" *Chafer Theological Seminary Journal* (spring/ summer 1996), 6–8, 12; Gordon D. Fee, *God's Empowering Presence* (Peabody, Mass.: Hendrickson, 1994), 718–23; Timothy D. Crater, "The Filling of the Spirit in the Greek New Testament" (Th.M. thesis, Dallas Theological Seminary, 1971); Dwight Allen Ekholm, "The Doctrine of the Christian's Walk in the Spirit" (Th.M. thesis, Dallas Theological Seminary, 1973); David Spruance, "The Doctrine of the Filling of the Holy Spirit in Lukan Theology" (S.T.M. thesis, Dallas Theological Seminary, 1978); Darrell L. Bock, "A Theology of Luke-Acts," in *A Biblical Theology of the New Testament*, ed. Roy B. Zuck and Darrell L. Bock (Chicago: Moody, 1994), 98; Mike Stallard, "Being Filled with the Spirit," *Baptist Bible Seminary Expositor* 5 (fall 1994): 5; and Stanley D. Toussaint, "The Filling of the Spirit," in *Basic Theology: Applied*, ed. Wesley Wills, Elaine Willis, John Master, and Janet Master (Wheaton, Ill.: Victor, 1995), 210–18.

   For a survey of the diversity of positions on the doctrine of Spirit-filling, see Terry L. Skalland, "The Meaning and Application of Being Filled with the Spirit in Ephesians 5:18" (Th.M. thesis, Western Conservative Baptist Seminary, 1987), 2–7; Crater, "Filling of the Spirit in the Greek New Testament," 5–13; and Spruance, "Doctrine of the Filling of the Holy Spirit in Lukan Theology," 11–15.

8. Bock, "Theology of Luke-Acts," 98.

9. We are not told whether the Spirit that "filled" Elizabeth and Zacharias continued with them throughout their lives or departed after they prophesied. Probably the Holy Spirit "filled" them only for that occasion and then departed.

10. James A. Sanders, "Isaiah in Luke," *Interpretation* 36 (April 1982): 144–55, Sanders says, "Luke's knowledge of Scripture was rather remarkable. His RSV, so to speak, was a Greek text of what the Old Testament was to that point. There is abundant evidence in Luke and Acts that Luke knew his ancient RSV very well indeed," 146.

11. The compound *empimplēmi* is used, but this does not negate the point. The only times *plēroō* is used of anything *close* to Spirit-filling is in Daniel 2:35 and Haggai 2:7. In the case of Daniel, it is "the stone that struck the statue [which] became a great mountain and *filled* the whole earth." The Haggai passage speaks of the Lord filling "this house with glory." Neither case has any relation to personal Spirit filling for the purpose of prophecy.

12. Wallace, *Greek Grammar Beyond the Basics*, 555.

13. John the Baptist appears to be an exception. By all indications, John's Spirit filling remained throughout his life (Luke 1:15). This, however, does not negate the potentially temporary nature of this special filling. First, it is a divinely sovereign work. Its duration may be limited or extended as the Spirit wills. Second, John's entire adult life is marked by prophetic activity. See Norval Geldenhuys, *Commentary on the Gospel of Luke*, NICNT (Grand Rapids: Eerdmans, 1951), 64–65.

14. Ice, "Filling of the Holy Spirit," 9, apparently following "Doctrine of the Christian's Walk," 37–46, uses the terms "special filling" and "normal filling." It is difficult to improve on these terms.

15. Gerhard Delling, "*pimplēmi*," in *Theological Dictionary of the New Testament*, trans. and ed. G. W. Bromily, ed. Gerhard Friedrich (Grand rapids: Eerdmans, 1968), 6:130.

16. Theo Preiss, "The Inner Witness of the Holy Spirit," *Interpretation* 7 (1953): 267.

17. Bock, "Theology of Luke-Acts," 99.

18. Ewert, *Holy Spirit in the New Testament*, 147.

19. Ibid.

20. Jack Deere, *Surprised by the Voice of God* (Grand Rapids: Zondervan, 1996), 167.

21. Ibid.

22. Ibid., 168.

23. Charles R. Smith, *Tongues in Biblical Perspective*, 2d ed. (Winona Lake, Ind.: BMH, 1973). Smith takes the view that tongues were unintelligible ecstatic utterances.

24. Deere speaks of a "trial and error" method of learning the "language of the Spirit" (*Voice*, 168–71), and of some who "try out" their new revelations or visions (ibid., 173). When in the New Testament did a prophet have to "try out" his vision or his prophecy?

25. Benjamin B. Warfield, *Miracles: Yesterday and Today* (Grand Rapids: Eerdmans, 1953), 6.

26. Arthur C. Custance, *The Silences of God*, Doorway Paper no. 23 (self-published, 1971), 21.

27. J. Lanier Burns, "A Reemphasis on the Purpose of the Sign Gifts," *Bibliotheca Sacra* 132 (July–September 1975): 249. For further study on the nature, purpose, and duration of tongues and the sign gifts see Thomas R. Edgar, *Miraculous Gifts* (New York: Loizeaux Brothers, 1983); idem, *Satisfied by the Promise of the Spirit* (Grand Rapids: Kregel, 1996); idem, "The Cessation of the Sign Gifts," in *Vital Contemporary Issues*, ed. Roy B. Zuck (Grand Rapids: Kregel, 1994); Ronald E. Baxter, *The Charismatic Gift of Tongues* (Grand Rapids: Kregel, 1981); Walter J. Chantry, *Signs of the Apostles* (London: Banner of Truth, 1973); Joseph Dillow, *Speaking in Tongues* (Grand Rapids: Zondervan, 1975); Robert Doyle, ed., *Signs and Wonders and Evangelicals: A Response to the Teaching of John Wimber* (Homebush West, Australia: Lancer, 1987); Richard B. Gaffin Jr., *Perspectives on Pentecost* (Phillipsburg, N.J.: Presbyterian and Reformed, 1979); Robert G. Gromacki, *The Modern Tongues Movement* (Philadelphia: Presbyterian and Reformed, 1967); Gerhard F. Hasel, *Speaking in Tongues* (Berrien Springs, Mich.: Adventist Theological Society, 1991); Harold W. Hoehner, "The Purpose of Tongues in 1 Corinthians 14:20–25," in *Walvoord: A Tribute*, ed. Donald K. Campbell (Chicago: Moody, 1982) 53–66; Anthony A. Hoekema, *What About Tongue-Speaking?* (Grand Rapids: Eerdmans, 1966); David E. Lanier, "With Stammering Lips and Another Tongue: 1 Cor. 14:20–22 and Isa. 28:11–12," in *Criswell Theological Review* 5 (spring 1991): 259–86; Richard Mayhue, *Divine Healing Today* (Chicago: Moody, 1983); Raymond H. Saxe, *The Battle for Your Bible* (Ann Arbor, Mich.: Grace Bible, 1975); Richard C. Schwab, *Let the Bible Speak . . . About Tongues* (Grand Rapids: Kregel, 1983); and Merrill F. Unger, *New Testament Teaching on Tongues* (Grand Rapids: Kregel, 1971).

A Verse-by-Verse Background Guide to the Book of Acts

1. A. T. Robertson, *Word Pictures in the New Testament* (Nashville: Broadman, 1930), 18.

2. F. F. Bruce, *The Book of the Acts* (Grand Rapids: Eerdmans, 1988), 46.

3. Charles Ryrie, *Basic Theology* (Wheaton, Ill.: Victor, 1986), 422.

4. John F. Walvoord, *The Holy Spirit* (Grand Rapids: Zondervan, 1991), 143.

5. Ibid., 139.
6. Henry Alford, *Alford's Greek Testament* (Chicago: Moody, 1852) II:3.
7. Ibid., 4.
8. William F. Arndt and F. Wilbur Gingrich, *A Greek-English Lexicon of the New Testament* (Chicago: University of Chicago Press, 1957), 559.
9. Ibid., 493–96.
10. Merrill F. Unger, *The New Unger's Bible Dictionary* (Chicago: Moody, 1988), 1116.
11. Martin Gilbert, *The Illustrated Atlas of Jewish Civilization* (New York: Macmillan, 1990), 124.
12. Josephus, *The Works of Josephus,* trans. and ed. W. Whiston (Peabody, Mass.: Hendrickson, 1987), 265.
13. Merrill C. Tenney, *New Testament Survey,* rev. ed. (Grand Rapids: Eerdmans, 1985), 111.
14. Josephus, *Works of Josephus,* 476.
15. Cecil Roth, *A History of the Jews* (New York: Shocken, 1989), 101.
16. Gilbert, *Illustrated Atlas of Jewish Civilization,* 47.
17. Henry C. Thiessen, *Introduction to the New Testament* (Grand Rapids: Eerdmans, 1958), 294.
18. J. D. Douglas, ed., *New Bible Dictionary* (Wheaton, Ill.: InterVarsity, 1987), 617.
19. James Hastings, ed., *A Dictionary of the Bible* (Peabody, Mass.: Hendrickson, 1988), 3:305.
20. R. C. H. Lenski, *The Interpretation of the Acts of the Apostles* (Minneapolis: Augsburg, 1946), 52–53.
21. John Gill, "Acts," in *Exposition of the Old & New Testaments* (Paris, Ark.: Baptist Standard Bearer, 1989) 8:147.
22. Simon J. Kistemaker, *Exposition of the Acts of the Apostles,* New Testament Commentary (Grand Rapids: Baker, 1990), 67–68.
23. John MacArthur Jr., *The MacArthur New Testament Commentary: Acts 1–12* (Chicago: Moody, 1994), 44.
24. Douglas, *New Bible Dictionary,* 880–81.
25. W. White Jr., "Media," in *The Zondervan Pictorial Encyclopedia of the Bible,* ed. Merrill C. Tenney (Grand Rapids: Zondervan, 1976), 4:148.
26. Carl E. DeVries, "Mesopotamia," in *Zondervan Pictorial Bible Dictionary,* 528.
27. Unger, *New Unger's Bible Dictionary,* 116.
28. Ibid., 116.
29. Tenney, *New Testament Survey,* 3.
30. Josephus, *Works of Josephus,* 621.
31. Robert Young, *Analytical Concordance to the Bible* (Peabody, Mass.: Hendrickson), 57.
32. Eusebius, *The History of the Church* (New York: Barnes and Noble, 1965), 165.
33. Douglas, *New Bible Dictionary,* 937.

34. Horatio Hackett, *Commentary on Acts* (Grand Rapids: Kregel, 1992), 182.

35. John MacArthur Jr., *The MacArthur New Testament Commentary: Romans 1–8* (Chicago: Moody, 1991), 18–19.

36. Lenski, *Interpretation of the Acts of the Apostles*, 338–39.

37. C. L. Feinberg, "Proselyte," in *Zondervan Pictorial Encyclopedia of the Bible*, 4:908–9.

38. Richard H. Longenecker, "Acts," in *The Expositor's Bible Commentary*, ed. Frank E. Gaebelein (Grand Rapids: Zondervan, 1981), 9:385.

39. A. Duane Litfin, "Titus," in *The Bible Knowledge Commentary, NT*, ed. John F. Walvoord and Roy B. Zuck (Wheaton, Ill.: Victor, 1983), 763.

40. MacArthur, *New Testament Commentary: Acts*, 83.

41. H. G. Anderson, "Beautiful Gate," in *Zondervan Pictorial Encyclopedia of the Bible*, 1:501.

42. J. Barton Payne, "Solomon's Porch," in *Zondervan Pictorial Encyclopedia of the Bible*, 5:479.

43. Bruce, *Book of the Acts*, 80.

44. J. A. Alexander, *Commentary on the Acts of the Apostles* (Grand Rapids: Zondervan, 1956), 113.

45. L. T. Johnson, *The Acts of the Apostles* (Collegeville, Minn.: Liturgical, 1992), 69.

46. Lenski, *Interpretation of the Acts of the Apostles*, 47.

47. Arnold G. Fruchtenbaum, *Israelogy: The Missing Link in Systematic Theology* (Tustin, Calif.: Ariel Ministries, 1992), 75.

48. Hackett, *Commentary on Acts*, 65.

49. Ryrie, *Basic Theology*, 633.

50. Hackett, *Commentary on Acts*, 65.

51. Unger, *New Unger's Bible Dictionary*, 1034.

52. Hackett, *Commentary on Acts*, 65.

53. Roth, *History of the Jews*, 84.

54. Josephus, *Works of Josephus*, 477.

55. Lenski, *Interpretation of the Acts of the Apostles*, 157.

56. Ibid., 376.

57. Philip Sigal, *Judaism: The Evolution of a Faith* (Grand Rapids: Eerdmans, 1988), 29–30.

58. Bruce, *Book of the Acts*, 91.

59. Matthew Henry, *The NIV Matthew Henry Commentary* (Grand Rapids: Zondervan, 1992), 456.

60. Eusebius, *History of the Church*, 61.

61. Robertson, *Word Pictures in the New Testament*, 50.

62. Unger, *New Unger's Bible Dictionary*, 80.

63. Josephus, *Works of Josephus*, 478.

64. Robertson, *Word Pictures in the New Testament*, 50.

65. Hackett, *Commentary on Acts*, 67.

66. Josephus, *Works of Josephus*, 297.

67. Lenski, *Interpretation of the Acts of the Apostles*, 181.
68. Ryrie, *Basic Theology*, 1675.
69. Hackett, *Commentary on Acts*, 180.
70. G. B. Stevens, *The Theology of the New Testament* (Edinburgh: T & T Clark, 1968), 484.
71. Unger, *New Unger's Bible Dictionary*, 1128–29.
72. E. H. Plumptre, "Acts," in *Commentary on the Whole Bible*, ed. Charles John Ellicott (Grand Rapids: Zondervan, 1959), 7:29.
73. Longenecker, "Acts," 319.
74. MacArthur, *New Testament Commentary: Acts*, 198.
75. Lenski, *Interpretation of the Acts of the Apostles*, 552.
76. Ibid., 217.
77. Tenney, *New Testament Survey*, 105.
78. Roth, *History of the Jews*, 84.
79. Herbert Lockyer, *All the Men in the Bible* (Grand Rapids: Zondervan, 1958), 326–27.
80. Josephus, *Antiquities of the Jews* 20.5.1.
81. Hackett, *Commentary on Acts*, 82–83.
82. Josephus, *War of the Jews*, 2.8.1.
83. Harold W. Hoehner, "Hellenism, Hellenists," in *Zondervan Pictorial Encyclopedia of the Bible*, 3:117.
84. Arndt and Gingrich, *Greek-English Lexicon of the New Testament*, 486.
85. Ibid., 298.
86. W. T. Dayton, "Stephen," in *Zondervan Pictorial Encyclopedia of the Bible*, 5:515.
87. Ibid., 5:516.
88. Charles Ryrie, *Ryrie Study Bible* (Chicago: Moody, 1986) 1659.
89. Longenecker, "Acts," 360.
90. Roth, *History of the Jews*, 87.
91. Unger, *New Unger's Bible Dictionary*, 444.
92. Robertson, *Word Pictures in the New Testament*, 75–76.
93. "Cilicia," in *Microsoft Encarta '96 Encyclopedia*.
94. Ryrie, *Ryrie Study Bible*, 1691.
95. Clyde E. Harrington, "Haran," in *Zondervan Pictorial Bible Dictionary*, 335.
96. Eugene H. Merrill, *Kingdom of Priests* (Grand Rapids: Baker, 1992), 50.
97. Ibid., 58.
98. Arthur B. Fowler, "Midian," in *Zondervan Pictorial Bible Dictionary*, 532.
99. Ibid., 71, 75.
100. Steven Barabas, "Aaron," in *Zondervan Pictorial Bible Dictionary*, 1.
101. Unger, *New Unger's Bible Dictionary*, 489.
102. Bruce, *Book of the Acts*, 149.
103. Unger, *New Unger's Bible Dictionary*, 1197.
104. Lenski, *Interpretation of the Acts of the Apostles*, 318–19.
105. Bruce, *Book of the Acts*, 175.

106. Eusebius, *History of the Church*, 74.

107. Longenecker, "Acts," 363.

108. Unger, *New Unger's Bible Dictionary*, 203.

109. Francis Brown, ed., *The New Brown-Driver-Briggs Gesenius Hebrew and English Lexicon* (Peabody, Mass.: Hendrickson Publishers, 1979), 78.

110. A. Bowling, "Damascus," in *Zondervan Pictorial Encyclopedia of the Bible*, 2:7–8.

111. Longenecker, "Acts," 373.

112. Unger, *New Unger's Bible Dictionary*, 1223.

113. Douglas, *New Bible Dictionary*, 1166.

114. J. W. McGarvey, *New Commentary on Acts of Apostles*, (Delight, Ark.: Gospel Light, n.d.), 194–95.

115. Everett F. Harrison, "Acts," in *The Expanding Church* (Chicago: Moody, 1978), 164.

116. Lenski, *Interpretation of the Acts of the Apostles*, 402–4.

117. Ibid., 438.

118. "Cyprus," in *Microsoft Encarta '96 Encyclopedia*.

119. Stanley D. Toussaint, "Acts," in *Bible Knowledge Commentary*, 383.

120. Ryrie, *Ryrie Study Bible*, 1675.

121. Plumptre, "Acts," 7:75.

122. Merrill F. Unger, *Unger's Bible Dictionary* (Chicago: Moody, 1981), 578.

123. F. F. Bruce and W. E. Vine, eds., "Prophecy, Prophesy, Prophesying," in *Vine's Expository Dictionary of Old and New Testament Words* (Old Tappan, N.J.: Revell, 1981), 3:221.

124. "Claudius I," in *Microsoft Encarta '96 Encyclopedia*.

125. Josephus, *Antiquities* 2.5.51–53.

126. Ibid., 3.15.320–21.

127. *"Claudius I."*

128. Unger, *New Unger's Bible Dictionary*, 242.

129. *"Claudius I."*

130. Harrison, "Acts," 189.

131. Ibid., 195–196.

132. Toussaint, "Acts," 387.

133. Ryrie, *Ryrie Study Bible*, 1753.

134. Unger, *New Unger's Bible Dictionary*, 959.

135. Toussaint, "Acts," 388.

136. Robertson, *Word Pictures in the New Testament*, 179.

137. Merrill F. Unger, *Archeology and the New Testament* (Grand Rapids: Zondervan 1962), 188.

138. Longenecker, "Acts," 9:422–23.

139. Alexander, *Commentary on the Acts of the Apostles*, 483–84.

140. Unger, *Unger's Bible Dictionary*, 964.

141. Alexander, *Commentary on the Acts of the Apostles*, 505.

142. George Howe and G. A. Harrer, *A Handbook of Classical Mythology* (England: Oracle, 1996), 297.

143. Bruce, *Book of the Acts*, 275.

144. Robertson, *Word Pictures in the New Testament*, 210.

145. Howe and Harrer, *Handbook of Classical Mythology*, 128.

146. Robertson, *Word Pictures in the New Testament*, 210.

147. W. E. Vine, *Vine's Expository Dictionary of Biblical Words* (Nashville: Nelson, 1985), 330.

148. Arndt and Gingrich, *Greek-English Lexicon of the New Testament*, 771–72.

149. Ibid., 339.

150. W. T. Dayton, "James, Epistle of," in *Zondervan Pictorial Encyclopedia of the Bible*, 3:396.

151. Josephus, *Works of Josephus*, 550.

152. Ibid., 640.

153. Bruce, *Book of the Acts*, 225.

154. W. J. Conybeare and J. S. Howson, *The Life and Epistles of St. Paul* (Grand Rapids: Eerdmans, 1980), 433.

155. E. M. Blaiklock, "Galatia," in *Zondervan Pictorial Encyclopedia of the Bible*, 2:624–26.

156. "Mysia," in *Microsoft Encarta '96 Encyclopedia*.

157. Longenecker, "Acts," 9:457.

158. "Bithynia," in *Microsoft Encarta '96 Encyclopedia*.

159. Pliny the Younger, *Letters* 10. 96–97; see Longenecker, "Acts," 9: 457.

160. A. Rupprecht, "Macedonia," in *Zondervan Pictorial Encyclopedia of the Bible*, 4:24.

161. Unger, *New Unger's Bible Dictionary*, 780.

162. A. Rupprecht, "Philippi," in *Zondervan Pictorial Encyclopedia of the Bible*, 4:759.

163. M. G. Easton, *The New Illustrated Dictionary* (New York: Crescent Books, 1989), 546.

164. Bruce, *Book of the Acts*, 331.

165. Rupprecht, "Philippi."

166. Alexander, *Commentary on the Acts of the Apostles*, 580.

167. Ibid., 584.

168. Hastings, *Dictionary of the Bible*, 4: 750.

169. Unger, *New Unger's Bible Dictionary*, 1089.

170. Robert L. Thomas, "I Thessalonians," in *Expositor's Bible Commentary*, 11:247.

171. Henry Alford, *The Greek Testament* (Chicago: Moody, 1958), 2:190.

172. Hastings, *Dictionary of the Bible*, 1:197.

173. Simon Blackburn, *The Oxford Dictionary of Philosophy* (Oxford, N.Y.: Oxford University Press, 1996), 122.

174. Robertson, *Word Pictures in the New Testament*, 280.

175. George and Donald Sweeting, *The Acts of God* (Chicago: Moody, 1986), 143.

176. Howe and Harrer, *Handbook of Classical Mythology*, 35.

177. Alexander, *Commentary on the Acts of the Apostles*, 611.

178. Ibid., 143.

179. Bruce, *Book of the Acts*, 331–32.

180. Unger, *New Unger's Bible Dictionary*, 1317–18.

181. Bruce, *Book of the Acts*, 340.

182. Ibid., 343.

183. John B. Polhill, "Acts," in *The New American Commentary* (Nashville: Broadman, 1992), 374.

184. Ibid.

185. Arndt and Gingrich, *Greek-English Lexicon of the New Testament*, 155.

186. Longenecker, "Acts," 9:478.

187. Unger, *New Unger's Bible Dictionary*, 304–5.

188. John MacArthur Jr., *New Testament Commentary: 1 Corinthians* (Chicago: Moody, n.d.), 7–8.

189. D. E. Hiebert, "Aquila and Priscilla," in *Zondervan Pictorial Encyclopedia of the Bible*, 1:232.

190. Unger, *New Unger's Bible Dictionary*, 1229.

191. Ryrie, *Ryrie Study Bible*, 1680.

192. McGarvey, *New Commentary on Acts of Apostles*, 140–41.

193. William Ramsey, *St. Paul the Traveler*, 259.

194. Ryrie, *Ryrie Study Bible: Expanded Edition*, 1765.

195. *Harper's Bible Dictionary* (New York: Harper and Row, 1985), 167.

196. D. E. Hiebert, "Apollos," in *Zondervan Pictorial Encyclopedia of the Bible*, 1:215.

197. Toussaint, "Acts," 408.

198. Hiebert, "Apollos," 216.

199. Merrill F. Unger, *Biblical Demonology* (Grand Rapids: Kregel, 1994), 80.

200. Longenecker, "Acts," 9:498.

201. James Orr, gen. ed. *The International Standard Bible Encyclopedia* (Grand Rapids: Eerdmans, 1957), 969.

202. Longenecker, "Acts," 9:502.

203. Ryrie, *Ryrie Study Bible*, 1683.

204. Howe and Harrer, *Handbook of Classical Mythology*, 39–41.

205. Tenney, *New Testament Survey*, 65.

206. *Eerdman's Handbook to World Religions* (Grand Rapids: Eerdmans, 1994), 414.

207. John R. W. Stott, *The Message of Ephesians* (Downers Grove, Ill.: InterVarsity, 1979), 23.

208. Robertson, *Word Pictures in the New Testament*, 3:331.

209. Hastings, *Dictionary of the Bible*, 1:141.

210. Robertson, *Word Pictures in the New Testament*, 3:327.

211. Bruce, *Book of the Acts*, 376–77.

212. Unger, *New Unger's Bible Dictionary*, 44.

213. Conybeare and Howson, *Life and Epistles of St. Paul*, 12–13.

214. Hastings, *Dictionary of the Bible*, 4:821.

215. Unger, *Unger's Bible Dictionary*, 961.

216. E. M. Blaiklock, "Miletus," in *Zondervan Pictorial Bible Dictionary*, 532.

217. Arndt and Gingrich, *Greek-English Lexicon of the New Testament*, 655.

218. Lenski, *Interpretation of the Acts of the Apostles*, 850.

219. Charles Pfeiffer and Vos, *The Wycliffe Historical Geography of Bible Lands* (Chicago: Moody, 1967), 372–74.

220. "Rhodes," in *Microsoft Encarta '96 Encyclopedia*.

221. Unger, *Archeology and the New Testament*, 291.

222. Clifton T. Allen, gen ed., *Broadman's Bible Commentary* (Nashville: Broadman, 1970), 10:120.

223. A. F. Rainey, "Acco," in *Zondervan Pictorial Encyclopedia of the Bible*, 1:32.

224. McGarvey, *New Commentary on Acts*, 202.

225. Josephus, *Antiquities* 20.8.169–72.

226. Lenski, *Interpretation of the Acts of the Apostles*, 909.

227. John F. Walvoord and Roy B. Zuck, eds., *The Bible Knowledge Commentary, New Testament* (Wheaton, Ill.: Victor, 1983), 419.

228. Ibid.

229. Bruce, *Book of the Acts*, 434.

230. Robertson, *Word Pictures in the New Testament*, 408.

231. Bruce, *Book of the Acts*, 436.

232. Eusebius, *History of the Church*, 95.

233. Unger, *New Unger's Bible Dictionary*, 564.

234. Bruce, *Book of the Acts*, 457.

235. Josephus, *Works of Josephus*, 519.

236. Ibid., 534.

237. Unger, *New Unger's Bible Dictionary*, 564.

238. Lenski, *Interpretation of the Acts of the Apostles*, 1056–57.

239. Hackett, *Commentary on Acts*, 290–91.

240. "Cnidus," in *Microsoft Encarta '96 Encyclopedia*.

241. As quoted by Merrill F. Unger, "Fair Havens," in *Unger's Bible Dictionary* (Chicago: Moody, 1985), 340.

242. *Interpreter's Dictionary of the Bible* (New York: Abingdon, 1962), 3:72.

243. Robertson, *Word Pictures in the New Testament*, 3:464.

244. Longenecker, "Acts," 9:563.

245. *Unger's Bible Dictionary*, 1050.

246. Walvoord and Zuck, *Bible Knowledge Commentary, New Testament*, 431.

Appendix 1

1. Roland de Vaux, *Ancient Israel*, vol. 2, *Religious Institutions* (New York: McGraw-Hill, 1965), 449, 416.

2. D. W. Wead, "Laying on of Hands," in *The International Standard Bible*

Encyclopedia, 4 vols. revised, ed. Geoffrey W. Bromiley (Grand Rapids: Eerdmans, 1982), 2:611.

3. Ibid.

4. Ardel B. Caneday, *"The Significance and Relationship of the Laying on of Hands and the Bestowal of Spiritual Gifts,"* (M. Div. thesis, Grace Theological Seminary, 1976), 12.

5. Henry Barclay Swete, *The Holy Spirit in the New Testament* (London: Macmillan, 1910; reprint, Grand Rapids: Baker, 1964), 85. Swete says this symbol was "once employed by Jesus in an act of benediction."

6. The apostles also performed miracles and healings in the Gospels, but we are not told whether the laying on of hands was involved (Matt. 10:1–8; Luke 9:6; 10:9, 17).

7. Caneday, "Significance and Relationship," 14.

8. Frank Thielman, "Laying on of Hands," in Walter A. Elwell, ed., *Evangelical Dictionary of Biblical Theology* (Grand Rapids: Baker, 1996), 472.

9. H. L. Strack and G. Stemberger, *Introduction to the Talmud and Midrash*, trans. M. Bockmuehl (Minneapolis: Fortress, 1992), 15.

10. Ibid.

11. Ibid.

12. John Lightfoot, *A Commentary on the New Testament from the Talmud and Hebraica: Matthew–I Corinthians*, vol. 4, *Acts-I Corinthians*; reprinted from the 1859 Oxford University Press ed., *Horae Hebraicae Et Talmudicae* (Grand Rapids: Baker, 1979), 111. Philip Blackman, *Mishnayoth*, vol. 4, *Order Nezikin*, 2d ed. (New York: Judaica, 1963), 236, translates the passage: "The laying on of the hands by the elders, and the breaking of the neck of the heifer [are decided] by three [judges]."

13. Lightfoot, *Talmud and Hebraica*, 111.

14. Ibid. Lightfoot surely intended to include an index of abbreviations for his commentary on the New Testament. But he apparently died before he could complete it. Part of the work was published during his lifetime, and part posthumously.

15. Dan Cohn-Sherbok, *The Blackwell Dictionary of Judaica* (Oxford: Blackwell, 1992), 365, places the compilation of the *Mishnah* by Judah ha-Nasi in the second century. However, Richard N. Soulen, *Handbook of Biblical Criticism*, 2d ed., rev. and augmented (Atlanta: Knox, 1981), 123, places it in the early decades of the third century. Strack and Stemberger, *Introduction to the Talmud*, 123, date it at c. A.D. 200.

16. R. Laird Harris, introduction to *Commentary on the New Testament from the Talmud and Hebraica: Matthew–1 Corinthians* by Lightfoot, 1:vii.

17. Cohn-Sherbok, *The Blackwell Dictionary of Judaica*, 339.

18. Strack and Stemberger, *Introduction to the Talmud*, 2–8; Herbert Danby, *The Mishnah, Translated from the Hebrew with Introduction and Brief Explanatory Notes* (Oxford: Oxford University Press, 1933), xiv, states that

"the accepted hypothesis was that it [the oral law] was delivered at Mount Sinai at the same time as the Written Law, and preserved by word of mouth, generation after generation, until it found permanent expression in the Mishnah." In a footnote (n. 1 on p. xiii) Danby defines the *Mishnah* as "both teaching and the substance of the teaching passed on from teacher to pupil by word of mouth. It is used of the teaching of a single teacher or *tanna*, either in the sense of a single tenet held by him or as a collection of oral laws taught by him. 'The Mishnah,' as used without qualification, signifies the collection of oral laws made by Rabbi Judah the Patriarch." David Bridger, ed., *The New Jewish Encyclopedia* (New York: Behrman House, 1962), 438–39, says, "In the days of the Second Commonwealth, and later during the Talmudic period, one generation of teachers would grant *Semikhah* to future teachers, who were thus ordained to exercise religious and legal authority." He then adds, "Technically, Semikhah ceased some two thousand years ago, and was not established anew until the 14th or 15th century." This latter statement, however, is incongruent with his first statement, unsupported by the evidence, vague and indefinite, and counter to the consensus.

19. M. E. Manton, *A Dictionary of Theological Terms* (London: Grace, 1996), 116.

20. Nicholas Turner, *Handbook for Biblical Studies* (Philadelphia: Westminster, 1982), 131. According to F. B. Huey Jr., and Bruce Corley, *A Student's Dictionary for Biblical and Theological Studies* (Grand Rapids: Zondervan, 1983), 184, the Hebrew word *tanna* means "teacher" or "transmitter." Danby's definition is, "lit. 'repeaters,' teachers of the oral law," *The Mishnah*, xiii.

21. Joachim Jeremias, *Jerusalem in the Time of Jesus* (Philadelphia: Fortress, 1969), 235.

22. Ibid.

23. Cohn-Sherbok, *Blackwell Dictionary of Judaica*, 408.

24. Ibid.

25. J. Coppens, "Imposition of Hands," in *New Catholic Encyclopedia*, 15 vols. (New York: McGraw-Hill, 1967), 7:401.

26. *Encyclopedia Judaica*, 1971 ed., s.v. "Semikhah." Presumably, the author meant that the rite of laying on of hands continued into the Talmudic period, but his language makes it difficult to be certain.

27. David Daube, *The New Testament and Rabbinic Judaism*, Jordan Lectures 1952 (London: Athlone, 1956; reprint, Salem, N.H.: Ayer, 1984), 229; see also 230ff.

28. Ibid., 231.

29. Ibid., 232.

Appendix 2

1. Richard Chenevix Trench, *Notes on the Miracles and Parables of Our Lord* (Old Tappan, N.J.: Revell, 1953), 49–50.
2. C. S. Lewis, *Miracles;* cited in John A. Witmer, "The Doctrine of Miracles," *Bibliotheca Sacra* 130 (April–June 1973): 132.
3. Witmer, "The Doctrine of Miracles," 132.
4. Joseph Dillow, *Speaking in Tongues: Seven Crucial Questions* (Grand Rapids: Zondervan, 1975), 96.
5. Ibid., 97.
6. Jack Deere, *Surprised by the Voice of God* (Grand Rapids: Zondervan, 1996), 223; cf. 249.
7. Dillow, *Speaking in Tongues,* 129.

Appendix 3

1. Craig A. Blaising and Darrell S. Bock, *Progressive Dispensationalism* (Wheaton, Ill.: Victor, 1993), 206.
2. Ibid., 84–85.
3. Ibid., 177.
4. Ibid., 178.
5. Charles C. Ryrie, *The Basis of the Premillennial Faith* (New York: Loizeaux Brothers, 1953), 107.

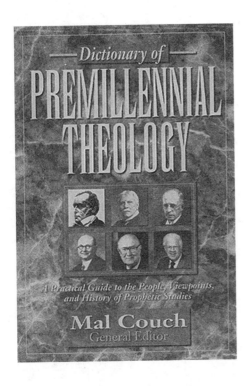

Dictionary of Premillennial Theology

Mal Couch, general editor

More than fifty scholars, authors, and Bible teachers have combined their expertise to present a historical and topical dictionary of premillennial theology. Included are articles on the major figures of prophetic studies such as Darby, Scofield, Chafer, Ladd, and Walvoord, as well as historical figures such as Augustine, Edwards, and Spurgeon. Additional articles cover major terms and concepts in premillennial theology as well as the eschatology of individual Bible books, Scripture passages, and extra-canonical writings.

Contributors include Robert Gromacki, Thomas Ice, Edward Hinson, John Hannah, Robert Lightner, Charles Ryrie, Tim LaHaye, and H. Wayne House.

Comprehensive in scope yet concise in its entries, *Dictionary of Premillennial Theology* will serve the needs of both the academic and lay reader as a practical reference book for prophetic studies.

448 pages
0-8254-2351-1 / hardcover

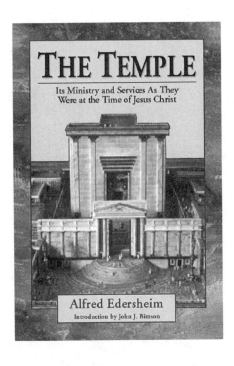

ALSO BY KREGEL PUBLICATIONS

Josephus: The Essential Works

translated with commentary by Paul L. Maier

Dr. Paul L. Maier's award-winning translation and condensation of the essential works of Josephus has now been expanded and improved. As the primary source of information about the first century outside of the New Testament, the *Jewish Antiquities* and *The Jewish War* of Josephus take on a brilliant new dimension with full-color photographs of first-century places and artifacts.

In addition to Dr. Maier's eminently readable and engaging text are newly-included discussions on the historical and chronological issues raised by Josephus. Key features of this new edition include:

- 91 full-color photographs
- 21 maps, illustrations, and charts
- 19 sidebar discussions

Thoroughly indexed and keyed to the Loeb Classical Library's numbering of the Greek text of Josephus, this new edition will be the standard resource for first-century study.

416 pages
0-8254-3260-x / hardcover

ALSO BY KREGEL PUBLICATIONS

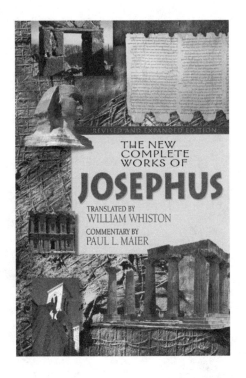

The New Complete Works of Josephus

translated by William Whiston with commentary by Paul L. Maier

The primary source outside the Bible for information on the first century is coming with a new look and new insights! *The New Complete Works of Josephus* has been reset in easy-to-read type with:

• Introduction by Paul L. Maier, internationally recognized scholar in ancient history

• Over 50 pages of new commentary by Dr. Maier throughout the text on the crucial references that make an impact on Christian history

• Cross-reference numbers in each paragraph to the standard Loeb edition of the Greek text

This new edition is destined to become the English standard for referencing the collected works of Josephus.

1,152 pages
0-8254-2948-x / paperback
0-8254-2924-2 / hardcover